THE Complete Healthy Dog Handbook

THE Complete Healthy Dog Handbook

The Definitive Guide to Keeping Your Pet Happy, Healthy & Active

BETSY BREVITZ, D.V.M.

WORKMAN PUBLISHING • NEW YORK

Design by Lisa Hollander with Sophia Stavropoulos
Front cover photograph by GK Hart/Vikki Hart/Getty Images
Back cover photographs by Hans Wretling/age fotostock (dog) and Shutterstock (ball)

Library of Congress Cataloging-in-Publication Data is available.
ISBN 978-0-7611-5412-9

Originally published as *The Hound Health Handbook*—now revised and updated.
Some of the material in this book is adapted from the website www.urbanhound.com,
or from the book *Urbanhound: The New York City Dog's Ultimate Survival Guide*,
by Nina Munk and Nadia Zonis.

Workman books are available at special discounts when purchased in bulk for premiums and sales
promotions as well as for fund-raising or educational use. Special editions or book excerpts can be
created to specification. For details, contact the Special Sales Director at the address below.

Workman Publishing Company, Inc.
225 Varick Street
New York, NY 10014-4381
www.workman.com

Printed in the United States of America
First printing: March 2009
10 9 8 7 6 5 4 3 2 1

To dogs,
who love with their whole hearts;
and to my "home pack,"
whom I love doggedly.

• • • • • •

Contents

The Rollover Test, page 16

• Home Care for Vomiting • Bloat •
Eating the Inedible • Liver Problems •
Pancreatitis • Gall Bladder Disease

The Head Collar, page 183

Tennis-Ball Mouth, page 81

The Chihuahua, page 25

Foreword to the New Edition

In the four years since the original *Hound Health Handbook* was published, notable events, trends, and discoveries have changed dog ownership and veterinary medicine alike. The two most significant events were Hurricane Katrina in August 2005 and the widespread pet food contamination of spring 2007. Hurricane Katrina rapidly increased the numbers of dogs being moved from one area of the country to another, or even from one country to another, in search of homes. When dogs relocate, so do diseases. Heartworm disease is much more prevalent in the Northeast now that so many southern and Gulf Coast dogs have found homes here, and vets everywhere have had to expand their diagnostic lists of "usual suspect" diseases to include newcomers from other parts of the country. In 2007, pet food recalls shook consumer trust, raised awareness of what's in pet food and where it comes from, and created tremendous interest in home cooking for dogs and cats.

Trends that have influenced the canine world include the skyrocketing popularity of "designer dog" breeds; the increased availability of such once-rarefied procedures as CT and MRI scans, joint replacement, and radiation therapy for cancer; and the rising cost of veterinary care. Designer dogs have raised and sometimes dashed consumer expectations, provided lots of work for vets due to their inherited diseases, and raised profits for puppy mills. The spread of high-tech care means that almost anywhere in the country, you can now spend thousands of dollars diagnosing and treating a dog's illness or injury. You *can*, but should you? Financial pressures are affecting practically every dog-care decision these days. The current economic downturn has forced many dog owners to postpone or forgo preventive health care measures, and added to the difficulty of deciding what to do if their dogs get sick.

On a brighter note, the past four years have provided some handy new tools for the veterinary toolbox. An anti-vomiting drug that can be used for car sickness and other stomach upsets, a new injectable antibiotic that lasts for two weeks, and a vaccine against malignant melanoma that significantly increases dogs' survival time after tumor removal are a few of the useful new innovations.

Of course, the essentials of our relationships with dogs have *not* changed in the past four years, and I take great comfort in that. People remain devoted to their dogs, and their dogs to them. We veterinarians remain committed to giving your animals the best possible care, and are fully aware of the economic pressures facing so many of us these days. As for the future, I look forward to taking care of dogs and cats for a good many years to come—learning, growing, and appreciating the pleasures that animals bring to our lives.

Betsy Brevitz, D.V.M.
January 2009

Introduction

In my first job as a veterinarian, I was a nervous wreck. I loved medicine, I loved animals—so why was it all so overwhelming? My boss coddled me by having the front desk schedule only three appointments an hour for me, even though the more experienced vets at our practice had four. Still, my clients got backed up in the waiting room, and I was frazzled.

I had 20 minutes to talk to each owner about the animal's symptoms, do a complete physical exam, make at least a tentative diagnosis and an initial plan for testing and treatment, and then explain to the owner what I wanted to do and why. I would have dismissed that pace as impossible, except that I saw my colleagues keeping up, or at least not falling as far behind as I did.

Fortunately, follow-up phone calls gave me more time to get things right. When the evening's appointments were over, I would sit down with a stack of medical files and phone messages and call clients to discuss test results or simply to ask how their animal had been doing in the few hours since I'd seen him. During those phone calls, I sometimes discovered that a client hadn't really understood why I wanted to do a particular blood test or diagnostic procedure. So I would explain it all again, trying even harder to make sense. Often people had questions they had thought of after they'd left the office. Sometimes I had questions *I'd* thought of only after they'd left. Many times, in talking again with an animal's owner, I would hear a detail or focus on a symptom I had missed during the initial exam. I relied on those phone calls to explain whatever I hadn't made clear, to add any information I'd forgotten to give, and to make sure I'd understood all the owner's concerns.

ANIMALS AND THEIR PEOPLE

No one becomes a veterinarian for the money or the glamour—the profession doesn't offer much of either. For the most part, people decide to become veterinarians because they're interested in medicine and enjoy working with animals. But on that heady day when senior veterinary students first walk into an exam room on their own, it becomes clear to them—if they hadn't realized it before—that they are going to be working with people, too. Those dogs, cats, and guinea pigs don't amble into the veterinary hospital on their own. Attached to every animal is a human being, and the vet has as much to learn from listening and talking to the person as she does from examining the patient.

Watching my fellow students as we made our way through vet school at Tufts University, I realized that the talking-to-people part of the job can be just as difficult to learn as the medicine part, especially for students who are fresh out of college. But I was lucky: I was 35 years old when I entered vet school, and I'd spent a decade as a magazine writer and editor before that. Communicating with people came fairly easily to me.

TALK THERAPY

I had always hoped to write an "Ask the Vet" column for the local newspaper, or at least to put together a few concise handouts on common diseases that I could give to my clients to cover any gaps in my whirlwind exam-room explanations, but I never got around to it. Then an ideal forum for combining my veterinary and writing skills materialized. Nina Munk, a writer for publications like *Vanity Fair* and *The New York Times Magazine*, was launching a website for New York City dog owners, and she wanted a vet to answer health questions online.

Nina had come up with the idea for *Urbanhound.com* when she got her first "city dog," a handsome and charming Brittany puppy named Mack. Even with her formidable reporting skills, she had found very little useful and organized information about the ins and outs of dog ownership in New York City. And yet the city was filled with dogs—over a million of them. Recognizing an audience and a need, and being an archetypal New Yorker, Nina created the website *she* wanted to read. She designed *Urbanhound.com* to be sophisticated and sassy—Dogs for Smart People, not Dogs for Dummies.

The questions I received on the website echoed my experience in practice. The people who e-mailed me wanted clear, complete, understandable information about what was going on with their dogs. In many cases, they already had a diagnosis from their own vets—they just hadn't understood all the details, and they wanted to know more. Other times, they had questions they were too embarrassed to bring up in the exam room, such as "Why does my dog scoot her bottom on the rug?" or "Is it normal for my female dog to mount other dogs—and Aunt Ethel's leg?"

WHY I WROTE THIS BOOK

I wrote *The Complete Healthy Dog Handbook* to answer as many canine health questions as I possibly could, clearly and completely. I wanted a crib sheet I could refer to in the exam room when time or words (or both) failed me as I was trying to explain a complicated disease to a concerned dog owner. I wanted to teach dog owners how to use their powers of observation so they could be the best possible health advocates for their pets. I wanted to save people from making unnecessary trips to the vet, and yet rush them in when their dogs really needed to be there. And yes, I wanted to tell people that tapeworms in a dog's feces are not an emergency, and please don't call your vet in the middle of the night if you see them.

HOW TO USE THIS BOOK

If you don't have a dog yet but are thinking about getting one, start by reading Chapter 1, "Choosing a Healthy Dog or Puppy." Along with describing how to assess a dog's health and temperament, the chapter discusses how to integrate a dog with a career, kids, a dog-allergic family member, and other aspects of your life. The chapter ends with a Health Checklist for 130 Popular Breeds and 13 "Designer Dogs." Before you set your heart on a certain breed, find out about its potential health problems and your potential veterinary expenses.

If you already have a dog and he's less than a year old, start by reading Chapter 2, "Raising a Healthy Puppy." It will tell you everything you need to know about puppy vaccines, illnesses, spaying and neutering, and other first-year concerns. If your puppy is a purebred, look up his breed in the Health Checklist in Chapter 1 to see whether you should be on the lookout for particular health problems. And because puppies can be accident-prone, flip through Part 3, the Quick Reference section on first aid and injuries, and fill out the Emergency Numbers chart on page 496 so you'll know where to find help in a hurry.

If your dog is more than a year old, start with Chapter 3, "Keeping Your Adult and Senior Dog Healthy." Along with addressing the new vaccine protocols, nutrition, and dental care, the chapter also describes how to keep the older dog happy and comfortable. After you've boned up on preventive care and wellness, you probably will want to read up on your dog's specific health concerns in Part 2, Common Canine Illnesses. Part 2 covers everything from allergies and other skin diseases (Chapter 4) to end-of-life issues (Chapter 17).

Owners of adult dogs should also familiarize themselves with Part 3, the Quick Reference section, and fill out the Emergency Numbers chart on page 496 before a crisis arises. Chapter 18, "First Aid Basics and Poison Control," covers such topics as taking your dog's temperature, heart rate, and respiratory rate; stocking a canine first-aid kit; clipping and cleaning wounds; and common household toxins. Chapter 19, "ABC Guide to Injuries and Emergencies," gives clear and concise instructions for coping with more than 70 emergencies, from bee stings to choking to toad poisoning.

Finally, Part 4, Healthy Dog Resources, provides information on pet health insurance, alternative and complementary medicine, veterinary specialists, and the best health-related dog websites.

A caution for those of you who have cats as well as dogs: don't assume that *anything* in this book applies to cats. As we're taught in vet school, "Cats are not small dogs." Their systems, nutritional needs, and reactions to medication differ in significant ways from those of dogs, and treating a cat the same way you would a dog can be disastrous.

Finally, please understand that this book is not a substitute for your own vet. Don't try to diagnose and treat your dog single-handedly. Rather, use the book as a guide for keeping your dog healthy and for working with your vet when your dog is ill. When you and your vet are partners, your dog will be healthier, your vet can do the highest-level work, and you, I hope, will get to experience the best my profession has to offer.

Betsy Brevitz, D.V.M.

Part 1
Preventive Health Care

CHAPTER 1

Choosing a Healthy Dog or Puppy

IT'S LIKE FALLING IN LOVE. Deciding to get a dog is exciting and joyful, and you won't want to slow down even for a moment to think through the details. But sharing your home with a dog is not just love, it's marriage—a commitment to stand by and care for another creature for a lifetime. So do your research, take your time, and look beyond that adorable face and those delightful puppy antics to consider whether the two of you will be happy and healthy together over the long run.

GETTING A DOG

"I really want a dog—I think. I love them, and my family always had dogs when I was a kid, but I know that having a dog as well as an office job may be a challenge. What do you think? And how do I decide what kind of dog would be best for me?"

A re dogs wonderful? Yes. Is everyone who has a dog always glad he does? Not necessarily. Will you be happy if you get a dog, and if so, what kind should it be? Those are questions only you can answer, but thinking about the following canine compatibility factors can help you decide.

Your daily grind. How many hours of the average day will your dog be home alone? If the answer is more than four hours, an adult dog would do better than a puppy. If it's more than eight hours a day, even an adult dog is likely to become lonely and bored, which may translate into barking, howling, chewing on furniture and other objects, or urinating or defecating in the house. Dog walkers and dog daycare centers can provide a lonely dog with companionship and exercise, but to get a dog just to keep you company for the few hours that you're home in the evening doesn't seem fair to the dog. If you're gone all day but still desperately want a dog, consider either "sharing" a friend's dog—by arranging to walk or play with the dog for an hour several times a week—or volunteering to walk dogs for a local animal shelter.

Fitness fiend or couch potato? Some people like to spend their free time hiking, biking, or skating, while others are happiest reading or relaxing at home. Look for a dog with an energy level that matches yours. A Newfoundland or Greyhound is more likely to be content puttering around the house with you than is a Border Collie or Weimaraner, who prefer to be on the go all the time.

Experience counts. Consider your background in training and handling dogs. Some breeds simply aren't good "starter dogs." Rottweilers, for example, are wonderful when they're paired with a calm, steady, seasoned owner, but they can be 120 pounds of trouble in the hands of a novice. And don't be fooled by size—many Jack Russells and other terrier breeds are "too much dog" for many people. If you're interested in a purebred dog, research the breed's personality. If you're interested in a mixed-breed dog, learn how to do some basic temperament testing (see page 16), or ask a trainer to help you find a suitable dog.

Maintenance and upkeep. Some dogs require daily brushing or combing to keep their coats from becoming matted. If this is not your idea of a good time, stay away from breeds with long, silky hair, such as Maltese, Old English Sheepdogs, and Afghan Hounds. Dogs whose coats are clipped—such as Poodles, Schnauzers, and Kerry Blue Terriers—need a haircut about every six weeks, plus twice-weekly brushing and frequent face washing to keep their beards and eyebrows from getting crusty. Short- to medium-haired dogs are the easiest to keep clean: figure on brushing them thoroughly once a week and bathing them once a month or so.

The kid factor. Some dogs get along great with kids, and others do not. If you have children, or if children visit your home frequently, a kid-compatible dog will make your life simpler (see page 12).

WHAT'S WRONG WITH
THAT PUPPY IN THE WINDOW?

Please don't buy a dog from a pet store. Buy all the supplies you need there, but get your dog from a shelter or a top-notch breeder. Here's why:

❏ **A dog should not be an impulse buy.** The decision to get a dog should not be prompted by a window display of eight-week-old Pugs. If you haven't given serious thought to how a dog will fit into your life, wait.

❏ **Dogs in pet stores are not the best of show.** Pet stores sell dogs purely to make a profit. Good breeders, on the other hand, are also in the business for the love of the breed—they work hard to produce healthy puppies free of genetic disorders, and they also breed for sound temperament.

❏ **Buying a dog from a pet store supports puppy mills.** Because pet stores need a consistent supply of animals, they get their dogs mainly from large commercial breeders known as puppy mills, which churn out dogs without regard to breed standards, health, or temperament. Dogs bred in puppy mills are more likely to suffer from malnutrition, disease, genetic defects, and overall poor quality.

❏ **Service counts.** Few pet stores have the knowledge, time, or inclination to help you after you take your dog home. A good breeder, by contrast, is an invaluable source of information. She can help you pick the right breed, and she'll stay in touch with you and your dog forever, offering information and help each step of the way. A conscientious breeder will even take back a dog at any time if you feel you can no longer care for him. Well-run shelters are also great resources. They'll help you choose a dog that is well suited to you, and will often provide free or low-cost spaying or neutering, microchipping (see page 15), and even obedience classes.

PUPPY OR ADULT?

"My husband and I have agreed to get a dog, but he thinks we should adopt an older dog and I really want a puppy. Now what?"

Puppies and adult dogs each have their points. To settle your impasse, you and your husband could discuss the advantages and disadvantages of each, described below, until you reach an agreement; or you could keep an open mind while looking at both puppies and adult dogs, and then get the one neither of you can resist.

Puppies are adorable—but like babies, they require a tremendous amount of care. They can't be left alone for more than two or three hours in a row. They may nip your hands and chew your furniture. They need to be house-trained and socialized. And veterinary bills for the first year of a puppy's life can really add up: puppies need vaccine boosters every three weeks until they're between three and four months old, and they should be spayed or neutered at around six months.

An adult dog, on the other hand, is likely to be calmer and better behaved than a puppy. She may already be house-broken and even obedience trained. And adopting an adult dog can mean fewer surprises, because maturity reveals many health and temperament problems that may be hidden in a puppy. But be aware that although some dogs come up for adoption because their owners died or moved someplace that doesn't allow dogs, others are given up because of health or behavior problems.

PUREBREDS VS. MIXED BREEDS

"I'm torn between buying the purebred dog of my dreams and waiting to find the right mixed-breed dog in a shelter."

Both mixed breeds and purebreds can be wonderful, so there's no right or wrong choice here. Weigh the advantages and disadvantages in the lists below—and then visit a few shelters to give fate a vote in your decision.

MIXED-BREED PROS
❑ If you adopt from an animal shelter, you're providing a home to a dog that really needs one.
❑ You may be saving a dog from being killed because no one wants him.
❑ You're not contributing to pet overpopulation.
❑ You're getting a dog for a low price, and if the dog's from a shelter, you're probably eligible for free or low-cost spaying or neutering and obedience classes.
❑ Your dog will be one-of-a-kind. To find

out exactly *what* kind, you can even have his DNA analyzed, for around $150 (*www.wisdompanel.com*).

MIXED-BREED CONS
❑ You may not be able to predict your dog's eventual size and temperament.
❑ You won't know your dog's background; he may not have been cared for properly and could have health or behavior problems.
❑ Although there's a popular perception that mixed breeds are healthier than purebreds because mutts are not inbred, a mixed-breed dog can have any of the health problems seen in a purebred, including hip dysplasia, allergies, and heart disease.

PUREBRED PROS
❑ You can do research to choose a breed that matches your preferences in looks, personality, and aptitudes.
❑ If you buy from a skilled and conscientious breeder, your dog will have been bred to high standards of appearance, health, and disposition.
❑ If you buy from a skilled and conscientious breeder, the puppy and her mother will have received excellent prenatal and postnatal care.
❑ If you buy from a skilled and conscientious breeder, you'll always have someone to turn to for help with your dog.

PUREBRED CONS
❑ The breed you want may be prone to certain genetic disorders.
❑ You may have to wait for the right dog to become available, because good breeders don't churn out puppies on demand.
❑ Your dog may cost hundreds to thousands of dollars.

BREED BASICS

Whether you want a purebred or a mixed breed, knowing breed characteristics can help you find the right dog (you can usually guess at least one or two of the breeds in a mutt's ancestry). A dog's breed makeup influences not only his appearance but also his personality and aptitudes.

The 150 or so breeds recognized by the American Kennel Club (new breeds are admitted periodically) are divided into seven broad groups: sporting, hound, working, terrier, toy, herding, and nonsporting, a catch-all group for dogs that don't fit into the other categories. Because the dogs in each group (except for nonsporting) were bred for a certain purpose, they usually share such general traits as energy level, tendency toward aggression, and trainability, as outlined in the table below.

AKC GROUP	BRED TO ...	COMMON TRAITS	BREEDS INCLUDE	POSSIBLE DRAWBACKS
Sporting	... find and retrieve game.	Active, friendly, alert	Retrievers, spaniels, setters	Without plenty of exercise, sporting dogs can become bored and destructive.
Hound	... track game.	Hardy and brave	Beagles, Dachshunds, Greyhounds	Hounds can be stubborn and hard to train. Driven by tracking instinct, they may roam if let off the leash. Some have a loud, baying bark that can be annoying.
Working	... guard, pull sleds, and rescue.	Intelligent and strong-willed	Rottweilers, Siberian Huskies, Great Danes	Working dogs are large and strong, and they can be aggressive and territorial.
Terrier	... hunt and kill rats and other vermin.	Scrappy, self-confident, relentless	Jack Russells, Westies, American Staffordshires	Stubborn and focused, terriers can be hard to train. Originally bred to fight to the death, they rarely back down—even when their owners want them to.
Toy	... be companions.	Small and affectionate	Pugs, Toy Poodles, Maltese	Toys may be fragile and prone to yapping.
Herding	... herd livestock.	Intelligent, alert, energetic	German Shepherds, Border Collies, Welsh Corgis	Without plenty of exercise and stimulation, herding dogs may become bored and destructive. May chase and bark at children in an attempt to herd them.

BREED RESCUE

"I'd like to adopt an older purebred dog. How can I find one?"

You can find purebred dogs through breeders, animal shelters (yes, people give up purebreds as well as mutts), or breed rescue organizations. Breed rescue is a matchmaking service for purebred dogs in need of a good home and people who know and understand the breed's needs and temperament.

Rescue groups for American Kennel Club breeds can be found on the AKC website: *www.akc.org/breeds/rescue.cfm.* To find rescue groups for non-AKC breeds, use a good Internet search engine. Petfinder is an online database of animals available from more than 10,000 adoption groups throughout the United States and Canada. You can search for dogs by age, gender, size, location, and breed at *www.petfinder.com.*

FINDING A GOOD BREEDER

"I'm guessing the best way to find a good purebred dog is to find a good breeder, but how do I do that?"

Anyone can call himself a dog breeder (after all, the dogs do most of the work). The trick is finding a skilled and responsible breeder, and there's no simple way to do that. For example, the American Kennel Club (AKC) doesn't monitor breeders or certify the quality of their dogs, so knowing that a breeder's puppies are "AKC registered" tells you only that they're purebred.

To find a good breeder, get recommendations from people you trust. Other resources include dog shows (where you can talk to breeders and meet their dogs),

breed clubs (whose officers can recommend reputable breeders in your area), and breed rescue organizations. Online directories of breeders, like those listed below, can provide leads, but remember that the breeders haven't been screened:

❑ American Kennel Club Breeder Referral Contacts
  www.akc.org/breederinfo/breeder_search.cfm
❑ InfoDog's National Breeders Directory
  www.infodog.com/brag/breedbystate/
❑ Breeders.net
  www.breeders.net/search.php

Once you've narrowed your search to three or four breeders, interview them by phone and then, if it seems worthwhile, in person. Make sure that they breed for temperament and health as well as for appearance, screen for breed-related health problems, assess whether you will be a responsible dog owner, and have friendly dogs and clean, orderly kennels. Don't be in a rush to buy a dog—a good breeder is likely to have a waiting list of people who want puppies.

THE UNICORN AND THE DOG THAT DOESN'T SHED

"My husband really wants a dog. I'm not much of an animal person, but I wouldn't mind getting a dog as long as it wasn't too messy. Are there dogs that don't shed?"

Dogs that don't have hair don't shed, but that would pretty much limit you to a Chinese Crested or a Mexican Hairless. Otherwise, every hair on a dog is going to fall out every few months and potentially wind up on your rug, sofa, and clothing.

Certain dogs do shed more than others, however. A dog's follicles produce two types of hair: longer, coarser primary hairs and thinner, finer secondary hairs. Depending on the type of hair coat, a dog may have a lot of primary hairs, a lot of secondary hairs, or a lot of both. Primary hairs, being longer and thicker, are the most noticeable when they attach themselves to your best wool pants or billow in the corners of the living room. German Shepherds, Bernese Mountain Dogs, and other breeds that were developed to work outdoors in cold weather have huge amounts of both types of hair, so you'll probably want to stay away from those.

Dogs who have few primary hairs and many secondary hairs usually feel soft or silky, like a Soft-Coated Wheaten Terrier or certain spaniels. When fanciers of a breed say their dogs "don't shed" or "have hair, not fur," they're referring to a coat with a lot of secondary hairs. You may want to steer your husband toward a dog with that type of coat.

A second option for keeping your house neater is a dog with a curly or kinky coat that is clipped every six weeks or so, like a Poodle or Wire Fox Terrier. The regular clipping and bathing will remove much of the loose hair, leaving less to accumulate in the house.

Third, you can adopt a huge and hairy beast but keep ahead of the mess by giving him a few swipes with a brush or comb every day and bathing him about twice a month to remove loose hair. Or alter your perspective and regard the fuzz the way I do: "It's not dirt, it's just dog hair."

By the way, shedding, no matter how excessive it may seem, is almost never the result of illness or a nutritional deficiency, so adding supplements to a dog's diet won't help.

DESIGNER DOG BREEDS

"I'm preparing to get a dog, and I've done a lot of research online. A Labradoodle or a Puggle sounds perfect, but I've gotten conflicting advice on these breeds. What do you think?"

Cute and popular though they may be, in my opinon "designer dogs"—crosses between two established breeds—are overpriced, inconsistent in quality, and prone to all the health problems of their parent breeds. The current designer dog craze, which started with the Labradoodle (Labrador Retriever/Poodle cross) and Puggle (Pug/Beagle cross) around the year 2000, has gone on long enough now for most vets to have treated many dogs from each of the most common crosses, including Goldendoodles (Golden Retriever/Poodle), Jugs (Jack Russell Terrier/Pug), Labbes (Labrador Retriever/Beagle, also called mini Labs), Malti-Tzus (Maltese/Shih Tzu), Cavachons (Cavalier King Charles Spaniel/Bichon Frisé), and Chorkies (Chihuahua/Yorkshire Terrier). Here's what we've learned:

1. There is no breed consistency within any designer breed, whether you're talking first generation, second generation, or beyond. These dogs can look like either parent or neither parent. You can't accurately predict their adult size, body type, color, coat type, or temperament.

The strangest Labradoodle I've seen so far was shipped from Australia and cost my clients several thousand dollars. He was around 12 weeks old when I first saw him, unrecognizable as a Labradoodle or any other breed, and so subdued I thought he was ill. As he grew to adulthood neither his looks nor his

THE 25 MOST POPULAR BREEDS IN AMERICA

What makes a breed popular? Partly its looks and disposition, and partly fashion. The Labrador Retriever has ranked No. 1 in American Kennel Club registrations since 1991, probably due to its versatility as a family pet, hunting dog, and service dog. But back in the early 1930s, Boston Terriers were the most popular. Then came Cocker Spaniels, Beagles, and from 1960 to 1982, Poodles.

Fashion is fickle, and just as quickly as a breed becomes popular, it can drop right out of favor. In 1990 there were 105,642 Cocker Spaniels registered with the AKC; in 2003, the number fell to 19,036. It's important to note that the more popular a breed is, the higher the percentage of poor-quality puppies there will be for sale, bred by people who know more about marketing trends than they do about dogs.

Below are the top 25 AKC breed registrations for 2007. For updates, visit the AKC's website: *www.akc.org.*

1. Labrador Retriever
2. Yorkshire Terrier
3. German Shepherd
4. Golden Retriever
5. Beagle
6. Boxer
7. Dachshund
8. Poodle
9. Shih Tzu
10. Bulldog
11. Miniature Schnauzer
12. Chihuahua
13. Pomeranian
14. Pug
15. Rottweiler
16. Boston Terrier
17. Cocker Spaniel
18. German Shorthaired Pointer
19. Maltese
20. Shetland Sheepdog
21. Doberman Pinscher
22. Pembroke Welsh Corgi
23. Great Dane
24. Siberian Husky
25. Cavalier King Charles Spaniel

Left to right, 5 of the 10 perennially favorite breeds: Beagle, German Shepherd, Golden Retriever, Labrador Retriever, Dachshund

temperament matched those of a Lab or a Poodle—he looked a bit like a miniature Afghan Hound, and was unusually quiet. And then his hair started to fall out (most likely from an irreversible hair follicle disorder). "I paid a lot of money for this dog!" protested the owner. And so she had, but she didn't get what she wanted or expected.

If your goal in buying a purebred dog is knowing what he will look and act like, then forget all designer dog breeds for at least the next 20 years. By then, those that are still around may have become true breeds, with their undesirable traits weeded out and their desirable traits made consistent and reproducible.

2. Designer dogs do not display hybrid vigor, the better health that is said to result from not being inbred. Rather, they combine the health problems of their constituent breeds. In other words, Labradoodles are prone to problems affecting both Labs and Poodles, among them ear infections, allergies, and joint problems; Malti-Tzus are prone to collapsing trachea, knee problems, and bladder stones; and so on. Consult the Health Checklist starting on page 19 for problems to watch for in 13 designer breeds as well as 130 established breeds.

3. You can't design a hypoallergenic dog. A major selling point for Labradoodles and Goldendoodles has been that they allegedly won't cause symptoms in people who are allergic to dogs. If one of these crosses happens to have a Poodle-type coat, and if you have that dog bathed and clipped every six to eight weeks, which reduces the amount of hair and dander that collects in your house, then that dog might be less of an allergic trigger to a particular person. Maybe, but maybe not (see "Allergic to Dogs," right, for more on this topic).

4. The traits that make designer dogs appealing are not exclusive to those breeds. Say you're looking for an attractive, medium-size, family-friendly dog. Many breeds (Portuguese Water Dog, Soft-Coated Wheaten Terrier, and Bearded Collie, among many others) and non-designer mixed breeds can match your specifications.

5. The majority of designer dogs for sale today come from "commercial breeders" (the polite term for puppy mills). Puppy mills are quick to capitalize on canine fads, and designer dogs are a hugely lucrative one. The typical puppy mill churns out several different breeds anyway, so mixing them—on purpose or accidentally—is simple. Breeders advertising puppies for sale in magazines and over the Internet often are fronts for puppy mills—you have no way of knowing unless you go to their kennels and see the pups, their parents, and their living conditions in person. Missouri, Pennsylvania, Iowa, Kansas, Nebraska, Arkansas, and Oklahoma are notorious havens for puppy mills. If your local pet store sells dogs with registration papers from those states, they are almost certainly the products of puppy mills. (To find out more about puppy mills, go to the Humane Society of the United States website at *www.hsus.org*).

The bottom line: when searching for a great dog, don't be fooled by the hype.

ALLERGIC TO DOGS

"Our son really wants a dog, but my wife is allergic. I've heard that some breeds are hypoallergenic—they don't bother people who are allergic to other dogs. Is this true?"

No, I'm sorry to report, there's no such thing as a universally hypoallergenic dog. Different people can be allergic to proteins in a dog's hair, skin, saliva, or all three—making each individual's allergic profile slightly different. Some people are more allergic to fluffy hair, others to coarse hair; some react strongly to Labrador Retrievers or German Shepherds and less to other breeds; and so on. Therefore, it's possible that a certain breed—say, a Coton de Tulear—might not bother some dog-allergic people but could make your wife miserably itchy or congested. The only way to know for certain would be to put her in close contact with different breeds or types of dogs until you found one that didn't bother her, which would require a wife who's an extremely good sport as well as access to a lot of dogs.

Pet-supply stores sell sprays and rinses that can be applied to dogs regularly to lessen the allergic symptoms of people around them, but they don't provide 100 percent relief. Bathing the dog once a week with regular dog shampoo will remove loose hair and skin flakes and make the dog less "allergenic." Keeping the dog off the furniture and out of the allergic person's bedroom is helpful, as are air cleaners and super-filtering vacuum cleaners.

CHILDREN AND DOGS

"Our kids love dogs, and we'd like to get one. Which breeds are best with children?"

Dogs and children can be the best of friends, and many people first decide to get a dog "for the children." But good relationships between dogs and children are not automatic. Children are the victims of about 400,000 serious dog bites (those resulting in a visit to a doctor) each year, according to the Centers for Disease Control and Prevention. The rate of dog-bite injuries is highest for children ages five to nine years old. And a dog that's acquired to "teach the children responsibility" may wind up lonely and neglected on a chain in the backyard, or abandoned at an animal shelter.

Creating a mutually safe and rewarding relationship between dogs and children requires thought and planning. Here are some key issues to consider.

Whose dog is it, anyway? Parents often start to think about getting a dog because their children enjoy meeting dogs in the park or reading books or watching videos about dogs (Blue, Clifford, and the Disney Dalmatians being popular examples). But in reality, no child under the age of 12 can take any significant responsibility in caring for a dog, so if your children are younger than that, the dog will be yours, not theirs. Be very clear in your own mind that it

A large dog, no matter how gentle, may accidentally hurt a small child.

DOG-PROOFING YOUR CHILDREN

While you're busy choosing the perfect family dog, don't overlook the other side of the equation: your children. Teaching your children to be good to the dog is just as important as finding a dog that's good with children. Even if a dog "lets" a toddler flop down on top of him or pull his hair, or tolerates an older child yanking him around by the collar or teasing him with food, don't permit such behavior. First, it's unkind to allow a dog to be tormented. And second, even a dog with a very long fuse can one day reach the end of it and retaliate by biting. Don't let babies and toddlers manhandle your dog, and teach older children to be kind and respectful of dogs—your own and others—by following these guidelines:

❏ Never bother a dog when he's eating or sleeping. Leave his food dish alone, even when it's empty, and don't try to take anything out of his mouth.

❏ Don't talk to, pet, tease, or chase a dog that is behind a fence, in a parked car, or on a chain, even if he looks friendly or is wagging his tail.

❏ Always ask the person with a dog if it's OK to say hello to the dog before you walk up to him or pet him. Some dogs are shy or unfriendly and might bark or bite if startled.

❏ Many dogs don't like being touched around the face and ears. Pet them on the back or shoulder instead.

❏ Don't put your face close to a dog's face, stare into his eyes, or grab his neck. That's what dogs do when they're picking a fight with one another, so the dog might think you're being mean and snap at you.

❏ If a dog that's alone rushes up to you, stand as still as a tree. Don't scream, run, or hit or kick the dog. Stay calm and quiet, with your arms at your sides. When the dog loses interest in you and walks away, turn and walk slowly in a different direction.

❏ If a dog knocks you down and tries to bite you, be as still as a rock. Kneel with your head on the ground and cover the back of your head and neck with your arms. You're less likely to be injured if you're curled up with your face and neck protected.

will be your choice, your dog, and your responsibility, not your children's.

Size matters. Very large dogs and very small dogs generally are not good choices for families with preteen children. A child who is considerably smaller than the family dog is likely to have trouble earning the dog's respect and obedience to such safety-based commands as "Off" and "Sit." A very small dog may be intimidated by the rambunctious play and less-than-gentle handling of young children. Finally, to invoke the worst-case scenario, a large dog who attacks a small child will be able to inflict much more serious damage than a smaller dog could. Conversely, a child can seriously injure a small or fragile dog without meaning to.

Infants are different. Even dogs that are calm and friendly with children often don't know what to make of infants, so special vigilance is required when babies and dogs are together. For more about introducing a dog to an infant, see page 189.

Attributes of a kid-friendly dog. The dogs that get along best with children are people-friendly, calm, tolerant of being petted and handled, easygoing, and not shy or skittish. In many ways, they are "middle-of-the-road" dogs—neither fearful of children nor overly self-confident and independent. Fear and overconfidence (i.e., dominance) are the two main triggers for aggression in dogs, so they are qualities to be avoided in a family dog.

Breeds that are good or bad with children. It's tempting to think that "breed profiling" provides a foolproof way of choosing a dog who will be good with children. Breeds were developed for certain purposes and personality traits as well as for their appearance, so it seems reasonable to think that dogs of the same breed will have similar temperaments. But the differences in personality between two dogs of the same breed can be enormous, as can the dogs' upbringing and training.

Ultimately, you are choosing an individual dog, not a breed. Focus on the kid-friendly attributes listed above, and ask breeders and shelters for their advice on selecting an appropriate dog, but remember that temperament testing will tell you the most about an individual dog (see page 16).

Worms and germs. Can children catch diseases from dogs? Yes, they can, although "dog germs" are neither as numerous nor as easily contracted as many parents fear. People can catch worms and other intestinal parasites by ingesting microscopic amounts of feces from a contaminated animal. Parasites such as fleas, ticks, and scabies mites can feast on people as well as animals. Fortunately, preventing attacks by these parasites is straightforward, and is covered in detail in Chapter 6. (Note that pinworms and head lice, two banes of the preschool and elementary school set, are not spread by animals but rather from child to child.)

Of the bacteria and viruses to which both dogs and people are susceptible, strep throat, parvovirus, and Lyme disease seem to raise the most parental concerns, but leptospirosis and rabies are the real bad guys. Vets are sometimes asked by parents, at the behest of their pediatrician, to swab the family dog's throat and do a bacterial culture to determine whether the dog is the source of a child's recurring strep infection. This is a waste of time. Many dogs naturally carry Group G strep, but it is not infectious to people. Many people naturally carry Group A strep, the agent of strep throat, often without being ill themselves. So the kid is almost certainly catching strep from another person, not from the dog.

Similarly, the parvovirus responsible for fifth disease, which can cause miscarriages in pregnant women and a rash, fever, and joint swelling in children, is completely different from the parvo that causes severe bloody diarrhea in dogs, and they don't cross between the two species. And people can catch Lyme disease only by being bitten by an infected deer tick, not through contact with an infected dog.

Lepto and rabies, on the other hand, are deadly diseases that are spread through contact with infected urine (in the case of lepto) and animal bites or scratches (in the case of rabies). For more on the risks and prevention of those two diseases, see pages 63 and 320.

IDENTIFICATION, PLEASE

"Should I have my dog microchipped or tattooed? Are the microchips harmful in any way?"

"Microchips cause cancer!" That was the message being passed around dog websites in September 2007, after an Associated Press article reported that cancer had been found in a few research mice at the site of their microchips. The reality is that millions of dogs and cats have been microchipped over the past 15 years, and apart from one or two documented cases, vets simply aren't seeing cancer associated with microchips in companion animals.

A microchip is an electronic label about the size of a grain of rice that is inserted under the skin, usually between a dog's shoulder blades. It is a safe and virtually permanent form of identification. (Rarely, a microchip will work its way back out through the skin and be lost.)

Each microchip is imprinted with a number that can be read by a scanner. All animal shelters and most veterinarians' offices have scanners, and all found animals are scanned for microchips. A national database matches the microchip number with your name, address, and phone number (you provide that information by mail or online after the microchip is inserted).

Find out more through American Kennel Club Companion Animal Recovery, 800-252-7894, *www.akccar.org;* Avid Micro-Chip ID Systems, 800-434-2843, *www*

.microchipidsystems.com; or HomeAgain, 888-466-3242, *www.homeagain.com.* A growing number of places, including Singapore and the United Kingdom, require that all dogs entering the country have a microchip.

Tattoos are another virtually permanent form of identification—"virtually" in this instance because they may fade or blur over time and become difficult to read. Dogs are usually tattooed on a thinly haired part of the body, such as the inside of the ear or thigh. Tattooing is mildly uncomfortable but not particularly painful—mainly dogs resent having to hold still for the procedure. Like microchips, tattoos must be registered with a national database in order to be useful.

For more information on tattoo registry, contact American Kennel Club Companion Animal Recovery, 800-252-7894, *www.akccar.org;* National Dog Registry, 800-637-3647, *www.nationaldog registry.com;* or Tatoo-A-Pet, 800-828-8667, *www.tattoo-a-pet.com.*

Even if your dog has a microchip or tattoo, also keep a collar and ID tag on him at all times. Unexciting and low-tech though it is, a collar and tag is still the best and fastest way to reunite a dog and his owner within the same neighborhood or town. Anyone who finds your dog can read who he belongs to and call you, or even walk or drive your dog back home. The collar should be strong, comfortable, and adjusted so it doesn't pull over your dog's head easily. Use a leather or nylon nonsliding collar for the ID tag, not a choke chain—a sliding collar or choke chain could get caught on something and strangle your dog. When you travel with your dog, add a temporary tag to his collar listing a local phone number where you can be reached.

(continued on page 18)

CHOOSING MR. OR MS. CONGENIALITY

You may know what qualities you're looking for in a dog, but how do you pick out those traits in a rambunctious litter of puppies, or a lineup of madly barking dogs at an animal shelter? You talk to the people who care for the dogs; you compare the dogs' behavior with one another; and then you give each dog you're interested in a simple temperament test. Following are two basic tests a novice dog owner can use to check out a potential canine companion: one for puppies up to about six months old, the other for puppies and dogs older than six months.

PUPPY TEST: Take the puppy to a quiet area, away from his mother and littermates. Most novice dog owners will find a dog that is neither too skittish nor too dominant the easiest to train and bond with. In each example below, the responses are ordered from fearful to dominant. The "moderate," or preferred, response is in italics.

1. Set the puppy down and let him walk away from you, then crouch down and call him back to you in a friendly, happy voice. Does he put his tail down and stay away? *Walk over to you and wag his tail?* Run over to you and jump up or bite playfully at your hands or feet? Ignore you and explore the room on his own?

2. Pet the puppy from his head to his tail. Does he cringe? Roll over on his back? *Nuzzle your hand or wag his tail?* Nip at your hand? Walk away?

3. Roll the puppy gently onto his back and hold him there with a hand on his chest for 8 or 10 seconds. Does he yelp, cringe, or tremble? *Struggle to stand up for a few seconds and then calm down?* Flail and struggle wildly and bite or growl?

In the rollover test (Step 3), look for a puppy who accepts gentle restraint.

4. Drop a set of keys on the floor to make a sudden noise. Does the puppy cringe and cower? *Startle, then look curiously toward the noise?* Bark loudly or "attack" the keys? Ignore the noise?

5. Gently squeeze one of the puppy's toes. Does he yelp or jerk his foot back wildly? *Pull his foot back calmly?* Growl or bite at your hand?

6. Put a small amount of canned dog food in a dish and set it in front of the puppy. When he smells the food or starts to eat it, pick up the dish. Does he shy away from your hand? *Look up at you?* Jump up at the dish? Growl or bark?

ADULT DOG TEST: The goal is to find a dog that is friendly and trainable without being skittish or aggressive. Cross off your list of potential adoptees any dog that reacts aggressively to you or anyone else at any stage of the temperament test. Aggressive behavior includes staring; standing stiffly at attention, possibly with a raised, slightly wagging tail; lifting or twitching the lips to show the teeth; growling, even if the tail is wagging; and snapping or biting. If you are unsure of yourself around dogs, ask an experienced dog handler to evaluate the dogs for you.

In each example below, the responses are ordered from fearful to dominant. The "moderate," or preferred, response is in italics.

1. When you first look at the dog—in a dog run, or brought to you by another person—does the dog back away from you? *Approach you in a friendly manner, with a slightly lowered head and wagging tail?* Stand stiffly at attention and watch you?

2. Put the dog in a flat collar (not a choke collar) attached to a four-foot leash. Walk around the room and see if the dog will follow you. Does he plant his feet and refuse to move? *Move toward you when you call him in a friendly voice?* Lunge against the leash or bark wildly?

3. Stroke the dog's back. Does he flinch or cower? *Wag his tail and stay close to you?* Move away from your touch or ignore you?

4. Ask someone to make a sudden noise, such as by hitting a metal desk or chair. Does the dog cower and try to run? *Startle, then look toward the noise or at you?* Bark wildly or lunge at the noise?

5. While petting the dog, run your hand down each leg to the foot and pick the foot up for a moment. Run your hands up the dog's neck to his ears and stroke them. Does he flinch and jump when you try to touch his feet or ears? *Allow you to touch them without making a big fuss?* Struggle or growl when you try to touch them?

6. Put a small amount of canned dog food in a dish on the floor. Let the dog smell or start to eat the food, then push the dish away from him with a broom or long stick. Does he cower? *Watch the dish move or follow it to continue eating?* Growl, bark, or attack the stick?

7. Take the dog for a walk outside with a flat collar and short leash. Does he seem skittish or frightened? *Happy and excited?* Does he lunge against the leash or bark continuously?

Observe his reactions to other people, cars, and animals. Is he nervous? *Interested but controllable?* Hyperactive or threatening?

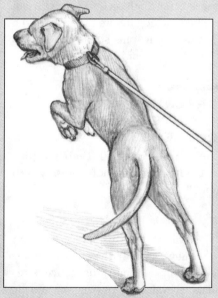

Training a dog who pulls wildly on the leash will require skill and patience.

(continued from page 15)

PUPPY LEMON LAWS

"After I spent $1,000 on a 12-week-old puppy, my veterinarian discovered he has a serious heart defect—one that could potentially be corrected with expensive surgery. What's the breeder's financial responsibility to me in this situation?"

Many states have "puppy lemon laws," which address the seller's responsibility in such situations. Your vet or your state's consumer affairs office can tell you whether your state has such a law and exactly what it covers. In general, puppy lemon laws require that a seller exchange the unhealthy dog for a healthy one; take back the dog and refund the purchase price; or pay veterinary costs for treating the condition, up to the purchase price of the dog. Written confirmation from a veterinarian of the dog's illness or defect is required. Usually there is a time limit on how long you can have had the dog before discovering the problem, but in some states that limit is as long as one year.

SCREENING FOR INHERITED HEALTH PROBLEMS

"Can't breeders check their puppies for health defects before they sell them?"

Most breeders want to produce the healthiest, best examples of their breed they can. For that reason, many breeders have their prospective sires and dams evaluated for common genetic health problems. Puppies can also be checked for some—but not all—genetic problems before they are sent to new homes. For the prospective owner, it's important to understand what the health tests are, what the scores mean, and what such tests can and can't predict about the dog you are thinking of buying. Following are three of the most common screening tests.

Orthopedic Foundation for Animals (OFA) screening for hip dysplasia. The OFA keeps records on adult dogs whose hips have been x-rayed and graded for signs of hip dysplasia. The x-rays are evaluated independently by three certified veterinary radiologists, whose scores are averaged. A dog must be two years old or older before being given an official score, because hip conformation can change as a dog grows. The OFA passing scores are Excellent, Good, and Fair. Dogs whose x-rays show signs of dysplasia are ranked Borderline, Mild, Moderate, or Severe Dysplasia. Only dogs that receive a passing score should be bred.

If you're thinking about buying a puppy whose breed has a high incidence of hip dysplasia—such as a Labrador Retriever, Rottweiler, or German Shepherd—it's wise to ask the breeder whether the parents' hips were screened and what their OFA scores were. Hip dysplasia is not a single-gene, yes-or-no, black-and-white disease, however. A puppy whose parents' hips were rated Good or Excellent is *less* likely to develop hip dysplasia than one whose parents' scores were Fair, but that is not an absolute guarantee that he will not have the disease.

The OFA also compiles information on elbow dysplasia (which often accompanies hip dysplasia), knee problems, thyroid problems, and inherited heart defects. Information about a particular dog can be found online by entering the dog's name and breed or its OFA or AKC registration number on the OFA website: *www.offa.org/search.html*.

PennHIP screening for hip dysplasia. In the PennHIP method, outward pressure is applied on the hip joints while they are x-rayed to determine how loose they are, rather than x-raying them in a neutral position as in OFA screening. (The dog is anesthetized for the x-rays, so the procedure isn't painful.) The amount of laxity in the hip joints is measured on the x-rays and assigned a percentile score according to the dog's breed. PennHIP x-rays can be done on puppies as young as four months old, and the amount of laxity has been shown to correlate closely with the development of arthritic hips later on. If you're thinking about buying a puppy or adult whose breed has a high incidence of hip dysplasia, ask whether the dog or her parents have had PennHIP x-rays. A veterinarian must be specially trained and certified to do PennHIP x-rays. To find such a veterinarian, go to the PennHIP website: *www.pennhip.org*.

Canine Eye Registration Foundation (CERF) screening for eye defects. A CERF exam is a comprehensive eye exam performed by a certified veterinary ophthalmologist. CERF exams can uncover a wide range of inherited eye problems, including conditions affecting the eyelids, cornea (surface of the eye), iris (colored portion of the eye), lens, and retina and optic disc (in the back of the eye). Cataracts in young dogs and "Collie eye" (see page 217) are two of the specific conditions evaluated on a CERF exam.

Puppies and dogs of any age can have a CERF exam. Breeders often have their breeding stock "CERFed" so they can avoid passing along genetic eye diseases. More about CERF and inherited eye diseases can be found at *www.vmdb .org/cerf.html*.

Health Checklist for 130 Popular Breeds and 13 "Designer Dogs"

By definition, purebred dogs come from a more limited gene pool than the average mixed-breed dog. The same goes for Labradoodles and other "designer dogs"—intentional crosses between two established breeds. Sometimes efforts to achieve a certain coat color or body type inadvertently pass along undesirable traits at the same time. That doesn't mean all purebred and designer dogs have congenital defects, or that no mixed-breed dogs do—I've seen plenty of Labs with perfect hips and mutts with hip dysplasia or bad knees. The checklist below includes significant health problems that have been reported more

Definitions and references for the health problems listed appear at the end of the checklist.

frequently in certain breeds than in other dogs, as well as a "veterinary cost index." The veterinary cost index is my subjective ranking of the breed's likely veterinary expenses over the dog's lifetime, based on how expensive various disorders are to treat.

$ Routine veterinary expenses, such as vaccinations, heartworm prevention, and dental care.

$$ Likely to incur expenses for one significant medical problem.

$$$ Likely to incur expenses for two or more significant medical problems.

AFFENPINSCHER Patent ductus arteriosus (blood vessel defect); brachycephalic airway syndrome (respiratory disorder); luxating kneecaps; von Willebrand's disease (blood clotting disorder) $$

AFGHAN HOUND Elbow dysplasia, osteochondrosis (joint disorders); immune-mediated skin disease; hypothyroidism; cataracts, glaucoma, lens luxation, progressive retinal atrophy, retinal dysplasia (eye disorders); hemophilia A, von Willebrand's disease (blood clotting disorders) $$

AIREDALE TERRIER Obsessive-compulsive skin injury (behavior disorder); immune-mediated skin disease; cerebellar atrophy (brain disorder); hypothyroidism;

entropion, pannus, progressive retinal atrophy, retinal dysplasia (eye disorders); hemophilia B, von Willebrand's disease, hemolytic anemia (blood disorders) $$

AKITA Bloat, irritable bowel disease (digestive tract disorders); hip dysplasia, osteochondrosis (joint disorders); amyloidosis (joint and kidney disorder); deafness; Cushing's disease (adrenal disorder); hypothyroidism; myasthenia gravis (muscle disorder); lysosomal storage disease (brain disorder); dominance aggression (behavior); allergies, immune-mediated skin disease; cataracts, entropion, glaucoma, progressive retinal atrophy, retinal dysplasia, uveodermatologic syndrome (eye disorders); hemolytic anemia, platelet deficiency, von Willebrand's disease (blood disorders) $$$

ALASKAN MALAMUTE Hip dysplasia, osteochondrosis (joint disorders); kidney dysplasia; laryngeal paralysis (respiratory disorder); diabetes mellitus; nerve atrophy; hermaphroditism (reproductive disorder); hypothyroidism; cataracts, glaucoma, progressive retinal atrophy, uveodermatologic syndrome (eye disorders); hemophilia A, hemophilia B, von Willebrand's disease (blood clotting disorders) $$$

AMERICAN ESKIMO DOG Allergies; hypothyroidism; Cushing's disease (adrenal disorder) $

AMERICAN STAFFORDSHIRE TERRIER Allergies; osteochondrosis (joint disorder); deafness; hypothyroidism; mast cell tumor; cataracts, entropion, progressive retinal atrophy (eye disorders) $$

ANATOLIAN SHEPHERD DOG Hip dysplasia; hypothyroidism; bloat (digestive tract emergency); entropion (eyelid disorder) $

AUSTRALIAN CATTLE DOG Portosystemic shunt (blood vessel defect); hip dysplasia; deafness; epilepsy, lysosomal storage disease (brain disorders); inguinal hernia; cataracts, lens luxation, progressive retinal atrophy, retinal dysplasia (eye disorders); hemophilia A (blood clotting disorder) $$

AUSTRALIAN SHEPHERD Hip dysplasia, osteochondrosis (joint disorders); epilepsy; deafness; hypothyroidism; cataracts, retinal dysplasia, progressive retinal atrophy, uveodermatologic syndrome (eye disorders); von Willebrand's disease (blood clotting disorder) $$

AUSTRALIAN TERRIER Diabetes mellitus; Legg-Calvé-Perthes disease (hip disease); luxating kneecaps; progressive retinal atrophy, cataracts (eye disorders) $$

BASENJI Kidney dysplasia; hypothyroidism; inguinal hernia; inflammatory bowel disease; progressive retinal atrophy, retinal dysplasia (eye disorders); hemolytic anemia, pyruvate kinase deficiency (blood disorders) $$

BASSET HOUND Addison's disease (adrenal disorder); bloat, intussusception (digestive tract emergencies); elbow dysplasia, osteochondrosis, luxating kneecaps (joint disorders); panosteitis (bone disorder); wobbler syndrome (spinal cord disorder); undescended testicle; cystine urine crystals; epilepsy, lysosomal storage disease (brain disorders); hypothyroidism; inguinal hernia; foot infections, immune-mediated skin disease; entropion, glaucoma, lens luxation, progressive retinal atrophy (eye disorders); hemophilia A, hemolytic anemia, von Willebrand's disease (blood disorders) $$$

Basset Hound

BEAGLE Pulmonic stenosis, tetralogy of Fallot, ventricular septal defect (heart defects); amyloidosis (joint and kidney disorder); kidney dysplasia; deafness; epilepsy, cerebellar atrophy, lysosomal storage disease (brain disorders); hermaphroditism (reproductive disorder); hypothyroidism; spinal disk disease; diabetes mellitus; exocrine pancreatic insufficiency (digestive disorder); bladder cancer; allergies; cataracts, glaucoma, lens luxation, progressive retinal atrophy, retinal dysplasia (eye disorders); hemophilia A, hemolytic anemia, von Willebrand's disease, pyruvate kinase deficiency (blood disorders) $$$

BEARDED COLLIE Aortic stenosis (heart disorder); Addison's disease (adrenal disorder); hip dysplasia; hypothyroidism; cataracts, retinal dysplasia (eye disorders); hemolytic anemia, platelet deficiency (blood disorders) **$$**

BEDLINGTON TERRIER
Copper storage disease (liver disease); kidney dysplasia; cataracts, progressive retinal atrophy, retinal dysplasia (eye disorders) **$**

BELGIAN MALINOIS Hip dysplasia; epilepsy; hypothyroidism; progressive retinal atrophy (eye disorder) **$$**

BELGIAN TERVUREN
Osteochondrosis (joint disorder); epilepsy; hypothyroidism; cataracts, pannus, progressive retinal atrophy (eye disorders) **$$**

BERNESE MOUNTAIN DOG Portosystemic shunt (blood vessel defect); elbow dysplasia, hip dysplasia, osteochondrosis (joint disorders); cerebellar atrophy (brain disorder); hypothyroidism; inflammatory bowel disease; immune-mediated skin disease; cataracts, entropion, progressive retinal atrophy, retinal dysplasia (eye disorders) **$$$**

BICHON FRISÉ Ciliary dyskinesia (respiratory disorder); epilepsy, little white shaker syndrome (brain disorders); luxating kneecaps; foot infections; cataracts, entropion, retinal dysplasia (eye disorders); hemophilia B (blood clotting disorder) **$$**

BLOODHOUND Bloat (digestive tract emergency); hip dysplasia, osteochondrosis (joint disorders); hypothyroidism; ectropion, keratoconjunctivitis sicca (eye disorders) **$$**

BORDER COLLIE Deafness; epilepsy; hip dysplasia, osteochondrosis (joint disorders); ciliary dyskinesia (respiratory disorder); lens luxation, progressive retinal atrophy, retinal dysplasia (eye disorders) **$$**

Border Collie

BORDER TERRIER Ventricular septal defect (heart defect); brain or spinal cord tumor; undescended testicle; luxating kneecaps; cataracts, lens luxation, progressive retinal atrophy, retinal dysplasia (eye disorders) **$$**

BORZOI Bloat (digestive tract emergency); hip dysplasia; hypothyroidism; cataracts, pannus, progressive retinal atrophy, retinal dysplasia (eye disorders); von Willebrand's disease (blood clotting disorder) **$$**

BOSTON TERRIER Patent ductus arteriosus (blood vessel defect); Cushing's disease (adrenal disorder); deafness; brachycephalic airway syndrome (respiratory disorder); esophageal stenosis, pyloric stenosis, intussusception (digestive tract disorders); cardiac tumor (cancer); hydrocephalus, pituitary tumor (brain disorders); hypospadias (male urinary tract disorder); hypothyroidism; inguinal hernia; luxating kneecaps; allergies, tail-fold dermatitis (skin disorders); cataracts, entropion, glaucoma, kerato-conjunctivitis sicca, progressive retinal atrophy (eye disorders) $$$

BOUVIER DES FLANDRES Aortic stenosis (heart defect); hip dysplasia, osteochondrosis (joint disorders); hypothyroidism; laryngeal paralysis (respiratory disorder); dominance aggression (behavior); cataracts, entropion, glaucoma (eye disorders); von Willebrand's disease (blood clotting disorder) $$

BOXER Portosystemic shunt (blood vessel defect); aortic stenosis, atrial septal defect, dilated cardiomyopathy (heart disorders); undescended testicle; cystine urine crystals; deafness; epilepsy; mega-esophagus, inflammatory bowel disease, pyloric stenosis (digestive tract disorders); hypothyroidism; osteochondrosis (joint disorder); mast cell tumor, cardiac tumor, testicular tumor, squamous cell carcinoma (cancers); allergies, facial-fold dermatitis, foot infections (skin disorders); cataracts, corneal ulcer, entropion, progressive retinal atrophy (eye disorders); hemophilia A, von Willebrand's disease (blood clotting disorders) $$$

BRIARD Panosteitis (bone disorder); hypothyroidism; cataracts, progressive retinal atrophy (eye disorders); von Willebrand's disease (blood clotting disorder) $

BRITTANY Osteochondrosis (joint disorder); cerebellar atrophy

(brain disorder); hypothyroidism; cata-racts, lens luxation, progressive retinal atrophy, retinal dysplasia (eye disorders); hemophilia A (blood clotting disorder) $

BRUSSELS GRIFFON Hip dysplasia, Legg-Calvé-Perthes disease, luxating kneecaps (joint disorders); brachycephalic airway syndrome (respiratory disorder); hydrocephalus (brain disorder); cataracts, progressive retinal atrophy (eye disorders) $

BUGG (BOSTON TERRIER/ PUG) Patent ductus arteriosus, portosystemic shunt (blood vessel defects); brachycephalic airway syndrome, collapsing trachea (respiratory disorders); allergies, ear infections, facial-fold dermatitis, tail-fold dermatitis (skin disorders); hip dysplasia, Legg-Calvé-Perthes disease, luxating kneecaps (joint disorders); mast cell tumor (cancer); Cushing's disease, Addison's disease (adrenal gland disorders); hypothyroidism; diabetes mellitus; urinary tract infections, urinary stones, hypospadias, bladder cancer (urinary tract disorders); inguinal hernia; deafness; epilepsy, hydrocephalus, encephalitis, pituitary tumor (brain disorders); hermaphroditism (reproductive disorder); spinal disk disease; esophageal stenosis, pyloric stenosis, intussusception, irritable bowel disease (digestive disorders); entropion, pannus, cataracts, glaucoma, keratoconjunctivitis sicca, progressive retinal atrophy (eye disorders) $$$

BULLDOG (ENGLISH BULLDOG) Brachycephalic airway syndrome (respi-ratory disorder); valve disease, pulmonic stenosis, ventricular septal defect (heart defects); pyloric stenosis (digestive tract disorder); hip dysplasia; hydrocephalus (brain disorder); brain or spinal cord tumor, cardiac tumor; undescended testicle; cystine urine crystals; facial-fold dermatitis, deep bacterial skin infections, foot infections, tail-fold dermatitis (skin disorders); hypothyroidism; cataracts, cherry eye, entropion, keratoconjunctivitis sicca (eye disorders); von Willebrand's disease (blood clotting disorder) $$$

BULLMASTIFF Bloat (digestive tract emergency); wobbler syndrome (spinal cord disorder); elbow dysplasia, osteochondrosis (joint disorders); dominance aggression (behavior); cerebellar atrophy (brain disorder); hypothyroidism; entropion, glaucoma, progressive retinal atrophy, retinal dysplasia (eye disorders) $$

BULL TERRIER Osteochondrosis (joint disorder); obsessive-compulsive skin injury, obsessive-compulsive disorder (behavior disorders); laryngeal paralysis (respiratory disorder); inguinal hernia; squamous cell carcinoma (cancer); deep bacterial skin infections; deafness; entropion, lens luxation (eye disorders) $$

BULL TERRIER, MINIATURE Collapsing trachea (respiratory disorder); hypothyroidism; entropion, lens luxation (eye disorders) $

CAIRN TERRIER Portosystemic shunt (blood vessel defect); cerebellar atrophy, hydrocephalus, lysosomal storage disease (brain disorders); undescended testicle; inguinal hernia; cystine urine crystals; hypothyroidism; cataracts, glaucoma, lens luxation, progressive retinal atrophy (eye disorders); hemo-

philia A, hemophilia B, von Willebrand's disease (blood clotting disorders) $$

CANAAN DOG Elbow dysplasia, hip dysplasia (joint disorders); epilepsy; hypothyroidism $

CAVACHON (CAVALIER KING CHARLES SPANIEL/BICHON FRISÉ) Valve disease (heart disorder); ciliary dyskinesia (respiratory disorder); diabetes mellitus; epilepsy, little white shaker syndrome (brain disorders); luxating kneecaps (joint disorder); cataracts, entropion, retinal dysplasia (eye disorders) $$

CAVALIER KING CHARLES SPANIEL Valve disease (heart disorder); diabetes mellitus; epilepsy; hypothyroidism; luxating kneecaps; cataracts, entropion, progressive retinal atrophy, retinal dysplasia (eye disorders); platelet deficiency (blood clotting disorder) $$

CHESAPEAKE BAY RETRIEVER Hip dysplasia, osteochondrosis (joint disorders); epilepsy; hypothyroidism; cataracts, entropion, progressive retinal atrophy, retinal dysplasia (eye disorders); von Willebrand's disease (blood clotting disorder) $$

CHIHUAHUA Portosystemic shunt (blood vessel defect); valve disease, pulmonic stenosis (heart disorders); hydrocephalus, lysosomal storage disease (brain disorders); collapsing trachea, ciliary dyskinesia (respiratory disorders); undescended testicle; cystine urine crystals; hypoglycemia; neck instability; hypothyroidism; myasthenia gravis (muscle disorder); osteochondrosis,

Chihuahua

luxating kneecaps (joint disorders); entropion, glaucoma, keratoconjunctivitis sicca, lens luxation, progressive retinal atrophy (eye disorders); hemophilia A (blood clotting disorder)   **$$$**

CHINESE CRESTED Luxating kneecaps; skin cancer; allergies, bacterial skin infections, contact hypersensitivity, immune-mediated skin disease, seborrhea (skin disorders); undescended testicle; hypothyroidism
$$

CHOW Bloat, inflammatory bowel disease (digestive tract disorders); diabetes mellitus; elbow dysplasia, hip dysplasia, osteochondrosis (joint disorders); kidney dysplasia; hydrocephalus (brain disorder); deep bacterial skin infections, immune-mediated skin disease, foot infections; hypothyroidism; ciliary dyskinesia (respiratory disorder); dominance aggression (behavior); cataracts, entropion, glaucoma, pannus, progressive retinal atrophy, retinal dysplasia (eye disorders)   **$$$**

CHORKIE (CHIHUAHUA/ YORKSHIRE TERRIER) Portosystemic shunt, patent ductus arteriosus (blood

vessel defects); valve disease, pulmonic stenosis (heart disorders); hydrocephalus (brain disorder); collapsing trachea (respiratory disorder); Legg-Calvé-Perthes disease, luxating kneecaps (joint disorders); neck instability (spinal cord disorder); Cushing's disease (adrenal gland disorder); hypothyroidism; seborrhea (skin disorder); undescended testicle; cystine urine crystals; cataracts, entropion, keratoconjunctivitis sicca, progressive retinal atrophy, retinal dysplasia (eye disorders)   **$$$**

COCKER SPANIEL, AMERICAN
Patent ductus arteriosus, portosystemic shunt (blood vessel defects); dilated cardiomyopathy, pulmonic stenosis (heart disorders); deafness; elbow dysplasia, hip dysplasia, osteochondrosis, luxating kneecaps (joint disorders); epilepsy, cerebellar atrophy, hydrocephalus, lysosomal storage disease (brain disorders); kidney dysplasia; hermaphroditism; hypothyroidism; inguinal hernia; spinal disk disease; breast adenocarcinoma, anal gland adenocarcinoma (cancers); fear aggression (behavior); allergies, ear infections, foot infections, seborrhea (skin disorders); blocked tear ducts, cataracts, corneal ulcers, entropion, glaucoma, inward-growing eyelashes, keratoconjunctivitis sicca, lens luxation, progressive retinal atrophy, retinal dysplasia (eye disorders); hemophilia A, hemolytic anemia, platelet deficiency, von Willebrand's disease (blood disorders)   **$$$**

COCKER SPANIEL, ENGLISH Patent ductus arteriosus (blood vessel defect); hip dysplasia, osteochondrosis (joint disorders); undescended testicle; deafness; epilepsy;

kidney dysplasia; hermaphroditism (reproductive tract disorder); hypothyroidism; cataracts, entropion, glaucoma, lens luxation, progressive retinal atrophy, retinal dysplasia (eye disorders); von Willebrand's disease (blood clotting disorder) $$

COLLIE Patent ductus arteriosus (blood vessel defect); hip dysplasia, osteochondrosis (joint disorders); bladder cancer; deafness; immune-mediated skin disease, foot infections; epilepsy, cerebellar atrophy (brain disorders); hypothyroidism; cataracts, entropion, pannus, progressive retinal atrophy, retinal dysplasia (eye defects); hemophilia A, von Willebrand's disease (blood clotting disorders) $$

DACHSHUND Cushing's disease (adrenal disorder); diabetes mellitus; spinal disk disease; megaesophagus (digestive tract disorder); undescended testicle; cystine urine crystals, kidney dysplasia (urinary tract disorders); deafness; epilepsy, lysosomal storage disease (brain disorders); hypothyroidism; bacterial skin infections, immune-mediated skin disease, foot infections; cataracts, corneal ulcers, entropion, glaucoma, keratoconjunctivitis sicca, lens luxation, pannus, progressive retinal atrophy (eye disorders); hemolytic anemia, platelet deficiency, von Willebrand's disease (blood disorders) $$$

DACHSHUND, MINIATURE Cushing's disease (adrenal disorder); diabetes mellitus; spinal disk disease; cystine urine crystals, kidney dysplasia (urinary tract disorders); deafness; bacterial skin infections, immune-mediated skin disease, foot infections; hypothyroidism; cataracts, pannus,

progressive retinal atrophy (eye disorders); hemolytic anemia, platelet deficiency, von Willebrand's disease (blood disorders) $$$

DALMATIAN Dilated cardiomyopathy (heart disorder); urate urine crystals; deafness; hip dysplasia, osteochondrosis (joint disorders); laryngeal paralysis, ciliary dyskinesia (respiratory disorders); copper storage disease (liver disorder); nerve atrophy; lysosomal storage disease (brain disorder); inflammatory bowel disease, megaesophagus (digestive tract disorders); squamous cell carcinoma (skin cancer); hypothyroidism; allergies, deep bacterial skin infections, immune-mediated skin disease (skin disorders); entropion, glaucoma, pannus, progressive retinal atrophy (eye disorders) $$$

DANDIE DINMONT TERRIER Hip dysplasia, luxating kneecaps (joint disorders); hypothyroidism; spinal disk disease; cataracts, entropion, glaucoma (eye disorders) $$

DOBERMAN PINSCHER Vascular ring anomaly, portosystemic shunt (blood vessel defects); dilated cardiomyopathy (heart disorder); hip dysplasia, osteochondrosis (joint disorders); panosteitis (bone disorder); Addison's disease (adrenal disorder); diabetes mellitus; wobbler syndrome, spinal disk disease (spinal cord disorders); ciliary dyskinesia (respiratory disorder); deafness; kidney dysplasia; hemangiosarcoma (cancer); hypothyroidism; exocrine pancreatic insufficiency (digestive disorder); copper storage disease (liver disorder); nerve atrophy; obsessive-compulsive skin injury, dominance aggression, fear aggression (behavior); foot infections, immune-mediated skin disease; cataracts, entropion, progressive retinal atrophy, retinal dysplasia (eye disorders); hemophilia A, hemolytic anemia, von Willebrand's disease (blood disorders) $$$

ENGLISH SETTER Bloat (digestive tract emergency); hip dysplasia, osteochondrosis (joint disorders); hypoglycemia; hypothyroidism; hemangiosarcoma, cardiac tumor (cancers); ciliary dyskinesia (respiratory disorder); lysosomal storage disease (brain disorder); deafness; cataracts, entropion, keratoconjunctivitis sicca, progressive retinal atrophy (eye disorders); hemophilia A, von Willebrand's disease (blood clotting disorders) $$

ENGLISH SPRINGER SPANIEL Patent ductus arteriosus, portosystemic shunt (blood vessel defects); elbow dysplasia, hip dysplasia, luxating kneecaps, osteochondrosis (joint disorders); Addison's disease (adrenal disorder); diabetes mellitus; epilepsy, hydrocephalus, lysosomal storage disease (brain disorders); spinal disk disease; myasthenia gravis, nerve atrophy (nerve disorders); phosphofructokinase deficiency (muscle and blood disease); ciliary dyskinesia (respiratory disorder); breast or anal gland adenocarcinoma (cancer); dominance aggression (behavior); hermaphroditism (reproductive disorder); hypothyroidism; inguinal hernia; allergies, ear infections, immune-mediated skin disease, seborrhea (skin disorders); cataracts, ectropion, glaucoma, progressive retinal atrophy, retinal dysplasia (eye disorders); hemophilia A, hemolytic anemia, von Willebrand's disease (blood disorders) $$$

FLAT-COATED RETRIEVER Epilepsy; hip dysplasia; hypothyroidism; cataracts, entropion, progressive retinal atrophy (eye disorders) $

FOX TERRIER, SMOOTH Vascular ring anomaly (blood vessel defect); pulmonic stenosis (heart disorder); Legg-Calvé-Perthes disease, osteochondrosis (joint disorders); myasthenia gravis (muscle disorder); deafness; esophageal stenosis (digestive tract disorder); hypothyroidism; allergies; cataracts, glaucoma, lens luxation (eye disorders); von Willebrand's disease (blood clotting disorder) $$

FOX TERRIER, TOY Pulmonic stenosis (heart disorder); luxating kneecaps, Legg-Calvé-Perthes disease (joint disorders); allergies $

FOX TERRIER, WIRE Vascular ring anomaly (blood vessel defect); pulmonic stenosis, tetralogy of Fallot (heart disorders); Legg-Calvé-Perthes disease (hip disorder); myasthenia gravis (muscle disorder); deafness; epilepsy; esophageal stenosis (digestive tract disorder); hypothyroidism; cataracts, entropion, glaucoma, lens luxation, progressive retinal atrophy (eye disorders); von Willebrand's disease (blood clotting disorder) $$

FRENCH BULLDOG Allergies, seborrhea; elbow dysplasia (joint disorder); brachycephalic airway syndrome (respiratory defect); cardiac tumor; cataracts, entropion (eye disorders); hemophilia A, hemophilia B, von Willebrand's disease (blood clotting disorders) $$

GERMAN SHEPHERD Patent ductus arteriosus, vascular ring anomaly (blood vessel defects); aortic stenosis, dilated cardiomyopathy, valve disease (heart disorders); elbow dysplasia, hip dysplasia, osteochondrosis (joint disorders); panosteitis (bone disorder); esophageal stenosis, exocrine pancreatic insufficiency, irritable bowel disease, megaesophagus (digestive tract disorders); cystine urine crystals; deafness; diabetes mellitus; epilepsy, lysosomal storage disease (brain disorders); hemangiosarcoma, osteosarcoma (cancers); nerve atrophy, cauda equina syndrome (nerve disorders); kidney dysplasia; systemic lupus erythematosus (immune-mediated disease); dominance aggression, fear aggression, separation anxiety (behavior); hypothyroidism; allergies, ear infections, immune-mediated skin disease, deep bacterial skin infections (skin disorders); cataracts, entropion, lens luxation, pannus, progressive retinal atrophy, retinal dysplasia (eye disorders); hemophilia A, hemophilia B, von Willebrand's disease (blood clotting disorders)   **$$$**

GERMAN SHORTHAIRED POINTER
Aortic stenosis (heart disorder); hip dysplasia, osteochondrosis (joint disorders); Addison's disease (adrenal disorder); fibrosarcoma (cancer); hermaphroditism (reproductive disorder); lysosomal storage disease (brain disorder); hypothyroidism; myasthenia gravis (muscle disorder); cataracts, entropion, pannus, progressive retinal atrophy (eye disorders); platelet deficiency, von Willebrand's disease (blood clotting disorders)   **$$**

GERMAN WIREHAIRED POINTER
Hip dysplasia, osteochondrosis (joint disorders); hypothyroidism; cataracts, entropion, retinal dysplasia

(eye disorders); von Willebrand's disease (blood clotting disorder)   **$**

GOLDEN RETRIEVER
Portosystemic shunt (blood vessel defect); aortic stenosis (heart disorder); diabetes mellitus; elbow dysplasia, hip dysplasia, osteochondrosis (joint disorders); epilepsy; hypothyroidism; lymphoma, hemangiosarcoma, cardiac tumor (cancers); myasthenia gravis (muscle disorder); laryngeal paralysis, ciliary dyskinesia (respiratory disorders); irritable bowel disease; kidney dysplasia; nerve atrophy; obsessive-compulsive skin injury (behavior abnormality); allergies, deep bacterial skin infections, ear infections, foot infections, immune-mediated skin disease (skin disorders); cataracts, entropion, inward-growing eyelashes, progressive retinal atrophy, uveodermatologic disorder (eye disorders); hemophilia A, hemolytic anemia (blood disorders)   **$$$**

German Shorthaired Pointer

GOLDENDOODLE
(GOLDEN RETRIEVER/POODLE)
Portosystemic shunt (blood vessel defect); aortic stenosis (heart disorder); elbow dysplasia, hip dysplasia, osteochondrosis (joint disorders); allergies, ear infections, obsessive-compulsive skin injury, immune-mediated skin disease (skin disorders); diabetes mellitus; hypothyroidism; Addison's disease, Cushing's disease (adrenal gland disorders); epilepsy; lymphoma, hemangiosarcoma, stomach cancer (cancers); bloat (digestive tract emergency); cataracts, entropion, glaucoma, inward-growing eyelashes, lens luxation, pannus, progressive retinal atrophy, retinal dysplasia (eye disorders) $$$

GORDON SETTER
Bloat (digestive tract emergency); epilepsy; hip dysplasia, osteochondrosis (joint disorders); cerebellar atrophy (brain disorder); hypothyroidism; cataracts, entropion, progressive retinal atrophy, keratoconjunctivitis sicca, retinal dysplasia (eye disorders) $$

GREAT DANE
Vascular ring anomaly (blood vessel defect); dilated cardiomyopathy, valve disease (heart disorders); elbow dysplasia, hip dysplasia, osteochondrosis (joint disorders); panosteitis (bone disorder); Addison's disease (adrenal disorder); bloat, megaesophagus (digestive tract disorders); wobbler syndrome (spinal cord disorder); cystine urine crystals; deafness; hypothyroidism; hemangiosarcoma, osteosarcoma (cancers); obsessive-compulsive skin injury (behavior disorder); foot infections; cataracts, entropion, glaucoma, progressive retinal atrophy, retinal dysplasia (eye disorders); von Willebrand's disease (blood clotting disorder) $$$

GREAT PYRENEES
Elbow dysplasia, hip dysplasia, osteochondrosis (joint disorders); deafness; hypothyroidism; cataracts, entropion, progressive retinal atrophy, retinal dysplasia (eye disorders); hemophilia B, platelet deficiency (blood clotting disorders) $$

GREATER SWISS MOUNTAIN DOG
Hip dysplasia, osteochondrosis (joint disorders); bloat (digestive tract emergency); epilepsy; platelet deficiency (blood clotting disorder) $

GREYHOUND
Osteochondrosis (joint disorder); epilepsy; esophageal stenosis (digestive tract disorder); hypothyroidism; cataracts, lens luxation, pannus, progressive retinal atrophy (eye disorders); hemophilia A, von Willebrand's disease (blood clotting disorders) $

HAVANESE
Allergies, immune-mediated skin disease; luxating kneecaps; cataracts, progressive retinal atrophy, retinal dysplasia (eye disorders) $$

IBIZAN HOUND
Undescended testicle; deafness; hypothyroidism; allergies; cataracts, retinal dysplasia (eye disorders); platelet deficiency (blood clotting disorder) $

IRISH SETTER
Vascular ring anomaly, portosystemic shunt (blood vessel defects); bloat, megaesophagus, exocrine pancreatic insufficiency (digestive tract disorders); hip dysplasia, osteochondrosis (joint disorders); wobbler syndrome (spinal cord disorder); epilepsy, cerebellar atrophy (brain disorders); hypothyroidism; obsessive-

compulsive skin injury (behavior disorder); allergies, deep bacterial skin infections, immune-mediated skin disease, foot infections, seborrhea (skin disorders); cataracts, entropion, lens luxation, progressive retinal atrophy, uveodermatologic syndrome (eye disorders); hemophilia A, hemolytic anemia, platelet deficiency (blood disorders) $$$

IRISH TERRIER Cystine urine crystals; progressive retinal atrophy (eye disorder) $

IRISH WATER SPANIEL
Hip dysplasia; epilepsy; hypothyroidism; cataracts, progressive retinal atrophy (eye disorders); von Willebrand's disease (blood clotting disorder) $$

IRISH WOLFHOUND
Portosystemic shunt (blood vessel defect); dilated cardiomyopathy (heart disorder); elbow dysplasia, hip dysplasia, osteochondrosis (joint disorders); panosteitis (bone disorder); hypothyroidism; allergies, foot infections (skin disorders); cataracts, entropion (eye disorders); von Willebrand's disease (blood clotting disorder) $$$

ITALIAN GREYHOUND
Vascular ring anomaly (blood vessel defect); undescended testicle; epilepsy; cataracts, glaucoma, progressive retinal atrophy (eye disorders); platelet deficiency (blood clotting disorder) $

JACK RUSSELL TERRIER (PARSON RUSSELL TERRIER)
Allergies; epilepsy; myasthenia gravis (muscle disorder); corneal ulcers, lens luxation (eye disorders); von Willebrand's disease (blood clotting disorder) $

JAPANESE CHIN Lysosomal storage disease (brain disorder); cataracts, entropion, progressive retinal atrophy (eye disorders); undescended testicle $

JUG (JACK RUSSELL TERRIER/ PUG) Portosystemic shunt (blood vessel defect); Addison's disease (adrenal gland disorder); epilepsy, encephalitis (brain disorders); spinal disk disease; hip dysplasia, Legg-Calvé-Perthes disease, luxating kneecaps (joint disorders); collapsing trachea, brachycephalic airway syndrome (respiratory disorders); allergies (skin disorder); hypothyroidism; diabetes mellitus; urinary tract infections, urinary stones; mast cell tumor (cancer); hermaphroditism (reproductive disorder); corneal ulcers, entropion, pannus, progressive retinal atrophy (eye disorders) $$$

KEESHOND Portosystemic shunt (blood vessel defect); pulmonic stenosis, tetralogy of Fallot, ventricular septal defect (heart defects); Cushing's disease (adrenal disorder); diabetes mellitus; epilepsy; hypothyroidism; kidney dysplasia; cataracts, glaucoma, progressive retinal atrophy (eye disorders); von Willebrand's disease (blood clotting disorder) $$$

KERRY BLUE TERRIER
Hermaphroditism (reproductive disorder); cerebellar atrophy (brain disorder); hypothyroidism; cataracts, entropion, keratoconjunctivitis sicca, progressive retinal atrophy (eye disorders); hemolytic anemia, platelet deficiency, von Willebrand's disease (blood disorders) $$

KOMONDOR Hip dysplasia; hypothyroidism; cataracts, entropion (eye disorders) $

KUVASZ Hip dysplasia, osteochondrosis (joint disorders); deafness; hypothyroidism; cataracts, entropion (eye disorders); von Willebrand's disease (blood clotting disorder) **$$**

LABBE (LABRADOR RETRIEVER/ BEAGLE) Pulmonic stenosis, tetralogy of Fallot, ventricular septal defect (heart defects); portosystemic shunt (blood vessel defect); elbow dysplasia, hip dysplasia, osteochondrosis (joint disorders); spinal disk disease; hypothyroidism; obsessive-compulsive skin injury, allergies, ear infections, seborrhea (skin disorders); Addison's disease (adrenal gland disorder); laryngeal paralysis (respiratory disorder); deafness; diabetes mellitus; epilepsy, cerebellar atrophy (brain disorders); hemorrhagic gastroenteritis, exocrine pancreatic insufficiency (digestive tract disorders); hypoglycemia; amyloidosis (joint and kidney disorder); kidney dysplasia, bladder cancer (urinary tract disorders); hermaphroditism (reproductive disorder); hemolytic anemia (blood disorder); cataracts, entropion, lens luxation, glaucoma, progressive retinal atrophy, retinal dysplasia (eye disorders) **$$$**

LABRADOODLE (LABRADOR RETRIEVER/POODLE) Portosystemic shunt (blood vessel defect); elbow dysplasia, hip dysplasia, osteochondrosis (joint disorders); panosteitis (bone disorder); hypothyroidism; obsessive-compulsive skin injury, allergies, ear infections, seborrhea, immune-mediated skin disease (skin disorders); Addison's disease, Cushing's disease (adrenal gland disorders); laryngeal paralysis (respiratory disorder); deafness; diabetes mellitus; epilepsy; hemorrhagic gastroen-

teritis, exocrine pancreatic insufficiency, bloat, stomach cancer (digestive tract disorders); hemangiosarcoma (cancer); hypoglycemia; cataracts, entropion, inward-growing eyelashes, lens luxation, pannus, glaucoma, progressive retinal atrophy, retinal dysplasia (eye disorders) **$$$**

LABRADOR RETRIEVER Portosystemic shunt (blood vessel defect); elbow dysplasia, hip dysplasia, osteochondrosis (joint disorders); panosteitis (bone disorder); Addison's disease (adrenal disorder); laryngeal paralysis; deafness; diabetes mellitus; epilepsy; hemorrhagic gastroenteritis, exocrine pancreatic insufficiency (digestive tract disorders); hemangiosarcoma (cancer); hypoglycemia; hypothyroidism; obsessive-compulsive skin injury (behavior disorder); allergies, ear infections, seborrhea (skin disorders); cataracts, entropion, progressive retinal atrophy, retinal dysplasia (eye disorders); hemophilia A, hemophilia B, von Willebrand's disease (blood clotting disorders) **$$$**

LHASA APSO Kidney dysplasia; hydrocephalus (brain disorder); inguinal hernia; luxating kneecaps; hypothyroidism; allergies, immune-mediated skin disease (skin disorders); cataracts, entropion, keratoconjunctivitis sicca, progressive retinal atrophy, retinal dysplasia (eye disorders); von Willebrand's disease (blood clotting disorder) **$$**

MALTESE Collapsing trachea (respiratory disorder); luxating kneecaps (joint disorder); encephalitis, hydrocephalus, little white shaker syndrome (brain disorders); undescended testicle; deafness;

hypoglycemia; hypothyroidism; immune-mediated skin disease; blindness, glaucoma, progressive retinal atrophy, retinal dysplasia (eye disorders); hemolytic anemia, platelet deficiency, von Willebrand's disease (blood disorders) $$$

MALTI-TZU (MALTESE/SHIH TZU)
Portosystemic shunt (blood vessel defect); luxating kneecaps; kidney dyplasia, calcium oxalate bladder stones (urinary tract disorders); brachycephalic airway syndrome, collapsing trachea (respiratory disorders); hypothyroidism; allergies, immune-mediated skin disease (skin disorders); encephalitis, hydrocephalus, little white shaker syndrome (brain disorders); deafness; undescended testicle (reproductive disorder); hypoglycemia; hemolytic anemia (blood disorder); blindness, glaucoma, cataracts, corneal ulcers, entropion, inward-growing eyelashes, keratoconjunctivitis sicca, progressive retinal atrophy, retinal dysplasia (eye disorders) $$$

MANCHESTER TERRIER
Cataracts, lens luxation, progressive retinal atrophy (eye disorders); hypothyroidism $

MASTIFF
Bloat (digestive tract emergency); osteochondrosis (joint disorder); hypothyroidism; entropion, progressive retinal atrophy, retinal dysplasia (eye disorders) $$

MINIATURE PINSCHER
Collapsing trachea (respiratory disorder); Legg-Calvé-Perthes disease (hip disorder); diabetes mellitus; inguinal hernia; immune-mediated skin disease; cataracts, entropion, keratoconjunctivitis

sicca, pannus, progressive retinal atrophy (eye disorders) $$

NEWFOUNDLAND
Patent ductus arteriosus (blood vessel defect); aortic stenosis, dilated cardiomyopathy, ventricular septal defect (heart defects); elbow dysplasia, hip dysplasia, osteochondrosis (joint disorders); Addison's disease (adrenal disorder); myasthenia gravis (muscle disorder); cystine urine crystals; hypothyroidism; allergies; cataracts, entropion (eye disorders); hemolytic anemia, von Willebrand's disease (blood disorders) $$$

NORFOLK TERRIER
Portosystemic shunt (blood vessel defect); valve disease (heart disorder); epilepsy; hypothyroidism $$

NORWEGIAN ELKHOUND
Hip dysplasia; kidney dysplasia; hypothyroidism; seborrhea (skin disorder); cataracts, entropion, glaucoma, lens luxation, progressive retinal atrophy (eye disorders) $$

NORWICH TERRIER
Hypothyroidism; lens luxation (eye disorder); von Willebrand's disease (blood clotting disorder) $

OLD ENGLISH SHEEPDOG
Portosystemic shunt (blood vessel defect); dilated cardiomyopathy (heart disorder); Addison's disease (adrenal disorder); hip dysplasia, osteochondrosis (joint disorders); inflammatory bowel disease; ciliary dyskinesia (respiratory-tract disorder); deafness; diabetes mellitus; immune-mediated skin disease, foot infections; hypothyroidism; cataracts, entropion, progressive retinal atrophy, retinal dysplasia (eye disorders);

hemolytic anemia, hemophilia B, platelet deficiency, von Willebrand's disease (blood disorders) **$$$**

PAPILLON Luxating kneecaps; deafness; hypothyroidism; cataracts, entropion, progressive retinal atrophy (eye disorders); von Willebrand's disease (blood clotting disorder) **$$**

PEKINGESE Neck instability, spinal disk disease (spinal cord disorders); Legg-Calvé-Perthes disease (hip disorder); hydrocephalus (brain disorder); irritable bowel disease; inguinal hernia; undescended testicle; testicular tumor; facial-fold dermatitis; hypothyroidism; cataracts, entropion, keratoconjunctivitis sicca, blocked tear ducts, lens luxation, pannus, progressive retinal atrophy (eye disorders); hemolytic anemia, platelet deficiency (blood disorders) **$$$**

PHARAOH HOUND Allergies; hypothyroidism; platelet deficiency (blood clotting disorder) **$**

POINTER Hip dysplasia; ciliary dyskinesia (respiratory tract disorder); irritable bowel disease; deafness; epilepsy; hypothyroidism; nerve atrophy; allergies, immune-mediated skin disease (skin disorders); cataracts, entropion, pannus, progressive retinal atrophy (eye disorders); von Willebrand's disease (blood clotting disorder) **$$$**

POMERANIAN Portosystemic shunt, patent ductus arteriosus (blood vessel defects); luxating kneecaps; collapsing trachea (respiratory disorder); hydrocephalus, lysosomal storage disease (brain disorders); neck instability (spinal cord disorder); undescended

testicle; immune-mediated skin disease; hypothyroidism; cataracts, entropion, blocked tear ducts, inward-growing eyelashes, lens luxation, progressive retinal atrophy (eye disorders) **$$$**

POOCHI (POODLE/CHIHUAHUA) Patent ductus arteriosus (blood vessel defect); ventricular septal defect, valve disease, pulmonic stenosis (heart disorders); osteochondrosis, luxating kneecaps (joint disorders); collapsing trachea, ciliary dyskinesia (respiratory disorders); spinal disk disease, neck instability (spinal cord disorders); hypothyroidism; allergies, ear infections, immune-mediated skin disease (skin disorders); myasthenia gravis (muscle disorder); diabetes mellitus; Cushing's disease (adrenal gland disorder); deafness; ectopic ureters, cystine urine crystals (urinary tract disorders); squamous cell carcinoma (cancer); epilepsy, hydrocephalus, cerebellar atrophy (brain disorders); fear aggression (behavior); hemolytic anemia (blood disorder); cataracts, entropion, glaucoma, blocked tear ducts, inward-growing eyelashes, lens luxation, pannus, keratoconjunctivitis sicca, progressive retinal atrophy, retinal dysplasia (eye disorders) **$$$**

POODLE, MINIATURE Patent ductus arteriosus (blood vessel defect); ventricular septal defect (heart defect); osteochondrosis, luxating kneecaps (joint disorders); collapsing trachea (respiratory disorder); spinal disk disease; myasthenia gravis (muscle disease); diabetes mellitus; Cushing's disease; deafness; ectopic ureters (urinary tract defect); squamous cell carcinoma (cancer); epilepsy, cerebellar atrophy, lysosomal storage disease (brain disorders); fear aggression (behavior);

hypothyroidism; allergies, ear infections, immune-mediated skin disease, foot infections (skin disorders); cataracts, entropion, glaucoma, blocked tear ducts, inward-growing eyelashes, lens luxation, pannus, progressive retinal atrophy, retinal dysplasia (eye disorders); hemolytic anemia, hemophilia A, platelet deficiency, von Willebrand's disease (blood disorders) $$$

POODLE, STANDARD

Addison's disease, Cushing's disease (adrenal disorders); bloat (digestive tract emergency); epilepsy; hip dysplasia, osteochondrosis (joint disorders); hypothyroidism; allergies, ear infections, immune-mediated skin disease; hemangiosarcoma, stomach cancer; cataracts, entropion, glaucoma, blocked tear ducts, inward-growing eyelashes, lens luxation, pannus, progressive retinal atrophy, retinal dysplasia (eye disorders) $$$

POODLE, TOY

Portosystemic shunt, patent ductus arteriosus (blood vessel defects); ventricular septal defect (heart defect); collapsing trachea (respiratory disorder); osteochondrosis, luxating kneecaps (joint disorders); spinal disk disease; diabetes mellitus; Cushing's disease (adrenal disorder); squamous cell carcinoma (skin cancer); epilepsy, hydrocephalus, lysosomal storage disease (brain disorders); deafness; ectopic ureters; fear aggression (behavior); hypothyroidism; allergies, ear infections, immune-mediated skin disease (skin disorders); cataracts, entropion, glaucoma, blocked tear ducts, inward-growing eyelashes, lens luxation, pannus, progressive retinal atrophy, retinal dysplasia (eye disorders); hemolytic anemia, hemophilia A, platelet deficiency, von Willebrand's disease (blood disorders) $$$

PORKIE (POMERANIAN/ YORKSHIRE TERRIER)

Portosystemic shunt, patent ductus arteriosus (blood vessel defects); Legg-Calvé-Perthes disease, luxating kneecaps (joint disorders); hydrocephalus (brain disorder); neck instability (spinal cord disorder); collapsing trachea (respiratory disorder); seborrhea, immune-mediated skin disease (skin disorders); hypothyroidism; Cushing's disease (adrenal gland disorder); undescended testicle; cystine urine crystals; cataracts, entropion, lens luxation, keratoconjunctivitis sicca, progressive retinal atrophy, retinal dysplasia (eye disorders) $$$

PORTUGUESE WATER DOG

Addison's disease (adrenal disorder); lysosomal storage disease (brain disorder); cataracts, progressive retinal atrophy (eye disorders); hypothyroidism $

PUG

Portosystemic shunt (blood vessel defect); Addison's disease (adrenal disorder); spinal disk disease; hip dysplasia, Legg-Calvé-Perthes disease, luxating kneecaps (joint disorders); collapsing trachea; irritable bowel disease; diabetes mellitus; urinary tract infections, urinary stones; brachycephalic airway syndrome (respiratory disorder); encephalitis, epilepsy (brain disorders); mast cell tumor (cancer); hermaphroditism (reproductive disorder); hypothyroidism; allergies, facial-fold dermatitis, tail-fold dermatitis (skin disorders); entropion, pannus, progressive retinal atrophy (eye disorders) $$$

PUGGLE (PUG/BEAGLE)

Pulmonic stenosis, tetralogy of Fallot, ventricular septal defect (heart defects);

portosystemic shunt (blood vessel defect); spinal disk disease (spinal cord disorder); hip dysplasia, Legg-Calvé-Perthes disease, luxating kneecaps (joint disorders); collapsing trachea, brachycephalic airway syndrome (respiratory disorders); deafness; epilepsy, cerebellar atrophy, encephalitis (brain disorders); diabetes mellitus; hypothyroidism; allergies (skin disorder); mast cell tumor (cancer); Addison's disease (adrenal gland disorder); irritable bowel disease, exocrine pancreatic insufficiency (digestive disorders); hermaphroditism (reproductive disorder); amyloidosis (joint and kidney disorder); kidney dysplasia, urinary tract infections, urinary stones, bladder cancer (urinary tract disorders); cataracts, entropion, glaucoma, pannus, lens luxation, progressive retinal atrophy, retinal dysplasia (eye disorders)   **$$$**

PULI Hip dysplasia; cataracts, progressive retinal atrophy, retinal dysplasia (eye disorders)   **$**

RHODESIAN RIDGEBACK
Hip dysplasia, osteochondrosis (joint disorders); wobbler syndrome (spinal cord disorder); deafness; cerebellar atrophy (brain disorder); hemangiosarcoma (cancer); hypothyroidism; cataracts, entropion, progressive retinal atrophy (eye disorders); hemolytic anemia, von Willebrand's disease (blood disorders)   **$$**

ROTTWEILER Aortic stenosis (heart disorder); elbow dysplasia, hip dysplasia (joint disorders); panosteitis (bone disorder); Addison's disease (adrenal disorder); lymphoma (cancer); deafness; diabetes mellitus; irritable

bowel disease; nerve atrophy; dominance aggression (behavior); hypothyroidism; cataracts, entropion, progressive retinal atrophy, retinal dysplasia (eye disorders); hemolytic anemia, platelet deficiency, von Willebrand's disease (blood disorders)   **$$**

SAINT BERNARD
Portosystemic shunt (blood vessel defect); dilated cardiomyopathy (heart disorder); bloat, exocrine pancreatic insufficiency (digestive tract disorders); hip dysplasia, osteochondrosis (joint disorders); wobbler syndrome (spinal cord disorder); laryngeal paralysis (respiratory disorder); osteosarcoma (cancer); epilepsy; dominance aggression (behavior); hypothyroidism; immune-mediated skin disease; cataracts, ectropion, entropion, uveodermatologic syndrome (eye disorders); hemophilia A, hemophilia B, von Willebrand's disease (blood clotting disorders)   **$$$**

SALUKI Lysosomal storage disease (brain disorder); hypothyroidism; cataracts, entropion, progressive retinal atrophy, retinal dysplasia (eye disorders); hemolytic anemia, platelet deficiency, von Willebrand's disease (blood disorders)   **$**

SAMOYED Portosystemic shunt (blood vessel defect); atrial septal defect, pulmonic stenosis (heart disorders); hip dysplasia, osteochondrosis (joint disorders); diabetes mellitus; kidney dysplasia; cerebellar atrophy (brain disorder); immune-mediated skin disease; hypothyroidism; cataracts, entropion, glaucoma, progressive retinal atrophy, retinal dysplasia, uveodermatologic syndrome (eye disorders); hemophilia A, hemolytic anemia, platelet

deficiency, von Willebrand's disease
(blood disorders) $$$

SCHIPPERKE Legg-Calvé-Perthes
disease (hip disorder); diabetes mellitus;
hypothyroidism; immune-mediated skin
disease; cataracts, entropion, progressive
retinal atrophy (eye disorders) $$

SCHNAUZER, GIANT
Hip dysplasia, osteochondrosis (joint
disorders); panosteitis (bone disorder);
hypothyroidism; seborrhea (skin
disorder); cataracts, glaucoma, progressive retinal atrophy, retinal dysplasia
(eye disorders); hemolytic anemia,
platelet deficiency (blood disorders) $$

SCHNAUZER, MINIATURE
Portosystemic shunt (blood vessel
defect); pulmonic stenosis, arrhythmia
(heart disorders); collapsing trachea
(respiratory disorder); Legg-Calvé-
Perthes disease, osteochondrosis
(joint disorders); undescended testicle;
Cushing's disease (adrenal disorder);
diabetes mellitus; hypothyroidism;
urinary tract infections, urinary stones,
kidney dysplasia; esophageal stenosis,
hemorrhagic gastroenteritis, mega-
esophagus, pancreatitis (digestive tract
disorders); allergies; cataracts, entro-
pion, progressive retinal atrophy, retinal
dysplasia (eye disorders); hemophilia A,
hemolytic anemia, platelet deficiency,
von Willebrand's disease (blood
disorders) $$$

SCHNAUZER, STANDARD
Pulmonic stenosis (heart disorder);
Addison's disease (adrenal disorder);
Legg-Calvé-Perthes disease, osteochondrosis (joint disorders); anal sac
adenocarcinoma (cancer); hypothyroidism; cataracts, blocked tear ducts,

retinal dysplasia (eye disorders);
hemophilia A, von Willebrand's
disease (blood clotting disorders) $$

SCOTTISH TERRIER Cystine
urine crystals; lymphoma, squamous cell
carcinoma, bladder tumor, cardiac tumor
(cancers); allergies, immune-mediated
skin disease (skin disorders); myasthenia
gravis (muscle disorder); cataracts, lens
luxation, progressive retinal atrophy (eye
disorders); deafness; hypothyroidism;
hemophilia B, von Willebrand's disease
(blood clotting disorders) $$

SEALYHAM TERRIER
Deafness; hypothyroidism; cataracts,
glaucoma, lens luxation, progressive
retinal atrophy, retinal dysplasia
(eye disorders) $

SHAR-PEI Brachycephalic airway
syndrome (respiratory disorder);
amyloidosis (joint and liver disorder);
hip dysplasia, osteochondrosis, luxating
kneecaps (joint disorders); irritable
bowel disease, megaesophagus (digestive
tract disorders); allergies, deep bacterial skin infections, ear infections, foot
infections, seborrhea (skin disorders);
entropion, glaucoma, lens luxation,
progressive retinal atrophy, retinal
dysplasia (eye disorders); hypothy-
roidism $$$

SHETLAND SHEEPDOG
Patent ductus arteriosus (blood vessel
defect); hip dysplasia; systemic lupus
erythematosus (immune-mediated
disease); undescended testicle;
epilepsy; deafness; hypothyroidism;
Cushing's disease (adrenal gland
disorder); immune-mediated skin
disease; cataracts, corneal ulcers,
progressive retinal atrophy, retinal

dysplasia, uveodermatologic syndrome (eye disorders); hemophilia A, hemophilia B, von Willebrand's disease (blood clotting disorders)   **$$$**

SHIBA INU Allergies; hypothyroidism; epilepsy; luxating kneecaps; glaucoma, progressive retinal atrophy (eye disorders)   **$**

SHIH TZU Portosystemic shunt (blood vessel defect); kidney dysplasia, calcium oxalate bladder stones; brachycephalic airway syndrome (respiratory disorder); hypothyroidism; cataracts, corneal ulcers, entropion, inward-growing eyelashes, keratoconjunctivitis sicca, progressive retinal atrophy, retinal dysplasia (eye disorders); hemolytic anemia, platelet deficiency, von Willebrand's disease (blood clotting disorders)   **$$**

SHORKIE (SHIH TZU/ YORKSHIRE TERRIER) Portosystemic shunt, patent ductus arteriosus (blood vessel defects); collapsing trachea, brachycephalic airway syndrome (respiratory disorders); Legg-Calvé-Perthes disease, luxating kneecaps (joint disorders); neck instability (spinal cord disorder); hydrocephalus (brain disorder); hypothyroidism; allergies, seborrhea (skin disorders); Cushing's disease (adrenal gland disorder); undescended testicle (reproductive disorder); kidney dysplasia, calcium oxalate bladder stones, cystine urine crystals (urinary tract disorders); cataracts, corneal ulcers, entropion, keratoconjunctivitis sicca, progressive retinal atrophy, retinal dysplasia (eye disorders); hemolytic anemia, von Willebrand's disease (blood disorders)   **$$$**

SIBERIAN HUSKY
Portosystemic shunt (blood vessel defect); hip dysplasia, osteochondrosis (joint disorders); ectopic ureter (urinary tract disorder); laryngeal paralysis (respiratory disorder); epilepsy; hypothyroidism; immune-mediated skin disease; hemangiosarcoma; cataracts, entropion, glaucoma, lens luxation, pannus, progressive retinal atrophy, retinal dysplasia, uveodermatologic syndrome (eye disorders); hemophilia A, von Willebrand's disease (blood clotting disorders)   **$$$**

Siberian Husky

SILKY TERRIER Diabetes mellitus; Legg-Calvé-Perthes disease, luxating kneecaps (joint disorders); undescended testicle; hydrocephalus, lysosomal storage disease (brain disorders); cataracts, progressive retinal atrophy (eye disorders); platelet deficiency (blood clotting disorder)   **$$**

SKYE TERRIER Irritable bowel disease; myasthenia gravis (muscle disorder); hypothyroidism; lens luxation (eye disorder); von Willebrand's disease (blood clotting disorder)   **$$**

SOFT-COATED WHEATEN TERRIER
Kidney dysplasia; irritable bowel disease; Addison's disease (adrenal disorder); allergies; hypothyroidism; cataracts, progressive retinal atrophy, retinal dysplasia (eye disorders); von Willebrand's disease (blood clotting disorder)   **$$**

STAFFORDSHIRE BULL TERRIER
Hip dysplasia; epilepsy; cataracts, cherry eye, entropion, progressive retinal atrophy (eye disorders)   **$**

TIBETAN SPANIEL
Epilepsy; cherry eye   **$**

TIBETAN TERRIER
Nerve atrophy; lysosomal storage disease (brain disorder); cataracts, entropion, lens luxation, progressive retinal atrophy, retinal dysplasia (eye disorders)   **$**

VIZSLA
Hip dysplasia, osteochondrosis (joint disorders); hemangiosarcoma, lymphoma (cancers); epilepsy; facial-nerve paralysis; hypothyroidism; immune-mediated skin disease; cataracts, entropion, progressive retinal atrophy (eye disorders); hemophilia A (blood clotting disorder)   **$$$**

WEIMARANER
Elbow dysplasia, hip dysplasia; panosteitis (bone disorder); bloat (digestive tract emergency); hermaphroditism (reproductive disorder); myasthenia gravis (muscle disorder); immune-mediated skin disease, foot infections (skin disorders); hypothyroidism; entropion, progressive retinal atrophy (eye disorders); hemophilia A (blood clotting disorder)   **$$$**

WELSH CORGI, CARDIGAN
Cystine urine crystals; spinal disk disease; entropion, glaucoma, lens luxation, progressive retinal atrophy, retinal dysplasia (eye disorders)   **$$**

WELSH CORGI, PEMBROKE
Patent ductus arteriosus (blood vessel defect); cystine urine crystals; spinal disk disease; epilepsy; dominance aggression (behavior); hypothyroidism; cataracts, lens luxation, progressive retinal atrophy, retinal dysplasia (eye disorders); von Willebrand's disease (blood clotting disorder)   **$$$**

WELSH TERRIER
Hypothyroidism; cataracts, glaucoma, lens luxation (eye disorders); von Willebrand's disease (blood clotting disorder)   **$**

WEST HIGHLAND WHITE TERRIER
Addison's disease, Cushing's disease (adrenal disorders); diabetes mellitus; Legg-Calvé-Perthes disease (hip disorder); inguinal hernia; little white shaker syndrome, lysosomal storage disease (brain disorders); copper storage disease (liver disorder); deafness; allergies, deep bacterial skin infections,

West Highland White Terrier

ear infections, foot infections, seborrhea (skin disorders); cataracts, keratoconjunctivitis sicca, retinal dysplasia (eye disorders); pyruvate kinase deficiency (blood disorder) **$$$**

WHIPPET Osteochondrosis (joint disorder); diabetes mellitus; hemangiosarcoma (cancer); undescended testicle; hypothyroidism; cataracts, lens luxation, progressive retinal atrophy (eye disorders); von Willebrand's disease (blood clotting disorder) **$$**

YO-CHON (YORKSHIRE TERRIER/BICHON FRISÉ)

Portosystemic shunt, patent ductus arteriosus (blood vessel defects); neck instability (spinal cord disorder); collapsing trachea, ciliary dyskinesia (respiratory disorders); hydrocephalus, epilepsy, little white shaker syndrome (brain disorders); Legg-Calvé-Perthes disease, luxating kneecaps (joint

disorders); hypothyroidism; allergies, seborrhea (skin disorders); Cushing's disease (adrenal gland disorder); undescended testicle; cystine urine crystals; cataracts, entropion, keratoconjunctivitis sicca, progressive retinal atrophy, retinal dysplasia (eye disorders) **$$$**

YORKSHIRE TERRIER

Portosystemic shunt, patent ductus arteriosus (blood vessel defects); Legg-Calvé-Perthes disease, luxating kneecaps (joint disorders); Cushing's disease (adrenal disorder); undescended testicle; hydrocephalus (brain disorder); cystine urine crystals; neck instability (spinal cord disorder); collapsing trachea (respiratory disorder); seborrhea (skin disorder); hypothyroidism; cataracts, entropion, keratoconjunctivitis sicca, progressive retinal atrophy, retinal dysplasia (eye disorders); von Willebrand's disease (blood clotting disorder) **$$$**

Definitions and References

Here are brief descriptions of the medical problems listed in the Health Checklist beginning on page 19, plus the page numbers where those problems are discussed in detail.

ADDISON'S DISEASE: a serious adrenal-gland deficiency requiring lifelong hormone supplementation; see page 304.

ALLERGIES: reactions to inhaled substances or food; see page 94.

AMYLOIDOSIS: abnormal protein deposits in joints, kidneys, and other

organs, causing lameness, fever, and kidney failure; see page 245.

ANAL GLAND ADENOCARCINOMA: malignant tumor; see page 377.

AORTIC STENOSIS: partial blockage of the aorta; see page 259.

ARRHYTHMIA: erratic heartbeat; see page 261.

ATRIAL SEPTAL DEFECT: a hole between the upper two chambers of the heart; see page 255.

BLADDER CANCER: malignant tumor of the urinary bladder; see page 386.

BLOAT: potentially fatal emergency in which the stomach distends with gas and twists out of position; see page 136.

BLOCKED TEAR DUCTS: malformed ducts between the eye and nose, leading to runny eyes and tearstains; see page 203.

BRACHYCEPHALIC AIRWAY SYNDROME: one or more respiratory abnormalities common in dogs with pushed-in faces, such as constricted nostrils, an elongated soft palate, or a narrow trachea; see page 282.

BRAIN OR SPINAL CORD TUMOR: cancer of the brain or spinal cord; see page 367.

BREAST ADENOCARCINOMA: malignant breast tumor; see page 384.

CALCIUM OXALATE BLADDER STONES: a type that have to be removed surgically; see page 334.

CARDIAC TUMOR: cancer of the heart; see page 270.

CATARACTS: cloudiness of the lens that can impair vision; see page 216.

CAUDA EQUINA SYNDROME: compression of nerves in the lower spine causing lameness and incontinence; see page 249.

CEREBELLAR ATROPHY: breakdown of a part of the brain leading to tremors or loss of balance; see page 318.

CHERRY EYE: protruding gland of the third eyelid; see page 208.

CILIARY DYSKINESIA: failure of microscopic "hairs" lining the respiratory tract to move properly, leading to recurring respiratory infections; see page 286.

COLLAPSING TRACHEA: flattened tracheal cartilage that makes it harder to breathe; see page 280.

CONTACT HYPERSENSITIVITY: itchy rash caused by a substance contacting the skin; see page 100.

COPPER STORAGE DISEASE: defect in copper excretion resulting in liver damage; see page 144.

CORNEAL ULCER: painful erosion on the surface of the eye; see page 204.

CUSHING'S DISEASE: overproduction of cortisol by the adrenal glands; see page 299.

CYSTINE URINE CRYSTALS: abnormal mineral deposits in the urine that can form urinary stones; see page 335.

DEAFNESS: hearing defect in one or both ears; see page 225.

DIABETES MELLITUS: insufficient insulin production by the pancreas, which causes problems with glucose metabolism; see page 291.

DILATED CARDIOMYOPATHY: disease that causes weakened heart contractions and arrhythmias; see page 267.

DOMINANCE AGGRESSION: a bullying personality that can make a dog aggressive or more difficult to train; see page 183.

EAR INFECTION: ear inflammation often associated with allergies or other skin diseases; see page 219.

ECTOPIC URETERS: tubes from the kidneys that connect with the urethra rather than the bladder, sometimes causing urinary incontinence or urinary tract infections; see page 331.

ECTROPION: loose lower eyelid that predisposes to eye irritation; see page 203.

ELBOW DYSPLASIA: a malformed elbow joint, causing variable degrees of lameness; see page 234.

ENCEPHALITIS: brain inflammation, often causing seizures, abnormal behavior, or difficulty walking; see page 324.

ENTROPION: a turned-in eyelid that rubs against the eye; see page 203.

EPILEPSY: brain disorder causing recurrent seizures; see page 308.

ESOPHAGEAL STENOSIS: narrowing of the esophagus where it joins the stomach, potentially causing regurgitation; see page 132.

EXOCRINE PANCREATIC INSUFFICIENCY: pancreas that produces lower than normal amounts of digestive enzymes; see page 129.

FACIAL-FOLD DERMATITIS: recurrent skin infections in dogs with deep folds on their faces; see page 102.

FACIAL-NERVE PARALYSIS: a nerve problem that often leads to dry eye, or keratoconjunctivitis sicca; see page 316.

FEAR AGGRESSION: shyness or timidity that can make a dog aggressive or more difficult to train; see page 184.

FIBROSARCOMA: highly invasive malignant tumor; see page 382.

GLAUCOMA: increased fluid pressure within the eye leading to pain and potentially loss of vision; see page 213.

HEMANGIOSARCOMA: malignant tumor most often found on the spleen or the heart; see pages 380 and 270.

HEMOLYTIC ANEMIA: abnormal destruction of red blood cells; see page 351.

HEMOPHILIA A: a blood clotting deficiency; see page 361.

HEMOPHILIA B: a blood clotting deficiency; see page 361.

HEMORRHAGIC GASTROENTERITIS: severe, potentially fatal vomiting and bloody diarrhea; see page 126.

HERMAPHRODITISM: having "mixed" reproductive organs, such as a vagina and testicles; see page 346.

HIP DYSPLASIA: malformed hip joints, causing variable degrees of lameness; see page 229.

HYDROCEPHALUS: accumulation of cerebrospinal fluid within the skull, potentially causing vision problems, seizures, or mental retardation; see page 316.

HYPOGLYCEMIA: low blood sugar, potentially leading to seizures; see pages 295 and 299.

HYPOSPADIAS: urethral opening on the underside of the penis rather than at the end, sometimes leading to urinary incontinence; see page 346.

HYPOTHYROIDISM: thyroid hormone deficiency; see page 298.

IMMUNE-MEDIATED SKIN DISEASE: sores, scaling, or hair loss caused by an immune-system attack on the skin; see page 107.

INGUINAL HERNIA: a gap in the abdominal muscles that must be closed surgically; see page 346.

INTUSSUSCEPTION: emergency in which part of the intestine contracts into the adjacent part, causing a blockage; see page 121.

INWARD-GROWING EYELASHES: eyelashes growing from the underside of the eyelid or curving toward the eye that cause eye irritation; see page 203.

IRRITABLE BOWEL DISEASE: inflammation of the intestines, causing diarrhea, vomiting, or both; see page 125.

KERATOCONJUNCTIVITIS SICCA: a deficiency in tear production that can lead to damaged corneas; see page 211.

KIDNEY DYSPLASIA: malformation of one or both kidneys, potentially leading to kidney failure; see page 336.

LARYNGEAL PARALYSIS: failure of the larynx to open fully, causing breathing problems; see page 283.

LEGG-CALVÉ-PERTHES DISEASE: disintegration of the hip joint; see page 235.

LENS LUXATION: displacement of the lens of the eye, causing eye inflammation, pain, and glaucoma; see page 216.

LITTLE WHITE SHAKER SYNDROME: brain disorder causing severe head and body tremors; see page 318.

LUXATING KNEECAPS: kneecaps that slide out of place, causing variable degrees of lameness; see page 236.

LYMPHOMA: a blood cell cancer affecting the lymph nodes, bone marrow, or other organs; see page 374.

LYSOSOMAL STORAGE DISEASE: enzyme deficiency that causes nerve-cell damage and tremors, stumbling, seizures, or other nerve and brain disorders; see page 317.

MAST CELL TUMOR: a malignant tumor of the skin, liver, or bone marrow; see page 383.

MEGAESOPHAGUS: an esophagus that doesn't contract properly, leading to regurgitation and often pneumonia; see page 132.

MYASTHENIA GRAVIS: inability of nerve signals to control muscles, causing weakness and megaesophagus; see page 323.

NECK INSTABILITY: disorder of the upper spine that can lead to pain or paralysis; see page 246.

NERVE ATROPHY: breakdown of nerve cells, leading to muscle weakness; see page 319.

OBSESSIVE-COMPULSIVE BEHAVIOR: spinning, tail-chasing, or other obsessive behavior; see page 198.

OBSESSIVE-COMPULSIVE SKIN INJURY: obsessively licking the skin to the point of creating wounds; see page 198.

OSTEOCHONDROSIS: malformed cartilage in a joint, causing variable degrees of lameness; see page 238.

OSTEOSARCOMA: a bone cancer; see page 383.

PANCREATITIS: inflammation of the pancreas, causing severe abdominal pain and vomiting; see page 142.

PANNUS: an inflammatory disease of the eyes; see page 210.

PANOSTEITIS: bone inflammation in growing dogs; see page 237.

PATENT DUCTUS ARTERIOSUS: an abnormal connection between the pulmonary artery and the aorta; see page 258.

PHOSPHOFRUCTOKINASE DEFICIENCY: blood disease causing exercise intolerance, muscle cramps, and anemia; see page 355.

PITUITARY TUMOR: tumor in the part of the brain that regulates glands, such as the thyroid and adrenals; see pages 292 and 367.

PLATELET DEFICIENCY: blood disorder potentially leading to bruising or bleeding; see page 357.

PORTOSYSTEMIC SHUNT: blood vessel defect in the digestive tract that affects the brain: see page 263.

PROGRESSIVE RETINAL ATROPHY: a breakdown of the retina that leads to blindness; see page 215.

PULMONIC STENOSIS: a partial blockage of the pulmonary artery; see page 259.

PYLORIC STENOSIS: narrowing of the opening between the stomach and small intestine, potentially leading to vomiting; see page 135.

PYRUVATE KINASE DEFICIENCY: a condition causing anemia; see page 355.

RETINAL DYSPLASIA: malformation of the retina that can cause vision problems; see page 217.

SEBORRHEA: skin disease causing severe skin flaking and, sometimes, skin infections or hair loss; see page 106.

SEPARATION ANXIETY: fear of being alone; see page 179.

SKIN CANCER: any of several malignancies that target the skin; see page 382.

SPINAL DISK DISEASE: disk degeneration leading to pain, weakness, or paralysis; see page 248.

SQUAMOUS CELL CARCINOMA: a type of skin cancer; see page 382.

STOMACH CANCER: an often untreatable tumor; see page 385.

SYSTEMIC LUPUS ERYTHEMATOSUS: an immune-system attack on various organs; see page 244.

TAIL-FOLD DERMATITIS: skin irritation caused by moisture and bacteria accumulating in the folds around a docked tail; see page 102.

TESTICULAR TUMOR: cancer of a testicle; see page 387.

TETRALOGY OF FALLOT: a severe heart defect; see page 257.

UNDESCENDED TESTICLE: testicle that remains in the abdomen and is at higher risk of becoming cancerous; see page 346.

URATE URINE CRYSTALS: mineral deposits in the urine that can form urinary stones and cause blockages; see page 333.

URINARY STONES: rocklike mineral deposits in the kidneys or bladder that can cause pain and urinary blockages; see page 333.

URINARY TRACT INFECTION: an infection of the bladder or kidneys that often causes pain, blood in the urine, or straining to urinate; see page 329.

UVEODERMATOLOGIC SYNDROME: immune-system attack on the eyes and the skin, potentially leading to blindness; see page 210.

VALVE DISEASE: malformation or malfunction of one or more of the four heart valves; see pages 260 and 266.

VASCULAR RING ANOMALY: blood vessel defect that can constrict the esophagus and lead to regurgitation and pneumonia; see page 133.

VENTRICULAR SEPTAL DEFECT: a hole between the lower two chambers of the heart; see page 255.

VON WILLEBRAND'S DISEASE: a blood clotting deficiency; see page 358.

WOBBLER SYNDROME: instability of the neck vertebrae leading to pain, leg weakness, or paralysis; see page 247.

Raising a Healthy Puppy

WATCH THAT PUPPY GROW! If you've just adopted a puppy, get ready for some big changes. In a single year, a puppy grows and matures from infancy to adolescence or even to young adulthood, depending on her eventual size. You'll probably spend a lot of time in your vet's office that first year, because puppies need a series of vaccine boosters between the ages of 8 and 17 weeks. Your puppy will also be tested and treated for intestinal parasites, started on heartworm prevention, and spayed or neutered. You can avoid additional trips to the vet by following this chapter's guidelines on puppy nutrition, health, and safety.

PUPPY VACCINATIONS

"Why do puppies get so many shots, and which vaccines does my puppy really need?"

Puppies are vaccinated every 3 to 4 weeks, starting at age 7 or 8 weeks and finishing at 16 or 17 weeks. They are vaccinated several times rather than just once because the antibodies they receive from their mothers at birth interfere with their ability to produce their own antibodies in response to a vaccine. Exactly when the maternal antibodies lose their effectiveness varies with each puppy, so to avoid leaving a puppy unprotected during his vulnerable early months, vaccinations are started as early as maternal antibodies may begin fading and continued until the puppy's own immune system is fully functional.

Every puppy should be vaccinated against parvovirus, distemper, infectious hepatitis, and rabies: the first three because they're widespread, highly contagious, and often fatal; and rabies because it's widespread, always fatal,

and contagious to people as well as other animals. Despite a growing trend toward reducing the number of vaccinations given to adult dogs, it's still recommended that puppies receive a full series of these core vaccines, followed by boosters when they're one year old.

Depending on their environment, some puppies may also benefit from vaccines against upper respiratory diseases (parainfluenza and *Bordetella bronchiseptica*, or kennel cough), leptospirosis, or Lyme disease. Read the questions about those vaccines starting on page 63, and discuss with your veterinarian whether they're advisable for your puppy.

Vaccinating puppies against coronavirus, which causes mild diarrhea, is unnecessary because puppies develop antibodies against it naturally without becoming seriously ill. However, many boarding kennels still require the vaccine. Vaccinating dogs against giardia, a protozoal parasite that also causes diarrhea, is ineffective and is not recommended.

To keep track, refer to the typical puppy vaccination schedule below.

AGE	CORE VACCINES	OPTIONAL VACCINES
7 to 8 weeks	Parvo, distemper	Parainfluenza, *Bordetella bronchiseptica* (kennel cough)
10 to 11 weeks	Parvo, distemper, infectious hepatitis	Parainfluenza, *Bordetella bronchiseptica* (kennel cough)
13 to 14 weeks	Parvo, distemper, infectious hepatitis	Leptospirosis, Lyme
16 to 17 weeks	Parvo, rabies	Leptospirosis, Lyme
1 year	Parvo, distemper, infectious hepatitis, rabies	Parainfluenza, *Bordetella bronchiseptica* (kennel cough), leptospirosis, Lyme

11 TIPS FOR A HEALTHY, HAPPY PUPPY

When you bring home a puppy, you begin a lifelong friendship. Here are some tips for giving that relationship the best possible start.

1. Choose a vet before you get the puppy, and schedule a vet visit for the first week after you bring the pup home. The vet will check for health problems, discuss vaccines and deworming, and advise you on nutrition, house-training, and other puppy issues. See page 60 for advice on finding the right vet for you.

2. Make sure your puppy wears a collar and ID tag at all times, even when she's inside, because puppies can slip out a door in an instant. Adjust a buckle collar—not a slip collar—so it's snug enough not to pull over her head. Inexpensive nylon collars are a good choice for the first few months because your puppy will probably outgrow several before reaching adult size. The ID tag should include your address and a phone number.

3. Set aside two half-hour blocks every day for exercise and obedience training. Start teaching your puppy to come, sit, lie down, stay, and walk quietly on a leash right away. Enroll in puppy training classes if you need help.

4. Teach your puppy not to jump up on people or chew on their hands. These behaviors may seem charming in a young pup, but they'll quickly become annoying as she gets bigger, stronger, and more persistent.

5. Provide your puppy with a comfortable place to rest—a bed in a crate or on the floor—in the area where she'll be spending most of her time, and respect her need for "quiet time" when she's relaxing there.

6. Give your puppy two or three dog toys that are safe to chew on (see page 51), and replace them when they get worn out.

7. Brush your puppy's teeth once a day. This may sound excessive, but plaque hardens into tartar within about 36 hours, so it's important to get into the habit. See page 82 to learn how to brush.

8. Yelling and hitting simply don't work as training methods. If you need help teaching your puppy to do (or stop doing) something, work with a trainer and use positive reinforcement (praise, petting, a food tidbit, or a toy) rather than punishment.

9. Once she's fully vaccinated, introduce your puppy to a wide variety of people, places, and other dogs so she'll be comfortable and well-behaved in different situations.

10. Unless you're showing or breeding your dog, spay her (or neuter him) before she's one year old.

11. Supervise children when they play with the puppy, and teach them not to tease her or encourage undesirable behaviors, such as chasing and barking.

VACCINE REACTIONS

"I recently adopted a 10-week-old puppy, and I'm taking him to the vet this week for shots. Do the shots hurt? Will he feel sick afterward?"

Some puppies squirm or yelp a bit when they're vaccinated, and others don't even seem to notice. Based on that observation, I'd say the shots hurt a little but not much.

Most puppies bounce back from their vaccinations as if nothing happened. A few puppies will be sore at the injection site, run a low fever, and have less energy than usual for a day or two after being vaccinated. Those symptoms go away on their own and need not cause worry. Your puppy should be able to follow his usual routine after being vaccinated.

It's possible but exceedingly rare for a vaccine to trigger a severe allergic reaction called anaphylactic shock. No study of the mathematical risk of a vaccine causing anaphylactic shock has been done, but anecdotal evidence from veterinarians suggests that severe vaccine reactions occur in fewer than 1 in 1,000 dogs. Symptoms usually appear within one hour of receiving the vaccine (in an early-onset reaction) or within two days (in a delayed-onset reaction) and can include vomiting, hives, a swollen face, weakness, or collapse. Anaphylactic shock can be fatal, so if your puppy vomits, develops hives or a swollen face, or is weak or very lethargic after being vaccinated, call your vet or a veterinary emergency hospital immediately. The reaction can be treated with epinephrine, antihistamines, steroids, and oxygen.

If a puppy who has not completed his vaccine series has an allergic reaction, the remaining vaccines can be given, extremely cautiously, using the following protocol: (1) the puppy is given an antihistamine two hours before receiving a vaccine; (2) vaccines are given one at a time in two-week intervals, in part so that the specific vaccine causing the reaction can be identified; and (3) the puppy remains at the vet clinic for several hours after receiving a vaccine for observation and immediate treatment if necessary.

PICKING A PUPPY FOOD

"What's the best food for my puppy?"

There's no single best brand, and all puppy foods—from the least expensive to the most expensive—are formulated to the same basic nutritional standards. So feel free to choose any good-quality commercial brand whose label states the following, usually in tiny type near the ingredient list: "Animal feeding tests using AAFCO procedures substantiate that [Brand X] provides complete and balanced nutrition for the growth of dogs."

Just what does that mean, and why is it important? Here's the translation:

AAFCO is the Association of American Feed Control Officials, an organization that sets standards for the nutritional content of commercial dog foods sold in the United States. Those standards include the minimum (and sometimes maximum) levels of protein, fat, carbohydrates, vitamins, and minerals a dog or puppy needs to remain healthy.

"Animal feeding tests" means the food was fed to a group of test dogs for several months rather than simply analyzed in a chemistry lab to determine its nutrient content. AAFCO allows dog-food manufacturers to use either feeding tests or laboratory tests, but because feeding tests take longer, cost more, and provide more information, to me they're a sign that the manufacturer has put more time and effort into developing a good product.

"Complete and balanced" means the food provides all the nutrients a dog needs, aside from water. A food that's "complete and balanced for growth" is designed for puppies; one that's "complete and balanced for the maintenance of dogs" is for adult dogs, and one that's "complete and balanced for the growth and maintenance of dogs" is appropriate for both puppies and adults.

Unexciting and eye-straining though it may be, that AAFCO certification statement is the single most important piece of information you'll find on a dog food label. The catchy product name, cute dog photo or appealing graphics, and restaurant-worthy flavor descriptions are pure marketing razzle-dazzle. For more tips on deciphering dog food labels, see page 68.

Once you've picked a brand, your next choice is canned or dry. Personally, I'll always choose dry food (kibble) because it's less expensive (with canned, three-quarters of what you're paying for is water), creates less garbage, and is, arguably, a bit healthier for the dog's teeth over a lifetime. Many people feed their dogs dry food with a bit of canned added for variety.

What about adding cooked meat, vegetables, grains, and fruit to your puppy's diet? That's a fine idea—within limits. Your puppy's diet should be at least 80 percent commercial puppy food, because that contains the proper balance of nutrients. The remaining 20 percent can be *healthy* fresh food—there's no sane reason to give your puppy junk food, such as potato chips or cookies. Also avoid giving your puppy more than a dash of dairy products, such as milk, cheese, or yogurt—the extra calcium can actually contribute to joint problems, especially in large-breed puppies. See page 74 for other "people foods" that aren't good for dogs of any age.

MILK AND OTHER SUPPLEMENTS

"My puppy is only eight weeks old. Should I give her milk as well as puppy food? How about vitamins?"

Don't give your puppy formula, milk, or vitamins. At eight weeks, she is completely weaned and doesn't even need her own mother's milk, much less cow's milk, which is completely different. Milk can give a puppy diarrhea, and the extra calcium can actually predispose her to hip dysplasia and other joint problems (see page 50). Vitamin supplements are unnecessary at best (puppy food contains the appropriate levels of vitamins and minerals) and harmful at worst (if they push your puppy's intake of calcium and fat-soluble vitamins over healthy limits).

WHY NOT A HOMEMADE DIET?

"I just brought home a 10-week-old Doberman Pinscher puppy. The breeder gave me the recipe for the homemade diet she feeds all her puppies. When I showed it to my veterinarian, he said I should switch the puppy to a high-quality commercial puppy food immediately. What's wrong with feeding what the breeder recommends?"

I agree with your vet: buy, don't make, your puppy's food. Save the home cooking for after he's full-grown, when his nutritional needs will be easier to fulfill. The consensus among veterinary nutritionists is that the nutrient requirements of puppies are too exacting to be met by any home-cooked diet. Even slight errors in the formulation and preparation of a puppy's daily diet can have permanent health consequences.

Calculating the appropriate levels of protein, carbohydrates, fat, and fiber for a puppy diet is fairly simple; getting the micronutrients right is not. Commercial puppy foods that are labeled as "complete and balanced for the growth of dogs" contain precise amounts of 10 amino acids; 2 essential fatty acids; 12 minerals; and 12 vitamins (see "Picking a Puppy Food," page 48). Dog food manufacturers are able to analyze the nutrients in the raw ingredients they use, as well as in the finished food. Because they prepare large batches of food at once, they add vitamins and minerals by the gram or kilogram, not the thousandth or even millionth of a gram a home cook would have to calculate.

Simply adding a standard multivitamin and mineral supplement won't solve the problem. If you read the fine print on the puppy vitamin/mineral supplements sold at pet stores, you'll see that they are to be given *in addition* to a balanced commercial diet, not to correct dietary deficiencies.

What are the potential consequences of a homemade diet for puppies? Severe bone and joint deformity is the most common. Puppies require a precise ratio of calcium to phosphorus in their diet—in addition to appropriate total amounts of those minerals—for normal bone development. Throw that ratio off, and a puppy's bones will become soft and weak,

leading to curved bones, fractures, and collapsed joints. Abnormal brain development, iron-deficiency anemia, and skin abnormalities are other disorders that can result from deficiencies or excesses in trace nutrients.

Clearly, the stakes are too high to risk making your puppy's food at home. Instead, choose from among the many fine large-breed growth formulas on the market, to help him grow into a strong and healthy adult Doberman.

FEEDING TO PREVENT HIP DYSPLASIA

"I have a Rottweiler puppy, and I've heard that what you feed a puppy can influence whether he gets hip dysplasia. Is this true?"

Yes, what you feed your large-breed puppy can affect whether he gets hip dysplasia. Three factors are known to contribute to the development of this joint disorder: heredity, nutrition, and exercise. Your puppy's heredity is already fixed, but you still have control over the other two factors.

To lessen the likelihood that your puppy will develop hip dysplasia, avoid overfeeding him or giving him extra calcium or vitamin D. Excess calories promote too-fast growth, which strains a puppy's developing bones and joints, and excess calcium interferes with normal bone growth and cartilage development. Feeding a puppy "rocket fuel" may make him grow faster, but it won't make him grow bigger: his adult stature is determined by genetics, and he'll reach the same size whether he grows rapidly or slowly.

Large-breed puppies—those who will weigh 50 pounds or more as an

PUPPY HEALTH HAZARDS

The No. 1 risk to your puppy's health is what he'll put in his mouth. When you're puppy-proofing your house and yard, focus on things he might chew or eat, such as the following:

Electric cords. Biting an electric cord can cause mouth burns, lung damage, or even death. Keep your puppy away from electric cords until he outgrows the "mouthy" stage.

Kitchen garbage. Getting into the garbage can cause anything from a nasty bout of vomiting and diarrhea to an intestinal obstruction that requires surgery to unblock (if your puppy gulps down something like part of a corncob or a wooden grilling skewer, which puppies have been known to do).

Small balls and dog toys that can be chewed into pieces. Most pieces of dog toys will pass through the digestive tract uneventfully, but once in a while a piece gets stuck, requiring a vet to go in there and get it out. Balls

small enough to fit inside your puppy's mouth are dangerous because they can get stuck in the back of his throat and block the air from getting into his trachea. If this should happen, do the Heimlich maneuver immediately (see page 429).

Socks, underwear, and other clothing. Although cloth may seem like a benign substance, it can easily get hung up in the digestive tract. Trapped cloth or string is often difficult to see on x-rays, and it may even cut through the intestines as they contract.

Chew toys and other objects that are hard enough to break teeth. A puppy or dog can break a tooth chewing on sterilized bones, cow hooves, rocks, or other hard objects. Give your puppy hard rubber toys (such as Kong or Nylabone) or rawhide to chew on instead. Supervise your puppy closely when you give him rawhide—if he gnaws off large pieces and tries to swallow them, take away the rawhide to prevent choking.

adult—should not be given unlimited access to food. Instead of setting out a bowl of dry food and refilling it whenever it gets low, give your large-breed puppy a measured amount of food, divided into three meals per day. Use the amount suggested on the food package as a starting point, then increase or decrease the amount as needed to keep your puppy lean but not bony.

Several manufacturers now sell food designed for large- or giant-breed pup-

pies, or you can feed your large-breed puppy a good-quality adult food instead. Read the "Guaranteed Analysis" section of the label and choose a food that contains between 28 percent and 32 percent protein, between 8 percent and 15 percent fat, and between 1 percent and 1.5 percent calcium.

Overly strenuous exercise can strain developing bones and joints and worsen any inherited tendency toward hip dysplasia. So don't run your puppy for hours

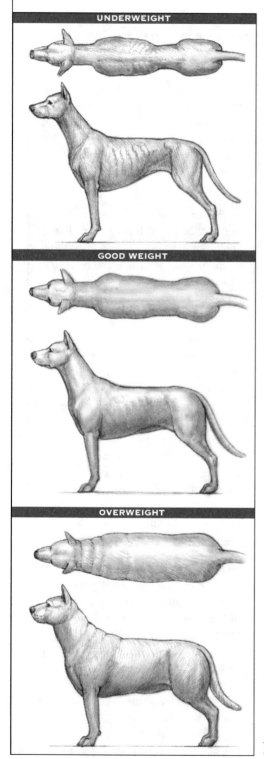

UNDERWEIGHT

GOOD WEIGHT

OVERWEIGHT

on end, and don't go roller blading or jogging with him until he is full-grown. Be especially careful to avoid activities that involve jumping—postpone the frisbee catching and agility classes until he's around 18 months old.

PUPPY FAT

"How can I tell how much food my puppy needs?"

Weigh your puppy and use the feeding guidelines on the puppy food package as a starting point. Then check her ribs once a week to determine whether she's underweight, overweight, or just right.

❑ If you can see her ribs, she's underweight. Increase the amount you feed her by about one-fourth, and continue checking her body condition each week and increasing her food as needed.

❑ If you can feel her ribs easily with the flat of your hand but not see them, her weight is just right, and you can continue feeding the same amount.

❑ If you have to push through a thin layer of fat to feel her ribs distinctly with the flat of your hand, she's overweight. Decrease her food by about one-fourth and continue monitoring her body condition once a week. Unless she's really fat, you shouldn't need to decrease her food again, because she'll grow into some of the extra weight.

Divide your puppy's daily food ration into three meals per day until she's about four months old, then switch her to two meals a day (breakfast and dinner).

Ribs should be easy to feel—but not see—in both puppies and adult dogs (left).

Unless they are underweight, puppies should be switched to adult food when they're six to eight months old.

THE POTBELLIED PUP

"My 10-week-old puppy has a round tummy, and my neighbor says that means he has worms. Is that true?"

Not necessarily. Most puppies have a bit of a potbelly, especially right after they eat, because their abdominal muscles are weaker and their abdominal organs are proportionally larger than an adult dog's. However, many puppies also have roundworms, because these parasites are passed along from the mother while the pups are in utero or nursing. The best way to find out for sure whether your puppy has worms is to have your vet do a fecal test, which involves checking a small sample of the feces microscopically for worm eggs.

For information on diagnosing and treating all kinds of intestinal parasites, see Chapter 6.

TO PEE OR NOT TO PEE

"What's the best way to housebreak a puppy?"

Take advantage of the puppy's natural eat/poop, drink/pee reflex. A puppy will get the urge to urinate and defecate 10 to 20 minutes after drinking or eating, so feed him three meals a day rather than leaving food out all the time, and take him outside to his "bathroom" about 10 minutes after he finishes eating. His bathroom should be a small area in your yard or, if you're paper-training, a small section of your kitchen or bath-

room floor covered in newspaper or housebreaking pads. When you think he needs to relieve himself, take him straight to his bathroom so he can learn to associate the site with the desired action.

It's also helpful to come up with a verbal cue for what you want him to do—take him to his spot and say "Bathroom" or any other word of your choosing. Just as racehorses are taught to urinate when a whistle is blown (to facilitate post-race drug testing), so too can your puppy learn to do his business when you say "Business," or whatever.

Stay at the bathroom spot for five minutes or so. If your puppy doesn't urinate and defecate within that time, take him back inside and put him in his crate (if you're crate-training him) or keep him tethered to you by his leash (so you can rush him back outside if he squats or looks like he's about to) for 20 minutes. Then take him back outside to his bathroom and try again. Repeat until he urinates or defecates, then praise him extravagantly and reward him with a short walk or playtime.

Aside from right after he eats or drinks, your puppy will need to urinate as soon as he wakes up (in the morning or after a nap), right before you go to bed, and at appropriate intervals throughout the day. A puppy can hold his urine for roughly one hour per month of his age, so take an 8-week-old puppy out every two hours, a 12-week-old puppy every three hours, and so on.

Using these guidelines, your puppy should be reliably housebroken by the time he's five months old. If he isn't, ask your vet whether there could be a physical cause, and if there isn't, work with a trainer to fine-tune your housebreaking routine.

HIGH-RISE HOUSEBREAKING

"I've heard that puppies shouldn't come in contact with other dogs until they've had all their shots. As I don't have an enclosed yard—I live on the 11th floor of an apartment building—does this mean I have to paper-train my puppy indoors?"

It's true that it's best to keep a puppy away from other dogs and their feces and urine until she has had all her vaccines, usually at 16 or 17 weeks. If you're a city dweller who can't create a dog-free zone near your apartment building, you can paper-train your puppy as directed in the previous Q&A; and then retrain her after she's had all her shots by taking her and some newspaper or a housebreaking pad outside and placing it where you want her to go. Before long, your puppy will get the hang of going outdoors and you'll be able to skip the newspaper.

VAGINAL DISCHARGE IN A PUPPY

"My six-month-old Lab mix has started licking her vulva constantly. Does this mean she's coming into heat or has an infection?"

She may be coming into heat, or she may have what's known as puppy vaginitis. Females first come into heat sometime between the ages of 6 and 24 months, smaller dogs earlier than larger dogs (because smaller dogs mature faster). But rising hormone levels long before that first heat can trigger a heavy vaginal discharge in some puppies. This discharge may be thin and clear or thick and whitish or yellowish, and it often persists for several weeks. Owners may notice only their dog's constant licking, not the discharge itself.

If she's in heat, her vulva will be swollen, the discharge may be streaked with blood, and male dogs will be obsessively interested in her (see page 338 for more about the heat cycle).

The best treatment for puppy vaginitis is to wait it out. The discharge may contain some bacteria or yeast that have hopped on for the ride, but antibiotics or antifungal medications won't eliminate the problem because the discharge is set off by hormones, not by an infection. Once a puppy has gone through her first heat, her hormones level out and the vaginitis usually disappears for good.

Because that first heat is the most reliable cure, it's often recommended to let a dog with puppy vaginitis go through one heat before being spayed. Waiting through one heat increases her risk of breast cancer in later life (from 0.5 percent in dogs spayed before their first heat to 8 percent in dogs spayed between their first and second heat) and the risk of an unwanted pregnancy, but it decreases the possibility that she'll have vaginitis as a lifelong problem.

A NEW ADDITION TO THE PACK

"I have an adult dog and will be getting an eight-week-old puppy soon. Do I need to separate the puppy and the adult at first, or can they be together immediately?"

It's a good idea to keep the puppy quarantined at least until you've had a chance to take her to your vet and verify that she's healthy and up-to-date with her vaccines and deworming. Otherwise, the puppy could potentially transmit roundworms or another contagious condition to your adult dog. Be sure to keep your adult dog away from the new pup's feces as well as the puppy herself until you've verified that the puppy doesn't have worms.

There's also a chance your adult dog could transmit a virus or parasite to your puppy. This is unlikely if the adult dog has been vaccinated and is in good health, but ask your vet about the possibility if you're concerned.

Finally, it's best to give any new dog or cat its "own room" for a while to give the resident animals a chance to adjust to the smells and sounds of someone who may be perceived as an interloper. Don't leave your puppy and your adult dog alone together in one room until you're sure they can get along peacefully in your absence. For tips on preventing sibling rivalry between dogs, see page 192.

THE TOOTH FAIRY

"My four-month-old puppy's teeth are falling out! What could be wrong?"

Probably nothing. Like children, puppies have "baby teeth" that fall out and are replaced by adult teeth. Some owners never see the shed baby teeth because the puppies swallow them, but they may notice a drop of blood on a chew toy now and then.

The last adult teeth to come in are the canines (fangs) in the upper jaw. Those appear by the time a dog is six months old. (Shelter workers determine whether "mystery" pups are older or younger than six months by looking for those adult canine teeth.)

Occasionally a baby tooth doesn't fall out by six months, and the adult tooth will crowd in next to it. Retained baby teeth should be removed because they

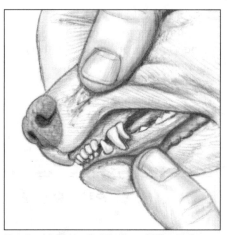

Retained baby teeth, like the smaller canine tooth above, can cause a misaligned bite and tooth-root infections.

interfere with the alignment of the permanent teeth and can cause tooth-root infections. Retained baby teeth are commonly removed while a young dog is anesthetized for spaying or neutering.

DEWCLAW REMOVAL, TAIL DOCKING, AND EAR CROPPING

"At what age are a puppy's dewclaws, tail, and ears operated on? What are the medical pros and cons?"

There is no medical reason to dock a puppy's tail or crop his ears. Those procedures are done purely for appearance's sake, and it's the owner's choice whether to have them done or not. Dewclaws are sometimes removed for medical reasons, but most often it's cosmetic surgery as well.

A dewclaw is the innermost toe (of five) on each foot. Dewclaws are found up around the ankle or not at all—some dogs are born without them. There's medical justification for removing them if the nails curve close to the skin and will be difficult to keep trimmed, or if the hair on the puppy's legs will be clipped and the dew-claws are likely to get nicked repeatedly by the clippers or scissors. Otherwise, removing dewclaws is a cosmetic choice. Certain breeds, such as Great Pyrenees, Bernese Mountain Dogs, and Briards, are supposed to have *double* rear dewclaws, and theirs are never removed.

Tail docking and dewclaw removal are usually done when puppies are three to five days old. The puppies are not anesthetized because the anesthetic risk at that age is felt to outweigh the pain the puppies feel during the 30-second procedure. The tails and dewclaws are amputated with surgical scissors or a scalpel. The skin of the tail is closed with surgical glue or a couple of sutures. The skin on the

---

PUPPY SKIN PROBLEMS

When people think of puppy skin, they picture soft folds and velvety fur, not pimples, scabs, and bumps. But puppies are susceptible to infections that can temporarily mar that soft skin.

Puppy pyoderma is a mild infection of the thinly haired skin on the belly of puppies between 2 and 16 weeks old. The infection looks like bumps, pimples, or scabs and is usually associated with a damp, dirty, or crowded environment. The treatment consists of keeping the puppy's environment (such as the kennel or crate) clean and dry, and washing the infected areas of the skin with a few drops of chlorhexidine or povidone-iodine (Betadine) anti-bacterial cleanser diluted in water. Pat the skin dry after washing. Wash the skin twice a day at first, tapering off to once a day and then every other day as the infection clears up. Oral antibiotics usually aren't needed, and the infection should disappear within 10 days. If it doesn't, have your vet take a look.

Pimples can pop up on an adolescent dog's face, believe it or not. See page 102 for how to treat canine acne.

Puppy warts are small fleshy or knobby lumps that suddenly sprout on a dog's lips, muzzle, or mouth. They are caused by a virus that is transmitted from one dog to another by close contact, such as play-fighting. They typically appear in dogs who are 6 to 12 months old, but they can also occur in older dogs who haven't previously been exposed to the virus. (The virus is dog-specific, so you can't catch the warts from your puppy.) Warts may be single or multiple, and they typically enlarge over a few weeks, then disappear over a month or two as the dog's immune system gears up against the virus. No treatment is necessary unless the warts

Puppy warts are caused by a virus and go away on their own.

feet may be glued, sutured, or left alone if there isn't much bleeding. Complications are rare and primarily cosmetic—the end of the tail may feel lumpy or bony after it's healed, and it may be slightly longer or shorter than desired.

Ear cropping is most often done when puppies are between 8 and 12 weeks old. The pup is put under general anesthesia, the ear cartilage and skin are cut to the desired shape, the skin is sutured together along the cut edges, and the ears are taped upright using cardboard tubes, tongue depressors, gauze rolls, a disposable coffee cup, or various other contraptions for support. The stitches are removed 7 to 10 days after surgery, but the ears usually need to be taped and supported for weeks to months after that before they will stay upright on their own.

Potential medical complications include persistent bleeding, swelling, or infection in the first week or two after surgery. The main source of dissatisfaction for owners, however, is the cosmetic outcome: sometimes the ears won't stand upright despite months of taping, or the tips may twist or bend, or the shape of the ears may not be to the owner's liking. Many vets don't crop ears because they feel it isn't worth the aggravation. To find a vet who is experienced in ear crops in your breed of dog, ask breeders in your area for their recommendations.

SPAYING AND NEUTERING

"At what age should a puppy be spayed or neutered?"

A dog can be safely spayed or neutered anytime from the age of eight weeks through old age. Spaying or neutering at six months is optimal for preventing unwanted pregnancies, roaming, and hormone-related aggression between dogs. To reduce the risk of breast cancer, a female dog should be spayed before her first heat, which usually occurs between the ages of 6 and 18 months. If she has severe puppy vaginitis, however, it's advisable to wait until she has gone through one heat (see page 54).

---

are numerous (I once heard of a dog with 23 of them), continually become irritated and bleed, or interfere with the dog's ability to eat. In such cases, giving the dog immune-system boosters (such as antioxidant vitamins) and cimetidine (Tagamet) may help—consult your vet for the proper dose.

Demodex mites can create thin patches in a puppy's fur, especially around the eyes or elsewhere on the face. For more on diagnosing and treating mange mites, see page 167.

Puppy strangles is a swelling and inflammation of the face, usually accompanied by swollen lymph nodes in the neck, in a young dog (usually less than six months old). It's caused by a temporary misfiring of the immune system, and is believed to be hereditary because it's seen more often in certain breeds (such as Dachshunds, Golden Retrievers, yellow Labrador Retrievers, Lhasa Apsos, setters, and pointers) than in others. One puppy or several in a litter may be affected. The treatment is corticosteroids (to calm the immune system) and also antibiotics (to fight off any secondary bacterial infection).

CHAPTER 3

Keeping Your Adult and Senior Dog Healthy

WHERE HAS YOUR PUPPY GONE? Once a dog has reached the one-year mark, the pace of physical changes slows dramatically. You may miss that rambunctious baby, but look at the bright side. If you continue to focus on preventive health measures such as good nutrition, exercise, safety, and home dental care, you may now be able to limit your vet visits to once a year. The senior years—beginning anywhere from age 8 in an extra-large dog to 12 in a small dog—often bring an increase in medical concerns, but your continued good care will have an enormous impact on your older dog's health and well-being.

CHOOSING A VET

"How can I find the best vet in my area?"

Start by listing the qualities you find most important in a veterinarian. These can include anything from personality traits to location to office hours to philosophies on such things as diet and vaccines.

Then ask dog-owning friends and acquaintances which vets they recommend. Seek referrals especially from people whose dogs are at a similar life stage (such as puppy or senior), have similar medical issues (such as hip dysplasia, skin problems, or seizures), or have similar temperaments (very nervous, very dominant, and so on) as your dog. Remember that no vet is loved by every client all the time—we're just like the rest of humanity that way—so don't expect any vet to get straight As across the board. Focus on the issues that are the most important to you.

Once you have some recommendations, drop by the more promising practices during office hours and see if they seem like the kind of place you'd feel comfortable bringing your dog. Note whether the office is clean and whether the staff (receptionist, technicians, assistants) seems friendly, efficient, and well-trained.

If you have a clear favorite, schedule an office visit for your dog. Tell the veterinarian that you're "auditioning" to find a permanent vet. Ask for the vet's opinion about your dog's medical issues and any other care issues you feel strongly about. Observe how you, the vet, and your dog all interact. Are you a good match? If so, great. If not, better to keep looking.

While you're looking for a long-term veterinary relationship, remember that unexpected illnesses and emergencies do crop up, so be sure you have a backup plan of a vet or a veterinary emergency clinic to call if your dog should suddenly become ill. Also, if you find your veterinary soul mate at a large practice, remember that he or she may not be the vet who will care for your dog during an emergency: someone else may be on call that day.

THE VACCINE CONTROVERSY

"Do adult dogs need vaccine boosters every year?"

No, they don't. That short-and-sweet answer reflects a major change in thinking among veterinarians, one that merits a detailed explanation.

Giving dogs yearly vaccine boosters against the Big 3 viral diseases—distemper, parvo, and infectious hepatitis—was accepted veterinary practice until the late 1990s. Why? Because exactly how long the vaccines protected dogs against those diseases was unclear. Vaccine manufacturers typically tested their products' effectiveness under laboratory conditions to a year or two postvaccination, and then stopped testing. Veterinarians wanted to be certain dogs remained protected, and the vaccines themselves were considered perfectly safe, so we adopted a practice of giving boosters every year.

Then our conviction that dog and cat vaccines were absolutely safe was rocked. In the late 1990s, it was discovered that vaccinations had caused malignant tumors at the injection sites in a small number of cats (estimated at 1 or

11 TIPS FOR A HEALTHY, HAPPY ADULT DOG

Once your dog has reached adulthood, your relationship will probably settle into a routine. Make sure it's a mutually rewarding one by following these guidelines.

1. Give your dog at least a half hour of your undivided attention every day. Play with him, brush him, or practice obedience commands or tricks.

2. Give him plenty of exercise every day.

3. Make sure he wears a flat collar and up-to-date ID tag at all times, even indoors, to help bring him home safely if he should escape or get lost.

4. Keep practicing basic obedience commands: "Come," "Sit," "Down," "Heel," and so on. Sign up for a refresher course if your dog or you need it.

5. Take him to the vet once a year for a thorough physical exam and discussion of any new or ongoing health issues.

6. Brush his teeth once a day. That may sound like a lot, but you have to stay ahead of the tartar. See page 82 for the easy way to brush.

7. Keep him on heartworm prevention during mosquito season.

8. Bathe him whenever he's dirty, smelly, or itchy.

9. If your dog is home alone all day, consider putting him in "doggie daycare" or hiring a dog walker to take him out during the day. Dogs are intensely social animals, and they become bored, lonely, and destructive without companionship.

10. Provide your dog with a comfortable place to rest in the area where he spends most of his time, and respect his need for "quiet time" when he's napping or relaxing there.

11. Supervise children when they play with your dog, and teach them not to tease him or encourage undesirable behaviors, such as chasing and barking.

---

2 per 10,000 vaccinated cats). Although this vaccine/cancer connection was seen only in cats, not in dogs, veterinarians and animal owners alike began to question the more-is-better philosophy of vaccine boosters.

Researchers started compiling statistics on the long-term effectiveness of vaccines. The data came mainly from vaccine manufacturers' tests, measurements of antibody titers in vaccinated dogs, and natural disease outbreaks, rather than new "challenge" studies in which vaccinated dogs were deliber- ately exposed to viruses to see whether they would become ill. One influential report by veterinary researcher R. D. Schultz, published in 2000, stated that the currently available vaccines against parvo, distemper, and infectious hepatitis remained effective for at least seven years in more than 90 percent of dogs.

Rabies is a separate issue. Schultz's data indicated that the rabies vaccine is effective for at least three years (not seven years) in 85 percent of dogs (rather than 90 percent). In addition, rabies is a public-health issue for people as well as for animals, and states regulate how often cats and dogs must receive a rabies booster. The frequency ranges from every year to every three years, depending on how prevalent rabies is among the wildlife in that state.

Vaccines against kennel cough, Lyme, and leptospirosis are another exception. Those diseases are bacterial (or partly bacterial, in the case of kennel cough), and vaccines against bacteria are protective for only 6 to 12 months, so dogs who need those vaccines need them at least once a year.

In 2006, the American Animal Hospital Association, whose members include more than 6,000 companion-animal practices in the United States and Canada, released its canine vaccine guidelines. Those guidelines recommend giving booster vaccines against distemper, infectious hepatitis, and parvo every three years or even less often, at the veterinarian's discretion. To date, however, the American Veterinary Medical Association, with a membership of more than 76,000 veterinarians, has not endorsed any specific vaccine intervals. The AVMA's position is that individual veterinarians should set their own vaccine protocols based on local and individual risk factors.

In the real world of small-animal practice, that is just what veterinarians are doing. Some still recommend boosters every year. Some advise annual blood tests to check antibody levels, or titers, against distemper and parvo, followed by boosters if the titers are too low to be considered protective. (The correlation between an antibody titer and what would happen if the dog encountered the virus in the real world isn't exact.) Others give boosters or check antibody levels every three years. Antibody tests are

more expensive than vaccines, so some dog owners choose to skip the blood test and simply give their dog the shot.

If you're uncomfortable with your vet's vaccine policy, ask for the reasons behind it and whether the practice offers any alternatives to the usual protocol. If you're not satisfied with the explanations you get, you'll probably be happier finding a vet whose thinking about vaccines is closer to your own.

Some things have not changed during this shift in thinking about vaccines. It's still recommended that puppies receive a series of vaccines, followed by boosters when they're one year old, as outlined on page 46. Adult dogs whose vaccine history is unknown, such as those adopted from shelters, should either have their antibody titers checked or receive booster vaccines twice, three weeks apart, against distemper, parvo, and infectious hepatitis. And all dogs should be on heartworm prevention and have a physical exam once a year so that illnesses can be detected and treated sooner rather than later.

ADVERSE EFFECTS OF VACCINES

"Some of the dog owners I see in the park are convinced that vaccines are dangerous. Is this true?"

Vaccines protect dogs against common and potentially deadly diseases. They also carry a small risk of causing harm. Here's what's known and what's being investigated about vaccine side effects.

❑ **Overall risks.** A 2005 study of 1.2 million dogs vaccinated at 360 animal hospitals reported 38 "adverse events" per 10,000 dogs vaccinated. These adverse events occurred within 72 hours of vaccination and included everything from pain at the injection site to vomiting or diarrhea, hives, or anaphylactic shock (see "Severe vaccine reactions," below). Reactions were most common in smaller dogs (those weighing less than 22 pounds) receiving more than one vaccine at the same time.

❏ **Vaccines and cancer.** Vaccines have caused malignant tumors at the injection site in approximately 1 or 2 cats per 10,000 vaccinated. Studies have found no connection between vaccines and cancer in dogs.

❏ **Severe vaccine reactions.** A small number of dogs—probably fewer than 1 in 1,000—go into anaphylactic shock after receiving a vaccine. Anaphylactic shock is a severe allergic reaction that can be fatal if not treated immediately (see page 48). Vaccines against leptospirosis seem to carry the highest risk of provoking such reactions, but any vaccine could be the trigger for a particular dog. There's no way to test dogs beforehand for their likelihood of having a severe allergic reaction to a vaccine. A dog who has had a mild allergic reaction to a vaccine—such as swelling at the injection site or a swollen face—is considered high risk for having a more severe reaction in the future.

❏ **Vaccines and immune-mediated diseases.** Diseases caused by a misfiring of the immune system—for example, antibody attacks against a dog's own thyroid hormone or red blood cells—seem to have increased over the past 20 years, but whether this is an increase in diagnosis or in actual occurrence of those diseases isn't clear. Immune-system diseases are *occasionally* triggered in dogs (and in people) by an infection, drug,

or vaccine. Most often, however, those diseases appear "out of the blue" and have no identifiable cause.

A 1996 study of 58 dogs who had developed immune-mediated hemolytic anemia—an antibody attack on red blood cells—showed that 26 percent had been vaccinated in the previous four weeks. However, no research has ever found a direct cause-and-effect relationship between vaccines and hemolytic anemia.

Other studies have shown that dogs produce more anti-thyroid-hormone antibodies—which could potentially lead to immune-mediated hypothyroidism—after being vaccinated, but a connection between vaccines and full-blown hypothyroidism has not been documented so far.

Research into the subject is ongoing, but as of this writing, no direct connection between vaccines and immune-mediated diseases has been uncovered.

VACCINATING AGAINST LEPTOSPIROSIS

"The breeder I bought my puppy from says the leptospirosis vaccine is dangerous. My vet says dogs who are at high risk for getting the disease should have the vaccine. Who's right?"

They're both right. The leptospirosis (lepto) vaccine is somewhat more likely than other vaccines to cause a serious allergic reaction, but the risk is still extremely small for an individual dog. The risk is highest in very young puppies, so a puppy should be at least 12 weeks old before being vaccinated against lepto.

Leptospirosis is caused by bacteria that are spread by the urine of infected animals (wildlife and livestock as well as dogs). It causes severe kidney and liver damage. The bacteria can live for a long time on wet soil and in standing water, such as ponds and lakes. Dogs who are at high risk for getting lepto are those who wade in, swim in, or drink from ponds or stagnant pools of water in areas of the country where the disease is common (such as the Northeast and Midwest). Urban and suburban wildlife that can harbor lepto include rats, skunks, squirrels, opossums, and raccoons, so a dog who chases and kills those animals is also at risk. People can catch leptospirosis by swimming in contaminated water or coming into contact with the urine of infected animals.

The specific strains of bacteria that cause the majority of lepto cases in dogs have shifted over the past 20 years. A lepto vaccine introduced in 2000 protects against the two "newer" strains (*Leptospira grippotyphosa* and *L. pomona*) as well as the two "older" strains (*L. icterohaemorrhagiae* and *L. canicola*). The vaccine doesn't offer 100 percent protection against lepto, but it significantly reduces the likelihood a dog will contract the disease and, if he does, the severity of the symptoms.

What does lepto look like in dogs? Symptoms usually appear one to two weeks after the dog has been exposed to the bacteria and can include fever, lethargy, weakness, loss of appetite, drinking and urinating more than usual, vomiting, or jaundice (yellowing of the skin, gums, or whites of the eyes). Lepto is diagnosed by checking blood samples for rising levels of antibodies against the bacteria, or by examining a tissue sample from the liver or kidneys for the bacteria.

Leptospirosis can be fatal, and a dog who comes down with the disease needs prompt, aggressive treatment. Lepto is treated with antibiotics, often two weeks of penicillin followed by two weeks of doxycycline. Dogs usually remain in the hospital on IV fluids for several days or more to combat the liver and kidney damage.

Now that you're armed with the facts about leptospirosis, you and your vet can discuss whether your dog is in the high-risk category and should be vaccinated against the disease.

VACCINATING AGAINST LYME DISEASE

"I live in the Northeast, and last fall my dog got two ticks on her. Should she be vaccinated against Lyme disease?"

Probably not. If a dog picks up a tick only occasionally, I recommend using a reliable tick-killing product rather than the Lyme vaccine. Products that are effective against deer ticks—the type that can transmit Lyme disease—include amitraz (found in some tick collars and sprays) and fipronil (found in some spot-ons). Read labels carefully. If a product is effective against deer ticks, it will say so. Use the tick product according to label instructions during times when your dog may encounter ticks.

Dogs are most likely to encounter ticks in wooded areas or meadows—ticks like to hang out in underbrush, leaf piles, and tall grass. They're less fond of mowed lawns and other exposed places that don't provide much protection from the sun. The young deer ticks that are best at transmitting Lyme disease are especially active during the weeks

HOW OLD IS THAT IN PEOPLE YEARS?

You may be surprised to hear that a dog's relative age is based on his size: small dogs mature faster but also live longer than large dogs. So multiplying a dog's age by seven isn't accurate most of the time. The table below provides a more precise reckoning of your dog's relative age.

4 TO 20 POUNDS		21 TO 50 POUNDS		51 TO 85 POUNDS		OVER 85 POUNDS	
Dog Years	People Years	Dog Years	People Years	Dog Years	People Years	Dog Years	People Years
1	18	1	16	1	15	1	14
2	24	2	22	2	20	2	19
3	28	3	28	3	30	3	32
4	32	4	33	4	35	4	37
5	36	5	37	5	40	5	42
6	40	6	42	6	45	6	49
7	44	7	47	7	50	7	56
8	48	8	51	8	55	8	63
9	52	9	56	9	61	9	70
10	56	10	60	10	66	10	77
11	60	11	65	11	72	11	84
12	64	12	69	12	77	12	91
13	68	13	74	13	82	13	98
14	72	14	78	14	88		
15	76	15	83	15	93		
16	80	16	88	16	99		
17	84	17	93				
18	88	18	98				
19	92						
20	96						

when the weather shifts from warm to cold and vice versa—for example, October/November and March/April in the Northeast. So be sure to use a tick protectant on your dog when she may be roaming through meadows or woods, especially in the fall and spring.

If a dog in a Lyme-infested area routinely gets a lot of ticks, or if any of the people she lives with have been diagnosed with the disease, then I recommend a belt-plus-suspenders approach: tick protectant plus the Lyme vaccine.

VACCINATING AGAINST KENNEL COUGH AND CORONA VIRUS

"Should my dog be vaccinated against kennel cough and corona?"

Only if a boarding kennel, dog show, or other event your dog will be attending demands it. Kennel cough is a mild illness—basically a cold with a cough—that is unlikely to cause serious harm in a healthy adult dog (see page 278). Corona is a virus that can cause mild diarrhea, but virtually all adult dogs have been exposed to it and are immune.

WHAT'S IN THE CAN?

"I always buy the canned dog foods that look like a real dinner—with meat slices, rice, peas, and carrots in gravy—for my Bichon Frisé. They look much more appetizing than the stuff that comes out of the can in one big lump. Are they better?"

Nope, you've been fooled by the magic of marketing and technology. Try this experiment: empty a small can of this stew-type dinner into a strainer, wash off all the sauce or gravy under running water, and spread out what's left on a plate. Now take a close look at those "meaty chunks" or "slices." They are probably soy (textured vegetable protein) pressed into meat shapes. There's nothing wrong with feeding a dog soy protein, but if you think you're feeding him roast beef, you're mistaken. The gravy? Mostly gluten, water, and salt. The peas and carrots? Sure, there are a few bits in there, but they're adding more visual appeal to you than they are nutritional value to your dog.

If meat and vegetables are what you're looking for in a canned dog food, choose a variety that's named for the meat only (just "Beef," not "Beef Entree" or "Beef Dinner"—see page 68) and add a variety of cooked vegetables from your own refrigerator.

PET FOOD POISONING

"The news of contaminated pet food killing thousands of dogs and cats in 2007 was shocking. Even some varieties of the premium food I buy were recalled, although fortunately my dog didn't get sick. Given what happened, how can I feel confident that any commercial pet food is safe?"

The scope of the contamination and the damage caused were indeed horrific: more than 180 varieties of dog and cat food and treats sold under more than 100 brand names were recalled between March and May of 2007. They were contaminated with melamine (a chemical used to make plastic and fertilizer) and cyanuric acid (a chemical often used in swimming pools). When eaten, these chemicals can combine to form crystals that damage the kidneys.

The kidney damage in affected animals ranged from mild to fatal. Symptoms included vomiting, lethargy, loss of appetite, increased thirst, and increased urination. Some animals were able to regain adequate kidney function after being given fluids (either intravenously or subcutaneously) for days to weeks. Others died despite treatment. About 4,000 dog and cat deaths were reported to the U.S. Food and Drug Administration. The actual toll was undoubtedly higher, since many dogs and cats may have died without being diagnosed, and not all suspicious deaths were reported to the FDA. In addition, thousands more animals got sick but didn't die, and thousands of others had blood and urine tests to determine whether they had been harmed by eating the contaminated foods.

The source of the 2007 contamination was wheat gluten and rice protein concentrate produced by two companies in China. These ingredients are commonly added to dog and cat foods to thicken gravy, bind dry mixtures, or boost protein levels. The Chinese manufacturers allegedly added the nitrogen-rich melamine and cyanuric acid to their products to make it look like they contained more protein than they actually did (crude protein is commonly determined by measuring nitrogen levels). The intent apparently was to increase profits by selling a cheaper product, not to deliberately poison animals.

The contaminated protein concentrates were imported into the U.S. by ChemNutra and sold to Menu Foods and about a dozen other pet food manufacturers in the United States and Canada. Menu Foods plants make "cuts and gravy" style pouch and canned foods for many other pet food companies.

In October 2008, a settlement was approved in a class-action suit brought by pet owners against about 35 companies involved in manufacturing or selling the tainted foods. The settlement provided $24 million to reimburse pet owners for their economic losses, including what they paid for the recalled food and their animals' medical tests and treatment, as well as the purchase price, "fair market value," or replacement cost of the animal. An additional $8 million had already been paid by pet food companies to settle individual lawsuits.

After this catastrophe, what assurances do we have that pet food is now safe? Inspection and testing of raw ingredients has definitely increased, but we can't be sure a particular package of dog food is 100 percent safe any more than we can be sure that no bag of organic spinach or package of ground beef in the grocery store is contaminated with *E.coli*. We still have to rely on the FDA's ability to monitor pet food production and detect problems as quickly as possible.

I was encouraged by the speed with which the FDA and pet food producers announced the 2007 contamination, recalled products, and identified the toxins and their sources. Since then, the FDA has inspected all vegetable protein products (including wheat gluten, rice protein concentrate, and corn gluten) from China before they enter the U.S. food supply. In addition, many pet food companies have stepped up their testing of ingredients and finished products. Most companies already routinely screened ingredients for such contaminants as heavy metals, bacteria, antibiotics residue, pesticides, herbicides, and mold toxins.

Ideally, consumers, too, will increase their scrutiny of what they feed their dogs and cats. To evaluate a specific food, study the label closely—especially what's printed in small type on the back and sides. Read the ingredient list. Look into any ingredients you're unfamiliar with or concerned about (to start, check the glossary starting on page 69 and "Food Myths" on page 71). The package should include a toll-free number, a website, or both, so that consumers can ask the company directly about the product. Who manufactures the food, and where are they located? Pet food sold outside of the state in which it is manufactured is bound by AAFCO (Association of American Feed Control Officials), FDA, and USDA rules. A food that has passed an AAFCO feeding trial, as opposed to a nutrient analysis only, has undergone an additional level of testing (see page 48). Manufacturers who use only USDA-inspected meat, follow FDA Good Manufacturing Practices (GMPs), or are

Hazard Analysis and Critical Control Point (HAACP) certified, have implemented extra levels of quality control.

I'm still feeding my own dog and cat commercially prepared pet food, but I'm also monitoring the FDA website, product recall lists, and pet food company news more closely than before. These are things everyone can do to help them make informed choices about what to feed their animals.

READING DOG FOOD LABELS

"I'd like to understand exactly what I'm getting when I buy dog food, but I don't know what half the ingredients are. For example, what's 'poultry digest,' and is it a bad thing to feed a dog?"

Dog food labels contain an enormous amount of information about what's in the can, pouch, or bag—if you can decipher the lingo. The U.S. Food

Meat should be the first ingredient listed in canned food, and one of the first three in dry food.

and Drug Administration's Center for Veterinary Medicine regulates the content and wording of pet food labels, but those rules are far from self-evident to the average buyer. Below are explanations and translations of the three most important sections of a dog food label: (1) the variety or flavor name; (2) the guaranteed analysis; and (3) the ingredient list. For even more on dog food labeling, go to the FDA's website: *www.fda.gov/cvm/petlabel.htm.*

THE VARIETY OR FLAVOR

More modifying words mean less of the main ingredient, according to the FDA's naming rules.

❏ To be called **Beef,** a food must contain at least 70 percent beef by weight. Only three or four superpremium canned foods contain this much meat.
❏ To be called **Beef & Liver,** a food must contain at least 70 percent beef and liver by weight, and there must be more beef than liver.
❏ To be called **Beef Dinner, Entree, Platter, Nuggets, Formula,** or a similar name, a food must contain at least 25 percent beef by weight.
❏ Something called **Dog Food with Beef** needs to contain only 3 percent beef by weight.
❏ Something called **Beef Flavor Dog Food** must only have a detectable beef flavor.

The take-home message? The simpler the name, the more beef (or chicken, lamb, or turkey) you're getting.

THE GUARANTEED ANALYSIS

This lists the minimum amounts of protein and fat and maximum amounts of fiber and moisture the food contains.

❏ More protein and fat aren't necessarily better—the best levels for your dog depend on his age, activity level, and ideal weight. For example, puppies require a minimum of 22 percent protein and 8 percent fat, but the diet of a large-breed puppy at risk of developing hip dysplasia should contain a maximum of 32 percent protein and 15 percent fat, even though some puppy foods have higher levels than that.

❏ Adult dogs require a minimum of 18 percent protein and 5 percent fat. An extremely active dog—think sled dog here—may need a lot more protein and fat than that for muscle repair and energy, but an overweight couch potato does not.

❏ The fiber level isn't a major concern for most dogs. But canned-food buyers, take note of your food's moisture level—it's probably between 72 and 78 percent. So when you buy canned food, three-quarters of what you're paying for is water. That's why dry food is a more economical choice.

THE INGREDIENT LIST

Here's where it really gets interesting. The ingredients are listed in descending order by their weight in the finished product, just like in people food. Two key facts to remember here: (1) "wet" foods, like fresh meat, weigh more than dry foods, like ground corn, so wetter foods will naturally wind up near the top of an ingredient list; and (2) manufacturers can downplay how much of a particular ingredient is in the food by using different forms of it. A food whose ingredient list includes flaked corn, ground corn, and cornmeal, for example, contains a lot more corn than you might have thought at first glance.

What ingredients are good and bad in dog food? First, the generalities. Meat provides all the amino acids (the building blocks of protein) a dog needs, so meat should be one of the first three ingredients in a dry dog food and the first ingredient in a canned dog food. (It is possible, however, to devise a healthy vegetarian diet for a dog—see page 73.) Second, dogs don't need sweeteners (such as corn syrup or molasses) or artificial colors in their food, so avoid foods that include them.

Now the specifics. Here's a glossary that explains some common dog food ingredients.

❏ Meat and other animal products provide protein, fat, and calcium. Beef is used below as an example, but the definitions also apply to the other meat sources.

Animal fat. Fat from any combination of cattle, pigs, sheep, and goats.

Beef. The muscle tissue of cattle. Along with the kind of muscle we know as steak and ground beef, it may include the tongue, heart, and muscle from the esophagus and diaphragm. Fat and skin (minus the hair) that are attached to the muscle and blood vessels, nerves, and connective tissue within the muscle can be included.

Beef by-products. The non-muscle tissue of cattle, which may include the internal organs (liver, kidneys, spleen, lungs, intestines, and brain), udder, bone, blood, blood vessels, cartilage, and tendons.

Bone meal. Cooked and ground bones. A source of calcium.

Casein. The main protein in milk.

Chicken. The muscle, skin, and bones of chickens, minus the feathers, heads, feet, and internal organs.

Chicken by-products. The heads, necks, feet, and internal organs of chickens.

Digest. Meat and organs that are partially digested with enzymes and used as a flavor coating on dry food.

Dried egg product. Dried whole eggs, minus the shells; a source of protein and fat.

Dried whey. The portion of milk that remains after cheese is made, in dried form. A source of protein and minerals.

Meal. Any ingredient that has been ground or otherwise reduced to small particles.

Meat. Muscle tissue from any combination of cattle, pigs, sheep, and goats. A dog food that contains meat from another source must list it explicitly: "venison," "rabbit," or "horsemeat," for example.

Poultry. The muscle, skin, and bones of a variety of poultry, including chickens, turkeys, ducks, and so on.

Poultry by-products. Like chicken by-products but from a variety of poultry, such as chickens, turkeys, and ducks.

❏ Non-animal protein sources are used because they're less expensive. They don't contain as broad a range of amino acids as meat does, so they shouldn't be the only protein source (except in a vegetarian diet; see page 73).

Alfalfa meal. The high-protein portion of the grain alfalfa.

Brewer's dried yeast. Yeast that is filtered from a fermented beverage and dried. A source of protein and B vitamins.

Brewer's rice. The high-protein fraction of rice after most of the starch has been fermented away in brewing.

Germ. The innermost portion of grain seeds, often removed when grains are ground into flour. A source of protein and fat.

Gluten. The protein fraction of a grain, with most of the carbohydrate and fiber removed.

Soy flour, soybean meal. The high-protein portion of soybeans, often used to make textured vegetable protein, which can be formed into the "meaty chunks" or "carved slices" that resemble meat in canned dog food.

❏ Non-animal fat sources include flaxseed and vegetable oils, such as corn, safflower, soybean, or sunflower oil.

❏ Grains and vegetables provide mainly carbohydrates, fiber, or both. Many are commonly eaten by people as well as dogs, so I've listed only the less familiar.

Bran. The outer coating of grain seeds. A source of fiber.

Cellulose. The fiber portion of plants.

Dried beet pulp. The material that remains after sugar is extracted from beets. A source of moderately fermentable fiber.

Dried kelp. A source of carbohydrates.

Flaxseed, flaxseed meal. A source of carbohydrates and fat.

Mill run. The hulls of grain that are removed when it is ground into flour. A source of fiber.

Pomace. The skins and seeds of vegetables or fruits after they have been juiced. A source of fiber.

❏ Preservatives prevent mold and bacteria from growing in the food.

BHA, BHT. Preservatives widely used in human food as well as pet food.

Citric acid. An antioxidant that is a natural preservative.

Ethoxyquin. A preservative that in the 1990s was the focus of a widespread myth that it could cause health problems ranging from allergies to cancer. Studies have found no connection between ethoxyquin and cancer or any other health problem in dogs, and it continues to have FDA approval.

Potassium sorbate. Prevents mold growth.

Tocopherols. Antioxidants that are a natural preservative.

FOOD MYTHS

"Why do so many dog foods contain corn and wheat? I thought dogs can't digest grains."

What you've heard is one of many myths suggesting that certain foods are allergenic, indigestible, toxic, or otherwise bad for dogs. (For foods that truly are dangerous, see "Table Food" on page 74.) Here are the facts about some of the most commonly cited food culprits.

Meat by-products. These can include internal organs (such as the heart, lungs, kidneys, stomach, intestines, and brain), bone, cartilage, tendons, blood vessels, and other animal parts that people rarely eat. It's true that they contain less high-quality protein than does meat, which is defined as the muscle tissue of an animal. However, under FDA rules, meat by-products do *not* contain hair, horns, teeth, hooves, roadkill, or dog and cat carcasses. They can be a good natural source of such nutrients as glucosamine and calcium, and dogs find meat by-products very tasty.

Some meat by-products come from plants that are USDA certified to process meat for human consumption. Others come from plants that produce pet food only. So-called "4D meats" are those that have been rejected for human consumption because the animals were disabled, diseased, dying, or dead at the time of inspection. The FDA does allow the use of meat from certain disabled animals in pet food if it is processed to destroy potential disease-causing microorganisms. The thought of sick animals being turned into pet food is disturbing, it's true. In reality, most of the 4D animals that are rerouted to pet food processors are cattle that have broken a leg on their way to the meatpacking plant or in a holding pen, and dairy cows who can't walk because their blood calcium levels are depleted from making milk. If you want to avoid any chance that your dog food contains meat from such animals, look for a food that says it uses "only USDA-certified meat." "Human-grade" is meant to convey the same idea but has no regulatory meaning.

Wheat. Veterinary dermatologists estimate that 10 to 20 percent of dogs who are itchy year-round have a food allergy (see page 99). Some of those food-allergic dogs may be allergic to wheat. The vast majority of dogs are *not* allergic to wheat and can digest it perfectly well.

Corn. This is an ingredient that's often condemned on dog enthusiast websites as "filler," meaning a cheap ingredient that is indigestible or has little or no nutritional value. Cracked corn, cornmeal, and the like may be less expensive than meat, it's true, but they do have nutritional value: they contain complex carbohydrates, linolenic acid, and essential amino acids. Most dogs digest corn just fine, and most dogs are not allergic to it. If you are concerned about the amount of "filler" in a particular dog food, just check the fiber content on the back label: the percentage of fiber is the percentage of indigestible material. Note that all dogs need some fiber, especially fermentable fiber (see "Beet pulp," below), so the food that contains the least fiber isn't necessarily the best food. Reduced-calorie dog foods, designed to help dogs lose weight, usually contain more fiber and less fat than the regular versions.

Soy. A few dogs are allergic to soy, but most are not. Soy is a digestible and less expensive source of protein than meat. It does not cause bloat (see page 136). The worst thing about soy, in my opinion, is that it can be used to trick dog owners into thinking they are buying a food that contains a lot of meat when it doesn't (see page 66).

Pork. Lean, unseasoned pork is a good protein source for dogs. It is no more allergenic than any other meat.

Gluten. Following the melamine poisonings of 2007, gluten got a bad rap. But unless it has been adulterated, gluten is neither toxic nor unhealthy. It is the purified protein fraction of a grain, such as wheat or corn.

Preservatives. Some people believe that preservatives cause cancer, but most scientists say that by preventing the oxidization of fat and fat-soluble vitamins in food, preservatives protect health rather than harming it. See page 71 for more about specific preservatives.

Mill run. This is the hulls of grains that remain after they are ground, cracked, or flaked. It is added to dog food as a source of fiber.

Brewer's rice. This is the dried extract of rice that remains after brewing. It is commonly used in pet food because it is higher in protein than whole rice. It is digestible and safe to eat.

Beet pulp. This is the material that remains after sugar is extracted from sugar beets. It is added to dog food as a source of moderately fermentable fiber. When fermentable fiber reaches the large intestine, it is broken down and used for food by the "good" bacteria, or probiotics (such as *Lactobacillus* and *Enterococcus*), living there. It does not contain sugar, and it does not produce gas in the stomach or cause bloat.

Peanuts and peanut butter. Unless they are contaminated with mold toxins or bacteria, or a dog is allergic to them, peanuts and peanut butter are safe to eat.

HOMEMADE DIETS

"I avoid processed foods in my own diet as much as possible, and after the massive pet food recalls of 2007, I am committed to cooking for my three dogs as well. What is the best way to create a balanced homemade diet? Can I feed all of them the same thing, or will each require a separate recipe?"

The widespread pet food contamination in 2007 led to a huge spike in interest in homemade dog and cat food. You can find recipes in scores of books and on scores of websites, but beware: almost none meet the basic AAFCO standards for a complete and balanced maintenance diet. They are fine for feeding occasionally, but they will not keep a dog or cat healthy when fed every day for months or years.

If you're going to feed your dogs a homemade diet every day, not just once in a while, you need a recipe that's complete and balanced for the long term. Three resources for such recipes are Balance IT (*www.balanceit.com*), PetDiets (*www.petdiets.com*), or a veterinary nutritionist (consult the American College of Veterinary Nutrition, *www.acvn.org*, or any veterinary school's clinical nutrition department for a referral). Note that homemade diets are safe *only* for adult dogs. No reputable nutritionist will create one for a growing puppy (see "Why Not a Homemade Diet?" on page 49).

At Balance IT and PetDiets, you'll be asked to select one protein and one carbohydrate source from lists of 8 to 10 of each. Vegetarian and vegan recipes are available (using eggs, cottage cheese, or tofu as a protein source). You will also need to buy one or more specific vitamin and mineral supplements to use in the recipe. All commercial dog foods that are labeled "complete and balanced" include precise amounts of 10 amino acids, 1 essential fatty acid, 12 minerals, and 12 vitamins. These nutrients are equally necessary for a healthy homemade diet and can't be omitted or approximated.

Each recipe is tailored to the age, weight, and health of the individual dog. The websites prompt you to enter your dog's vital statistics before creating the recipe. If your three dogs have similar health profiles, then a single recipe may be appropriate for all three. However, if one or more has specific health considerations—such as obesity or kidney disease, for example—then you'll need to prepare separate formulas, although you'll probably be able to use the same protein and carbohydrate sources.

When feeding a homemade diet exclusively, plan on weighing your dogs and assessing their body condition monthly in order to make any necessary changes to the recipes, and on having your dogs examined by your vet twice a year, to make sure their health and nutritional needs haven't changed.

You'll spend more time and money making food for your dogs than you would buying a high-quality commercial dog food. But if you have the resources and motivation to cook, then both you and your dogs are likely to enjoy the results.

THE VEGETARIAN DOG

"I am a committed vegetarian, and I would prefer not to feed meat to my dog either. Is a vegetarian diet healthy for dogs, or do they need meat?"

Dogs can be healthy vegetarians, as long as their diet is carefully devised to provide all the nutrients they need. It's even possible to make or buy a nutritionally complete vegan diet (one that uses no animal products at all, including eggs and dairy) for dogs. Royal Canin, Natural Balance, AvoDerm, and Wysong are four of the companies that sell vegetarian or vegan dog food. If you buy a commercially prepared food, look for one that has passed an AAFCO feeding trial (the best choice) or at minimum conforms to the AAFCO nutrient standards (see page 48).

If you make your dog's vegetarian diet yourself, make sure you include enough protein. Many dogs love carbohydrates and will happily eat a vegetarian meal that contains no protein at all, but for optimal health, an adult dog's diet should contain a minimum of 18 percent protein. For recipes for vegetarian dog food, go to the Balance IT or PetDiets website (*www.balanceit.com* or *www.petdiets.com*).

TABLE FOOD

"Why are vets so against giving dogs table food?"

Our objection to table food is based on how often it causes obesity and vomiting or diarrhea. Frankly, a lot of the food we eat isn't particularly good for us, much less for our dogs.

But I'm no longer as dogmatic on the topic of people food as I once was. I now believe that lean meats, grains, vegetables, and fruits can be healthy additions to a high-quality commercial dog food. If you're interested in adding fresh foods to your dog's diet, keep them to 25 percent of his total intake, and study the guidelines that follow for foods that are dangerous and those that are generally safe for dogs.

Eating fatty "people food" can pack on the pounds, or even make a dog sick.

Some dogs have "sensitive stomachs" and will vomit, have diarrhea, or simply develop knock-you-down gas with almost any change in their diet. Such dogs are not good candidates for a lot of variety in their food. Also, slipping food to your dog from the table while you're eating is a surefire way to create a begging nuisance, so feed your dog only from his own dish at his own mealtimes.

DANGEROUS FOR DOGS

Some of the foods in this list are outright toxic to dogs, and others are unhealthy for the reasons given. More about the toxic effects of the foods marked with an asterisk (*) can be found starting on page 411.

Chocolate.* Chocolate in large doses is toxic to dogs and can cause tremors and heart arrhythmias. But chocolate in any dose—even a single Oreo cookie—is junk food and not healthy for dogs.

Macadamia nuts.* Bizarrely, as little as an ounce or two of macadamia nuts can cause temporary paralysis in dogs.

Tomatoes and tomato plants.* These contain atropine, which can cause dilated pupils, tremors, and heart arrhythmias.

Onions and garlic.* Eating large amounts of them can cause hemolytic anemia.

Grapes and raisins.* For unknown reasons, eating grapes or raisins can cause kidney failure in dogs.

Any food that has mold on it or may be even slightly spoiled. Dogs can get severe food poisoning from moldy or spoiled food. The consequences can include persistent vomiting, diarrhea, or even shock and death (see page 139). Remember, any food that's not fresh enough for you to eat isn't fresh enough for your dog either.

Raw meat, raw bones, and cooked bones. A few vets advocate feeding these to dogs, but I'm not one of them because I think they can make dogs sick. See page 77 for more on bones-and-raw-food diets.

Cookies, cake, ice cream, and candy. These have zero nutritional value, make dogs fat, and may make them vomit or have diarrhea.

Sugarless gum, candy, desserts, or toothpaste sweetened with xylitol.* Even small amounts of xylitol can cause hypoglycemia, seizures, or liver disease in dogs.

Fried, greasy, or fatty foods. High-fat foods can trigger pancreatitis in dogs (see page 142).

Beer or other alcoholic beverages. Giving alcohol to a dog is animal abuse, pure and simple.

Corncobs, peach pits, apple cores, and the like. Never underestimate a dog's ability to swallow things whole and have them get stuck somewhere in the digestive tract.

SAFE FOR MOST DOGS

Cooked lean meat, fish, and eggs.

Raw or cooked vegetables and fruits other than those on the "Dangerous" list above. But remember that not all dogs can tolerate all fruits and vegetables, so eliminate any that give your dog an upset stomach.

Rice and other cooked grains.

Plain low-fat yogurt.

Small amounts of bread. I say "small amounts" because bread contains carbohydrates and very little else, so it's not a particularly healthful addition to a dog's diet.

TOO FAT

"My shepherd mix is chubby. I think I need to cut back on her kibble rations, but she already seems to be hungry all the time. How can I slim her down?"

Dogs are professional eating machines and people-trainers. Your dog may seem hungry all the time because she's learned that if she stares at you while you're eating, paces by her food bowl, or keeps looking at the cabinet where the dog treats are kept, you'll give her something to eat. So first and foremost, you must break your training and stop responding to your dog's cues to overfeed her. Then try the following methods for getting her slim and trim:

1. The average adult dog requires one 8-ounce cup of dry dog food per 20 pounds of body weight per day. If you're feeding more than that, cut back.

2. Divide her food into three meals a day. This way she can eat more often without eating more. You could give her breakfast, lunch, and dinner if this works with your daily schedule, or breakfast, early supper, and a bedtime snack.

3. Strictly limit the biscuits and other treats. Many dog treats are loaded with calories, and it's easy to lose track of how many your dog is getting a day, especially if you're using them for training or for comfort while you're gone. Set a sane limit on treats (such as two small pieces a day), and make sure your significant other, children, and dog walker are aware of the limit. Try a raw baby carrot, a bite of apple, or a single piece of kibble as a treat instead of a salty, fatty dog snack.

4. Supplement her kibble with low-calorie vegetables and fruits. Add just a

SUMMER HEALTH HAZARDS

Summer is a great time to enjoy being outdoors with your dog, but be aware of the following hot-weather hazards.

Breathing problems. Hot, humid weather is especially hard on dogs with pushed-in faces, like English Bulldogs, Pugs, and Lhasa Apsos. Keep these dogs indoors with the air-conditioning on as much as possible when it's really hot outside. For more on breathing problems in flat-faced dogs, see page 282.

Heat stroke. Dogs can cool themselves only by panting, so they can easily become overheated in hot weather. Don't leave your dog in the car—even with the windows cracked open—in hot weather. For symptoms and treatment of heat stroke, see page 430.

Drowning. Even a dog who loves to swim can become overtired or get trapped in a swimming pool he's forgotten how to climb out of. Never let your dog swim unattended. Keep him out of swimming-pool enclosures when you're not there to watch him. For emergency treatment for drowning, see page 427.

Fleas. Unless you live in the South, where fleas are a year-round problem, you'll have the most trouble with the bloodsuckers at the tail end of summer—usually August and September. For information on preventing and treating flea infestations, see page 160.

Always supervise your dog when he swims.

tablespoon or so of veggies to her kibble at a time until you're sure her system tolerates them. Many dogs enjoy carrots (cooked or raw), green beans, winter squash, and raw apple. Fresh or frozen vegetables are fine, but stay away from canned because they're heavily salted. The vegetables and fruits will add fiber to help your dog feel full.

5. Gradually switch her to the lower-calorie version of her kibble. Almost all dry dog foods these days come in a "reduced calorie" or "less active" formula. She'll be able to eat the same volume of food while getting fewer calories. Always make dietary changes gradually, mixing increasing amounts of the new food with the old food over 10 days or so, to give her system a chance to adjust.

6. Make sure your dog gets plenty of exercise. Walk or play fetch with her for a minimum of an hour every day. She'll be healthier and happier, and so will you.

What about Slentrol, the canine weight-loss drug introduced in 2007? Slentrol is a prescription-only liquid that is given by mouth once a day. It decreases a dog's appetite and partly blocks the absorption of dietary fat. Some dogs vomit or have diarrhea briefly while taking the medication, and some become lethargic. The benefit of using Slentrol is that it allows owners to reduce the amount of food their dogs eat without having them beg for more. The drawbacks are the expense of the drug, the monthly vet visits required to adjust the dosage, and the impermanence of the solution. Slentrol can be given for a maximum of one year, and once you stop giving it, your dog's appetite will increase, putting her at risk of regaining weight. Making the changes outlined above is a less expensive, longer lasting answer to the problem of obesity.

TOO THIN?

"My three-year-old Rottweiler seems very thin. He is large-boned, tall, and very active. Two different vets said not to worry, but I do anyway."

Most Rottweilers are more square than streamlined, it's true, but even purebred dogs can have significant individual variations in their build and metabolism. If your dog has no signs of illness—such as diarrhea, vomiting, poor energy, or a dull, thin coat—and two vets have found nothing amiss, it seems reasonable to conclude that he's simply a lean, rangy individual.

How much does he eat? Is it about what's recommended for his current weight, or is it significantly more or less? If your dog is extremely active and athletic, he will burn a lot of calories. It's OK to feed him more of a well-balanced diet to see if he'll gain a little weight, but be realistic. Even if you could turn a long, lean marathon runner into a muscle-bound linebacker, it wouldn't necessarily be in his best interest. If your dog doesn't seem sick, then his weight is probably fine for him.

THE BONES-AND-RAW-FOOD DIET

"Are you familiar with the BARF (bones-and-raw-food) diet, espoused by Dr. Ian Billinghurst, and other natural or homemade diets that include raw meat? If so, what is your opinion on their safety and benefits?"

Like all vets these days, I'm aware of the popularity of such feeding plans with some dog owners, and I try to keep up with the arguments for and against the diets. As far as I know, there is no thorough, unbiased study comparing the health effects of a raw-food diet with a commercial diet in a large population of healthy dogs. That's a shame, because we need detailed information to determine whether raw-food diets are healthier than commercial dog food or not. In the meantime, however, my view is that for the average dog and dog owner, the potential benefits of a raw-food diet are outweighed by the drawbacks. My reasoning is given below. But first, for dog owners who aren't familiar with these types of feeding plans, here are the basic features of four popular variations. (Please note that these descriptions cannot be used to formulate a balanced diet for your dog; they are merely an overview of their proponents' approaches.)

1. BARF. Developed by Australian veterinarian Dr. Ian Billinghurst. The diet is 60 percent raw, meaty bones and

40 percent a changing variety of vegetables, fruits, meat, organ meat, yogurt, and eggs.

2. Ultimate Diet. Developed by Kymythy R. Schultze, a certified clinical nutritionist. The diet includes raw meat, raw bones, vegetables, and nutritional supplements (such as kelp, vitamin C, and essential fatty acids). Schultze believes dogs should not be fed grains or dairy products.

3. Volhard Natural Diet. Developed by Wendy Volhard, a well-known trainer and the coauthor (with veterinarian Dr. Kerry L. Brown) of *The Holistic Guide for a Healthy Dog*. Breakfast is oats, buckwheat, millet, rice, vegetables, oil, egg, vitamins, molasses, and kefir or yogurt. Dinner is raw meat, raw liver, fruit, herbs, and vitamin and mineral supplements. Bones are given about twice a week as a treat. Volhard suggests pouring boiling water over raw poultry and fish before feeding them to dogs to "kill any bacteria."

4. Pitcairn's natural diets. Developed by American veterinarian Dr. Richard H. Pitcairn. He advocates feeding a wide variety of foods and provides numerous recipes in his book *Dr. Pitcairn's Complete Guide to Natural Health for Dogs & Cats*. Ingredients he uses include raw meat, raw eggs, raw milk, cottage cheese, yogurt, whole grains, legumes, raw and cooked vegetables, vegetable oil, and vitamin and mineral supplements.

Here are the potential benefits and drawbacks of such diets as I see them:

BENEFITS FOR THE DOG

❏ **He obtains vitamins and minerals from foods as well as from supplements.** Research in people has shown that eating a variety of fruits and vegetables provides more health benefits than taking vitamin and mineral supplements. Perhaps there are subtle interactions among the nutrients in blueberries or broccoli, or perhaps they contain healthful substances we haven't yet identified. Dogs also may benefit from getting vitamins and minerals from whole foods. But note that homemade diets must include vitamin and mineral supplements as well, to ensure that they are not deficient in any essential nutrient.

❏ **He obtains nutrients from a variety of foods rather than from the unvarying ingredients of a commercial diet.** A homemade diet may provide a larger variety of whole-food nutrients than a commercial dog food does. However, if the homemade diet is based on the same six ingredients week-in and week-out, it isn't particularly varied.

DRAWBACKS FOR THE DOG AND DOG OWNER

❏ **Creating a complete and balanced raw diet isn't simple.** Owners need to meticulously follow formulas created by a nutritionist. Studies have established the minimum and, in some cases, maximum levels of nutrients required for a dog to remain healthy. These levels include specific amino acids, as well as protein in general; fat and essential fatty acids; a dozen minerals; and a dozen vitamins. Commercial dog foods are formulated to provide the appropriate amounts of these nutrients. Feeding a dog raw chicken wings, raw beef bones, carrots, apples, and rice every day would not provide appropriate levels of all of these nutrients.

❏ **Raw meat and bones can make you and your dog sick.** Noting the rise in popularity of raw diets for dogs and cats, the FDA in 2004 published guidelines addressing the health risks of such diets for animals and their owners. The main risk is the viruses, bacteria, and parasites that can be transmitted by eating or handling raw meat and bones. The FDA recommends using only meat and bones that are USDA certified as safe for human consumption. Raw meat and poultry should be stored separately from other foods to prevent cross-contamination. Countertops, utensils, cutting boards, bowls, and hands should be washed thoroughly with warm soapy water after touching raw meat or poultry. Meat that is frozen, including commercially prepared raw diets, should be kept frozen until ready for use, then thawed in a refrigerator or microwave. The FDA also points out that many commercially prepared raw diets are not complete and balanced, and so should be fed only occasionally or as a supplement to a dog food that meets AAFCO standards (see page 48).

❏ **Puppies have especially complicated nutritional needs.** Feed a puppy too much calcium and vitamin D and you predispose him to hip dysplasia. Feed him too little and he'll get rickets (soft, deformed bones). Homemade diets of any kind are not recommended for puppies (see page 49).

❏ **Changes in diet or particular foods make some dogs sick.** Some dogs get gas, vomit, or have diarrhea when they eat almost any new food; others, when they eat a particular food. The trigger foods are individual—some dogs are fine with peas, others get tre-mendously gassy and uncomfortable when they eat them. A dog may gradually acclimate to the problem food, but only time will tell.

❏ **Vitamin and mineral excesses or deficiencies can make dogs sick.** *Deficiencies* of the following nutrients are known to cause illnesses: calcium (bone deformity or fractures); zinc (scaly skin, poor wound healing); iron (anemia); vitamin A (eye diseases, muscle weakness); and vitamin D (bone deformity or fractures). *Excesses* can also cause illnesses: calcium (bone and joint problems); vitamin D (diarrhea, weight loss, calcium overload in the blood); vitamin A (loss of appetite, bone deformity); and zinc (blocks absorption of calcium).

DOG BREATH

"My dog has terrible breath. Is there anything I can do?"

Dental disease is the most common cause of "dog breath." Bits of food and bacteria form soft deposits called plaque on the teeth, which eventually hardens into tartar. Tartar irritates the gums and gives bacteria access to the tooth roots, which leads to infection, pain, and tooth loss as well as bad breath. The bacteria can even wind up in the bloodstream and infect a dog's heart valves or kidneys.

To assess the general condition of your dog's teeth (assuming she doesn't bite), gently push up her upper lip, one side at a time, and look along the gum line. Check the base of the upper canines (fangs) and the first large teeth in the back (the upper fourth premolars). Do you see yellowish, brownish, or grayish gunk on the teeth? That's tartar. Does the gum line look red rather than pink?

WINTER HEALTH HAZARDS

Wolves may be able to handle subzero temperatures without a whimper, but they aren't acclimated to houses with central heating the way our dog companions are. When the weather outside is frightful, protect your dog against the following hazards.

Bitter cold weather. If you're freezing even in your winter coat, your dog probably is freezing in his, too. Shorten your walks in really severe weather, and keep a towel by the back door to dry the melting snow and ice off your dog's coat and feet.

Eating snow. Some dogs love to do this, but eating a lot of snow can lower a dog's body temperature and possibly even lead to hypothermia. During winter hikes, take some lukewarm water in an insulated bottle for your dog to drink so he doesn't have to slake his thirst with snow.

Ice-melting salt. The regular kind stings chapped paws like crazy, and the "paw-safe" kind works well but is very expensive. Other options to protect your dog's feet include strap-on boots (Muttluks is one popular brand) and foot waxes (such as Musher's Secret). Boots can pull off in deep snow, so they're best for plowed roads and sidewalks. The waxes are rubbed onto a dog's pads and between the toes before he goes outside. Some dog owners say petroleum jelly also works—it doesn't stay on as well as the wax, but it's much cheaper. Remember that any salve you put on your dog's feet should be safe to eat, because he's certain to lick it off.

Even if your dog's feet don't seem sore after a winter walk, it's a good idea to rinse them with plain warm water and dry them as soon as you get home. This will keep your dog from licking road salt off his feet.

Antifreeze. You've heard it before, but here it is again: *antifreeze is a deadly poison.* Small amounts can make a dog sick or even kill him (see page 411). Keep your dog away from antifreeze spills in your garage or on the road.

Flaky, itchy skin. Many dogs get flaky skin in the winter, and some dogs are allergic to mold spores in heating systems or to dust mites.

To combat flaky, itchy skin, bathe your dog regularly even during the winter. It's fine to bathe a dog indoors during cold weather as long as you keep him warm until he's dry.

Boots protect against ice-melting salt.

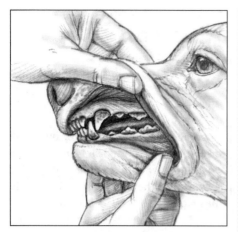

The tips of the teeth may be shiny, but check for tartar along the gum line.

That's gingivitis (inflamed gums). Are there sores or crusts on her lips? All of these are signs of dental disease.

The symptoms of dental disease aren't restricted to the mouth. Infection from an abscessed upper canine tooth may break through into the dog's nasal passages and produce a yellowish or whitish discharge from the nose. The infection from an abscessed upper premolar or molar may cause a swelling or a draining wound below the dog's eye.

If your dog has tartar on her teeth or signs of an infection, make an appointment with your vet. Once tartar has hardened, it's almost impossible to remove at home. A dental cleaning under anesthesia is required. Vets clean a dog's teeth using the same types of instruments your dental hygienist uses on your teeth: hand scalers (the crooklike metal instruments) followed by ultrasonic scaling, polishing, and a fluoride treatment. The vet also checks for gum recession, infections, loose teeth, and growths in the dog's mouth. Loose teeth often are removed, but a veterinary dental specialist sometimes can do a root canal instead to save the tooth.

Once your dog's teeth have been professionally cleaned, you should start brushing them every day (see page 82).

TENNIS-BALL MOUTH

"My dog is only four years old but her teeth are very worn, especially the lower canines. Another dog owner said the wear could be caused by playing with a tennis ball, which my dog does all the time. Is there any validity to this?"

Yes, absolutely. In fact, this pattern of worn teeth is sometimes called "tennis-ball mouth." Tennis balls are very abrasive—sort of like dish-scrubbing sponges—and they will erode the teeth, especially if a dog carries one in her mouth for several hours a day.

If the wear is gradual, the teeth will lay down a protective layer of dentin from the inside as they are eroded from the outside. However, if the teeth are sanded down more rapidly, they can wear right through to the pulp cavity, which is painful and can lead to serious tooth-root infections and abscesses.

Tennis balls are abrasive, and chewing on them all day can wear down the teeth.

TOOTHBRUSHING 101

A dog's mouth is host to many of the same factors and processes as our own—bacteria producing plaque, plaque hardening into tartar, and tartar causing gum irritation and recession, tooth-root infections, and tooth loss. It shouldn't be surprising, then, that regular tooth-brushing is the best first line of defense for dogs as well as for people.

Happily, brushing a dog's teeth is usually easier than you might think. But there are a couple of situations in which you shouldn't attempt it. One is with a dog who is likely to bite if you come near his mouth with a toothbrush: clean teeth simply aren't worth getting bitten over. The other situation is when a dog already has lots of tartar on his teeth. Tartar can't be removed by simple brushing, and brushing could be uncomfortable for a dog whose gums are very irritated. If your dog's teeth are funky, schedule a dental cleaning by your vet before you begin the following home dental-care regimen.

1. Plan on brushing your dog's teeth once a day. Plaque hardens into tartar within about 36 hours, so you need to remove it every day.

2. Buy a soft-bristle toothbrush that's an appropriate size for your dog's mouth and a tube of dog toothpaste. A "people" toothbrush is fine, but don't use people toothpaste—it contains foaming agents that might make a dog vomit, and the enzymes in dog tooth-paste do a better job of cleaning.

3. A dog has 42 teeth, but you can begin by brushing the outside surfaces (the lip side) of just 4 of them: the upper canines (fangs) and the upper fourth premolars (the first large teeth in the back of the mouth). Those are the four teeth that accumulate the

To clean the back teeth, slide the brush under the lip to below the eye.

You may see brownish dots in the middle of the biting surface of the worn teeth. These aren't necessarily "cavities" or signs that the teeth have worn through to the pulp cavity—the dentin itself is brownish. To determine whether a brown spot is a hole into the pulp cavity or just dentin, your vet can poke the area with a dental probe. Don't try this at home, though, because if it is a hole, it will hurt.

To prevent excessive wear of the teeth, don't let your dog chew on a tennis ball all day long. Give her a dog-safe rubber ball, Nylabone, or Kong toy instead. Keep the tennis balls hidden away until you're ready to play fetch.

most tartar, so brushing them alone will contribute significantly to your dog's dental health.

4. Wet the toothbrush, put a tiny dab of toothpaste on it, and brush gently using a circular motion at the gum line of one of the upper canines for about five seconds. Repeat with the upper canine on the other side.

5. Next, brush the upper fourth premolars. The upper fourth premolars are far back in a dog's mouth, but you can brush them without cranking your dog's lip back all the way, which can be uncomfortable for both of you. Picture a vertical line running straight down from your dog's eye. Where that line meets his mouth is where his upper fourth premolar is. Push back your dog's lip to take a peek—it's the biggest triangular tooth. Once you have an idea of where your target is, let go of the lip, wet the toothbrush, put a tiny dab of toothpaste on it, and slide the toothbrush gently along the inside of his mouth until the head of the toothbrush is about even with his eye. Then brush with a circular motion at the gum line for about five seconds. Repeat with the upper fourth premolar on the other side.

6. Your dog will probably chew on the toothbrush as you're brushing his teeth. That's fine, and it will even help brush other tooth surfaces.

7. You may notice some blood on the toothbrush when you first start brushing your dog's teeth. This is a sign either that his gums are inflamed or that you're brushing too hard or with a sawlike back-and-forth motion at the gum line. Ease up on the pressure, but don't stop brushing. You should notice less bleeding within a week or so of daily brushing, as your efforts make your dog's gums healthier.

8. Once you're comfortable brushing the four teeth described above, expand your efforts to include the outer surfaces of the other teeth. With practice, you'll be able to brush all 42 in just one or two minutes. Focus your efforts at the gum line, because that's where the plaque builds up.

If brushing your dog's teeth is impossible, ask your vet whether using an enzyme or antibacterial mouth spray instead would help reduce the plaque and irritation in your dog's mouth. Another option is Science Diet t/d, a prescription dry dog food that scrapes the sides of a dog's teeth as he eats. Rawhide or other chew toys may help clean a dog's teeth a little, but they are nowhere near as thorough or effective as daily brushing.

If your dog is drooling more than usual, having trouble eating, or seems to be in pain, have your vet examine her teeth soon. If her mouth doesn't seem to bother her, worn teeth are not a medical emergency, but you should mention them to your vet and have them checked out the next time your dog has a physical exam.

A BROKEN TOOTH

"I noticed about a week ago that the entire point of one of my dog's canines is gone. I'm worried because the top of the tooth looks brown, and an acquaintance told me that cracked teeth can become infected."

If a tooth breaks all the way down to the pulp canal, bacteria can get inside the tooth, possibly forming a tooth-root abscess, and into the bloodstream as well. The brown you're seeing on the broken surface of your dog's tooth may be dentin—the layer directly under the enamel, which is darker than enamel but still quite hard—or it may be the pulp canal. Your best bet is to have your vet take a look. The vet will determine whether the tooth is loose and whether the broken surface is hard (dentin) or soft (pulp canal).

If the pulp canal is exposed, your dog should either have a root canal or have the tooth removed, because the exposed pulp is painful and infection is likely.

OVERCOMING CAR SICKNESS

"Is there anything I can do for my dog who always gets car sick? I've tried Dramamine about an hour before a trip, and no food for at least four hours before, but the poor thing still gets sick a half hour into the drive. Any suggestions?"

Dramamine and no food for 6 to 8 hours before a trip work very well for many dogs with car sickness, but since your dog isn't one of them, here are some other things to try.

1. Move her up front. Like people, dogs with car sickness feel better if they can sit in the front seat and look forward. But you can't have an unrestrained dog burrowing under your feet or slamming against the dashboard when you brake. Put her in a crate or carrier belted into the front seat. Keep the windows open a couple of inches so she gets lots of fresh air.

2. Make it short and sweet. You say that she invariably gets sick after she's been riding for 30 minutes. Desensitize her (see page 180) by giving her some shorter, more pleasant car experiences. Take her on a 15-minute drive to a park or a friend's house, then go for a walk or do something else fun for 15 minutes or so, then drive home. (Don't give her any Dramamine, but do make sure she hasn't had any food for four hours beforehand.) Do this a couple of times a week, if you can manage it. The idea is to end the car ride *before* she gets sick—if 15 minutes is too long, try 10 minutes, or even 5 minutes.

3. Stop and smell the roses. If you're going to be in the car for an hour or more, stop and take a short walk every half hour or so. This is impractical if you're driving all the way across the country, of course, but it's helpful for uneasy travelers on trips of an hour or two.

4. Give it time. Young dogs sometimes outgrow car sickness, just like children can.

5. Upgrade the medication. The prescription anti-vomiting drug Cerenia, introduced in 2007, can be given once a day to prevent car sickness, for one or two days in a row. Note that it prevents vomiting but not necessarily panting, whining, pacing, or other symptoms of anxiety. If anxiety is your dog's main symptom and a long car trip is unavoidable, talk to your vet about giving a prescription anti-anxiety medication instead (see page 185). Some dog owners feel that Rescue Remedy or herbs help relieve car sickness; see page 196.

6. Let her be a homebody. If she continues to be miserable in the car, and she's not all that happy when you get where you're going anyway, consider leaving her at home with a pet sitter while you hit the open road.

FEEDING THE OLDER DOG

"Should I change what I feed my dog now that she's turned 12? What's the best food for older dogs?"

You don't need to switch an older dog to a different food if she is healthy and maintaining a good weight on her current diet. A "senior" food may be appropriate if she is underweight or overweight, but don't choose one without carefully comparing the label to that of the food she's currently eating, because some senior diets are higher calorie and others are lower calorie than maintenance foods.

A special diet may be appropriate if your dog has heart disease, kidney disease, diabetes, or another major health concern—consult your vet if that's the case.

SENIOR DENTAL CARE: NOW MORE THAN EVER

"My 14-year-old Toy Poodle has lost many teeth over the years. Is there any point in brushing the ones she has left? Will she still be able to eat if she loses all her teeth?"

A dog is never too old for the best dental care you can manage. Yes, you should continue to brush the teeth your dog has left, starting after they've been professionally cleaned by your veterinarian. A small, soft toothbrush designed for babies is a good choice for a tiny dog like yours. Ask your vet whether you should use an antibacterial mouth spray as well. Brushing and once-

or twice-a-year checkups by your veterinarian are your best bet for saving your dog's remaining teeth and—more important—keeping them pain-free. Even a dog who has no teeth will manage to eat, but it would be nice to prevent your dog from going through the pain and infection that can accompany tooth loss.

ANESTHESIA RISKS

"My dog is 13 years old and in good health for her age, but I'm sorry to say that I've neglected her dental care for most of her lifetime. I'd like to have her teeth cleaned, but I'm concerned about her going under anesthesia. What are the risks in anesthetizing an older dog? Can her teeth be cleaned without anesthesia?"

A dog's teeth can't be cleaned properly when she's awake. It's crucial to remove the tartar beneath the gum line, using handheld instruments followed by an ultrasonic scaler, and although that's not necessarily painful, it's simply not something a dog will sit quietly for—with her mouth wide open, no less. So general anesthesia is absolutely required.

A dog whose teeth are being cleaned is given an inhaled anesthetic plus oxygen through a tube placed in her trachea. In addition to delivering the anesthetic gas and oxygen, the trach tube has a secondary benefit of preventing fluid and debris from getting into the dog's lungs during the dental cleaning.

Anesthetizing a dog of any age is never 100 percent risk-free, because there's always a small chance of an unpredictable reaction to the anesthetic. That risk is minimized by monitoring the breathing, heart rate, and sometimes blood oxygen levels, temperature, and

(continued on page 89)

TRAVELS WITH FIDO

Taking your dog on vacation can be fun for both of you, but plan ahead to keep him safe and comfortable. Bring your dog's usual food to help prevent stomach upsets. Only give him water that you would drink yourself—don't let him drink from ponds, streams, or dubious water sources. Make sure he wears his collar at all times, and attach an additional temporary tag that gives a local phone number, contact, or location.

Traveling by car. The safest place for your dog to ride is in a carrier or crate secured by a seatbelt or anchor strap. Tragedies can occur when cars are in minor fender benders and unsecured dogs smash into the dashboard or flee, terrified, into oncoming traffic when the driver opens the car door to check for damage. A dog seatbelt is a good alternative to a crate unless your dog is a squirmy noodle who will tangle herself upside down in the belt before you even get out of the driveway. And if your dog suffers from car sickness, try the measures described on page 84.

Traveling by plane. This involves a different set of risks, because unless your dog is very small and will fit in an airline-approved carrier under the seat in front of you, you won't be able to directly supervise him and ensure that he's safe throughout the trip. For that reason, air travel with a dog shouldn't be undertaken lightly. Consider whether your dog would be better off being boarded at home while you're away, and check the specific airline's rules and fees for carrying a dog before you make your decision. If you must fly with your dog, take the following precautions:

❑ Unless you have no other choice, and even if it's more expensive, take a nonstop flight. This sharply reduces the risk that your dog will escape while being loaded and unloaded or wind up on the wrong plane.

❑ If you must change planes or take a flight with a layover, make sure the airline will let you claim and then recheck your dog yourself, and schedule a long enough layover to take your dog for a walk.

❑ If the airline permits dogs to fly in the summer (many don't), travel only early or late in the day to avoid high temperatures while your dog is being loaded onto the plane and before it takes off.

❑ In very cold weather, travel in the middle of the day. The live-cargo compartments of planes are pressurized and kept between 50 and 70 degrees Fahrenheit, but your dog's crate might be on the runway or in another exposed area for a while before being loaded, especially if there's a flight delay.

❑ To avoid extra delays and confusion, don't fly when the rest of the world is trying to get away on a holiday. Leave at least one day earlier or later than the masses.

❏ Don't give your dog food or water for four hours before he's crated for the flight. This will help keep him from vomiting or needing to urinate or defecate while he's in the crate.

❏ Don't give your dog a tranquilizer before a flight unless he's likely to injure himself trying to break out of the crate. A groggy, sedated dog is less able to adapt to changes in temperature and other environmental conditions than an untranquilized dog would be.

❏ Don't leave anything in the crate your dog might tear up or choke on.

❏ Clearly mark your dog's crate, using stickers or permanent markers, with the following information: (1) your dog's name, age, breed, special medical concerns, special behavior concerns (for example, "Bites when frightened!" or "Very friendly"), and a physical description (size, color, hair length) or photograph; (2) the travel date, airline, and flight number; (3) your name, home address and phone number, and cell phone or pager number; (4) the names and phone numbers of other people to contact in case of an emergency—one in your departure city and one in your arrival city.

❏ Make sure your kennel closes tightly and securely. If your dog somehow got out of his kennel, he could be lost forever. Just above the kennel door, write: "Do not open this door without the permission of the owner or a veterinarian."

❏ Arrive at the airport early and check in, but keep your dog with you until the last possible moment (usually 30 minutes before departure). If there's time, take your dog for a quick walk outside the terminal to urinate or defecate.

❏ Once you're at the gate, watch out the window for your dog's crate to be loaded into the live-cargo hold. If you don't see the crate being put on the plane before the last call for boarding, ask the gate attendant to call the baggage area to make sure your dog is on board. Usually a gate attendant will do this happily, reporting back that, yes, your dog is on board. If you get any flak, refuse to board until someone confirms that your dog is on the plane.

A seatbelt or crate will keep both you and your dog safe in the car.

11 TIPS FOR A HEALTHY, HAPPY SENIOR DOG

Make sure your dog's later years are as golden as possible by following these guidelines:

1. Continue to give your older dog at least a half hour of your undivided attention every day. Don't stop going for walks just because your dog moves more slowly now. She still needs the mental and physical stimulation of touring the neighborhood.

2. Take an older dog out to urinate every three or four hours during the day, to keep her comfortable and maintain her housebreaking skills.

3. Take her to the vet at least once a year for a thorough physical exam and discussion of any new or ongoing health issues.

4. Don't assume an older dog's decline in health is "just old age" and nothing can be done about it. Tell your vet about symptoms such as lethargy, weight loss, reluctance to climb stairs, or increased panting so the vet can determine what's causing them and suggest remedies.

5. Dogs with weak hind legs can slip and fall on bare floors. Place carpet runners with a nonskid backing on slippery floors your dog must cross frequently.

6. Provide an older dog with a thick but fairly firm bed to cushion her joints while still allowing her to climb in and out easily.

7. If your dog has trouble climbing stairs, set up an area on the main level of the house where she can eat, sleep, and spend most of her time. Use baby gates to block stairways if she might fall down them.

8. You can use a bath towel as a sling under a larger dog's abdomen to help support her hind legs as she climbs stairs or gets into the car.

9. A stand that raises dishes to the height of your dog's chest will make eating more comfortable if she has an arthritic back or weak legs.

10. Keep her clean and tidy. If she needs clipping but has trouble standing for long periods of time, find a considerate groomer who will clip her while she sits or lies down.

11. Touch and warmth are especially soothing to the sometimes achy joints and muscles of older dogs. Pet your dog, brush her, or gently massage her neck, back, and legs every day to improve her circulation and make her feel good all over.

Use a simple sling to help a dog with weak hind legs climb stairs.

(continued from page 85)

EKG of the dog while she is under anesthesia. The risk that an anesthetized dog will develop a breathing or circulatory problem that could lead to organ damage or even death is significantly increased in dogs who have heart, lung, kidney, or liver disease. For that reason, older dogs are carefully checked for underlying problems—with blood tests, stethoscope exams of their heart and lungs, and sometimes chest x-rays or an EKG—before they are scheduled for a procedure that requires anesthesia. Often a dog with a medical condition such as a heart arrhythmia or kidney insufficiency can be given medications to make anesthesia safer for them.

After 13 years without dental care, your dog's teeth are undoubtedly in need of a thorough professional cleaning. If your vet has carefully examined your dog, checked her for hidden health problems, and given her the OK to go under general anesthesia, then I recommend you go ahead with the dental cleaning. If you commit to brushing your dog's teeth once a day after that, maybe she'll never need another professional cleaning.

URINATING IN THE HOUSE

"My 14-year-old dog has started urinating in the house. She smells bad, the house smells bad, and my husband just wants to get rid of her. Is there anything I can do?"

An older dog who loses her housebreaking may have a disease that's making her drink and urinate more, a weak urinary sphincter, or "doggie Alzheimer's," all of which are treatable. To help you home in on the problem, see page 336, then make an appointment with your vet for a precise diagnosis and treatment.

In the meantime, give your dog plenty of opportunities to urinate outside during the day (every three or four hours); pick up her water bowl after dinner; and take her outside one last time before you go to bed, even if you have to wake her up to do so. Bathe her and wash her bedding as often as necessary to keep her from smelling bad—keeping her clean and dry will also help prevent skin infections from the urine. You can buy "doggie diapers" from any large pet-supply store or pet-supply catalog. If need be, you could restrict her to a single room of your house—one with an uncarpeted floor—by blocking the doorways with baby gates.

SEE ME, HEAR ME?

"My dog doesn't seem to see and hear as well as he used to. Do dogs lose their eyesight and hearing as they get older?"

Sometimes. Some of the problems that can cause a decline in vision, such as cataracts or glaucoma, are treatable; others are not. Most causes of hearing loss are not reversible. (For more on diagnosing and treating vision and hearing problems, see the eye Q&As beginning on page 211, and the deafness Q&A on page 225.)

Fortunately, dogs don't read, drive cars, or talk on the telephone, so they can get along quite well despite a decline in vision or hearing. The important things for you to do are to tell your vet what you've noticed during your dog's regular physical exam—or sooner, if the problem has come on suddenly or your dog's eyes or ears seem painful—and take extra precautions to protect your dog from hazards he may not see or hear as clearly as before, such as stairways and traffic.

Part 2

Common Canine Illnesses

CHAPTER 4

Allergies, Itching, and Other Skin Diseases

ITCH, ITCH, SCRATCH, SCRATCH. Skin problems account for a disproportionate number of the "sick visits" dogs make to the vet each year. If that surprises you, consider how much territory the skin covers and how difficult its distress signals can be to interpret. Take itching: a dog who scratches all the time may have allergies, a bacterial infection, a fungal infection, or fleas—to name just a few of the possibilities. By learning the diagnostic details that distinguish each itch, lump, rash, or bald spot, you can reduce your dog's skin-related visits to the vet and make any necessary trips more productive.

EMERGENCY!

Does your dog need immediate veterinary care? Check this list to help you decide.

TAKE IMMEDIATE ACTION!

Call your vet or an emergency veterinary clinic *now* if your dog is showing any of the following symptoms:

❏ Her **face is swollen or puffy;** this is a symptom of a potentially dangerous allergic reaction.

TAKE A MINUTE . . .

Read further in this book and then call your vet during office hours as needed if your dog is showing any of the following symptoms:

❏ He **licks his feet excessively;** see the Q&A below.

❏ She is **scratching a lot;** see page 96.

❏ He has **dandruff;** see page 106.

❏ She has **lumps or bumps** on her skin; see page 108.

❏ His **toenails are breaking** at the quick; see page 105.

❏ She **smells bad;** see page 104.

❏ He **scoots his bottom** on the rug; see page 100.

❏ She has **food allergies;** see pages 96 and 99.

❏ He **sheds excessively;** see pages 8 and 110.

❏ Her **foot pads are hard, dry, or cracked;** see page 113.

Remember, it's never wrong to call your veterinarian if you have a question about your dog's health, or if you're worried about a symptom or your dog's overall condition. That's what we're here for.

THE CONSTANT PAW LICKER

"My three-year-old Soft-Coated Wheaten Terrier licks her paws incessantly. I've examined her feet carefully and found no injuries or other obvious problems. Is this some kind of nervous tic?"

The No. 1 cause of persistent paw-licking is allergies. Unlike people, dogs with allergies tend to get itchy skin rather than a stuffed-up nose. An allergic dog often will rub her face on the rug, lick her paws, or lick her belly. Licking as a "nervous tic"—a form of obsessive-compulsive disorder—is possible but far less likely (see page 198).

Dogs can be allergic to substances they inhale or absorb through the skin, such as pollen, dust, mold spores, or flea saliva; to substances found in food; or to both. About 10 to 15 percent of dogs are allergic to inhaled or absorbed substances, a condition known as atopy or atopic dermatitis. About 1 to 5 percent of dogs have food allergies.

Certain breeds appear to be predisposed to atopy, including Beagles, terriers, Labrador Retrievers, Shih Tzus, Shar-Peis, Dalmatians, English Bulldogs, Golden Retrievers, Irish Setters, Lhasa Apsos, Miniature Schnauzers, and Pugs.

For information on how atopy is treated, read on.

DIAGNOSING AND TREATING ALLERGIES

"We've been treating our two-year-old West Highland White Terrier for allergies ever since we adopted her a year ago. The couple who owned her previously said she never had allergies when she lived with them, so the problem has to be in our home. What are the most common causes of skin problems in Westies?"

The problem isn't necessarily in your home. Allergies often first appear in young adulthood, so it may be that your dog simply hadn't "grown into" her allergies before you got her.

Although a tendency toward allergies can be inherited, it's just the tendency—not the specific allergy—that is passed along genetically. In other words, Westies aren't more likely to be allergic to molds or Beagles to ragweed; it's individual.

Blood tests and skin tests provide two ways of determining what your dog is allergic to. If she's had one type of test and the results were inconclusive, try the other type. Once the offending substances are identified, you can avoid them or limit your dog's exposure to them.

Besides avoiding known allergens, the treatment plan for allergies includes the following: (1) weekly baths with a colloidal oatmeal shampoo during flare-ups; (2) essential fatty acid supplements, which can reduce itching; (3) antihistamines; and perhaps (4) a corticosteroid injection or tablets for *rare* use in a dog who is extremely itchy.

If your dog has been on one antihistamine and it hasn't helped, talk to your vet about trying another. Different antihistamines work better for different dogs. Diphenhydramine (Benadryl), hydroxyzine (Atarax), clemastine (Tavist), and cetirizine (Zyrtec) are four antihistamines that work well for many dogs. Check with your vet for the appropriate dose.

Hyposensitization therapy (allergy shots) is another option. The principle is to periodically inject under the skin minute amounts of the purified substance or substances your dog is allergic to, so she'll develop an increased tolerance to them. Your dog would have to be tested to identify exactly what she is allergic to, and a formula would be created for her specific allergies. Hyposensitization can be expensive and time consuming, and it doesn't take effect immediately, so your dog would still need antihistamines during the interim.

(continued on page 98)

THAT AWFUL ITCH

Vets' offices are overrun with itchy dogs. A dog whose skin itches may scratch his ears, face, or body with a hind foot; rub his face with his front feet or on a rug, sofa, or his owner's leg; or persistently lick his paws, belly, or genitals. The fur of a light-colored dog who licks his feet constantly will be stained a rusty color from his saliva. A dog who chronically licks his abdomen will develop lacy or patchy black pigment in the skin. Dogs who scratch or lick excessively may lose their hair in those areas or develop skin infections.

Recognizing that a dog is itchy is easy. Determining *why* is not so simple—itching can be a symptom of literally every skin disorder in the book. But details can help you and your vet zero in on a diagnosis: when the itching started; how severe it is; whether there are signs of external parasites or a skin infection; whether the dog has had this problem before, and if so, whether it was linked to a particular season or environment; whether the itching has responded, partly or completely, to antihistamines, cortico-steroids, antibiotics, or medicated shampoos; and so on.

Here is a guide to some of the more common skin conditions that can cause itching, their key symptoms, and suggested treatments.

INHALANT ALLERGY

Key symptoms: Itchiness at first linked to a season or environment that may later become constant; often starts in young adulthood (ages one to four); paw-licking, face-rubbing, belly-licking, and recurrent ear infections are common.

Treatments: Essential fatty acid supplements; oral antihistamines; weekly baths with colloidal oatmeal shampoo; antihistamine or corticosteroid sprays; hyposensitization therapy (allergy shots); corticosteroid injection or tablets; Atopica.

For more information: See page 95.

FOOD ALLERGY

Key symptoms: Itchiness not linked to a season or environment; paw-licking, face-rubbing, and recurrent ear infections are common; may develop suddenly even if the dog has eaten a particular food for a long time.

Treatment: Novel food trial for 6 to 12 weeks; avoid trigger food(s).

For more information: See pages 99 and 101.

CONTACT HYPERSENSITIVITY

Key symptoms: Sudden onset of itching; feet, chest, and abdomen may be itchy if the substance is on the ground, floor, or dog's bedding; dog may be itchy all over if a shampoo, rinse, or spray is responsible; redness, a rash, or bumps may accompany the itch.

Treatment: Eliminate the offending substance from the dog's environment; bathe the dog with a colloidal oatmeal shampoo; corticosteroid spray, injection, or tablets.

For more information: See page 100.

SKIN PARASITES

Key symptom: Exposure to fleas, ticks, or mites, such as scabies, demodex, or cheyletiella.

Treatment: Parasite-killing shampoo, spray, dip, or spot-on; eliminate parasites from the home; prevent recurrence; corticosteroid injection or tablets if itching is severe.

For more information: See pages 160, 167, and 169.

EAR INFECTION

Key symptoms: Head shaking, ear scratching, smelly ears, heavy accumulation of wax and debris deep in ear canals.

Treatment: Thorough ear cleaning; antibacterial, antifungal, or anti-inflammatory ear drops or ointment; address underlying factors.

For more information: See pages 219 and 220.

ANAL GLAND IRRITATION

Key symptoms: "Scooting" of the anal area on rugs or grass; biting or licking excessively at the anal area.

Treatment: Express anal glands if overfull; lance gland, flush, and treat with antibiotics if impacted or infected.

For more information: See page 100.

BACTERIAL INFECTION

Key symptoms: Sores, bumps, pimples, or scabs.

Treatment: Antibiotics, medicated baths.

For more information: See page 102.

FUNGAL INFECTION

Key symptoms: Sores, redness, or oozing and crusting, often on feet or in skin folds or other moist areas; often bad-smelling; may cause gradual hair loss.

Treatment: Antifungal medication, medicated baths.

For more information: See page 103.

SEBORRHEA

Key symptoms: Scaly dandruff; skin and hair may be either dry or oily; may lead to gradual hair loss.

Treatment: Essential fatty acid supplements; medicated baths; corticosteroid tablets or injection if itching is severe.

For more information: See page 106.

ENDOCRINE DISEASE

Key symptoms: Gradual hair loss; bumps or pimples; scaly skin; darkened skin; thinning skin; increased thirst and urination, recurrent urinary tract infections, or enlarged abdomen (in diabetes mellitus or Cushing's disease).

Treatment: Treat underlying disease; medicated baths; antibiotics if infections are present; avoid corticosteroids.

For more information: See pages 112, 298, and 299.

IMMUNE-MEDIATED SKIN DISEASE

Key symptoms: Bumps or sores on the face and ears, feet, or body; scaly skin; toenails that split and break off at the quick; or hair loss.

Treatment: Corticosteroids or chemotherapy-type immunosuppressants; antibiotics if infections are present; medicated baths.

For more information: See pages 105 and 107.

SKIN CANCER

Key symptoms: Appearance varies widely; may be a bump or sore, single or multiple, painful or nonpainful.

Treatment: Surgical removal, chemotherapy, or radiation.

For more information: See pages 108 and 382.

OBSESSIVE-COMPULSIVE LICKING

Key symptom: Licking an area to the point of creating deep sores.

Treatment: Antibiotics and bandages until the sore heals; anti-obsessive medication such as clomipramine (Clomicalm) or fluoxetine (Prozac).

For more information: See page 198.

(continued from page 95)

Atopica (cyclosporine), introduced in 2003, is an oral medication for atopy (allergies) that suppresses T cells, a type of white blood cell that plays a major role in inflammation. The benefit of Atopica is it can reduce or eliminate a dog's need for corticosteroids to control severe itching. The downsides are its high cost, especially for a large dog, and its potential side effects. It can cause loss of appetite, vomiting, or diarrhea, especially when first started. Because it is an immunosuppressant, Atopica can also predispose dogs to bacterial or fungal infections.

ALLERGIC TO FLEAS

"Last September my Golden Retriever was so itchy, she tore at her skin with her hind feet and her teeth and got a horrible skin infection. My vet thinks the itching was set off by a flea-bite allergy. How is that possible when my dog is on Sentinel and we saw no sign of fleas?"

Sentinel is a monthly heartworm preventive that also contains lufeneron, an "insect growth regulator" that prevents the eggs a flea lays *after* biting your dog from developing into adult fleas. Lufeneron doesn't deter fleas from biting your dog, however, and a single flea bite can be all it takes to set off a dog who is flea-allergic.

How can a dog be allergic to fleas, you might wonder? Dogs who live with fleas all the time seem to develop a tolerance to them, but dogs who are bitten only occasionally can develop a full-blown, violent allergy to components in flea saliva. Flea-bite allergies are therefore extremely common among dogs who live in areas where fleas are primarily a seasonal (usually late summer) concern.

Flea-bite allergy is usually diagnosed by circumstantial evidence. The lower back, the base of the tail, and the abdomen are the areas most often affected. A flea or flea dirt may be found on the dog, or the exposure may be assumed simply because the dog has been outdoors during flea season.

The treatment for a flare-up of a flea-bite allergy includes twice-weekly baths with a medicated shampoo until the skin clears up; oral antibiotics if the skin is infected; and corticosteroid tablets for two weeks to calm the intense itch. Apply a flea-killing spot-on, such as Frontline or Revolution, to each dog and cat in the household. If people are getting bitten by fleas as well, then the house should be treated as described on page 161.

HOT SPOTS

"What are hot spots, and what causes them?"

"Hot spot" is the common name for what veterinary medical books call acute moist dermatitis or pyotraumatic dermatitis. It's a red, oozing, hairless, angry-looking sore that seems to pop up overnight on a dog's skin.

Thick-coated, long-haired breeds (such as Golden Retrievers, Newfoundlands, German Shepherds, and Bernese Mountain Dogs) are particularly susceptible. Hot spots develop when something causes such severe itching or irritation that a dog scratches and licks his skin raw. Often, this licking and scratching goes on at night or while the people in the house are at work or school, so the sudden appearance of the raw, oozing wound can come as a shock to the dog owner. The most common cause of hot spots is a flea-bite allergy. Other allergies, other parasites, a chemical irritant, or a skin infection are other possible causes.

Hot spots are treated by clipping the hair down to the skin at least 1 inch all around the sore, so the sore can be thoroughly washed with an antibacterial solution (such as Betadine or chlorhexidine) and exposed to the air. Oral antibiotics for the skin infection, a soothing spray or ointment, and corticosteroid tablets to relieve the extreme itch may also be required. A dog may need to wear an Elizabethan collar or a foot bandage to keep him from inflicting further damage to the area while it heals (see page 427).

THE TRUTH ABOUT FOOD ALLERGIES

"My Bichon Frisé rubs her face and licks her paws constantly. The groomer said she probably has a food allergy and I should switch her to an organic diet. What do you think?"

Your dog may have a food allergy, but switching her to an organic diet won't help you find out. If she is allergic, it's almost certainly to a natural component of the food itself and not to hormones, pesticides, or preservatives used in growing or preparing it.

Food allergies are widely misunderstood. People think they are common in dogs, but allergies to inhaled substances are actually far more common. People think vomiting, diarrhea, or other digestive problems are the main symptoms of canine food allergies, but the most common symptoms are actually non-seasonal itchiness (manifested by paw-licking, face-rubbing, and scratching) and recurrent ear infections. People

think dogs are born with a particular food allergy and it never changes. In fact, an allergy to a particular food develops only after a dog has eaten it one or more times, and a food allergy can develop at any point, even if the dog has eaten the food without any problem for years.

Diagnosing food allergies is equally complicated. The blood or skin tests that are used to diagnose allergies to inhaled substances are not accurate for food allergies. Sometimes such tests will state that a dog is allergic to beef even though she shows no symptoms when she eats beef, or the tests may detect no allergy to eggs even though eating eggs clearly makes her itchy. What's known as a novel food trial produces much more meaningful results and is therefore the best way to diagnose food allergies.

In a novel food trial, a dog is placed on a special diet that contains a "novel" protein and carbohydrate—in other words, ones she has never eaten before. It's those main ingredients, and not the brand, type, or variety of food, that must be entirely new to your dog. Organic dog food, a homemade diet, and lamb-and-rice foods do not qualify as novel if your dog has eaten the same ingredients before (see page 101).

A novel food trial lasts a long time—6 to 12 weeks. During that time, a dog must not eat *any* other food—no dog biscuits, table food, rawhide, or other treats. If the dog's allergy symptoms clear up significantly in those 6 to 12 weeks, then it's likely that she does have a food allergy.

Precisely what food your dog is allergic to won't be revealed by the novel food trial, but you may be able to narrow the possibilities by reading the label of the food your dog was eating when she developed symptoms. The most common documented food allergies are to beef, dairy, or wheat, but allergies to egg, chicken, lamb, soy, and other ingredients have also been reported.

Avoiding the problem food or foods is the only effective treatment for food allergies. Antihistamines and allergy shots do not help.

Over time, a dog can become allergic to what was once novel, so she may have to be switched at some point from, say, Royal Canin Potato & Duck Formula to Iams Response KO (kangaroo and oats). There are also hypoallergenic prescription foods whose ingredients have been digested into molecules too small to trigger an allergic reaction, such as Hill's Prescription Diet z/d Ultra, Purina CNM HA, and Royal Canin HP, but they are relatively expensive and don't work well for all dogs.

A RAGING RUG RASH

"In a fit of spring housecleaning, I washed my Labrador Retriever's bed, gave her a bath, and used a dry carpet freshener on the rug. I also dusted the dog's bed with a little of the carpet powder to keep it smelling nice. A couple of days later, my dog got a scabby red rash on her belly, and she's licking and scratching constantly. What should I do?"

It sounds as though your dog may have a contact hypersensitivity—a localized allergic reaction—to something in the carpet freshener. Dogs can be hypersensitive to something that's used indoors (like a cleaning product), outdoors (like a lawn fertilizer or pesticide), or on the dogs themselves (like a flea or tick product).

The first step is to bathe your dog using a colloidal oatmeal shampoo,

focusing on the irritated area and rinsing thoroughly. Then wash her bed again to remove the carpet freshener, using an unscented laundry detergent. Vacuum the rug again to remove as much of the carpet-freshener residue as possible, and move the dog's bed to an area where you didn't use the carpet freshener, if possible. If her belly hasn't started to clear up and she's still itchy the following day, take her to your vet. She may need antibiotics for a skin infection and corticosteroid tablets for the itch.

THOSE PESKY ANAL GLANDS

"My dog drags his behind on the rug, and sometimes when he does that there's a really foul odor. Is there something wrong with his bottom?"

Dogs scoot when their bottoms feel itchy or irritated. The source of that irritation is often the anal glands (or anal sacs). These are marble-size glands located beneath the skin that have tiny openings into the anus. They produce an oily, skunky substance that is supposed to squeeze out in small amounts

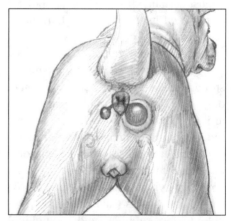

An infected anal gland may look like a swelling or draining wound on the dog's bottom.

WHAT'S SO NICE ABOUT LAMB AND RICE?

The way dog foods containing lamb and rice are advertised, you'd think those two ingredients had miraculous effects on a dog's skin. Not so. There's nothing about lamb or rice that's inherently better than any other protein or carbohydrate source for a dog with food allergies or any other type of skin problem. The proliferation of lamb-and-rice foods on grocery and pet-store shelves is a fad based on those ingredients' long-ago use in "novel food trials" to diagnose food allergies in both people and dogs.

A "novel" food is one the dog (or person) has never had before. Thirty years ago, lamb and rice were essentially never used in commercial dog foods in the United States (though lamb and mutton were found in dog food in Australia, where they're relatively inexpensive and plentiful). For that reason, a dog that was suspected of having food allergies could be placed on a 6- to 12-week trial diet of lamb and rice (with a fat source, vitamins, and minerals added) with the assumption that he'd never eaten those ingredients before and therefore could not have developed an

allergy to them. If his skin symptoms improved noticeably while he was on the lamb-and-rice diet, then he probably had a food allergy to something in his previous diet, such as beef or wheat.

Nowadays, of course, lamb is in every other food in the dog food aisle, so it can no longer be used in a novel-food trial. Instead, veterinarians prescribe novel-food diets that contain venison, duck, fish, or even kangaroo. Once any of those ingredients becomes trendy and crosses over into mainstream dog food, however, its usefulness in diagnosing and treating food allergies will disappear.

Lamb-and-rice foods may not be a miracle cure, but neither is there anything wrong with feeding them to your dog if you choose to do so. Rice is highly digestible, so it's often recommended for dogs who have a "sensitive stomach" or are recovering from a bout of vomiting or diarrhea. In addition, many lamb-and-rice diets are fortified with essential fatty acids, which help reduce skin inflammation and can make a dog feel less itchy.

---

each time the dog defecates, as a scent-marking system. In some dogs, however, the glands and their openings become inflamed, the secretions build up, and the dog feels pressure or pain in the rectal area. Bacteria can overrun the anal glands, filling them with pus. Sometimes

an infected anal gland will burst, creating an open wound near the anus.

If the anal glands are simply overly full, your vet or a vet technician or groomer can empty (or "express") them. This is a stinky business involving a latex glove and petroleum jelly, so vets often whisk a dog out of the exam room and into the treatment area to do the squeezing. But if you'd really like to learn to express your dog's anal glands yourself, just say the word and your vet will be happy to show you how it's done.

If your dog seems *very* uncomfortable, or if you see a swelling, wound, or wet or crusty discharge near his anus, then an infected or ruptured anal gland might be the cause. Your vet will need to flush the gland with an antiseptic solution and apply an antibiotic ointment. Oral antibiotics are often prescribed as well. Surgery is sometimes required to remove infected tissue from the wound. Anal glands can be surgically removed altogether, but this is seldom necessary unless a dog has repeated infections.

THE BROKEN-OUT BOXER

"My three-year-old Boxer has pimples on his chin. Do dogs get acne? What can I use to clear it up?"

Yes, some dogs do get acne, with pimples on the chin and around the mouth. Clean the area gently twice a day, after your dog eats, using a dab of a human facial cleanser containing benzoyl peroxide on a wet paper towel. Don't scrub vigorously, pat dry after washing, and don't squeeze or pick at the pimples. You can dab pimples on the chin with a benzoyl peroxide lotion after washing, but be careful not to get it on your dog's lips, where it can be irritating.

Wash your dog's food and water dishes thoroughly at least once a week. Stainless steel dishes are easy to clean and harbor fewer bacteria than plastic or porous ceramic bowls.

If the pimples don't clear up with twice-daily washing, have your vet take a look to rule out demodex mites or a fungal or deep bacterial infection. Also call your vet if the pimply area seems irritated, painful, or swollen; your dog might have a deep infection that warrants oral antibiotics.

BACTERIAL SKIN INFECTIONS

"My Boston Terrier is on antibiotics for a skin infection. What causes skin infections? Can they be related to allergies? My apartment is very clean and so is my dog, so I'm perplexed."

A dog who is damp and dirty most of the time is indeed a good candidate for a bacterial skin infection, but hygiene isn't the only predisposing factor. As you've surmised, a bacterial skin infection can be secondary to allergies; fleas or mites; moisture-trapping skin folds on the face, tail, or neck; obesity (which can lead to moisture and friction); seborrhea; or conditions that suppress the dog's immune system, such as hypothyroidism, diabetes, or Cushing's disease.

A bacterial skin infection can look like pimples, bumps, or open sores. The hair may be matted in the area or it may fall out. Often the infection will spread or worsen as the dog licks or scratches at the area (contrary to myth, dog saliva is not a good antiseptic). Bacterial infections are treated with medicated baths every other day or twice a week—often with a shampoo containing tea tree oil, sulfur, salicylic acid, or benzoyl peroxide—and oral antibiotics. The antibiotics should be taken for a minimum of one week past the complete healing of the infection, so a deep or extensive infection may require six weeks or more of antibiotics.

Infections in skin folds on the face, neck, or tail can be especially persistent. The constant dampness and difficulty in keeping the folds clean predispose these areas to fungal infections. Cleaning skin folds daily with medicated wipes is helpful. Plastic surgery may even be recommended to "flatten out" skin folds that become infected over and over again.

Although most bacterial skin infections are confined to the uppermost layers of skin, they occasionally spread deep into the skin and are extremely painful and persistent. Extensive oozing sores, abscesses, hair loss, and thickened, dark, scarred skin are the result. For some reason, German Shepherds and shepherd mixes, Bull Terriers, Golden Retrievers, Irish Setters, Doberman Pinschers, and Great Danes are predisposed to these deep skin infections. The treatment is essentially the same as for a more superficial skin infection—medicated baths and antibiotics—but clearing the infection is likely to require months rather than weeks, and a painstaking search should be undertaken to eliminate all underlying factors, including allergies, parasites, and immune-system disorders. The drug Atopica (see page 98) is often given along with antibiotics when there is an allergic or immune-system component to the infection.

Some dogs with recurring skin infections are hypersensitive to staphylococcus bacteria, which are normal inhabitants of the skin surface and cause most dogs no problems. Dogs who are hypersensitive to these bacteria may benefit from periodic injections of staphage lysate. Like allergy shots, these injections build up a dog's tolerance to a foreign substance—in this case, his own normal skin bacteria.

YEASTY BEASTIES

"I'm fostering an English Bulldog who has skin problems, mainly on his feet. The vet suspects a yeast infection. What's the best treatment?"

The yeasts that infect skin are part of the fungus family. Malassezia is the most common type of yeast that causes skin problems in dogs. It grows well in moist areas, such as the ear canals, the feet, the "armpits," and skin folds. Skin infected by malassezia often will be greasy and smelly.

Vets can sometimes find malassezia by pressing a piece of clear tape against the skin, then sticking the tape on a slide, staining it, and examining it under a microscope for the characteristic peanut-shaped yeast. This method doesn't always work well with the feet, however, because the yeast can be hidden deep within the cracks of the foot pads rather than on the surface.

The first line of defense against malassezia is antifungal shampoos, rinses, and creams. These usually contain chlorhexidine; povidone-iodine; boric acid and acetic acid; or one of the "zole" antifungals, such as miconazole. Soak the feet twice a day in an antifungal rinse, and dry them well afterward. Moisture contributes to yeast infections, so use an Elizabethan collar if necessary to keep your dog from licking his feet. Bulldogs' skin folds make them susceptible to fungal infections elsewhere on the body as well, so bathe the entire dog at least twice a month with an antifungal shampoo during warm weather, and clean his ears on the same schedule with an ear cleaner that contains chlorhexidine, povidone-iodine, or acetic acid.

Persistent or recurrent fungal

DEBUNKING BATHING MYTHS

One of the most persistent myths in canine care is that baths are bad for a dog's skin. I think a dog must have started that rumor, or perhaps people got bad results when they used to wash their dogs using laundry detergent and ice-cold water from the garden hose.

The truth? Baths are not harmful. In fact, they are an important component of the treatment for virtually every skin problem. Moreover, dogs who don't have a skin problem can—and should—be bathed whenever they are dirty, greasy, smelly, flaky, or itchy. Even puppies as young as eight weeks old can be bathed (as long as they are kept warm and dried thoroughly afterward), but usually a sponge bath with a damp washcloth or baby wipes will suffice for a young pup.

Use a mild shampoo formulated for dogs, not a baby shampoo or other "people shampoo" that is formulated for our slightly acidic skin rather than the neutral to slightly alkaline skin of a dog. Make sure the water's lukewarm, keep the suds out of the dog's eyes (unless it's "tearless," shampoo can damage the cornea—see page 204), and rinse well. Gently dry the insides of your dog's ears with cotton balls or a soft towel after a bath, because excess moisture can promote an ear infection.

If you bathe your dog once a week or every other week and he's still greasy, smelly, or itchy, it's time to visit your vet. A clean dog who smells bad or scratches excessively probably has parasites, a skin infection, or seborrhea (see page 96).

If your dog does have a skin disease, then a medicated dog shampoo will be part of the treatment. There are hundreds of different brands, but most of them make use of the same dozen or so active ingredients. Here's what those active ingredients do:

Colloidal oatmeal. Soothes and lightly moisturizes itchy skin. Often recommended for dogs with allergic skin disease or mild itchiness.

Tea tree oil. Mildly antibacterial, mildly antifungal, and a mild itch reliever.

---

infections are usually treated with oral antifungal medications, such as ketoconazole, as well. For a fungal foot infection, a dog may be given ketoconazole every day for a month to six weeks, then two or three times per week long-term to reduce the likelihood of recurrence.

Ringworm is another member of the fungus family that can occasionally cause itching, hair loss, or a rash in dogs.

It's much more common in cats, and cats can be carriers of the fungus without showing itching or hair loss themselves. People can also catch ringworm, so it's one of the diseases your vet will want to consider—along with fleas and scabies—if both you and your dog are itchy.

Ringworm is diagnosed with a Wood's lamp or a ringworm culture. A Wood's lamp is an ultraviolet light that's

Sulfur. Reduces excessive skin flaking; mildly antibacterial and antifungal, and a mild itch reliever.

Salicylic acid. Reduces excessive skin flaking; mildly antibacterial, and a mild itch reliever.

Coal tar. Reduces excessive skin flaking and cleans greasy skin; a mild itch reliever.

Selenium sulfide. Reduces excessive skin flaking and cleans greasy skin (may be too drying or irritating if used frequently).

Benzoyl peroxide. Antibacterial; helps unclog pores and cleans greasy skin (may be too drying or irritating if used frequently).

Chlorhexidine. Antibacterial and antifungal.

Povidone-iodine. Antibacterial and antifungal.

Boric acid. Antifungal and drying.

Acetic acid. Antifungal.

Clotrimazole, ketoconazole, miconazole, thiabendazole. Antifungal.

shined on the skin or some plucked hairs. If *Microsporum canis*—one of the three main species of fungus that cause ringworm in dogs—is present, it will show up as an apple-green fluorescence about 50 percent of the time. The other varieties of ringworm fungus never fluoresce under a Wood's lamp, however, so it's useless in diagnosing those. Alternatively, plucked hairs can be placed in a special culture medium and checked for fungal growth after 10 to 14 days.

Ringworm is treated by clipping long-haired dogs or cats, bathing them weekly using a chlorhexidine or miconazole shampoo, and giving an oral antibiotic for one to three months—griseofulvin for dogs, and itraconazole for cats. All cats and dogs in the household must be treated, and the house must be thoroughly cleaned as well because the ringworm fungus can live in the environment. Bedding should be washed in hot water, carpets steam-cleaned, and hard surfaces cleaned with a 1:10 dilution of chlorine bleach.

SLOUGHING TOENAILS

"My five-year-old Dachshund used to have perfectly normal toenails, but then they began softening, splitting, and breaking off at the quick, leaving painful, bloody stubs. About half the nails on her front feet are gone, and the ones on her back feet are starting to split. Why is this happening, and what can I do about it?"

If the nails on just one foot had broken, then an infection by a fungus, bacteria, or demodex mites would be likely. Because all four feet are involved,

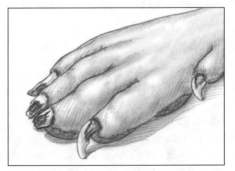

Splitting, broken nails can be caused by skin mites, an infection, or an immune disorder.

however, the most likely diagnosis is an immune-system attack on the nails. The medical term for this is lupoid onchyodystrophy. The treatment is as drawn-out as the name: an antibiotic and two vitamins (tetracycline, vitamin E, and niacinamide, a B vitamin) given by mouth for two to three months. This combination reduces the inflammation of the cells in the nail bed. The treatment continues for so long because it takes about two months for a healthy new nail to grow from the nail bed.

Your dog's remaining toenails will most likely continue to break even after you start the treatment, because it takes weeks to reach full effect. Carefully trim partially broken nails and normal-appearing nails that are overlong, or have your vet or groomer do this. A partially broken nail that catches and snags every time your dog takes a step is even more painful than a stump. If your dog is in pain—limping, refusing to walk, perhaps losing her appetite—talk to your vet about giving her enteric-coated aspirin, carprofen (Rimadyl), or another pain reliever. In cases where the tetracycline-vitamin treatment doesn't halt the breakage and the dog's feet are extremely painful, amputation of the last bone in the most severely affected toes (the nails grow, essentially, directly from this bone) can be done as a last resort to relieve the pain.

A FLAKY MESS

"My 10-year-old shepherd mix has what looks like the world's worst case of dandruff. Some of the flakes are as big as a dime. He also smells so bad no one wants to get near him. What can I do?"

With its flakes, scabs, and thinning hair, seborrhea is unsightly and uncomfortable. Medicated baths—lots of them—are the answer.

If you've ever paid close attention to magazine ads for dandruff shampoo, you've probably seen the word "seborrhea," the medical term for a skin irritation whose primary symptom is flaky skin. From your description, it sounds like your dog has seborrhea.

A dog with seborrhea is usually itchy as well as flaky. He might have small scabs, bumps, or pimples on the skin. His hair may be thin in some areas, or he may have patches that are almost totally bald. Seborrhea comes in two main forms: oily and dry. You'll know which type your dog has by rubbing a flaky area of his skin and hair and seeing whether it feels greasy or not.

Breeds that are prone to oily seborrhea include Cocker Spaniels, Basset Hounds, English Springer Spaniels, Labrador Retrievers, Shar-Peis, and West Highland White Terriers. Breeds that are prone to dry seborrhea include Dachshunds, Doberman Pinschers, German Shepherds, and Irish Setters.

Pair a dog with seborrhea with an owner who believes that dogs shouldn't be bathed, and you have a real mess. In fact, frequent bathing is critical to treating seborrhea. A dog who has "the world's worst dandruff" should be bathed *every other day* for a week or 10 days, however long it takes to remove the majority of the flakes and debris from the skin. The baths should then be tapered off to twice a week, once a week, and when the disease seems to be completely under control, a minimum of once a month. What's important is getting rid of the flakes and other skin debris; not only are they extremely itchy, but they also create a perfect environment for secondary bacterial or fungal skin infections.

A dog who has dry seborrhea should be bathed with a shampoo that contains sulfur or salicylic acid. One who has oily seborrhea should be bathed with a shampoo that contains coal tar, benzoyl peroxide, or selenium sulfide, which degrease the skin. When bathing a dog with seborrhea, wet him thoroughly with warm (not hot) water; lather him well, using plenty of shampoo and concentrating on the flaky areas of his skin; leave the lather on for 10 to 15 minutes, using whatever judo holds or distracting maneuvers you can think of to keep him in the tub; then rinse him with luke-warm water until all traces of shampoo are gone. If his skin is dry, apply a soothing rinse or spray after bathing—something that contains colloidal oatmeal, essential fatty acids, urea, or glycerin. Essential fatty acid supplements given orally also help relieve the itch in some dogs with seborrhea.

Other treatments for seborrhea depend on the underlying factors, if any. In some dogs, seborrhea is a symptom of allergies, a bacterial or fungal skin infection, or parasites. (If a dog has "walking dandruff"—small flakes that move—he has a skin mite; see page 169.) In other cases, seborrhea is a stand-alone prob-lem. Have your vet take a look at your dog's skin to determine whether he needs antibiotics for a skin infection, corticosteroids for extreme itchiness or inflammation, treatment for parasites, or other adjuncts to the bathing regimen.

IMMUNE-MEDIATED SKIN DISEASES

"When my four-year-old Collie mix got some sores on the top of her muzzle, I thought maybe she'd got-ten a sunburn. Then the sores got worse and started spreading to the rest of her face, so I took her to the vet, who wants to take skin biopsies to check for an immune disease. Is this the right thing to do?"

Yes, a skin biopsy is the appropri-ate way to check for an immune-mediated skin disease—one where the dog's immune system starts attacking her own skin cells. Skin biopsies are usu-ally taken by lightly sedating the dog, if necessary, then numbing the skin with a local anesthetic and removing four or five snips of skin from the affected areas using a biopsy punch, which is like a tiny,

Immune-mediated skin diseases often target the face, producing sores, hair loss, or changes in skin color.

(continued on page 110)

LUMPS, BUMPS, AND GROWTHS

Dogs can sprout a variety of lumps, bumps, and skin growths, especially as they get older. Fortunately, most are merely unsightly or messy rather than harmful. Here is a guide to some typical skin growths in dogs. No growth can be definitively diagnosed by its appearance alone, however, so point out such lumps and bumps to your veterinarian during your dog's annual physical exam, and be sure to consult your vet if your dog has a lump that grows rapidly, oozes and doesn't heal, or otherwise bothers you or your dog.

Warts. These firm, bumpy growths occur in both young dogs and middle-aged to older dogs. "Puppy warts" are caused by a virus, appear around a young dog's mouth, and go away on their own. Older dogs often grow warts on their heads or bodies. Warts should be surgically removed if they routinely bleed or become irritated, or if they grow on the eyelid margin and rub against the eye.

Pimples and blackheads. Dogs can get "clogged pores" just like people do, and these may form pimples or blackheads. Facial acne in dogs usually responds well to frequent cleaning with a benzoyl peroxide cleanser. Pimples or blackheads elsewhere can be a symptom of a bacterial skin infection or seborrhea (see page 106).

Sebaceous cysts. These lumps are oil-producing (sebaceous) glands that have become blocked and enlarged, ranging from mosquito-bite-sized to an inch or two in diameter. They contain a whitish, greasy, pastelike combination of oil, bacteria, and skin cells. Sebaceous cysts will sometimes open and ooze their contents on their own, or the material can be squeezed out, but usually they will simply fill up again over time. If a sebaceous cyst is particularly messy or in an area where it constantly becomes irritated, it can be surgically removed.

Lipomas. Although these are commonly referred to as "fatty tumors," they are benign, not malignant, and so are not "tumors" in the cancer sense. Rather, they are lumpy accumulations of fat—

Many older dogs develop lipomas, or fatty lumps, beneath the skin.

sort of the canine equivalent of cellulite. They usually appear in middle-aged and older dogs and can range from 1 inch in diameter to 8 inches or more, growing slowly over months to years. If your dog has lipomas, your vet should (1) measure them during your dog's yearly physical exam and note their location and size on your dog's medical chart; and (2) when each new lipoma appears and if one enlarges rapidly, do a fine-needle aspirate (FNA) of the lump. An FNA takes only a few seconds, can be done during a regular exam, and is virtually painless. The vet inserts a needle into the lump and extracts a drop of its contents to examine under a microscope. If the contents are just fat, you can be reasonably certain the lump is a lipoma. If the contents include other types of cells, then the lump may not be a lipoma, and it would be prudent to remove it surgically and have it checked by a pathologist to make sure it's not cancer. Lipomas that are large enough to make a dog uncomfortable or interfere with his ability to walk should also be removed.

Elbow calluses. Large, heavy dogs often develop thick, dark, hairless calluses on the parts of their bodies that contact hard surfaces when they lie down, such as their elbows, hocks, or even over the breastbone. Sometimes these calluses crack and bleed or become infected. They can be treated by providing thickly padded areas for resting; using warm compresses or soaks two or three times a day; applying petroleum jelly, lanolin, or another softening and soothing agent (make sure it's safe to eat if the dog can reach the area and lick it off); and oral antibiotics if the area is infected.

Hives or facial swelling. Hives are fluid-filled, blisterlike swellings that crop up in groups when a dog has been exposed to something she is hypersensitive to, such as a spider bite, bee sting, or, rarely, a medication or vaccine. They can range from about ¼ inch to 2 inches or more in diameter. Facial swelling—in which the dog's face becomes puffy—is a similar hypersensitivity reaction. If your dog suddenly sprouts hives, give her the antihistamine Benadryl (diphenhydramine) at a dose of 1 mg per pound of her body weight (that's 10 mg for a 10-pound dog, 25 mg for a 25-pound dog, and so on). If she's very itchy or the hives are still spreading one hour later, call your vet. If your dog has a swollen or puffy face, call your vet or a vet emergency clinic immediately, because in severe cases the windpipe may swell shut, leaving the dog unable to breathe and in need of emergency care.

Skin cancer. Dogs can get a variety of skin cancers, including melanomas, mast-cell tumors, and squamous cell carcinomas. They can look like anything at all: a lump, sore, or discoloration. Skin cancer may itch, hurt, or not bother the dog at all. Always point out new skin growths to your vet during your dog's annual physical exam, and have your vet check out sores that take more than 10 days to heal, lumps that grow rapidly or swell and shrink, or any other skin growth that's worrisome to you or your dog. For more on individual types of skin cancer, see page 382.

(continued from page 107)

sharp cookie cutter. Each snip is about ¼ inch in diameter and is closed with a single stitch of suture material.

The biopsies are sent to a veterinary pathologist for microscopic analysis. If your dog's skin problem is immune-mediated, the pathologist will see a characteristic pattern of broken skin cells plus an accumulation of white blood cells within the skin, but none of the bacteria, fungi, parasites, or other agents that can sometimes cause similar signs.

Your vet probably will also want to run some blood tests to make sure the skin sores aren't merely one symptom of systemic lupus erythematosus (SLE), an immune-mediated disease that can attack the joints, kidneys, and blood as well as the skin.

The immune-mediated skin diseases include cutaneous lupus erythematosus and several forms of pemphigus. They target the face, causing sores, crusting, hair loss, and changes in skin color in and around the nose, mouth, and eyes. One variant, pemphigus foliaceus, often begins on the head and then spreads to the body and feet.

The treatment for immune-mediated skin diseases is corticosteroids (such as prednisone) to calm the immune system. In more severe cases that don't respond to corticosteroids, stronger, chemotherapy-type immunosuppressant drugs are used. Your dog will probably also need oral antibiotics for any secondary bacterial skin infection. Sunlight makes immune-mediated skin diseases worse, so it's advisable to keep your dog indoors during peak sunlight hours—10 A.M. to 2 P.M.—and to apply a 15 SPF sunscreen to your dog's face (rub it into the fur and dab it on the edges of her nose) when exposure to the sun is unavoidable.

Sometimes immune-mediated skin diseases are induced by exposure to a virus, fungus, medication, or food. Other times they crop up for no known reason. Heredity appears to be a factor, because these diseases are seen more frequently in certain breeds, including Collies, German Shepherds, Shetland Sheepdogs, Brittanys, and Siberian Huskies. Pemphigus foliaceus is seen most commonly in Akitas, Bearded Collies, Chows, Doberman Pinschers, English Springer Spaniels, Finnish Spitz, Newfoundlands, Schipperkes, and Shar-Peis.

HAIR, HAIR, EVERYWHERE

"My three-year-old Doberman/German Shepherd mix sheds quite a bit. I feed him a supermarket brand of dry dog food, and I have been told that a premium dog food might reduce his shedding. Is that true?"

It's doubtful that a better diet would reduce shedding. Most shedding, as excessive as it may seem, is normal and not a sign of a nutritional deficiency or illness. If the skin is scaly or scabby, or he's actually becoming bald in places, then a disease of some sort might be involved, but it doesn't sound like that's the case with your dog.

Many of the higher-quality dog foods are fortified with antioxidants and essential fatty acids, but these would most likely just make all that hair wafting through your apartment extra shiny. Of course, there is no harm in trying a different type of dog food or adding a fatty-acid supplement to your dog's diet. Just be sure to switch the food gradually, over a week or more, because some dogs' digestive tracts are sensitive to any kind of change.

The best anti-shedding advice I can give you is to brush and bathe your dog frequently, so you can throw that hair away in big bunches rather than seeing it pile up in the corners. Brush him at least a few strokes every day. And it's OK to bathe him as often as once a week when he's shedding heavily, as long as you use a mild dog shampoo and rinse it out thoroughly.

Some short-haired dogs develop bald patches on their ears or body as they get older.

BALDING DOGS

"The hair on the edges of my Dachshund's ears is very thin. My husband jokes that the dog is going bald. Will the hair grow back?"

Your husband is correct. Thin hair on the ears is a form of "baldness" that's common in Dachshunds and other short-haired dogs. They may also lose hair on their sides, chest, and rear end, in a symmetrical pattern (the same on the left and right sides of the body). The hair is unlikely to grow back because some of the hair follicles in those areas have disappeared, and others have converted to producing only short, soft, downy hairs.

A few other patterns of hair loss or hair thinning are also seen in dogs. One is symmetrical hair loss on the body, often accompanied by bumps, blackheads, flaking, or other mild skin irritation. This can be a sign of Cushing's disease or hypothyroidism, so consult your vet if your dog is showing signs of those problems.

Some hair loss is breed- or even color-specific. Greyhounds often shed and later regrow the hair on their thighs. An irreversible form of hair-thinning is seen in dogs that are "blue" (actually a shade of gray) or "fawn" (light tan) in color, especially the blue Doberman Pinscher and fawn Irish Setter. The hair loss usually begins when the dog is one to three years old and may be accompanied by mild skin irritation. The irritation can be treated with medicated baths, but the hair loss is permanent.

A few dogs lose hair on the sides of the body and then regrow the hair three or four months later. Often the skin darkens noticeably in the areas of thinning hair, and the hair may grow back a somewhat different color or texture than before. Giving the dog melatonin supplements can help speed the regrowth of hair in this type of seasonal or cyclic hair loss.

One form of immune-mediated skin disease targets the hair follicles, causing patchy hair loss. Dogs who are more than one color may lose the hair of one color only. This type of hair loss, called alopecia areata, can be diagnosed by skin biopsy and treated by corticosteroid injections into the skin in the affected areas, but unless the skin is also irritated or infected, the best course may be to simply leave matters alone. The hair sometimes regrows on its own in alopecia areata.

When should you take a balding dog to the vet? If your dog is itchy or smells bad, if the skin appears irritated or infected, or if your dog seems ill or not quite right aside from the hair loss, then a vet visit is in order to check for a bacterial or fungal infection, parasites, or another problem requiring treatment. A dog you're planning to breed should also be checked out in case the hair loss is hereditary.

HORMONES AND HAIR

"My four-year-old Keeshond's coat has gotten thinner and thinner over the past couple of years, to the point where he now has almost no hair on his sides. I read on a website that Keeshonds can lose their hair because of a hormone problem. Is it serious? Can it be treated?"

Keeshonds are prone to two adrenal-gland diseases that can cause hair loss: Cushing's disease and a form of atypical Cushing's called alopecia X. In Cushing's disease, the adrenals produce too much cortisol. This predisposes a dog to infections, interferes with blood-sugar regulation, and leads to increased thirst and urination, muscle wasting, weakness, and sometimes hair loss. In atypical Cushing's, the adrenal glands produce more sex hormones—such as progesterone or testosterone—than normal, which can lead to similar symptoms. Alopecia X usually begins in young dogs, between the ages of one and four, and primarily causes hair loss. It is seen most often in Pomeranians, Keeshonds, Poodles, Samoyeds, and Chows.

Has your dog been tested for Cushing's? If not, he should be, because if he has it, he should be treated to prevent the more severe consequences of the disease (see page 299 for more about treating Cushing's). The blood samples drawn to check for Cushing's can also be tested for abnormally high levels of sex hormones in order to diagnose alopecia X.

Although both neutered and unneutered dogs can suffer from alopecia X, neutering or spaying an intact dog with alopecia X often causes the hair to regrow. If your dog is already neutered, melatonin supplements or melatonin implants can sometimes trigger hair regrowth. Your vet can calculate the proper dose.

A few other hormone problems can also cause hair loss in unneutered dogs. One is testicular cancer. Many testicular tumors—especially those in undescended testicles (those found in the abdomen rather than in the scrotum)—secrete high levels of estrogen, which can cause hair loss and darkening of the skin. More rarely, a testicular tumor can secrete high levels of testosterone, which can cause aggressive behavior, oily and scaly skin, and occasionally hair loss and darkening of the skin. Testicular tumors are treated by neutering, and the skin and hair usually return to normal within three to four months.

Unspayed female dogs can develop ovarian tumors or cysts that secrete high levels of estrogen. Symptoms can include an enlarged vulva, enlarged nipples, oily and scaly skin, and hair loss on the sides and hindquarters. Ovarian tumors or cysts are treated by spaying, and the skin and hair usually return to normal within three to four months.

DUDLEY NOSE

"My three-year-old yellow Lab's nose has gradually changed from black to pinkish brown. I don't think he ever injured his nose, and it doesn't look sore. What could have caused the color change?"

It sounds like what's known as Dudley nose, a fading of the pigment in the nose and sometimes the eyelid margins as well, common in light-colored dogs like yellow Labs, Golden Retrievers, and Bichon Frisés. Dudley nose does the dog no harm but may reduce his breeder to tears, because it's considered a conformation fault and will lower his score in the show ring. There's no medical treatment to restore the black pigment, although the color sometimes waxes and wanes on its own. "Snow nose" is a seasonal version of Dudley nose in which the nose fades during winter—apparently in reaction to the cold—and regains color in the spring.

A nose that changes color and is also swollen, crusty, lumpy, or sore should be checked out by a vet to rule out infection, an immune-mediated disease, or even skin cancer.

DRY FOOT PADS

"My dog's foot pads are hard, dry, and cracked. Should I soak them or put moisturizer on them?"

A dog's foot pads are supposed to be dry and leathery for protection against rough pavement, rocks, and so on. You may also notice shallow cracks on the surface. This is normal. Unless your dog is limping or otherwise seems uncomfortable, you should leave the feet alone. Remember not to apply anything to your dog's feet that isn't safe for her to eat, because she'll inevitably lick it off.

Here are some symptoms that do warrant attention: sores on the pads or between the toes; bleeding, oozing, or crusting at the base of the toenails; thick calluses or corns that push the toes out of position; and deep cracks that ooze or bleed. Foot wounds and infections can be difficult to clear up, so it's best to consult your vet about those problems.

If ice-melting salt irritates your dog's feet in the wintertime, you can use boots (Muttluks are a popular brand) or a special foot wax (see page 80) when you take your dog outdoors, and rinse and dry the feet when you come back inside.

CHAPTER 5

Vomiting, Diarrhea, and Other Digestive Ailments

ANOTHER DAY, ANOTHER UPSET STOMACH.
As most dog owners know firsthand, vomiting and diarrhea are exceedingly common in dogs—which, considering what the average dog will eat, is not surprising. "Something he ate" is the No. 1 cause of gastrointestinal distress in dogs, and in simple cases it can be treated successfully at home. But before you prescribe that daylong fast followed by a bland diet, learn how to assess your dog's symptoms and situation so you'll know when you need to call the vet instead.

EMERGENCY!

Does your dog need immediate veterinary care? Check this list to help you decide.

TAKE IMMEDIATE ACTION!

Call your vet or an emergency veterinary clinic *now* if your dog is showing any of the following symptoms:

❏ He is retching or clearly very uncomfortable, and his **sides or belly looks bloated** or swollen.

❏ She is a female dog who has not been spayed, was **in heat a month or two ago,** is **lethargic,** and has **lost her appetite.**

❏ He may have lapped up some **antifreeze,** a deadly poison.

❏ She is taking **digoxin or digitoxin** for heart disease, is **diabetic,** or has **kidney disease** or **cancer.** Vomiting and diarrhea require special care in animals with these conditions.

❏ He has eaten something that may be **stuck in the digestive tract,** especially cloth, string, or rope.

❏ Her **vomit is bloody or looks like it has coffee grounds** in it.

❏ His **diarrhea looks like it's almost all blood.**

❏ She is a puppy or recently adopted dog who has **diarrhea,** is **weak or lethargic,** and **has not yet completed her vaccine series against parvo.**

❏ He has **lost his appetite,** is **vomiting,** or has **diarrhea,** and you gave him **ibuprofen** (Motrin or Advil), **naproxen** (Aleve), or **aspirin** in the past week.

❏ She seems to have **severe abdominal pain,** along with **persistent vomiting** and a **loss of appetite.**

❏ He is an adult dog who has been vomiting or having diarrhea and seems **too weak to walk,** or he is a puppy less than six months old who seems **weak and lethargic.**

❏ Her temperature, taken with a rectal thermometer, is **103°F or higher.**

❏ The **whites of his eyes, the insides of his ears, or his gums look yellow;** jaundice is a symptom of a liver or blood disease.

TAKE A MINUTE . . .

Read further in this book and then call your vet during office hours as needed if your dog is showing any of the following symptoms:

❏ His feces or diarrhea contains **streaks of blood or mucus;** this is a symptom of colitis (see page 125).

❏ She is taking **antibiotics and has diarrhea** (see page 127).

❏ He is vomiting up **yellow or orange liquid;** this is bile, from the gall bladder, and indicates that your dog is continuing to vomit even though his stomach is empty (see pages 130 and 134).

Remember, it's never wrong to call your veterinarian if you have a question about your dog's health, or if you're worried about a symptom or your dog's overall condition. That's what we're here for.

WHY DO DOGS GET DIARRHEA?

"My dog has a bout of diarrhea every other month or so. Do I need to take her to the vet every time, or can I treat it at home?"

Diarrhea is the bane of many a dog owner's existence. Sometimes, it's nothing to be overly concerned about and can be treated at home, but other times it does warrant a call or visit to your veterinarian. Here's how you can decide which category you're facing this time.

The four most common causes of diarrhea in dogs are dietary indiscretion ("something she ate"), intestinal parasites, stress, and digestive-tract viruses. If you think your dog may have intestinal parasites, take her to the vet—along with a small, fresh sample of her feces. (For more on intestinal parasites, see page 149.)

If you think your dog's diarrhea is probably caused by something she ate or by a stressful situation, then treating her at home may be an option. To be sure, ask yourself the following questions:

❏ Is your dog basically healthy, or does she have other health problems, such as heart or kidney disease? If your dog has other major health issues or is on any medicine other than monthly heartworm prevention, call your vet right away.

❏ Is your dog vomiting as well? If your dog has vomited more than once or twice along with having diarrhea, call your vet.

❏ Is your dog lethargic? Has she lost her appetite? Call your vet.

❏ Does she just seem really miserable or sick? Call your vet.

❏ Is she passing watery diarrhea every hour or two? Call your vet.

❏ Is there blood or mucus in the diarrhea? Trick question. A small amount of blood or mucus is simply a sign that the colon is irritated. That's not an emergency, and if your dog checks out OK on the other questions, you can try home treatment. However, if there's a lot of blood, or if the diarrhea is almost entirely blood, call your vet immediately. Severely bloody diarrhea can be a symptom of parvovirus (see page 121), hemorrhagic gastroenteritis (see page 126), or another serious illness.

❏ Has your dog eaten table food or a different brand of dog food in the past couple of days? If you think a change in diet may have precipitated a bout of diarrhea, it's probably safe to treat it at home.

Dietary indiscretion—eating something they shouldn't—is one of the most common causes of canine diarrhea.

❏ Did your dog recently get into the garbage or eat something that's not meant to be eaten (toy, TV remote, rock)? Call your vet immediately. Plastic packaging, a bone, or some other object might be stuck in the intestines.

❏ Might your dog have eaten something poisonous, such as antifreeze or mouse bait? Call your vet immediately.

❏ Diarrhea can be a response to stress. Have you been away recently? Has your dog just returned from boarding? Did you recently move? If so, it's probably safe to treat the diarrhea at home.

❏ Is your dog less than six months old? Call the vet, because puppies can dehydrate quickly. Many puppies have intestinal parasites that cause diarrhea (and are easily treatable with the proper dewormer). They also are more likely to eat things that can get stuck in their GI tract, have parvo, or develop a potentially fatal intussusception (see page 121).

If your dog doesn't show any of the danger signs described in the above questions, try the treatment for diarrhea outlined on page 122. If the diarrhea doesn't improve within one day of home treatment, or isn't at least 80 percent better by the end of three days, then you should call your vet.

TABLE FOOD AND DIARRHEA

"My terrier mix has a sensitive stomach. He gets diarrhea all the time and sometimes vomits. We give him special food for his stomach, but he doesn't like it very well, so we usually give him some of whatever we're eating too."

The problem here may be not your dog's stomach, but rather the table food he's putting into it. Although conditions such as irritable bowel disease certainly can cause recurring diarrhea, in your dog's case I think you should first rule out the effects of eating what sounds like a smorgasbord of table food. Many dogs, especially those with sensitive stomachs, will vomit or get diarrhea after eating the kinds of foods and snacks that people do. This is a form of food "intolerance" rather than food "allergy" (see the following Q&A for details on the difference).

To determine whether table food is the culprit in your dog's digestive problems, make him go cold turkey for one month: no table food or treats. You'll have to enlist the cooperation of everyone in your household—spouse, children, babysitter, in-laws, dog walker, and so on. Tell them that your dog loves his treats but they may be making him sick, and that the only way to find out is to stop giving them to him.

For one month feed him only his special diet, half in the morning and half at dinnertime. Leave the food in his bowl for half an hour, and if he hasn't eaten it by then, throw it away and try again at his next meal. Do leave a bowl of fresh water out at all times, but don't give him any table food or even dog biscuits, rawhide, cow hooves, or other treats.

Your dog is certain to miss his customary handouts, but be firm. This is a long-ingrained habit you're trying to break. Shut him out of the kitchen or dining room during meals, and resist all begging and moping. He may not eat his dog food for a couple of days, but don't give in—he won't starve. When he needs to eat, the dog food will start to look rather tasty.

If the diarrhea and vomiting are much improved after a month of this regimen, then you have pretty good evidence that table food makes your dog sick. Present that diagnosis to your household, followed by the treatment: no more people food. If you'd like to reintroduce one or two dog treats—such as rawhide chews or plain dog biscuits—you can do so one at a time, in *small* amounts. You want him to eat his well-balanced diet, not to fill up on doggie junk food. But if the diarrhea returns after he starts getting rawhide, for example, you should eliminate it permanently. And stay away from fatty dog snacks like pig's ears and bacon-flavored thingamajigs.

Alternatively, if your dog has diarrhea and vomits just as much when he's not eating table food as he did before, then it's time to dig deeper for a cause: see page 128.

FOOD ALLERGY AND FOOD INTOLERANCE

"My spaniel mix has loose stools all the time and vomits once a week or so. Couldn't this be a food allergy? How would I find out?"

True food allergies do exist in dogs, but they are rare, affecting roughly 1 to 5 percent of the canine population. In addition, most canine allergies—including food allergies—produce skin symptoms, such as itching and ear infections, rather than digestive-tract symptoms.

Food *intolerances* are somewhat more common than food *allergies*. What's the difference? With an allergy, the body's white blood cells coordinate an attack against the offending substance, which is most often a protein molecule. The white blood cells trigger the release of substances that cause inflammation, itching, or swelling in one or more areas of the body. A food intolerance, on the other hand, is what many people mean when they say a particular food, such as cucumbers or garlic, "doesn't agree" with them. They may find the food hard to digest, and it may give them gas or even diarrhea, but they are not, strictly speaking, allergic to it.

So could your dog have a food allergy or a food intolerance? Yes, it's possible, and if you've ruled out the more common causes of diarrhea (see page 117), it's worth exploring. For details of how food allergies are diagnosed and treated, see page 99.

FACTS ABOUT FLATULENCE

Gassy hounds abound. Flatulence isn't usually a sign of a serious illness, but the symptoms are distressing enough to lead many a gassed-out dog owner to ask what can be done about the problem.

The first step is to make sure you're just talking about gas, and not vomiting or diarrhea as well. If a gassy dog vomits or has diarrhea frequently, then read this chapter to learn about the underlying causes of overall digestive-tract distress, and consult with your vet as needed to diagnose and solve the problem.

If your dog has gas and, perhaps, a rumbly tummy, then food ingredients or swallowed air are the most likely contributors to the gas blast.

Dogs swallow excessive amounts of air if they gobble their food rapidly or anxiously. If this describes your dog, try the measures outlined on page 135.

Certain foods can give certain dogs gas. You'll have to be a detective on this one because the potential causes are numerous. Some dogs have problems with legumes, such as peas or soybeans. Others have trouble digesting particular carbohydrates (grains such as corn, wheat, oats, and rice, or potatoes). Still others find certain proteins hard to digest (such as beef, cheese, chicken, lamb, or pork). Every dog is likely to get gas (or worse) from eating fatty food or spoiled food. If you suspect a food allergy or food intolerance may be making your dog gassy, see the previous Q&A.

If your dog's gas attacks began at the same time you started giving him a nutritional supplement or medicine, that might be the culprit. Ask your vet whether it's safe to stop giving the supplement or medicine, or whether you need to switch to a different type. Watch out, too, for treats such as pig's ears, cow hooves, and rawhide—these can wreak havoc on some dogs' digestion, causing gas or diarrhea.

If changing the diet doesn't help, try over-the-counter simethicone (Gas-X is one of many brand names). Simethicone is generally quite safe, but ask your vet for an appropriate dose for your dog's weight.

THE DREADED PARVOVIRUS

"My five-month-old puppy has diarrhea with some blood in it. I'm scared to death she might have parvo. What should I do?"

If your puppy is weak or lethargic and her diarrhea has a lot of blood in it, you should put down this book and call your vet or an emergency veterinary clinic immediately. But if the diarrhea has just a streak or two of blood in it, your puppy is bright and bouncy, and she has finished the three- or four-shot series of puppy vaccines against parvo, then chances are the blood you're seeing is caused by whipworms (see page 152) or colitis (see page 125), not parvo.

Parvo is one of the deadliest viruses that cause diarrhea. Dogs with parvo often have severe watery or bloody diarrhea and a fever of 103°F or higher. They quickly become dehydrated, weak, and lethargic. They can die from dehydration, shock, or a bacterial infection attacking through the ravaged intestines. Treating parvo requires hospitalization on IV fluids for a minimum of several days, plus antibiotics to ward off bacterial infections, and other supportive care as needed. Even with prompt, intensive care, some puppies still die of parvo.

Parvo is highly contagious between dogs—an unvaccinated dog can easily catch it through contact with an infected dog or infected feces. (Dog parvo is not contagious to people. The mild fever-and-rash form of parvovirus that children get, called fifth disease, is caused by a different member of the parvo family.) In the hospital, dogs with parvo are strictly quarantined from other dogs, and a bleach solution is used to kill the

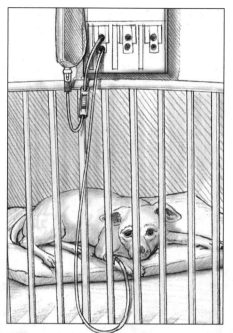

Parvo can be fatal even if it's treated promptly with IV fluids and medication.

virus on their cages, dishes, and other equipment.

Fortunately, vaccines against parvo are widely available and are used in puppy shots and adult vaccine boosters. These vaccines are highly effective.

Distemper is another often-deadly virus that can cause vomiting and diarrhea in unvaccinated puppies and dogs. Usually distemper starts with a fever, runny nose, and watery eyes, then progresses to vomiting or diarrhea, weakness, and lethargy. Like parvo, it does not strike fully vaccinated puppies and dogs. For more about distemper, see page 278.

TELESCOPING INTESTINES

"My puppy was really sick with diarrhea for a couple of days. When I took him to the vet, she did an ultrasound exam of his belly and said that part of his intestine had collapsed

into itself, and he needed surgery right away to fix it. How did this happen?"

When diarrhea is severe—as when a puppy has parvo or a heavy infestation of intestinal parasites—the contractions that move material from the stomach through the intestines sometimes go into overdrive, and part or parts of the intestine can be pushed into each other like a collapsing telescope. The medical term for this is intussusception. Intussusceptions are more common in puppies, but they can happen in older dogs as well.

Your vet may have felt a suspicious lump in your puppy's belly and then confirmed that the lump was an intussusception by looking at it via ultrasound. Intussusceptions may also be visible on x-rays.

The danger with intussusceptions is that blood flow to the telescoped section of the intestine is cut off, and the tissues in that section can die and break open, leaking bacteria and fluid into the abdomen. Shock, infection, and death can quickly result. Immediate surgery is the best option for treating an intussusception.

During surgery, the veterinarian examines the intestine to determine

HOME CARE FOR DIARRHEA

If your dog has diarrhea but doesn't show any of the warning signs of a serious illness (see page 117), then it's generally safe to treat the diarrhea at home, using the following plan.

First, don't give your dog any food at all for 12 to 24 hours, but give him all the fresh, clean water he'd like (unless he's also vomiting; in that case, see page 134).

After that fast, start feeding him a bland diet of 3 parts cooked rice mixed with 1 part boiled chicken. Salt the mixture lightly, but make sure it contains no fat (skin the chicken pieces *before* you cook them), no spices, and of course no bones.

Feed small amounts of this bland diet three or four times a day for three days. If the diarrhea doesn't improve within one day or isn't at least 80 percent better by the end of three days, then you should call your vet. If his

diarrhea is at least 80 percent better by the end of three days, start mixing increasing amounts of his regular food into the rice-and-chicken mixture over another three or four days, until he's eating just his regular food.

Human over-the-counter diarrhea medicines, such as Imodium (loperamide), Pepto-Bismol (bismuth subsalicylate), or Kaopectate (attapulgite), can *sometimes* be used safely in dogs, but don't try them without talking to your vet to get an appropriate dose and to make sure you're not overlooking a more serious problem.

Finally, don't give your dog an over-the-counter dewormer when he has diarrhea. That's a wasted effort unless you *know* that your dog has intestinal parasites (based on a current fecal exam) *and* you know that the dewormer on the shelf is effective against those particular parasites.

whether the tissues have been damaged by a loss of blood flow. If so, she will cut out the damaged area of intestine and suture the healthy portions back together. If the tissues look healthy and the intussusception can be undone by gentle pulling, however, then the vet can instead unfold the intestine and tack it into place with a few sutures to prevent it from telescoping in that area again.

Either way, the puppy has undergone major abdominal surgery and will need to be closely monitored in the hospital for a few days. Meanwhile, the underlying cause of the diarrhea (such as intestinal parasites) will also need to be treated to prevent another intussusception from occurring elsewhere in the intestines.

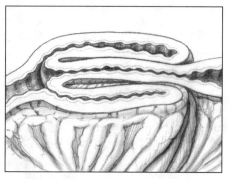

In an intussusception, part of the intestine pushes into itself, cutting off blood flow.

STRESS BELLY

"My five-year-old spaniel mix comes home with diarrhea every time I board her. Is the kennel doing something wrong? Is there any way to stop this from happening?"

The diarrhea is probably triggered by stress, not by anything the kennel is doing wrong. "What does a dog have to be stressed about?" you may ask. Well, when she's boarding, no matter how kind

and competent the caretakers are, she's away from home, she's away from you, her daily routine is different, she is with dogs she doesn't know, there may be lots of barking, and she may not be sleeping well. For many dogs, that equals stress.

How can you lessen the chances that your dog will have stress-induced diarrhea when you go away? If you can find a reliable dog-and-house-sitter who can stay with your dog in your home while you're away, that's ideal. If your dog must board outside your home, the following measures may help:

❏ Take a supply of your dog's regular food to the boarding facility so she's not on an unfamiliar diet.

❏ Have them feed your dog on the same schedule she's used to at home. Some kennels feed once a day, but if your dog is used to being fed twice a day, ask them to do the same while she's boarding.

❏ If your dog is sociable with other dogs, she may be more comfortable in a run where she can see and hear her neighbors. If she's nervous, aggressive, or not sociable, she may be more comfortable in a quieter, more private location. Try to fit the accommodations to her personality.

❏ Schedule an individual daily walk, playtime, or petting time for your dog. The added cost will be worth it.

❏ Avoid tranquilizers for boarding. Often the dose required to make a dog "calm" is high enough to make her sleepy and zoned-out. In my opinion, it's better to have a slightly edgy dog with mild diarrhea than a dog who's drugged out for days at a time. If your dog is already taking a prescription drug for separation anxiety or a similar condition, however, then she should stay

PAINT YOUR VET A PICTURE

Use all your descriptive powers to describe your dog's digestive-tract upset to your vet—details will provide important clues to what's going on. Here are some of the things your vet will want to know:

❑ What does the diarrhea look like? Is it mostly water; runny, like pancake batter; or just a little softer than usual? Is it jellylike? Does it contain streaks of blood, clots of blood, or mucus? Is it an unusual color? Is there undigested food in it? Is there foreign material in it, such as pieces of bone, wood, fabric, or plastic? How often is your dog having diarrhea? How much is there each time she goes? Is she having trouble holding it long enough to get outside? Does she sometimes strain to defecate but nothing comes out?

❑ What does the vomit look like? Does it contain food? Does it contain blood or something that looks like coffee grounds (digested blood)? Does it contain yellow, greenish, or orange liquid (bile)? Does it contain foreign material, such as pieces of bone, string, or plastic? How many times has she vomited? When does she vomit: right after eating or drinking, on an empty stomach, at night, during the daytime, or at random?

❑ Has your dog had this problem before?

❑ Are any other animals in the household sick?

❑ Are there any new animals in the household?

❑ Are any people in the household sick?

❑ When was the last time your dog's feces were examined for intestinal parasites?

❑ Is your dog on monthly heartworm prevention? What kind? (Many heartworm preventives also protect against certain intestinal parasites.)

❑ Has your dog had a recent change in diet, eaten table food, or gotten into the garbage?

❑ Was your dog recently in a different environment, such as on vacation, at the beach, hiking near a lake, in a boarding kennel, or staying with friends?

❑ Is your dog taking medicine for anything?

❑ How have you treated the vomiting or diarrhea at home? What has your dog eaten and drunk over the past 24 hours? Have you given her any medicine for the vomiting or diarrhea?

❑ Does your dog have any other symptoms, such as lameness, a cough, a rash, a fever, or listlessness?

on the prescribed dose while she's boarding.

❏ If you've had success with homeopathic or herbal stress remedies, do ask the boarding facility to give them while your dog is boarding. Just stay away from any remedy that makes your dog excessively groggy or that isn't labeled as safe for daily use.

IRRITABLE BOWEL DISEASE

"My six-year-old Bichon Frisé has diarrhea quite frequently, and my vet thinks he has irritable bowel disease (IBD). Do dogs really get this? How is it diagnosed and treated?"

IBD is seen in dogs. It can affect one area of the digestive tract or multiple areas. Depending on the location, it can cause intermittent diarrhea, vomiting, or both.

In IBD, inflammatory white blood cells multiply within the lining of the intestines, and the intestines become hypersensitive to proteins and other substances that normally wouldn't bother them. Why the white blood cells migrate into the intestinal tissues in the first place usually is impossible to determine.

IBD is diagnosed by first ruling out the more common causes of recurrent diarrhea, such as intestinal parasites, overgrowth of clostridium or campylobacter bacteria in the large intestine, or eating table food. The most precise test for confirming IBD is endoscopy plus biopsies of the affected areas of the digestive tract (see page 128). Large numbers of white blood cells are seen microscopically in biopsies of dogs with IBD. Vets can also get a general impression that a dog has IBD by feeling thickened intestinal walls on physical exam or seeing them on ultrasound exam.

Treatment for IBD starts by placing the dog on an easily digestible diet to avoid triggering flare-ups of diarrhea. Paradoxically, though, if the dog's colon is affected, adding fiber to the diet often helps calm the diarrhea. Fiber sources like bran, psyllium (Metamucil), and canned pumpkin are used by the "good" bacteria in the large intestine to produce short-chain fatty acids, which are natural anti-inflammatories for the colon.

Depending on the severity of the symptoms—such as diarrhea, vomiting, and weight loss—prescription medicines such as steroids, metronidazole (Flagyl), sulfasalazine, and tylosin (Tylan) are sometimes used as well. Most of them can cause serious side effects, so vets use the lowest dose that's effective and monitor dogs closely while they're taking the drugs.

BLOOD AND MUCUS IN THE FECES

"My dog has had diarrhea for a couple of days, and now there are streaks of blood and mucus in it. I'm really worried, but my vet doesn't seem overly concerned. Why not?"

Your dog probably has colitis, or an inflamed colon. Even mild bouts of diarrhea can trigger an inflamed colon in dogs, and small amounts of blood and mucus in the feces are often the result. That may seem scary, but it's seldom a sign of serious disease.

The treatment for this type of colitis is to treat the cause of the underlying diarrhea. In addition, metronidazole (Flagyl) is sometimes prescribed for its anti-inflammatory properties.

Colitis that lasts for more than five to seven days or recurs frequently may be a sign of IBD (see the previous Q&A).

ANOTHER BAD BLOODY-DIARRHEA DISEASE

"My dog had bloody diarrhea, so I took him and a fecal sample to the vet. She took one look at my dog and the fecal sample and admitted him to the hospital right away. She said he has hemorrhagic gastroenteritis. Will he be OK?"

Hemorrhagic gastroenteritis (HGE) is a scary disease, but fortunately, most dogs recover well if they're treated promptly.

What causes HGE is mysterious. It is not due to anything the dog ate, or to any poison. It appears to be set off by the immune system: for unknown reasons, a dog suddenly starts making antibodies against his own intestinal cells. The damaged cells lose their ability to prevent bacteria and toxins from crossing the intestinal wall into the bloodstream, and large amounts of fluid pass from the

WHAT ABOUT CONSTIPATION?

Dogs get diarrhea at the drop of a chicken bone, but do they get constipated? Only rarely.

True constipation means extremely hard stools that are painful to pass. It has nothing to do with how often a dog has a bowel movement. Constipation almost never strikes dogs that have adequate exercise and water and are given at least three opportunities per day to relieve themselves outside.

One thing that *can* cause big-time constipation in a dog, however, is chewing up and eating a large bone or bones. The minerals from the bone can form an almost concrete-like stool that can be very painful to pass. In such cases, an enema can be helpful—call your vet.

Other factors that can make a dog strain or feel pain when attempting a bowel movement are inflamed anal sacs (see page 100), an object

blocking the colon (see page 137), a tumor or mass blocking the colon, an enlarged or infected prostate (see page 346), or a hernia. If your dog seems to be in pain when he tries to defecate, call your vet.

If your dog vomits or has diarrhea for a couple of days and then doesn't defecate at all for a couple of days, that is not constipation. The most likely explanation is that he's emptied his digestive tract and won't need to defecate again until he has eaten normally for a couple of days.

If your dog has diarrhea and sometimes strains to defecate but nothing comes out, he may simply have intestinal cramps that make him feel like he needs to go, but he might also have an object blocking the colon. Call your vet immediately if you think your dog may have swallowed something that could be blocking the colon.

MEDICINES THAT CAN CAUSE VOMITING OR DIARRHEA

Many medicines, both prescription and over-the-counter, have the potential to cause stomach upset, vomiting, or diarrhea in dogs, even at appropriate doses. If your dog is taking any medicine and develops digestive-tract problems, call your vet right away and ask whether the medicine could be causing the problem and, if so, whether you should stop giving it, give it with a meal, switch to a different medicine, or bring your dog in for an exam.

Here are some drugs that can cause vomiting or diarrhea:

❏ **Pain relievers** such as aspirin, Rimadyl (carprofen), Metacam (meloxicam), Deramaxx (deracoxib), EtoGesic (etodolac), and Butazolidin (phenylbutazone).

❏ **Dog-toxic pain relievers** such as Advil or Motrin (ibuprofen) and Aleve (naproxen). *Never* give a dog any over-the-counter medicine containing these ingredients—not even a child's dose. They can damage a dog's kidneys and liver, sometimes fatally (see page 412).

❏ **Antibiotics** such as amoxicillin, Clavamox, cephalexin, Antirobe (clindamycin), Flagyl (metronidazole), and tetracycline.

❏ **Digoxin or digitoxin** (Cardoxin, Lanoxin) for heart disease.

❏ **Steroids** in high doses, like those used to treat severe spinal cord inflammation and paralysis. Low doses of steroids (like those sometimes used to control severe allergic diseases) don't usually cause stomach upsets.

❏ **Lysodren** (mitotane) for Cushing's disease.

❏ **Chemotherapy drugs** for cancer.

---

blood and lymph systems into the colon and out of the body as diarrhea. The fluid loss is so great that a dog can go into shock and die of dehydration if not treated quickly.

HGE is diagnosed from two factors. One is the history and clinical signs: sudden onset of vomiting and diarrhea not connected with anything the dog has eaten; weakness; and bloody, gelatinous, horrible-smelling diarrhea. (The classic HGE diarrhea is described as looking like raspberry jam.) The second diagnostic factor is the dog's dehydration from fluid loss. Vets determine this with a quick in-house blood test to measure the dog's packed cell volume (PCV) or hematocrit, which is the percentage of the blood that's made up of cells (mostly red blood cells) rather than fluid. A dog's normal PCV is 35 to 45 percent, but in HGE, a dog loses so much fluid that his PCV rises to 60 or even 80 percent, indicating a life-threatening degree of dehydration.

Treatment centers on rehydrating the dog as quickly as possible using IV

DIAGNOSING PERSISTENT OR RECURRING DIGESTIVE PROBLEMS

Many dogs have occasional bouts of vomiting or diarrhea, usually because of dietary indiscretion, intestinal parasites, stress, or digestive tract viruses. But if your dog vomits or has diarrhea frequently—say, twice a month or more—and you and your vet haven't been able to pinpoint a cause through physical exams, fecal exams, and eliminating obvious risk factors (such as eating table food or taking antibiotics or pain relievers on an empty stomach), then further testing may be needed to get to the root of the problem.

Here is a guide to some of the tests your vet may recommend, and what those tests look for. Which tests should be done, and in what order, depends on your dog's specific symptoms and physical exam findings.

Blood chemistry test to assess the liver, gall bladder, kidneys, electrolytes, and blood sugar. To help diagnose diseases of the liver (see page 143), gall bladder (see page 144), kidneys (see page 335), and adrenal glands (see page 304), and diabetes mellitus (see page 291).

Blood test for pancreatic enzymes. To diagnose pancreatic insufficiency (see the following Q&A) or pancreatitis (see page 142).

Plain x-rays of the chest. To help diagnose megaesophagus or a hiatal hernia (see page 132).

Plain x-rays of the abdomen. To look for bloat (see page 136); a foreign object or blockage of the stomach or intestines (see page 137); or abdominal tumors (see page 385).

Barium x-rays of the abdomen. To look for a motility disorder (see page 135) or a foreign object or blockage in the stomach or intestines (see page 137).

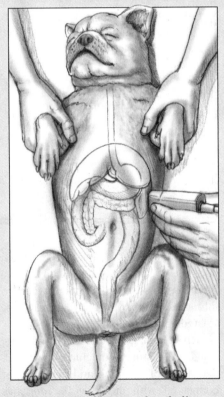

An ultrasound exam can explore the liver, intestines, and other abdominal organs.

Fluoroscopy (motion x-ray) of the esophagus. To diagnose regurgitation or swallowing problems, such as megaesophagus (see page 132) or a vascular ring anomaly (see page 133).

Ultrasound exam of the abdomen. To look for foreign material in the digestive tract; an inflamed pancreas; areas of potential infection or tumors in the abdominal organs (liver, kidneys, stomach, pancreas, spleen, intestines, and bladder); or fluid in the abdominal cavity.

Endoscopy and biopsy. To diagnose stomach ulcers (see page 139); stomach or intestinal cancer (see page 385); foreign objects; or irritable bowel disease (see page 125). An endoscope is a tiny video camera on a thin, flexible tube. The dog is anesthetized and the endoscope is passed from the mouth into the esophagus, stomach, and small intestine, or from the rectum into the colon. Biopsies can be taken of the inner surfaces of the digestive tract through the endoscope.

Novel food trial. To diagnose a food allergy (see pages 99 and 119).

Special fecal tests. To confirm parvovirus (see page 121), giardia (see page 154), or bacterial infection by clostridium, toxic forms of *E. coli*, salmonella, campylobacter, or yersinia.

Blood test for lead. To check for lead poisoning (see page 415).

fluids, plus giving antibiotics to prevent further damage from bacteria crossing the intestinal wall. Dogs with HGE usually remain in the hospital on IV fluids for several days, but most do recover with no lasting damage.

DIGESTIVE ENZYME DEFICIENCIES

"My German Shepherd puppy seemed fine until he hit 10 months old, but now he has soft, very stinky feces, and he's eating all the time but seems to be getting skinnier instead of filling out the way he should. My vet wants to test him for a pancreas problem. Why?"

The pancreas has two main functions: the first is producing insulin, which ushers glucose from the bloodstream into cells, and the second is producing enzymes that help digest food so that nutrients can be absorbed by the small intestine.

Some dogs have an inherited problem in which the pancreas cells responsible for producing these digestive enzymes die and are not replaced. This condition—called exocrine pancreatic insufficiency, or EPI—is seen more often in German Shepherds than in other breeds, so it makes sense, given your dog's symptoms, that your vet wants to test for it.

When too little of these pancreatic enzymes are produced, the food your puppy eats isn't digested fully, and he can't extract all the nutrients from it. He's hungry and eats well but loses weight because the nutrients are passing right through him, which often results in large, smelly stools.

EPI is diagnosed with a blood test that measures trypsin, one of the pancreatic enzymes, in the blood. In dogs with EPI, the trypsin level is much lower than normal because the pancreas is producing so little of it.

Dogs with EPI are given pancreatic enzyme supplements, vitamin supplements, highly digestible low-fat food, and sometimes antacids (to help prevent the enzyme supplements from being deactivated in the stomach). Most gain weight and do well, but the enzyme supplements are expensive, and EPI must be treated for life.

The tendency to develop this type of EPI is present from birth and usually appears when a dog is between six months and two years old. EPI can also develop in dogs of any age and breed if the pancreas is damaged by recurrent pancreatitis, cancer, or other diseases. In that type of EPI, the underlying cause is treated and the dog is also given enzyme and vitamin supplements and highly digestible food.

INTESTINAL CANCER

"My 14-year-old Poodle gets diarrhea sometimes. Could it be cancer?"

Dogs do get cancers of the digestive tract, but that shouldn't be your first worry in an older dog with diarrhea. Other causes—including dietary indiscretion, a reaction to medicine, or irritable bowel disease—are much more common. Schedule an appointment with your vet, and describe your dog's digestive-system problems in detail (see page 124). Tell your vet you're worried that the diarrhea may signal a serious problem, and the vet will tell you how that possibility can be ruled out.

For more about digestive-tract cancers, see page 385.

THE VOMITING HOUND

"My dog vomited three times today. Should I take her to the vet or wait it out?"

Like diarrhea, vomiting can be caused by serious problems (including pancreatitis, kidney disease, and liver disease) or not-so-serious problems (such as eating too fast or eating grass). Here are some questions to help you assess how urgent the problem is:

❏ Is your dog less than six months old? A puppy can quickly develop dangerously low blood sugar and dehydration, plus she is more likely to have intestinal parasites, parvo, a birth defect, or something blocking the stomach or intestines. Call your vet right away.
❏ Are there worms, plastic, cloth, or other nonfood material in the vomit? Call your vet right away.
❏ Did your dog recently chew up or swallow a dog toy, cloth, rocks, or some other inedible object? Call your vet right away.
❏ Is there blood or digested blood (this looks like coffee grounds) in the vomit? Call your vet right away.
❏ Could your dog have eaten something toxic? Call your vet right away.
❏ Is your dog very uncomfortable, retching and heaving as if she wants to vomit, and swollen in the sides or belly? Call your vet or an emergency vet clinic *immediately*—she may have bloat, a life-threatening emergency.
❏ Does she have other health problems such as heart disease, diabetes, or kidney disease? If your dog has other health issues or is taking any medicine other than monthly heartworm

HACK, GAG, REGURGITATE, VOMIT: WHICH IS IT?

A dog who is "bringing up stuff" from his mouth may be doing one of several different things that have different potential causes. Observe your dog closely, compare his actions to the following definitions, and then use the appropriate word or description when consulting this book or talking to your vet.

Vomiting often starts with drooling and retching or gulping. (Drooling is often a sign of nausea.) The key sign that a dog is vomiting rather than regurgitating is that his belly muscles heave noticeably when he brings up the solid or liquid material. Vomiting is an active process—the material doesn't just "blurp" out of his mouth with no effort. Vomiting can originate with the digestive tract, from the stomach down; with a disease that affects the whole body, such as diabetes or kidney failure; or rarely, with the "vomiting center" in the brain.

Dog owners often confuse **regurgitating** with vomiting. In regurgitation, solids or liquids simply blurp out of the dog's mouth with little or no effort. The dog may gag or cough as the material comes up, but you won't see his belly heave. Regurgitation is caused by a problem with the throat, the esophagus, or the valve between the esophagus and the stomach.

A dog that is **hacking** or **gagging** may be coughing rather than vomiting or regurgitating. He may hack up fluid, mucus, or foamy material. His belly muscles will not heave, but his chest—the area covered by his ribs—may move noticeably. Coughing is caused by a problem with the esophagus; the respiratory system, from the nasal sinuses through the lungs; or the heart, because a heart that isn't pumping effectively may allow fluid to seep from blood vessels into the lungs, triggering a cough.

Dropping food or water from the mouth or making repeated efforts to swallow is caused by a problem with the teeth; the nerves that control the muscles for picking up food, chewing, or swallowing; or the brain, which coordinates the nerves for chewing and swallowing.

prevention, it's best to call the vet about vomiting.

❏ Has your dog had pancreatitis in the past? This can be a recurring problem, so call your vet right away.

❏ Is she weak or lethargic, or does she just seem very sick? Call your vet right away.

❏ Has she been vomiting repeatedly for more than four hours even though she hasn't had any food, water, or medication during that time? Call your vet.

If your dog does not display any of the red flags described above, try the home treatment outlined on page 134.

REGURGITATING PUPPIES

"I thought my three-month-old Great Dane puppy was throwing up every time she ate, but my vet says it's not her stomach. He wants to test her for megaesophagus. What's that?"

The esophagus is the tube that carries food from the mouth to the stomach. Megaesophagus literally means "large esophagus." It is large (in diameter) because it's got poor muscle tone—the nerves or muscles that control the contractions that move food to the stomach don't work properly. When a dog with megaesophagus eats, the food doesn't pass quickly down to the stomach, and it may "blurp" back up after being swallowed. Technically, this is called regurgitation, not vomiting, and points to a problem in the throat or esophagus, not the stomach (see page 131).

Megaesophagus can be a birth defect or it can develop later in life. The birth defect is more common in certain breeds, including Great Danes, than in others. In adult dogs, it can develop from diseases affecting the nerves or muscles, such as myasthenia gravis (see page 323).

Fluoroscopy (motion x-rays) of the dog swallowing food mixed with barium (the barium makes the swallowing process visible on x-rays) is often used to diagnose megaesophagus. Fluoroscopy can also reveal other causes of regurgitation, such as an object stuck in the esophagus; blood vessels compressing the esophagus (see the following Q&A); stenosis, or narrowing, of the esophagus; or a hiatal hernia, in which a tear or abnormally large opening in the diaphragm lets part of the stomach slip up into the chest.

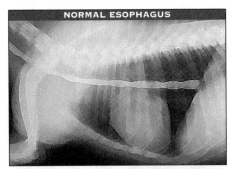

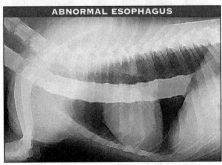

Barium outlines a normal esophagus (top) and an abnormal one (bottom) on x-rays.

Treatment centers on changing the way the puppy is fed, to help get as much of the food into her stomach as possible. This includes raising the food and water dishes on a step stool so that the puppy keeps her head up while eating and gravity can help the food move down; feeding smaller amounts of high-calorie food several times a day rather than larger amounts of lower-calorie food once or twice a day; and feeding whatever type of food the particular puppy can most easily swallow, which can range from a liquid gruel to soft food to dry kibble.

A common and potentially life-threatening complication of megaesophagus is pneumonia. Because the dog doesn't move food from her mouth to her stomach efficiently, food can easily be inhaled into the windpipe and lungs, where it can cause severe pneumonia. Dogs with megaesophagus are watched closely for respiratory trouble and given chest x-rays and antibiotics as needed.

No medication has been shown to reliably improve esophageal contractions in dogs with the birth defect. Surgery on the esophagus is sometimes done, but it's difficult and often ineffective. Unfortunately, the overall prognosis for a puppy with inherited megaesophagus is generally poor.

Megaesophagus that develops in adult dogs secondary to a disease of the nerves or muscles can sometimes be managed more successfully, by treating the underlying disease as well as using the feeding regimen described above. These dogs are also at risk of developing pneumonia, however, and require careful monitoring.

A RING AROUND THE ESOPHAGUS

"My eight-week-old German Shepherd puppy was spitting up his food every time he ate. The vet took barium x-rays and discovered a birth defect—an abnormal blood vessel wrapped around the esophagus so tightly that it can't expand to let food pass through. Is surgery the only answer?"

This birth defect is called a vascular ring anomaly. A fetus's circulatory and digestive systems start out as side-by-side tubes with branches coming off them. The circulatory tube develops into the heart, arteries, and veins, and the digestive tube develops into the esophagus, stomach, and intestines. Occasionally the blood vessels develop abnormally so that the esophagus becomes encircled in a "vascular ring" that will not allow food to pass normally. This birth defect

is seen more often in German Shepherds and Irish Setters than in other breeds.

Symptoms of a vascular ring anomaly appear when a puppy starts to eat solid food, at four to six weeks old. The abnormal blood vessel constricts the esophagus at the level of the heart, making it difficult for food to squeeze past, so the puppy brings the food back up after it's been swallowed. Although spitting up is normal in human infants, it isn't in puppies, and a puppy that routinely regurgitates after eating should be evaluated by a vet for the possibility of a vascular ring anomaly or megaesophagus (see the previous Q&A).

The best treatment for a vascular ring anomaly is surgery to free the esophagus from its entrapment. (The abnormal blood vessel is unnecessary and can be tied off without depriving anything of its blood supply.) The prognosis is best when surgery is done while the puppy is still very young. The longer the esophagus remains entrapped, the more likely it is to remain abnormally stretched in front of where it was constricted, and the more likely the puppy is to inhale regurgitated food or water into the lungs and develop pneumonia.

For a few weeks after surgery, the puppy will need to eat a "mush" of puppy food mixed with water (to make it easier to swallow), from dishes raised to the height of his head (so gravity will help push the food into the stomach). Often the puppy can switch to regular food after a month or two, but it's best to continue feeding from raised dishes for life.

The prognosis for puppies who don't have surgery to correct a vascular ring anomaly is poor. They usually don't grow well because of their difficulty getting food into the stomach, and they are at high risk for developing pneumonia from inhaling food into their lungs.

HOME CARE FOR VOMITING

If your dog has vomited once or twice today, is older than six months, and does not show any of the warning signs of a serious illness (see page 130), it's generally safe to try home treatment for one to two days, using the following plan.

First, and most important, give your dog absolutely nothing to eat *or drink*—no rice, no water, no ice cubes, no heartworm pill, no chicken broth, *nothing*—for 12 to 24 hours after she has vomited. For the vomiting to stop, the digestive tract needs to rest completely. If your dog is older than six months and is healthy otherwise, she will not become severely dehydrated from a 12- to 24-hour fast. If she continues to vomit repeatedly or hasn't stopped vomiting by four hours into the fast, call your vet.

Then, 12 to 24 hours after the last episode of vomiting, give your dog a small amount of water: about 2 table-spoons for a dog that weighs less than 20 pounds, about ¼ cup for a dog that weighs 20 to 50 pounds, and about ½ cup for a dog that weighs more than 50 pounds.

Wait 30 minutes, and if she hasn't vomited, give her twice that amount of water.

Wait one hour, and if she hasn't vomited, offer her a small amount— about 2 tablespoons for a small dog, ¼ cup for a medium dog, and ½ cup for a large dog—of the following bland diet: 3 parts cooked rice mixed with 1 part boiled chicken (no skin, no fat, no bones, no spices), lightly salted.

If she does not vomit after that, continue to offer her that small amount of the bland diet along with a small amount of water every three hours or so.

If at any point she begins to vomit again, call your vet. Otherwise, the following day you can double the amount of the bland diet fed each meal and decrease the number of meals to three, plus give her unlimited water.

After three days on the bland diet, start mixing increasing amounts of her regular food into the rice-and-chicken mixture over another three or four days until she's eating just her regular food.

There are no over-the-counter medicines for vomiting in dogs. A prescription drug such as Cerenia (page 85), Reglan (metoclopramide), or chlorpromazine can be used to stop vomiting, but they can be dangerous if a dog has something blocking the stomach or intestines or other health problems, so your vet will need to examine your dog before administering it.

VOMITING ON AN EMPTY STOMACH

"Our dog vomits almost every day, usually in the morning before she has breakfast. She brings up frothy stuff and yellow liquid. Otherwise, she seems just fine. What could be going on?"

The yellow (or sometimes orange) liquid is probably bile, from the gall bladder, and indicates that there's no food in the stomach to come up. Some otherwise healthy dogs who vomit on an empty stomach seem to have a form of acid indigestion or acid reflux. They are fine when they've eaten recently, but become nauseated and vomit when they haven't, usually early in the morning.

Talk to your vet to make sure you're not overlooking any other symptoms. If your dog is suffering from what's sometimes called "bilious vomiting" and nothing else, then a few treatments may help. The first is to divide your dog's food into three or four meals per day, feeding the first meal as soon as your dog gets up and the last meal about two hours before she goes to bed. Second, an antacid can also be given at bedtime—ask your vet for an appropriate product and dose. Finally, the prescription drug metoclopramide (Reglan) is sometimes given before a meal as a "motility modifier" to help keep the stomach's and small intestine's contractions pushing food in the right direction—down, not up. Because the feeding changes and antacid alone may work just fine, try those first before moving up to the stronger stuff.

SPEED EATERS ANONYMOUS

"I feed my two dogs together, and the smaller one seems to gobble her food without chewing it and then throws it back up a few minutes later. Why does she do this?"

She may be worried that if she doesn't wolf down her food, your other dog will get some of it. This is a rational fear, but her coping strategy isn't ideal.

How about feeding your dogs in separate rooms so the little one feels less pressured by the presence of the bigger dog? If she still eats so fast that she vomits even when she eats in private, then spread out her food over a large surface (such as a cookie sheet) or in several small bowls in different parts of the room so she can't hoover up her entire meal in one breath. And if you now feed your dogs only once a day, divide the food into two or three smaller meals per day instead. Knowing that her next meal is just around the corner may help your gobbler to relax and enjoy her food less anxiously.

If these measures don't work and the vomiting continues, make an appointment with your vet to check into the possibility that she's regurgitating (see page 131) rather than vomiting.

VOMITING HOURS AFTER A MEAL

"My four-year-old English Bulldog often throws up his food a few hours after he's eaten. He also seems to belch a lot. Does he need Alka-Seltzer or something like that?"

When a dog regularly vomits up food hours after he's eaten, it's a sign that his stomach isn't emptying into the small intestine as quickly and efficiently as it should. He should be checked by your vet to determine why not. The dog could have an object trapped in his stomach, polyps (growths) in the lower part of the stomach, abnormal thickening of the pylorus (the outflow tract from the stomach to the small intestine), or rarely, weak or ineffective contractions of the stomach. Dogs with pushed-in faces, like your Bulldog, are more likely than other

WHY DO DOGS EAT GRASS?

Because they like to. Some dogs consider grass a salad bar and like to snack on it from time to time. Other dogs seem to have a taste for grass only when they're nauseated.

If your dog vomits every time he eats grass, *don't let him eat it.* He does not "need" to eat grass to help him vomit. If he's going to vomit, he'll manage just fine on his own, without the grass's help.

Also, if you know or even suspect that grass has been treated recently with pesticides or fertilizers, don't let your dog graze. If you use pesticides or fertilizers on your own lawn, read package labels carefully to find out how dangerous they are. Follow directions precisely, noting how long to keep children and pets off the lawn, and whether a thorough watering will help lessen the danger. Finally, tips on growing more grass and fewer weeds without using any pesticides or fertilizers are widely available in books and on the Internet.

breeds to be born with a thickened pylorus, but any kind of dog could develop that thickening over time.

Problems with how the stomach empties itself are diagnosed by feeding the dog a meal mixed with barium (the barium allows the stomach contents to be seen on x-rays), then x-raying the dog's abdomen periodically over several hours to see how long it takes the stomach to empty its contents into the small intestine. Food remaining in the stomach for longer than about eight hours is considered abnormal. The barium x-rays may also reveal a stomach that's abnormally large for the amount of food the dog has eaten, a growth or foreign object in the stomach, or a pylorus that's obviously constricted or narrow.

Ultrasound or endoscopy can also be used to look for polyps, foreign objects, and an unusually thick-walled or narrow pylorus. If the pylorus is abnormal, the treatment is surgery to widen it. If no structural cause is found, and it's believed that the dog has a motility disorder (weak stomach contractions), then medicine to promote more effective contractions may be tried, along with multiple small meals of a low-fat/low-fiber diet.

PREVENTING BLOAT

"A Bernese Mountain Dog I used to see in the park just died of bloat. What is bloat? How would I know if my dog had it?"

Bloat is the common name for gastric dilatation and volvulus (GDV). It's a serious, often fatal medical emergency that happens more frequently to large, deep-chested dogs than to smaller dogs.

In GDV, the stomach rapidly distends with gas (that's the dilatation) and then twists into an abnormal position (that's the volvulus). The twisting pinches shut the openings to the esophagus and small intestine, trapping food and gas inside the stomach. Meanwhile, blood flow is hampered by the twisting of blood vessels and by pressure from the ballooning stomach, and the dog goes into shock.

If GDV is not treated immediately, the dog will die from shock or a ruptured stomach.

How would you know that your dog was bloating? The earliest signs are often restlessness and anxiety. Hit with a massive bellyache, a dog with GDV will pant and pace, unable to get comfortable in any position. Early on a dog may vomit, but as the esophagus twists shut she'll more likely drool and retch without bringing anything up. Her sides, just behind the ribs, might bulge or look swollen. In later stages, she will go into shock and be unable to walk or stand.

What should you do if you think your dog is bloating? Call your vet or a veterinary emergency hospital immediately. Be prepared to take your dog to the clinic as soon as you hang up the phone, because every minute counts.

To help combat shock in a dog that's bloating, a vet will immediately start administering IV fluids and medications. To release gas from the stomach, he will try to pass a tube from the dog's mouth down the esophagus and into the stomach. Sometimes this works, sometimes it doesn't. If the tube won't go into the stomach, the vet may poke a sterile, hollow needle through the dog's side and into the stomach to tap off some gas and relieve the pressure.

Once the dog can safely be put under anesthesia, she's prepped for emergency abdominal surgery. During surgery, the vet examines the stomach to see if any part of it has ruptured or is damaged from interrupted blood flow. Damaged areas of the stomach are cut out and the edges sutured together. Often the dog's stomach is tacked to the abdominal wall in a couple of places (this is called gastropexy) to help keep it from twisting out of position again.

Even after all that, the dog is still not out of danger. GDV can trigger a bout of cardiac arrhythmia, so dogs who have bloated are monitored in the hospital for a few days after surgery.

Some dogs are more likely to bloat than others. Dogs with deep and narrow chests (for example, Great Danes and Irish Wolfhounds) have the highest risk. Bloat also is related to eating habits: dogs that eat one large meal a day (rather than two or more smaller meals) and dogs that wolf down their food are more likely to get GDV. So don't put out a big bowl of food for a hyperactive, food-inhaling shepherd as you head out the door for a 10-hour workday; feed her at least an hour before you leave so she'll be calmer and you can check on her after she eats. And don't let your dog engage in strenuous activity (running, playing fetch, swimming, and so on) right after a meal.

EATING THE INEDIBLE

"We use old socks to play tug-of-war with our Lab puppy, and a friend of ours says that's dangerous. Is it?"

Yes, chewing on socks can be dangerous. If your puppy chewed up and swallowed part of a sock, it could become stuck in his esophagus, stomach, or intestines, causing major medical problems and potentially requiring abdominal surgery.

Many dog owners feel that dogs—or their dog in particular—can "eat anything" without ill effects, but unfortunately, that's not true. The medical term for an inedible object trapped in a dog's digestive tract is a "foreign-body obstruction," and removing such objects is one of the more common surgeries veterinarians perform. Most vets keep a mental

"I Can't Believe He Ate the Whole Thing" list of objects they've removed from dogs' digestive tracts. Here are some of the more common ones:

- ❏ Pantyhose, underwear, socks
- ❏ Pieces of rugs, towels, bedding
- ❏ Dog toys
- ❏ Children's toys
- ❏ Diapers, disposable or cloth
- ❏ Corncobs
- ❏ Apples, mango pits, avocado pits
- ❏ Rocks
- ❏ Wooden grilling skewers, teriyaki sticks
- ❏ Bones
- ❏ Sticks, wood
- ❏ Plastic food packaging

And that's just a small sample. The strangest foreign-body case I've seen so far involved a six-month-old Lab who had surgery to remove a 2-inch-diameter rock from his small intestine and then, ten days later, ate a C battery that also got stuck in his small intestine. He had to have a second surgery, in which about a foot of small intestine was removed along with the battery. He did, fortunately,

Socks are dangerous toys, since pieces of cloth can get stuck in a dog's digestive tract.

recover from this double whammy of dietary indiscretion.

Symptoms of a foreign-body obstruction depend on where the object is lodged and whether the obstruction is total or partial. Dogs with an object stuck in their esophagus often will gulp or cough, and they may not want to eat or drink. If a dog has a foreign body in his stomach, he will usually vomit, but the vomiting may not be continuous and the dog may still be able to eat and drink. An obstruction of the small intestine is often very painful, and the dog may vomit and refuse food and water.

Vets diagnose foreign bodies from the owner's knowledge of missing or frequently chewed objects; feeling an unusual mass in the esophagus or intestines (objects in the stomach usually can't be felt); and x-rays, barium x-rays, or ultrasound. Using an endoscope (a tiny video camera on a long, flexible tube), vets can sometimes retrieve objects from the esophagus or gently push them into the stomach, where they can either pass on their own or be surgically removed more safely than from the esophagus. Foreign-body obstructions in the stomach and small intestine must be surgically removed. The prognosis in all cases depends on how long the object has been stuck, how severely damaged the area where it was lodged is, and whether infection or other complicating factors are present.

Cloth, rope, and stringlike objects are particularly dangerous because they can partially pass through the intestines and then saw through them when one end becomes stuck and the intestines keep contracting against it. Cloth and stringy things also can be more difficult to detect than denser objects because they are harder to feel and liquid digestive-tract contents may continue to pass around and through them.

To avoid these problems, use careful prevention. Throw away any dog toys your dog can chew apart, or any that are small enough for him to swallow. Keep your garbage and dirty laundry under lock and key if your dog has a taste for them. Make sure your dog can't swipe corncobs or teriyaki sticks at backyard cookouts. Be especially cautious with puppies, who are notorious for eating things they shouldn't. And if you suspect your dog may have eaten something inedible, call your vet immediately.

GARBAGE-CAN POISONING

"My dog ate some moldy cottage cheese I'd thrown in the garbage. I thought it was no big deal at first, but then she started shaking all over, collapsed, and wound up in the hospital for a while. What happened?"

Most dogs that get into the garbage will vomit or have diarrhea for a couple of days and get better, but occasionally a dog will eat some spoiled food that essentially poisons them. Mold toxins or bacterial toxins in the food can cause tremors, seizures, and shock (dangerously low blood pressure and poor blood circulation), as well as vomiting and diarrhea. If they are not treated quickly, some of these dogs will die.

To treat "garbage-can poisoning," vets give a dog antiseizure medication, IV fluids, and antibiotics. The dog remains in the hospital until the tremors or seizures and shock are gone.

Awareness of the potential for garbage-can poisoning is key to preventing it from happening to your dog. Never give her any food that may be even a

---

THE PERILS OF THE DOGGIE BAG

The No. 1 cause of vomiting and diarrhea in otherwise healthy dogs is "dietary indiscretion"—the fancy medical term for "something he ate." If you want to make your dog vomit or have diarrhea, the easiest way to do so is to feed him table scraps or other people food. High-fat foods (such as fried food, gravy, chips, and sweets) are the worst offenders. Yes, your dog would love the fat off that steak and a little ice cream for dessert, but neither of you will love the morning after.

---

little spoiled. If it's not fresh enough for you to eat, it's not fresh enough for her to eat either. Do whatever it takes to prevent your dog from getting into garbage cans. And if she ever has an upset stomach and also just seems very sick—having trouble standing up, looking weak, shaking, or acting strange—call your vet or a veterinary emergency clinic immediately.

STOMACH ULCERS

"When my 12-year-old dog vomited the other day, there was bright red blood in it. The vet wants to run some blood tests and look at my dog's stomach using an endoscope. Isn't this most likely an ulcer? Can't I just give my dog antacids and skip the tests?"

Dogs don't get ulcers of the stomach or small intestine as easily as people

(continued on page 142)

MAKING SENSE OF LIVER TESTS

The first hint many dog owners *and* vets get that something may be amiss with a dog's liver is elevated liver enzymes on a blood test. This raises a warning—but of what? Unfortunately, not of any *specific* liver disease. Other tests are required to get an exact diagnosis and determine what treatment is needed. Here are some of those tests and what they can tell your vet.

Physical exam. By feeling your dog's abdomen, your vet can get an impression that the liver is smaller than normal, larger than normal, or sore. An unusually small liver in a young dog can be a sign of a birth defect called a portosystemic shunt (see page 263). A small liver in an older dog may mean that liver cells are dying and not being replaced. A large and sore liver may be inflamed by a virus, bacterium, toxin, parasite, or fungus. A large but pain-free liver may be a sign of Cushing's disease, diabetes, or phenobarbital use.

Some dogs with liver disease will show a yellow tinge to the whites of their eyes, their skin, or their gums. This is jaundice, a sign that the liver is unable to get rid of bilirubin (see below).

Blood tests for liver and gall bladder enzymes, glucose, albumin, bilirubin, and white blood cells. Liver enzymes are supposed to do their work *inside* liver cells. If those enzymes appear in the blood in higher than normal levels, it means that liver cells are breaking open and releasing their contents into the circulation. ALT, AST, and Alk Phos are the abbrevia-

tions for three liver enzymes measured on most routine blood-chemistry tests. Of the three, ALT is the most specific for liver damage, because the other two are found inside other types of cells as well.

GGT is the abbreviation for an enzyme found in bile, which is produced by the liver and stored in the gall bladder. An elevated GGT level may indicate an inflamed gall bladder or obstructed bile duct.

Glucose (blood sugar) is high in dogs with diabetes or Cushing's disease, which also can cause an enlarged liver and increased liver enzymes.

Albumin is a protein made by the liver that helps keep fluid from leaking out of blood vessels. If albumin levels are low, then either the liver is not working properly or albumin is being lost through the kidneys or small intestine.

Bilirubin is a pigment found in red blood cells. When red blood cells die (which they normally do when they're three to four months old), the liver breaks down the bilirubin. Higher than normal levels of bilirubin in the blood or urine mean that either the liver isn't working properly or large numbers of red blood cells are dying at once.

White blood cell counts can rise or fall with certain bacterial, viral, fungal, or parasitic diseases. Their numbers usually go up in Cushing's disease and diabetes.

Blood test for leptospirosis. Leptospirosis is a bacterial disease that can cause liver damage, kidney damage, or both (see page 63). The test looks for high levels of lepto antibodies in the blood.

Abdominal x-rays. X-rays show the relative size of the liver. An irregular shape can sometimes be seen on x-rays, but an ultrasound exam (see below) is more accurate for finding tumors, cysts, and irregularities within and on the surface of the liver.

Bile acid test. This reveals how well the liver is functioning. Bile acids are made by the liver, stored in the gall bladder, and released into the small intestine to aid in digestion. Once they've done their work in the small intestine, they are picked up by the liver from the blood stream and recycled.

In bile acid testing, a dog is given no food for 12 hours, and a blood sample is drawn to check for resting levels of bile acids. Then the dog is fed a meal, and a second blood sample is drawn 2 hours later to measure the rise in bile acids.

If the liver is working normally, bile acid levels in the first blood sample will be low, because the liver will already have recycled the bile acids from the previous meal. Bile acid levels in the second blood test should go up, but not too far up. If they are abnormally high, then blood isn't reaching the liver properly, or the liver is too sick to efficiently recycle its products.

Blood clotting tests. The liver makes proteins that enable blood to clot when a blood vessel is damaged. Tests measure how long it takes a blood sample to clot in a test tube or when a dog's skin is pricked with a needle. Inherited abnor-malities in clotting factors (see pages 358 to 361), severe liver damage, or eating mouse or rat poison (see page 412) can prolong clotting times.

Abdominal ultrasound exam. In the hands of an experienced person, an ultrasound exam can provide immense amounts of information. With ultrasound, you can scan the interior of the liver bit by bit, looking for tumors, fluid-filled cysts, inflammation, scarring, or a blocked gall bladder. The exam is painless. The dog's abdomen is shaved before the exam so that good contact can be made between the dog's skin, the ultrasound gel, and the ultrasound probe.

Liver biopsy. A biopsy is a small sample of tissue that's examined microscopically for signs of infection, cancer, dying cells, and scar tissue. It is the most definitive way to diagnose many liver diseases, including hepatitis and cancer.

Liver biopsies sometimes can be taken during an ultrasound exam. The dog is given a short-acting anesthetic just before the biopsy is taken. The skin is cleaned as if for surgery, and a sterile, needlelike punch pokes through the skin and plucks tiny samples of the liver.

The other way to biopsy the liver is during abdominal surgery. This, of course, requires the dog to be fully anesthetized throughout. If blood tests, x-rays, and ultrasound exams show that a disease is affecting more than just the liver—the spleen, kidneys, or stomach as well, for instance—then abdominal surgery is the best way to look directly at all the trouble spots and get biopsies of each.

(continued from page 139)

do, so your vet is smart to look for a predisposing factor rather than just treating the symptoms.

The stomach is normally well-protected against the digestive enzymes and acids it contains. Liver disease, kidney disease, anti-inflammatory pain relievers (such as aspirin), irritable bowel disease, and tumors of the stomach or pancreas are some of the things that can erode the stomach's defenses and lead to ulcers.

Blood tests can screen for liver or kidney problems, anemia caused by blood loss into the digestive tract, and pancreatitis. An endoscope allows the vet to see directly any damage to the stomach, locate any ulcers, and look for stomach tumors or other irregularities. During endoscopy, small "pinch" biopsies of the stomach are taken to be examined microscopically for evidence of malignant cells, irritable bowel disease, or helicobacter bacteria. (In people, helicobacter alone can cause stomach ulcers, but in dogs, some other contributing factor is usually present as well.)

The underlying cause of the ulcer is treated, and acid reducers and stomach-lining protectants are given for the ulcer itself. A dog with severe symptoms, such as persistent vomiting and weakness, will be hospitalized on IV fluids, fasted, and given acid reducers and stomach protectants until he is better.

AN INFLAMED PANCREAS

"After we went out to dinner, we gave our Miniature Schnauzer some leftover veal parmigiana, which he loved. That night, he woke us up with his vomiting, and when we took him to the vet, she said he'd have to stay in the hospital on IV fluids for a few days! What's going on?"

What's going on may be pancreatitis (an inflamed pancreas), which is painful and persistent and often does, indeed, require care in the hospital.

The pancreas is a humble but extremely important organ. Nestled next to the stomach and duodenum (the first part of the small intestine), it produces both insulin and digestive enzymes. Insulin allows the cells of the body to use glucose for energy. If the pancreas produces too little insulin, an animal has diabetes. Different cells in the pancreas produce digestive enzymes, which help break down food and allow the nutrients to be absorbed through the small intestine. In pancreatitis, those digestive enzymes spill over in the pancreas and surrounding tissues, causing pain and damage everywhere they go.

Pancreatitis occurs most commonly when overweight dogs are fed a high-fat meal or treat. The high-fat snack triggers the pancreas to produce and release lots of digestive enzymes, but the process goes haywire and the enzymes begin to digest the cells of the pancreas itself. This autodigestion spreads and worsens as long as the pancreas is signaled to release enzymes, which happens every time the dog eats or drinks.

A dog with a severe bellyache will sometimes adopt a "praying" position.

Pancreatitis can also be triggered by poor blood circulation to the pancreas or blocked pancreatic channels, but those scenarios are less common. In general, pancreatitis is rarely seen in thin, frequently exercised dogs who are fed a balanced, low-fat diet.

Dogs with pancreatitis often have severe abdominal pain, a loss of appetite, vomiting, and a fever of 103°F or higher. Occasionally a dog will even adopt a "praying" position (head down, front legs folded, and hind legs straight) to try to relieve the abdominal pain and pressure.

Pancreatitis is diagnosed by testing for higher than normal levels of digestive enzymes in the blood. Abdominal x-rays and ultrasound exams sometimes give clues that the pancreas is inflamed, but other times it may appear normal.

The key to treating pancreatitis is to rest the digestive tract completely—by hospitalizing the dog on IV fluids and giving no food, water, or medicine by mouth. The dog is monitored closely because the widespread release of digestive enzymes and other pancreatic products occasionally causes severe complications in the heart, lungs, or kidneys.

One to three days after the dog has last vomited, he will be offered small amounts of water and monitored for vomiting and pain. If the water doesn't cause any problems, next he will be offered a tiny amount of a low-fat, low-protein food. He must stay in the hospital until it's certain that he can eat and drink without suffering a relapse. The most common cause of an immediate relapse is drinking or eating too soon. Most dogs with pancreatitis will be hospitalized for several days to a week.

Unfortunately, pancreatitis also can recur weeks or months after the first episode if the predisposing factors are not eliminated. Take this illness as a wake-up call that your dog needs to slim down, eat a low-fat diet, stay away from table food and fatty snacks, and get more exercise in order to remain healthy.

LIVER DISEASES

"My eight-year-old Boxer hasn't had much of an appetite lately, and a couple of days ago, she started vomiting and having diarrhea. When I took her to the vet, he said my dog's belly seemed sore and the whites of her eyes looked a little yellow. He wants to do blood tests and an ultrasound exam to check my dog's liver. What does the liver have to do with the vomiting and diarrhea?"

The liver has a lot to do with just about every function of the body. It produces the substances that allow blood to clot when it needs to; breaks down certain medicines, toxins, and waste products; and packages, stores, and releases energy for the rest of the body. If the liver isn't working properly, toxins and waste products build up in the bloodstream, and virtually every organ in the body—including the stomach, intestines, kidneys, and brain—can be affected.

Toxins and waste products building up in the bloodstream can cause yellowing of the eyes and skin (jaundice), nausea, vomiting, and diarrhea. So those symptoms together give your vet ample reason to look for a liver problem.

Diseases affecting the liver are as numerous as the tasks the liver performs. Hepatitis (an inflamed liver) can be caused by viruses, bacteria, toxins (including ibuprofen), liver parasites, and fungal diseases. Excessive steroids or fats in the bloodstream, as seen in Cushing's disease and diabetes, can impair the liver. Liver damage can also be caused by inherited defects, such as a portosystemic shunt (see page 263) or copper storage disease, an inability to rid the body of excess copper seen most often in Bedlington Terriers. Then there are liver injuries—in dogs that have been hit by a car, for example—and liver cancers.

So your vet has a long list of possibilities to rule in or out. No single test can pinpoint the cause of a specific liver problem, but your vet will start with the most likely causes—given your dog's history, age, symptoms, and physical exam findings—and proceed from there. Meanwhile, he will treat your dog's symptoms and lighten the liver's load with IV fluids, special foods, and medicines.

Some liver damage is reversible, and some is not. Some liver diseases are readily treatable, especially in otherwise healthy dogs, and others are not. The liver's range of tasks, vulnerabilities, and responses to diseases and injuries is vast. Talk closely with your vet and ask lots of questions to make sure you understand what he sees and suspects in your dog's specific case. Once there's a diagnosis, ask more questions to understand the potential treatment and your dog's short- and long-term prognosis. You and your vet need to find out more before deciding what treatment to pursue.

GALL BLADDER DISEASE

"When my 8-year-old Sheltie had an upset stomach and didn't want to eat for a couple of days, I took him to the vet. The vet ran some blood tests, which she said showed that my dog's liver and gall bladder were inflamed. He is having an ultrasound exam of his belly today, and he might need to have his gall bladder removed. What kind of problems affect the gall bladder, and how serious are they?"

Problems affecting the gall bladder range from inflammation to blockages to rupture. The ultrasound exam your dog is having will show which issue your dog is facing and whether he needs surgery or medication.

The gall bladder is nestled between two lobes of the liver. It stores bile, produced by the liver, until the animal eats, then releases it through a duct into the duodenum (the section of the small intestine that connects to the stomach), where it helps digest food.

Any of the factors that cause hepatitis, or liver inflammation, can cause gall bladder inflammation as well (see the previous question). Gall bladder inflammation is often treated with antibiotics and ursodiol (Actigall), a synthetic bile acid that improves bile flow out of the gall bladder and helps relieve gall bladder inflammation.

Occasionally dogs form gallstones—hard accumulations of minerals within the gall bladder. If they are small and not obstructing the bile duct, they can be left alone, or treated with antibiotics and ursodiol. The treatment for larger stones or those causing obstruction is to remove the gall bladder.

Shelties have a high incidence of another type of obstruction: a mucocele, or gelatinous accumulation of mucus and other semisolid material within the gall bladder. These accumulations commonly enlarge until the gall bladder ruptures, spilling its contents into the abdomen, which results in peritonitis (widespread abdominal infection) and is often fatal.

Because a gall bladder rupture can be deadly, most vets recommend removing the gall bladder as soon as possible if a mucocele is detected on ultrasound.

The duct from the gall bladder into the duodenum can also be blocked from the outside by a tumor, inflammation, or infection of the liver, small intestine, or pancreas.

Along with Shelties, Cocker Spaniels, Miniature Schnauzers, and Poodles have a higher than average incidence of gall bladder disease. Symptoms include loss of appetite, vomiting, diarrhea, abdominal pain, or fever. Factors that can predispose a dog to gall bladder problems include pancreatitis (see page 142) or high levels of lipids (fats) in the blood, which in dogs occurs mainly with hypothyroidism, Cushing's disease, or diabetes mellitus. The best strategy for early detection of gall bladder disease in high-risk dogs is to do yearly blood tests to screen for the predisposing diseases listed above, followed by ultrasound exams if the test results indicate a potential problem.

OTHER CAUSES OF VOMITING

"My 13-year-old Shih Tzu recently started vomiting a couple of times a week. My vet wants to do some blood tests to look for other problems. Is she just fishing around for something else to treat?"

No, she's not. Many vets recommend that older dogs have a blood chemistry test and complete blood count *every year* to check for abnormalities and diseases that are common as dogs age. In this case, your Shih Tzu has a symptom—vomiting—that raises the suspicion of kidney problems or diabetes, both of which are diagnosed with blood and urine tests. Another possibility, though far less common, is that your dog has developed Addison's disease, an adrenal-gland problem.

Some dogs will vomit when they have vestibular disease—an inner-ear problem—but your vet evidently didn't see any signs of that on physical exam. Head injuries also can cause vomiting, but your dog's history and clinical findings didn't lead your vet in that direction either.

Whenever you don't understand why your vet wants to do a certain test, *ask*. She may not realize that she hasn't explained what she's looking for, or she may mistakenly believe that you're not interested in "the details." But it's to everyone's benefit for you to understand as much as possible about what's going on with your dog, and most vets are happy to explain what they're looking for and how they plan to find it.

CHAPTER 6

Worms, Fleas, Ticks, and Other Creepy-Crawlers

THERE'S NOTHING LIKE A FREE RIDE, which may explain why it's a rare dog who makes it through life without at least one run-in with a parasite. A parasite is any organism that finds food or shelter on or in a dog, usually to the dog's detriment. Fleas are a classic example: they drink a dog's blood and make him itch, sometimes severely. Then there are worms that stake out the intestines, worms that live in the bloodstream, ticks, mites, and a host of other freeloaders. This chapter covers all the major parasite players, from head to tail.

E M E R G E N C Y !

Does your dog need immediate veterinary care? Check this list to help you decide.

TAKE IMMEDIATE ACTION!

Call your vet or an emergency veterinary clinic *now* if your dog is showing any of the following symptoms:

❏ Your dog has **vomit or diarrhea with worms in it,** and he seems **weak or otherwise very ill.**

❏ You have used a **flea or tick product** on your dog and she is **weak, vomiting, twitching, or having a seizure.**

❏ He has **swollen joints** and a **fever of 103°F** or higher.

TAKE A MINUTE . . .

Read further in this book and then call your vet during office hours as needed if your dog is showing any of the following symptoms:

❏ She has vomited once or twice and the **vomit has worms in it,** but she

does not seem weak or otherwise very ill (see the following page).

❏ He has had diarrhea once or twice and the **diarrhea has worms in it,** but he does not seem weak or otherwise very ill (see the following page).

❏ She has **diarrhea that is streaked with a little blood or mucus;** this is a symptom of colitis (see page 125).

❏ You've just found one or more **ticks on his skin** (see page 170).

❏ She is **scratching herself raw,** or scratching so much that she (or you) can't sleep; this could be fleas (see page 160), a hot spot (see page 98), or sarcoptic mange (see page 167).

❏ He is **scooting his hind end** on the floor; this is caused occasionally by tapeworms (see page 154), but more often by an anal sac problem (see page 100) or itchy skin.

Remember, it's never wrong to call your veterinarian if you have a question about your dog's health, or if you're worried about a symptom or your dog's overall condition. That's what we're here for.

WORMS, WORMS EVERYWHERE

"I just took my new puppy to the vet, and he says the puppy has round-worms. This is not some stray— my puppy's a purebred from a top breeder. How can an $800 dog have worms?"

Almost all puppies have roundworms, regardless of their pedigrees, and it's not the fault of the breeder or shelter. Puppies get roundworms from their mothers while they're in utero or nursing. Dormant roundworm larvae can hide in a dog's muscles, where they can't be reached by deworming medicine. When the dog becomes pregnant, her hormones stimulate the larvae to develop; the roundworms then migrate into her developing puppies and her milk supply.

Puppies and dogs with roundworms may have no symptoms at all, or they may have slightly soft stools. In a more dramatic scenario, they may vomit up worms or pass them in diarrhea. If you see worms that are about 2 to 4 inches long and the diameter of spaghetti in your puppy's vomit or feces, they're probably roundworms. Revolting though this is, it's not a rush-to-the-vet emergency as long as the puppy is bright and bouncy and doesn't act sick—just call your vet during office hours to get the appropriate treatment.

Occasionally, worms will make a puppy very ill. A puppy that is weak or lethargic, vomits more than once or twice in one day, has watery diarrhea, or won't eat is in serious trouble and needs to be seen by a vet as soon as possible. The cause could be a heavy infestation of parasites or another ill-

ness, and your vet or a vet emergency clinic needs to diagnose the problem and correct it before the puppy becomes dangerously dehydrated.

Usually, puppies are given a dewormer that's effective against roundworms before they leave the breeder or shelter and again during their first two or three visits to the veterinarian. At those first visits to the vet it's important to test a fecal sample, and not just squirt the dog full of dewormer, because he may have other intestinal parasites that require a different medication than the one commonly used for roundworms.

ADULT DOGS AND WORMS

"I know that puppies often have worms, but how do adult dogs get them?"

Worms lay microscopic eggs that are passed with a dog's feces. Those eggs can live for months or even longer on the ground. When a dog sniffs another dog's feces, or even noses around the area where another dog has defecated, she can easily pick up a few of these eggs on her nose, then lick them into her mouth. Hookworm larvae can also burrow through the skin, and tapeworms are spread by flea bites. Once in the digestive tract, the eggs develop into adult worms and start laying eggs of their own. That's why many vets recommend a fecal test for parasites once a year—more often if your dog gets diarrhea. And that's also why it's important to clean up after your dog, in your own yard as well as on walks.

Fortunately, many of the once-a-month heartworm preventives also kill some intestinal worms.

TESTING, ONE, TWO, THREE

People taking their dogs to the vet for a yearly physical exam or because the dogs have been vomiting or having diarrhea are asked to bring a sample of their dog's stool. That raises the question: just what do vets do with that poop?

If the dog is sick, the vet looks at the color, consistency, and contents of the stool, then examines a small sample under a microscope to check for unusual bacteria, such as campylobacter or clostridium.

Whether a dog is sick or well, the vet (or, more likely, a technician or assistant) will do a "fecal float" in which a dab of stool is mixed with a salt solution in a small vial, and a microscope cover slip is balanced on top like a lid. The vial is left undisturbed for five minutes or so while any parasite eggs in the fecal sample float to the top of the salt solution, where they cling to the underside of the cover slip. Then the cover slip is lifted carefully and set on a clean microscope slide for examination.

The eggs of roundworms, hookworms, and whipworms are visible under low power (40x or 100x magnification). The eggs look different from one another and are easily identified with a little practice. Protozoal parasites, such as giardia and coccidia, are harder to find—they are much smaller and nearly transparent. High power (400x) is used to search for them on a microscope slide.

The fecal-float method of checking for intestinal parasites has limitations. Only a marble-size sample of feces is checked. Intestinal worms shed eggs intermittently, not constantly, so a particular sample may not contain any eggs even though the dog does have adult worms in its intestines.

The protozoal parasites are even more difficult to find, so hardly anyone is willing to declare that a dog absolutely, positively does *not* have giardia or coccidia if they don't see any of the organisms on one slide. If a dog has symptoms consistent with protozoal parasites and a likelihood of exposure, a vet may recommend treating for them without having absolute proof.

CHILDREN AND WORMS

"I have a two-year-old daughter. Can she get worms from our dog?"

It's possible for a person to catch intestinal parasites from a dog, and anyone who takes care of young children, in particular, should know the risk factors and what precautions to take.

Most intestinal worms are transmitted only via fecal-oral contact—a person has to swallow the worm eggs, which are passed in an animal's feces. Babies and toddlers crawl around on the ground, play in sandboxes, and put their fingers, toys, and other objects in their mouths whether they're dirty or not, so it is possible for them to ingest soil that contains a trace of dog or cat feces.

Hookworms are the exception to the fecal-oral rule. Hookworm eggs are found in feces, but in addition, the hookworm larvae that hatch from those eggs can penetrate the skin of someone who comes in contact with damp sand or soil. Hookworms are most prevalent in the Gulf Coast region of the United States. Builders working in damp sand or soil, sunbathers, and children walking barefoot or playing in damp areas are the most likely to become infected this way. Hookworm larvae leave a red, raised, itchy trail when they burrow into the skin.

Roundworms (*Toxocara* species) are extremely common in puppies and kittens, and older animals can be infected with them as well. No official tally is kept of the number of human cases of roundworms, but the Centers for Disease Control and Prevention (CDC) estimates that it may be as many as 10,000 *each year.*

If a child does catch roundworms from an animal, the results can be devastating. Rather than staying within the digestive tract, as they usually do in dogs and cats, roundworm larvae often migrate throughout the human body. They can damage the liver, lungs, eyes, or brain, sometimes irreversibly. Roundworms in children can be treated, but often they aren't diagnosed until symptoms appear.

There is a bit of good news about kids, worms, and pets: the type of worms that children get most commonly—pinworms—are not serious and are not transmitted by animals at all. Dogs and cats don't carry them. Pinworms are spread from person to person, not from pets to people.

To prevent other intestinal parasites from spreading from pets to people, take the following precautions:

❏ Have your vet test and treat your dogs (and cats) once a year for intestinal parasites, and more often if the animals vomit or have diarrhea.
❏ Pick up animal feces in your yard as frequently as possible and dispose of them in the trash.
❏ If animals sometimes defecate in your yard, don't let infants play directly on the grass; put them on a blanket or in a playpen instead.
❏ Wash your baby's or toddler's hands frequently, especially after she plays outdoors, after she pets a dog or cat, and before she eats or drinks.
❏ Dogs and cats sometimes use children's sandboxes as litter boxes. Keep your sandbox covered when your child isn't playing in it.
❏ Don't feed dogs or cats outdoors, or feed raccoons or other wildlife in your yard. Raccoon feces often contain *Baylisascaris*, a type of roundworm that is especially dangerous in people because the larvae often migrate to the brain.
❏ With older children, emphasize the importance of washing hands before eating anything, even just a snack.
❏ If you have a garden, wash all homegrown fruits and vegetables carefully before eating them.
❏ For more information on parasites and people, check the CDC website: *www.cdc.gov/healthypets/index.htm.*

HOOKWORMS

"I adopted a young dog from a shelter, and my vet did a fecal test and said he has hookworms. Then the vet did a blood test and said he was slightly anemic because of the worms. Will my dog be all right?"

Hookworms are a fairly common intestinal parasite with a very nasty habit: they literally hook onto a dog's intestines with their teeth and feed on the dog's blood. A dog that has a lot of hookworms can become anemic from blood loss, as your dog did, but if the dog is not malnourished or sick otherwise, it will recover from the anemia once the hookworms are eliminated.

Newborn puppies whose mother has hookworms, however, are at grave risk of dying from anemia in the first two or three weeks of life. They become infected with hookworms through their mother's milk, and because they are small and have no resistance to the hookworms, they can lose enough blood to kill them. Any female dog that is going to be bred should first be tested and treated for hookworms.

Older dogs are infected by sniffing around the feces of other dogs that have hookworms and ingesting the microscopic parasite eggs. These eggs can survive for years in the environment. In addition, hookworm larvae can live in damp sand or soil and burrow through the skin, usually on the dog's feet, before migrating to the dog's intestines and developing into adult worms. Hookworm larvae can burrow into people's skin but usually don't migrate any further.

Your vet will prescribe a dewormer that's effective against hookworms. If your dog spends a lot of time around lakes or the ocean, and hookworms are common in your area—as they are in the southeastern United States and Gulf Coast—you'd be smart to use Heartgard Plus, Interceptor, or Sentinel as a once-a-month heartworm preventive. Along with preventing *heart*worm infection, they also protect dogs against new *hook*worm infections.

WHIPWORMS

"My dog was passing soft stools with streaks of blood and mucus in them. A fecal test showed he has whipworms, and the medicine the vet prescribed is really expensive. Can't I use a cheaper over-the-counter dewormer instead?"

Whipworms are common in many parts of the United States, and they often cause colitis, or an inflamed colon. Diarrhea or soft stool, often with blood or mucus in it, is a symptom of colitis. Whipworm eggs are difficult to destroy in the environment and have been known to survive for many years.

The expensive dewormer your vet prescribed is probably Panacur (fenbendazole), to be given in nine doses: once a day for three days now, once a day for three days in three weeks, and once a day for three days in three months. This prolonged treatment is recommended because whipworm larvae can continue hatching out in your dog's body even after the adult whipworms are killed. The three-phase treatment is designed to wipe out the larvae as they mature.

The cheaper, over-the-counter dewormers don't kill whipworms, so that isn't an option for treating your dog. (Most of them contain pyrantel pamoate, which kills roundworms, or praziquantel, which kills tapeworms.)

Once your dog's current whipworm problem is cleared up, he'll be protected against picking them up again by the once-a-month heartworm pills Interceptor or Sentinel. These preventives are relatively expensive too (see page 155), but they're cheaper than treating whipworms repeatedly.

BELLY BUGS VS. HEARTWORMS

When most people hear "worms" and "dog" in the same sentence, they think of the types of worms that can infest a dog's digestive system. That can leave them confused about heartworms, which are not found in the digestive tract, and other parasites that are found in the digestive tract but are not worms. If you've ever assumed that your dog's fecal sample is being checked for heartworms, or that a negative heartworm test means your dog doesn't have intestinal parasites, read on.

Intestinal parasites live in a dog's digestive tract. They include several types of worms, including roundworms, hookworms, and whipworms, as well as microscopic organisms like giardia and coccidia. Adult worms are occasionally visible in a dog's vomit or feces, but usually they're diagnosed by checking a fecal sample microscopically for the worms' eggs. Giardia and coccidia also are diagnosed by checking a fecal sample microscopically. Tapeworms are yet another intestinal worm, one that is transmitted exclusively by fleas; they are diagnosed by finding their egg packets—white, wormlike, ½-inch-long segments that may wiggle—on a dog's feces, rectal area, or bedding.

Heartworms live in a dog's heart, lungs, and bloodstream. They are transmitted from dog to dog by the bite of a mosquito, and are diag-

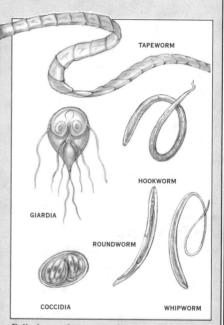

Belly bugs: these organisms are "the usual suspects" of the GI tract.

nosed via a blood test (heartworms don't live in the digestive tract and therefore are not found in feces). Unlike intestinal parasites, heartworms can be fatal to otherwise healthy adult dogs.

When a dog goes to the vet for an annual physical exam, he has a fecal test to check for intestinal parasites and a blood test to check for heartworms. One final confusing twist: some once-a-month heartworm preventives *also* prevent new infestations of the main three intestinal worms—roundworms, hookworms, and whipworms. The reverse is not true, however. Intestinal dewormers *do not* protect against heartworms.

Scooting can be a sign of an anal-gland problem, tapeworms, or simply an itchy bottom.

SCOOTING DOGS

"My dog scoots his bottom on the rug. My neighbor says that means he has worms. What should I do?"

Scooting proves that a dog's bottom is sore or itchy, but it does not prove that he has worms. What might make a dog's bottom sore or itchy? Full or infected anal sacs could do it (see page 100), or diarrhea, or an allergy. Once in a great while, scooting *is* caused by worms—specifically, tapeworms.

Tapeworms live in a dog's intestines and pass their egg packets with the dog's feces. These whitish egg packets are approximately ½-inch long. They wiggle around on the dog's feces and on his bottom, which is—not surprisingly—annoying and itchy and may make him scoot.

You'll know that your dog has tapeworms if you see these egg packets on his feces or bottom. Fleas transmit tapeworms to dogs and cats, so if your dog does have tapeworms, he also has fleas, or had them in the past. Tapeworms are not killed by the standard puppy and kitten dewormers, so it's possible for an animal to have had them for a long time before the owner notices any problem.

Fortunately, tapeworms seldom make dogs sick—usually the only symptom is the egg packets on the feces—and they're easy to get rid of once you know they're there. Your vet will prescribe a pill that contains praziquantel (Droncit) or epsiprantel (Cestex), and that will be the end of the tapeworms.

Be sure to check your dog for signs of fleas as well, however, because he could catch tapeworms again if he's bitten by more fleas.

BEAVER FEVER

"My dog and I had a wonderful time on vacation hiking in the mountains. Since we got home, however, we've both had diarrhea. The vet says my dog may have gotten 'beaver fever' from drinking from streams. What is that, and could I have it, too?"

Beaver fever is a colloquial name for giardiasis, diarrhea caused by the microscopic parasite giardia. Giardiasis is most often transmitted through lakes, ponds, and streams that contain traces of animal feces infected with the parasite. Beavers sometimes carry giardia, but so can people, dogs, and a variety of other wildlife.

The water source may be clear, clean-looking, and constantly moving (like a stream), which can lull people into assuming it doesn't contain any parasites. Dogs catch the illness most frequently by drinking the water. People can catch it from simply getting a little water in their mouths while swimming.

Infected dogs may have no symptoms at all, or they may have diarrhea. The diarrhea may come and go over a period of weeks. Giardiasis is diagnosed by examining a fecal sample microscopically, but the organisms are tiny and can be difficult to find. A veterinarian may suggest treating a dog based on the dog's symptoms and possible exposure (to a pond, lake, or stream) even if no giardia organisms are found in the feces.

Giardiasis is treated with the prescription drug metronidazole (Flagyl). Metronidazole also kills "bad" anaerobic bacteria, which can overrun the colon when a dog has diarrhea, and relieves colon inflammation (colitis), so it has other benefits in treating a dog with diarrhea as well.

Coccidia are similar microscopic parasites of the intestinal tract. Like giardia, they are tiny and can be difficult to find in a fecal sample. Unlike giardia, however, they usually are spread through feces directly, rather than through fecal contamination of lakes or ponds. The diarrheal disease coccidiosis is most common where large numbers of dogs are housed together, especially if feces are not removed promptly. A dog infected with coccidia may have no symptoms, but puppies and dogs who are weakened by other illnesses may have diarrhea, sometimes streaked with mucus or blood. Coccidiosis is usually treated with sulfadimethoxine (Albon).

HEARTBREAKING HEARTWORMS

"How common and how serious are heartworms? My vet says my dog should be on the monthly preventive all year long, but it's so expensive."

Vets do push hard to get dogs on monthly heartworm protection, because heartworms are (1) common, (2) potentially fatal, and (3) easily preventable. We vets feel really good when we can protect a dog against a serious disease with something as simple as a once-a-month pill.

To explain why heartworms are Public Enemy No. 1 in vets' offices, here are the facts. Heartworm larvae—a microscopic, immature form of the worms—are spread from one dog to another by mosquitoes. The disease is most common in places with many mosquitoes, but heartworms are found throughout the United States as well as in other parts of the world.

Once the heartworm larvae get into a dog's bloodstream, they take approximately four months to develop into microfilaria and then adult heartworms, which range from 2 to 10 inches long. The adults are carried by the bloodstream to the right side of the dog's heart and from there to the lungs. If both male and female heartworms are present, they can reproduce, so a single mosquito bite can lead to generations of heartworms living in the dog's bloodstream.

Heartworms can cause problems for dogs in several ways: by physically clogging the large blood vessels leading to the heart; by blocking blood flow to areas of the lungs; by causing inflammation of the blood vessels; and by blocking small blood vessels (capillaries) in other organs.

Most commonly, heartworms (and the body's reaction to them) block blood flow to parts of a dog's lungs, limiting the surface area where oxygen can cross over from the lungs to red blood cells. That oxygen deficit, in turn, forces the dog's heart to work harder than normal, which ultimately can lead to congestive heart failure (see page 270). Depending on how far the disease has progressed, symptoms could include loss of energy, loss of stamina, a cough, a heart murmur, difficulty breathing, or collapse. Of course, by the time these symptoms have appeared, your dog may already be very sick, which is why vets encourage dog owners to use heartworm preventives.

Heartworm preventives work by killing heartworm microfilaria—an intermediate lifestage of the worms—within a month after they develop from the larvae transmitted by a mosquito bite. Once the heartworm microfilaria are more than 45 days old, however, they aren't susceptible to the preventives at the monthly dose. That is why heartworm prevention must be given once a month without fail until at least one month past the last potential mosquito bite. This could be May through October in a place that has cold winters, like Minnesota, or year-round in warmer places, like the southern states. Because some dogs travel with their owners to warmer climates in the wintertime, and because it's possible for mosquitoes to live indoors even when it's freezing outside, many vets recommend year-round heartworm prevention in the northern states as well.

HEARTWORM TESTING

"Why does my dog have to be tested for heartworm every year before I can refill her heartworm prescription?"

A blood test that checks for substances produced by adult heartworms is done once a year to make sure the heart-

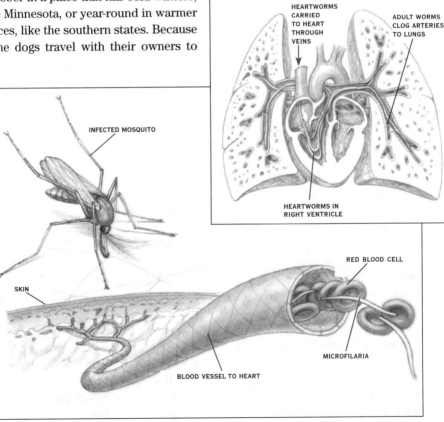

Heartworm larvae are transmitted by mosquitoes, then grow and reproduce in the blood vessels.

worm preventive worked the way it's supposed to. Occasionally dogs will spit out a pill without their owners' realizing it, or owners may forget to give the pill one month. Sometimes a dog that's on heartworm prevention only during the summer will travel to Florida with her owners for a couple of weeks in January and promptly get bitten by heartworm-carrying mosquitoes. By May, when the dog is due to start taking heartworm prevention again, the larvae would already have developed into adult worms.

There are two problems with refilling heartworm prevention without retesting a dog for heartworms. One is that it's possible for a dog that has large numbers of microfilaria (an immature stage of heartworms) in her bloodstream to go into shock if she's given a once-a-month heartworm preventive and masses of microfilaria die all at once. The other is that the heartworm prevention won't kill heartworms that are older than the microfilaria stage, so if a dog has managed to get infected despite being on the once-a-month pills, the disease can progress unless treatment is given to kill the adult worms that are reproducing.

PICKING A HEARTWORM PREVENTIVE

"Are all the once-a-month heartworm preventives—Heartgard, Interceptor, Revolution, and Advantage Multi—equally effective? Why the huge difference in cost?"

They are all effective at preventing heartworm infestation when given once a month as directed. All of them work by killing the immature heartworm microfilaria within a month after they develop from larvae transmitted by the bite of a mosquito. All are safe and have essentially no side effects.

So why the difference in cost? Because they are different drugs produced by different companies. Prices also vary according to the veterinarian or catalog selling the drug; some sellers are able to negotiate volume discounts or other reductions in wholesale prices from the manufacturers.

Here are the facts on the most commonly used heartworm preventives.

Heartgard is ivermectin, which has been used for once-a-month heartworm prevention for decades. Heartgard Plus is ivermectin plus pyrantel. The pyrantel protects dogs from two intestinal parasites, roundworms and hookworms. The manufacturer is Merial. (Heartgard went off patent in 2001, so generic versions may also be available.)

Collies are more sensitive to ivermectin than are other dogs, and many vets advise against giving them Heartgard (see the following Q&A).

Interceptor is a different microfilaria-killing drug, milbemycin. It is considered safe in all breeds of dogs. Milbemycin also protects against new infestations of three intestinal parasites —roundworms, hookworms, and whipworms. The manufacturer is Novartis.

Sentinel is Interceptor (milbemycin) plus lufenuron, which is a "flea growth regulator." Flea growth regulators are sort of like flea birth control: they don't kill adult fleas or prevent fleas from biting a dog, but they do prevent the flea's eggs—which fleas lay indoors as well as outdoors—from developing into adult fleas. Sentinel also is made by Novartis.

Revolution, introduced in 2000, is the drug selamectin. It's applied to the dog's skin as a topical liquid, or "spot-on," rather than given by mouth. Like heartworm pills, it must be used once a month to prevent heartworm infestation. Revolution also kills adult fleas, dog ticks (but not deer ticks, which carry Lyme disease), and sarcoptic mange mites (scabies mites); and it is a flea growth regulator.

Advantage Multi is another spot-on heartworm preventive. It contains moxidectin, which kills intestinal worms as well as heartworm larvae, and imidacloprid, which kills fleas. It was introduced in 2007 by Bayer.

Which heartworm preventive is best and most cost-effective for your dog depends on whether you also need protection against fleas, regular ticks, or deer ticks (the type that spread Lyme disease), or all of the above. To protect a dog against heartworms *and* Lyme disease, for example, you would need to use Revolution or Advantage Multi plus a Preventic collar, or one of the oral heartworm preventives plus Frontline (see "Sorting Out Spot-Ons," on page 164). Your dog's weight determines the dose and cost of these products, which you can look up online. If you're not sure which parasites are prevalent in your area, ask your vet.

"WHITE FEET— DON'T TREAT"

"My mixed-breed dog may be part Collie. I've always given her Heartgard for heartworm prevention, with no ill effects. Should I switch to something else?"

Collies, Collie mixes, and Collie "types" can be extra-sensitive to ivermectin, the active ingredient in Heartgard. The Collie category includes Border Collies, Bearded Collies, Shetland Sheepdogs (Shelties), Australian Shepherds, and Old English Sheepdogs. To keep that list

in mind, some clever vet came up with the mnemonic "White feet—don't treat."

Ivermectin can cause problems in those breeds because it crosses over from their bloodstream to their brain in higher concentrations than it does in most dogs. If a Collie is given a large dose of ivermectin—like that used to treat sarcoptic mange (see page 167)—she may develop neurological symptoms such as muscle twitches, staggering, blindness, or seizures. She could even become comatose or die.

However—and this is a big however, I admit—the dose of ivermectin in Heartgard is very low, and some Collies can tolerate it just fine. Vets advise against giving Heartgard to Collies to be extra-cautious, but if you've given it to your mixed-breed dog in the past and haven't seen any adverse symptoms, your dog may be fine with it. Just be sure to call your vet right away if you notice muscle twitching or odd behavior after your dog takes her monthly pill; ivermectin's effects on the nervous system can be treated if they're caught early.

THE HEARTWORM SHOT

"I remember seeing ads a few years ago for a heartworm preventive that was given by injection every six months. Is it still around? Does it work, and is it safe?"

ProHeart 6 is the product you remember. It was introduced in 2001, after being used for several years before that in Australia, then pulled off the market in 2004 amid fears that it may have been responsible for serious to fatal reactions—including hemorrhagic gastroenteritis, hemolytic anemia, and anaphylactic shock—in a small percentage

HOLD THE ESCARGOT, PLEASE

Like most other parts of the body, the lungs have their own special bugs. Lungworms are uncommon but they do exist, and once in a great while they can be the culprit in a coughing dog.

A specific environment is required for two of the four species of lungworm that occasionally infect dogs. Those two (*Paragonimus kellicotti* and *Crenosoma vulpis*) spend part of their life cycle in wildlife, such as foxes or raccoons; part in snails or slugs; and in the case of *Paragonimus*, part in crayfish. Practically speaking, this means that the only dog at risk of catching these two types of lungworms is one who spends time near rivers, ponds, or creeks, and eats the snails or crayfish he finds there. The other two species of lungworm are less restricted in their environment but nonetheless extremely rare.

Veterinarians diagnose lungworms by finding them in a dog's bronchi (the tubes that branch off the windpipe to the lungs). They can be found in bronchial secretions or by looking at the bronchi themselves with an endoscope. Sometimes lungworm eggs or larvae can be found in a dog's feces when they have been coughed up and then swallowed.

Fortunately, lungworms rarely cause dogs to become severely ill, and they can be treated with fenbendazole, praziquantel, or other antiparasitic drugs.

---

of the dogs who had received it. The manufacturer, Fort Dodge, reintroduced ProHeart 6 in 2008 with new label warnings and a requirement that vets who want to use the product complete a training program first.

ProHeart 6 contains moxidectin—the same active ingredient in Advantage Multi—in a slow-release injectable form. The advantage for dog owners is they don't have to remember to use a monthly heartworm preventive. The disadvantage is lingering concerns that it may be less safe than the other preventives. The new labeling states that ProHeart 6 should be used with caution in dogs with allergies, and should not be given within a month of vaccinations or to sick, debilitated, or underweight animals.

Some of the vets who used ProHeart 6 between 2001 and 2004 found it convenient and effective and did not see adverse reactions in their patients. They will probably start offering it again. Others didn't use it then and are unlikely to start using it now, when the market is well supplied with other heartworm preventives that have a longer history and fewer restrictions.

WHEN A DOG GETS HEARTWORMS

"What if I save the money I'd spend on monthly heartworm preventive, take my chances that my dog won't get heartworms, and treat him if he does?"

That's an unwise strategy, because preventing heartworm infestation is easy and safe, but treating the disease can be expensive, difficult, and dangerous. Assessing a heartworm-infected dog requires vet visits and tests, which can add up. Then there's the cost of hospitalization and the actual treatment. Finally, the drugs used to eradicate heartworms can be nearly as hard on the dog as they are on the worms.

Let's say you've just adopted an adult dog, and you take him to the vet for a heartworm test (which checks a blood sample for antigens produced by adult heartworms). Bad news: the blood test is positive. Next the vet will check a blood sample for microfilaria (an immature stage of heartworms). More bad news: that test, too, is positive.

After carefully evaluating your dog for symptoms of heartworm disease—such as a cough, difficulty breathing, a heart murmur, or lack of energy—the vet will run still more blood tests and a urinalysis to check for evidence of heartworm damage to the heart, lungs, kidneys, or liver. Your dog's chest will be x-rayed to look for an enlarged heart and damaged lungs. Finally, an ultrasound exam of the heart and surrounding large blood vessels will locate and get a rough count of the adult heartworms. All of this testing is required to see how much mayhem the heartworms have already caused, and whether your dog is healthy enough to withstand treatment to kill the heartworms.

When a dog is mildly to moderately affected by heartworms, Caparsolate (thiacetarsemide sodium) or Immiticide (melarsomine dihydrochloride) are commonly used to kill the parasites. These drugs are related to arsenic, and the dose must be carefully calculated. Even at appropriate doses, however, complications can occur. As the adult worms die, they can float downstream and cause additional circulatory blockages and lung inflammation. Occasionally this lung damage can be fatal. In addition, Caparsolate can cause kidney or liver damage. It is given in several small doses over a period of two or three days while the dog is monitored in the hospital and given IV fluids. Complete rest (meaning that the dog stays in a crate or a small room all day except for brief trips outdoors to urinate and defecate) is necessary before and for two to four weeks after treatment, to reduce strain on the lungs and heart while the heartworms are dying.

If a dog is severely affected by heartworms—he's already in congestive heart failure, or has adult heartworms blocking the vena cava or right atrium of the heart—then surgical removal of the worms is usually recommended as safer than drug therapy. The dog is anesthetized, a small forceps on surgical wire is threaded through the jugular vein to the vena cava or right atrium, and the forceps is used to "hook" and remove the worms one by one. Most often this is an emergency procedure, done in an attempt to improve a dog's heart and lung function enough to enable him to survive drug treatment a few weeks later to kill the remaining heartworms.

These gory details of heartworm infection and treatment have convinced you, I hope, that heartworm prevention is a wise investment financially as well as medically.

FINDING FLEAS

"How can I tell whether my dog has fleas?"

Check your dog's skin for fleas and flea dirt. Fleas look like small brown or black sesame seeds, but unlike sesame seeds, they move—fast. They're easiest to spot on a dog's belly, where the hair is thinner.

Flea dirt is actually flea excrement. It looks like flecks of pepper at the base of the dog's hair and often can be found on the back just in front of the tail. If you're not sure whether what you're seeing is flea dirt or regular dirt, comb some out of the hair with a fine-tooth flea comb, press the dirt on a wet paper towel, and wait a minute. If the paper towel turns red around the specks, you've got fleas: flea dirt contains blood, so when it gets wet, it bleeds red.

HIGH-RISE FLEAS

"I live in a 12-story apartment building in the city. How did my dog get fleas?"

Fleas can live outdoors when the weather is warm, and they can live happily indoors year-round in any climate. They get inside by hitching a ride on a furry animal—your dog or cat, for example—and then they hop off and set up housekeeping. Flea eggs can remain dormant in carpeting, cracks in the floor, and upholstery for months to years and then hatch when a suitable host, such as a cat or dog, appears on the scene.

FLEAS BY THE HOUSEFUL

"My dog has fleas. How do I get rid of them?"

A simple question with a not-so-simple answer. You actually have three tasks here: (1) getting rid of the fleas in your home, (2) getting rid of the fleas on your dogs and cats, and (3) preventing your dogs and cats from bringing home more fleas. These tasks must be performed more or less simultaneously, or your efforts will be doomed to failure.

Let's start with your home. How do I know there are fleas in your house? Because it's inevitable. Fleas don't live *on* an animal; they live *with* the animal, and jump on him only to suck his blood and lay eggs. The rest of the time, fleas and their larvae are lounging around in carpeting, the cracks of wood floors, and beds and upholstered furniture. The rule of thumb is that for every flea you see *on* a dog or cat, there are a hundred more in the house.

The simplest way to de-flea your house is to apply a spot-on, such as Frontline or Revolution, to each of your dogs and cats once a month until a month or two past a hard frost (see the following question). As the fleas hop on the animals to feed, they will be killed. This is a gradual approach, but as long as no people in the house are getting bitten by fleas, then there's no rush. If your animals are already on an over-the-counter monthly spot-on and you still have a flea problem, try upgrading to Frontline or Revolution.

If you have so many fleas that you're getting bitten as well, then a faster attack is warranted. Ridding a house of fleas is hard work: you need to treat every room that your dog or cat enters. You also need to treat your car if your dog rides in it, your office if your dog goes there, and so on. You can also hire an exterminator to do this job for you—after you realize what's involved, you may want to do just that.

Start with the beds. If your dog sleeps on your bed, launder all of your

FLEA-PRODUCT DANGERS

When you buy flea products, be sure to read the labels and follow all instructions *carefully*. A flea dip that is safe for adult dogs, for example, may be toxic to cats and too strong for puppies. Some flea repellents can be used once a week, but others can poison an animal if they're applied that frequently. If your dog or cat acts strangely or becomes weak or uncoordinated after you use a flea product, call your vet immediately.

bed linens (including the bedspread or comforter) in warm or hot water, or have them dry-cleaned. Also launder your dog's bed in hot water and detergent. Foam dog mattresses and other unwashable bedding should be thrown away (the best choice) or else vacuumed thoroughly and then lightly sprayed with a flea spray that's meant to be used *on the dog*. Your dog will be snuggled in that bed every day, so it's best to spray it with something that's safe for his skin.

Next, vacuum every square inch of your floors and your upholstered furniture, using a crevice attachment for baseboards and cracks in floors. Vacuum under the furniture as well. As soon as you're done, bag up the vacuum-cleaner bag and throw it away in an outdoor garbage can. Otherwise the fleas will jump right back out of the bag and into your house again.

Finally, apply a flea killer to all the floors you have just vacuumed. Here are advantages and disadvantages of the three basic types of flea killers designed for the house:

❏ **Sprays.** *Advantage:* You can apply them exactly where you want them. *Disadvantages:* Spraying is time-consuming and will make your hand very tired and sore.

❏ **Automatic foggers.** You place one fogger in each room, set the triggers, and then leave the house (taking all animals, including fish and birds, with you, of course) for as long as the label recommends. *Advantage:* They're easy. *Disadvantages:* You'll need to buy one for every room; they treat some areas that don't need it (tabletops) and miss other areas that do need it (under sofas and beds), so you'll still have to do some spraying; and you have to vacate the premises with your entire menagerie while they're working.

❏ **Boric acid, diatomaceous earth, and other mineral salts.** These are dusted onto rugs and floors and kill flea eggs and larvae. Many professional pest services carry them. *Advantage:* They're considered more "natural" and less toxic than sprays and foggers (see the following Q&A). *Disadvantages:* They don't kill adult fleas, just flea eggs and larvae, so they take a couple of weeks to knock back the flea population; and they are safe to walk on but not to eat, which could be a problem if a cat gets a lot on his paws and then licks it off, or if a toddler sticks her hand in the powder and then in her mouth.

If you use a spray or fogger, be sure to choose one that kills eggs and larvae as well as adult fleas.

One super-thorough vacuuming and treating of the house usually will clear it of fleas, but occasionally the whole process has to be repeated three or four weeks later.

DE-FLEAING FIDO

"I'm all set to de-flea the house. Now, what do I use to get rid of fleas on my dog?"

The current generation of spot-on flea killers works so well, I recommend spot-ons for every dog who isn't allergic to them (see "Spot-ons," below). Pet stores and pet supply catalogs, however, continue to carry many old-school flea products as well. Below are descriptions of how these products work. Some, but not all, can also be used safely on cats; read labels carefully.

Flea shampoos. *Advantages:* They clean the dog as well as killing the fleas, and they don't leave a bad odor. *Disadvantages:* Bathing your dog with a flea shampoo won't stop more fleas from jumping on him as soon as he gets out of the tub. *Tips:* Lather your dog's neck immediately to help prevent fleas from rushing to his head to hide. Don't get shampoo in his eyes—it can damage the cornea (surface of the eye). Use a washcloth to carefully wet the dog's face, then a flea comb to nab any fleas around the eyes and muzzle (swish the comb in the bathwater to drown the fleas). Once the dog is fully soaped up, the lather needs to stay on for 10 or 15 minutes (read the label) before being rinsed off.

Flea dips. A "dip" is diluted in water and poured or sponged on the dog, usually immediately after he has been bathed. *Advantages:* Flea dips are potent, and some have a "residual effect" that will prevent more fleas from jump-ing on the dog for a short time (check the label). *Disadvantages:* They're extremely messy and often smelly. *Tips:* Your dog needs to be drenched to the skin with the dip, which is easiest when he's still wet from a bath. Don't get the dip in his eyes or mouth. The dog needs to drip-dry after the dip is applied, so don't towel him off, and do shut him in a bathroom or other room that won't be damaged by the wet mess.

Flea foams. These have the texture of hair-styling mousse and are massaged into the fur. *Advantages:* You don't have to bathe or drench the animal, and they're far less messy than dips. *Disadvantages:* They won't get rid of flea dirt or any other kind of dirt, and they can leave the fur mussed or greasy. *Tips:* Use enough foam to leave the animal's fur damp all over.

Flea sprays. *Advantages:* You don't have to bathe or drench the animal, and they're far less messy than dips. *Disadvantages:* They won't get rid of flea dirt or any other kind of dirt, and they can leave the fur mussed or greasy. *Tips:* The spray needs to reach the roots of the hair to do its job. Brush the hair backward as you spray to get to the roots. Your dog should be damp all over when you're done. Don't spray the dog's face—dab on the flea spray with your hands so it doesn't get into his eyes or mouth.

Flea powders. *Advantages:* You don't have to bathe your dog, and powders are easy to apply. *Disadvantages:* They won't get rid of flea dirt, and they leave the coat dusty. *Tip:* Rub the powder into the coat well; it needs to get down to the skin.

Spot-ons. These little vials of oil are applied to one or two spots on the dog's head and back, and the active ingredient spreads over the skin to kill fleas over the dog's entire body. *Advantages:* They're easy to apply, they continue to kill fleas for one to three months, and some also kill ticks and heartworm larvae (check the label). *Disadvantages:* Some require a prescription; some are expensive; some take a day or two to start killing fleas; and most can't be used within a day or two of a bath, because they need some oil in the hair follicles to grab onto. So if you give your dog a flea bath, you'll have to wait at least 24 hours before applying a spot-on. *Tips:* The oil needs to be on the dog's skin, not the hair, so part the hair and drip the oil slowly along the part line. You can also clip the fur from a tiny area (about an inch square) and apply the oil to the clipped area. Put the first drop of oil on the top of the dog's head, because fleas (and ticks) often hide around the face. Apply the rest somewhere the dog can't reach to lick it off—between the shoulder blades is a good site. If your dog is large, put half of the oil on the back of his neck and half in the middle of his back. A few dogs are sensitive to the oily base of spot-ons. If the area where you applied the spot-on becomes itchy, red, sore, or scabby, wash the site with a mild dog shampoo and rinse well, then call your vet and describe the reaction to find out whether further treatment is needed.

SORTING OUT SPOT-ONS

"I used to buy Frontline for fleas and ticks from my vet, and it was quite expensive. Now there are a half-dozen spot-ons that you can buy over-the-counter, and they're much cheaper. What's the difference between them?"

The spot-ons may all look the same, but they contain different active ingredients. The less expensive ones generally contain permethrin, the same active ingredient found in many flea shampoos, sprays, and foams. Although permethrin theoretically is effective against fleas, deer ticks (which spread Lyme disease), and dog ticks, some fleas have become resistant to it. Insect growth regulators (IGRs) are sometimes added to permethrin products. IGRs gradually decrease the flea population in a home over a few weeks (by preventing flea larvae from developing further), but they do not kill adult fleas.

Permethrin-based spot-ons should not be used on cats—or on dogs that have close contact with cats. The concentration of permethrin in the spot-ons can be toxic to cats, causing tremors and seizures.

The active ingredient in the more expensive spot-ons is usually fipronil, imidacloprid, or selamectin (Frontline, Advantage Multi, K9 Advantix, and Revolution are four popular brands). Fipronil kills deer ticks (which transmit Lyme disease) and dog ticks as well as fleas. Selamectin is also a heartworm preventive and kills sarcoptic mange mites, dog ticks, and ear mites, but not deer ticks. A dog who's on Revolution or Advantage Multi can wear a Preventic collar for protection against deer ticks.

SPOT-ON DANGERS?

"A woman I see at the dog run insists that spot-ons for fleas and ticks are deadly poison and shouldn't be used on dogs. As evidence, she points out that the labels warn people to wear gloves when applying the spot-on so they don't get any on their skin. Are they really that dangerous?"

Spot-ons are safe and have no side effects in most dogs. The warning about not getting them on your own skin is based on the fact that the oily base soaks into the skin very quickly, so it's difficult to wash off. What will happen if you do get it on your skin? It might smell bad, it will taste bitter if you get any in your mouth, and it might itch a little if you have sensitive skin, but that's about it.

A few dogs are sensitive to the oily base of spot-ons and develop red, itchy, irritated skin where it was applied. Don't use any type of spot-on if your dog has had a skin reaction to one product.

The less expensive spot-ons often contain high concentrations of permethrin. Permethrin in high doses *is* toxic to *cats*, causing muscle tremors and seizures, and permethrin-based spot-ons should not be used either on cats or on dogs that snuggle up to cats.

PREVENTING FURTHER FLEA ATTACKS

"I gave my dog a flea bath last week, and he's scratching again already. What's going on?"

Even after you've de-fleaed your dog and your house, as soon as your dog sets foot outside, fleas can find him, bite him, and potentially hitch a ride back inside. So when you have a flea outbreak, it's wise to use preventive measures for the rest of the flea season. Here are your options:

❑ **Flea collars.** Flea collars are easy but they don't work well. Vets often see happy-looking fleas bouncing around on animals wearing flea collars.

❑ **Flea powders, foams, and sprays.** See page 163. These products usually need to be reapplied every one to two weeks for ongoing protection—check the label.

❑ **Spot-ons.** See the previous page.

❑ **Flea-growth-regulator pills.** Once-a-month flea pills prevent flea larvae from forming pupae, which is the last stage before the larvae become adult fleas. Program contains flea growth regulator only, and Sentinel has flea growth regulator plus the heartworm preventive milbemycin. They're not messy and they're easy to give, but they require a prescription and don't kill adult fleas.

NATURAL FLEA PREVENTION

"I don't like using pesticides on my dog. Is there a less toxic approach to flea control?"

Some dog owners, depending on their environment, can get good results with natural flea prevention. Here are some popular products and techniques.

❑ **Knowing where and when to watch out.** Although fleas can live anywhere, indoors or out, they are most numerous in grassy or wooded areas (such as parks and lawns) and most active in hot, humid weather. Be extra vigilant in those environments and during those weather conditions.

❑ **Preventing fleas from biting your dog.** Flea repellents containing natural ingredients are available in many pet-supply stores and online catalogs. Sprays, foams, or rinses are more effective for flea prevention than flea collars. Do not apply undiluted essential oils to your dog (they can burn the skin). Don't use these products on cats unless they are labeled as safe for cats. And be sure to read labels carefully and apply the following products appropriately.

Citronella is an insect-repelling oil derived from a fragrant grass (*Cymbopogon nardus*) of southern Asia. **d-Limonene** is a flea-repelling compound found in citrus oils and tea tree oil. **Natural pyrethrins** are extracted from chrysanthemums and related flowers.

Garlic, brewer's yeast, and **ultrasonic flea collars** do *not* work, so don't waste your money on them.

❏ **Removing fleas from your dog.** If you flea-comb your dog every day, you can stay ahead of flea problems. This is most practical, of course, with short-haired dogs. You'll need a flea comb (these have very finely spaced teeth) with a long handle, a bowl of soapy water, and a towel. Comb through your dog's fur, swishing any fleas you catch into the soapy water and then wiping the comb on the towel. Pay special attention to your dog's head and neck (be very gentle around the face, of course), belly, and the base of the tail. When you're done, flush the soapy flea water down the toilet.

Regular bathing also can keep fleas at bay, especially if you combine it with regular housecleaning (see below). You don't even need to use a flea shampoo for the baths, but you do need to be thorough and patient. For flea prevention, bathe your dog once a week during hot and humid weather. Use a mild dog shampoo. Get your dog thoroughly wet, then lather

Thoroughly soak and lather your dog's neck first, to prevent fleas from running up to her head.

a big collar of shampoo around her neck (to help stop fleas from zooming to her head, where they're harder to wash off). Lather the rest of her body, rinse lightly, and lather her again. Let the second lather stay on for 10 minutes, then rinse, rinse, rinse. The fleas will be washed down the drain with the lather.

❏ **Removing fleas from your house.** Fleas jump on their "hosts" only to take a blood meal. The rest of the time, the fleas and their offspring (eggs and larvae) are hanging out on your floors, rugs, couches, beds, and so on. The free-breeding freeloaders need to be evicted. Here are some ways to do that.

Vacuum thoroughly twice a week, and immediately put the bag in your outside garbage. Vacuum all floors and upholstered furniture. Be sure you vacuum under the furniture, not just around it.

Wash bedding—yours and your dog's—twice a week in warm water and detergent.

Consider applying boric acid. This can be dusted into rugs or cracks in floors. The powder dehydrates flea larvae and kills them. Boric acid is not safe to eat, however, so don't leave piles of it where children or animals might get into it.

Finally, I have seen "flea traps" advertised. They're basically a lightbulb over a tray of flypaper. Supposedly the heat and light attract fleas and the flypaper traps them. Although it's conceivable that the trap might attract fleas from a foot or two away, I doubt that it would be effective at curbing the flea population within an entire room.

THE MANGY DOG

"My nine-month-old terrier has demodectic mange. The vet says it's nothing to worry about, but it sounds horrible. Can my kids catch it from the dog?"

Sarcoptic mange, or scabies, is so itchy that it may make a dog scratch his skin raw.

It can be a shock to find out that "mangy dog" is not just an expression but an actual medical diagnosis. In fact, mange is a general term for a skin disease caused by a microscopic bug in the mite family.

Two types of mange commonly afflict dogs: demodectic mange, caused by demodex mites, and sarcoptic mange (or scabies), caused by sarcoptes mites. Vets diagnose mange by scraping skin flakes from itchy or patchy areas and checking them under a microscope for mites. (Demodex are cigar-shaped and sarcoptes are round, so they're easy to tell apart.) The two types of mange behave differently and are treated differently, as follows:

Demodectic mange, which your puppy has, is fairly common in young dogs. The symptoms are mild: thinning of the fur, especially around the eyes or elsewhere on the face, and sometimes, but not always, mild itchiness. Dogs can catch demodectic mange from close contact with other dogs that have it, but this type of mange is not contagious to people, so you needn't worry that your children will catch it.

Some puppies simply "outgrow" demodectic mange once their immune systems gear up against the mites, but if your puppy is itchy or has patches of mange all over its body, your vet may prescribe a daily dose of Interceptor (milbemycin) or ivermectin or weekly dips in amitraz until four weeks after skin scrapings of the affected areas are free of mites.

Sarcoptic mange, on the other hand, is extremely itchy. Dogs with sarcoptic mange will sometimes scratch their skin raw—hence its common name, red mange. Dogs who roam in areas with a lot of wildlife (foxes, raccoons, and so on) can catch sarcoptic mange by rolling in the carcass of an animal that had it.

Vets commonly treat sarcoptic mange with Revolution (selamectin) applied to the skin every two weeks for three to six treatments, or two or three injections of ivermectin over several weeks. Often the dog will also need medicine for the itch, and any skin wounds caused by scratching need to be cleaned and treated.

Ivermectin should not be given in large doses to Collies and similar dogs (see page 158). In Collies, sarcoptic mange is treated with Revolution and demodectic mange with Interceptor.

Unlike demodectic mange, sarcoptic mange is contagious to people, in whom it is called scabies. If you or your children have an itchy rash and have been in close contact with a dog that has sarcoptic mange, talk to your physician so you can be checked and, if needed, given appropriate medication.

PERSISTENT DEMODECTIC MANGE

"My three-year-old Shar-Pei has had recurring demodex mites since she was a puppy. I keep dipping her with amitraz, but a few days later she starts scratching again. Isn't there another treatment? My vet said that because the demodectic mange persisted after she was a year old, she will probably have it for life."

Shar-Peis have an inherited predisposition to demodectic mange and other skin problems. Even worse, their skin folds make it difficult to treat mites effectively with topical medica-tions. Fortunately, though, you have at least two other options: ivermectin (Heartgard tablets or a generic formulation) and milbemycin (Interceptor). Either is given orally once a day for at least six to eight weeks.

While your dog is taking the medication, your vet will do periodic skin scrapings to check for mites. Veterinary dermatologists recommend that treatment be continued for four weeks after no mites are found on skin scrapings. (This means no mites at all—neither dead nor alive.) Shar-Peis have very thick skin, so the skin scrapes, which are done with the edge of a scalpel, have to be deeper than with other breeds. If your dog finds this very uncomfortable, your vet may recommend sedating her for the scrapes.

While you are giving your dog milbemycin or ivermectin, you should also bathe her weekly with a benzoyl peroxide shampoo. Demodex mites live in the hair follicles, and benzoyl peroxide makes the cells lining the follicles slough faster, which helps the skin purge itself of the live and dead mites. You'll need to use a moisturizing conditioner after the baths, because benzoyl peroxide can be very drying. If your dog also has a skin infection from scratching at the mites, she should be treated with antibiotics as recommended by your vet.

Factors that suppress the immune system can predispose a dog to demodectic mange. Has your dog been taking steroids, such as cortisone, for itching or other problems? Does she have any signs of diabetes, Cushing's disease, or hypothyroidism? Discuss with your vet whether these or other immunosuppressive factors might be contributing to the recurring mange.

EAR MITES

"My Golden Retriever scratches at her ears, and I noticed that she has brown stuff in them. Does she have ear mites?"

Ear mites are much more common in cats than in dogs. Unless your dog has had close, friendly contact with a cat, she's unlikely to have ear mites. Your vet can find out easily by swabbing some of the brown stuff from your dog's ears and looking at it under a microscope—the mites are unmistakable when magnified (though not, unfortunately, to the naked eye). If ear mites aren't the problem, your dog probably has an ear infection or allergies (see page 219).

DANDRUFF ON THE MARCH

"My new puppy is itchy, and when I looked at her skin I thought she had dandruff, but then I saw the dandruff moving! Is it some kind of bug?"

Sounds like cheyletiella, also known as the "walking dandruff" mite. These mites can live on dogs, on cats, and unfortunately, on people. (If you develop an itchy rash after handling your infected puppy, tell your physician that you may have mites so that you can get the proper treatment.)

Cheyletiella mites generally are easy to get rid of using flea treatment: either a flea bath, dip, foam, or spray. Treat not only your affected puppy but also any other animals in the household, whether they have symptoms or not. Remember to read labels carefully to make sure the product is safe for puppies the age of the one you're treating, for cats if you have cats to treat, and so on.

Wash your pets' bedding and thoroughly vacuum the area where they sleep, sealing the vacuum cleaner bag and throwing it away in an outdoor garbage can as soon as you're finished. Unlike fleas, cheyletiella mites can live for only a few days off their animal host, so spraying or treating your entire house shouldn't be necessary to get rid of them. Mites and fleas can coexist on the same dog, though, so check your puppy carefully for fleas as well.

LICE—NOT NICE

"My five-year-old daughter has head lice. Could she have gotten it from our dogs?"

No, the dogs are not to blame for this one. The lice that people get don't like dogs, and vice versa. Your daughter got the lice from another person, or a hat or comb or pillowcase used by someone who has head lice. Dogs and cats can get their own types of lice, but lice in pets are far less common than fleas.

Pets are not responsible for the recent upsurge in bedbug (*Cimex*) infestations, either. Bedbugs live on and around mattresses and furniture, and come out to feed on their unwitting hosts at night. Bedbugs may bite dogs as well as people, but they don't live on animals and aren't spread by them.

If you've seen some sort of critter on your dogs, or you think they're being "bugged" by something because they're scratching a lot, take them to your vet so the bug or problem can be identified and treated appropriately.

A WORM THAT ISN'T

"Our neighbor's new kitten has ringworm. The kitten has been in our yard. Does this mean we should deworm our dog?"

No. Despite the name, ringworm is not a worm at all—it's a fungal infection of the skin. For more about symptoms and treatment of ringworm, see page 104.

MAGGOTS

"There's an old dog that lies around the stable where I board my horse. Yesterday he was gone, and the stable owner said he was at the vet's being treated for maggots! How does a dog get maggots?"

If an animal has a skin wound that goes untreated, flies may be attracted to the wound and lay their eggs there. The eggs hatch into fly larvae, or maggots, and the maggots feed on fluid and tissue in the wound. Dogs that live outdoors and are not handled or looked at regularly are the ones most likely to have this happen.

The maggots can be plucked off or killed with ivermectin, and by themselves they do no lasting harm. The real problem is the wound that attracted them in the first place, which sometimes can be difficult to treat if it's gone unnoticed for days or weeks. Your barn dog may have been lying around all the time because his hind legs were partially paralyzed from a spinal disc problem or other nerve injury. He may have been urinating and defecating where he lay and developed an infected skin wound from contact with the urine and feces.

Maggots are not something that's going to attack a dog that lives indoors and

is closely observed, handled, and petted each day. If you see a stray dog that has an obvious injury, or a "yard dog" that seems disabled, unkempt, or badly neglected, you would be doing that dog a great kindness by asking your local animal-control authorities to look into the situation.

GETTING RID OF TICKS

"My dog and I went hiking, and he came back covered with ticks—all different sizes and colors. What should I do?"

The easiest way to get rid of ticks, especially when there are a lot of them, is to put a Preventic collar or Frontline on your dog immediately. They will poison the ticks and make them all fall off within a day. Note that you need a *tick collar* that contains the active ingredient amitraz—a flea collar won't work—or a spot-on that's labeled for deer and dog ticks.

Of course, some of those poisoned ticks are going to fall off inside your house. So don't let your dog sleep on your bed for a couple of nights, and plan on vacuuming around his bed and washing his bedding a couple of times over the next few days to get rid of dead and dying ticks.

If a dog has just one or two ticks, then pulling them off manually is an option (see the following page). It's important to get ticks off your dog within 24 hours to prevent them from transmitting Lyme or other diseases.

LOOKING OUT FOR LYME

"My dog was bitten by some ticks while I was clearing brush out of our yard. How will I know whether she got Lyme disease?"

TICKED OFF!

If your dog has just two or three ticks and you want to pull them off, here's the best way to do it.

You'll need a pair of disposable vinyl or latex gloves (many supermarkets carry these, as well as drugstores), cotton balls, hydrogen peroxide, a pair of tweezers or a tick remover, rubbing alcohol, and a jar with a lid. Pour a half-inch of rubbing alcohol in the jar, and put on the gloves. Using cotton balls, soak the skin with hydrogen peroxide where the tick is attached. (This doesn't do anything to the tick but helps kill some of the bacteria on the skin.)

Using the tweezers or tick remover, gently grasp the tick as close to the dog's skin as possible, and pull steadily until the tick comes off. Do your best not to squeeze the tick's body while you're pulling, because you want to avoid squishing tick fluids into the dog's skin. Put the tick in the jar with the alcohol and cap it. Wipe the area where the tick was attached with a little more hydrogen peroxide to clean it.

Go over your dog carefully to make sure you haven't missed any ticks, and don't forget to check the head and face. Even if you think you've gotten all the ticks, it's not a bad idea to put a Preventic collar or Frontline on your dog afterward, just in case. Throw away the sealed tick jar when you're finished.

A bump or welt may appear on the dog's skin after you pull off the tick.

People often worry that this means the tick's head is stuck in the skin, but more often the bump is inflammation, like a mosquito bite. If the bumps seem to bother your dog, you can put cool compresses on them for five minutes at a time a couple of times a day until they subside. Don't apply any creams or ointments to bumps that your dog can lick, because lick them she will, which prevents the ointment from doing any good and may give her an upset stomach.

What if there *are* tick mouth parts stuck in the skin? Normally no special treatment is needed. Check the area once a day, and if the bump should become hot or painful, get considerably larger, or ooze blood or fluid, then have your vet take a look.

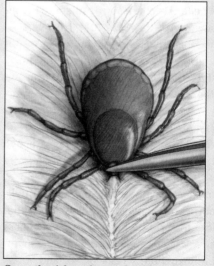

Grasp the tick as close to the skin as possible, and avoid squeezing as you pull.

WHICH TICK IS WHICH?

Not all kinds of ticks transmit Lyme disease. If you live in an area where Lyme disease is common, it's good to know what deer ticks—the ones that transmit Lyme—look like. But be aware that although all ticks don't carry Lyme disease, they can transmit other illnesses, such as anaplasmosis, Rocky Mountain spotted fever, ehrlichiosis, and babesiosis.

	AMERICAN DOG TICK		DEER TICK	
	PRE-FEEDING	ENGORGED	PRE-FEEDING	ENGORGED
ADULT				
NYMPH				

If you saw the ticks yourself, you can check the chart above to see whether they were the size of deer ticks—the ones that carry Lyme disease—or whether they were the larger dog ticks, which don't carry Lyme but can transmit other diseases (see page 173).

Also, if you managed to get the ticks off soon after they bit your dog, she's in good shape: ticks need to be attached and feeding for at least 24 hours in order to transmit Lyme.

If you're not sure what kind of ticks they were or how long they were on your dog, don't panic. Keep a close eye on her energy level, appetite, and behavior for the next three weeks or so, and whisk her to your vet if it seems like she's ADR (ain't doin' right). Common signs of Lyme disease include loss of energy, loss of appetite, fever, limping, or swollen joints. The disease can be confirmed with a blood test, and because it's caused by bacteria (*Borrelia burgdorferi*), it can be treated with antibiotics.

Lyme disease in dogs often can be cured if detected and treated early. Many vets run a 4Dx blood test annually to check dogs for exposure to heartworms, *Borrelia*, and two other bacteria transmitted by tick bites, *Ehrlichia canis* and *Anaplasma* (see page 174). A 4Dx test may be negative if a dog was bitten by an infected tick recently and hasn't yet developed antibodies against those organisms, so if your dog is limping and has a fever, your vet is likely to put her on an antibiotic regardless of the test result.

One severe potential complication of Lyme disease is kidney damage leading to protein loss in the urine. This is most often seen in dogs who were not diagnosed or treated within the first few months of infection. When a dog tests positive for exposure to Lyme, a vet will often check the urine for protein. Medications can help improve blood flow to the kidneys and slow the protein loss, but sometimes the kidney damage progresses to kidney failure and can be fatal (see page 335).

If your dog gets ticks more than once in a blue moon, you'd be smart to use an anti-tick product—such as a spot-on, spray, or collar—to protect her against the diseases that ticks carry. In areas where Lyme disease is a concern, make sure the product is labeled as effective against deer ticks and not just dog ticks. Ask your vet what times of the year ticks are most active in your part of the country, and use tick prevention during those months. A vaccine against Lyme disease is available and may be a good idea for dogs that frequently get ticks (see page 64).

BULL'S-EYE RASH

"Does a dog get a bull's-eye rash with Lyme disease, like people sometimes do? My Lab has a small red target on his stomach—no evidence of a tick, just the mark."

Occasionally, a dog will get a bull's-eye rash from a tick bite, but such a mark can have other causes too, ranging from minor (such as a mosquito bite, flea bite, or infected hair follicle) to more worrisome (such as a blood disorder). Your options are (1) watch your dog closely for spreading of the rash, more spots, or signs that he isn't feeling well; or (2) have your vet take a look at the bull's-eye (and the rest of the dog too, of course!)

and determine whether he needs testing or treatment. If your dog seems perfectly well otherwise—good energy, good appetite, no lameness—then waiting and watching for a few days is appropriate. If you're worried or just not sure that your dog is feeling well, however, by all means have your vet take a look.

TICKS THAT AREN'T

"I tried to pull a tick off my Sheltie's belly, and he yelped and tried to bite me. Now what?"

The first thing to do is make sure it's actually a tick. You'd be surprised how many people have taken tweezers to scabs, freckles, or nipples (yes, male dogs have nipples too, just like male people do). Identifying bumps can be especially difficult in furry dogs, like your Sheltie. So put down the tweezers and take a closer look, if your dog will let you.

Still sure that spot or bump is a tick? Or alternatively, not at all sure what the heck it is? Then apply Rule No. 1 for taking care of your dog at home: Don't get hurt. He's already tried to bite you once, so it's time to turn the job over to a professional. Call your vet's office and tell them that your dog *may* have a tick and that if it is, you'd like them to take it off. They won't mind a bit as long as you tell them *before* they reach for the dog that he may try to bite.

MORE TICK TROUBLE

"My dog got some ticks on him two weeks ago, but they weren't deer ticks so I didn't worry about Lyme. Then he got really sick, and the vet said it's tick-related. What other diseases do ticks carry?"

Ticks can cause several nasty problems other than Lyme disease. Fortunately, tests are available to confirm most of these diseases, and they can be treated. Symptoms usually appear one to four weeks after a tick bite. Here are the facts about six additional tick-borne diseases:

❏ **Rocky Mountain spotted fever (RMSF).** The name is highly misleading—many dogs don't get spots with RMSF, and it doesn't occur only in the Rockies. In fact, it's more common in the eastern states. RMSF is caused by bacteria (*Rickettsia rickettsii*) that attack the lining of blood vessels and make the blood vessels leaky. Symptoms can include fever, weakness, heavy breathing or a cough, a swollen face or legs, red eyes, or red or purplish bruises on the skin. (These bruises, which can be pinhead-size or larger, are the "spots" of RMSF, but not all dogs get them.) Blood tests are used to help confirm the disease. Dogs with RMSF often become severely ill, but the disease can be treated with antibiotics, and dogs often recover well if treated early.

❏ **Ehrlichiosis.** Like RMSF, this disease is caused by bacteria that affect the blood. Ehrlichiosis is most common in the southern and midwestern states, but it can occur anywhere. The symptoms are usually milder than those of RMSF. A dog may have a fever, lethargy, a loss of appetite, or sometimes a runny nose or eyes. The main signs are seen in the blood itself: a significant drop in the numbers of red blood cells, white blood cells, and platelets. A separate blood test confirms the disease, which is treated with antibiotics.

❏ **Anaplasmosis.** Dog owners may have heard of this disease via the 4Dx blood test, which many vets run as part of a dog's yearly physical exam. The 4Dx test checks for exposure to heartworms and three tick-borne infections: Lyme, anaplasmosis, and ehrlichiosis (specifically, the type caused by *Ehrlichia canis*). Often dogs who test positive for exposure to *Anaplasma* have no symptoms at all, or none that the owner has noticed. In other cases, anaplasmosis can cause a fever, sore joints, and decreased platelet and white blood cell counts. The disease usually responds well to treatment with the antibiotic doxycycline.

❏ **Southern Tick-Associated Rash Illness (STARI).** At this writing, STARI is primarily a human disease, but it has potential to spread to dogs as well. In people, STARI causes a rash, fever, and muscle and joint pain. It is caused by bacteria in the same family (*Borrelia*) as those that cause Lyme disease, and is spread primarily by the Lone Star tick. Lone Star ticks are most prevalent in the South and Southwest, but they have started to appear in the Northeast and other areas as well. All of the standard tick preventives (amitraz, fipronil, permethrin) are effective against Lone Star ticks.

❏ **Babesiosis.** This disease is caused by babesia—protozoa (one-celled organisms) that damage red blood cells—and is seen most often in the southern and southwestern states. Symptoms may include fever, weakness, loss of appetite, anemia, vomiting, or jaundice (a yellow tinge to the dog's skin or the whites of his eyes). Babesiosis is treated with an antiprotozoal drug such as imidocarb, along with intravenous fluids and occasionally blood transfusions. Treatment often can't clear all of the protozoa from a dog's body, and relapses can occur.

Two types of dogs are especially likely to have been exposed to babesia: Pit Bull Terriers in the South and Southwest, and former racing Greyhounds. The Greyhounds are believed to pass around babesia-infected ticks during their racetrack careers. Pit Bulls are more susceptible to infection with the protozoa for unknown reasons. Unless a Pit Bull or Greyhound is sick, is going to be bred, or is going to donate blood, there is no need to test the dog for babesia.

❏ **Tick paralysis.** Some ticks secrete a toxin that causes a dog to become progressively paralyzed from the hind legs forward over a few days. If the tick is not found and removed, the diaphragm and chest muscles may become paralyzed, and the dog will be unable to breathe on his own and will die unless he is placed on a ventilator. If the tick is removed, the dog usually recovers and is able to walk within a few days.

SALMON POISONING

"My dog and I just moved from the Midwest to Oregon. I've heard I have to watch out for something called salmon poisoning, but I'm not sure what it is."

Salmon poisoning is a well-known problem in the Pacific Northwest but is virtually unheard of anywhere else. Dogs can catch it from eating fresh-caught raw salmon or trout. Like the tick-borne diseases discussed above, it's caused by a parasite of a parasite: a protozoan parasite called *Neorickettsia* infecting a fluke (a wormlike parasite) that infects the fish. Symptoms are seen about a week after the dog eats the raw fish, and they are severe: vomiting, bloody diarrhea, and fever. Salmon poisoning can be fatal, especially if it's not treated right away with intravenous fluids, antibiotics, and other medicines as needed to control the symptoms.

How do you prevent salmon poisoning? By keeping your dog away from fresh-caught fish or fish parts. Cooking the fish kills the parasites, so only raw fish is a problem.

CHAPTER 7

Mental Health and Behavior Problems

DOGS ON PROZAC—who'd have guessed it would come to this? Only a few years ago, the notion of dogs with mental health issues was laughable. Now we know better. Part of this chapter addresses what are more commonly thought of as behavior problems, such as separation anxiety, barking, and biting. But some canine "behavior" problems have obvious parallels to human psychological issues—including obsessive-compulsive disorder and Alzheimer's—and these days, psychiatric medication may be part of the treatment plan. Considering the psychological aspects of your dog's behavior will help you to better understand his bad habits and counteract them before they drive both of you crazy.

NOISES OFF

"My Cocker Spaniel is petrified of thunderstorms and fireworks. She trembles and whines before I can even hear the thunder, tries to burrow into the closet, and urinates. I used to give her acepromazine when I knew a storm was coming and on the Fourth of July, but that makes her groggy without seeming to really ease the fear. Is there anything else I can do?"

Fear of loud noises, such as thunderstorms and fireworks, is the most common canine phobia. Like other phobias, it is best treated by desensitization: rewarding your dog for remaining calm as you slowly and gradually get her accustomed to the noise.

You can use a CD or video of a thunderstorm or fireworks for desensitization. You'll need to start with the volume extremely low—perhaps even lower than *you* can hear—and turn it up gradually over many sessions (see page 180 for more details on this process). Play with your dog or otherwise reward her

A dog with a noise phobia may cower, hide, or urinate during thunderstorms and fireworks displays.

for remaining calm, but be sure you're not "reassuring" her when she trembles or otherwise shows fear. Dogs interpret someone fussing over them and saying "It's OK, it's OK, don't be scared" as a reward for being frightened.

Acepromazine is a heavy-duty tranquilizer that was the best veterinary medicine had to offer for many years for relief of thunderstorm phobias, car sickness, and so on. These days, however, antianxiety medications are a much better choice (see page 185). Unlike acepromazine, an antianxiety medication such as alprazolam (Xanax) doesn't sedate the dog. Antianxiety medications should be given one hour before the "aversive stimulus" (the thunderstorm or fireworks display) whenever possible. At a minimum, they have to be given *before* a dog begins to show signs of anxiety (such as trembling, whining, or hiding) in order to have any effect. Antianxiety medications work best when combined with desensitization, as described above.

For alternative-medicine options for treating noise phobias, see page 196.

A MOUNTING CONCERN

"My parents recently adopted a young female terrier mix from a shelter. But when I visited their house recently, the dog mounted my leg. I thought only male dogs did that. Do you think there's something wrong with this dog?"

Probably not. Mounting is a dominance behavior as well as part of the sex act, and normal female dogs will sometimes mount another dog—or a person's leg—and perform very convincing pelvic thrusts. Even puppies who haven't yet reached puberty can show this behavior.

The best way to stop a leg-humper is to distract him or her with another activity. Try tossing a toy across the room for the dog to retrieve, or call her into the kitchen and ask her to sit or lie down for a dog treat.

THE VELCRO DOG

"Help! My dog is going to get me kicked out of my apartment. My neighbors have complained that whenever I leave her in the apartment, she barks, howls, and scratches at the door nonstop. When I'm home, she follows me from room to room as if she were stuck to my leg. What can I do?"

Your dog has separation anxiety, which is epidemic these days because so many dogs are left home alone while their human companions go to work or school. Dogs are social creatures—pack animals—and they're not naturally equipped to handle being left behind.

If you have to leave your dog home every day when you go to work, for example, first brainstorm whether you can provide her with companionship at least part of the time. Can you enroll her in "doggie daycare," where she'll have other dogs to play with? Can she stay with a friend or relative while you work? Can a dog walker take her out for an hour in the middle of the day? Adopting another dog or cat to provide your dog companionship is not an appropriate option at this point; your dog's separation anxiety has already become a habit, and the presence of another dog isn't going to change her behavior. In fact, the second dog might simply chime in with his own barking and howling.

Regardless of whether you can find alternatives for leaving your dog alone regularly for long stretches of time, you should also implement the following behavior modification plan. She is going to have to be alone at least some of the time, and you, she, and your neighbors will all be happier if you can ease her anxiety.

❏ Give your dog 30 minutes to 1 hour of aerobic exercise each day (see page 192).

❏ Work on basic obedience commands (come, sit, sit-stay, down, down-stay) for 15 or 20 minutes each day. Use rewards for compliance (praise, a quick pat on the chest, a food treat) rather than reprimands or punishment for lack of compliance. If you need help getting consistent obedience from your dog, work with a professional trainer.

❏ Wean your "Velcro dog" from being attached to you at all times when you're home. Use a baby gate to barricade her in a separate room for part of the time when you're home.

❏ Provide her with a delicious distraction, such as a Kong toy stuffed with a food treat (peanut butter is a popular Kong stuffer) while she's by herself. You can also use a "down-stay" or "get in your bed" command to put some distance between you.

❏ Ignore her for 20 minutes before you leave and 20 minutes after you return. Effusive goodbyes and hellos make a dog with separation anxiety feel worse.

❏ When you leave her alone, don't give her the run of the house or apartment. Instead, use a baby gate to confine her to one room, such as the bedroom, bathroom, or kitchen—wherever she's least likely to do damage or disturb the neighbors. Leave a radio or TV on

UNLEARNING FEARS AND PHOBIAS

Like people, dogs can develop a seemingly infinite number of fears and phobias. Technically speaking, a fear is based on direct personal experience, while a phobia is not: a dog who was once left outdoors during a violent storm may have a *fear* of thunderstorms, but any dog can have a thunderstorm *phobia*. Fortunately, the treatment is essentially the same for fears and phobias, so we don't need to explore a dog's memories of puppyhood before we can help. I'll use the word "fear" from here on as shorthand for fear or phobia.

Before addressing the mental part of a fear, it's important to consider whether there's any physical component. A dog who is frightened of stairs, especially one who develops that fear later in life, may have arthritis or a sore back that makes navigating stairs difficult and painful. A dog who is suddenly afraid of dark rooms or shadows may have developed a vision problem. In such cases, treating the physical component is the first step in treating the fear.

Unlearning the fear is next. Psychologists describe two basic methods for this: flooding and desensitization.

Flooding is immersing the dog in the very thing he fears in hopes that he'll realize it's not so scary. This is like putting a child who is afraid of clowns on a float in the middle of a clown parade: the child will either decide clowns are not so bad, or he'll freak out completely. Flooding should never be used when a dog is afraid of something that is, in fact, dangerous. In other words, don't throw a dog who's afraid of water into the deep end of a swimming pool. I recommend flooding primarily as a treatment for separation anxiety (see page 179).

Desensitization is slow, gradual exposure to the feared object or situation. It takes time and patience on the dog owner's part but can be wonderfully effective. The basic idea is to bring the dog closer and closer to what he fears—usually over days or weeks—while rewarding him for remaining calm. Ideally, desensitization sessions are held once or twice a day for about a half hour. Each session should end while the dog is still comfortable and not frightened.

For example, desensitization for a dog who is afraid of men might go like this: the dog's owner would take him to

very low to provide distracting background noise.
- Do not leave a dog with separation anxiety in a closed crate. Many dogs with separation anxiety have panic attacks when crated and will injure their mouths or front feet trying to bite or claw their way out of the crate.
- Don't use an anti-bark collar (see page

193). It's unlikely to work on a dog with separation anxiety.
- Start a program of desensitization or "flooding" (see the box above). Flooding for separation anxiety would involve setting aside several hours on a weekend during which you enter and leave your apartment so often that you essentially wear the dog out. Leave

a pleasant spot, such as a quiet bench in the park. By prior arrangement, a male friend of the dog's owner would walk past at a distance and say hello: "Hi, Susan. Hi, Sparky." "Hi, Tom." Tom should be far enough away that it's unlikely Sparky will be alarmed, and Susan should be relaxed and calm and pet Sparky quietly as long as Sparky remains calm. Tom can pass by a few more times at the same distance, then the first session is over.

In subsequent sessions, Tom passes by a little closer each time. Ultimately, he sits on the opposite end of the park bench and gives Susan a delicious dog treat to give to Sparky.

Extreme caution must be used in desensitizing a dog who is afraid of people. The human assistants in such situations should be adults who are familiar with dogs and dog training and are comfortable with your dog. You can hire a professional trainer as an assistant if need be. Settle on a reasonable goal before starting desensitization. If your dog is afraid of children or infants, that goal might be for the dog to sit beside you calmly while a child runs past six feet away. Asking a child-averse dog to tolerate a bear hug from a three-year-old is neither safe nor necessary.

the apartment every few minutes, on a varying schedule, for a minute or two at a time, then come back. Be sure not to return *while* your dog is barking or howling, or else you will be rewarding her for that behavior. If it's impossible to walk out the door without having your dog bark, you might have a friend remain in the apartment while you go in

and out. Desensitization for a dog with separation anxiety involves giving her your customary cues that you're leaving—such as picking up your car keys or briefcase, opening the coat closet, putting on your "work shoes," and so on—without actually leaving.

❏ A DAP diffuser or collar may help calm an anxious dog (see page 197).
❏ An antidepressant may be helpful for a dog with separation anxiety (see page 185). Clomicalm (clomipramine) is widely used for that purpose. In severe cases and for occasional use, an anti-anxiety medication can also be given one hour before your departure. No drug can extinguish separation anxiety on its own, however. Desensitization is essential.
❏ For alternative-medicine remedies for separation anxiety, see page 196.

"ALZHEIMER'S" IN DOGS

"Do some dogs get senile when they get older? What are the symptoms? Is there any treatment?"

Some dogs do develop a sort of Alzheimer's disease as they get older. The veterinary term for it is canine cognitive dysfunction (CCD). The symptoms can include failure to recognize familiar locations or people, wandering or pacing, restlessness at night, and loss of housebreaking. Because there aren't any practical ways to test a dog's thinking ability, CCD is diagnosed by ruling out physical explanations for the symptoms, such as failing eyesight or blindness, a urinary tract infection, or pain that causes the dog to feel irritable and distracted.

The drug Anipryl (selegiline/deprenyl) reduces the symptoms of CCD in some dogs. Other dogs are either not helped by Anipryl or show an increase in symptoms such as restlessness and trembling. Anipryl should not be given to a dog who is taking either phenylpropanolamine (for urinary incontinence) or an antidepressant, because the combination of drugs can produce extreme restlessness and agitation. A dog taking Anipryl should not use a Preventic collar or other products that contain amitraz.

Melatonin is a natural supplement that's often recommended for dogs who display sleeplessness, restlessness, or agitation at night, but it shouldn't be used in diabetic dogs. See page 196 for other alternative-medicine options for treating canine cognitive dysfunction.

There's also a prescription dog food designed to fight aging changes in the brain. Hill's Prescription Diet Canine b/d contains antioxidants, brain-specific fatty acids, and other nutrients to help slow the breakdown of brain cells. A research study showed that normal dogs fed b/d were able to learn new tasks more quickly than dogs fed a regular diet. At this writing, b/d was too new on the market for its success rate in dogs with CCD to be clear-cut, but its freedom from side effects puts it in the "couldn't hurt, might help" category.

UNDERSTANDING AGGRESSION

"When I took my Chihuahua to the vet for a nail trim, the assistant asked me whether he was aggressive. I said of course not, she tried to pick him up, and he growled and snapped at her. The girl jerked her hand back and said to me, 'Not aggressive, huh?' in a nasty tone, and I got mad and left. What was her problem?"

To quote from *Cool Hand Luke*, "What we have here is a failure to communicate." It sounds as though the assistant thought she was asking you whether your dog might try to bite her, and you thought she was asking whether he was a vicious beast—so you said no. Then he growled and snapped, and she was startled and angry at you for not warning her.

This sort of misunderstanding over canine aggression is extremely common in vets' offices and, I'm sure, anywhere else that strangers are called upon to handle dogs. Aggression is a natural canine personality trait—all dogs have it to some degree and will show it under certain circumstances. Yet because people tend to equate aggression with dogs that are "mean" or "bad," they sometimes misinterpret or downplay the signals their own dogs send. If you ignore an aggressive signal, such as a growl, and you continue the behavior the dog is objecting to, he may escalate to a nip to get his point across. For the record, then, the following are all signs of aggression:

❑ Lifting a lip, snarling, or growling.
❑ Snapping (without making contact).
❑ Nipping (biting without breaking the skin).
❑ Biting.
❑ Barking and lunging at a person or animal.
❑ Refusing to let a person approach or pick up a food dish, toy, treat, or other prized possession.

These behaviors need to be put in context to fully understand what the dog is saying. Under what specific circumstances does the dog growl, snap, or bite? Toward which people or animals is the behavior directed? The context determines what category the aggression falls into, and the category determines the treatment.

The five most common categories of canine aggression are described in the following Q&As: (1) dominance aggression ("Who's the Boss?"); (2) fear aggression ("Sneak Attack"); (3) territorial aggression ("Protectiveness Run Amok"); (4) predatory aggression ("Like Cats and Dogs" and "Bringing Home Baby"); and (5) "sibling rivalry," or aggression between dogs in one household ("Cain and Abel"). A dog can show more than one type of aggression—for example, a dominant-aggressive dog can also be territorial. In such cases, either the treatments for the two types of aggression can be combined, or the type that's causing the most serious problems can be treated first, and the other later if it is still a concern.

WHO'S THE BOSS?

"Our two-year-old Husky is friendly and easygoing most of the time, but when my wife tries to push him off the couch or our bed he growls, and

A head collar won't prevent biting but does make many dogs calmer and more obedient.

once, when she went to put something in his food bowl while he was eating, he snapped at her. How should we handle this?"

Your dog is showing classic signs of dominance aggression. He's a happy, friendly guy as long as he's getting what he wants, but when your wife tries to horn in on his territory, no more Mr. Nice Guy.

Dogs don't understand equality or democracy; they're accustomed to a linear power structure. Your dog has decided that he's either No. 2 in your household (after you and before your wife) or possibly even No. 1 (before both you *and* your wife). You need to change the way you treat him so he realizes he's not the boss of anyone in your house.

Notice I didn't say you need to "show him who's boss." Punishing him, yelling, or engaging in a battle of wills will make matters worse: a dominant-aggressive dog will interpret the escalating conflict as an invitation to full-scale warfare for the position of top dog. Instead, implement the following behavior modification program:

❑ Give your dog at least one hour of aerobic exercise each day (see page 192). Avoid games that are battles for control, however, such as wrestling or playing tug-of-war with dog toys.
❑ Consider using a head collar (two brands are Gentle Leader and Halti) with your dog (see page 188).
❑ You and your wife should each work with your dog separately on obedience commands (come, sit, sit-stay, down, down-stay) for 15 or 20 minutes each day. Use rewards for compliance (praise, a quick pat on the chest, a food treat) rather than reprimands or

punishment for lack of compliance. If you need help getting consistent obedience from your dog, work with a professional trainer.

❏ Institute a "no free lunch" policy. Ask your dog to perform a simple task (come-sit, or sit-stay) before you feed him, pet him, play with him, or take him outside. This emphasizes that you are the boss of all the goodies in your house.

❏ Your wife should feed the dog (requiring a come-sit or sit-stay first) to show him that she's in charge of the food and does in fact outrank him.

❏ Don't allow the dog on the couch or your bed—this "elevates" his status. Rather than reprimanding him or pushing him off, however, distract him by asking for a different, pleasant behavior, such as going outside, coming into the kitchen for a food treat, or playing with a toy.

❏ Avoid overtly challenging your dog, such as by trying to take away his food dish while he's eating. If a situation should arise where he growls or threatens you anyway, don't scold or punish him—instead, turn and leave the area quietly and ignore him completely.

❏ Don't pet him when he asks you to by leaning against your leg or nuzzling your hand. He's not politely asking for your attention, he's *demanding* it, which reinforces his dominance. Instead, surprise him by calling him to you for a pat when he's not expecting it.

❏ If a dominant-aggressive dog engages in power struggles with children, remember that most children don't have the maturity, consistency, and strength to work with a difficult dog. The adults in the household should work with the dog on behavior modification, and the

A basket muzzle allows a dog to breathe, pant, and even drink water, but not bite.

children should be taught to leave the dog alone. If you have any concerns that your dog might snap at a child, he should wear a basket muzzle whenever contact with children can't be avoided (see page 188).

❏ A DAP collar or diffuser may help calm a dominant dog (see page 197).

❏ An antidepressant or anti-obsessive drug helps some dominant-aggressive dogs respond better to behavior modification (see the box on the following page).

SNEAK ATTACK

"My five-year-old Peke-a-Poo is the sweetest dog in the world to me and my roommate, but if anyone else comes over, she barks hysterically at the door and then runs and hides. She has even hidden under the dining room table and nipped at our guests' feet! How can we get her to stop?"

What you're describing is fear aggression. A fear-aggressive dog will cower, hide, growl, snap, or bite when people approach her, reach for her, or touch her.

DOES THAT PUPPY NEED PROZAC?

Talking to people about psychiatric drugs for dogs tends to provoke a strong response of one kind or another. Some people think giving a dog an antidepressant or anti-anxiety pill is ridiculous. Others believe it borders on animal abuse. And yet a third group are thrilled to imagine there's a pill out there that could magically cure their dogs' behavior problems.

Here's the reality: there are no magic pills for behavior problems. Resolving a behavior problem requires, first and foremost, behavior modification—for the dog *and* for the owner. As an adjunct to behavior modification, certain psychiatric drugs can help *some* dogs with *some* behavior problems, but no drug can work a miracle cure on its own.

The Q&As in this chapter provide behavior-modification plans and list types of drugs that may be helpful in treating those behavior issues. Below are examples of psychiatric drugs that are used in dogs. They should be used only as prescribed by your veterinarian.

Anti-anxiety medications: Alprazolam (Xanax), buspirone (BuSpar), diazepam (Valium)

Antidepressants: Fluoxetine (Reconcile, Prozac), amitriptyline (Elavil), clomipramine (Clomicalm), sertraline (Zoloft), paroxetine (Paxil)

Anti-obsessives: Clomipramine (Clomicalm), fluoxetine (Reconcile, Prozac), naltrexone

"Canine Alzheimer's" medication: Selegiline/deprenyl (Anipryl)

Some fear-aggressive dogs are scared of all strangers; others are frightened of a specific category of people, such as children, men, or even people of a certain skin color or people wearing hats.

To get your dog to stop barking and biting, you need to help her overcome her fear of people. Use the following behavior-modification plan:

❑ Make sure she gets 30 minutes to 1 hour of vigorous exercise each day.

❑ Work with your dog on obedience commands (come, sit, sit-stay, down, down-stay) for 15 or 20 minutes each day. Use rewards for compliance (praise, a quick pat on the chest, a food treat) rather than reprimands or

punishment for lack of compliance. If you need help getting consistent obedience from your dog, work with a professional trainer.

❑ Begin desensitizing your dog to people coming into your home, using the guidelines on page 180. Until she can calmly accept visitors, use a baby gate to keep her in a separate room when you have company.

❑ A DAP diffuser or collar may help calm a fearful dog (see page 197).

❑ If your dog's fear aggression is severe, an antidepressant may be helpful during behavior modification, plus an anti-anxiety drug to be given as directed by your vet—for example, one hour before you are expecting guests for a dinner party. For alternative-medicine options for treating fear, see page 196.

❑ Don't scold or punish a fear-aggressive dog or force her to let someone pet her. Doing so will increase her fear rather than decrease it, and may make her bite.

PROTECTIVENESS RUN AMOK

"I used to leave my four-year-old Lab in my fenced yard during the day, but my neighbors complained that he would run along the fence barking at anyone who walked past. So I put him inside, and then he broke my living room window by jumping against it when he saw the FedEx guy across the street. Now what?"

Your dog is displaying territorial aggression by launching a vociferous attack against anyone who comes near your yard or house. Some territorial-aggressive dogs also overreact to other dogs walking past, or even to cars driving by too slowly. Many territorial-aggressive dogs also go berserk when they're left in a parked car and someone walks past.

Guarding is a natural behavior for some dogs. Many dog owners appreciate being warned of legitimate threats, but wish to narrow their dogs' definition of an intruder or scale back the response. Use the following behavior-modification plan for the territorial-aggressive dog:

❑ Give your dog at least one hour of *accompanied* vigorous exercise each day. Letting him run around your fenced yard, barking at the neighbors, doesn't count as exercise.

❑ Work with your dog on obedience commands (come, sit, sit-stay, down, down-stay) for 15 or 20 minutes each day. Use rewards for compliance (praise, a quick pat on the chest, a food treat) rather than reprimands or punishment for lack of compliance. If you need help getting consistent obedience from your dog, work with a professional trainer.

❑ Don't leave him alone in the yard or car.

❑ When you leave him in the house alone, shut him in a quiet room—perhaps at the back of the house—where he'll be less likely to hear or see passersby. If the room has windows he can reach, you can block them with sheets of plywood or fiberboard. Leave a radio or TV on quietly to help block outside noise, and leave your dog with a delicious treat, such as a Kong toy stuffed with a little peanut butter or Cheez Whiz.

❑ Start a desensitization program to reward your dog for remaining quiet and calm as people, dogs, or cars come closer to your yard and house (see page 180).

❑ If your dog barks excessively when the doorbell rings, reward the initial bark by quickly saying, "Good dog! Come get a biscuit," and giving him a treat. Your goal is to get him to bark once or twice and then wait quietly for his treat.

❑ Don't yell at a barking dog to "be quiet" or "shut up." Your shouts sound like barking to him, and he'll simply think you're joining in the attack on the intruder.

❑ Some territorial-aggressive dogs become even more violent when their owners have them on a leash or grab them by the collar, again because the

FOLLOW THE LEADER

Canine social structure is much simpler than human social structure. One dog is in charge, followed by the second in command, third in command, fourth in command, and so on. Each dog defers to all the dogs who outrank him, and takes precedence over all the dogs he outranks, in terms of valuable commodities such as food. The pack leader—also known as the top dog, or alpha dog—makes decisions for the pack, and the other pack members follow. Squabbles among dogs in the ranks are minor once the basic chain of command is established.

Dogs are amenable to forming the same type of social structure with their human companions. The key to having a well-behaved dog is to make sure *you*—not the dog—are the pack leader. Both you and your dog will be more relaxed and content when it's clear exactly who's in charge.

People fortunately have some built-in advantages to help them claim alpha status. We provide our dogs with food; we're the ones who open doors to permit them access to the fabulous outdoors; and we're taller than they are. Basic obedience training, such as teaching a dog to come, walk calmly on a leash, sit, and stay, solidifies our position as pack leader. Establishing a "no free lunch" policy also helps get the point across: require your dog's attention and obedience to a simple command, such as "Sit," before feeding him, petting him, playing with him, or opening the door to let him outside.

All the people in the household—not just the pack leader—need to outrank the dog so that he doesn't bully or otherwise disrespect them (see page 183). If there is more than one dog in the household, they will get along best if their own chain of command is clear, so it's best not to expect or try to enforce equality of rank between dogs. Instead, support the most likely candidate for "top dog" (see page 192).

dogs think their owners are joining them in the fight. If your dog reacts that way and you are expecting guests, for example, put the dog in a room with a baby gate across the doorway *before* your guests arrive so you won't have to haul your dog away from the door by the collar when the doorbell rings.

❏ A DAP collar or diffuser may help calm a territorial dog (see page 197).

❏ An antidepressant or anti-obsessive drug helps some territorial dogs respond better to behavior modification (see page 185).

LIKE CATS AND DOGS

"I'm moving in with a wonderful guy who has two indoor cats. My five-year-old shepherd mix has never been around cats, but she's obsessed with chasing squirrels. Do we have to worry about her hurting the cats? What's the best way to introduce them to one another?"

EQUIPPED FOR SAFETY

Behavior problems require behavior modification, which is nothing more than super-smart, super-targeted dog training. Depending on the dog's specific behavior issues, certain equipment can make the training easier and safer for all concerned. People sometimes misunderstand the function or purpose of such hardware, however, so here's an explanation of how these tools are used to treat behavior problems:

BABY GATE. A baby gate is a 30-inch-high barrier that can be used to block a doorway or stairs. It can be used to separate a predatory-aggressive dog from a baby or the household cats or to confine dogs with separation anxiety to a smaller area when they're alone. If your dog is tall enough or athletic enough to vault over a standard baby gate, you can find extra-tall gates in most dog-supply catalogs.

MUZZLE. A comfortable, well-fitted muzzle is an essential piece of equipment for any dog who has unavoidable encounters with people or animals she might bite. Behavior modification can lessen the likelihood of a dog's biting someone, but the consequences of a dog bite—physical, psychological, and legal—are simply too grave to take any risk. A basket muzzle is the type that's needed. These have a metal or plastic basket that fits loosely over the dog's nose and mouth and fastens with a strap around the neck (see illustration on page 184). A dog wearing a basket muzzle can still open her mouth a little, pant, and even drink water, but can't bite through the mesh. A potential biter should wear a basket muzzle whenever she might come in contact with an infant, child, or other likely target. Basket muzzles come in a variety of sizes and can be found in some pet-supply stores and virtually all pet-supply catalogs.

The other type of muzzle—a fabric or leather cuff that fits tightly around the jaws—isn't comfortable or safe for a dog to wear for more than 10 minutes or

Many dogs get along just fine with cats, and vice versa, but it's best to be cautious about the introduction just in case. Certain dogs seem to regard cats as prey rather than housemates, and unfortunately, you can't predict what your dog's reaction will be without direct experience. Many dogs will chase squirrels, a cat, or any other animal that darts across their path, but that alone doesn't tell you how strong their predatory drive is or how they regard cats overall. Some dogs will even go after "stranger" cats outside but get along fine with their "own" cats indoors. So you should plan on making the introduction and acclimation safe and gradual. Keep in mind the worst-case scenario—otherwise sweet-tempered dogs have been known to kill a cat—and you won't take the situation for granted. Here are some guidelines for preparing your dog to meet her new housemates:

so at a time. In order to stop a dog from biting, it has to be tight enough to prevent her from opening her mouth at all, which means she can't pant and could become dangerously overheated.

HALTER-TYPE HEAD COLLAR. Gentle Leader and Halti are two brand names for these nylon collars that fit on a dog's head like a horse halter (see illustration on page 183). Their original purpose was to help train "pullers" to walk quietly on a loose leash. Then trainers and dog behaviorists discovered a beneficial side effect: wearing a head collar seems to make some dogs calmer and more responsive to obedience commands even when there's no leash attached. The head collar must fit properly, and both the dog and the person on the other end of the leash must be trained how to use it, but the head collars come with detailed instructions, or the dog owner can learn the ropes from a dog trainer. Remember that a head halter is *not* a muzzle, so although it may have a calming effect on a dog with aggressive leanings, it will not prevent the dog from biting.

1. Outfit your dog with a head collar (see the box above) and have her wear it indoors as well as outside.
2. Work with your dog on obedience commands (come, sit, sit-stay, down, down-stay) for 15 or 20 minutes each day. Use rewards for compliance (praise, a quick pat on the chest, a food treat) rather than reprimands or punishment for lack of compliance.
3. Give your dog an hour of aerobic exercise each day.

4. Before you move in together, take your dog to your boyfriend's house, keeping her on a leash the whole time, and see how she reacts to the cats. If she's interested but not stalking them or lunging or snapping at them, that's a positive beginning.
5. Establish a "dog's room" when you move in and—for the first couple of weeks at least—confine your dog in that room, with a baby gate across the door, anytime you aren't holding her leash and supervising her interactions with the cats. Use a baby gate rather than a solid door so that your dog can see the cats walking around, and you can observe her reactions to them. Using a DAP collar or diffuser for the dog and placing a Feliway diffuser near the dog's room for the cats may help calm and soothe the new housemates (see page 197).
6. If after a couple of weeks the dog and cats are pretty much ignoring each other, then you can cautiously give your dog more freedom by letting her off the leash inside while you're still supervising her.
7. If after a couple of weeks your dog is stalking, lunging at, or otherwise menacing the cats whenever she sees them, she is a definite threat to them, and you have a tough decision to make. For the cats' safety, either your dog must wear a basket muzzle in the house at all times, or you must find a good home elsewhere for one or the other.

BRINGING HOME BABY

"I'm pregnant with my first child, and my mother-in-law is scared to death that our dog, a lovable and well-trained Rottweiler, might hurt the baby. Do we need to be concerned

about this? What should we do to prepare the dog for our baby's arrival?"

The problem with dogs and infants is that dogs don't see infants as people, exactly. Infants look different, smell different, sound different, and move differently than older children and adults. They don't even stand on two legs like people do, so for all a dog knows, an infant could be some interesting variety of squirrel or rabbit. For that reason, *all* dog owners should be cautious when introducing a baby into the household. It's possible, though blessedly rare, for even a well-behaved family dog to display predatory aggression toward an infant, so don't take your dog's acceptance of the new arrival for granted. Here's what you can do to prepare, starting now, before the baby is born:

❑ Outfit your dog with a head collar and have him wear it even indoors when you're home.

❑ Give him at least one hour per day of aerobic exercise.

❑ Practice obedience commands (come, sit, sit-stay, down, down-stay) for 15 or 20 minutes each day. Use rewards for compliance (praise, a quick pat on the chest, a food treat) rather than reprimands or punishment for lack of compliance. If you need help getting consistent obedience from your dog, work with a professional trainer.

❑ Put a baby gate across the door to the baby's room while you're still pregnant so your dog gets used to the idea that the room is off-limits to him. A DAP diffuser near the baby's room or a DAP collar may help calm him (see page 197).

❑ While you're in the hospital with the new baby, have your husband take home a shirt the baby has worn for the dog to smell so the dog can work out some of his new-odor interest before the baby gets home.

❑ When you arrive home with the new baby, have your husband carry the infant into the house so that you are unencumbered and can greet your dog the way you ordinarily would if you'd been away from home for a couple of days.

❑ To introduce the dog to the baby, sit on the couch holding the baby comfortably in your arms while your husband brings the dog over on a leash. Talk to the dog and pet him while he smells the baby's feet. Don't encourage him to nuzzle or lick the baby; the less contact between a dog and a newborn, the better.

❑ If your dog clamors for attention when you feed or change the baby, for example, keep some pleasant distractions—such as a Kong toy stuffed with a little peanut butter or Cheez Whiz—nearby, ask your dog for a "down-stay," and give him the treat to occupy him while you take care of the baby.

❑ Never turn your back on the baby when she's on the floor, the couch, or anywhere else the dog could reach her.

❑ If your dog should show any signs of aggression toward the baby—stalking, prolonged staring, growling, or incessant efforts to get close to the baby or into the baby's room—call a veterinary behaviorist for an emergency appointment and make doubly sure to keep your dog and the baby apart until your appointment.

❑ A dog who is known to be fearful or anxious around babies or small children would also benefit from desensitization (see page 180), and possibly an antidepressant starting two months or so before the baby's arrival (see page 185).

THAT "GUILTY LOOK"

Two of the most common negative assumptions people make about dog behavior are that (1) dogs know when they've done something wrong, and (2) dogs sometimes do bad things on purpose to get back at their owners. In fact, the human emotions guilt and spite are not part of the canine repertoire. Understanding what your dog is *really* telling you with that "guilty look" or misbehavior will defuse your anger and help you deal with the situation more appropriately.

Say you come home from the movies to discover that your dog has strewn the contents of the kitchen garbage can all over the floor. Your dog greets you at the door with his head down, his ears back, and his tail low and wagging slowly. He's telling you he feels guilty, because he knows he shouldn't have gotten into the garbage, right?

Wrong. What his posture is really saying is he's happy to see you, but he knows you're angry at him—from your tense, jerky body movements, explosive sigh, or tone of voice, or because you've been mad at him before when you first get home. He doesn't know *why* you're angry at him this time, nor does he understand and remember everything you don't want him to do.

Can you explain the problem to him by pointing angrily at the mess and saying "Bad dog!"? Nope. "The evidence" and the behavior that put it there aren't connected in a dog's brain. That's why it's pointless to pun-ish a dog for a misdeed after the fact. He won't make the connection.

So what should you do when you come home to find garbage on the floor? Remember that your dog doesn't know what he did wrong, greet him neutrally, clean up the mess, and resolve to lock up the kitchen garbage can more securely the next time you go out.

Then there's the "spite" scenario. You return to your apartment after a rare evening out, greet your Yorkshire Terrier with a cuddle and a dog biscuit, and climb into bed—only to sit squarely on the wet spot where your Yorkie has urinated while you were out.

The dog urinated *on your bed*. Clearly she's getting back at you for leaving her home alone, right? Wrong again. She may dislike being left alone, it's true, but she did not consciously choose a medium (urine) and a location (your side of the bed) to get her point across. A more likely interpretation is that she got on your bed because it's comfortable and comforting, and she urinated out of separation anxiety, not spite.

What should you do about a dog who urinates, defecates, or is destructive when left alone? Remember that the dog is not doing it to get back at you. Remember that punishing her for something she did as little as five minutes ago is pointless. And use the behavior modification plan for dogs with separation anxiety described on page 179.

CAIN AND ABEL

"I recently adopted a younger dog to keep my five-year-old Lab mix company, but instead, they're constantly getting into fights. Both are neutered males. I scold the older dog and try to protect the younger one, but it doesn't seem to help."

It's often called "sibling rivalry"—dogs living together in one household who frequently and persistently fight over food, toys, being petted, and other desirable commodities. The underlying problem is that the dogs haven't figured out which of them is "top dog" in their relationship. By favoring and supporting the newer, younger, smaller member of the pack, you have inadvertently confused the situation further.

People often feel they should root for the underdog in such conflicts, but that is precisely the *wrong* thing to do. Instead, you should reflect on which dog is the likely pack leader and support *him* by feeding him first, petting him first, putting on his leash first, and taking his part in any petty squabbles between the

Standing stiffly and staring are signs of dominance; a lowered head and a sidelong glance signal submission.

dogs. Your vote of confidence in the top dog will help stabilize the pack structure and minimize fighting between the dogs.

Which of your dogs is the top dog? Usually it's the dog who is more dominant and persistent and is in the bloom of adult health—neither a puppy nor a senior dog. Because your Lab mix is larger, in his prime, and was there first, I'm guessing he's the more dominant of the two, but if you're not sure, you can ask an experienced dog trainer or veterinary behavior specialist to observe the dogs and decide.

DAP diffusers or collars may help calm the siblings (see page 197). If one or both dogs is naturally fearful or anxious, an antidepressant might also help (see page 185). For alternative-medicine remedies for anxiety, see page 196.

Unfortunately, sometimes two dogs simply will not get along despite their owner's best efforts at stabilizing the situation. In such situations, a dog can be seriously injured or even killed by a rival housemate. If your dogs continue to fight "for keeps" and not just for show—inflicting deep bite wounds rather than just snarling, barking, posturing, and nipping at one another—then you must keep them strictly separated when you are not there to supervise their interactions, or else find a more congenial home for one of them.

TOO TIRED FOR TROUBLE

"My three-year-old Border Collie mix is basically a nice dog, but sometimes he practically bounces off the walls. Is there any way I can tone down his energy a notch?"

I have the perfect treatment for you. It's highly effective, widely available, and costs next to nothing. What's this miracle cure, you ask? Exercise.

A tired dog is a good dog, but most dogs get nowhere near enough exercise to keep them content. Depending on his age, fitness, and energy level, even a relative couch potato of a dog should get a minimum of 30 minutes of aerobic exercise each day, such as jogging, swimming, or playing tag or fetch. The average Lab, Border Collie, or terrier—to name just a few high-energy breeds—will do better with one to two hours of vigorous exercise per day. (Large-breed puppies who are still growing, however, need low-impact exercise to protect their joints—see page 50.)

Exercise can help reduce virtually every behavior problem in the book. If you have a dog who's hyperactive, neurotic, or troubled and you feel you can accomplish nothing else, give him plenty of vigorous exercise and a 10-minute obedience lesson every day. You'll both be happier and more relaxed for the effort.

THE SHOCKING TRUTH

"Our dog barks constantly. I'd like to try a shock collar to stop the barking, but my wife says they're cruel. What do you think?"

Collars that deliver electric shocks are widely marketed for a variety of purposes: as an "invisible fence" to keep a dog from leaving his yard, a deterrent to nuisance barkers, or an aid to obedience training. If a shock collar cured bad behavior as easily as flipping a light switch, every dog owner would want one, despite the often hefty price tag. But the results are far from instantaneous or universal. Before you shell out

the money for a shock collar, be sure you understand the behavior you're trying to extinguish and what the collar might or might not accomplish.

First, a word about safety. Invisible fences and shock collars are not physically harmful for most dogs. But a handful of dogs have died from them, either because a too-powerful charge was accidentally delivered to an invisible fence by an outside electric source, such as a downed power line, or because a dog had a heart arrhythmia no one knew about that was fatally triggered by a jolt from a shock collar.

Invisible fence. The dog wears a collar that delivers a shock if he crosses an established boundary line. For this to work, the dog must learn and remember where the boundary is. Some dogs have a high threshold of pain and are undeterred by the shocks, especially if they see a cat, deer, or bicyclist on the other side. This type of fence doesn't prevent other animals or people from entering the yard, so your dog remains exposed to outside dangers, and it won't stop a territorial dog from making a nuisance of himself by barking and dashing furiously along the boundary line. There are two better alternatives, one free and one expensive: (1) don't leave your dog outside unattended, or (2) put up an attractive, dog-proof, visible fence.

Anti-bark collar. The collar delivers a shock when the dog barks more than two or three times in a row. Some anti-bark collars issue a warning beep before giving a shock, in hopes that the dog will learn to pipe down when she hears the beep in order to avoid a shock. The strength of the shock can be adjusted on some collars. Anti-bark collars work on some, but not all, "recreational" barkers—dogs who are bored or simply enjoy vocalizing. Dogs with a high threshold of pain and deep love of barking will keep on despite the shocks. Anti-bark collars almost never work on dogs who bark because of separation anxiety. These dogs either switch to howling, which doesn't set off the collar, or they're so distressed they're undeterred by the further misery of being shocked every three barks.

Anti-bark citronella collar. More humane than shock collars, anti-bark citronella collars spray citronella oil as a negative deterrent or distraction. Like shock collars, citronella collars may work on some recreational barkers but are unlikely to deter hardier barkers or those with separation anxiety.

Obedience-training collar. The dog handler has a transmitter for delivering a shock when the dog doesn't obey a command. The principle is punishment for unwanted behavior. In order for this to work, the handler needs to have exquisite timing, and the dog must make the mental connection between what he did and what happened afterward. This is harder for dogs than you might think. The major drawback for punishment as a training strategy is that it doesn't teach the dog what you want, only what you *don't* want. Positive reinforcement—rewarding the desired behavior with praise, pats, or food—works better for dogs.

If you think you need a shock collar to gain control over your dog, a better place to invest your time and money would be in an evaluation by and lessons with a dog trainer who's experienced in using positive reinforcement.

DOG SMARTS

"What's the smartest breed of dog, and what's the average dog's IQ?"

I know of no accurate way to measure a dog's IQ, but you know what? I don't think a number like that would be meaningful anyway. Dogs are smart at what they need to be smart at. Different breeds have different aptitudes, and I don't think a simple number could begin to express that.

People are fascinated with the concept of animal intelligence, and when someone asks me how smart dogs are, I like to say they're "dog smart." By this I mean they're intelligent, but they don't think the same way people do. Here are some examples of dog smarts:

❏ Dogs are adept at learning their owners' routines and habits. Your dog knows that when you pick up your keys, you're leaving the house; when you put a suitcase on the bed, you'll soon be going away somewhere; and when you put on your sneakers first thing in the morning, it's Saturday and you're taking him to the bagel shop and the park.

❏ Dogs understand the words they've been taught, but they don't understand long, involved discussions or diatribes. If you've worked on "Scooter, *come!*" your dog knows what that command means, but he's not going to respond to "Scooter! Scooter! *Scooter!* Get over here now! Stupid dog . . . *Scooter!* Come *here!* If you make me chase you, I swear I'll . . ."

❏ Your dog knows when you're angry at him, even if you don't say a word, from your body language. This leads some people to imagine their dogs are "acting guilty" about something, when in reality the dogs know the people are angry but don't know why (see page 191).

❏ Dogs talk. They use different sounds to mean different things: a short, high-pitched bark to greet or attract the attention of a person they know; lower-pitched, longer barks to protect their territory against a stranger; howling, mournful barks when they're lonely; whines to seek attention; and whining yawns when they're anxious or frustrated.

❏ Dogs grieve. Because they are pack animals, they prefer the company of others to being alone, and they will perceive and mourn the loss of a person or animal they felt close to.

HOUSEBREAKING HORRORS

"I recently adopted a male dog. He's housebroken, but he lifts his leg indoors anyway, especially on the kitchen cabinets. What can I do? It's driving me crazy."

Urinating in the house can have a variety of causes, some of them physical (a urinary tract infection, Cushing's disease or diabetes, incontinence) and some mental (lack of housebreaking,

If your dog urinates submissively when greeting you, ignore her for the first few minutes after you get home.

submissive urination, marking behavior). Physical problems are discussed on page 336. Assuming that your dog doesn't have any of those, he may be urinating to "mark his territory," even indoors. Here's what you can do:

❏ If you have more than one dog, read up on sibling rivalry (see page 192) and use the behavior modification method described there to support the "top dog" in your house.

❏ Use an enzyme-based odor eliminator, available from any pet store or pet-supply catalog, to completely and thoroughly remove the urine odor from any surfaces your dog has marked.

❏ If the new dog has not been neutered, that may be contributing to the problem. If the marking is a longstanding habit, however, it won't be eliminated by lowering his hormone levels.

❏ If the dog who's marking seems anxious, anti-anxiety medication may help (see page 185). For holistic remedies, see the following page.

A dog who urinates indoors when greeting someone, often while crouching or even rolling over on his back, is displaying submissive urination. That can be treated as follows:

❏ Ignore the dog, and advise visitors to ignore the dog, when you come in the door if the peeing is part of a greeting ritual.

❏ Don't reprimand a dog who pees submissively; it will only increase his submissiveness and make the problem worse.

❏ Work with your dog on obedience commands (come, sit, sit-stay, down, down-stay), using positive rewards, for 15 or 20 minutes each day to help boost his confidence.

(continued on page 198)

HOLISTIC HELP
FOR MENTAL HEALTH PROBLEMS

Maybe it's because behavior problems in dogs are so common and so distressing to their owners, or because so many people have incorporated alternative medicine into their own health regimens. Whatever the reason, more and more Americans are using alternative medicine to treat their dogs' mental health or behavior problems.

Bach's Rescue Remedy, which is now sold in just about every pet-supply store and catalog, is perhaps the best example of this trend. One of 38 homeopathic flower-based remedies developed in the early 1900s by Dr. Edward Bach, Rescue Remedy is immensely popular as an antidote for both human and canine stress, anxiety, and emergencies of almost every description.

For all its popularity, however, the question remains: does Rescue Remedy really ease a dog's anxiety? More broadly, is alternative medicine effective in treating canine mental-health problems? A body of anecdotal evidence from holistic veterinary practitioners and dog owners suggests that certain alternative remedies may work. What's more, since the alternative-medicine treatments described here are generally safe and have few side effects, that to me places them in a "couldn't hurt, might help" category for dog owners who are interested in exploring them.

Before you try these remedies, remember that you first need to accurately diagnose your dog's behavioral problem, and you will also need to

modify his behavior through training. All medications used for behavioral problems, whether alternative or traditional, are an adjunct to treatment, not a cure-all. Read this chapter for insights into why your dog behaves as he does and ways to untrain those behaviors. If your dog's behavior doesn't fit any of the profiles in this chapter, or if you're unsure what the essential problem is, consult with a behaviorist, veterinarian, or trainer.

Here is a guide to some of the more commonly recommended holistic remedies for various mental-health symptoms. Specific acupuncture points and traditional Chinese medicine (TCM) treatments are not included because their use relies on factors (such as pulse quality, energy, and dryness) separate from the symptoms listed below.

For more on holistic medicine and finding a holistic veterinarian, see Appendix B, starting on page 453.

ANXIETY

Herbs: Valerian (*Valeriana officinalis*), passionflower (*Passiflora incarnata*), kava (*Piper methysticum*), oats (*Avena sativa*). Kava can cause inflamed skin or liver damage, so stop using it immediately and consult with a veterinarian if your dog's skin becomes irritated or if he vomits, has diarrhea, or loses his appetite. Hops (*Humulus lupulus*) should not be given to dogs because it can cause fever and shock. Skullcap (*Scutellaria lateriflora*) and Saint-John's-wort (*Hypericum* *perforatum*) are not thought to be effective in dogs.

Dog-appeasing pheromone (DAP) products: DAPs are the pheromones female dogs secrete after giving birth, which promote calmness and contentment in the mother and pups. Synthetic versions of DAPs are available as plug-in diffusers (akin to room fresheners), collars, and sprays. There are also feline pheromone diffusers and sprays (Feliway is one brand).

Acupuncture and TCM: As determined by the practitioner.

FEARS AND PHOBIAS

Herbs: Valerian (*Valeriana officinalis*), passionflower (*Passiflora incarnata*), kava (*Piper methysticum*). See potential adverse side effects of kava under "Anxiety," above.

Supplements: Melatonin. Melatonin can disrupt blood-sugar regulation and should be used with caution in diabetic dogs.

Bach flower remedies: Aspen (*Populus tremula*); mimulus (*Mimulus guttatus*); Rescue Remedy, which contains cherry plum (*Prunus cerasifera*), clematis (*Clematis vitalba*), impatiens (*Impatiens glandulifera*), rockrose (*Helianthemum nummularium*), and star-of-Bethlehem (*Ornithogalum umbellatum*).

Homeopathics: Aconite or monkshood (*Aconitum napellus*), phosphorus, belladonna (*Atropa belladonna*), gelsemium (*Gelsemium sempervirens*), Natrum Muriaticum.

DAP products: See above.

Acupuncture and TCM: As determined by the practitioner.

SLEEPLESSNESS, RESTLESSNESS AT NIGHT, OR HOUSE SOILING AT NIGHT

Herbs: Valerian (*Valeriana officinalis*).

Supplements: Melatonin. Melatonin can disrupt blood-sugar regulation and should be used with caution in diabetic dogs.

DAP products: See above.

Acupuncture and TCM: As determined by the practitioner.

CANINE COGNITIVE DYSFUNCTION (CCD)

Herbs: Ginkgo (*Ginkgo biloba*), qian ceng ta (*Huperzia serrata*), curcumin (*Curcuma longa*). Ginkgo should not be used in dogs that are taking Anipryl (Selegiline/deprenyl) for CCD or phenylpropanolamine for urinary incontinence because the combination can cause extreme restlessness or agitation; and ginkgo should be stopped two weeks before surgery because it interferes with blood clotting.

Supplements: Acetyl-L-Carnitine; melatonin; vitamins C and E. See potential adverse side effects of melatonin under "Sleeplessness," above.

Acupuncture and TCM: As determined by the practitioner.

OBSESSIVE LICKING (OBSESSIVE-COMPULSIVE DISORDER)

Homeopathics: Belladonna (*Atropa belladonna*), hyoscyamus (*Hyoscyamus niger*).

Supplements: Melatonin. See potential adverse side effects of melatonin under "Sleeplessness," above.

DAP products: See above.

Acupuncture and TCM: As determined by the practitioner.

(continued from page 195)

OBSESSIVE LICKING

"About six months ago, my five-year-old Golden Retriever started licking her left front leg so persistently that she created a deep sore. The vet bandaged the leg to let it heal, but my dog tore off one bandage after another to go after the leg, even when we coated the bandage with pepper sauce. Help!"

Chronically licking the skin to the point of injury is a form of obsessive-compulsive disorder that's fairly common in dogs, especially Akitas, Doberman Pinschers, Shar-Peis, Golden and Labrador Retrievers, Weimaraners, Dalmatians, and German Shepherds. Favorite sites are a front leg or the tail, but a dog may obsessively lick any part of the body she can reach. Doberman Pinschers, for example, are known for a variant of this behavior called flank sucking. Spinning in circles, tail chasing, obsessions with toys, and other unusual behaviors can also be manifestations of obsessive-compulsive disorder if they are persistent, repeated, and virtually impossible to interrupt.

It's important to distinguish between licking that's purely obsessive and licking caused by an injury or itch. Many dogs who have allergies lick both front paws or all four feet, often leaving them stained brown from saliva, because their skin feels itchy. This should be treated as an allergic skin problem, not a mental health issue (see page 94). A fungal infection, bone pain, or foreign material embedded in the skin (such as a wood splinter or glass fragment) can cause a dog to lick obsessively, so a meticulous physical exam, x-rays, fungal cultures, and other tests should be done before approaching it as a purely mental problem.

If the diagnosis is in fact obsessive-compulsive disorder, then the following steps should be taken:

❏ As always, give your dog at least one hour of vigorous exercise each day.
❏ As always, work with your dog on obedience commands (come, sit, sit-stay, down, down-stay) for 15 or 20 minutes each day.
❏ Provide your dog with a rotating stock of delightful things to chew on, such as a Kong toy stuffed with peanut butter, rawhide, and so on.
❏ Don't reprimand your dog or focus a lot of attention on her when you see her licking. Your response may be part of her positive feedback.
❏ A DAP diffuser or collar may help relax an obsessive dog (see page 197).
❏ Obsessive-compulsive disorder is the one canine mental health issue that almost always requires drug treatment. Clomipramine (Clomicalm) or

Most licking is a response to itching or pain, but occasionally it's a form of obsessive-compulsive behavior.

fluoxetine (Reconcile, Prozac) is commonly used as an anti-obsessive drug. An opioid blocker such as naltrexone is sometimes used in addition, in order to blunt the "high" that an obsessive licker gets from the behavior.

❏ For alternative-medicine options for obsessive-compulsive disorder, see page 196.

FECES EATERS

"Why does my dog eat her feces, and how can I make her stop?"

As revolting as it is to humans, eating feces is fairly common among dogs. Horse manure and deer droppings are irresistible, and cat poop is considered a tasty snack by many. Some dogs like to eat dog feces, be it their own, their friends', or their neighbors'.

Coprophagia (the official term for eating feces) is not usually a sign of illness; in fact, mother dogs normally eat the feces of their young pups. Once in a great while, it can be a symptom of malnutrition, in a dog who is having trouble digesting and absorbing her food (see page 129) or one who has been starved. If your dog's coprophagia were caused by malnutrition, you would probably see other symptoms: loss of weight and energy; a poor hair coat; or greasy, loose stools, for example. But most of the time, eating feces is simply a bad habit. It's also unhealthy—it can transmit intestinal parasites, contribute to tooth decay, and cause stomach problems.

Some people recommend sprinkling a feces-eater's food with veterinary products called For-Bid or Deter, a flavor enhancer like Accent, or a meat tenderizer like Adolph's. The monosodium glutamate in these products supposedly makes a dog's own stool less appealing. Pouring pepper sauce on a dog's feces is another favorite tactic.

To me, however, preventing opportunities to eat feces is a more sensible idea. For one thing, even if Accent discourages your dog from eating her own stool, it won't make her any less interested in another dog's. Here's how to break the feces-eating habit:

❏ Always clean up after your dog; get to her feces before she can.

❏ Keep her on a leash during the training period, and if she makes a beeline for a pile of poop, say "Leave it!" in a stern voice and move her along. Reward her with a small treat whenever she listens to you.

❏ Be patient. If your dog is a puppy, coprophagia may be a passing phase. Use these training tips anyway, however, so a passing phase doesn't become a persistent habit.

CHAPTER 8

Eye and Ear Diseases

CATARACTS, DRY EYE, GLAUCOMA—dogs get many of the same eye diseases that people do. Some seemingly minor eye problems can cause pain and vision loss if not treated promptly, while other scarier-looking conditions, like cherry eye, aren't really emergencies at all. Then there are ear infections, to which dogs are uniquely susceptible. Those deep vertical ear canals, wax-trapping ear hair, and moisture-sealing ear flaps make canine ears an ideal petri dish for irritating organisms of all kinds. Even if you feel like an old hand with the ear cleaner, cotton balls, and ointment, there's more to learn about the underlying causes of ear problems and ways to prevent them.

EMERGENCY!

Does your dog need immediate veterinary care? Check this list to help you decide.

TAKE IMMEDIATE ACTION!

Call your vet or an emergency veterinary clinic *now* if your dog is showing any of the following symptoms:

❑ His **eyeball looks swollen.**

❑ Her eye has popped **out of the socket.**

❑ He is **suddenly blind.**

❑ She is **squinting** or holding an **eye closed.**

❑ He is **pawing or rubbing** at one or both eyes as if they were **extremely uncomfortable.**

❑ She may have gotten a **caustic substance** in the eye.

TAKE A MINUTE . . .

Read further in this book and then call your vet during office hours as needed if your dog is showing any of the following symptoms:

❑ He has clear, brown, yellowish, or greenish **eye discharge,** but he is not scratching or rubbing at his eyes and doesn't seem sick (see page 207).

❑ Her **pupils look cloudy** (see page 216).

❑ He's newly **hesitant of dark places,** such as poorly lit stairs (see page 215).

❑ Her **third eyelid** is showing in one or both eyes (see page 208).

❑ He has **cherry eye,** a red blob of tissue protruding from the inner corner of the eye (see page 208).

❑ Her **ear is puffy** (see page 225).

❑ He is **shaking his head** or **scratching his ears** a lot (see page 225).

❑ Her **ears smell bad** (see page 219).

❑ He's got **brown stuff** in his ears (see page 223).

❑ She gets **frequent ear infections** (see page 219).

Remember, it's never wrong to call your veterinarian if you have a question about your dog's health, or if you're worried about a symptom or your dog's overall condition. That's what we're here for.

INWARD-GROWING EYELASHES

"My two-year-old Pekingese has one eye that's always been goopy. The vet says she has an eyelash growing from the underside of her eyelid that rubs against the eye, and she should have it removed surgically. Why can't we just pluck the eyelash?"

Because the hair follicle will grow another eyelash in the same place no matter how many times you pluck it. An eyelash that grows beneath the lid or pokes toward the eye from the edge of the lid should be fixed permanently so that it doesn't damage the surface of the eye. To prevent the hair from regrowing, your vet will probably surgically remove a tiny snip of skin containing the hair follicle. Other options include freezing the follicle or zapping it with a laser.

TURNED-IN EYELIDS

"My Chow's lower eyelids turn in slightly, and his eyes are always red and runny. My vet suggested I think about plastic surgery. Is he kidding?"

He's not kidding. Plastic surgery is a legitimate cure for turned-in eyelids that rub against and irritate the eyes. This defect, which is called entropion, is especially common in Chows, Pugs, Bulldogs, Maltese, Pekingese, and Poodles. The surgery removes a thin slice of skin below the eye and rotates the eyelid outward slightly so the eyelashes or skin folds don't rub against the surface of the eye. If a dog's entropion is severe enough to cause eye irritation, surgery is the only permanent solution.

DROOPY LOWER EYELIDS

"My St. Bernard has huge bags under his eyes, and the tears run out and leave his face constantly brown and crusty. Is there any way to fix this?"

Maybe. There's a little duct in the inner corner of each eye that is supposed to funnel tears and eye secretions into the nose, where they evaporate or are swallowed. Because your St. Bernard's lower lids are so loose and floppy, the tears are probably missing these ducts and dripping down his face instead.

Most owners of Bloodhounds, St. Bernards, and other droopy-eyed dogs live with the problem by cleaning their dog's eyes and faces daily (see page 206) and using eye drops or ointment if the eyes become irritated. If the problem is severe, plastic surgery may be an option, but it should be considered a last resort: it's difficult to predict exactly how surgery will alter your dog's appearance and whether the tear duct can be repositioned precisely enough to fix the overflow of tears.

BLOCKED TEAR DUCTS

"My husband bought the cutest tea-cup Maltese puppy from a pet store because she looked like she was crying. We've had her for two weeks, and she still has tears running down her face. What's going on?"

Your puppy may have blocked tear ducts. These ducts are supposed to funnel tears from a tiny opening in the inner corner of the eye to the nose. The opening to this duct may be covered by a layer of skin—this is a birth defect sometimes seen in Poodles, Samoyeds,

Light-colored dogs with runny eyes naturally will develop dark tearstains.

Golden Retrievers, Cocker Spaniels, and other breeds. Other possibilities include unusually taut lower eyelids, inflammation from an eye or respiratory infection, and long hair that wicks tears onto the face.

Tell your vet about the problem and have him check your puppy's eyes closely to determine the cause. If the opening to the tear duct is blocked, it can be surgically opened, with good results in most cases. If the eyes are inflamed, your vet can diagnose and treat the cause (see page 207). Taut eyelids or hair that wicks the tears onto the face can't be easily corrected, so if one of those is the problem, you may have to live with the tearstaining (see page 206).

DAMAGED CORNEAS

"My Poodle is squinting and rubbing her left eye, and there's some sticky discharge. It started after she went to the groomer's a few days ago. Should I call the vet or wait?"

C all your vet right away. Your poodle may have gotten shampoo in her eye.

Unless it's "tearless," shampoo can damage the cornea (the clear surface of the eye) and cause a corneal ulcer. If your dog does have a corneal ulcer, it's best to treat it as soon as possible. Your vet will place a drop of fluorescent dye on the eye and look at it with an ophthalmoscope to check for a corneal ulcer. If the cornea is damaged, the ulcer will grab onto the dye and glow when a light is shone on it.

Simple corneal ulcers are treated with antibiotic drops or ointment several times a day. Your poodle will need to wear an Elizabethan collar to prevent her from rubbing the eye. Atropine drops may also be prescribed to prevent painful eye spasms while the ulcer is healing.

Small, uncomplicated corneal ulcers —which are most often caused by chemical or mechanical irritants such as shampoo, an inward-growing hair, or something caught under the eyelid, like sand or plant material—will heal in three to five days. Your vet will want to recheck the eye during that time to make sure the ulcer is healing well. Deep corneal ulcers—ones that weren't treated immediately, or ones infected by unusual bacteria—can require four to six weeks of treatment.

When corneal ulcers don't heal quickly, it's important to search for a reason. Sometimes there is an almost invisible hair growing under the eyelid. Or a corneal ulcer may be infected by bacteria that are resistant to the antibiotic that's being used (a bacterial culture can identify the bacteria and determine which antibiotics they are sensitive to). When corneal ulcers are slow to heal, a vet may need to scrape damaged tissue from the cornea one or more times to help the healthy cells "stick" better. A contact-lens-like shield may be placed on the cornea to protect the ulcer while it heals.

THE STRAIGHT SCOOP ON EYE GOOK

All dogs produce eye secretions, also known as tears, sleep, or eye gook. So what's the difference between normal eye secretions and secretions that indicate illness?

Normal eye discharge is clear. As it dries, however, natural pigments turn the secretions a rusty brown to blackish color. So clear, brownish, or blackish eye gook is normal for a dog and isn't usually a sign of illness.

Eye discharge that is yellowish to greenish is a sign of eye irritation or infection. Depending on a dog's age, medical history, and other symptoms, possible causes include (1) irritation caused by swimming; shampoo or flea spray in the eyes; or pollen-type allergies; (2) a bacterial, viral, or fungal eye infection or upper-respiratory infection; (3) inward-growing eyelashes; or (4) the onset of an eye disease such as dry eye (keratoconjunctivitis sicca) or glaucoma.

If your dog has yellowish or greenish eye discharge and her eyes also seem uncomfortable (if she's rubbing them or squinting, or if her eyes or eyelids seem swollen), call your vet immediately. If you're bathing your dog and you get shampoo in her eyes, flush them immediately with plain saline eyewash or plain water. Call your vet if your dog's eyes seem uncomfortable even after you've flushed them.

If your dog has yellow or green eye discharge but otherwise seems comfortable and well, rinse the eyes with a sterile plain saline eyewash from the drugstore. Squirt copious amounts of the eyewash into each eye, and gently wipe away the discharge with a clean tissue. Do this two or three times a day for a day or two. If the discharge goes away and doesn't recur, the irritation has passed. If it doesn't go away or flares up again quickly, make an appointment with your vet to find out the underlying cause.

BALD PATCHES AROUND THE EYES

"My four-month-old Pit Bull is losing the hair around his eyes. What's wrong?"

He probably has demodex mites, which live in the hair follicles and can make the hairs break off. Your vet can do a skin scraping to check for mites and prescribe the appropriate treatment (see page 167).

ONE BULGING EYE

"I just noticed that my 12-year-old dog's right eye seems to be bulging out more than the other eye. The eye doesn't seem to bother him. What could be wrong?"

Look carefully to see whether (1) the upper eyelid is swollen, (2) the eyeball itself is swollen (bigger than the other eyeball), or (3) the eyelid and eyeball are normal-size but seem to be

WHITE FUR, BROWN TEARSTAINS

Many dogs with white or light-colored faces are plagued with rusty brown tearstains under their eyes. An oft-repeated myth is that the brown color is caused by preservatives or dyes in dog food. In fact, the color of these tearstains is produced by natural pigments, called porphyrins, in the dogs' eye secretions.

The more eye discharge a dog produces, the more likely she is to develop tearstains. If your dog has tearstains and you'd like to minimize them, the first question to address is whether she has excessive amounts of eye discharge. Does she rub at her eyes, or do they seem to bother her in any way? Does she have allergies to airborne substances, like pollen or mold, or to food? Has your vet ruled out potential causes of increased or excessive eye discharge, such as blocked tear ducts, inward-growing eyelashes, turned-in eyelids, glaucoma, and dry eye (keratoconjunctivitis sicca)? If a dog has allergies or an eye problem, treating the condition helps reduce the amount of eye discharge, and therefore the tearstaining.

If her eyes and the amount of discharge are normal, then gently cleaning the area two or three times a day is the best way to reduce the staining. You can rinse the eyes with plain saline eyewash from the drugstore, and you can clean the fur under the eyes with wipes sold for that purpose in pet-supply stores and catalogs. Be careful not to get these under-eye cleaners in the eyes themselves, because they can sting and irritate.

Tearstains can sometimes be reduced by giving a dog tetracycline or tylosin—both antibiotics—daily or every other day. But should dogs be given antibiotics to treat a minor cosmetic problem? I say they shouldn't, to avoid contributing to the spread of antibiotic-resistant bacteria and drug residues in the soil and groundwater. In any case, tetracycline shouldn't be given to puppies less than six months old, because it can stain their developing permanent teeth.

pushed forward. If it's the eyelid that is swollen, conjunctivitis, an eye injury, or an allergic reaction are the most likely causes. If the eyeball itself is swollen, glaucoma (fluid buildup within the eye) is the most likely cause, and you should call your vet or an emergency veterinary clinic *immediately*—the high pressure of the fluid in the eye can cause permanent blindness if it's not treated quickly. If the eyelid and eyeball are pushed forward, an abscess or tumor behind the eye could be the cause. The roots of a dog's upper molars are close to the eye socket, and an infected tooth will sometimes produce an abscess behind the eye. Your vet will examine your dog's mouth carefully and take skull x-rays if an abscess or tumor is suspected.

EYE OUT OF THE SOCKET

"Someone told me that a big dog grabbed a Boston Terrier by the neck in the park, and the terrier's eye popped out of the socket! Is this possible? Can anything be done if it happens?"

Dogs with bulgy eyes, like Boston Terriers, Pugs, and Pekes, can indeed have an eye pop out of the socket in an accident or fight. The eye can be put back in, so the dog should be rushed to a vet or veterinary emergency clinic as quickly as possible. Keep the eye moist by holding a clean cloth soaked in water or saline eyewash over it. The vet will put the eye back in the socket and temporarily stitch the eyelid closed to hold it in place while it heals. If the eye and optic nerve aren't severely damaged, it's possible that the dog will regain some vision in the eye, but that won't be certain until the eye has healed and the inflammation has subsided, in about one month.

RED EYES

"My three-year-old dog's eyes are runny, and the whites of the eyes seem kind of red. Does she have conjunctivitis?"

Yes, she has conjunctivitis, but that's a description rather than a diagnosis. Inflamed eyes, or conjunctivitis, can be caused by dozens of things, including irritants such as smoke or pollen; bacteria; viruses; dry eye (keratoconjunctivitis sicca); cataracts; glaucoma; or fungal infections like blastomycosis, cryptococcosis, or histoplasmosis (see page 284).

The most common cause of conjunctivitis in a young dog like yours is irri-

THE DREADED LAMPSHADE

Dogs that have an eye infection or other eye problems often need to wear an Elizabethan collar, or E-collar, a lampshade-like contraption that dogs (and their owners) almost universally detest. For eye injuries, an E-collar is indispensable because it keeps the dog from pawing at his eyes or rubbing them against rugs or other surfaces. Such pawing or rubbing can cause severe eye damage.

For it to do any good, an E-collar must fit properly and be worn at all times—even at night. The cone must be long enough to prevent the dog from reaching around it with a front or hind paw, and it must be secured snugly around the upper neck so he can't push the collar back toward his shoulders to get at his eyes (see page 427).

How can you ease the annoyance of an E-collar for your dog? Make sure his food and water dishes are the right shape to fit inside the collar so he can eat and drink while wearing it. If necessary, guide the E-collar for him when he goes up and down stairs and through doorways. Take him for long walks to distract him. And remember that the collar is performing an important function, and he won't have to wear it forever.

tants or allergies. If she doesn't seem sick otherwise, and she's not rubbing her eyes or squinting as if they were painful, rinse the eyes with a plain saline eyewash from the drugstore. Squirt copious amounts of the eyewash into each eye, and gently wipe away the discharge with a clean tissue. Do this two or three times a day for a day or two. If the redness and discharge go away in that time and don't recur, the irritation has passed. If the conjunctivitis doesn't go away or flares up again quickly, make an appointment with your vet to find out the underlying cause.

EYELID GROWTHS

"A growth like a skin tag has appeared on my 14-year-old dog's upper eyelid. Is it harmful? Should I have it removed?"

Many dogs sprout small bumps or skin tags on their faces as they get older. Most of these are not harmful, but it's always wise to have your veterinarian take a look and note in your dog's medical chart how big the growth is and what it looks like.

A growth on the margin of the eyelid may rub against the eye and irritate it, in which case the growth should definitely be removed. Don't wait for an eyelid growth to become huge before deciding to have it removed—the surgery is less complicated and less likely to change the dog's appearance when the growth is smaller.

Any time your veterinarian removes a lump, bump, or growth from your dog, it makes good sense to send the tissue to a veterinary pathologist so it can be positively identified and checked for cancer. The pathology fee is extra, and most growths are *not* cancer, but the only way to know for certain is to look under a microscope.

CHERRY EYE

"This morning my one-year-old Cocker Spaniel woke up with a pea-size red thing on his lower eyelid. Did he injure the eye? It looks awful."

THE THIRD EYELID

When a dog is sick or in pain, you will sometimes see a whitish or pinkish triangle of tissue covering the inner corner of his eye. This is called the third eyelid. If you see the third eyelid in one eye, that eye may be injured or painful, or a nerve may be damaged. If you see the third eyelid in both eyes, both eyes may be painful, or the dog may be sick or in pain from some other cause. Call your vet to discuss what the cause may be and whether your dog needs to be seen right away.

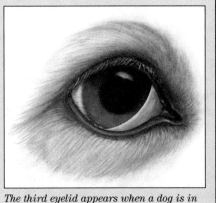

The third eyelid appears when a dog is in pain or has a nerve injury.

The blob on the dog's lower right eyelid is cherry eye, an inflamed tear-producing gland.

He has what's commonly called cherry eye, a condition seen most frequently in Cocker Spaniels, Lhasa Apsos, Pekingese, Bulldogs, Boston Terriers, and Beagles. The "red thing" is a tear-producing gland that has become inflamed and popped out of its normal position behind the third eyelid. Although it looks awful, cherry eye isn't usually painful. The swelling normally subsides by itself within a day or two, but it's almost certain to happen again because the gland isn't well-anchored beneath the third eyelid. Eventually the gland may remain out permanently. Make an appointment with your vet to discuss the situation. Surgery to tack the gland under the eyelid is the recommended treatment for recurrent cherry eye.

A SUNKEN EYE

"Our old hound's left eye looks a little sunken, and there's a triangle of tissue showing in the corner of his eye. Did he have a stroke?"

The triangle of tissue is the third eyelid. Your dog may have an eye injury, or he may have something known as Horner's syndrome. Horner's syndrome occurs when one of the nerves that controls the muscles around the eye is damaged or becomes inflamed.

Call your vet. She will examine the eye to see whether it's injured. If the eye isn't injured, then the vet will look for the underlying cause of the Horner's syndrome. The nerve involved in Horner's syndrome travels a long pathway, arising from the spinal cord at the level of the first or second rib, traveling up the neck to the head, and passing close to the middle ear before ending at the eye muscles. An ear infection, a neck wound, or very rarely, a tumor somewhere along the nerve's route from the upper chest to the eye can damage it and cause Horner's syndrome.

Horner's syndrome is not painful. There is no treatment for the changes in the eye, but if the nerve inflammation or damage is mild, it can heal on its own, and the dog's appearance will return to normal.

FRECKLES AND SPOTS ON THE IRIS

"My dog's eyes have always been light brown, but lately I've noticed a couple of darker spots. Is this anything to worry about?"

Probably not, but point out the dark spots to your vet, and tell her when you first noticed them and whether they've gotten any bigger since then. Most "freckles" on the iris (the colored part of the eye) are pigment cells, not cancer, but even benign spots sometimes spread rapidly and affect a dog's vision. They can be treated by a veterinary ophthalmologist if they are spreading. Occasionally a spot on the eye is cancer, such as melanoma, but this too may be treatable (see page 368).

The eyes of pop-eyed dogs—Pugs, Pekes, Shih Tzus, Lhasa Apsos, and so on—occasionally protrude so much that the dog can't close his eyelids all the way. The eyes are partly visible even when the dog is sleeping. This constant exposure to the air irritates the surface of the eye, and the cornea responds to the irritation by producing dark pigment. Eventually the pigment can cover so much of the eye that the dog can't see well. Bulgy-eyed dogs who are producing extra pigment in this way need eyedrops to protect the eyes or, occasionally, plastic surgery to enable the eyelids to close all the way.

AN IMMUNE ATTACK ON THE EYE

"My three-year-old German Shepherd had conjunctivitis in one eye. The vet prescribed an antibiotic ointment, but the eye seemed to get worse, not better. Now there is pinkish stuff growing on the surface of the eye. What's going on?"

From your description, this sounds like an eye disease called pannus. Pannus is a misfiring of the immune system in which white blood cells damage the eye rather than help it heal. What triggers the white blood cells to do this is unknown. (When the same process inflames the third eyelid, it's called plasmoma.)

Pannus is most common in young German Shepherds, Shepherd mixes, Greyhounds, and dogs that live at high altitudes (because of increased exposure to ultraviolet light). It begins with conjunctivitis—inflammation and reddening of the whites of the eyes—and a watery or mucous eye discharge. Over days to weeks, fleshy pink areas appear on the surface of the eye. This is essentially scar tissue that's created in an abnormal response to the inflammation. Over months to years, if it's untreated, the scar tissue can spread to cover the entire surface of the eye, leaving the dog blind.

Pannus is diagnosed by microscopically examining a tissue sample scraped from the cornea. (The eye is numbed first, and the process isn't painful or damaging to the eye.) The tissue is checked for bacterial growth, fungal spores, white blood cells, and other unusual cells. If the sample contains many white blood cells but no bacterial infection or other contaminants, the diagnosis is pannus.

It's important to rule out bacterial, fungal, and other infections because pannus is treated with steroids. The steroids calm the white blood cells' overreaction, but they would make an infection worse. Unfortunately, pannus can't be completely cured, and the inflammation may flare up periodically. It's important to treat pannus and then keep it under control, because of the potential for blindness.

AN IMMUNE ATTACK ON THE EYES AND SKIN

"When my six-year-old Akita suddenly developed horribly itchy sores around her eyes, I thought it was mange or some kind of allergic reaction. But the vet noticed that my dog's eyes were affected as well, and he diagnosed a serious autoimmune disease whose name I can't even pronounce. Can you tell me more about this disease and its prognosis?"

Your description sounds like uveodermatologic syndrome, an immune-system malfunction that targets the eyes ("uveo") as well as the skin ("dermatologic"). I'll call it U.D. syndrome for short. Certain breeds—including Akitas, Irish Setters, Siberian Huskies, and Samoyeds—are predisposed to this disease, for unknown reasons. A similar condition in people is sometimes referred to by the equally unwieldy name Vogt-Koyanagi-Harada syndrome.

In U.D. syndrome, the body's immune system begins to attack pigment cells in the eyes and skin of the face. The eyes become extremely inflamed, and the skin is often severely itchy and raw. Over time, the hair and skin in the affected areas turn white as the pigment cells die and are not replaced. Even worse, U.D. syndrome can quickly lead to glaucoma, detached retinas, cataracts, or blindness. The disease is diagnosed by examining biopsies of the skin and cornea.

U.D. syndrome is treated with high doses of steroids to calm the immune system. It's a very tough disease to get under control, and even stronger, chemotherapy-type immunosuppressive drugs are often required. The goal is to relieve the extreme discomfort and save your dog's eyesight if at all possible. If glaucoma or cataracts develop, they are treated as well.

DRY EYE

"For a while now my 12-year-old dog has had a lot of sticky discharge from both eyes. When I took her to the vet, the vet measured her tear production with little strips of paper and said she has 'dry eye.' How can it be dry eye when the eyes are so goopy?"

The full name of dry eye—which occurs frequently in people as well as in dogs—is keratoconjunctivitis sicca, or KCS. In KCS, the eyes produce less than adequate amounts of the tears that normally lubricate and protect the eyes.

The eyes become irritated, and they may develop a thicker, mucous discharge that doesn't look "dry" but does not protect the eyes. If left unchecked, KCS leads to pain and progressive corneal damage, sometimes to the point of blindness.

Tear production is measured by tucking the end of a specially designed, match-size strip of absorbent paper under the eyelid for 60 seconds and measuring how many millimeters of the paper are wet after that time. (The process isn't painful.) Normal eyes will wet 16 to 24 millimeters per minute. In KCS, the eyes wet less than 10 millimeters per minute.

Most cases of KCS are caused by a misfiring of the immune system: for unknown reasons, the body's white blood cells attack the tear glands and hamper their ability to produce tears. Sulfa antibiotics (such as trimethoprim/sulfadiazine) and facial nerve damage are two less common causes of KCS. The disease can occur in any dog, but it is the most common in Bulldogs, West Highland White Terriers, Lhasa Apsos, Pugs, Cocker Spaniels, Yorkshire Terriers, and Pekingese.

KCS is treated by cleaning the eyes with saline eyewash, using artificial tears and eye lubricants (often a gel or ointment) to keep the eyes moist and protected, and using prescription cyclosporine eyedrops or ointment to increase tear production by the tear glands. Treatment almost always must continue for life. Cyclosporine, which is most effective at increasing tear production in dogs with the immune-triggered form of the disease, takes several weeks to reach full effect. Artificial tears and lubricants must be applied four to six times a day at first, but in cases where the cyclosporine works well, that often can be decreased to one or two times a day.

APPLY EYE MEDICATIONS LIKE A PRO

Many people are intimidated at first about putting ointment or drops in their dogs' eyes, but with a little practice, it's usually a breeze.

You'll need a couple of cotton balls, some plain saline eyewash, the eye medicine you're using, and if your dog is squirmy, an assistant to hold the dog.

First, squirt some eyewash on a cotton ball and clean any discharge from the inner corner of your dog's eye and eyelid. Use a separate, clean cotton ball for each eye to avoid spreading any infection from one eye to the other.

Next comes the medicine. The most important thing to remember is not to touch the tip of the ointment tube or eyedrop bottle to anything, including your finger or the dog's eye. This is to avoid contaminating the tube or injuring the eye. Keep the cap clean, too—set it on a clean tissue on the counter or table while you're applying the medicine.

Take a practice squeeze of the tube of ointment or bottle of eyedrops to see

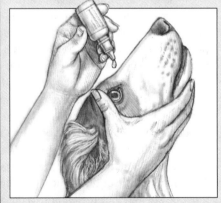

Tilt the dog's nose up so the drops will fall squarely on the eye.

how much pressure you need to dispense the prescribed amount. Often a vet will tell you to put a "dot" or "quarter-inch" of ointment in the eye, or 1 or 2 drops of liquid. Some drops come out fast, others slow. More is not better, but it is more expensive, so use only as much as prescribed.

Drops are easiest, so let's talk about them first. Hold the bottle of drops in your "good" hand. With your dog sitting in front of you and facing away from you, use your other hand to gently tip up his nose until his eye is basically a horizontal surface. Holding the bottle about 2 inches above the dog's eye, squeeze the bottle to allow the appropriate number of drops to fall onto the eye. If your dog squeezes his eye shut, gently push up the upper eyelid with the thumb of your other hand while you dispense the drops. Repeat with the other eye (if you need to medicate both eyes). Cap the bottle right away to keep it clean.

Ointments are a little trickier because you have to somehow get the blob onto the eye without touching the tip of the tube. Hold the ointment in your "good" hand. With your dog sitting in front of you and facing away from you, gently lift his chin with your other hand. With the thumb of your chin-holding hand or a finger of the tube-holding hand, push the upper eyelid up a bit until you see the white of the eye, then drip the correct amount of ointment onto the white of the eye. Let go of the eyelid and let the ointment melt and distribute itself on the eye surface.

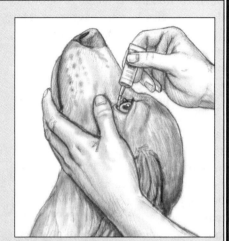

Push the lower lid down to make a pocket for ointment.

If the ointment sticks to the tip of the tube rather than dropping into the eye, gently swish the ointment against the edge of the eyelid to get the ointment off. Do your best to touch only the ointment (and not the tip of the tube) to the eyelid to avoid contaminating the tube.

Instead of pushing up the upper eyelid, you can also push down the lower eyelid to make a pocket to squeeze the ointment into, or put the ointment in the outer corner of the eye. As long as it gets somewhere on the eye or inner eyelid, it will melt and spread to where it needs to go. Avoid poking the tube or ointment directly at the center of your dog's eye, because he's more likely to be startled and jerk away if he sees it coming straight at him.

If you're working with an assistant, the assistant should hold the dog's body steady and put a forearm across the dog's front legs (so he can't reach up with his paws) while you guide the dog's head and apply the medicine.

GLAUCOMA

"Do dogs get glaucoma? What are the symptoms?"

Yes, dogs get glaucoma, a disease in which increased fluid pressure within the eye can lead to pain and eventually blindness. The symptoms of glaucoma can be vague, especially early on. Some dogs will have red eyes (conjunctivitis). Some will have increased eye discharge. The pupil may be larger than normal. One eye or both may be affected by any of these symptoms. Rarely, a dog's eyeball will become noticeably larger (see page 205). If the pressure inside the eye is very high, the dog may show that the eye is painful by squinting and rubbing at it. Other times dogs don't reveal the pain directly but may become withdrawn or snappish or lose their appetite.

Glaucoma is diagnosed by measuring the fluid pressure within the dog's eye with a device called a tonometer. (Anesthetic eyedrops are applied beforehand so this isn't uncomfortable.) A dog's normal eye fluid pressure is 15 to 25 mm Hg (millimeters of mercury). Glaucoma is defined by a pressure of 30 or higher. Pressures of 40 or higher can lead to blindness by damaging the retina and the optic nerve.

The goals of treating glaucoma are relieving pain and protecting vision. People with glaucoma often can keep the disease under control and maintain their vision by using eyedrops to reduce the pressure. The underlying cause of the disease is different in dogs, however, and it progresses more quickly and is more difficult to treat. Most dogs have what is called "closed-angle" glaucoma, in which fluid is produced normally but can't drain from the eye properly. Medications to decrease the production of fluid within the eye are used when the pressure is slightly to moderately elevated, but often those medications can't hold the disease completely in check. Surgery to destroy the fluid-producing cells within the eye is more effective and permanent but also complex and expensive. Another option is surgery to implant tiny shunts within the eye to drain the fluid, a procedure that's even more difficult and costly. If you're interested in discussing surgical options for glaucoma, your vet can refer you to a veterinary ophthalmologist who performs those procedures.

If glaucoma causes a dog to lose vision in one or both eyes and the fluid pressure remains high, pain relief becomes the primary concern. In humans, high pressure within the eye is extremely painful and can feel like a migraine headache. Presuming that the pain for dogs with glaucoma is just as intense as it is for people, veterinarians usually recommend removing an eye that is blind but still has high pressure. Dog owners often are reluctant to agree to the surgery at first, but the dog will be pain-free, and he will look fine once he has healed—you'll see closed eyelids, not an empty socket.

Most glaucoma is hereditary. Breeds that have a higher than average incidence of the disease include Beagles, Poodles, Basset Hounds, Bouviers des Flandres, Chihuahuas, Giant Schnauzers, Fox Terriers, Samoyeds, Chows, and Shar-Peis. Like all hereditary diseases, however, glaucoma can appear in a dog of any breed or mixture.

SUDDEN BLINDNESS

"One day my ten-year-old Dachshund woke up and started walking into the walls and furniture. At first I thought she was having some kind of seizure, but it turned out she had gone blind. My vet wants her to have a special test to determine whether the blindness is permanent. Can you tell me more about possible causes?"

Sudden blindness is terrifying to dogs and to their owners. In otherwise healthy dogs with no other symptoms, it is most often caused by a sudden breakdown of the retina or by inflammation of the optic nerve. Both are in the back of the eye. The retina is the surface that contains the light-sensing rods and cones; the optic nerve is the large nerve that collects signals from the rods and cones and transmits them to the brain for interpretation.

Blindness caused by a sudden breakdown of the retina is irreversible. Blindness caused by optic-nerve inflammation sometimes gets better. The back of the eye, when viewed through an ophthalmoscope, looks essentially normal in *both* diseases. Your vet has recommended that your dog have an electroretinogram (ERG) to distinguish between the two diseases. An ERG measures nerve impulses emitted by the retina. In sudden retinal degeneration, the graph of the retina's response is a flat line. In optic-nerve inflammation, the graph has its normal hills and valleys.

The cause of sudden retinal degeneration is unknown. Optic-nerve inflammation may be caused by infectious diseases; by severe eye injury, such as having the eyeball pop out (see page 207); by cancer; or by unknown factors. The last scenario—"unknown"—is the most common, especially in a dog with no other symptoms. Because it may be caused by an immune-system attack, optic neuritis of unknown cause is treated with steroids, and often the dog regains at least partial vision.

What if your dog remains permanently blind? Fortunately, blindness is not painful. Dogs also are blessedly free of self-consciousness and self-pity. And because they have excellent senses of smell and touch and are attuned to changes in air currents and pressures, most dogs adjust very well to blindness.

Of course, a dog that suddenly goes blind needs to relearn her environment. Place baby gates at the tops and bottoms of stairs until she has a chance to learn her way around again. When you or other family members are home, put a leash on her and guide her through her usual routes and routines indoors. Don't carry her—she can't learn where to walk if she's in your arms. She will quickly learn to use sound, smell, and air-current cues to guide her from her bed to the kitchen, the back door, her favorite resting places, and so on. Tidy the house, if need be, to remove such unexpected obstructions as shoes or backpacks, a laundry basket, and children's toys from the floor. Push in the chairs around your kitchen and dining room table as soon as you're finished with them. Don't move furniture around—let your dog memorize the layout, then leave it as is as much as possible.

Outdoors, it's important to keep your dog in a safe, fenced yard or on a leash. If she enjoys leash walks, don't deprive her of that pleasure now that she's blind. She has you on the other end of the leash to show her which way to go and keep her safe. Before you let her explore a fenced yard, do a dog's-eye-level survey to make sure it doesn't contain hazards for a blind dog, such as sharp branches or fence wires.

GRADUAL LOSS OF VISION

"My three-year-old Golden Retriever has started to get funny about going upstairs when the hall light isn't on or walking into the dark garage from the sunlight. He also seems to bump his nose into things more often than he used to. Could he be losing his vision at such an early age?"

Dogs can gradually lose their vision from cataracts, glaucoma, or a few other causes. A young purebred dog, like yours, could have a disease called progressive retinal atrophy, or PRA. In PRA, the light-sensing rods and cones in the retinas of both eyes gradually break down and stop working. The dog's vision deteriorates over months to years until he becomes blind. Night blindness is often the earliest sign.

Signs of PRA can be seen by examining the back of the eye with an ophthalmoscope. Depending on how far the disease has progressed, a veterinarian may be able to see thinning blood vessels, clumps of pigment on the retina, or changes in the shape and contour of the optic nerve where it joins the retina. An electroretinogram, or ERG, is used to definitively diagnose the disease (see the previous Q&A). In PRA, the ERG's hills and valleys become progressively flattened.

PRA is an inherited disease, carried on a recessive gene. It's rare in mixed-breed dogs because they are far less likely to receive this gene from both parents. If a dog receives one normal gene and one PRA gene from each parent, that dog will not develop PRA, but he is a carrier of the disease. Dogs with PRA or a family history of PRA should be neutered so they do not pass on the gene.

There is no treatment for PRA. Let me emphasize again, however, that even totally blind dogs can adapt beautifully to their environments and continue to live happy lives. A dog with PRA loses his vision gradually, which helps him adapt. For ways that owners can help their dogs adjust, see the previous Q&A.

A LENS ADRIFT

"I noticed one of my 11-year-old dog's eyes looked funny—I couldn't pinpoint it any better than that—so I took him to my vet, who said the lens of that eye had shifted out of position. What could have caused this, and what's the best treatment?"

The lens is normally held firmly in place behind the iris, where it can be seen by looking through the pupil with an ophthalmoscope. Occasionally the fibers holding the lens in place break down, allowing it to move. If it shifts up, down, or sideways a bit, you might see a crescent-moon shadow in the pupil. In more severe cases, the lens pops forward through the pupil and winds up in front of the iris, or pops backward into the fluid-filled chamber in the back of the eye. A minor shift is called a subluxation, and a complete displacement is called a luxation. Eye irritation often accompanies this shift, so the white part of the dog's eye may look red or he may have some eye discharge.

CLOUDY EYES OR CATARACTS?

Most dogs' pupils start to look cloudy as they reach middle age, and sometimes owners assume their dogs are developing cataracts. Most often, however, this cloudiness is a thickening of the fibers that make up the lens of the eye, rather than the more severe changes in the lens that occur with cataracts. The "normal" cloudiness of older dogs' eyes probably blocks some of the light reaching the retina and decreases their vision a bit, but since dogs don't need to read or drive cars, this slight handicap doesn't affect their normal activities. Cloudy-looking pupils in puppies or young dogs, however, are *not* normal and should be checked by a veterinarian.

The difference between true cataracts and cloudy pupils is apparent when a veterinarian examines your dog's eyes with an ophthalmoscope.

There are two general categories of cataracts: those that occur in young dogs (usually less than six years old) and those that occur in older dogs (usually more than eight years old). Cataracts of young dogs almost always are an inherited problem. They may be present at birth or first appear when a dog is a few months to a few years old, and they may progress very quickly. Cataracts of older dogs also can be hereditary, or they can be caused by diabetes.

Cataracts progressively decrease a dog's vision, sometimes to the point of blindness, and in later stages they can irritate the eye and become painful. Surgery is the only cure, although vets usually recommend waiting to have surgery until the cataracts have developed to a "mature" stage. During the surgery, which is performed by a

Some breeds, including Wirehair, Sealyham, Tibetan, and Jack Russell Terriers and Border Collies, have an inherited predisposition to lens displacement. Sometimes lens displacement can be precipitated by glaucoma (increased pressure within the eye) or severe inflammation of the lens or other parts of the inner eye. Trauma, such as being hit by a car, normally cannot jar the lens out of position.

Slight shifts of the lens may be treated with steroid eyedrops to calm any associated inflammation. Your vet will also check the pressure in both your dog's eyes for signs of glaucoma, and treat that if necessary.

veterinary ophthalmologist, the lens is either broken up using sound waves and removed through a tiny incision in the cornea, or removed intact through a larger incision. Sometimes the lens is replaced with an artificial one, but that's not absolutely necessary—a dog's distance vision is good even without a lens, and his near vision is bolstered by his nose and other senses.

If cataracts are so opaque that a veterinarian can't see through them to the retina, an electroretinogram (ERG) should be done before deciding on surgery. The ERG measures nerve impulses emitted by the retina to check whether the retina is working properly. In some instances, a dog with cataracts may also have a retinal problem that would leave him blind or nearly so even if the cataracts were removed. In such cases, surgery is recommended only if the cataracts are causing pain, not to restore eyesight.

A lens that has popped through the pupil into the front of the eye can trigger glaucoma (by blocking fluid flow within the eye) and intense irritation, so it should be surgically removed by a veterinary ophthalmologist. A lens that has luxated into the back of the eye can be left there if it isn't causing irritation. Eyedrops that keep the pupil constricted are used to keep the lens from migrating to the front of the eye. A dog with a luxated lens has poorer vision but usually maintains some sight in the eye.

A COLLIE EYE DISEASE

"I'm thinking of buying a Collie puppy, and the breeder I'm talking to says she checks all her pups for 'the Collie eye disease.' Now I'm worried—what is the Collie eye disease?"

"Collie eye" is a group of related eye problems seen primarily in Collies, Australian Shepherds, Border Collies, and Shetland Sheepdogs (Shelties). The problems, which affect the retina and the optic nerve, range from mild to severe. These abnormalities are visible only with an ophthalmoscope. Because Collie eye is so widespread, many breeders have their puppies' eyes checked at the age of six weeks.

Mildly affected dogs have small areas of the retina that appear pale because they did not develop properly. The optic disc (the part of the optic nerve that can be seen using an ophthalmoscope) may be slightly misshapen. Severely affected dogs have partially detached retinas or very small, undeveloped optic discs. Partially detached retinas almost always become fully detached over time, leaving the dog blind in that eye. Severely underdeveloped

EYES THAT GLOW IN THE DARK

Have you ever seen an eerie greenish flash from your dog's eyes when it's dark? Dogs, cats, and many other animals have a reflective area, called the tapetum, on their retinas that helps them make the most of low levels of light. At night, when the angles between you, your dog, and a light source are just right, you may see a green or yellow glow reflecting off the tapetum. This is completely normal (though it may be spooky enough to make you swear off Stephen King novels at bedtime).

optic discs cause poor vision or blindness. Collie eye can't be cured or treated.

Mild forms of Collie eye do not become worse over time, and such dogs have normal or nearly normal vision. They should not be used for breeding, however, because their offspring could have severe forms of the disease.

Collie eye is not more common in dogs of a particular coat color or sex. However, it is more challenging to diagnose in Collies with blue eyes—often seen with a blue merle coat—because such dogs normally have paler retinas than dark-eyed collies do. A veterinary ophthalmologist can be called upon to distinguish between normal blue eyes and "Collie eye" if there is any question about the diagnosis.

There's no reason not to buy or adopt a puppy that has the mildest form of Collie eye, because his vision

shouldn't be affected, but do neuter the puppy to avoid passing on the condition.

CHECKING FOR GENETIC EYE PROBLEMS

"I have a three-year-old, unneutered male Havanese whose eyes failed a CERF exam. What does this mean?"

CERF stands for Canine Eye Registration Foundation. These exams are done by certified veterinary ophthalmologists to check for genetic eye problems that breeders do not want to pass on to future generations.

CERF exams look for a wide range of inherited eye problems, including conditions affecting the eyelids, cornea, iris, lens, and retina and optic disc (in the back of the eye). Cataracts in young dogs and "Collie eye" (see the previous Q&A) are two of the specific conditions evaluated on a CERF exam.

The abnormalities found can range from mild—something that won't ever affect the dog's eyesight—to very serious, such as partially detached retinas, which often progress to blindness. Dogs with even mild problems should not be bred because they can pass along more serious versions of the defects to their offspring, but there's no reason not to buy or adopt such a dog as a companion animal.

The most common inherited eye problem in the Havanese breed is cataracts, but your dog may have failed the CERF exam for some other reason. His CERF report should state exactly what defect was found; you can request a copy of the report from the breeder. For more information about CERF, cataracts, and other inherited eye diseases, go to *www.vmdb.org/cerf.html*.

When you get the CERF report, ask your vet to read it and interpret the information for you. She can monitor the condition with periodic eye examinations and prescribe treatment if necessary. Also, it's best to neuter your dog now, so there's no risk of his passing along the eye problem.

SMELLY EARS

"I have a four-year-old King Charles Spaniel, and for a while now I have noticed that her ears smell bad. Could it be health-related?"

Clean, healthy dog ears shouldn't smell bad. Normal canine earwax is brown and smells a little waxy, but not foul. Do you or a groomer clean her ears regularly—say, once a month or so? If not, you should start; see page 220.

If you are cleaning her ears regularly and they *still* smell bad, then she probably has an ear infection. Ear infections can be caused by bacteria, yeast (especially malassezia), or other fungi. Take her to your vet for a proper diagnosis and the appropriate medication.

TREATING EAR INFECTIONS

"Every summer my dog gets an ear infection, and my vet prescribes the same antibiotic ointment every time. My dog's ears are flaring up again this year. Can I get an antibiotic ointment over-the-counter, or must a vet prescribe it?"

Ear-cleaning solutions and ear-mite remedies are sold over-the-counter, but antibiotic ear ointments are not. Vets prescribe different ear medications depending on the cause of the infection: bacteria, malassezia (yeast), other fungi, or a combination. The ointment you have used in the past may contain an antibiotic, an anti-inflammatory, an antifungal, or all three.

When a dog gets an ear infection, even if he's had "the same thing" before, it's definitely worthwhile to have a vet swab the ear and identify the organisms responsible for the infection; look at the ear canals for inflammation, thickening, or other changes; see whether the eardrum is ruptured; and flush the ears thoroughly—as well as prescribing the appropriate medication and frequency of cleaning.

The fact that your dog gets an ear infection every summer points to a seasonal factor, such as pollen allergies or swimming. If allergies are a likely suspect, your vet may recommend antihistamines as well as more-frequent ear cleaning starting in the spring to head off your annual problem next year.

FREQUENT EAR INFECTIONS

"My Lab mix seems to get one ear infection after another. Why is this? Is there any way to stop the cycle?"

Many factors can predispose dogs to recurrent ear infections. The keys to breaking the cycle are identifying your dog's risk factors, eliminating or managing those risk factors, treating the current ear infection with the appropriate medication for the appropriate length of time, and then cleaning your dog's ears properly (see page 220) once every two weeks to head off future infections. Below are some of the most common factors that can lead to recurrent ear infections.

Swimming and bathing. Ear canals are already warm and dark, and when you add moisture, you have the ideal environment for growing bacteria and

(continued on page 222)

EAR CLEANING 101

It happens every day in vet clinics. Mr. and Mrs. Devoted Dog Owners bring in their three-year-old Golden Retriever, Bud. On their previous visit, they were advised to start cleaning Bud's ears at home twice a month to help head off ear infections. But the instructions weren't quite clear, and they certainly didn't want to hurt Bud's ears, so at home they dutifully swabbed the creases on the inside of Bud's ear flaps with a cotton ball moistened with ear-cleaning solution, never venturing down into the ear canal with cotton or cleaner. The result? Bud has the cleanest ear flaps in town, but his ear canals are stuffed with brown wax and, sure enough, he's got a yeast ear infection.

The moral of the story: good technique is as important as good intentions when it comes to ear cleaning. Here's a step-by-step guide to getting the wax out.

1. LOCATION. Dogs do not like having their ears cleaned. Your dog will try to worm out of your clutches when you try to clean his ears. Therefore, work in a small room (such as a bathroom) to make it harder for your dog to get away from you, and have an assistant hold the dog while you work on the ears.

2. SUPPLIES. You'll need a bottle of ear-cleaning solution, tissues or cotton balls, and a few cotton swabs. A flashlight is handy for peering into the ear canals to make sure you've done a thorough job. Ear-cleaning solution is essential to break up the earwax and debris and float it up from the depths

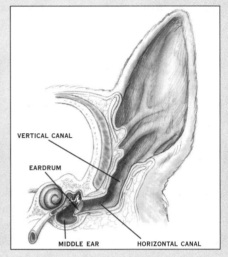

VERTICAL CANAL

EARDRUM

MIDDLE EAR   HORIZONTAL CANAL

Ear cleaner loosens the debris that collects deep in the ear canal, and floats it up.

of the ear canal. Choose a product that doesn't contain alcohol—alcohol stings inflamed skin. Don't use hydrogen peroxide or a homemade concoction for cleaning the ears (see page 222).

3. SAFETY. If your dog might snap or bite, put a muzzle on him (see page 188) before cleaning his ears, or have a veterinarian or groomer clean his ears for you. Clean ears are not worth getting bitten over.

4. ANATOMY. Dogs have long, L-shaped ear canals. The outer part of the canal extends down vertically, then makes almost a 90-degree bend in toward the head. The eardrum is at the far end of this horizontal section. You will not hit the eardrum with your cotton or swabs if you're careful to clean vertically and avoid poking in horizontally toward the dog's head.

5. PLUCKING. Some types of dogs (such as Poodles) have hair growing deep inside the ear canal. Because the hair can trap wax, dirt, and moisture, which promote the growth of bacteria and yeast, plucking it is often recommended. If you're a wizard with tweezers and have a cooperative dog, ask your vet or groomer to show you which hair needs to be plucked. (The short hair growing around the edge of the canal, for example, doesn't need to be plucked, and that area is loaded with nerve endings, so plucking there would really hurt. Also, long hair growing on the underside of the ear flap, like Cocker Spaniels have, should be trimmed with an electric hair clipper if it's matted or dirty, but not plucked.) Otherwise, ask your vet or groomer to do it for you.

6. CLEANING. Grasp one ear firmly and hold the flap straight up. Without letting go of the ear, squirt between 1 teaspoonful (for a small dog) and 1 tablespoonful (for a large dog) of ear cleaner into the ear canal (the hole leading straight down into the ear). Before he can shake his head, let go of the ear flap and vigorously massage the base of the ear for a few seconds. (This helps distribute the ear cleaner and break up the wax.) You should hear the ear cleaner squishing around inside the ear. Let go of the dog's head and let him shake out the excess ear cleaner. Repeat the squirt-massage-shake routine with the other ear.

Go back to the first ear. With a cotton ball or tissue, gently wipe out the wax in the ear canal, using an upward-scooping motion. Remember, you want to bring the debris up and out, not pack it farther down into the canal. If you'd like to, you can use the cotton swabs to clean debris out of the creases on the ear flap. Use the flashlight to look for any lumps of debris you may have missed. Make sure the ear canal and ear flap are dry when you're finished (leaving the ear canal wet promotes the growth of yeast and bacteria). Clean the second ear with tissues or cotton in the same manner.

The one time you *don't* want to display your ear-cleaning prowess is right before you take your dog to the vet for a suspected ear infection. Hold off on the ear cleaning for two or three days before the vet visit. Your vet will want to see how much ear discharge there is, and what it looks like, in order to properly diagnose and treat the infection.

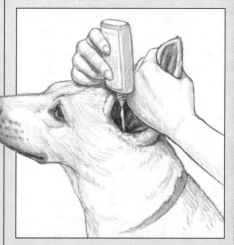

Hold the ear firmly while you squeeze in the cleaner, then massage the base of the ear.

(continued from page 219)

fungi. If your dog is a swimmer, be sure to dry her ear canals and ear flaps carefully with cotton balls or a soft towel after she swims, and clean her ears with ear cleaner at least once a week during swimming season. Also be sure to dry your dog's ears thoroughly after a bath.

Heavy or hairy ears. Some dogs, like Bloodhounds and Cocker Spaniels, have heavy, pendulous ears that seem to seal in moisture and wax, which provide a perfect growth medium for bacteria and fungi. In addition, some dogs have hair growing deep inside their ear canals, which also traps crud. Dogs with heavy or hairy ears often benefit from having their ears cleaned every two weeks or so. It also doesn't hurt to flip the dog's ears back when you think of it to let air in and moisture out. Pluck hair growing inside the ear canals and, for longhaired dogs, carefully trim the hair on the underside of the ear flaps with electric hair clippers to make it easier to keep the ears clean and dry inside.

Breed predispositions. Cocker Spaniels are notorious for ear infections, and vets tend to see a lot of Golden Retrievers, Labrador Retrievers, and terriers with ear problems as well. Most often, these "breed tendencies" toward ear infections result from one or more of the other factors discussed here: allergies (Goldens and terriers); other skin diseases (Cockers); swimming (Labs and Goldens); heavy, hairy ears (Cockers); and so on.

RECIPES FOR DISASTER

For some reason, otherwise sensible people will pour the darnedest things into their dog's ears in an attempt to clean them. Hydrogen peroxide, rubbing alcohol, vinegar, dish soap, and mineral oil are a few of the more popular ingredients. Are these homemade ear cleaners a good idea? Absolutely not. Could they hurt the dog's ears? Definitely.

Rubbing alcohol and vinegar sting like crazy on inflamed skin, and a dog that has an ear infection is likely to have inflamed skin or even open sores in the ear canals.

Mineral oil makes a big, greasy mess that's very difficult to remove. Besides, bacteria and fungi can live very happily in the mineral oil that gets left behind in the dog's ears.

Soap is an irritant and is very difficult to completely remove from the ear canal. Hydrogen peroxide crackles so loud in the ears that your dog is likely to be terrified.

It's worth spending a few dollars to buy a commercially prepared ear cleaner. Ear cleaners contain ingredients that break up clumps of wax in the lower ear canals. They make the canal slightly acid, to discourage the growth of yeast, and are gentle and sting-free on inflamed ears.

When you're shopping for an ear cleaner, buy one that just cleans, not one that contains an antibiotic or ear-mite killer as well. In most cases those extra ingredients are unnecessary.

Allergies. This is the No. 1 predisposing factor to ear infections. Allergies are widespread among dogs, both pure-bred and mixed-breed. In dogs, allergies commonly cause itching and inflamed skin. When the skin lining the ear canals is inflamed, it produces more wax. Excess wax provides a breeding ground for bacteria and fungi. It's wise to evaluate any dog with recurring ear infections for allergies, and to treat any allergies that are found (see page 95).

Diseases that affect the immune system. Hypothyroidism and Cushing's disease (see pages 298 and 299) can affect both the skin and the body's ability to fight infection, so occasionally they can be a factor in ear infections. Both diseases are treatable, and treating them can help get ear infections under control.

Ear mites. Dogs don't often get ear mites unless they have close, friendly contact with a cat, but ear mites can make the ears irritated or infected (see page 169).

Other skin diseases. Any disease that affects the rest of the skin can also affect the ears. Seborrhea—which occurs when skin cells go into overdrive—is one example. In most cases, medications used to treat specific skin conditions are also available in ear preparations. For more about seborrhea and other skin diseases, see pages 102 and 106.

WAXY BUILDUP

"My dog never had much earwax when she was a puppy, but now that she's a year and a half old, she seems to have a lot. Does this mean she's likely to get ear infections?"

Dogs often start to produce more earwax when they become adults, so this is not necessarily a sign of a problem. However, earwax production also increases when the ear canals are inflamed or irritated, as with allergies or ear infections. Normal earwax is brown and smells waxy but not foul. If your dog's ears smell bad, she may have an ear infection, and you should take her to the vet. If they don't smell bad, try cleaning them every two to four weeks.

EAR LICKING

"I have two dogs, and one likes to lick the other's ears. Is this harmful?"

Probably not. But you should check the ears of the dog who's being licked to make sure that it's not an ear infection that's attracting all the interest from his housemate. Do his ears smell bad? Does he scratch or rub at them a lot? Are they very dirty or waxy? If they smell bad or are itchy, have the vet check him for an ear infection. If they're dirty or waxy, clean them every two to four weeks, because licking alone won't do the trick.

SENSITIVITY TO EAR OINTMENT

"I've been using an ointment in my dog's ears for an ear infection, and yesterday I noticed that his ear flap has red bumps on the underside. Is he allergic to the antibiotic?"

He may have developed a sensitivity to the antibiotic or to the ointment base (such as petrolatum). Have your vet take a look. If it seems that the ointment is causing a rash, you can often switch to a liquid formula instead.

SURGERY FOR SEVERE EAR INFECTIONS

"I adopted a six-year-old Cocker Spaniel who was given up by his previous owners because of recurring ear infections. He constantly has a foul-smelling ear discharge, and his ears are very sore. My vet says the ears are in such bad shape, he recommends surgery to remove the ear canals altogether. This sounds so drastic—and what about my dog's hearing?"

The surgery your vet has recommended, ear-canal ablation, sounds so Frankensteinian that many dog owners are reluctant to agree to it at first. But consider the pain your dog is living with now. Imagine the pain of a severe ear-ache. Now imagine having that earache continuously for the rest of your life. The key benefit of the surgery is that it eliminates that pain completely.

Ear-canal surgery is only recommended for dogs that have severe, recurrent ear infections. Your dog is probably in so much pain that cleaning and medicating his ears is a real challenge. Plus, the chronic ear inflammation and infection have probably scarred and thickened his ear canals so much that it's extremely difficult to get the ear cleaner and medication where they need to be. A dog with chronic, severe ear infections may have ruptured eardrums, which allow the infection to spread to the middle ear. In some cases, the infection goes even deeper, and can eat away nerves or bone.

As for your dog's hearing, with a history of chronic, severe ear infections,

---

APPLY EAR MEDICATIONS LIKE A PRO

In order for ear medications to do their job, the ears must be clean, the medicine must get deep into the ear canal, and it must be distributed well.

First, clean the ears. If the ear canals are coated with wax, discharge, and yesterday's ear ointment, what you put in the ear today will never reach the skin surface, where it needs to be to do its work. Ears that are waxy or have a lot of discharge should be cleaned with an ear cleaner. If the ears are clean except for previously applied medication, then you can simply wipe the canals thoroughly with cotton balls.

Next, apply the medicine. Ear medications can be an ointment, a liquid, or a powder. Remember that the dog's ear canal is very long and L-shaped. You want to get the medication as close to the bottom of the L as possible. Give the medicine tube or bottle a practice squeeze to see how much pressure you need to apply the amount your vet told you to use. Then hold the flap of the dog's ear straight up with one hand, insert the tube or bottle vertically into the ear canal with the other hand, and give your premeasured squeeze. Before your dog can shake his head, massage the base of the ear for a few seconds to distribute the medicine on the inner surface. Repeat the process with the other ear.

he's probably living with significant hearing loss already. Dogs that have had ear-canal ablation surgery can still feel vibrations and may still respond to some loud or low-frequency sounds. Certainly, dogs can adapt much more comfortably to deafness than to constant pain. And although the surgery may sound drastic, the outward appearance of the ear is very much the same once the incision has healed and the hair has grown back.

There is one serious potential risk to the surgery, however. The facial nerve, which runs close to the ear canal, can accidentally be damaged. If that happens, a dog can lose the ability to close his eye on that side, and he may require eyedrops and careful monitoring for eye injuries for the rest of his life. To lessen the risk of damage to the facial nerve, it's best to have ear-canal ablation surgery performed by a veterinarian who has lots of experience with the procedure.

A SWOLLEN EAR

"My dog has been shaking her head a lot, and now one of her ears is swollen like a balloon. What happened? Can it be fixed?"

Sometimes a dog shakes her head so hard that she breaks a small blood vessel in the ear flap and it fills up with blood. Or a bite wound on the ear can become infected and the ear flap can become swollen with pus. Whatever caused the head shaking—ear mites, an ear infection, something stuck in the ear, a bite wound—needs to be treated. The fluid can be drained from the ear flap, but if it's blood, more will often accumulate and the process will have to be repeated. A swollen ear sometimes will scar and have a slightly crinkled appearance after it heals.

THE DEAF DOG

"Our 15-year-old Poodle mix doesn't seem to hear as well as she used to. Do dogs go deaf?"

Some dogs start to lose their hearing as they get older when nerve cells and other cells in the inner ear break down. Chronic ear infections—especially if the eardrum is ruptured—also can lead to deafness. Antibiotics in the gentamicin family can cause deafness, particularly if they're used in high doses or in dogs that have kidney disease. (The kidneys help break down gentamicin.) Have your vet check your dog for signs of ear infection. Hearing loss caused by infection will often improve with treatment, and that caused by gentamicin may resolve after the drug is discontinued.

Other forms of deafness are not reversible, but fortunately, dogs can function very well with hearing loss. To ensure her safety, keep your dog away from cars—even in your own driveway. She may not be able to hear well enough to move away from a car backing out of the garage. And to ensure your own safety, be careful not to "sneak up on her," especially when she's dozing—she might be startled enough to bite.

Dogs can also be born deaf. This disorder is seen most often in Dalmatians; dogs with a merle (dappled) coat, such as some Australian Cattle Dogs; and dogs whose coats are mostly white, such as Old English Sheepdogs and Bull Terriers. Most dog breeders routinely test puppies of these breeds for deafness before selling them. Beware of buying a Dalmatian or merle dog from a pet store without checking his hearing, however. A deaf puppy may be difficult to train and may react aggressively when startled.

CHAPTER 9

Bones, Joints, and Arthritis

WITH A HOP, SKIP, OR LIMP, your dog is telling you something—but what? That his foot, back, or leg hurts, that's what. The problem could be something as simple and easily remedied as an acorn top stuck between his pads, or it could be something more serious, from an inherited bone or joint disease (like hip dysplasia) to a "sports injury" (like a torn knee ligament) or even a ruptured spinal disk. When it's working well, the canine skeletal system supports the body and allows free movement. If your dog's support system isn't working properly, this chapter will help you pinpoint the cause, as well as give you insight into the full range of treatment options for the dog with bone or joint problems.

EMERGENCY!

Does your dog need immediate veterinary care? Check this list to help you decide.

TAKE IMMEDIATE ACTION!

Call your vet or an emergency veterinary clinic *now* if your dog is showing any of the following symptoms:

❏ She is **unable to move a leg;** paralysis can be a sign of a spinal-cord injury.

❏ He has suddenly started to **drag a foot** along the ground when he walks; this can be a sign of a spinal-cord injury.

❏ She is **reluctant to move her head** or her **neck or back seems very painful;** these could be signs of a spinal-cord injury.

❏ He has an **obviously broken bone.**

TAKE A MINUTE . . .

Read further in this book and then call your vet during office hours as needed if your dog is showing any of the following symptoms:

❏ She has suddenly started **limping** (see page 232).

❏ You think he may have **hip dysplasia** (see page 230).

❏ You think she may have **arthritis** (see page 238).

❏ Your dog is taking medication for arthritis but is still **stiff and sore** (see page 239).

❏ He is becoming increasingly **unsteady on his feet;** this could be a sign of a spinal cord problem (see page 247).

❏ She is a small dog who sometimes **skips** on one hind leg when she walks; this could be a knee problem (see page 236).

❏ He is a young, large-breed dog with **sore or swollen leg bones;** this could be panosteitis (see page 237).

Remember, it's never wrong to call your veterinarian if you have a question about your dog's health, or if you're worried about a symptom or your dog's overall condition. That's what we're here for.

CAUSES OF HIP DYSPLASIA

"I want to get a Labrador Retriever puppy, but I've heard that a lot of Labs have hip dysplasia. How common is hip dysplasia, and how can I find a puppy that doesn't have it?"

Hip dysplasia (simply put, a poorly formed hip joint) is very common in dogs, especially in large purebreds, although small dogs and mixed breeds can certainly have it as well. Labs, Goldens, Rottweilers, and German Shepherds have traditionally had a high incidence of hip dysplasia, but a better understanding of the contributing factors has helped decrease that incidence in recent years.

In a normal hip, the head of the femur (the thigh bone) and the pelvis fit together in a snug ball-and-socket joint. In hip dysplasia, the socket is too shallow, or the ball is too small or too flat, or the ligaments holding the joint together are too loose. This allows the ball to slide around in the socket, causing a wobbly gait and pain. The problem can be so mild it's virtually undetectable, or it can be so severe that a puppy will limp even at a walk and have trouble pushing himself to a standing position when lying down. Over time, the wear and tear of the hip sliding back and forth causes arthritis to develop in the joint. Arthritis can start when a dog is as young as one year old, or it can take much longer to set in.

Three factors are known to contribute to hip dysplasia: heredity, nutrition, and exercise. Understanding these factors will help you to minimize the risk of hip dysplasia when choosing and raising your Lab puppy.

1. Heredity. Genetics plays a part in hip dysplasia, but it's not a single-gene, all-or-nothing relationship. A sire and dam who do not have hip dysplasia are less likely to produce a puppy that has the disease, but they still could. Most breeders of large-breed dogs have their sires' and dams' hips x-rayed and graded by either the OFA (Orthopedic Foundation for Animals) or PennHIP (The University of Pennsylvania Hip Improvement Program). The OFA passing scores are Excellent, Good, and Fair. PennHIP scores are given as a number, with lower numbers (tighter hips) being better than higher numbers (looser hips). When you're looking for a large-breed

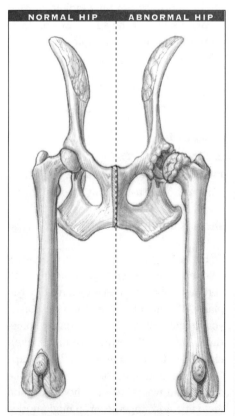

NORMAL HIP · ABNORMAL HIP

A normal hip has a tightly fitting ball-and-socket joint. In hip dysplasia, the joint is loose and unstable, the cartilage becomes damaged, and arthritis sets in.

puppy, ask the breeder whether the parents' hips have been screened and what their scores were. Ask whether the parents have been screened for elbow dysplasia as well—about 50 percent of dogs with dysplastic hips also have dysplastic elbows.

For more information on these hip-screening tests, see page 18.

2. Nutrition. Overfeeding large-breed puppies, or giving them calcium or vitamin D supplements, *increases* the likelihood they will develop hip dysplasia. Excess calories promotes too-fast growth, which strains a puppy's developing bones and joints. Feeding puppies "rocket fuel" doesn't make them any bigger as adults, either; a puppy's ultimate height is determined by genetics, not by how fast he grows. Excess calcium or vitamin D interferes with normal bone growth and cartilage development.

Large-breed puppies—those who will weigh 50 pounds or more as an adult—should not be fed free-choice or allowed unlimited amounts of food. They should be given a measured amount of food, divided into two or three meals per day. Choose a food that has between 28 percent and 32 percent protein, between 8 and 15 percent fat, and between 1 and 1.5 percent calcium (see page 50).

3. Exercise. Too much exercise can also strain developing bones and joints and worsen any inherited tendency toward hip dysplasia. Remember that puppies are babies. They need lots of rest, and the exercise they get should be gentle and fairly brief. Don't take a puppy hiking for hours, and don't Rollerblade or jog with a puppy until he is full-grown. Be especially careful to avoid anything that involves jumping. Save the agility and endurance events for after your puppy has finished growing.

CHECKING FOR HIP DYSPLASIA

"Can't breeders simply x-ray their puppies to check for hip dysplasia before they sell them?"

Not unless the puppies are at least four months old, and even then only if they use the PennHIP x-ray method (see page 19). The PennHIP method measures how much looseness, or play, there is in the hip joint, and it can diagnose hip dysplasia at a younger age than plain x-rays can.

Hip dysplasia develops as a puppy grows, and large-breed dogs continue growing until they're about two years old. A puppy whose hips looked normal on plain x-rays at the age of two or three months—when most puppies are sold—could still develop hip dysplasia later on. The Orthopedic Foundation for Animals won't give an official score to any dog that is less than two years old.

SYMPTOMS OF HIP DYSPLASIA

"My six-month-old Rottweiler has a goofy, bouncy walk. Does that mean she has hip dysplasia?"

A lot of puppies—especially big, gangly ones—have a clumsy, bumbling gait, and this does not mean they have hip dysplasia. If your puppy had hip dysplasia, you might notice that she limps sometimes, especially after strenuous exercise. You might hear or feel her hips "click" in and out, or notice that she stands and walks with her hocks or hind feet very close together. You might notice her struggling to push herself up into a standing position when she's lying down, or she might have trouble climbing stairs.

The way vets assess a puppy for hip dysplasia is by looking for a limp as the puppy walks and runs, then checking whether the hip can easily be pushed out of position in the socket (this feels like a "click" and is called the Ortolani sign).

If there's a suspicion of a problem—or if owners simply want more information—x-rays can be taken to check for hip dysplasia. Although a six-month-old puppy whose hips looked normal on plain x-rays might still develop hip dysplasia later, signs of the disease are often visible at this age. These x-rays are taken with the dog lying on her back in a frog-leg position. The puppy is sedated for a few minutes while the x-rays are taken. Sedation is required to relax the hip and thigh muscles and keep the dog in the proper position for accurate x-rays. These x-rays can also be taken while a pup is under anesthesia for spaying or neutering.

On the x-rays, the vet will look at whether the head of the femur is smooth and round and fits snugly into the pelvis. In a puppy with severe hip dysplasia, the head of the femur may be out of the socket, or it may be obviously flat or misshapen.

Looseness in the hip joint—another sign of dysplasia—is measured by PennHIP x-rays (see page 19). Very loose hips are a sign of dysplasia, and a good indication that a dog will develop arthritis over time.

You have a puppy of a breed that is known to have a high incidence of hip dysplasia, and you're obviously concerned about it. If you haven't already asked your vet to evaluate the puppy for hip dysplasia, I encourage you to do so. If her hips are normal, you'll be reassured, and if they are abnormal, you'll have surgical options for correcting the problem before arthritis sets in (see the following Q&A).

TREATING HIP DYSPLASIA

"What can be done for a dog who has hip dysplasia?"

Many treatments are available for a dog with hip dysplasia. Which is best for your dog depends on the severity of his problem, his size, and whether he already has arthritis in the hip joints, among other factors.

Surgery to correct the anatomical defect in the hips is one option. Other treatments for hip dysplasia address the arthritis that inevitably results from it.

Arthritis treatments—including lifestyle changes, joint supplements, anti-inflammatory medications, acupuncture, and physical therapy—are described in the box on page 240. Below are the four main types of surgery for dogs with hip dysplasia.

Juvenile pubic symphysiodesis (JPS). This is a relatively new procedure for puppies five months old or younger who have moderate to severe hip dysplasia. In a JPS, a small incision is made in the lower abdomen, and the growth plate of the pubic bone is cauterized using a surgical cautery probe. This stops the pubic bone from growing, and as the rest of the pelvis continues to grow, the hip sockets wind up rotating slightly outward and downward. The repositioned hip sockets hold the head of the femur more firmly, reducing or eliminating hip dysplasia. The advantages of a JPS over a TPO (see below) are that it's less painful and less expensive, and the puppy recovers very quickly. The disadvantages are that a JPS can be done only in a young puppy with an actively growing pelvis, and there is a small risk of damaging the urethra or other structures in the lower abdomen with the cautery probe.

THE LIMPING HOUND

A limp or skip in a dog's gait is caused by pain or restricted motion somewhere in the foot, leg, or back. The pain could be from a new injury, or it could be from a flare-up of a chronic condition, such as arthritis. If your dog develops a limp, look for a simple, obvious cause before calling your vet.

First, think about the onset of the problem. What was your dog doing when you first noticed the limp? Did he jump or yelp as if he had a sudden injury? Can you tell at a glance what part of the foot, leg, or back is bothering him? Has he injured or shown signs of a problem in that area before?

Next, do a systematic physical exam to home in on the problem. Start with a close look at your dog's overall posture. When he's standing still, is his weight balanced on both hind legs, or is he resting one leg? Does his back look level? Is he hunching his back, extending his neck stiffly, or otherwise holding himself any differently than usual? Does the affected leg have any obvious lumps or bumps the other leg doesn't have?

If your dog is in so much pain that he may snap at you if you touch his feet or legs, stop there, call your vet, report your findings, and arrange to bring your dog in for an exam. If your dog is not so uncomfortable that you're at risk of getting bitten, you can take a closer look yourself.

Start with the foot of the affected leg. Common foot problems include a broken toenail, something sharp stuck between the pads, sores between the toes, or a broken toe. Do any of his toes look swollen? Does he have a broken toenail? If so, see page 425 for how to apply first aid. Does he have anything stuck between his toes (on top) or between his pads (underneath)? If so, remove the object and check closely for cuts or sores. If there are cuts or sores, soak the foot for five minutes in warm water with a drop of mild soap or shampoo added, then dry the foot carefully, especially between the toes. If the foot continues to bother your dog, call the vet. If your dog has a swollen toe or other signs of a possible broken bone, call your vet.

If there's nothing wrong with the foot, place one hand on the ankle of that leg and your other hand on the

Triple pelvic osteotomy (TPO). This is for young dogs (usually less than one year old) who have moderate to severe hip dysplasia but have not yet developed arthritis in the hip joint. In a TPO, the bones of the pelvis are cut, angled, and anchored with bone plates to create a hip joint that holds the femur more firmly. TPOs are expensive, costing thousands of dollars, and are not appro-priate for all dogs with hip dysplasia (a veterinary orthopedic surgeon can tell you whether your dog is a good candidate), but under the right circumstances, they can allow normal function in a young dog that would otherwise become crippled by arthritis.

Total hip replacement. This is for large dogs who have become debilitated by hip dysplasia and arthritis. The dog's

ankle of the opposite leg, and gently run your hands up the front of the legs all the way to the top, feeling for a bump, swelling, warmth, or pain in a specific location. Repeat while running your hands up the back of the legs. If your dog doesn't flinch and you don't feel any difference between one leg and its opposite, then very gently flex and extend the joints in the leg, starting with the foot and working your way up. Stop immediately if your dog growls, snaps, or otherwise acts distressed, and call your vet to tell him where the problem seems to be. The most common problems in the knee are a ligament tear or a dislocated kneecap (see page 236). The most common problem in the hip is hip dysplasia (see page 230). The most common problems in the elbow and shoulder are elbow dysplasia (see page 234) and osteochondrosis dissecans, or OCD (see page 238).

If you think your dog's neck or back is painful, do *not* bend the neck or prod the back to try to locate the problem; if your dog has a spinal disk problem or wobbler syndrome (see page 248), such pressure could be excruciating and might even damage the spinal cord. Call your vet instead.

hip joint is removed and replaced with an artificial hip joint, much like those used in people with hip fractures. "Total hip" surgery is usually done in dogs who weigh 40 pounds or more. In smaller dogs, a femoral head ostectomy (see below) is often recommended instead.

Femoral head ostectomy (FHO). In an FHO, the head of the femur is removed but not replaced by an artificial

joint. The dog's hip and thigh muscles hold the hip and thigh bone in place, and the dog can walk comfortably despite not having a hip joint. This works well in smaller dogs—those weighing less than 40 pounds or so—and is designed mainly to eliminate the pain of severely arthritic hip joints.

VITAMIN C AND HIP DYSPLASIA

"I recently heard that hip dysplasia can be prevented by—or maybe it was treated with—vitamin C and baby aspirin. Is this true?"

People have given vitamin C to puppies in the hope of preventing hip dysplasia and to adult dogs in the hope of slowing the development of arthritis secondary to hip dysplasia. The theory is that vitamin C's antioxidant properties will lessen the damage to cartilage in the hip joints. I have not seen any controlled studies that show that vitamin C is effective in preventing or treating hip dysplasia or other forms of arthritis. That said, C is a relatively safe vitamin, so there is little harm in trying it if you're so inclined. Doses range from 250 to 1000 mg per day, depending on the size of the dog or puppy, divided and given with meals. The most common side effect, if any, is loose stools; if this happens, reduce the dose or stop giving the vitamin.

If vitamin C plus baby aspirin seems to help a dog with arthritis, it's the aspirin that's producing the effect. Buffered or enteric-coated aspirin is often used as an anti-inflammatory to reduce the pain of arthritis in dogs. You should always consult your vet, however, for an appropriate dose before starting a dog on aspirin, and it should not be given to a dog who is already on another pain reliever, such as Rimadyl or EtoGesic. Aspirin will not "prevent" hip dysplasia or arthritis in young dogs and should not be given for that purpose, because it can cause bleeding in the stomach or intestines.

ELBOW DYSPLASIA

"I have an 11-month-old Lab puppy with terrible elbow dysplasia. He has developed arthritis, and the elbow is quite swollen. Should I make him take it easy, and can I expect him ever to stop limping?"

Elbow dysplasia is a general term for several specific problems affecting the bones and cartilage of the elbow joint. (A dog's elbow is the backward-pointing joint at the top of the front leg, by the "armpit.") The ends of the bones forming the joint may not have fused properly during growth, the cartilage may be damaged, the joint may be misshapen, or

a dog may have a combination of these problems. One possible result is that pieces of cartilage or even fragments of bone can break off inside the joint, causing additional pain.

Over time, all dogs with elbow dysplasia will develop arthritis in the affected joints. Here's the bad news: elbow dysplasia is a lifetime problem. It is not going to go away. So yes, you should be making your dog take it easy, and no, he may never stop limping altogether.

What else can you do about elbow dysplasia? Surgery may be an option. Total elbow replacement is the newest, and most expensive, type of surgery. Alternatively, surgery to remove loose bits of cartilage or bone fragments in the elbow joint can relieve pain and allow the joint to move more freely. Take your dog and his x-rays to a veterinary orthopedic surgeon to discuss whether surgery can help your dog, and if so, how much it can help. Be very specific in your questions so that you fully understand

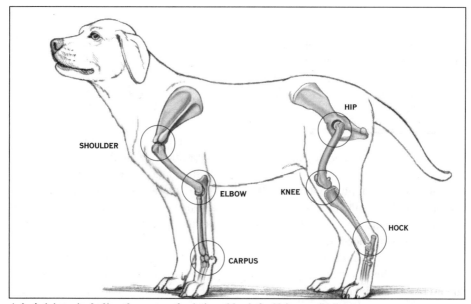

A dog's joints, including the carpus (wrist) and hock (ankle), are similar to ours.

the prognosis. Will surgery decrease your dog's pain? If so, by how much—25 percent? Or 50 percent? Will his exercise need to be restricted to leash walks forever, whether or not he has surgery? Is he likely to need anti-inflammatory medication even after surgery? Can the surgery slow down the progression of the arthritis?

It's possible that you and the orthopedic surgeon will decide that surgery will *not* help significantly in your dog's case. If surgery can help, it will be up to you to decide whether the degree of potential benefit makes the effort and cost worthwhile.

Be sure to have your dog's other elbow and his hips x-rayed before you make a decision about surgery. More than 50 percent of dogs that have dysplasia in one elbow have it in the other elbow or the hips as well. The number of joints affected and which are affected most severely are important factors in deciding whether to have surgery and, if so, on which joint or joints.

The other way to manage elbow dysplasia is to treat the resulting arthritis. These treatments are described on page 240.

Elbow dysplasia, like hip dysplasia, is partly hereditary. If you got your dog from a breeder, tell the breeder that your dog has this condition. A good breeder would not want to breed a sire or dam again if their pups had elbow dysplasia. And of course, you should not breed your dog either. If he hasn't already been neutered, it's a good idea to do so.

THE LITTLE-DOG HIP DISEASE

"Over the past month, my Yorkshire Terrier, who's just one year old,

started limping worse and worse on a hind leg. The vet took some x-rays and said my dog has a bad hip disease—something with a French name—and needs surgery. Will my dog be crippled for life?"

That bad hip disease with a French name is Legg-Calvé-Perthes, and it afflicts mainly toy and small breeds. In this disease, for unknown reasons, the bone in the head of the femur dies and breaks down. The result is pain and, eventually, collapse of the hip joint. In 15 percent of the dogs with Legg-Calvé-Perthes disease, both hips are affected.

There are two pieces of good news about this otherwise nasty disease. First, it is fairly rare—much less common than hip dysplasia, for example. Second, the small dogs who most commonly get Legg-Calvé-Perthes are good candidates for a femoral head ostectomy (FHO), or surgical removal of the head of the femur, which relieves the pain of the dying bone and speeds the dog's return to normal activity. This procedure is the same as that used for smaller dogs with debilitating hip dysplasia (see page 233).

Legg-Calvé-Perthes is seen most often in Miniature Poodles, Miniature Pinschers, Pugs, Dachshunds, and small terriers, such as Yorkies, Jack Russells, Westies, and Cairns. It affects puppies and young dogs, most between the ages of 3 and 18 months, and is believed to be at least partly hereditary. In most cases, dogs with the disease had no known history of injuring the leg or hip or any other predisposing factors.

The main symptoms are hip pain and lameness in a young dog that worsen over a few weeks. Legg-Calvé-Perthes is diagnosed by hip x-rays, which show moth-eaten bone in the head and neck of the femur and, eventually, collapse of the affected bone. At this time, no treatment is known to halt or reverse the progression of the disease, and the best treatment is an FHO. Anti-inflammatory drugs or other pain medication can be used before and after surgery to relieve pain. Most dogs recover well and have essentially normal function after surgery, so you needn't worry about your dog being "crippled." The affected leg may be slightly shorter than the other hind leg, so your dog may always have a slight limp, but he will be able to get around normally and will not be in pain once he recovers from the surgery.

KNEE LIGAMENT INJURIES

"My three-year-old Lab was playing off-leash in the park when he suddenly yelped and held up his left hind leg. He's still barely using the leg. The vet suspects a cruciate ligament injury. Is this common? What's the best treatment?"

Injuries to the anterior cruciate ligament (ACL) are *very* common in large, active dogs. The ACL is the key ligament that allows dogs to bear weight on their knee joints. (A dog's knee is the joint in the hind leg closest to the belly that bends the same direction our knees do.) Similar injuries are common among people who jog or play sports.

The ACL can be partially or completely torn, and cartilage in the knee can also be damaged. An ACL injury is diagnosed by physical exam and x-rays. The vet will check whether the top of the tibia (the lower bone in the knee joint) can be pulled forward abnormally. This motion is called the drawer sign—as in

opening a drawer—and is only possible if the ACL is torn. X-rays do not show ligaments or cartilage clearly, but they sometimes show an obviously displaced tibia or a swollen joint capsule. They will also show whether your dog has hip dysplasia as well, which will influence the treatment and prognosis.

The best treatment for a torn ACL is surgery to stabilize the knee joint. The prognosis with surgery is excellent, but the recovery can be prolonged: it may be six months or more before the dog walks and runs as well as he did before the injury. The other option for a dog with a torn ACL is pain medication and rest—in other words, no exercise off-leash for a month or more. Dogs who weigh less than 40 pounds or who hardly ever run may recover adequate mobility without surgery. Arthritis will develop in the affected knee, but that can occur even with surgery. Glucosamine/chondroitin sulfate supplements may be helpful in easing the arthritis.

If your dog tears the ACL in one knee, be aware that he has a better than 50-50 likelihood of tearing the ACL in the *other* knee within the next couple of years. By blowing out the first knee, he has demonstrated that he possesses all the risk factors—he's big, he's active, and his knees are a vulnerable point.

WOBBLY KNEECAPS

"My Pomeranian skips on her hind legs sometimes. I thought this was cute, but my new vet says my dog has dislocated kneecaps. Should I be concerned?"

This condition is called luxating patellas ("patella" is the medical term for "kneecap"). It is extremely common in toy and small breeds like your Pomeranian. Usually the tendency is present from birth, but an injury to the knee (such as getting hit by a car) can dislocate the kneecap in a dog of any size. The severity of the condition varies widely, so it's important to discuss with your vet just how bad your dog's knees are and whether anything needs to be done to correct the problem.

The anatomy of a dog's knee is essentially the same as that of a person: the femur (thigh bone) and tibia (lower leg bone) meet in a hinge joint. The patella is a small, round bone imbedded in the tendon that passes over the knee to connect the large muscles at the front of the thigh to the tibia. The patella is supposed to move up and down smoothly in a groove in the lower end of the femur. In patellar luxation, the kneecap occasionally or permanently pops out of this groove to one side or the other, making it difficult for the dog to flex and extend the leg smoothly.

Patellar luxation is graded according to its severity. Grade I is a kneecap that occasionally pops out of position but usually stays where it belongs. A dog with Grade I patellar luxation will walk normally most of the time, and occasionally skip or limp briefly when the knee pops out of place.

Grade II is a kneecap that pops out of position easily when the knee is flexed and straightened but returns to the proper position on its own. A dog with Grade II patellar luxation will skip or limp frequently but not constantly, and may have slight curving of the lower leg bones because the slipping patella and tendon put abnormal pressure on the bone.

Grade III is a kneecap that is usually dislocated but can be pushed back into normal position. A dog with Grade III patellar luxation limps or skips all the time and has curved lower leg bones because of the abnormal pressure of the patellar tendon.

Grade IV is a kneecap that is permanently dislocated and can't be pushed back into position. A dog with Grade IV patellar luxation is obviously lame and may even walk with her hips in the air and most of her weight shifted to the front legs. The lower leg bones are curved or bent.

Grades I and II usually don't need to be treated. Surgery is recommended for most dogs with Grades III and IV patellar luxation. Doing surgery early—before the dog is six or eight months old—can prevent the lower leg bones from becoming deformed. The surgery is tailored to the dog's specific abnormality. The groove the patellar tendon rides in can be deepened so the patella doesn't pop out as easily. If the leg bones are angled or bent in such a way that the patella is forced out of position, then the bones can be cut and pinned to correct the angle and keep the patella in place.

"GROWING PAINS" IN YOUNG DOGS

"The puppy I adopted from the local shelter is really tall and long legged—he looks like he may be part Great Dane. He's nine months old now and has started limping off and on. The vet thinks he has something called panosteitis. What's the treatment?"

Panosteitis is a painful but temporary inflammation of the leg bones in growing puppies. It affects mainly large breeds, such as German Shepherds, Saint Bernards, Great Danes, Airedales, and Irish Setters, perhaps because large dogs' leg bones grow so rapidly. Panosteitis usually shows up between the ages of 6 and 18 months, and male dogs are affected about four times as often as females.

Dogs with panosteitis will limp and show pain when the leg bones are squeezed. Areas of the bone may feel swollen as well. The symptoms often shift from one leg to another as different bones flare up and recover. X-rays show exuberant bone growth and sometimes swelling at the affected areas.

Injuries (such as a bone fracture or torn ligament) or joint problems (such as elbow dysplasia or Lyme disease) can also make a large-breed puppy limp, so your vet probably ruled out those possibilities before diagnosing panosteitis. Panosteitis affects the middle of the bones, not the joints, so a careful physical exam and perhaps x-rays usually can confirm the diagnosis.

The treatment for panosteitis is pain medication (such as corticosteroids, enteric-coated aspirin, or Rimadyl) and rest as needed. Puppies outgrow panosteitis as they reach maturity, and there are no lasting ill effects.

CARTILAGE PROBLEMS IN YOUNG DOGS

"My 15-month-old Golden Retriever was limping on a front leg. The vet took x-rays and said my dog has a loose piece of cartilage in his shoulder joint that should be removed. Could he have injured the shoulder without my knowing it?"

The loose cartilage isn't necessarily the result of an injury. Osteochondrosis dissecans (OCD) is a condition in which cartilage doesn't form properly in a joint. The cartilage may erode, causing joint pain, and small pieces or flaps of cartilage may break free. OCD is most common in fast-growing, large-breed dogs, such as Rottweilers, Great Danes, Irish Wolfhounds, and Newfoundlands.

A limp and possibly swelling of the joint are the symptoms an owner might notice. Symptoms usually appear between the ages of 6 and 18 months. The shoulder is the joint most commonly affected, followed by the elbow (OCD can be one factor in elbow dysplasia—see page 234), hock, and knee.

Definitively diagnosing OCD can be a challenge, because the defective cartilage is apparent on x-rays only if there are obvious loose fragments, joint swelling, or changes in the underlying bone.

The treatment for OCD is surgery to remove unhealthy cartilage and thereby prevent its ongoing breakdown within the joint. Some degree of arthritis is likely to affect the joint even after surgery, but it will be less severe than if nothing was done. Treatments for arthritis (see page 240) can help relieve the pain of OCD.

THOSE ACHY JOINTS

"What causes arthritis in dogs, and how is it diagnosed?"

The most common form of arthritis in dogs is osteoarthritis, also known as degenerative joint disease (DJD). This type of arthritis—which is extremely common in dogs, increasing as they get older—is a progressive breakdown of the cartilage in one or more joints. (Cartilage is the smooth, tough material that covers the ends of bone and cushions the bone against the friction of the moving joint.) DJD probably begins with some sort of injury to the cartilage—anything from a sprain or broken bone involving the joint to microscopic, cumulative wear and tear. The most common sites of DJD in dogs are the hips (because of hip dysplasia), the knees (because of anterior cruciate ligament injuries), the elbows (because of elbow dysplasia), and the lower back (because of stress and strain).

A different kind of arthritis—an inflammatory form—also affects dogs but is much less common; it's most often caused by a blood-borne infection or an immune-system overreaction involving the joints (see pages 243 and 244).

DJD is diagnosed by symptoms, physical exam, and sometimes x-rays. The symptoms of DJD are gradually increasing pain and stiffness in one or more joints. Dogs with DJD often have the most pain after rest, and then "warm out of it" as they move about. On physical exam, the affected joint may feel thicker than normal. The joint's normal range of motion is likely to be restricted, and fully flexing and extending the joint is painful to the dog. The vet may feel "crunchiness," or crepitus, when flexing the joint, caused by abnormal bone remodeling in the joint. X-rays may show this remodeling—called osteophytes or bone spurs—and either swelling or partial collapse of the joint, depending on how severe and longstanding the problem is.

Many treatments are available to relieve the pain of DJD. They are described beginning on page 240.

HIND-LEG STIFFNESS

"My dog seems very stiff in the hips when she gets up. Would the human glucosamine/chondroitin sulfate joint supplements help her?"

Has your dog been previously diagnosed with hip dysplasia? Hip dysplasia leads to arthritis in the hip joints, and arthritic hips can cause stiffness in the hind legs. If so, glucosamine/chondroitin sulfate supplements might help. It's OK to give human glucosamine/chondroitin supplements to dogs, but you need to scale down the dose to your dog's size (see page 240). The supplements made specifically for dogs are easier to use because they're dosed appropriately and many of them are flavored, so you can give them as a treat rather than having to make your dog swallow a pill every day.

If, however, your dog has never been diagnosed with hip dysplasia or arthritic hips, then have your vet examine her to be sure her difficulty in getting up is caused by arthritis and not something else, such as a spinal cord problem (see page 247).

RIMADYL FEARS

"I've heard that Rimadyl can be deadly, and I'm scared to give it to my arthritic dog. How dangerous is it?"

In 1998, Rimadyl—a prescription anti-inflammatory for dogs—was reported to have caused liver damage in approximately 0.2 percent of the dogs who had taken it. Nonetheless, veterinarians have continued to prescribe Rimadyl (the brand name of carprofen), because it's an excellent pain reliever for arthritis in dogs and is safe for more than 99 percent of them. I wouldn't hesitate to use it for my own dog, as long as I followed the same precautions that my colleagues and I now advise all dog owners to take.

Those precautions are to (1) run a blood test checking the dog's liver enzymes before starting on Rimadyl; (2)

(continued on page 242)

TREATING ARTHRITIS

Arthritis is common among dogs—so common that it may seem as though every other dog is on some treatment for it. Still, many people don't understand the range of treatments and how they work.

The most common form of arthritis is degenerative joint disease (DJD), which is caused by a breakdown of the cartilage in one or more joints. DJD can't be cured, but the pain can be relieved by the following treatments.

❏ **Lifestyle changes.** Weight loss and regular, low-impact exercise are key treatments for dogs with arthritis. Excess weight places extra strain on the joints and makes it more difficult for a dog to move comfortably. Regular, mild-to-moderate exercise—such as leash walks or swimming—is excellent therapy for arthritic dogs, both physically and mentally. Daily exercise that is not so strenuous as to cause limping is best. Two or more shorter walks per day are better than one long walk. Avoid exercise that involves sudden stops, starts, and pivots, such as playing fetch.

Slippery floors can be treacherous for arthritic dogs. Consider putting down carpet runners on slick floors.

Stairs are often difficult for dogs with arthritis. Set up your dog's bed and eating area on the first floor so he doesn't have to climb stairs as often. A firm mattress-type dog bed will cushion arthritic joints. Small dogs can be carried on stairs, and large dogs can be supported with a sling (see page 88).

❏ **Joint supplements.** Glucosamine and chondroitin sulfate are nutrients that cartilage cells use to repair themselves. Roughly half of dogs with arthritis seem to be in less pain when they take glucosamine/chondroitin sulfate supplements. These supplements can be used along with an anti-inflammatory (although giving both together will make it impossible to determine which one is producing results). The usual dose is 20 mg of glucosamine and 16 mg of chondroitin sulfate per pound of bodyweight per day. In other words, a 50-pound dog would get 1,000 mg of glucosamine and 800 mg of chondroitin sulfate per day. If your dog shows no improvement after taking the supplements for six weeks, then you may as well stop giving them; they don't work for all dogs.

Adequan is the brand name of a compound called polysulfated glycosaminoglycan (PSGAG). Adequan helps the cartilage in the hip joints produce more lubricating fluid, which makes movement less painful. The injections (which are given in the thigh muscle, not in the joints themselves) work well for some dogs but not for others. The injections are usually given twice a week for four weeks, then once a week for four weeks, then once every two to four weeks as needed. If Adequan worked for your dog, you would see significant improvement after four weeks.

❏ **Anti-inflammatory medications.** These can be used either intermittently (after strenuous exercise) or daily (when a dog has difficulty climbing stairs or walking) to relieve the pain of arthritis. Buffered or enteric-coated aspirin, Rimadyl, EtoGesic, Metacam, Previcox, and Deramaxx are the anti-inflammatories used most commonly in dogs. Ask your veterinarian for an appropriate dose. Always give anti-inflammatories with a meal, to lessen the chances of stomach irritation. Never give a dog two different anti-inflammatory medications (such as Rimadyl and aspirin) simultaneously. If your dog vomits, loses her appetite, or has diarrhea after you start giving an anti-inflammatory, stop giving it and call your vet. Never give a dog ibuprofen (Motrin or Advil) or naproxen (Aleve), as these can be toxic to dogs in relatively low doses (see page 412). Acetaminophen (Tylenol) doesn't work well as a pain reliever for dogs.

❑ **Acupuncture.** Acupuncture increases blood circulation and the release of natural pain-killing substances by the body. For that reason it can be helpful in treating chronic pain in dogs, such as that from arthritis. Acupuncture treatments are given once a week for six weeks, and once every two to four weeks after that. The treatments are not painful—in fact, many dogs seem to find them relaxing. If no improvement is seen within the first four to six weeks, then acupuncture is unlikely to help your dog (it works in about 50 percent of dogs with arthritis). Your vet can refer you to a veterinary acupuncturist, or see page 453.

❑ **Physical therapy.** Therapists in many areas of the country now provide post-surgical rehabilitation, hydrotherapy, and massage for dogs. These treatments increase blood circulation and joint flexibility. Most dogs love to be touched, and such treatments often make them feel better both mentally and physically. Your vet or a veterinary orthopedic surgeon can refer you to physical therapists who work with dogs.

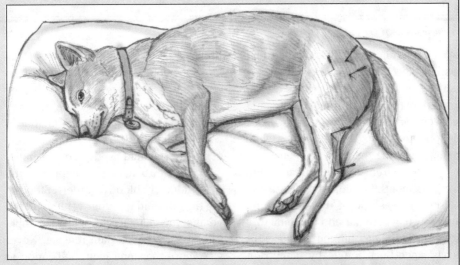

Acupuncture provides pain relief for about half of the dogs who have arthritis.

THE EXPENSE OF SURGERY

Orthopedic surgery is one of the most expensive categories of veterinary treatment. When all the tests, hospitalization, and follow-up visits are tallied, a triple pelvic osteotomy to correct hip dysplasia, or spine surgery to prevent paralysis from a ruptured disk, can cost thousands of dollars.

When faced with the prospect of spending that much money, the first thing the owner should do is to decide as clearheadedly as possible whether the cost is worth it. Note that I don't mean whether the dog is worth fixing; I mean whether the procedure in question is worth going into debt over. Is there a less expensive procedure that might work well for your dog? Could he potentially get better with pain medication, physical therapy, or other less costly treatment? With back surgery in particular, what is the likelihood your dog will remain paralyzed even after surgery? Setting aside the current problem, what is your dog's life expectancy? Are you comfortable with spending thousands of dollars to gain only months or a year of quality time with your dog? Alternatively, is your dog young and likely to live another 10 years if this problem can be fixed, making the expense a long-term investment?

Discuss these questions with your family, close friends, the surgeon, and other veterinarians. If you decide to go forward with an expensive treatment, look into the following resources for ways to manage the cost:

If you already have **pet health insurance,** it may pick up most or all of the tab for surgery. However, pet health insurance companies often refuse to cover treatment for inherited health problems, and if they include hip dysplasia in this category, they probably won't pay for your dog's hip surgery.

(continued from page 239)

avoid prescribing Rimadyl to a dog that has elevated liver enzymes, which may indicate preexisting liver problems; (3) stop giving Rimadyl immediately and recheck the liver enzymes if a dog loses his appetite, vomits, or has diarrhea while taking it; and (4) check the liver enzymes one month after starting Rimadyl and every six months while the dog is taking it. Rimadyl was one of the earliest prescription nonsteroidal anti-inflammatory drugs (NSAIDs) to hit the market, but it has since been joined by many others. EtoGesic (etodolac), Deramaxx (deracoxib), Metacam (meloxicam), and Previcox (firocoxib) are some of the mostly widely used for canine pain. Like most drugs, they are processed by the liver and excreted by the kidneys.

Most NSAIDs have the potential to cause stomach ulcers and affect blood cells. None should be given on an empty stomach or to a dog with preexisting liver, kidney, or blood disorders. Stop giving the pills and call your vet if your dog vomits, has diarrhea, or loses his appetite after starting a pain reliever. Never give more than one pain medication at the same time unless your vet authorizes the combination, because combining

(For more about pet health insurance, see page 438.)

All vets accept **credit cards,** of course, so you could charge the surgery and pay it off over time, with interest. Some vets also offer a less expensive option: **interest-free extended payment plans.** Others participate in **CareCredit,** an interest-free loan program to cover veterinary expenses that's backed by the American Animal Hospital Association (AAHA). ASPCA hospitals, veterinary-school hospitals, and other large veterinary institutions often have **donor programs** to help cover veterinary expenses for people who couldn't otherwise afford it.

If an expensive procedure is what's best for your dog but you simply can't foot the bill, be frank with your veterinarian, and ask if she knows of any program or group that can help with the cost. Such programs don't trumpet their existence, but they're out there, working quietly to help dogs and dog owners in need.

pain medications increases the risk of adverse side effects tremendously.

In addition to the known risks of prescription pain relievers for dogs, there are the unpredictable, idiosyncratic reactions an individual dog can have to a drug of any kind. If you have any suspicion that a medication may be causing an unwanted side effect in your dog, stop giving it and talk to your vet as soon as possible about continuing the drug or choosing an alternative.

Many of the prescription NSAIDs are formulated as tasty chewable tablets that a dog may regard as treats. Be sure to keep the bottle locked away where your dog can't reach it so he doesn't chew the bottle open and eat all the tablets. Call your vet or a veterinary emergency clinic immediately if you discover that your dog has eaten more than two or three doses of the prescription at one time.

Note that over-the-counter pain relievers are NOT safer for dogs than the prescription NSAIDs described above. Aspirin is at least as likely to cause stomach ulcers, which is why only buffered or enteric-coated versions should be given to dogs, and ibuprofen (Motrin, Advil) and naproxen (Aleve) are toxic to dogs even in low doses. Acetaminophen (Tylenol), which is highly toxic to cats, can also be toxic to dogs if given in high enough doses, and doesn't work well as a canine pain reliever anyway.

ARTHRITIS CAUSED BY AN INFECTION

"My dog is limping on a front leg, and it looks a bit swollen. He had some ticks on him after we went camping last week. Does he have Lyme disease?"

It's possible. The most common symptoms of Lyme disease in dogs are lameness, one or more swollen leg joints, and fever. Lethargy, muscle stiffness, and loss of appetite are other possible symptoms.

Lyme is a bacterial disease transmitted by deer ticks, and it usually appears between one and four weeks after a tick bite. A deer tick must be attached and feeding for about 24 hours in order to transmit the disease, which is diagnosed with a blood test and treated with antibiotics. If treated promptly, most dogs recover well.

Lyme disease is probably the most common type of infective arthritis in dogs. Other bacteria, fungi, viruses, and similar organisms also can enter joints from the blood and cause inflammation and arthritis. Two other tick-borne bacterial diseases—Rocky Mountain spotted fever and ehrlichiosis—occasionally cause lameness and swollen joints in dogs (see page 174). The fungal diseases blastomycosis and coccidioidomycosis also can cause infective arthritis (see page 284).

These types of arthritis are diagnosed either by blood tests, which may show an increased white blood cell count and antibodies to the organism involved, or by tests on joint fluid, which may contain white blood cells and bacteria or other organisms. Once the organism is identified, the appropriate antibiotic is given, and usually the arthritis clears up completely.

IMMUNE-MEDIATED ARTHRITIS

"When my five-year-old Standard Poodle got swollen joints and a fever, my vet thought she had Lyme disease. Antibiotics didn't help, though, and I finally took her to the vet school upstate, where they diagnosed a form of lupus. It's funny—I had wondered whether it was an immune problem, because I have rheumatoid arthritis myself, but I didn't know dogs got those diseases."

Dogs do get immune-mediated diseases —those triggered by a misfiring of the immune system—and they are among the most mysterious and difficult to diagnose. Your dog apparently has systemic lupus erythematosus (SLE), an immune-system attack on multiple organs. Dogs also get rheumatoid arthritis (RA), which primarily targets the joints. Neither is common in dogs, but some studies have shown higher rates of immune-mediated diseases in Shelties, Old English Sheepdogs, Afghan Hounds, Collies, Beagles, German Shepherds, and Poodles.

SLE can cause a variety of problems, including arthritis in multiple joints, fever, sores on the skin or in the mouth, red blood cell or platelet deficiencies, and kidney disease. It's diagnosed by the presence of two or more of those indicators, plus a positive antinuclear antibody (ANA) blood test, and negative tests for diseases that could cause similar symptoms, such as Lyme or another tick-borne bacterial disease.

Rheumatoid arthritis causes lameness and joint swelling, and often fever, lethargy, and loss of appetite. It's diagnosed based on the symptoms plus a positive blood test for rheumatoid factor, x-rays showing small erosions of bone in multiple joints, and the absence of other diseases that can cause lameness and fever.

Like other immune-mediated diseases, SLE and rheumatoid arthritis are treated with medication to calm the immune system. Corticosteroids such as prednisone are given, and chemotherapy-type drugs may be added if the disease doesn't respond to prednisone within a week or so. Gold injections are sometimes used to treat dogs with rheumatoid arthritis, as they are for people.

The prognosis for dogs with immune-mediated arthritis is variable. Dogs with SLE who have kidney disease and those with rheumatoid arthritis so severe that they have difficulty standing and walking have a poor prognosis. Overall, about half to two-thirds of the dogs with SLE or rheumatoid arthritis respond well to treatment and are able to return to normal activities.

THE IMPORTANCE OF REST AND REHAB FOR ORTHOPEDIC INJURIES

Cage rest is often prescribed following surgery for bone or joint problems. Since many such problems occur in young, active dogs, strict confinement can be a challenge. Once their bouncy young patients seem to feel OK, dog owners sometimes abandon efforts to confine them to their beds. But allowing a dog to be too active too soon after surgery can undo the work that has been done. So carefully follow your vet's instructions for postsurgical rest and rehab, and call your vet for advice if you have any problems carrying out the instructions.

Cage rest means that a dog should be confined in an area just large enough for him to stand up, turn around, and lie down comfortably. A crate is ideal for cage rest. For very large dogs, a small closet with a baby gate blocking the door can also work well. This confinement is for 24 hours a day, except for quick trips on a leash to just outside the door to urinate and defecate. Otherwise, the dog should sleep, eat, and rest in this small space for as long as your vet has recommended. Note that confining your dog to the kitchen or bathroom does not qualify as cage rest—unless your bathroom is minuscule and your dog is a Great Dane. Will your dog go bonkers being confined like this? Maybe, but it really is important. Do your best to distract him with a cheese-stuffed Kong toy and lots of petting. Call your vet if your dog absolutely will not tolerate the confinement. Occasionally, vets will prescribe a sedative (for the dog, not the owner!).

Range-of-motion exercises are often prescribed for dogs who have had surgery on their spine or legs. Your vet will tell you whether you should do such exercises with your dog, on which leg or legs, and how many times each day. The basic movement of such exercises is to hold the dog's foot in your hands and gently flex and extend the toes, then the foot, then the hock or wrist, and so on up the leg to the hip or shoulder. These exercises are done to prevent joints from healing in a rigid position and to encourage good blood circulation in the leg. The exercises should not be painful, and most dogs seem to enjoy the attention. You can also gently squeeze and massage the dog's leg muscles, starting from the foot and working your way up.

SHAR-PEI FEVER

"My six-month-old Shar-Pei lost his appetite and started limping on his hind legs. The vet took one look and said, 'Shar-Pei fever.' Can you tell me more about this disease and its prognosis?"

Shar-Pei fever is the common name for familial renal amyloidosis, an inherited disease in Shar-Peis. Lameness, swelling of the hocks (see the illustration on page 234), and fever are often the first signs. This inflammatory arthritis goes away by itself in a few days, but unfortunately, it is an early warning sign of amyloidosis, the progressive formation of abnormal protein deposits in the kidneys and elsewhere. Over months to years, amyloidosis disrupts the normal functioning of the kidneys and causes kidney failure. The drugs DMSO and colchicine are sometimes given in the hope of slowing the accumulation of amyloid, but the prognosis for long-term health and survival is poor.

NECK INSTABILITY IN SMALL DOGS

"The day after playing with my friend's two Pugs, my Toy Poodle started holding her head and neck funny. The vet x-rayed my dog's neck and said the top two bones in her spine were abnormal and may have pinched the spinal cord. He says she should wear a neck brace for six weeks. Is it really that serious?"

The spine is supposed to protect the spinal cord from being squeezed or bent. Occasionally the top two vertebrae in a dog's neck are malformed and do not interlock and support the head properly, allowing the upper part of the spinal cord to bend or compress when the dog moves her head. This condition is called atlantoaxial instability and is seen most often in toy and small breeds, such as Chihuahuas, Pekingese, Pomeranians, Poodles, and Yorkshire Terriers.

The severity of the problem varies. Often it isn't discovered until a slight injury or strain makes the vertebrae shift and pinch the spinal cord. Then the symptoms can range from neck pain and stiffness, as

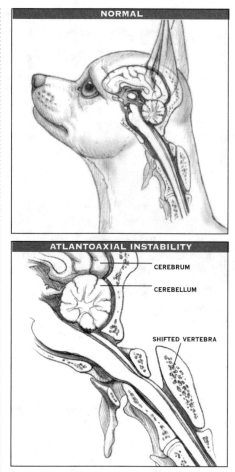

If the top two bones in the spine don't interlock properly, the spinal cord can become pinched, causing pain or even paralysis.

in your dog, to progressive weakness of the legs or even sudden paralysis.

Atlantoaxial instability is diagnosed by x-raying the upper neck. Care must be taken not to flex or extend the dog's neck too far when examining and x-raying her, because that can further damage the spinal cord. Another condition that can cause similar symptoms (neck pain, leg weakness, or paralysis) is a spinal disk problem. The uppermost vertebrae of a dog with a disk problem will look normal on x-rays, unlike those of a dog with atlantoaxial instability.

A range of treatments are available for dogs with atlantoaxial instability. First, any dog with symptoms of pain, leg weakness, or paralysis is assumed to have some degree of damage to the spinal cord and is given high doses of corticosteroids to reduce the swelling around the cord and preserve blood circulation to the area. Minor injuries or minor degrees of instability can then be treated by placing the dog in a neck brace or splint for six to eight weeks. More severe injuries—those where the dog's legs are weak or paralyzed—are best treated by surgery to pin or wire the vertebrae into position and prevent further pressure on the spinal cord.

The prognosis for dogs with atlantoaxial instability varies with its severity. Some dogs that are paralyzed do not regain the ability to stand and walk even if they have surgery. Dogs with only intermittent neck pain or stiffness can do very well with exercise restriction and use of a neck brace when they seem sore.

WOBBLER SYNDROME

"I'm a new Doberman Pinscher owner, and I've been told I need to watch out for something called wobbler syndrome. How serious is it? What are the symptoms?"

Wobbler syndrome is a catch-all name for a group of problems affecting the neck vertebrae of large-breed dogs, especially Dobermans and Great Danes. The common feature of these problems is they result in compression of the spinal cord, which can cause neck pain, leg weakness, or leg paralysis. Twice as many male dogs as female dogs are affected, for unknown reasons.

Dogs with wobbler syndrome usually become progressively uncoordinated, especially in the hind legs, over months to years: they wobble when they walk. Sometimes the neck will also be stiff or painful. Occasionally, a dog with wobbler syndrome will suddenly become paralyzed.

The disease is diagnosed by a myelogram of the spinal cord in the neck, or by an MRI or CT scan. In a myelogram, dye is injected into the fluid surrounding the spinal cord to make it stand out in silhouette on x-rays. (The spinal cord is soft tissue and would not otherwise show up clearly on x-rays.) The spinal cord of dogs with wobbler syndrome is compressed in two or more areas along the neck. If it is compressed in just a single area, a single displaced disk is the more likely cause of the symptoms.

Mild cases of wobbler syndrome—in which the dog has neck pain and slight incoordination or weakness of the hind legs—are treated with corticosteroids to reduce swelling and improve blood circulation around the spinal cord, plus strict cage rest (see page 245) and a neck brace for four weeks. If a dog has severe weakness or paralysis or does not improve with cage rest, then surgery to widen the space around the spinal cord and prevent the vertebrae from shifting is recommended.

DACHSHUND BACK TROUBLE

"I have a Dachshund, and I've been told I shouldn't let her jump on furniture or climb stairs because the length of her back makes it weak and easily injured. Is this true?"

Long-backed dogs, such as Dachshunds, Pekingese, Lhasa Apsos, Corgis, and

Basset Hounds, do have a higher incidence of disk problems than other dogs, but that doesn't mean they need to be treated like invalids.

The best way to protect your Dachshund against back injury is by keeping her slim and fit. Excess weight puts strain on the back and should be strictly avoided in Dachshunds and other long-backed dogs. Good muscle tone will help support the back, so make sure your Dachshund stays fit with lots of exercise.

Jumping up or down from a height and climbing stairs do put stress on the lower back. They needn't be banned entirely if it's important to you to have your Dachshund snuggle up with you on the couch or bed. But beware of letting her turn into an overweight couch potato, because then you really are piling on the risk factors.

SPINAL DISK DISEASE

"I have a somewhat arthritic 12-year-old Beagle, and when he started dragging a hind leg, I didn't think too much of it. But the vet was very concerned about a spinal disk problem, and wanted him to have a myelogram right away. Are disk problems common in dogs? How serious are they?"

Spinal disk problems are quite common, and they can be very serious indeed, progressing to irreversible paralysis in some cases. So it's wise to pursue a diagnosis without delay if your dog has symptoms of a possible disk problem: severe neck pain, front leg weakness or paralysis, or lower back pain and weakness or paralysis of one or both hind legs.

The bones of the spine form a canal that shields the spinal cord from bending and pressure. Beneath the canal that houses the spinal cord, the vertebrae are separated and cushioned by intervertebral disks, which have a gelatinous core and a rubbery outer layer. These disks can break down over time, becoming less elastic and flexible. Occasionally these disks rupture or expand upward into the vertebral canal, putting pressure on the spinal cord and causing pain, leg weakness, or paralysis.

A spinal disk problem is diagnosed by a physical exam and a myelogram or an MRI or CT scan. Plain x-rays of the spine (without contrast dye) can sometimes provide clues to the location of the problem, but a myelogram is much more precise and definitive.

On physical exam, a dog with a spinal disk problem may show neck or lower back pain; exaggerated reflexes (like our knee-kick reflex) in the affected leg or legs; a failure to sense where his feet are, possibly causing him to knuckle a foot over or drag it; paralysis of a leg or legs; loss of superficial pain sensation in the leg (as from a pinprick); or loss of deep pain sensation (as when a toe is pinched hard with forceps). The progression of these symptoms—from dragging a foot to not feeling deep pain—reflect how deeply the spinal cord has been affected and what the prognosis is.

Like neck instability and wobbler syndrome, spinal disk problems are treated with corticosteroids to reduce swelling and inflammation around the spinal cord, plus strict cage rest. A dog that has a paralyzed leg or legs but still can feel deep pain should have surgery as soon as possible to remove part of the vertebra and disk material and relieve pressure on the spinal cord. The spinal cord of a dog who is paralyzed and hasn't had deep pain sensation for more than 24 hours is extremely unlikely to recover, so surgery is not beneficial in such cases. Such dogs will remain paralyzed for life. Some owners choose to care for a paraplegic dog at home, buying a dog wheelchair or using a towel or sling to help him move about, but others feel that the dog's quality of life is so diminished that they choose to euthanize him.

Compression of the spine by an unstable disk can be sudden or can progress slowly over time. Having your dog examined at the first sign of a problem—neck pain, back pain, or dragging a foot—will allow him to be treated before the condition progresses to irreversible paralysis.

FOOT-DRAGGING GERMAN SHEPHERDS

"When my nine-year-old German Shepherd started scuffing the toes of his hind feet when he walked, I figured he had arthritis. Then his tail got too limp to wag anymore. The vet said he had something called cauda equina syndrome. Can you tell me more about it?"

The cauda equina is a group of large nerves that fan out like a horse's tail from the end of the spinal cord, beginning in the lumbosacral area of the spine (just in front of the hips). When these nerves are damaged, the resulting symptoms are called cauda equina syndrome.

A dog with cauda equina syndrome may have lower back pain, difficulty lying down and getting up, weakness in the hind legs and tail, and pain when curving the lower back to defecate. If the condition worsens, which it often does without treatment, the dog may lose control of his bladder and bowels. It's most common in large-breed dogs, and is seen fairly frequently in German Shepherds.

The most common causes of cauda equina syndrome are a damaged disk, arthritis, a tumor in the lower spine, or an infection spreading from the bladder, prostate, or bloodstream. Back x-rays, a myelogram, blood and urine tests for bacteria and fungi, or a CT or MRI scan can be used to pinpoint the cause.

If a damaged disk is the problem, then surgery to remove the disk and relieve pressure on the cauda equina may be helpful. If a dog has a tumor putting pressure on the nerves, surgery or radiation may be recommended. Corticosteroids are usually given for arthritis, a damaged disk, or a tumor, to reduce swelling and pressure on the nerves.

An infected disk, which is called diskospondylitis, is treated with several months—not weeks—of antibiotics. Whatever the underlying cause of his cauda equina syndrome, a dog who has lost control of his bladder and bowels is unlikely to regain control even with treatment, so it's best to diagnose and treat the milder symptoms as soon as they appear.

CURVED LEG BONES

"I recently adopted a skinny young Doberman mix from a shelter. They said he was about six months old and probably had been out on the street for a while. With good food and TLC, he has gotten taller and even started to fill out a little, but the bones in his right front leg now seem to be curving to one side. Is this a nutritional deficiency?"

It's possible for a severely undernourished dog to get rickets—bones that are weak and deformed from a lack of calcium in the diet—but because your dog's leg started to curve *after* he was eating well and growing, the more likely explanation is a problem with the growth plate in a leg bone.

Growth plates are the regions toward the end of leg bones, near the joints, where most of the lengthening occurs as young dogs grow. Below the elbow, a dog's front leg contains two bones—the radius and the ulna—and if the growth plate in one shuts down while the other bone continues growing, curving of the leg toward the shorter bone results. A growth plate can be damaged by a crushing injury or bone fracture, but other times the cause of the premature shutdown is unknown.

X-rays can show whether the growth plates in your dog's right leg are active or closed, and whether there are any healing bone fractures or other abnormalities. If it appears that the affected leg will wind up much shorter than the other leg or put significant strain on the joints, then surgery to break and lengthen the short bone (using bone grafts) is recommended.

TMJ TROUBLE IN TERRIERS

"I have a six-month-old Scottish Terrier who suddenly stopped wanting to play with his tennis ball, then started having trouble eating. I thought maybe something was wrong with his teeth, but the vet thinks it's his jaw. What could have happened?"

Your Scottie may have bone inflammation affecting the temporomandibular joint (TMJ), the hinge joint that allows the mouth to open and close. This problem is quite rare, but when it does occur it affects mainly young terriers, often between the ages of three and eight months. Opening the mouth becomes painful, making the dogs reluctant to eat. Sometimes the jaw even feels warm or looks swollen.

What sets off the problem is unknown. The diagnosis can be confirmed with x-rays of the jaw, which will show characteristic changes in the bone around the TMJ, sometimes extending down into the lower jaw or up toward the ears as well. The treatment is anti-inflammatory medication to relieve the pain, and soft food or hand feeding as necessary to keep the dog well-nourished. Usually the inflammation goes away on its own in a few weeks and the dog is fine afterward.

BONE INFECTIONS

"My spaniel mix was hit by a car and broke a front leg in two places. The vet set the fractures using bone pins, and things seemed OK until a week later when my dog got listless, lost her appetite, and started running a fever. The vet suspects my dog has a bone infection. Is she going to be OK, or does this mean she's going to lose the leg, or even die?"

Bone infections can be very serious, to the point of requiring amputation or leading to sepsis (a whole-body infection) and death; but in your dog's case the infection was discovered and addressed quickly, so the odds are favorable for a full recovery.

Sometimes people are surprised to discover that bones can become infected, because they think of them as rocklike, inert material. But bones are living tissue with a blood supply. Organisms can enter and infect bones from the bloodstream or an injury to the bone or surrounding tissue. Blastomycosis and coccidioidomycosis are two fungal diseases that can infect bone via the bloodstream. A variety of bacteria can infect the bone as well, usually after a bone fracture.

Your vet will want to x-ray the leg again to see whether the bone pins have shifted and whether there is a fluid pocket within the tissue, as can happen with a bone infection. If so, your dog will need surgery to remove the infected fluid and tissue and reset the fracture. The vet will also biopsy the bone, removing a sliver of bone with a large hollow needle, for a bacterial culture and sensitivity test (C&S). Growing and testing the bacteria takes the lab a few days, so in the meantime your vet will probably start your dog on a broad-spectrum antibiotic. The antibiotic will be changed if the C&S results point to a better choice.

WEAKENED BONES

"X-rays of my 14-year-old Poodle mix showed thin, weak bones, and my vet is concerned. Couldn't this just be osteoporosis, like I have? Would calcium supplements help?"

Dogs don't get osteoporosis as easily as people do, so your vet undoubtedly wants to find the underlying cause. Calcium and phosphorus levels in the blood are regulated by parathyroid hormone (PTH), a substance produced by the parathyroid glands, which are embedded in the thyroid gland in the neck. If the parathyroid glands secrete excessive amounts of PTH, the body breaks down bone to free up calcium, leaving the bones thinner, weaker, and prone to fractures.

Oversecretion of PTH can be caused by a parathyroid tumor, a diet that contains almost no calcium, or kidney disease. Severe calcium deficiency is extremely rare, and generally occurs only in young, growing dogs who are fed nothing but meat rather than a balanced diet. Kidney disease causes an increase in blood phosphorus levels and a decrease in blood calcium levels, which triggers secretion of PTH and erosion of bones. This can make bones in the legs and spine thin and fragile, and bones in the skull thin or rubbery, which sometimes causes teeth to fall out.

The bones usually regain strength once the underlying problem is resolved. A parathyroid tumor can be removed surgically. A calcium deficiency in the diet can be corrected. High blood phosphorus and low blood calcium secondary to kidney disease can be treated with a low-phosphorus diet, phosphorus-binding medication, and calcium supplements.

SWOLLEN BONES IN OLDER DOGS

"When my older dog got stiff and sore on his front legs, I took him to the vet. She took x-rays and said she saw changes in the leg bones that made her concerned about lung cancer. Can you explain the connection?"

Cancer within the chest will sometimes trigger the leg bones to become active and create new layers of tissue. This process can cause swelling and pain. The changes are obvious on x-rays. Although bone proliferation does look similar to bone cancer (osteosarcoma), the difference is that it affects all the bones in both legs simultaneously, while osteosarcoma targets a single bone. If there is any doubt, a sliver of leg bone can be biopsied to check for cancer.

Chest x-rays will reveal the location of any lung tumors. The leg changes will go away by themselves once the cancer is treated. In the meantime, your vet may prescribe anti-inflammatory medication for pain relief.

CHAPTER 10

The Heart and Circulation

OUR HEARTS ARE NEARLY IDENTICAL, which explains why people and dogs share some of the same cardiac diseases. Like people, dogs can be born with a heart defect (such as a hole between two chambers) or develop one later in life (such as a leaky valve). But not all of our cardiac symptoms and risk factors are the same. For example, you don't need to worry about your dog's blood pressure or cholesterol, or fear that he'll have a heart attack. To monitor your dog's heart health, pay attention instead to such potential warning signs as a decrease in energy, an increase in panting, or a chronic cough.

E M E R G E N C Y !

oes your dog need immediate veterinary care? Check this list to help you decide.

If your dog has collapsed, is not breathing, and has no heartbeat, do chest compressions while rushing him to a vet (see page 426).

TAKE IMMEDIATE ACTION!

Call your vet or an emergency veterinary clinic *now* if your dog is showing any of the following symptoms:

❑ He is **unconscious.**

❑ She has **collapsed** and can't stand.

❑ He is **gasping for breath.**

❑ She is taking **digoxin** for heart disease and is **vomiting or having diarrhea.**

❑ He is having **trouble breathing** and his **gums look white, blue, or bright red** rather than pink.

TAKE A MINUTE . . .

Read further in this book and then call your vet during office hours as needed if your dog is showing any of the following symptoms:

❑ He is middle-aged or older and has a **persistent cough;** this could be any of several problems, including **kennel cough** (see page 278), **collapsing trachea** (see page 280), or **heart failure** (see page 269).

❑ She **pants** more than she used to, even at rest in cool weather (see page 262).

❑ His **heart rate** at rest is higher than normal (see page 258).

❑ She has **passed out** briefly one or more times; this could be a sign of heart disease or a seizure (see pages 262 and 308).

❑ He has gradually developed a **swollen abdomen and a cough;** these can be signs of congestive heart failure (see page 269).

❑ She **coughs when lying down;** this can be a symptom of heart disease (see page 262).

❑ He suddenly is **not able to play as hard or walk as far** as he used to (see page 262).

Remember, it's never wrong to call your veterinarian if you have a question about your dog's health, or if you're worried about a symptom or your dog's overall condition. That's what we're here for.

BIRTH DEFECTS OF THE HEART

"Are heart defects common in dogs? If so, why?"

Birth defects of the heart and major blood vessels are estimated to occur in 5 to 10 of every 1,000 births, or 0.5 to 1 percent of puppies. Some birth defects are hereditary, but others occur randomly and unpredictably during fetal development. A birth defect is often assumed to be genetic if it crops up at higher than average rates in a particular breed.

In the Q&As that follow, I name breeds that appear to have higher than average rates of certain birth defects. Such data should be interpreted cautiously, however, because a defect first noticed in a breed 30 years ago could since have been eliminated by removing carriers from breeding programs, or a veterinary cardiologist may see a high incidence of a certain disease in Golden Retrievers simply because Goldens are hugely popular and vets see a lot of them, period.

A HOLE IN THE HEART

"My 12-week-old Samoyed puppy has a soft heart murmur. The vet wants to do an ultrasound exam to check for a hole in his heart. My puppy is big, bright, and full of energy. What will happen if he does have a hole in his heart?"

Puppies can be born with a hole in the wall between the left and right atria (the upper chambers of the heart) or between the left and right ventricles (the lower chambers of the heart). A hole between the atria is called an atrial septal defect,

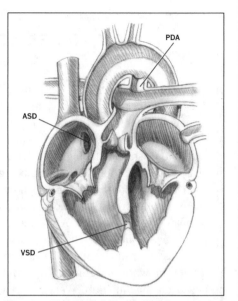

Some cardiac birth defects: a hole between the upper or lower chambers of the heart (an ASD or VSD), and an abnormal connection between major blood vessels (a PDA; see page 258).

or ASD. ASDs have been reported more in Boxers, Samoyeds, Doberman Pinschers, and Old English Sheepdogs than in other breeds. A hole between the ventricles is called a ventricular septal defect, or VSD. VSDs are more common than ASDs and have been reported more frequently in Keeshonds and English Bulldogs than in other breeds.

With either an ASD or a VSD, a puppy's prognosis depends on how large the hole is and how much blood is shunting through the hole from the left side of the heart to the right. (The left side of the heart ordinarily produces higher pressure, and blood is pushed from the higher-pressure side to the lower-pressure side.) A puppy who has a small hole in the heart with little blood passing through it may have no symptoms and lead a normal life with a normal lifespan. When the hole is large and a lot of blood passes through it, however, the lungs are overloaded with blood and the left side of the heart has to

MAKING SENSE OF MURMURS

Many heart problems are first noticed when a veterinarian hears a murmur (a sound other than the normal "lub-dub" of heart valves closing as the heart contracts) while listening to a dog's heart with a stethoscope. Blood being pushed through the heart normally flows smoothly and in one direction, with no turbulence or backwash. A murmur is caused by turbulence in the blood flow.

Most murmurs sound like a faint hissing or whooshing sound superimposed on the "lub-dub." Vets describe murmurs by how loud they are and by where on the ribcage they are heard the most clearly. Loudness is ranked using the Roman numerals I through VI: I for a murmur so soft it can barely be heard with a stethoscope, and VI for the loudest murmur, a murmur that can be heard without a stethoscope, by simply putting your ear against the dog's ribs, and that is palpable as a vibration of the ribs.

The loudness scale is, obviously, subjective. What some vets call a I, others might not hear at all; one vet's IV may be another vet's V; and so on, but the loudness ranking does at least put different listeners in the same ballpark. If your dog's medical chart says that last year Dr. X heard a grade I murmur and this year Dr. Y hears a grade IV murmur, both doctors can be certain that the murmur has gotten much louder. A louder murmur usually means the problem causing the turbulence has gotten worse.

A murmur can be caused by a leaky heart valve; a partially blocked aorta (the major artery carrying oxygenated blood from the heart to the rest of the body); a hole in the wall between the right and left sides of the heart; or an abnormal connection between the aorta and the pulmonary artery, which carries blood to the lungs. Holes in the heart and abnormal connections between blood vessels are birth defects, and those murmurs are present from birth. Leaky heart valves and partially blocked aortas can be birth defects or they can develop in adulthood, so those murmurs may be present from birth or begin later.

Occasionally, a young dog with a completely normal heart can have a murmur. These "innocent" or "func-

---

work harder than normal. Symptoms of a large hole in the heart can include a lack of energy, failure to grow normally, and panting or coughing.

The ultrasound exam will show the location and size of the hole and whether any other problems are present, such as malformed heart valves (see page 260). If your puppy has a small ASD with no symptoms and no other heart problems, then no treatment is necessary except for a physical exam every 6 to 12 months and an ultrasound exam every year or two to monitor the heart. If your puppy has a large ASD and the right side of the heart is already enlarged due to the oversupply of blood, however, then he is at risk of developing congestive heart failure and may have a shorter than normal lifespan.

tional" heart murmurs are heard when blood flow through the heart is increased because of excitement, pain, or exertion. The fast, hard blood flow produces turbulence and a soft murmur that goes away when the heart rate slows. Fever or anemia (a deficiency of red blood cells) can also raise the heart rate and produce a temporary murmur.

When a vet hears a murmur, what next? The best way to zero in on the problem is via an echocardiogram (see page 265).

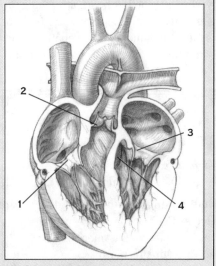

A leaky heart valve can produce a murmur. The valves are the tricuspid (1), pulmonic (2), mitral (3), and aortic (4).

As of this writing, open-heart surgery to close a hole in the heart is an experimental procedure done in only a handful of veterinary hospitals in the United States. VSDs are sometimes treated by surgically placing a band around the pulmonary artery—which leads from the right ventricle to the lungs—to reduce blood flow to the lungs to more normal levels. In other cases, vets rely on medi-cations such as ACE inhibitors, diuretics, and digitalis to ease the load on the heart if and when an ASD or VSD is severe enough to cause congestive heart failure (see pages 269 and 270).

TETRALOGY OF FALLOT

"First we were told that our puppy probably had a hole in his heart. Now we learn he's got four different heart defects that are apparently interconnected. Our vet has told us bluntly that our puppy may not live long. Can nothing be done?"

A hole in the heart can occur in conjunction with other abnormalities, and these usually worsen the prognosis. It sounds like your dog has a birth defect called tetralogy of Fallot ("tetra" for "four," and "Fallot" for the French physician who first described the defect in humans). The four abnormalities are a hole between the lower two chambers of the heart, a narrowed pulmonary artery, a malpositioned aorta, and an enlarged right heart. With this combination of defects, some blood is pumped directly to the body rather than first going to the lungs to pick up oxygen. Tetralogy of Fallot has been reported more in English Bulldogs and Keeshonds than in other breeds.

Puppies with this birth defect are often small and weak and have bluish gums. They also have an abnormally high red blood cell count: the body is starved for oxygen, and the bone marrow responds by churning out more red blood cells, which carry oxygen in the blood.

Treatment for tetralogy of Fallot includes drawing blood every few weeks to decrease the number of red blood cells, and low doses of aspirin, both to reduce the likelihood of circulation-impairing blood clots. At best, however, such treatments simply slow the deterioration of dogs with the defect, and most have a shortened life span. Surgery to reroute the blood vessels is occasionally done, but the risk of the dog dying during or shortly after the procedure is high.

A "WASHING-MACHINE" MURMUR

"When she listened to my new Pomeranian puppy's heart, the vet was so startled, she almost dropped her stethoscope. She said the puppy has a loud murmur that sounds like a washing machine, and the most likely cause is a birth defect that requires surgery. Is there any alternative to surgery?"

This sounds like patent ductus arteriosus (PDA), one of the most common cardiac birth defects in puppies. The ductus arteriosus is a connection between the pulmonary artery (which carries blood from the right ventricle to the lungs) and the aorta (which carries blood from the left ventricle to the body). This connection speeds the circulation of blood to the unborn pup from the placenta but is supposed to close within three days after birth. If the ductus arteriosus remains "patent," or open, after this time, then blood flows continuously from the aorta to the pulmonary artery, overloading the left heart, stretching the heart valves, and depriving the body of its full complement of oxygenated blood. Symptoms of a large PDA are a continu-

NORMAL HEART RATES

An abnormally fast heart rate signals a problem with the heart, lungs, or circulation. But how fast is too fast? That depends on a dog's size and age. Small dogs normally have faster heart rates than large dogs, and puppies have faster heart rates than adults. Below are some guidelines for what's normal in different dogs. See page 404 for how to measure your dog's heart rate.

Toy dogs (under 10 pounds, such as Yorkshire Terriers, Chihuahuas, and Maltese)
Normal resting heart rate:
100 to 160 beats per minute

Small dogs (10 to 25 pounds, such as Miniature Poodles, Miniature Schnauzers, and Boston Terriers)

Normal resting heart rate:
90 to 140 beats per minute

Medium dogs (25 to 50 pounds, such as Cocker Spaniels, Border Collies, and American Staffordshire Terriers)
Normal resting heart rate:
80 to 120 beats per minute

Large and giant dogs (over 50 pounds, such as Labrador Retrievers, Golden Retrievers, Rottweilers, and Newfoundlands)
Normal resting heart rate:
70 to 120 beats per minute

Puppies less than six months old
Normal resting heart rate:
at the upper range for their breed or predicted adult size

ous murmur and possibly poor growth, exercise intolerance, or panting.

PDAs are most common in female purebred dogs, especially Chihuahuas, Poodles, Maltese, Pomeranians, Shetland Sheepdogs, spaniels, Collies, and German Shepherds. Studies have shown that PDAs in Poodles are polygenic (determined by more than a single gene). The genetics of inheritance in other breeds is unknown.

A PDA is most easily diagnosed by an echocardiogram, or ultrasound exam of the heart. As your vet indicated, the best treatment for a PDA is to close it before the heart becomes damaged— most often before a dog is one year old, and preferably before the dog is four months old.

There are two techniques for closing a PDA. One involves opening the chest and tying off the vessel with suture material. The major risk in this technique is accidentally damaging the aorta or pulmonary artery and causing massive blood loss and death. The other technique, called coil embolization, does not require the chest to be opened. Rather, a large catheter is placed in an artery or vein, and a small coil is guided through the blood vessel to the ductus arteriosus and positioned there to block it. Occasionally the coil will move after it's placed and end up in the aorta or the pulmonary artery instead of the ductus arteriosus. If this happens, the coil can usually be removed or repositioned without serious harm to the dog. Coil embolization may not work for an unusually wide PDA, and if it doesn't, conventional surgery can be done instead.

When a PDA is not closed, heart failure develops quickly, and up to two-thirds of the dogs with a large uncorrected PDA will die within their first year of life. The heart failure caused by an uncorrected PDA is not reversible, so surgery is not usually recommended for dogs who do survive with a PDA past the age of one or two. Medication is used instead in those dogs to lower blood pressure and ease the load on the heart.

BLOCKED PULMONARY OR AORTIC BLOOD FLOW

"My six-month-old Boxer has a heart murmur, and my vet wants to check him for something called aortic stenosis. What exactly is this?"

The aorta is the large blood vessel that carries oxygenated blood from the left ventricle of the heart to the body. Stenosis means a constriction or narrowing. In aortic stenosis—also known as subvalvular aortic stenosis, or SAS— the flow of blood from the left ventricle to the aorta is partly blocked by a band of fibrous connective tissue. This partial blockage forces the left ventricle to work harder to eject blood. The muscular wall of the ventricle thickens with the strain, and the thickening can disrupt the transmission of electric signals within the heart, causing arrhythmias.

Aortic stenosis is known to be hereditary in Newfoundlands, and it also occurs more commonly in Boxers, German Shepherds, Golden Retrievers, Rottweilers, Bouvier de Flandres, Bernese Mountain Dogs, and German Shorthaired Pointers than in other breeds. When the blockage is mild, there may be no symptoms other than a murmur. When the blockage is more severe, weakness, exercise intolerance, fainting, or sudden death are possible. Fainting and sudden death in aortic stenosis may be caused by a burst of arrhythmia.

Aortic stenosis is diagnosed by an echocardiogram. A Holter monitor (see page 265) may also be used to diagnose intermittent arrhythmias in dogs with aortic stenosis.

Simply unblocking the aorta is, unfortunately, usually not an option. Balloon valvuloplasty—passing a balloonlike device through a blood vessel to the obstructed area and then inflating it—is only partially effective when the blockage is a wide, thick band of fibrous tissue below the aortic valve, as it is in most cases of aortic stenosis. Therefore, the mainstays of treatment for aortic stenosis are medicines to prevent arrhythmias and decrease the strain on the heart. Dogs with a significant degree of aortic stenosis almost always have a shortened life span. Sudden death caused by a run of arrhythmia is a common scenario.

Birth defects affecting the pulmonary outflow tract—from the right ventricle to the pulmonary artery—are also seen in dogs. In pulmonic stenosis, the pulmonic valve is often malformed. Other times, the pulmonary artery is partly blocked by a thick band of tissue below the pulmonic valve, as in aortic stenosis. Pulmonic stenosis is seen more often in English Bulldogs, Schnauzers, Beagles, Chihuahuas, terriers, Cocker Spaniels, and Samoyeds than other breeds of dogs.

As with aortic stenosis, symptoms of pulmonic stenosis depend on the degree of blockage. A dog might have a heart murmur and no other symptoms, or he might have occasional episodes of weakness and exercise intolerance. Severe pulmonic stenosis places a heavy strain on the right side of the heart and can lead to right-sided congestive heart failure, with distended jugular veins and an accumulation of fluid in the abdomen.

If pulmonic stenosis is caused by a "stuck valve" rather than a wide band of fibrous tissue, balloon angioplasty can be helpful. Otherwise medicine is used to reduce the symptoms of congestive heart failure and prevent arrhythmias. Dogs with mild pulmonic stenosis can have close to normal life spans, but those with severe stenosis may have a shortened life span.

FAULTY HEART VALVES

"I just found out my six-month-old Labrador Retriever has a deformed heart valve. The vet says that's probably why he has so much less energy than most Lab puppies. Can heart valves be replaced in dogs, the way they can in people?"

At present, valve replacement and surgical valve repair in dogs remain rare and expensive procedures, costing roughly $10,000. Only a few veterinary hospitals around the country are equipped with heart-lung bypass machines and have done valve replacement or repair. Colorado State University's College of Veterinary Medicine is one of the most experienced in open-heart surgery in dogs. (Lance Armstrong's Labrador Retriever puppy had a heart valve replaced there in 2005.) For most dogs and owners, treatment of a deformed heart valve will center on less-invasive surgery or medication to improve and lengthen his life.

First, some background: heart valves are flaps attached by thin cords to muscles on the inner walls of the heart. Normal valves open widely to let blood pass through with each heartbeat, then snap shut tightly to prevent blood from leaking backward. Abnormal valves don't

THE RHYTHM OF LIFE

Your dog's heartbeat is regulated by a natural pacemaker found in the right atrium of the heart. An electrical signal passes from this pacemaker to the muscles of the right and left atria (the upper chambers of the heart), which contract first. The signal continues from the atria to the right and left ventricles (the lower chambers of the heart), which contract second. The heart naturally speeds up a little as your dog inhales and slows a little as he exhales, because blood gets pushed into the atria a bit faster when the lungs expand.

This normal sequence is disrupted if the pacemaker fails to send regular signals, if the signals are blocked somewhere along their path, or if drugs or substances produced by the body trigger competing signals. The result is an arrhythmia—an erratic, ineffective heartbeat.

The problem with arrhythmias is they interrupt blood flow. In order to push blood through the body efficiently, the atria and ventricles need to contract in a coordinated way. If the ventricles suddenly contract before the atria have had a chance to fill them with blood, very little blood gets pushed to the body. A stray contraction may also make the heart pause briefly while the pacemaker recovers from the jammed signal. A prolonged burst of arrhythmia can bring blood flow to a standstill, depriving the brain, heart, and rest of the body of oxygen and killing the dog.

An arrhythmia can be heard with a stethoscope or felt as an interruption in a dog's pulse—if a veterinarian happens to be listening to the heart or feeling a pulse at the moment the arrhythmia occurs. Otherwise, arrhythmias are diagnosed using an electrocardiogram, or EKG. A vet will recommend doing an EKG on a dog that has had episodes of collapsing or passing out to determine whether an arrhythmia is responsible.

Arrhythmias can be caused by any disease that affects the heart muscle, such as dilated cardiomyopathy (see page 267) or a tumor (see page 270). Noncardiac diseases, such as severe damage to the stomach or spleen, can also trigger an arrhythmia. This is seen frequently in bloat, or gastric dilatation and volvulus (see page 136). Arrhythmias can often be treated successfully with medicine, such as lidocaine, procainamide, or propranolol.

open far enough to let blood through easily, don't close tightly enough to prevent blood from leaking, or both.

There are four valves in the heart: the tricuspid valve, between the right atrium and right ventricle; the pulmonic valve, between the right ventricle and the pulmonary artery; the mitral valve, between the left atrium and left ventricle; and the aortic valve, between the left ventricle and the aorta. Birth defects can occur in one or more of the valves and are seen more commonly in large-breed dogs, including Labs, German Shepherds, Weimaraners,

SYMPTOMS OF HEART DISEASE

To many people, "heart disease" is synonymous with "heart attack," and the main symptom is chest pain. But dogs don't have heart attacks (see page 268), and if they do experience chest pain, they have no good way of telling us about it. Owners are sometimes surprised when a vet diagnoses heart disease in their dog, because they either didn't notice any signs or attributed them to another cause, such as old age or being overweight. Here are some symptoms of heart disease that dog owners might see at home.

Small size or poor growth (in a puppy). Puppies with a birth defect of the heart or circulation may be smaller or thinner than average because they are unable to absorb and circulate oxygen and nutrients well enough for optimal growth.

Lack of energy or "slowing down." A young dog with a heart defect may be unusually lethargic and quiet, and an older dog with heart disease may have less energy for walks or play than he used to and spend more time resting.

Exercise intolerance. This is when a dog pants more with less exertion, needs to sit and rest during a walk, or stops playing or running much sooner than he used to.

Rapid breathing or panting at rest. When the left side of the heart doesn't pump as efficiently as it should, blood backs up in the blood vessels of the lungs, and fluid leaks out of the blood vessels and into the air spaces of the lungs, making it harder for them to take in oxygen and blow off carbon dioxide. In response, the dog breathes faster or pants even at rest.

Consistently rapid heart rate at rest. A failing heart moves less blood with each beat, so in an effort to maintain adequate blood flow, the body signals the heart to beat faster, even at rest (see page 258).

Cough when lying down or after awakening in the morning. Dogs with heart disease may cough because they have fluid in their lungs or because their hearts are enlarged and push on the trachea or bronchi, especially when they're lying down.

Swollen abdomen. When the right side of the heart isn't pumping well, blood backs up in the veins of the abdomen, and fluid can leak out, causing a swollen belly.

Sudden collapse. An arrhythmia can stop the heart from pushing blood to the brain and cause a dog to collapse or pass out. If the arrhythmia lasts for a few seconds or less, the dog will regain consciousness, but if it lasts longer than that, the heart may stop altogether.

and Great Danes. Dogs who are born with apparently normal valves also can develop valve problems later in life (see page 266).

Faulty valves hamper the heart's ability to push blood through the body efficiently. Symptoms can include exercise intolerance, lethargy, rapid breathing, or coughing. Over time, valve defects often lead to heart failure.

If the flaps of a valve are fairly normally shaped but partially fused together, balloon angioplasty may be effective in "unsticking" the valve. In this procedure, a balloonlike device is passed through a blood vessel to the valve, then inflated to pop the valve open. When the flaps are deformed rather than stuck, and if open-heart surgery to repair the valve is not an option (as it isn't for most dogs because of the scarcity of veterinary surgeons doing the procedure), then medication is used to treat heart failure if it occurs. Dogs with a deformed heart valve may have shorter than average life spans. Their quality of life depends on which valve is involved and how well or poorly it functions.

A DETOUR AROUND THE LIVER

"I have a 10-week-old Yorkshire Terrier puppy who sometimes acts dazed, bumps into things, and snaps at me if I try to pick her up. Other times she's fine. The vet ran some tests, and she suspects that my puppy has something wrong with a large blood vessel leading to the liver. Can you tell me more about this problem?"

The veins leading away from the intestines join up with a large blood vessel called the portal vein. The portal vein normally carries all the blood from the digestive tract to the liver, where the blood is filtered and nutrients and potentially toxic substances—such as ammonia—are processed for storage or safe removal from the body. In a birth defect called a portosystemic shunt (PSS), an abnormal blood vessel connects the portal vein with some other part of the circulatory system, shunting some of the blood that is supposed to be filtered by the liver directly to the heart, brain, and other organs. The ammonia and other

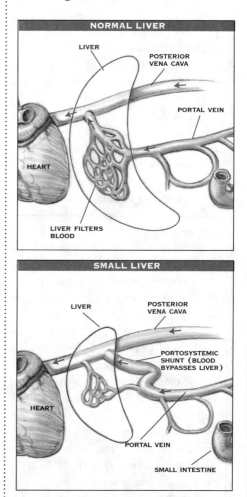

Blood that has picked up nutrients from the intestines is normally filtered by the liver (top). A PSS diverts blood past the liver (bottom).

(continued on page 266)

TOOLS OF THE TRADE

Cardiology may seem like the ultimate high-tech medical specialty, but even veterinarians in small neighborhood clinics have the tools needed to diagnose most heart problems. A thorough physical exam provides a wealth of information about how well the heart is functioning. Virtually all vet clinics are equipped to take chest x-rays and EKGs and measure blood pressure, and many also have ultrasound machines that can be used to investigate the cause of a heart murmur. Here are the tools of the trade and what your veterinarian can learn by using them.

Physical exam and history. Listening to your dog's chest with a stethoscope tells your veterinarian how fast the heart is beating, whether there are any murmurs, whether the heartbeat is regular or has an obvious arrhythmia, and whether there may be fluid in the lungs (a possible sign of heart failure).

Checking your dog's pulses tells the vet whether each heartbeat is propelling blood through the body effectively (pulses can be felt in the inner thighs and lower front legs). Pale or bluish gums indicate a lack of oxygen, which is usually caused by a heart or lung problem. Normal gums are pink and regain their color within three seconds after being pressed with a fingertip (this is the capillary refill time).

Jugular veins—on either side of the neck—that are swollen or pulse along with the heartbeat are most often a sign of a problem in the right side of the heart (such as a leaky valve, enlarged ventricle, or heartworm disease) or fluid filling the pericardium (the sac around the heart).

The history—your account of your dog's symptoms at home—is the best measure of how the dog actually feels. Does your dog cough? If so, when? After exercise? At night? Does he tire more easily when walking or playing than he did a year ago? Does he pant more than he did a year ago? Has he ever passed out or been unable to stand? Of course, coughing, panting, exercise intolerance, and episodes of weakness or fainting can be caused by other problems as well as heart disease, so symptoms must be compared with physical exam findings and other test results before a diagnosis can be made.

Chest x-rays. Heart disease often causes one or more chambers of the heart to enlarge. Chest x-rays are taken in pairs: one side-to-side view, and one back-to-front view. A normal dog heart is about three ribs wide on the side-to-side view, and about two-thirds the width of the chest on the back-to-front view. (The dog's body type also matters: the heart of a short, stocky dog, like a Pekingese, looks comparatively larger and rounder than that of a deep-chested dog, like a German Shepherd.) Sometimes a bulge will be seen where a single chamber of the heart, like the left atrium, is enlarged. Other times the whole heart may be enlarged and push the trachea closer to the spine than normal. Chest x-rays also show whether the lungs are more dense than normal, which can be a sign of congestive heart failure, pneumonia, or other diseases, and whether the arteries and veins supplying the lungs are larger than normal, as they are in some heart diseases.

EKG. The heart beats in response to an electric signal originating with the heart's natural pacemaker. An EKG, or electrocardiogram, records the path of this signal in graph form on paper. An EKG can reveal such problems as heart block, where some or all of the pacemaker's signals don't get through; enlargement of one or more heart chambers, which is usually a response to a valve problem or pressure overload; and arrhythmias (see page 261).

Holter monitor. A Holter monitor is a portable EKG transmitter, about the size of a deck of playing cards, that a dog wears taped to his back for one or more days to monitor his heart for arrhythmias. Some arrhythmias occur only sporadically and can be missed by a regular EKG reading, which lasts for only a couple of minutes. Holter monitors often are used on dogs that have had episodes of fainting or weakness to determine whether an intermittent arrhythmia could be the cause.

Blood pressure monitor. A dog's blood pressure is measured the same way a person's is: with a pressure gauge attached to an inflatable cuff. (The cuffs are much smaller than the ones used on people, because they need to fit snugly around a dog's lower leg.) Blood pressure readings are often used to monitor dogs while they're under anesthesia. If a dog's blood pressure drops below 100, the anesthesia is turned down and the dog is given more IV fluids. High blood pressure is uncommon in dogs, unlike in people (see page 268).

Echocardiogram. This ultrasound exam of the heart works the same way an ultrasound exam of a pregnant woman does: the probe emits harmless sound waves that bounce off structures inside the body and produce moving images on a computer screen. A dog's hair is clipped over the heart and a gel is applied to give good contact between the probe and the skin. The dog has to lie fairly still on his side for 15 minutes or so during the exam, but an echocardiogram is not painful, and no anesthesia is required (an assistant holds and soothes the dog during the exam). With an echocardiogram, a skilled operator can watch the heart contract and check each valve, chamber, and major blood vessel for abnormalities; measure the thickness of the walls of the heart (certain diseases can thin or thicken the walls); measure how effectively the heart contracts with each beat; measure the velocity of the blood leaving the heart; look for turbulence or backwash in blood flow (as when a valve is leaking); and look for adult heartworms. Some vets have ultrasound machines in their clinics, and others arrange for a veterinary ultrasound specialist to bring a portable machine to their clinics when needed.

(continued from page 263)

unprocessed substances in the shunted blood are toxic to cells. Brain cells are especially sensitive to these effects, so puppies with a portosystemic shunt may sometimes behave strangely, as your puppy does, or have seizures.

The severity of the PSS depends on how much blood returning from the digestive tract bypasses the liver. Sometimes the PSS detours only a small portion of the blood. Other times a large PSS diverts almost all of the blood from the portal vein away from the liver. In the latter case, the liver essentially can't do its job at all, and it is small and stunted from lack of use.

As the size of the shunt varies, so can the symptoms. Often dogs with a PSS will be unusually small or skinny because the liver can't process nutrients properly. Some dogs with a PSS may vomit or have diarrhea. Others will behave strangely an hour or so after eating, when toxic substances from the intestines begin to reach the brain.

Portosystemic shunts are more common in small dogs, especially Yorkies, Miniature Schnauzers, Miniature and Toy Poodles, Maltese, Shih Tzus, Pugs, and Dachshunds. In small dogs, the abnormal blood vessel usually diverts from the portal vein *before* it reaches the liver, which makes it easier to find and correct. When a PSS does occur in a large dog—such as an Irish Wolfhound, Golden Retriever, or Labrador Retriever—it's often hidden within the liver, which makes corrective surgery more difficult.

When a vet suspects that a puppy has a PSS, the first step toward confirming the diagnosis is to run blood tests looking for liver abnormalities. A puppy with a PSS often will have low levels of blood urea nitrogen and albumin (produced by the liver) and high levels of ammonia and bile acids (normally removed from the blood by the liver). An ultrasound exam is sometimes used to search for the PSS, but often the abnormal blood vessel is small and difficult to find on ultrasound. A definitive diagnosis is usually made by injecting a dye or radioactive marker into the blood and using x-rays or scintigraphy (a radioactivity scan) to trace the blood flow from the intestines to the portal vein and liver.

The best treatment for a PSS is surgery to close the abnormal blood vessel. The surgery can be long and complicated, depending on how difficult it is to find and close off the blood vessel, and in a small percentage of dogs the liver is too stunted to regain normal function after the shunt is eliminated. However, most puppies who have PSS surgery at an early age recover well and live normal lives.

If the owner of a puppy with a PSS chooses not to have surgery, then the puppy is usually kept on a low-protein diet, antibiotics, and lactulose for life to lessen the production and absorption of ammonia from the intestines. Such dogs almost always have shorter life spans than normal.

VALVE DISEASE IN OLDER DOGS

"I thought my seven-year-old Cavalier King Charles Spaniel was panting a lot because he's overweight, but my vet hears a murmur on his left side and says there's a good chance he has mitral valve disease. Can you tell me more about the prognosis?"

Deteriorating valves are the most common heart problem in dogs, and the mitral valve (between the left atrium and ventricle) is the one most often affected. Toy and miniature breeds are especially prone to valve disease when they reach middle age and older, and Cavalier King Charles Spaniels are known for developing valve problems early, so your dog has plenty of company.

In adult-onset valve disease, one or more of the four valves in the heart become thickened, bumpy, and stiff. Occasionally bacteria from elsewhere in the body, such as an abscessed tooth, infect the valves via the bloodstream and set off these changes, but most often no underlying cause is found—it's a "degenerative," or old-age, disease. The thickened valves don't close as tightly as normal valves, so some blood leaks backward instead of being pushed forward when the heart contracts. Over time, the backward flow stretches the affected chambers of the heart—which often makes the valves even more leaky—and forces the heart to beat faster to supply enough blood to the body.

The earliest sign of adult-onset valve disease is usually a heart murmur in a middle-aged or older dog. The murmur is loudest over the affected valve. The mitral valve is affected most often, followed by both the mitral and the tricuspid valves (between the right atrium and ventricle), and then the tricuspid valve alone.

When a dog develops a murmur, it's wise to do an echocardiogram to pinpoint the source and evaluate the backflow of blood, size of the chambers, strength of contractions, and so on. Chest x-rays are also useful to show backup of blood in the lungs, which can occur with mitral disease. Blood tests look for signs of bacterial infection and conditions such as kidney disease that would influence treatment.

Dogs with a murmur caused by adult-onset valve disease who have no other problems or symptoms are monitored but not started on medication until they show signs that their cardiac output isn't keeping up with demand. The monitoring may include physical exams once or twice a year and chest x-rays or echocardiograms every two or three years. Signs that a dog's cardiac output is flagging can include exercise intolerance, panting, lethargy, and coughing after exercise or when lying down.

It's impossible to predict how long and how well dogs with acquired valve disease will live. Some putter along quietly to a ripe old age. Others quickly begin to accumulate fluid in their lungs or abdomen and become uncomfortable and exhausted. Your vet's goal is to keep your dog feeling as well as possible, so keep track of your dog's symptoms and behavior and tell your vet if your dog is coughing more, has less energy, or seems uncomfortable. A change in medication may help put your dog back on track.

A BIG-DOG, BIG-HEART DISEASE

"My beautiful, healthy five-year-old Doberman was playing in the park when he suddenly collapsed. I got him to a vet within 15 minutes, but my dog's heart had stopped, and they weren't able to revive him. What happened? Was it anything I could have prevented?"

An autopsy would be required to say for certain, but based on your dog's breed and his sudden collapse, it's likely that he died from an arrhythmia brought on by a disease called dilated cardiomyopathy, or DCM. In DCM, the chambers

"DOC, WHAT ABOUT MY DOG'S CHOLESTEROL?"

Heart problems are almost as common in dogs as they are in people, and we're prone to some of the same diseases, such as leaky heart valves. But not all of the factors in human heart disease are the same for dogs. Here are some human health problems that usually aren't a concern in dogs.

High cholesterol. Many people are obsessed about their cholesterol numbers: high-density lipoprotein (HDL), low-density lipoprotein (LDL), and the ratio of the two. But because cholesterol and fat don't normally form fatty deposits in dogs' arteries, cholesterol is not linked with heart attacks and strokes in dogs. High cholesterol in a dog may, however, be a symptom of hypothyroidism, diabetes mellitus, Cushing's disease, or kidney disease.

Heart attack. A heart attack is a myocardial infarction: blood flow to the heart via the coronary arteries is blocked in one or more areas, and heart cells in those areas die. In people, the blockage is usually caused by fatty deposits in the coronary arteries. Dogs don't form these fatty deposits, so they don't have heart attacks. If a dog dies suddenly of a heart-related problem, the cause is most likely an arrhythmia, not a heart attack.

High blood pressure. Normal blood pressure in a dog ranges from about 120/70 to 160/90. High blood pressure is uncommon and is almost always secondary to another problem, such as severe kidney disease, diabetes mellitus, Cushing's disease, or an adrenaline-secreting tumor. However, drugs that lower blood pressure—such as beta blockers and ACE inhibitors—are frequently used in dogs with heart failure to enable their overtaxed hearts to push blood through the body with less resistance.

of the heart dilate, or stretch, and don't contract as strongly. The pacemaker's transmissions can be disrupted by the stretched muscle, and arrhythmias may develop. What sets off these changes is unknown, but they are more common in large and giant-breed dogs, particularly Dobermans, Boxers, Great Danes, St. Bernards, and Newfoundlands.

Could you have known that something was wrong with your dog before he collapsed? Not necessarily. Dogs with DCM often show no symptoms before they have a sudden crisis. Sometimes, however, owners of dogs with DCM will notice that their dogs have started to breathe rapidly even at rest, cough, pant, or tire out more easily than they used to. Such signs in a high-risk breed warrant a prompt visit to the vet for a thorough physical exam.

DCM is best diagnosed by an echocardiogram, which will show the dilated heart chambers and how strongly the heart is contracting. Chest x-rays can show the overall enlargement of the heart. An EKG should always be done in dogs with DCM because they frequently have life-threatening arrhythmias.

Emergency treatment for a dog who has collapsed from DCM includes IV medicines to stop arrhythmias (such as lidocaine) and strengthen contractions (such as dobutamine), plus oxygen. At home, dogs with DCM may be prescribed antiarrhythmics and drugs to improve cardiac output. Some Cocker Spaniels, Boxers, and Golden Retrievers with DCM are deficient in taurine and L-carnitine, so supplements of those nutrients are often recommended for those breeds.

The prognosis for dogs with DCM ranges from grave to fair. Some survive for only a few weeks after diagnosis— or die suddenly, as your dog did—and others live for years after diagnosis. Unfortunately, there is no way to screen puppies of the high-risk breeds to determine which are likely to develop DCM later on. Because DCM is so common in Doberman Pinschers, many veterinary cardiologists recommend screening them yearly for the disease (with an echocardiogram and a Holter-monitor EKG) starting when they are four or five years old.

CONGESTIVE HEART FAILURE

"I've been told that my 14-year-old Cocker Spaniel has congestive heart failure. Does this mean her heart will just stop one day soon and she'll die? What will the medicines she's been prescribed do for her?"

A diagnosis of congestive heart failure (CHF) means that a dog's heart is not pumping blood well enough to fully meet the body's needs for oxygen. The "congestion" of CHF is the accumulation of blood and fluid in organs or areas of the body, such as the lungs, liver, or abdomen.

Congestive heart failure is an end result, not a cause. The cause can be any of a number of primary heart problems, such as a birth defect, dilated cardiomyopathy, or heartworms. Adult-onset valve disease is the No. 1 cause of congestive heart failure in dogs.

In the early stages of CHF, a dog may have no symptoms at rest but quickly become tired, pant, or cough with stress or exertion. In later stages, many dogs pant and have a high heart rate even at rest. A vet usually diagnoses CHF based on a combination of ultrasound exam findings (such as thickened, leaky valves or an enlarged heart) and clinical signs (like a rapid heart rate, panting, and fluid in the lungs or abdomen).

Treatment for CHF centers on diuretics and drugs that improve cardiac output, such as ACE inhibitors and pimobendan (see the following page). A lower-salt diet and exercise restriction are often recommended for dogs with CHF. Dogs who have a persistent cough may be prescribed bronchodilators or cough suppressants as well.

The swollen belly of a dog in congestive heart failure is filled with fluid, not fat.

Periodic blood tests are done on dogs with CHF to check for dehydration and other drug-related problems. A dog with early CHF can live comfortably for months to years; dogs with severe CHF— those who have a high heart rate and difficulty breathing even at rest—may live for only weeks to months.

HEART TUMORS

"My eight-year-old Bernese Mountain Dog had been slowing down for a few weeks. Then she suddenly collapsed, and we rushed her to the vet, but she died within a few hours. We requested an autopsy, and it showed that she had a tumor on her heart. Was there anything we could have done had we known sooner?"

Sadly, there really are no good treatments for a tumor on the heart, so even if you had known a few weeks earlier, it's unlikely that your dog's life could have been prolonged significantly. Such tumors are fairly rare, but devastating when they do occur.

Of the cancers that can affect the heart, hemangiosarcoma is the most common. These tumors often grow on the right atrium and bleed into the pericardium (the sac surrounding the heart). A hemangiosarcoma may originate in the heart or spread from elsewhere in the body, such as the spleen. A chemodectoma is another tumor that can grow on the heart. Other types of cancer, such as lymphoma, carcinoma, and melanoma, occasionally spread to the heart from elsewhere in the body via the bloodstream.

There are no symptoms of a heart tumor until it begins to affect the heart's function, and then fatigue, lethargy, or weakness may occur. Collapse and sudden death from a tumor-induced arrhythmia or bleeding are also possible.

Veterinarians may suspect a heart tumor when they discover that an older dog has pericardial effusion (fluid in the pericardium). A dog with pericardial effusion will often have muffled heart sounds and a rapid heart rate with weak pulses, and the heart will appear rounded and enlarged on chest x-rays. The pericardial effusion, and sometimes the tumor itself, can be seen directly via ultrasound. The potential causes of pericardial effusion are few: a heart tumor (especially hemangiosarcoma or chemodectoma); occasionally congestive heart failure; inflammation (from infection or unknown causes); or trauma (such as being hit by a car).

Pericardial effusion prevents the heart from expanding normally to fill with blood, so the heart is unable to pump much blood to the body. It can be treated by draining the fluid from the pericardium, but this does not resolve the underlying problem, so the prognosis for a dog with pericardial effusion is fair at best.

DRUGS FOR HEART DISEASE

"The drugs used to treat heart disease in dogs sound like the same ones that are used in people. Do they work the same way?"

Yes, many of the same cardiac drugs are used in dogs and in people, and they work essentially the same way. Here are the main cardiac drugs and what they do.

ACE inhibitors. These lower the blood pressure by blocking one substance that causes blood vessels to constrict and another that causes the kidneys to reabsorb water. Although dogs rarely, if ever, have primary high blood pressure, ACE inhibitors are used in dogs with congestive heart failure to reduce blood pressure to low-normal levels, thereby giving their overtaxed hearts less resistance to push against. ACE inhibitors help delay the onset of heart failure in people with valve disease, but that protective effect unfortunately does not seem to occur in dogs, so in dogs they are used as a treatment for heart failure, not a preventive. Enalapril (Enacard, Vasotec) and captopril (Capoten) are two commonly used ACE inhibitors. *Side effects:* Because they have an indirect diuretic effect, ACE inhibitors can lead to dehydration in dogs who are also taking diuretics (see below), so the doses of those drugs may need to be lowered.

Other vasodilators. A vasodilator lowers blood pressure by dilating veins, arteries, or both. ACE inhibitors are one form of vasodilator. Other vasodilators that are sometimes used in dogs include pimobendan (Vetmedin), nitroglycerine, sildenafil (Viagra), and hydralazine. Nitroglycerine is usually used only as an emergency treatment for dogs with fluid in the lungs, because tolerance to the drug develops quickly, so it's not useful long-term. The others are usually used in addition to an ACE inhibitor and a diuretic. *Side effects:* Occasionally, vomiting or loss of appetite. Doses that are too high can drop a dog's blood pressure too low and result in shock.

Diuretics. These are the foundation of treatment for congestive heart failure. Diuretics reduce fluid buildup in the lungs and abdomen by triggering the kidneys to excrete more salt and water. Furosemide (Lasix), hydrochlorothiazide (HydroDiuril), and spironolactone (Aldactone) are three commonly used diuretics. *Side effects:* All of the diuretics can cause dehydration. Hydrochlorothiazide and spironolactone can cause vomiting and loss of appetite.

Beta blockers. In dogs, these are used primarily to block arrhythmias. Propranolol (Inderal), atenolol (Tenormin), and metoprolol (Lopressor) are three commonly used beta blockers. *Side effects:* Beta blockers occasionally cause loss of appetite, vomiting, or diarrhea. Overdoses can cause an abnormally low heart rate and shock. Propranolol can constrict the small airways in the lungs, worsening the symptoms of chronic bronchitis (see page 285). Atenolol and metoprolol do not have these effects on the lungs and are preferred for dogs who have both bronchitis and heart disease.

Other antiarrhythmics. Lidocaine is given intravenously as an emergency treatment for arrhythmias. Quinidine (Quinidex, Cardioquin), procainamide (Pronestyl), and tocainide (Tonocard) are three antiarrhythmics that can be used long-term. *Side effects:* All can cause vomiting and loss of appetite. Doses must be carefully regulated to avoid abnormally slow heart rates. Paradoxically, while suppressing some arrhythmias, these drugs can sometimes promote the development of different arrhythmias.

Digoxin. With its broad range of effects, digoxin (Cardoxin, Lanoxin) is in a category of its own. It's most often used in congestive heart failure when ACE inhibitors and diuretics alone are not sufficient. It slows and strengthens the heart's contractions, enabling the heart to push blood through the body more effectively, and suppresses some arrhythmias. *Side effects:* Loss of appetite, vomiting, diarrhea, and lethargy. Paradoxically, at higher doses, digoxin also can cause arrhythmias. These potential side effects are significant, and the appropriate dose of digoxin varies considerably with individual animals, so dogs taking digoxin need to be monitored carefully by their owners and vets. Dobermans may be particularly sensitive to digoxin. Blood levels of digoxin can be measured to check that a dog is receiving a safe and effective dose.

Medicines for chronic bronchitis or cough. When a dog has chronic bronchitis as well as heart failure, drugs to dilate the airways or calm coughing spasms are sometimes used to help him breathe more comfortably. Theophylline (Theo-Dur) dilates the airways. Hydrocodone (Hycodan) and butorphanol (Torbutrol) are cough suppressants. *Side effects:* Theophylline can cause a rapid heart rate, restlessness, and seizures, so the dose must be carefully monitored. Hydrocodone and butorphanol can cause loss of appetite, constipation, and sedation.

DIET AND EXERCISE IN HEART DISEASE

"Do dogs with heart disease need a special diet or exercise restrictions?"

A change in diet and activity may be advisable for some dogs with heart disease. Ask your vet what she recommends for your dog. Here are some of the measures she might suggest.

Salt restriction. Lowering the salt in the diet of a dog with heart disease is a "can't hurt, might help" measure recommended by many veterinarians. The theory is that extra salt makes the kidneys retain extra water, which increases the volume of blood a failing heart has to push through the body.

Prescription foods for dogs with heart disease include Hill's Science Diet h/d, Purina Veterinary Diets CV, and Royal Canin Early Cardiac EC. Another way to reduce the salt in a dog's diet is to cut out high-sodium table food and dog treats. Table foods high in salt include soup, gravy, and canned vegetables; hot dogs, bacon, cold cuts, and sausage; most cheeses; frozen dinners; and obviously, potato chips, flavored crackers, and similar snacks. Many dog treats, especially those flavored like bacon, sausage, or beef jerky, also are high in salt. Look for dog treats that are labeled "low sodium" or "low salt."

Weight loss. If a dog with heart disease is overweight, losing weight will lighten the load on his heart and help him feel better. But make sure that his big belly is fat, not fluid: dogs with congestive heart failure will sometimes leak fluid into their abdomen, making them look potbellied. Such dogs need a diuretic, not a diet.

Exercise. Exertion makes the heart work harder, and dogs with heart disease should not run, play fetch, or engage in other strenuous activity. This is especially true of dogs who have or are likely to develop arrhythmias, such as those with dilated cardiomyopathy (see page 269) or aortic stenosis (see page 259). However, most dogs with heart disease do benefit—both physically and psychologically—from daily walks, except in very hot weather.

NATURAL SUPPLEMENTS AND HEART DISEASE

"I've heard there are natural supplements that can help dogs with heart disease. Is this true?"

A variety of natural supplements have been investigated for their effects on dogs with heart disease. Here are some of the more common supplements and how they are used.

Taurine and L-carnitine. Some Cocker Spaniels, Boxers, and Golden Retrievers with dilated cardiomyopathy (DCM) are deficient in these protein components, so supplements are highly recommended for dogs of those breeds who have DCM (see page 267). Taurine and L-carnitine may be helpful in other breeds with DCM as well, but so far they haven't been shown to *prevent* DCM or to play a role in other types of heart disease.

Fish oil. The omega-3 fatty acids in fish oil increase appetite and decrease muscle wasting in some dogs with DCM or congestive heart failure (see page 269). They may also help suppress arrhythmias (see page 261).

Coenzyme Q10. This antioxidant reduces symptoms in some people with DCM, but so far these effects haven't been shown in dogs.

Other antioxidants. Antioxidants are believed to help prevent coronary artery disease, but dogs aren't susceptible to this condition (see page 268). Antioxidants may help relieve symptoms in dogs with congestive heart failure, but so far there's no direct evidence of this.

Hawthorn berry extract. This natural diuretic makes the kidneys excrete more water and minerals. Diuretics react with many other medications and can change the results of blood tests, so be sure to tell your vet if you are giving your dog hawthorn berry extract or other supplements.

Colds, Coughs, and Other Respiratory Problems

BREATHING IS FUNDAMENTAL, yet the inner workings of the respiratory system are not so simple. For example, all dogs pant, sneeze, and cough once in a while, and some dogs also honk, snort, snore, or snuffle. So when are these symptoms and noises normal, and when are they signs of disease? Does your coughing dog have a cold, bronchitis, a trachea problem, or heart disease? Learning what other clues to look for will help you decide whether your dog needs rest and chicken soup or an immediate visit to the vet.

EMERGENCY!

Does your dog need immediate veterinary care? Check this list to help you decide.

If your dog can't breathe and you know he has a small ball or other object stuck in his windpipe, do the Heimlich maneuver immediately (see page 429).

TAKE IMMEDIATE ACTION!

Call your vet or an emergency veterinary clinic *now* if your dog is showing any of the following symptoms:

❑ He is **gasping for breath.**

❑ She was **hit by a car;** the impact can damage the lungs even if a dog has no obvious wounds on the outside.

❑ He was in a **dog fight** and has **bite wounds** on his neck, ribs, or upper back; these wounds can puncture the trachea or the chest wall and cause breathing problems or infections.

❑ She has **heart disease** and is having **trouble breathing.**

❑ He has **collapsed** and is **breathing strangely.**

❑ She is **breathing strangely** and her **gums look white, blue, or bright red** rather than pink.

❑ He was in a house fire and **inhaled smoke.**

❑ She **almost drowned.**

❑ He bit an **electric cord.**

TAKE A MINUTE . . .

Read further in this book and then call your vet during office hours as needed if your dog is showing any of the following symptoms:

❑ He is **coughing;** this could be any of several problems, including kennel cough, collapsing trachea, or heart disease (see pages 278, 280, and 285).

❑ She makes **choking noises** when she gets excited or pulls even slightly on her collar; this could be collapsing trachea (see page 280).

❑ He is **pawing at his mouth and gagging or coughing;** he may have something stuck in his mouth. If you can do so without getting bitten, open your dog's mouth and look carefully for sticks, toys, bones, or other objects stuck (1) sideways across the roof of his mouth; (2) between his teeth, or between his teeth and lips;

or (3) in the back of his mouth. If you see an object and can remove it safely and easily, do so. If the object is in the back of the throat, be careful not to push it farther down. Try the Heimlich maneuver instead (see page 429). **If you don't see an object, or you see something but can't remove it safely, call your vet or an emergency veterinary clinic immediately.**

❑ She is a flat-nosed breed— like an English Bulldog, a Pug, or a Boston Terrier—and she has **trouble breathing** when it's hot and humid (see page 282).

❑ His **bark has changed** noticeably; this could be a sign of a larynx problem (see page 283).

❑ She has **blood** coming from one or both nostrils (see page 283).

❑ He has a **runny nose** (see the following Q&A).

Remember, it's never wrong to call your veterinarian if you have a question about your dog's health, or if you're worried about a symptom or your dog's overall condition. That's what we're here for.

THE COMMON CANINE COLD

"My dog seems to have a cold. She's sneezing and sounds a little congested. Can I give her something over-the-counter for it, or do I need to take her to the vet? Other than those symptoms she seems fine— she's playful and eating OK."

Dogs do get cold-type infections— "kennel cough" is one—that are contagious between dogs but not between dogs and people. As in people, they usually run their course within 10 to 14 days. If your dog is eating well, is energetic, and doesn't have any underlying major medical issues (such as heart disease), you can treat her at home with basic nursing care.

Don't give your dog any over-the-counter medicines for her cold—they're not necessary, and it's easy to overdose a dog on pain relievers (see page 412). But as your grandmother might say, How about a little chicken soup? Offer your dog some chicken soup that's lukewarm (you should be able to hold your finger in it comfortably), and not too oily or salty. She'll probably love it, the extra liquid will help keep her well hydrated, and it may help relieve her congestion the way it's been shown to do in people. You could also run a hot shower and hang out in the steamy bathroom with your dog for five or ten minutes once or twice a day to help loosen the congestion.

Clean gently around her eyes and nose with wet cotton balls a couple of times a day if she has mucus there, and make sure she gets plenty of rest and water. She's probably contagious, so she shouldn't have nose-to-nose contact with other dogs until she's completely well.

If she gets so stuffed up that she loses her appetite, if her eyes seem itchy or sore, or if she starts to cough so much that she (or you) can't sleep, then do take her to the vet.

KENNEL COUGH

"How serious is kennel cough? The place where I occasionally board my dog requires dogs to have had a kennel cough vaccine within the previous six months. Does the vaccine really keep dogs from getting sick?"

Kennel cough is basically a cold with a cough. The fancy medical name for it—infectious tracheobronchitis—is just as vague: "infectious" because it's caused by bacteria, a virus, or both; and "tracheobronchitis" because the trachea and bronchi are inflamed. (The bronchi are the two large airways that branch off from the trachea into the lungs.) When the bronchi are inflamed, they produce mucus, which makes a dog cough.

Several different upper-respiratory viruses and bacteria, singly or in combination, can produce the symptoms of kennel cough. One common factor—and

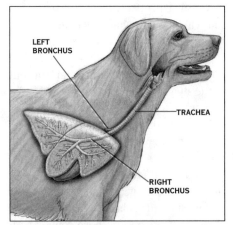

LEFT
BRONCHUS

TRACHEA

RIGHT
BRONCHUS

Kennel cough targets the large airways—the trachea and bronchi—rather than the lungs.

this is where the vaccine comes in—is the bacterium *Bordetella bronchiseptica.* Vaccinating a dog against bordetella will help prevent some cases of kennel cough and lighten the symptoms of others. It's like getting a flu shot: you may still get sick, but you won't get sick from that specific germ.

Kennel cough is most common in young dogs, because they haven't been exposed yet to many viruses and bacteria. It almost never makes a dog severely ill. The symptoms are coughing, possibly a stuffed-up or runny nose, and sometimes a mild fever. Usually it gets better on its own within 10 days or so. Occasionally, a dog will cough so hard he can't sleep, or he'll lose his appetite because his nose is so stuffed up he can't smell his food. In those cases, veterinarians will sometimes prescribe antibiotics (for the presumed bacterial part of the infection), expectorants, or cough suppressants.

If kennel cough isn't serious, why do kennels, groomers, dog daycare centers, and dog shows require the vaccine? Because bordetella is common and spreads very easily from dog to dog, and dog handlers want to do everything they can to prevent animals from getting sick while they're in their care. Immunity to bacteria—unlike immunity to viruses—lasts for only six months, so the vaccine is given twice a year to dogs who are regularly exposed to other dogs.

DISTEMPER AND THE MODERN DOG

"Why are dogs still vaccinated against distemper? I thought it had been wiped out."

Widespread vaccination has dramatically decreased the number of dogs—most of them puppies—who get distemper each year. But distemper is still very much present in the environment, and all puppies should be vaccinated against the disease.

The name "distemper" has such an old-fashioned sound that dog owners sometimes assume it's a figure of speech rather than a medical diagnosis. In fact, canine distemper is a specific disease caused by a paramyxovirus, similar to the one that causes measles in humans. The common name comes from the fact that as the disease progresses, it affects the brain and sometimes produces changes in a dog's behavior, making it seem out of temper, or "distempered." In earlier stages, however, the disease looks more like a bad cold, with a mucous nasal discharge, eye discharge, fever, loss of appetite, and coughing.

COUGH, GAG, SNORT:
GETTING SPECIFIC ABOUT THOSE STRANGE NOISES

If your dog makes strange noises when she breathes, describe them to your veterinarian. Most noises aren't serious, but they all mean something.

Cough. A cough can originate with the heart, the lungs, the bronchi, or the trachea. Tell your vet whether it occurs most often with exercise or excitement, when your dog is pulling on his leash, when he's eating, or just after he wakes up. Your vet will want to know whether it's a dry cough or a wet (phlegm-producing) cough. How can you tell? If it's a wet or "productive" cough, you may see the dog swallow after the cough, or the cough may end in a hacking gag.

Honk. Dogs with a collapsing trachea may make a honking noise when they're excited (see page 280).

Snoring. Dogs with flat noses, like English Bulldogs, often snore loudly. Snoring is caused by air being partially blocked in some part of the nose, throat, or trachea. If a dog has no breathing problems when he's awake, snoring is not a sign of a serious problem.

Snorting. Some dogs snort or grunt when they breathe. If the snort occurs on inhalation, this means the nose, throat, or upper trachea is constricted (see page 282). If the snort occurs on exhalation, the problem is more likely with the lungs, as in chronic bronchitis (see page 285).

Voice change. Dogs will temporarily "lose their voice" if they bark excessively. But if your dog's bark changes and it isn't because he's been barking a lot, tell your vet. A voice change usually originates in the larynx, and it can be caused by partial paralysis of the laryngeal muscles, something caught in the dog's throat, or a tumor putting pressure on the windpipe (see page 283).

The distemper virus lasts a long time in the environment and can spread easily from dog to dog, especially in places such as animal shelters, where dogs with uncertain health backgrounds are housed close together. Although all dogs in kennels and shelters are vaccinated against distemper as soon as they arrive, occasionally a dog will come into a shelter incubating the disease and spread it to other dogs before their vaccines have had a chance to take effect. If a dog has never been vaccinated against distemper before, it can take a couple of weeks for his immune system to produce an adequate level of antibodies to fight off the disease. Any puppy or adult dog that has already received the full series of vaccinations, however, is fully protected against distemper (see page 46).

What if you adopt a shelter puppy who develops a mucous discharge from his eyes or nose, a fever, and a cough a week or two after you bring him home? The most likely diagnosis is kennel cough rather than distemper, but it's best to have your vet check him out right away to make sure. The puppy may have received only one distemper shot so far (and that one quite recently), and he was exposed to dogs of unknown health status in the animal shelter.

Distemper can be fatal—especially if it has already spread to the nervous system, where it can cause muscle twitching or seizures—but in earlier stages it can sometimes be treated successfully. Dogs who are suspected of having distemper are often hospitalized (quarantined from other dogs, of course) and given plasma and antibiotics, to help combat any secondary bacterial infection. Distemper can be confirmed by tests on blood, tissue samples, or urine, but vets don't wait for confirmation before starting treatment of suspected cases.

HONKING SMALL DOGS

"My seven-month-old Chihuahua sometimes makes a strange coughing or honking sound, usually when he's excited. I was told this is normal for Chihuahuas because they have flat tracheas. Is this true, and if so, is it something to be concerned about?"

It's true that Chihuahuas and some other toy breeds (including Yorkies, Pomeranians, and Toy Poodles) have a higher incidence of collapsing trachea than other types of dogs. This doesn't mean it's normal for Chihuahuas to have a flat trachea; rather, it's a common abnormality.

The normal trachea is a tube supported by firm rings of cartilage. In collapsing trachea, the cartilage is weak and the trachea flattens in one or more areas along its length as the dog breathes, making it harder for him to move air in and out of the lungs. This narrowing of the trachea often produces a coughing or honking sound, especially when a dog exercises or is excited.

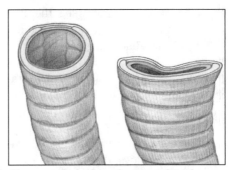

Air moves freely through a normal trachea (left) but not through one that's flattened because of weak cartilage (right).

A collapsing trachea tends to worsen over the years because the tissue lining the trachea becomes chronically inflamed and swollen, narrowing the airway even further. Occasionally the collapse is so severe that a dog will gasp for breath or pass out. This can be a life-threatening medical emergency.

If your puppy's cough is in fact due to a collapsing trachea, will he develop serious problems as he gets older? That's almost impossible to predict. Some dogs with the condition do fine and have a normal life span; others might require medication to decrease inflammation in the airways, or surgery to help support the trachea. Signs that a collapsing trachea is becoming worse include increased coughing, gagging, or shortness of breath when exercising.

Ask your vet what she thinks of your dog's respiration and overall condition. Depending on the severity of your dog's symptoms, your vet might recommend either waiting and watching to see whether the cough becomes more frequent, or chest x-rays or a tracheoscopy (examining the dog's trachea with a tiny video camera on a long, flexible tube) to further assess the problem. If the collapse is severe, surgery to place supporting rings around the trachea is sometimes recommended. That surgery is difficult and would need to be done by a surgeon who is experienced in the procedure.

THE HICCUPS

"My 16-week-old puppy seems to get the hiccups all the time—after eating and drinking, and sometimes when he's just lying around. Is this anything to be concerned about?"

Hiccups in puppies are almost always harmless. Usually the pup outgrows them by the time he's around six months old. Hiccups are often associated with eating or drinking, possibly because when the stomach is distended with food, it presses against the diaphragm, where the phrenic nerve (the major nerve controlling the hiccup reflex) is located.

Very rarely, hiccups can be associated with a disease or abnormality, such as a birth defect in the esophagus or diaphragm; distemper; migration of parasite larvae to the diaphragm; or an illness that has reduced the amount of calcium or potassium in the blood (such as pancreatitis or kidney disease).

If your puppy has received the routine vaccinations and deworming that most puppies get, you needn't worry that he has distemper or parasite migration. If, on the other hand, the puppy was rescued as a stray, you should discuss those possibilities with your vet.

Does your puppy also regurgitate after eating or drinking? Regurgitation means the food or liquid comes back up and falls from the dog's mouth without the abdominal heave of vomiting. If your puppy does regurgitate regularly, you should talk to your vet about whether a birth defect in the esophagus or diaphragm might be causing both the hiccups and the regurgitation (see page 132).

If your puppy had low blood calcium or potassium, which can cause hiccuplike contractions of the diaphragm with every heartbeat (sometimes called "thumps"), he would look and act sick, not like a normal puppy with the hiccups.

Persistent hiccups in dogs that are past puppyhood warrant a call to the vet, because the likelihood that they're a symptom of illness increases in older dogs.

THE FLAT-NOSED, SMUSHED-FACE BLUES

Much of the appeal of English Bulldogs, Pugs, Boston Terriers, Lhasa Apsos, and similar dogs lies in their flat faces, wrinkles, and comical expressions. Unfortunately, that cuteness factor may be accompanied by one or more respiratory problems.

Dogs with pushed-in faces are far more likely than longer-nosed dogs to have abnormally small nostrils, swollen tissue in the back of the throat that impairs breathing, or an unusually narrow trachea. These features make it difficult for the dog to move air in and out of his lungs. Sometimes the problem is minor, and the dog will simply snort and snore his way through life without major consequences. Occasionally, however, the problem is so severe that being outside in the summer heat or fetching a ball can leave a dog gasping for air.

When you first bring home a flat-nosed dog, it's a good idea to ask your vet to evaluate the dog's breathing. The vet will look at the nostrils and the back of the throat, watch the dog breathe, and listen with a stethoscope for rasps or wheezes that can indicate airflow obstruction. Mild breathing problems can often be managed by using a harness instead of a collar for walks, keeping the dog thin and fit, banning cigarette smoking in the house, and using an air conditioner in the summer.

For severe breathing problems related to a dog's facial features, surgery can sometimes help. Tightly pinched nostrils can be surgically widened, and excess tissue at the back of the throat can be removed so the flow of air is less obstructed.

Overheating, exercise, or excitement can trigger a life-threatening breathing crisis in a flat-nosed dog. If your dog becomes overtired or overheated and starts struggling for breath, cool him by moving him to an air-conditioned location or wetting him down, and calm him by talking to him and petting him gently. (The more agitated the dog gets, the more swollen the tissue in his nose and throat becomes and the more difficult it is for him to breathe.) Don't attempt mouth-to-nose respiration, because you will not be able to force air past the swollen tissue any better than the dog can, and your efforts would panic him further.

If cooling and calming the dog don't improve his breathing within 10 minutes, take him to a veterinarian, who can give him oxygen, steroids, or epinephrine, or even do a tracheotomy if necessary.

A cute pug-nosed profile and breathing problems often go together.

RASPY-SOUNDING BIG OLD DOGS

"My 11-year-old retriever gets tired on walks a lot easier than he used to. I thought it was just old age, but last week, when I was throwing a tennis ball for him, he started gasping for breath and slumped over. Also, the sound of his bark has changed. What could be wrong?"

Slowing down can be a normal sign of aging, but gasping for breath and falling over most definitely are not. In this case, your dog's voice change provides another clue to what may be going on. Older dogs—especially the larger breeds, like St. Bernards, Newfoundlands, and retrievers—sometimes develop a partial paralysis of the muscles that control air flow through the larynx, in the upper part of the trachea. Because the larynx is also the voicebox, dogs with laryngeal paralysis, or "lar par," can also have a voice change. Sometimes dogs with lar par will gag or cough when they eat or drink.

Call your vet for an appointment. The vet will listen to your dog's heart and lungs; feel his neck for enlarged lymph nodes, an enlarged thyroid gland, and other lumps and bumps; and look inside his mouth. If the vet suspects that your dog does in fact have lar par, the way to confirm it is by sedating him and then using a laryngoscope to look deep in his throat and watch the movement of the laryngeal folds.

Lar par can occur on its own, or it can be a sign of a generalized nerve problem, such as myasthenia gravis (see page 323). If your vet suspects a whole-body disease may be causing the lar par, she'll recommend further tests. Treating the underlying disease usually improves the lar par.

Avoiding exertion, losing weight, and keeping cool in the summertime may be all that's required for dogs who are mildly affected. If the paralysis is severe enough to make a dog gasp for breath, however, then surgery may be recommended to tie back the laryngeal folds so they remain open.

A BLOODY NOSE

"My dog has a little blood coming from one of his nostrils. Should I be concerned?"

It's a lot harder to make a dog's nose bleed than it is to make a person's nose bleed, so watch your dog carefully. If the bleeding does not stop within a half hour, if your dog seems sick or hurt in general, or if the bleeding starts up again a day or two later, call your vet. Common causes of nosebleeds in dogs include an infected tooth, a sharp object stuck in the nose or sinuses, a sinus infection, eating mouse poison (see page 412), a platelet problem (see page 357), or cancer in the nasal passages (see page 369).

Your vet will want to know whether the blood is coming from one or both nostrils; whether it's bright red, watery, or contains mucus; whether your dog has any other symptoms; and whether he may have eaten mouse or rat poison. Blood tests can check for a bleeding disorder, and an endoscope can be used to peer backward into the nose from the mouth to determine the source of the bleeding. Foreign material stuck in the nose must be removed, and infections can be treated by flushing the area, giving antibiotics, or both.

A FUNGUS AMONG US

Depending on where you live, your dog could encounter one or more fungal diseases affecting the respiratory tract. Fungi are microscopic, moldlike organisms. Often they are found in soil, and dogs can pick them up by inhaling or swallowing the spores or getting them in a wound. Once the spores have entered the body, they can spread via the bloodstream to other areas. Dogs who dig—especially in areas where birds, bats, or rodents hang out—are far more likely to be exposed to these fungi than are dogs whose feet touch only sidewalks and lawns.

Symptoms of a fungal infection of the respiratory tract may include a cough, a mucous discharge from the eyes or nose, a bloody nose, fever, or lethargy. Each of those symptoms could have a dozen causes, many of them more common than fungal diseases, so often a more oddball piece of information—such as a dog's recent exposure to bird or bat feces, or the presence of a skin infection along with pneumonia—is required to raise a veterinarian's suspicion that a fungus may be responsible. Some fungal diseases can be diagnosed through blood tests; others are diagnosed by finding the microscopic organisms in mucus or other fluids. Most are treated with the antifungal medications ketoconazole, itraconazole, or amphotericin. Here are the facts about the most common fungal diseases.

Blastomycosis. Found primarily in the Southeast and Midwest, especially along rivers and other waterways. Thrives in high humidity. Can cause a cough, harsh breathing sounds, eye inflammation, skin sores, or lameness. Very treatable if caught early.

Histoplasmosis. Found primarily in the Midwest, particularly in areas where birds and bats roost. Can cause pneumonia, diarrhea, or anemia. Disease ranges from mild to severe.

Coccidioidomycosis. Found primarily in the Southwest, especially in areas with rodent burrows. Sometimes called "Valley Fever." Outbreaks often occur after a rain in the desert (the moisture activates the fungal spores) or when excavation disturbs the soil. Can cause pneumonia, fever, lameness, or weight loss. Disease ranges from mild to severe.

Cryptococcosis. Found throughout North America, especially in areas where birds and bats roost. Much more common in cats than in dogs. Can cause eye inflammation, mucous discharge from the eyes or nose, stumbling, weakness, or seizures.

Aspergillosis. Found throughout North America. It frequently targets the nose and sinuses, causing a mucous or bloody discharge from the nose, sneezing fits, and sores around the nostrils.

THE HEARTFELT COUGH

"My spaniel mix has had a cough for a while now. I thought it was allergies, but the vet thinks it's his heart. How can heart disease make a dog cough?"

Several things can cause a "cardiac cough." One is an enlarged heart, which can push upward against the bronchi (the two large airways leading from the trachea into the lungs) and compress them, triggering a cough. Another is right-sided heart failure. The right side of the heart pumps blood to the lungs, where it picks up oxygen; if the heart is not able to pump blood efficiently, then fluid can leak from the blood vessels into the lungs, and the fluid makes a dog cough. A third is heartworms, which can also cause fluid to seep into the lungs.

Listening to the heart and lungs with a stethoscope, taking chest x-rays to look for an enlarged heart and signs of fluid in the lungs, running an EKG (electrocardiogram), and doing an echocardiogram (ultrasound exam of the heart) are some of the ways the heart and lungs can be evaluated. If your dog's cough is caused by a heart problem, treating the heart problem will help the cough.

PANTING

"Why does my dog pant so much? Does it mean he's sick?"

Dogs pant for four reasons: because they're excited, hot, short of breath, or in pain. A dog that pants when he's walking outside in 90° heat or when he's chasing a ball in the park is not sick, he's normal. Dogs with pushed-in faces, like English Bulldogs and Pugs, tend to pant more than other types of dogs because they have to work harder to move air in and out of their lungs. Not surprisingly, dogs with heavy coats, like Newfoundlands and St. Bernards, tend to pant during warm weather.

But what if your dog suddenly begins to pant a lot in situations where he wouldn't otherwise? Talk to your vet. Although most panting is normal, increased panting can be a sign of a breathing problem or heart disease, or even Cushing's disease (see page 299) or "doggie Alzheimer's" (see page 181). A good rule of thumb is to tell your veterinarian about any behavior that's unusual for your dog, and that includes panting for no apparent reason.

CHRONIC AND ALLERGIC BRONCHITIS

"My six-year-old Cocker Spaniel coughs every day, especially in the morning. My vet says she has chronic bronchitis. What can be done for her? I'm worried about this hacking cough."

Chronic bronchitis is a frustrating disease. The first step in diagnosing it is to rule out other possible causes for a persistent cough. Kennel cough or another infection, collapsing trachea, laryngeal paralysis, heart disease, heartworms, lungworms, fungal diseases, and lung tumors may be on the list of possible causes, depending on your dog's age, other symptoms, and environment. Those diseases are ruled out by measures such as blood tests, x-rays, and response to antibiotics.

Once the other cough-inducing diseases have been ruled out, chronic bronchitis can be confirmed by bronchoscopy and microscopic examination of tissue and secretions from the bronchi. Bronchoscopy involves passing a tiny video camera on a thin, flexible tube into the bronchi, so that the veterinarian can see inside them and take tissue and fluid samples. In chronic bronchitis, the veterinarian will see inflamed tissue and an abundance of white blood cells in the bronchial secretions, with no obvious bacteria or tumor cells present. In allergic bronchitis—one type of chronic bronchitis—there is an abundance of eosinophils, one type of white blood cells.

Chronic bronchitis is not cancer, and it's not pneumonia, but it can nevertheless be difficult to treat. It can't be cured, it can only be controlled. To that end, dogs with chronic bronchitis are advised to lose weight, if necessary; live in an environment free of cigarette smoke and other airborne irritants; and use steroids, antihistamines, and bronchodilators (medications that expand the airways) as needed. Deciding which steroid, antihistamine, or bronchodilator works best for a particular dog is where art and patience are required. Different medicines work better for different dogs. Ask your vet how long your dog needs to be on a particular drug before showing signs of improvement. If at the end of that time your dog is still not doing well, your vet will likely want to try a different drug.

The goal in treating chronic bronchitis is to give your dog a comfortable, normally active life. It is not to stop him from coughing, period. Coughing helps clear the bronchi and trachea of secretions, so it's expected and acceptable for a dog who is taking medicine for chronic bronchitis to still cough sometimes.

DOGS AND CIGARETTE SMOKE

"My grandmother smokes like a chimney, and she has a sweet little dog who never leaves her side. Is my grandmother going to make the dog sick with her smoking?"

Dogs who live with heavy smokers have a higher risk of developing chronic bronchitis than dogs who live with non-smokers do. And although no direct link has been documented between secondhand smoke and lung cancer in dogs, given what we know about secondhand smoke's effects on people, it certainly seems likely that a dog living with indoor air pollution has a higher risk of developing cancer somewhere along the respiratory tract (see page 370).

This much is certain: whenever veterinarians see a dog with a breathing problem who lives with smokers, they advise the people to not smoke indoors and to keep the dog's environment smoke-free. It wouldn't hurt to ask your grandmother to cut back on cigarettes or smoke only outdoors for her dog's sake, if she can't or won't do so for her own health.

A BIRTH DEFECT LEADING TO PNEUMONIA

"A friend of mine breeds Golden Retrievers, and I was going to buy a puppy from her latest litter. But then the entire litter—seven puppies—came down with bad coughs, runny noses, and fevers. The veterinarian suspects they have a birth defect that makes them susceptible to pneumonia. Is this common? Can it be cured?"

COLD NOSE, HEALTHY DOG?

One of the most common medical misconceptions about dogs is that feeling their noses will tell you whether they're sick. If only it were that simple.

The theory is that when a dog's nose is cool and moist, she doesn't have a fever, and when her nose is warm and dry, she does. But her nose could be cool and wet because she just drank some water, or it could be warm and dry because she's been lying in the sun. The only way to know whether a dog has a fever is to take her temperature, using a rectal thermometer (see page 404). A dog's normal temperature is between 101.5° and 102.5°F (three to four degrees higher than a person's), so the average dog will always feel warm to the average person.

If your dog's nose is usually cool and wet and today for some reason it's hot and dry, try offering her some water. But if her nose is hot and dry and she's also lethargic, has lost her appetite, is vomiting, coughing, or limping, or otherwise seems ill, then of course you should call your veterinarian.

The problem the vet is referring to is a defect in the cilia that line the trachea and bronchi. These cilia are microscopic hairs that move in sync to sweep secretions, bacteria, viruses, and other debris up and out of the lungs. In puppies with a birth defect called ciliary dyskinesia (CD), the cilia don't move properly, so normal debris gets trapped in the lungs, where it can cause pneumonia.

Happily, this inherited problem is extremely rare; unhappily, it cannot be cured. There is no way to fix the cilia so they work properly. Puppies with ciliary dyskinesia usually get one respiratory infection after another starting at a young age. Some owners try to manage these infections by keeping the dogs on antibiotics continuously, but often the dogs develop pneumonia or other severe breathing problems anyway. Most dogs with CD die or are euthanized at a young age because of recurrent pneumonia.

There are two ways to make a definitive diagnosis of ciliary dyskinesia. The easy way is to take an x-ray of the dog's chest and abdomen and look for a strange feature that accompanies CD 50 percent of the time: the position of the dog's organs is the mirror image of normal. In other words, the aorta comes from the right side of the heart, the duodenum is on the left side of the abdomen, and so on. The organs still function properly—they are simply reversed from their usual positions.

That sign is seen in only half of the dogs that have CD, however. The others can be diagnosed by taking a biopsy of nasal or tracheal tissue and sending it to a specialized diagnostic lab.

CHAPTER 12

Diabetes and Other Endocrine Diseases

IT'S COMPLEX BUT VIRTUALLY INVISIBLE, which helps explain why most people don't have a clue about what or where the endocrine system is—until some part of it malfunctions. But fear not if you can't locate the pancreas or don't know what the adrenal glands are supposed to do. This chapter will clear up those mysteries, while describing the major endocrine diseases (diabetes mellitus, hypothyroidism, Cushing's, and Addison's) and their treatments.

EMERGENCY!

Does your dog need immediate veterinary care? Check this list to help you decide.

TAKE IMMEDIATE ACTION!

Call your vet or an emergency veterinary clinic *now* if your dog is showing any of the following symptoms:

❏ He has been taking **mitotane** (Lysodren) for Cushing's disease and is **weak or uncoordinated.**

❏ She has been taking **insulin** for diabetes and is **weak or uncoordinated.**

TAKE A MINUTE . . .

Read further in this book and then call your vet during office hours as needed if your dog is showing any of the following symptoms:

❏ She is **drinking and urinating more than usual;** this is often seen with diabetes or kidney disease (see the following Q&A), or Cushing's disease (see page 299).

❏ He is **eating more but losing weight;** this can be a sign of diabetes.

❏ She has **frequent bladder infections or skin infections;** these can be signs of diabetes or Cushing's disease.

❏ He has developed a **potbelly;** this is sometimes a sign of Cushing's disease or heart disease (see page 272).

❏ She is **losing hair** on her back or sides; this can be a symptom of Cushing's disease.

❏ He is a toy or small-breed puppy who sometimes **staggers, seems weak, or acts strange;** these can be symptoms of low blood sugar (see page 295) or a birth defect in the blood vessels leading to the liver (see page 263).

Remember, it's never wrong to call your veterinarian if you have a question about your dog's health, or if you're worried about a symptom or your dog's overall condition. That's what we're here for.

INCREASED THIRST
AND URINATION

"I thought my 12-year-old Poodle might have a urinary tract infection because she was drinking a lot of water and peeing in the house. Along with checking her urine for bacteria, my vet wants to run some blood tests to check for diabetes and other diseases. What's the connection?"

Drinking and urinating more than usual, often with urinary accidents in the house, is the first symptom many owners notice when their dogs develop diabetes mellitus. And your dog is in the middle-aged-to-older stage at which dogs are more likely to develop diabetes, Cushing's, or kidney problems, the Big 3 diseases associated with increased thirst and urination. So it makes perfect sense to check for those diseases while also culturing your dog's urine to see whether she has a urinary tract infection.

Dogs with diabetes mellitus drink a lot because the glucose in their blood, which their cells can't use because they don't have enough insulin, is excreted by the kidneys into the urine. The glucose pulls more water than usual from the blood into the urine. The dog is dehydrated from losing extra water in the urine and feels thirsty, so she drinks as much water as she can to make up the deficit. But the spilling over of glucose into the urine is ongoing, so she keeps making excessive amounts of urine and drinking excessive amounts of water to try to catch up.

Any bacteria in the bladder feast on the glucose in the urine. And because the white blood cells of a dog with diabetes mellitus aren't able to fight infections as effectively as usual, it's quite common

for a dog with diabetes to get urinary tract infections.

To see whether your dog has diabetes, your vet will measure her blood glucose, urine glucose, and ketones. (Ketones are produced when the body breaks down fat to use as energy, which diabetic animals must do because they can't use glucose properly.) Normal blood glucose for a dog is 100 to 175, and normal urine contains no glucose or ketones. Diabetic dogs have blood glucose levels of 200 or higher, sometimes spiking as high as 600, and glucose or ketones in their urine.

While checking for diabetes, it's also important to run a full blood-chemistry profile to look for abnormalities suggestive of Cushing's disease and pancreatitis, because those diseases can accompany diabetes mellitus and should be treated simultaneously (see pages 299 and 142). The chemistry profile also will indicate whether the kidneys are working adequately, the other major concern in a dog who is drinking and urinating excessively (see page 335).

Other signs that are sometimes seen in dogs with diabetes mellitus are weight loss despite an increased appetite, fatigue, skin infections, vomiting or diarrhea, and cataracts.

COMPLICATIONS
OF DIABETES

"My dog was recently diagnosed with diabetes. I have an aunt who's a diabetic, and she has had problems with her eyes and her kidneys. Do diabetic dogs develop the same problems that diabetic people do?"

Diabetic dogs are susceptible to some of the complications seen in people,

A GUIDE TO GLANDS

The endocrine system is made up of organs and glands that secrete substances that help regulate processes such as metabolism (the body's use of energy). Hormones and insulin are two examples of such substances. Many endocrine glands are tiny, yet the substances they produce can have profound effects on the whole body. Here is a description of the key endocrine organs and glands discussed in this chapter.

❏ The **hypothalamus** is an area on the underside of the brain that is primarily responsible for regulating the secretion of hormones and other chemical messengers. It sends signals to the endocrine system via the pituitary gland.

❏ The **pituitary gland** is attached to the hypothalamus, deep within the skull. In a 40-pound dog, the pituitary is approximately a half inch long and a quarter inch wide. The pituitary receives signals from the hypothalamus and in response secretes hormones that turn other glands—such as the thyroid and the adrenals—on and off.

❏ The **thyroid gland** is in the neck, attached to the upper trachea. There is one lobe on either side of the trachea, each about 1½ inches long and ¾ inch wide. They secrete thyroglobulin, which speeds up the metabolism, heart rate, respiratory rate, and turnover of cells.

❏ The **parathyroid glands** are four pea-size structures, one on the outside and one on the inside of each lobe of the thyroid. They secrete parathyroid hormone, which maintains the proper

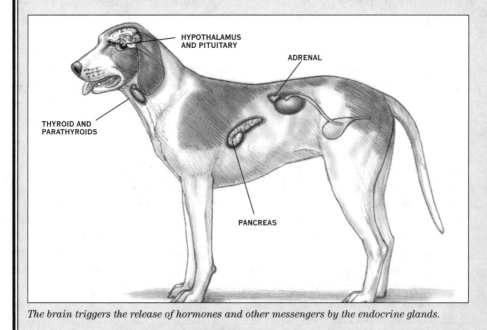

HYPOTHALAMUS AND PITUITARY

ADRENAL

THYROID AND PARATHYROIDS

PANCREAS

The brain triggers the release of hormones and other messengers by the endocrine glands.

level of calcium in the blood. Calcium regulates the contracting of muscle cells, including those in the heart. If blood levels of calcium are too high, the heart can beat erratically; if they are too low, muscles cramp and spasm and the heart rate is abnormally slow.

❏ The **pancreas** is in the abdomen, attached to the lower curve of the stomach. In a 40-pound dog, it's approximately 10 inches long and weighs about 1 pound. Some cells in the pancreas produce digestive enzymes that are secreted into the small intestine, and others produce insulin, which is released into the bloodstream and allows cells to pick up glucose and use it for energy.

❏ The two **adrenal glands** are in the abdomen, one next to each kidney. They are about ¾ inch long and ½ inch wide. The inner region of the adrenal glands produces epinephrine (adrenaline) and norepinephrine, the "fight or flight" hormones, which raise blood pressure and heart rate. The outer layers of the adrenal glands produce cortisol, aldosterone, and androgens. Cortisol stimulates the liver to produce glucose, reduces protein stores in the body, redistributes fat, reduces inflammation, and suppresses the immune system. Aldosterone regulates levels of sodium in the blood, which affects blood pressure, heart rate, and kidney function. Androgens are sex hormones, found in small amounts in females as well as in males, that promote muscle growth and red blood cell production.

but not all of them. Here are the main similarities and differences:

❏ **Eyes.** Cataracts are a common complication of diabetes mellitus in dogs. Diabetic cataracts form when glucose is converted to sorbitol within the lens of the eye. Sorbitol can't get out of the lens, and it attracts water from the bloodstream, which causes the lens fibers to swell and burst, creating cataracts. Cataracts can cause blindness, but they can be surgically removed.

Problems with the retina (the light-sensing surface on the back of the eye) are common in diabetic people but not in diabetic dogs.

❏ **Infections.** Diabetic dogs and people both are susceptible to skin infections, poor wound healing, urinary tract infections, and pneumonia.

❏ **Kidneys.** Kidney problems are not a common complication for diabetic dogs.

❏ **Pancreas.** Pancreatitis (an inflamed pancreas) can be a cause *or* an effect of diabetes mellitus in dogs (see page 142).

❏ **Nerve problems.** People with diabetes sometimes develop numbness in their hands or feet. Nerve complications are rare in dogs. Occasionally, however, a dog whose diabetes has not been controlled will have weakness in the hind legs, poor reflexes, or muscle wasting.

CAUSES OF DIABETES

"Does diabetes run in families? What causes it?"

Diabetes does seem to occur more in some breeds of dogs than in others.

It's found in higher than average numbers of Samoyeds, Miniature Schnauzers, Pugs, Beagles, and Miniature and Toy Poodles. Recurrent bouts of pancreatitis can destroy enough of the insulin-producing cells of the pancreas to result in diabetes. But in most cases, the underlying cause of the disease is not known.

ORAL MEDICATIONS FOR DIABETES

"People sometimes can control their diabetes through diet and oral medications, like Glucotrol and Glucophage, instead of insulin injections. Does this work for dogs?"

Unfortunately, oral medications for diabetes don't work for dogs. Those medications are for people who have Type II, or non-insulin-dependent, diabetes. Type II diabetics produce some insulin but not enough. Diabetic dogs are Type I; they produce essentially no insulin. So medications like Glucotrol (glipizide), which boosts the pancreas's secretion of insulin, and Glucophage (metformin), which boosts insulin's effectiveness by making cells more sensitive to it, are not helpful in dogs. Diabetic dogs require insulin injections.

Diet, however, does have a place in controlling diabetes in dogs. A high-fiber diet slows the absorption of simple carbohydrates from the digestive tract and helps smooth out the post-meal glucose spike. If your dog is diabetic, discuss his diet with your vet.

In dogs whose diabetes is difficult to control, other medications are sometimes used *with* insulin, though not in place of it. One such medication is acarbose, which slows the breakdown of carbohydrates into sugars in the digestive tract (but can also cause gas and diarrhea). Two others are the trace minerals chromium picolinate and vanadium, which may make insulin work "better," although they are not known for certain to be effective in dogs.

MONITORING DIABETES

"I just started giving my Lab mix insulin shots for diabetes. We got into a routine with the shots more easily than I expected, but what should I be looking for to know whether her diabetes is under control?"

Diabetic people test their blood glucose several times a day to know how much insulin they need at a given time. It's possible for dog owners to do the same, by pricking the dog's ear to get a drop of blood to test in a home glucose monitor, but such close monitoring in dogs is seldom necessary or desirable. Instead, owners should pay close attention to their dogs' appetite, water consumption and urination, energy level, and weight.

It's dangerous for an animal's blood sugar to drop too low, which can occur if a dog is given insulin but doesn't eat an adequate amount of food. When blood sugar drops too low, a dog can become weak and uncoordinated, then lose consciousness or have a seizure. For that reason, it's extremely important that a diabetic animal eats well. Ideally, a diabetic dog will be switched to a diet high in fiber and low in simple carbohydrates, but only if she likes the food and will eat it readily. If a diabetic dog won't eat or is just picking at her food, call your vet to ask whether to change food or change the amount of insulin you give that day.

Keep a daily record of how much your dog eats and drinks, how frequently she urinates, whether she has any accidents in the house, and whether she seems tired or has normal amounts of energy. A dog whose diabetes is well-controlled will (1) eat well, (2) drink and urinate less (if she was drinking and urinating excessively before), and (3) be bright and energetic.

Weigh your dog once a week. Diabetic dogs may be thin, normal, or overweight when they're first diagnosed. Often they're dehydrated, which lowers their weight somewhat. Call your vet if your diabetic dog was thin or normal to begin with and loses weight when she starts getting insulin injections. Slow weight loss in an overweight diabetic dog is OK, but call your vet if it's more than 1 percent of the dog's body weight per week.

Ask your vet whether you should use test strips to check your dog's urine for glucose once a day. Swish the paper strip through her urine stream to wet it, then check the strip's color change against the chart on the package. Although normal dogs have no glucose in their urine, vets like to see a *small amount* of glucose in a diabetic dog's urine, because that's a sign her blood sugar hasn't fallen too low. Low blood sugar is more dangerous than slightly high blood sugar, so the goal with diabetic dogs is to keep them in the slightly high range. If you do use urine glucose strips, test the urine at the same time each day, and write the results in your daily record. Don't change the amount of insulin you give based on a urine-strip reading unless you check with your veterinarian first.

Your vet will run blood tests periodically to monitor your dog's progress. About 10 to 14 days after she starts on insulin injections, your dog will spend a day at the vet clinic for a blood glucose curve. You will give her insulin and feed her as usual in the morning, then drop her off at the clinic, where her blood gluose will be checked every 1 to 2 hours for 8 to 12 hours to map the high and low points. Depending on the results, your vet may increase or decrease the amount of insulin your dog is getting.

Once a diabetic dog has achieved a good blood glucose curve (the ideal is one that goes no higher than 200 and no lower than 100), your vet can use a single blood test every two to three months to check whether the blood sugar is stable. A blood sample is checked for the level of either fructosamine or glycosylated hemoglobin. The levels of these compounds essentially reflect the average levels of blood sugar over the past three weeks. If the levels are normal, the diabetic dog continues on the same insulin regimen. If the levels are high, then a 12-hour blood glucose curve should be scheduled to determine what changes need to be made in the insulin regimen.

LOW BLOOD SUGAR IN PUPPIES

"I'm picking up a 10-week-old Yorkshire Terrier puppy from a breeder on Saturday, and she told me to make sure I have some honey or Karo syrup at home to give the puppy if he gets low blood sugar. How would I know that he had low blood sugar? Is this a common problem?"

Hypoglycemia (low blood sugar) *occasionally* occurs in puppies of small and toy breeds, but it's not nearly as common as you'd think, given how many people have heard they should keep a bottle of Karo syrup in the pantry just in case.

(continued on page 298)

"BUT I COULD NEVER GIVE MY DOG A SHOT!"

The biggest worry for most people whose dogs are diagnosed with diabetes is the thought of giving their dogs insulin injections (yes, with a needle and syringe) twice a day. Fortunately, the process is really not that bad, for the person or for the dog.

Is there any alternative to insulin shots for diabetic dogs? Not really. Insulin can't be taken by mouth; when it's swallowed, it's digested and doesn't reach the bloodstream in a usable form. Other oral medications sometimes used by diabetic people don't work in dogs (see page 294).

Pharmacies carry several different types of insulin for human diabetics, and the same types of insulin are used for dogs. Your veterinarian will write a prescription for the specific insulin your dog will be using, as well as for the syringes needed to give the insulin injections. (Syringes and needles are sold only by prescription to limit their potential use for illegal drugs.)

Insulin comes in a small glass bottle and must be stored in the refrigerator. The needles are already attached to the syringes, which are marked in units (U). Insulin is used in tiny amounts and injected just under the skin, so the needle is thin and small. A typical starting dose for a 20-pound dog is 10 U. That is only 0.1 milliliter—just a couple of drops. By contrast, when your dog is vaccinated against rabies, the vet injects 1 milliliter of vaccine, or 10 times as much.

Most diabetic dogs are given insulin and fed twice a day, ideally at 12-hour intervals, such as 7 A.M. and 7 P.M. The insulin is given first, then the food. Dogs who like to eat may actually be excited to see the insulin come out of the refrigerator, because they know that food comes next!

To give an insulin injection, get out a syringe and take the insulin out of the refrigerator. Turn the insulin

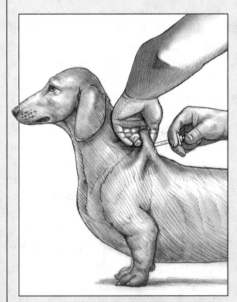

Most dogs don't mind insulin shots: a tiny prick, and they know that food is on its way.

vial upside down and roll it gently between your palms for about three seconds to mix it. Wipe off the top of the vial with a cotton ball soaked in rubbing alcohol. Take the cover off the needle, stick the needle through the rubber top of the insulin vial, and turn the vial upside down, keeping the tip of the needle "underwater." Pull back on the plunger to draw the proper amount of insulin into the syringe. If you get air in the syringe, that means the tip of the needle wasn't in the insulin. Push the plunger to inject the air back into the bottle, and reposition the needle tip so it draws up insulin instead. When you have the correct amount of insulin in the syringe, pull the needle and syringe out of the vial.

To give your dog an injection, pick up a small tent of skin on his neck or upper back. (Use a slightly different area each time so that one spot doesn't get sore.) Push the needle through the skin at the bottom of the "tent." You'll feel a slight pop as the needle goes through the skin. If your dog is small and thin-skinned, make sure you don't push the needle through both sides of the "tent," or you'll be injecting the insulin into the air.

Pull back on the plunger just a smidge, to make sure you haven't accidentally gotten into a blood vessel. If you see blood in the syringe, pull the needle out of the skin and poke it through again in a different spot. Then steadily push in the plunger to deposit the insulin under the skin. Pull the

needle and syringe out gently, praise your dog extravagantly, and give him his breakfast or supper. You'll need to keep a daily log of the time and dose of insulin, how much your dog eats and drinks, and what his attitude and energy level is like, so have your notebook or calendar nearby to jot down that information (see page 294).

Wipe off the top of the insulin vial again with the alcohol-soaked cotton and put the insulin back in the refrigerator.

People often jab themselves when trying to put the cap back on a needle, so you may want to invest in a syringe-disposal box that cuts the needle off the syringe. Alternatively, you can drop used syringes (needle and all) into an empty, heavy plastic bleach or laundry detergent bottle. Take the bottle to your vet's office for disposal as medical waste when it gets full.

Don't reuse syringes. Use a new one for each injection.

Most people find giving their dog insulin quite simple, and the dog seldom puts up a fuss. That makes scheduling the most difficult part of caring for a diabetic dog—he needs his insulin and a meal roughly every 12 hours, 7 days a week. If you know that work will occasionally interfere with this routine, look for a pet sitter who is experienced in giving injections, or board your dog for the day with your vet so he can get his insulin and food on time.

(continued from page 295)

Puppies have a slightly greater tendency than adult dogs to experience a dip in blood sugar for several reasons. They require more energy because they're growing rapidly, so they "use up" their meals more quickly than an adult dog would; they have less body fat to convert to energy in times of need; and their liver hasn't yet reached its full capacity to create glucose in response to demand.

Offsetting these predisposing factors, however, are the facts that puppies are fed more frequently than adult dogs are; puppy food is more calorie-dense than adult food; and puppies naturally conserve their energy by napping periodically throughout the day.

A puppy with low blood sugar might stagger or become weak. If this should happen, there's no harm in rubbing a little Karo syrup or honey on the puppy's gums or under his tongue (¼ teaspoon is plenty for a small puppy), but you should also call your vet or a veterinary emergency clinic to describe the problem and ask whether the puppy needs to be seen immediately.

Puppies with very low blood sugar may lose consciousness or have a seizure. An unconscious puppy can choke on anything put in his mouth, and a seizuring puppy may clench his jaws or bite down on your hand. It's OK to rub a dab of syrup or honey on an unconscious puppy's gums if you can, but your primary focus should be to call a vet and get the puppy to the vet's office as quickly as possible. Simply giving honey may not stop the seizure, and the puppy may have more going on than low blood sugar.

A puppy that seems dazed, staggers, or behaves strangely, particularly after eating, needs to be carefully evaluated by a vet. A birth defect of blood vessels leading to the liver, called portosystemic shunt, could be responsible (see page 263).

HYPOTHYROIDISM

"When I took my seven-year-old Golden Retriever for her annual checkup, I discovered that she'd gained 10 pounds in one year. Her hair is also thinner than it used to be, and she has some scaly and scabby areas on her skin. The vet wanted to check her thyroid. Why?"

The thyroid gland sets the baseline rate of metabolism for the body. Older cats sometimes become hyperthyroid—the thyroid produces too much thyroglobulin, and consequently their heart beats faster, they run around like kittens, and they lose weight despite eating voraciously. (A similar condition in people is called Graves' disease.) In older dogs, however, a malfunctioning thyroid gland almost always winds down rather than up, and they become *hypo*thyroid rather than *hyper*thyroid. Symptoms can include lethargy, weight gain, hair loss, and skin infections. When the levels of thyroid hormone are extremely low, dogs become weak and may even have trouble walking. Hypothyroidism in people is sometimes called Hashimoto's disease.

To evaluate what's going on with the thyroid, vets check a blood sample for levels of TSH (thyroid-stimulating hormone, produced by the pituitary gland) and thyroglobulin (the hormone produced by the thyroid gland). If thyroglobulin levels are lower than normal and TSH levels are higher than normal, it's evidence that the pituitary is signaling as loudly as it can for the thyroid to pro-

LOW BLOOD SUGAR IN ADULT DOGS

Hypoglycemia (low blood sugar) can occur in adult dogs, but it's rare. When a dog is eating normal amounts of food and expending normal amounts of energy, the pancreas (which produces insulin) and the liver (which can create glucose from other energy reserves when needed) work together to keep blood sugar in a normal range.

A scenario sometimes described as "hunting dog hypoglycemia" can occur when a dog expends more energy than his liver can readily mobilize. The name comes from the fact that pointers or retrievers whose owners took them out for long days of hunting sometimes would collapse, get the shakes, or have a seizure from low blood sugar. These dogs produce normal amounts of insulin and energy but simply "run out of gas" with pro-longed exercise. (Some also have an inherited deficiency in the enzymes used to convert glycogen—an energy source stored in the liver—to glucose.) The treatment is simple: rest, water, and a nutritious snack every couple of hours while they're working hard.

Low blood sugar in an adult dog also can result from an insulinoma, or tumor of the insulin-producing cells of the pancreas. The tumor doesn't respond to normal feedback mechanisms and continues to pour insulin into the bloodstream even when the dog's blood sugar is low. Weakness, staggering, collapse, or seizures can result. A high blood insulin level in an adult dog with low blood glucose is a sign of an insulinoma. Insulinomas can be surgically removed or treated with medication.

---

duce more thyroglobulin, but the thyroid gland is unable to respond. Diagnosis: hypothyroidism.

Hypothyroidism can be an immune-mediated disease, one that occurs when the body's own immune system mistakenly starts attacking the thyroid gland or thyroglobulin. Other times, the exact cause is not known. A malignant tumor of the thyroid gland can also cause it to malfunction, but this is rare in dogs (see page 373).

Hypothyroidism is treated with oral thyroid supplements. These are given daily for life. Blood tests are drawn every two or three months at first to reach the appropriate dose for the individual dog. After that, a blood test once or twice a year verifies that the dog's thyroglobulin levels are neither too high nor too low. Usually hypothyroid dogs will have more energy, lose weight, and have healthier skin and hair within a few weeks after starting thyroid supplements.

CUSHING'S DISEASE

"When my Miniature Poodle got thin hair and a potbelly and started panting a lot, I thought it was just old age. But my vet took one look at her and said we should test her for Cushing's disease. Can you tell me more about Cushing's?"

ushing's disease is the common name for a condition that's difficult to say, spell, and comprehend: hyperadreno-corticism. "Hyper" means "too much," "adreno" refers to the adrenal glands, and "corticism" refers to cortisol, one of the products of the adrenal glands. In Cushing's disease, a dog's adrenal glands produce too much cortisol.

Cortisol in normal amounts relieves inflammation, such as minor muscle or joint pain and skin irritation. In excessive amounts, however, cortisol thins and weakens the skin, leaves the body vulnerable to infections (bacterial, fungal, and viral), counteracts insulin's attempts to regulate blood sugar, promotes storage of fat, and weakens muscles. The most common symptoms of Cushing's disease are excessive hunger, excessive thirst, and excessive urination. Some dogs also get a potbelly, because their livers are enlarged, their abdominal muscles are weaker, and they are fatter. A dog's hair may become thin, and she may have a skin or urinary tract infection. Dogs with Cushing's may also pant more, because they have less energy and may have gained weight.

Cushing's disease is fairly common among middle-aged and older dogs.

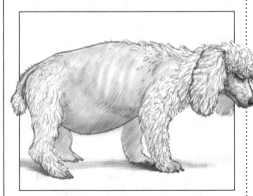

Symptoms of Cushing's, like weight gain, thinning hair, and lethargy, may be mistaken for normal aging changes.

Poodles, Dachshunds, Boxers, Beagles, terriers, and German Shepherds have higher than average rates of the disease.

Cushing's is caused by one of three factors: a tumor of the pituitary gland; a tumor of the adrenal gland; or long-term use of steroid medications, such as prednisone, for allergies or immune-system diseases. About 85 percent of the dogs with Cushing's have a pituitary tumor; these tumors are almost always benign. The tumor causes the pituitary to secrete excessive amounts of adrenocortico-tropic hormone (ACTH), which signals the adrenal glands to make more cortisol. About 10 percent of the dogs with Cushing's have an adrenal-gland tumor; 50 percent of adrenal tumors are benign and 50 percent are malignant. The tumor almost always is in one adrenal gland, not both. The remaining 5 percent of the dogs with Cushing's disease have been given too much steroid medication for too long.

All forms of Cushing's disease are treatable, but first the cause must be identified; see the following Q&A for how that is done.

TESTING FOR CUSHING'S DISEASE

"My vet explained the three types of Cushing's disease to me, but I still don't understand how the testing works. Why can't you just measure the cortisol in the blood, the way you can measure blood sugar to diagnose diabetes?"

iagnosing Cushing's disease is a step-wise project. A vet can't simply measure the amount of cortisol in a single sample of your dog's blood, because the adrenal glands secrete varying amounts of cortisol in pulses throughout the day. Therefore, a single blood sample won't give an accurate view of the total amount of cortisol the adrenals are producing.

Other clues that a dog may have Cushing's disease can be found on routine blood and urine tests, however. Dogs with Cushing's usually have elevated liver enzymes because cortisol stimulates liver cells to work harder at storing glycogen and other substances. They may also have high fasting blood glucose, as is seen in diabetes, because cortisol counteracts the effects of insulin on cells. They may have high cholesterol, because cortisol causes fat to be broken down and redistributed. They may have a low BUN (blood urea nitrogen) and dilute urine, because the kidneys are working overtime to eliminate excess water, and a urinary tract infection, because cortisol hampers the body's ability to fight infections.

Those test results can also be seen in dogs with other diseases—such as diabetes—so a more specific test is needed to definitively diagnose Cushing's. Vets use one of two tests for this: an ACTH response test or a low-dose dexamethasone suppression (LDDS) test. In essence, the ACTH test measures whether the adrenal glands are overexcitable, and the LDDS test measures whether they're irrepressible.

In an ACTH response test, a dog is fasted overnight and a blood sample is drawn in the morning to check the baseline level of cortisol. Then the dog is given an injection of ACTH (adreno-corticotropic hormone, produced by the pituitary gland) to stimulate the adrenal glands; one hour later, a second blood sample is drawn and the cortisol level is measured. If a dog has Cushing's disease caused by a pituitary or adrenal

tumor, the second cortisol level will be higher than a normal dog's. If a dog has Cushing's disease caused by overuse of steroids, the second cortisol level will be *lower* than a normal dog's, because the adrenal glands will have shut down from disuse.

In an LDDS test, a dog is fasted overnight and a blood sample is drawn in the morning to check the baseline level of cortisol. Then the dog is injected with a low dose of dexamethasone. Dexamethasone, a steroid, signals the pituitary to release less ACTH, which should signal the adrenal glands to release less cortisol. Blood samples are drawn four and eight hours later to check the cortisol levels. If the cortisol levels are higher than normal on both the four-hour and the eight-hour tests, then an adrenal-gland tumor is likely. If the cortisol level is low at four hours but elevated at eight hours, then a pituitary tumor is likely. An experienced ultrasonographer can then measure the dog's adrenal glands to verify the diagnosis. With an adrenal gland tumor, the affected gland is usually enlarged or has an obvious mass arising from its surface, and the opposite gland is usually smaller than normal. With a pituitary tumor, both adrenals will be enlarged overall.

TREATING CUSHING'S DISEASE

"My dog is being tested for Cushing's disease, and my vet said we should wait to talk about treatment until we have the results. I'd like to read up on the treatment now, though, so could you give me the details?"

When Cushing's disease is caused by an adrenal tumor, the treatment is to surgically remove the adrenal gland

AN ADRENALINE-PRODUCING ADRENAL TUMOR

A tumor of the outer layers of the adrenal glands can cause Cushing's disease. But what about a tumor of the inner core, which produces epinephrine? Called pheochromocytomas (or pheos, for short), such tumors are very rare—far less common, certainly, than the cortisol-secreting adrenal tumors that cause Cushing's disease—but they are found occasionally in older dogs.

Some pheos undoubtedly go undiagnosed, because they usually produce no symptoms that a dog owner would notice. Epinephrine, or adrenaline, is the classic "fight or flight" hormone. A dog with a pheo will experience periodic bursts of epinephrine. His heart rate and blood pressure will go up, but he may not show any outward signs, such as restlessness or agitation. Most pheos are diagnosed when an adrenal tumor is seen on abdominal x-rays or an ultrasound exam. (A pheo is usually larger than a cortisol-secreting adrenal tumor.) An adrenal mass paired with an increased heart rate (more than 100 beats per minute in a large dog, or more than 180 beats per minute in a small dog) and high blood pressure (more than 180/100 mm Hg) is consistent with a pheo.

Pheos are treated by removing them surgically. They can be invasive, punching through blood vessels and spreading to other sites in the body. Roughly half of the dogs with a pheo have malignant tumors elsewhere as well, so the prognosis is guarded.

that contains the tumor. Dogs that have one adrenal gland removed commonly need to take a steroid supplement—such as prednisone—for a few weeks after the surgery because the healthy adrenal gland will have shut down in response to the adrenal tumor's overproduction. In most cases, the remaining adrenal gland soon gears back up to produce enough cortisol. If it doesn't, the dog will need to take prednisone supplements for life.

The pituitary gland is deep within the skull and produces many hormones besides ACTH, so it can't be removed easily. The most common treatment for pituitary-dependent Cushing's is mitotane (Lysodren), a drug that kills cortisol-producing cells in the adrenal glands. Mitotane is given once a day for 5 to 14 days, until cortisol production (as determined by ACTH response tests) has decreased to normal levels. After that, mitotane is given once or twice a week for life.

Mitotane can have potentially serious side effects. About 25 percent of dogs vomit, have diarrhea, or become lethargic while taking mitotane. Those side effects are managed by dividing the daily dose into two or three parts, and giving it with food to make it easier on the stomach. The big risk, however, is that the mitotane will go too far, too fast, and the dog will develop *hypo*adrenocorticism, or Addison's disease (see page 304). Owners are advised of potential signs of Addison's (persistent vomiting and diarrhea, and being too weak or wobbly to walk) and given prednisone tablets to administer if their dog develops those signs.

Trilostane, a drug that inhibits production of cortisol by the adrenal glands, is currently available only from the United Kingdom. Vets in the United States can order trilostane from the U.K. if they first get an FDA letter of approval to use it in a specific patient. It's possible that the FDA will soon approve trilostane for sale and general use in the United States. The benefit of using trilostane rather than mitotane is that there is less risk of permanent adrenal-gland suppression. However, it is expensive (like mitotane) and has to be given daily, long-term.

Alternatively, selegiline HCl (Anipryl), a drug introduced in the late 1990s, reduces some symptoms of pituitary-dependent Cushing's disease—particularly excessive thirst, excessive urination, and overeating—although it does not lower cortisol levels to normal. Anipryl can have side effects (vomiting, diarrhea, restlessness, or trembling are occasionally seen), but they are less serious than the risk of an "Addisonian crisis" from mitotane. Anipryl is an attractive option for frail or elderly dogs with pituitary-dependent Cushing's disease whose owners want to stop the dog from urinating in the house but don't want to risk the side effects of mitotane. Anipryl, which is also used to treat canine cognitive dysfunction, or "dog Alzheimer's," should not be given to a dog who is taking antidepressants such as Prozac or Elavil.

OBSESSED WITH WATER

"A few months ago, my 10-year-old Collie developed an unquenchable thirst. He now drinks about five quarts of water a day and needs to urinate every couple of hours. Tests for kidney disease, diabetes, and Cushing's have all been negative, and now he's scheduled for something called a water deprivation test. Although my vet explained all this to me, I'm still not sure I understand. Please help."

Most older dogs who start drinking a lot have a reasonably straightforward problem, like kidney disease, diabetes mellitus, or Cushing's disease. Then there's the dog in a million who instead has a disease called diabetes insipidus (DI). Despite the confusing similarity in their names and one symptom—drinking and urinating a lot—DI has nothing to do with diabetes mellitus, the insulin deficiency. Rather, DI is caused either by a deficiency in antidiuretic hormone (ADH), which is produced by the hypothalamus and regulates urine concentration, or by the failure of the kidneys to respond to the hormone.

Rarely, a puppy will be born with a defect in ADH production or the kidneys that results in DI. But your dog wasn't born with the problem; he developed it at the age of 10. Once all other causes of excessive thirst and urination in an older dog are ruled out—and virtually anything affecting the kidneys in any way can produce those symptoms, so the search must be thorough—then and only then does a vet start to suspect DI.

The test for DI is risky, because it involves depriving the dog of water, and a dog with DI can become dehydrated so suddenly that he could go into shock and perhaps even die. In a water-deprivation test, the dog is hospitalized and given no food or water until his urine either becomes more concentrated or he loses 5 percent of his body weight from dehydration. The dog's urine and blood concentration and weight are measured every one to three hours so the test can be stopped before the dog becomes severely ill.

If a dog's urine doesn't become concentrated even when he's deprived of water, then he is strongly suspected of having DI. Whether the problem is in his hypothalamus or his kidneys is still in question. He may next be given synthetic ADH to test whether that brings his urine concentration closer to normal—a sign that the kidneys are OK but the hypothalamus isn't producing enough ADH. If so, synthetic ADH (also called desmopressin or DDAVP) can be given for life. If not, the dog must be allowed to drink and urinate as much as he wants in order to avoid potentially life-threatening dehydration.

ADDISON'S DISEASE

"My Portuguese Water Dog, who's three years old, always seemed to get sick easily—she would vomit, have diarrhea, and seem really ragged out. I thought maybe my kids were feeding her things they shouldn't. Then, over Christmas, she got so weak she passed out. The emergency-room vet did an EKG and some blood tests and discovered my dog's adrenal glands aren't working. How did this happen? Will she be all right?"

Your dog has hypoadrenocorticism, or Addison's disease. If people have heard of Addison's at all, it's usually in connec-

tion with the late John F. Kennedy, who had the disease but kept it quiet during his campaign for the presidency.

In Addison's disease, the adrenal glands stop producing enough cortisol and aldosterone, a hormone that regulates levels of sodium in the blood. When sodium levels go down, potassium levels go up and blood pressure goes down. When blood pressure goes down, the heart normally beats faster to compensate. But high levels of potassium prevent the heart's natural pacemaker from speeding the heart rate. Blood pressure and heart rate remain low, and the dog can go into shock. This is called an Addisonian crisis, and it can be fatal.

Your dog's EKG probably showed an abnormally low heart rate plus "heart block"—failure of the pacemaker's signals to get through. The blood tests probably showed low sodium paired with high potassium. Those two pieces of information would be enough to raise the strong suspicion of Addison's, and the emergency-room vet would have rushed to treat it with IV fluids containing sodium and glucose, and insulin (glucose and insulin lower the level of potassium in the blood). Once treatment was begun, Addison's probably was confirmed by an ACTH response test (see page 301). In Addison's, the baseline cortisol level is low and doesn't increase in response to ACTH.

Why Addison's happens is almost impossible to determine. It's seen mainly in young to middle-aged dogs, and in slightly more females than males. Standard Poodles, Labrador Retrievers, and Portuguese Water Dogs seem to have an inherited predisposition to Addison's, but it can affect other breeds and mixes of dogs as well. Symptoms arise when the adrenal glands atrophy. The cause of that atrophy usually is a mystery.

Dogs with Addison's often show waxing-and-waning signs of illness, the way your dog did. They may do OK until they are physically stressed, then become weak and lethargic, vomit, and have diarrhea, then get better with IV fluids or other nonspecific treatment.

Addison's is treated by giving a dog fludrocortisone acetate (Florinef) tablets or desoxycorticosterone pivalate (Percorten) injections as a replacement for aldosterone. Florinef tablets are given daily for life; Percorten injections are given every three to four weeks for life. About 50 percent of dogs on Florinef or Percorten also need to take prednisone to supplement their cortisol levels; the other half produce enough cortisol on their own. The main drawback to Florinef and Percorten is the expense—both can cost up to about $7 a day for a large dog with Addison's.

EXCESS CALCIUM IN THE BLOOD

"My vet did some blood tests as part of my dog's senior physical exam, and the calcium level was high. The vet wants to do some follow-up tests. Is high calcium a serious symptom?"

Calcium levels in the blood are regulated by the parathyroid glands (see page 292). High blood calcium is a red flag that a dog may have a parathyroid tumor, cancer elsewhere in the body, or a bacterial or fungal bone infection. A parathyroid tumor secretes too much PTH, which raises blood calcium levels. Several types of cancer—including lymphoma and anal-sac carcinoma—secrete PTH-like substances that also boost blood calcium levels. The third possibility is a bacterial or fungal infection that is eating away bones and releasing calcium into the bloodstream.

Perfectly healthy dogs may also have a single high blood-calcium reading for unknown reasons, so the first step is to check another blood sample a few days or a week after the first test to see whether the calcium is still high. (Extremely high blood calcium can cause the heart to beat erratically, but slight increases usually have no symptoms.) Your vet will also double-check your dog for any signs of cancer or a bone infection.

Whatever the underlying disease, treating it will correct the high blood calcium. Bone infections are treated with antibiotics and sometimes surgery to remove diseased areas of bone (see page 250). Parathyroid tumors are removed surgically. Because there are four parathyroid glands, removing one usually doesn't create a long-term problem with calcium regulation, but a dog may need to take calcium supplements and vitamin D for a few weeks to give his remaining parathyroid glands time to pick up the slack.

For more about diagnosing and treating lymphoma and anal-sac tumors, see pages 374 and 377.

CHAPTER 13

Seizures and Other Neurological Diseases

SUDDEN, SCARY, AND SURPRISINGLY COMMON. Those adjectives go a long way toward describing seizures in dogs. But then, there's also "frustrating," because you may have to get used to the idea that medication won't prevent your epileptic dog from ever having another seizure. In that way, seizures are emblematic of most neurological disorders: mysterious, complex, and sometimes difficult to treat. But diseases of the brain, spinal cord, and nerves do have their own logic, and understanding the ways of the nervous system will help you make sense of such problems, including epilepsy, meningitis, rabies, and paralysis.

EMERGENCY!

D oes your dog need immediate veterinary care? Check this list to help you decide.

TAKE IMMEDIATE ACTION!

Call your vet or an emergency veterinary clinic *now* if your dog is showing any of the following symptoms:

❏ He is **unconscious.**

❏ She suddenly **can't stand or is dragging a leg.**

❏ He has been having a **seizure** for **five minutes** or is having **one seizure right after another.**

TAKE A MINUTE . . .

Read further in this book and then call your vet during office hours as needed if your dog is showing any of the following symptoms:

❏ He is **having a seizure** (see page 310).

❏ Her **ear, eyelid, or lip is drooping** (see page 316).

❏ His **lower jaw is drooping or weak** (see page 316).

❏ She is **tilting her head to one side and falling or staggering** when she walks (see page 315).

❏ He seems **weak or unsteady on his feet** (see page 315).

❏ She has **tremors, "spells," or other odd behavior** (see page 311).

❏ He **walks differently or is clumsier** than he used to be (see page 319).

❏ She was **bitten** by an unknown animal (see page 320).

Remember, it's never wrong to call your veterinarian if you have a question about your dog's health, or if you're worried about a symptom or your dog's overall condition. That's what we're here for.

DEFINING A SEIZURE

"How do I know if my dog is having a seizure or a convulsion? And if he is having seizures, does he have epilepsy?"

"S eizure" and "convulsion" mean the same thing. Dogs most often have what are known in people as grand mal seizures. The dog loses consciousness, falls to his side, and holds his legs out stiffly, sometimes paddling them back and forth. He may make sounds, urinate, or defecate during the seizure, which lasts from a few seconds to a couple of minutes. Before the seizure, the dog may show a change in behavior—acting restless, seeking attention, or hiding—for anywhere from a few minutes to a few hours. After the seizure the dog may be temporarily blind, disoriented, anxious, weak, and uncoordinated for anywhere from a few minutes to a day or more. Less commonly, a dog may become temporarily irritable or aggressive after a seizure.

"Partial" or "focal" seizures are much rarer in dogs. In this type of seizure, the dog may or may not lose consciousness while a small area of his body—such as his face or one leg—twitches uncontrollably for a few seconds to a couple of minutes. A focal or partial seizure may spread to become a grand mal seizure.

Seizures are caused by abnormal bursts of nerve signals in the brain. Such bursts may have an identifiable underlying cause, such as low blood sugar, low oxygen, or a toxin. A dog who has recurrent seizures with no identifiable external cause is said to have epilepsy. Epileptic dogs are born with the problem and usually have their first seizure when they are young, often between the ages of six months and three years.

CAUSES OF SEIZURES

"My healthy three-year-old Lab mix had a seizure a couple of days ago, and my vet said we need to rule out some underlying factors before deciding it's epilepsy. Can you explain those factors?"

A head injury, exposure to a toxin, and low blood sugar are three factors that could cause a seizure in an otherwise healthy young dog like yours. To determine whether a dog has a hidden head injury, a vet will look for cuts, bruises, broken teeth, or bleeding from the nose, ears, or mouth; test the cranial nerves,

which transmit sensory and other signals to the head (see page 313); and use an ophthalmoscope to look at the backs of the eyes for bleeding, a detached retina, or optic nerve swelling.

Toxins that can trigger seizures include insecticides, tetanus, lead, strychnine, and antifreeze. If your dog had been exposed to one of those toxins, he would almost certainly have other symptoms in addition to the seizure, such as vomiting, diarrhea, or lethargy. Blood tests can check for exposure to lead or antifreeze, but if you had any reason to suspect that your dog might have ingested antifreeze—an often-deadly toxin—your vet would have begun treatment immediately without waiting for the results of a blood test.

A fasting blood glucose test can check for low blood sugar, which is occasionally seen in small-breed puppies (see page 294) or dogs with a glycogen storage disease or a pancreatic tumor (see page 299).

Certain serious viral diseases, such as distemper and rabies, can cause seizures; but a dog with those diseases would be ill or behave abnormally aside from having a single seizure. In addition, your dog has almost certainly been vaccinated against distemper and rabies and therefore is protected against catching them.

Certain birth defects also can cause seizures, but such defects usually become apparent before a dog is one year old: portosystemic shunt, a blood-vessel defect affecting the digestive tract and the brain (see page 263); hydrocephalus, a buildup of cerebrospinal fluid around the brain (see page 316); and lysosomal storage diseases, which are enzyme abnormalities that lead to the death of nerve cells in the brain and elsewhere (see page 317).

WHAT TO DO
WHEN A DOG HAS A SEIZURE

People often are terrified the first time they see a dog having a seizure. Fortunately, however, seizures are neither painful nor as devastating as they appear, and they almost never cause any lasting harm. If your dog has a seizure, stay calm and follow these steps:

❑ Look at your watch or a clock to see what time the seizure started, then check the clock again when the seizure stops so you know how long it lasted. Count only the time when the dog is unconscious and making involuntary movements (such as twitching or paddling her legs), not any unusual behavior before or after the seizure.

❑ **If your dog is unconscious and making involuntary movements for five minutes or more, or if three or more seizures occur one right after the other, she may need emergency treatment to stop the seizures.** Call your vet or the nearest veterinary emergency clinic and tell them what's happening. Be prepared to transport your dog to the vet clinic as quickly as possible after you hang up the phone.

❑ Don't put anything in a dog's mouth in an effort to prevent her from "swallowing her tongue." That won't happen, but you could get bitten severely by the dog's convulsing jaws.

❑ Don't move a seizuring dog unless she is in immediate danger—she's at the top of a flight of stairs and might tumble down them, for example, or she's in the road and could get hit by a car. If you do need to move a seizuring dog, the safest way is to pull her gently away from the danger by her hind legs or her tail. Again, you want to avoid the dog's mouth, because she may bite involuntarily while convulsing or while confused and disoriented after the seizure.

❑ A seizuring dog will often urinate or defecate while unconscious. If the dog is indoors, you may want to quickly grab some newspapers to place under her hindquarters, and some paper towels to clean up any mess.

❑ When the dog begins to regain consciousness, she will still be disoriented and unsteady. Try to keep her from standing up too quickly or exerting herself after the seizure. Keep her as quiet and calm as possible for the next few hours.

Stay calm and time the seizure. Most are over within a minute or two.

❏ If this was your dog's first seizure, call your vet to report the seizure, discuss potential underlying causes, and find out when you should bring your dog in for an exam. A single seizure is not a medical emergency, so unless your dog is otherwise ill or may have been exposed to a toxin, the vet may not need to see her immediately.

❏ If this was not your dog's first seizure, write down the details in her seizure diary. The seizure diary should include the following information for each episode:

• Length of seizure, in minutes or seconds (count only the time when the dog is unconscious and making involuntary movements).

• Day, date, and time of seizure (include possible seizures that you didn't directly observe, based on the dog's having urinated or defecated in the house or acting weak or disoriented afterward).

• Dog's activities in the hour or two before the seizure.

• Type and duration of altered behavior, such as weakness or disorientation, following the seizure.

• Current dose and time of antiseizure medication, if any.

• Most recent change in dose of antiseizure medication, if any.

• Suspected side effects of the antiseizure medication (such as sleepiness, lack of coordination, or vomiting), when they occur, and how long they last.

In older dogs, a brain tumor or advanced liver disease are included in the list of factors that can trigger seizures. Here again, a dog with liver disease would be obviously ill with vomiting, diarrhea, loss of appetite, weakness, or jaundice, and a dog with a brain tumor large enough to cause a seizure would behave abnormally all the time, not just when he was having a seizure. If there is any doubt, liver disease can be diagnosed with blood tests, an ultrasound exam of the abdomen, or a liver biopsy; and a brain tumor can be diagnosed with a CT or MRI scan (see page 321).

Once your vet is satisfied that no external factor was responsible for your dog's seizure, epilepsy is the diagnosis by exclusion.

STRANGE BEHAVIORS THAT CAN LOOK LIKE SEIZURES

"My five-year-old Pomeranian has what I call 'fits,' but they don't actually seem to be seizures; he just seems dazed or out of it sometimes. What causes these episodes?"

Several problems can be mistaken for seizures, which is why your vet will want to discuss in detail what your dog's "fits" are like, what seems to trigger them, how often they occur, how long they last, and so on. Fainting brought on by an irregular heartbeat that interrupts blood flow to the brain is one possibility. Trembling or shaking due to fear or pain is another. Some dogs, especially older ones, have bobbing heads or shaky legs, almost like a person with Parkinson's disease. Painful neck spasms can also look like a seizure. Finally, there are a few oddball conditions that can make a dog lose consciousness or twitch, such as narcolepsy, myoclonus, and myotonus. Narcolepsy is a birth defect that makes a dog suddenly fall asleep, usually when he's excited. Myoclonus is fast twitching of a muscle, and myotonus is a prolonged contraction of a muscle. Myoclonus is reportedly more common in Labrador Retrievers than in other breeds, and myotonus in Scottish Terriers (in whom it is called "Scottie cramp") and Dalmatians, but these conditions are so rare that they're almost never seen outside of veterinary neurology textbooks.

IS EPILEPSY INHERITED?

"Are certain breeds more prone to epilepsy?"

Yes. Epilepsy seems to run in certain families of Beagles, Dachshunds, German Shepherds, Belgian Tervurens, and Keeshonds. It also is seen commonly in Cocker Spaniels, Collies, Golden Retrievers, Irish Setters, Labrador Retrievers, Miniature Schnauzers, Standard Poodles, Miniature Poodles, St. Bernards, Siberian Huskies, and Fox Terriers. A genetic predisposition to epilepsy is suspected, but the specific gene or genes responsible have not been identified, so at this writing there is no genetic test for epilepsy.

FOOD ALLERGIES AND SEIZURES

"I told my chiropractor about my Golden Retriever, who started having seizures when she was about 18 months old, and the chiropractor said food allergies could be the cause. Is this possible?"

Many veterinary alternative-medicine practitioners believe allergies and seizures are connected in some dogs. The connection is considered most likely in dogs that have other allergic symptoms, such as itchy skin or frequent ear infections. If you'd like to check out the possibility that your dog's seizures are caused by a food allergy, ask your vet for a prescription hypoallergenic diet (see page 99). Don't decrease or stop your dog's antiseizure medication, however, until you see results from the diet change, such as less itchiness and fewer seizures.

TREATING EPILEPSY

"In the past six months my three-year-old Miniature Schnauzer has had two seizures, but my vet hasn't prescribed any medication. Why not? What is the usual treatment for epilepsy?"

Many vets don't recommend antiseizure medication unless (1) a dog is having seizures more than once a month; (2) the seizures last longer than five minutes; or (3) the seizures come in clusters of three or more, one right after the other. That's because one seizure a month is about the best control you can get even with antiseizure medication, which reduces the number and severity of seizures but doesn't eliminate them altogether. Your dog is having less than one seizure a month now, so the benefits of putting him on antiseizure medication wouldn't be worth the side effects, which are described below.

The most important thing you can do for a dog who has seizures, whether or not he is on medication, is to keep a seizure diary and let your vet know when

THE NEUROLOGIC EXAM

D ogs can't use words to tell us their head hurts, they feel dizzy or disoriented, or their leg is numb or tingly. So veterinarians rely on a number of physical tests to tell what's going on with a dog's nervous system.

The first clue is a dog's **stance and gait.** Does he stand normally, or is he wobbly, crooked, or weak? Does he stumble, scuff his toes, stagger, or walk in a circle or into the wall?

Next is his apparent **mental state.** Is he aware of his surroundings? Does he recognize his owner? Is he behaving oddly? Has his owner noticed any changes in behavior?

The **cranial nerves** control vision, hearing, and other sensory input and muscle control of the face and head. Vision and hearing are checked broadly in this part of the exam by dropping a cotton ball in front of one eye at a time and seeing whether the dog follows the motion, and observing whether the dog turns toward a sudden sound. A penlight is shined in the dog's eyes to see whether the pupils constrict normally with light. The dog's eyes are checked for an abnormal flickering movement, called nystagmus, or an eye that doesn't look straight ahead. The blink reflex is checked by touching the dog's eyelids and seeing if they close. A careful look at the dog's face will reveal whether it's symmetrical. The dog's gag reflex is checked by opening his mouth and pressing on the back of his tongue.

Finally, the **positioning sense, reflexes, and sensation** of the legs and tail are checked. When the dog is standing and you turn a foot knuckles-down, does he turn it back right away? Are his muscle reflexes normal, exaggerated, or weak? (A dog's muscle reflexes are checked the same way as a person's, with a rubber reflex hammer.) Is the tail limp? Can the dog feel a toe pinch on every foot?

The results of the exam help locate a neurologic problem precisely. Is a single nerve or closely associated group of nerves involved? Is the upper, middle, or lower spinal cord affected? Or are the signs generalized to more than one area of the body? Knowing *where* the problem is tells the veterinarian how to find out *what* it is and treat it appropriately.

your dog's seizure patterns change significantly (see page 310). The information in this diary is what your vet will use to determine whether to start, increase, decrease, or change an antiseizure medication.

If the number or duration of your dog's seizures increases, your vet may prescribe phenobarbital or potassium bromide, the two most common antiseizure medications for dogs. These drugs can be used individually or together. The side effects of phenobarbital are increased hunger, increased thirst, and increased urination. Dogs often will seem sedated or "out of it" when they first start taking phenobarbital, but that side effect goes away in a week or two as they adjust to the medication. Paradoxically, a few dogs become agitated when they start taking this drug. In such cases, the dose is lowered and then slowly increased to an effective level. Phenobarbital is processed by the liver, and long-term use makes the liver enlarge. This enlargement isn't dangerous, but it does mean that doses of some other drugs—some antibiotics, steroids, and some heart medications—may need to be increased in order for them to work properly. Phenobarbital comes in tablets and is usually given twice a day.

Potassium bromide is a liquid that's usually given once a day. The potential side effects include vomiting, loss of appetite, and sedation. When phenobarbital and potassium bromide are used together, their sedative effects combine, so dogs must be carefully monitored for excessive sleepiness, lethargy, or lack of coordination. Some vets recommend measuring the levels of phenobarbital and potassium bromide in a dog's blood every few months to make sure they're in an effective but not excessive range.

Veterinary alternative-medicine practitioners sometimes recommend a hypoallergenic diet or acupuncture as treatment for seizures. Although these therapies haven't been proven, they're in a "can't hurt, might help" category. If you're interested in pursuing alternative treatments for your dog's seizures, ask your vet for a prescription hypoallergenic diet or a referral to a veterinary acupuncturist.

STILL HAVING SEIZURES WHILE ON MEDICATION

"My four-year-old German Shepherd was having seizures about once a week, so two months ago the vet started him on potassium bromide and phenobarbital. But my dog is still having seizures, though now only about once a month. How can we get the seizures to stop?"

It's almost impossible to eliminate seizures entirely in an epileptic dog. The goal of antiseizure medication is to reduce the frequency and length of the seizures, not to abolish them altogether. Seizures are harder to control in large dogs—like Labs and German Shepherds—than in small dogs, so reducing the number of seizures from four per month to one per month is a major accomplishment.

Your vet may not realize that you were expecting the seizures to stop completely. Ask whether anything more can be done to reduce the frequency, such as increasing the dose of medication. Your dog may already be getting the highest dose that will do any good, so don't up the dose on your own.

EMERGENCY TREATMENT FOR SEIZURES

"My seven-year-old Poodle has had seizures for a long time, and my vet has advised me to call immediately if a seizure has lasted for five minutes. What's dangerous about a seizure longer than five minutes, and what would the vet do about it?"

There are two dangers: (1) a dog that's seizuring may stop breathing; and (2) occasionally a dog will start seizuring and not stop, a situation known as status epilepticus. A dog that does not stop seizuring will die.

If at all possible, it's best to call the vet clinic before you rush the dog there, for two reasons: to make sure it's open, and to alert them that you're coming so they can look up your dog's chart and prepare the appropriate medication.

Most prolonged seizures can be stopped by giving one or more of the following medications intravenously: diazepam (Valium), phenobarbital, or pentobarbital. Note that giving these drugs by mouth to a dog that is already seizuring will *not* work; they have to be given intravenously.

As soon as the seizure has been stopped, the dog will be given CPR or oxygen if necessary, plus IV dextrose in case low blood sugar played a part in the seizure. The dog will need to be monitored closely for several hours to make sure he doesn't go into another prolonged seizure.

THE SUDDENLY DIZZY OLD DOG

"Three days ago, my 12-year-old retriever mix fell over when she tried to get out of her bed in the morning. She was holding her head tilted to one side, and her eyes were flicking back and forth. I was terrified and rushed her to the vet, who said the condition wasn't serious, would get better on its own, and was fairly common in older dogs. Can this possibly be true?"

Yes. Old-dog vestibular syndrome is a bout of extreme dizziness that comes on suddenly and improves within a week or so. The symptoms are a head tilt, falling or staggering, and the flickering eye movement you noticed, which is called nystagmus. Often the dog will temporarily lose interest in food or vomit because she is dizzy.

The name comes from the vestibular system, a group of nerves that coordinate signals from the eyes, inner ear, and body to essentially tell the animal "which end is up." A glitch in the vestibular system will produce dizziness and nystagmus.

A severe ear infection can cause vestibular syndrome by affecting the inner ear and nearby nerves that are part of the vestibular system. Your vet was able to rule this out by looking in your dog's ears with an otoscope. An injury (such as getting hit by a car) or a brain tumor can also cause vestibular syndrome, but if your dog had one of those problems, she would also have other symptoms such as bleeding or bruising of the head, or extreme weakness or paralysis of one side of the body.

Dogs with old-dog vestibular syndrome get better gradually over one to two weeks. No medication is necessary. Some dogs have a slight head tilt permanently, but it doesn't affect their ability to get around.

Older dogs may get dizzy and develop a head tilt. Often they get better on their own.

An ear infection can damage the facial nerve, paralyzing the muscles on one side of the face.

A DROOPY FACE

"All of a sudden I noticed that one side of my 11-year-old Cocker Spaniel's face seemed droopier than the other. Did she have a stroke?"

It's probably not a stroke, but rather a problem with the facial nerve. The facial nerve controls the muscles of the ear, eyelid, and lip and affects tear production. The nerve can become inflamed and stop working properly because of an ear infection (it passes close to the middle ear) or for unknown reasons.

If your dog has an ear infection, it should be treated, and you will need to use artificial tears in the eye on the affected side for as long as the problem persists. The artificial tears will help prevent eye damage. The facial nerve starts working again (over several weeks) in about 50 percent of dogs; in the other 50 percent the paralysis is permanent. If it's permanent, your dog will need artificial tears for the rest of her life.

A DOG WHO CAN'T CLOSE HIS MOUTH

"For a couple of days, my 10-year-old hound mix was dropping food from his mouth when he tried to eat, and then I realized he can't close his lower jaw! What happened, and what can we do?"

Have your vet take a look to be sure, but it sounds as if your dog has trigeminal neuritis—inflammation of the nerve that controls the muscles of the lower jaw. This occurs for unknown reasons and gets better on its own within two or three weeks. In the meantime, you must help your dog drink and eat so he doesn't become dehydrated or malnourished. Fortunately, a different nerve coordinates swallowing, so if you can help your dog get food and water into the back of his mouth, he'll be able to swallow without choking. Do this by squirting a little water at a time toward the back of his mouth, using a turkey baster or a 10cc syringe from your vet. As for eating, you can form canned food into small meatballs and hand-feed those to your dog. Also provide food and water in the usual way so you'll know when he's able to eat and drink on his own again.

"WATER ON THE BRAIN"

"My cousin bred her Chihuahua to a friend's Chihuahua, and her dog had three puppies about five weeks ago. I'm a pediatric nurse, and the puppies don't seem right to me—they all have a huge soft spot on the top of their heads and don't respond much to what's going on around them. Could they have a birth defect?"

The puppies may have a birth defect called hydrocephalus, and they should be checked by a veterinarian to find out. Hydrocephalus literally means "water on the brain." The "water" is cerebrospinal fluid, which either isn't being reabsorbed normally, or is blocked from flowing normally around the brain and along the spinal cord. Hydrocephalus is a birth defect seen most often in toy breeds (such as Chihuahuas, Yorkshire Terriers, Toy Poodles, and Pomeranians) and breeds with round heads and flat noses (such as English Bulldogs, Boston Terriers, Pekingese, and Lhasa Apsos). Symptoms are caused by fluid pressure on the brain and can include mental retardation, seizures, blindness or deafness, and eyes that are directed slightly down and to the side rather than straight forward. An open fontanel (the large soft spot you noticed) and a dome-shaped head sometimes accompany the disorder, but they also can be seen in normal dogs of those breeds, so they are not proof of hydrocephalus.

Hydrocephalus can be diagnosed by doing an ultrasound exam of the brain through the puppy's open fontanel (this is not painful and doesn't require anesthesia) or an MRI scan, which does require anesthesia. The signs are unusual accumulations of fluid in the brain.

If the puppies do have hydrocephalus, their prognosis is uncertain. Some dogs who are born with hydrocephalus are mentally retarded but can survive when given corticosteroids to reduce the production of cerebrospinal fluid, antiseizure medication if necessary, and attentive care to prevent accidents and injuries. Others become progressively worse despite the medication and die suddenly or are euthanized when their quality of life deteriorates. Your cousin undoubtedly will want to find out whether the puppies have hydrocephalus before selling them or adopting them out. If the puppies do have the disorder, your cousin and her friend shouldn't breed their dogs again, because one or both may carry genes for hydrocephalus.

AN ENZYME BIRTH DEFECT

"Years ago, a coworker of mine had a Portuguese Water Dog that seemed normal when she got him at the age of 10 weeks, but he had some hereditary nerve disease that led to his being put to sleep before he was a year old. I'm wondering whether the disease is still a problem in Portuguese Water Dogs, because if it isn't, I'd like to get one."

From your description, the puppy probably had a lysosomal storage defect, a problem with the enzymes that are supposed to help rid cells of cellular junk. About a dozen different types of lysosomal storage defects have been identified in dogs. Puppies with these defects are normal at birth but develop neurological problems early in life because their nerve cells accumulate debris and stop working properly. Symptoms usually appear before the puppy reaches six months old and can include stumbling, weakness, tremors, blindness, and eventually paralysis or seizures. The signs get progressively worse, and there is no treatment.

Lysosomal storage diseases are hereditary and have been diagnosed in more than 20 breeds—including Portuguese Water Dogs, Cairn Terriers, Australian Cattle Dogs, and Poodles—and even a few mixed breeds. Fortunately, these invariably fatal diseases have always been rare and are becoming even rarer now that breeders are more aware of them. The genes for some types of lysosomal storage defects have been identified, and they are recessive, meaning that a dog can be a carrier of the disease without showing any symptoms. Carriers often can be identified with a blood test, which enables breeders to remove them from their breeding programs. If you're interested in getting a puppy of any breed that's had occurrences of lysosomal storage defects (see the breed Health Checklist starting on page 19), ask the breeder whether the puppy's parents have been tested.

STAGGERING PUPPIES

"Two months ago, a litter of terrier puppies appeared at the animal shelter where I volunteer. They had an unusual, high-stepping walk I found very cute. I was surprised when the vet who works with the shelter said we should observe the puppies for a month before putting them up for adoption. During that month, the puppies all began shaking, staggering, and falling down when they tried to walk, and the vet wound up putting them all to sleep. Was this a disease they had caught, or a birth defect?"

From the sounds of it, the puppies probably had a birth defect in the cerebellum, the part of the brain that coordinates balance and movement. In one form of birth defect, the cerebellum is normal at birth but begins to degenerate when the dog is a few weeks to a few months old. This defect is rare but occurs occasionally in about a dozen breeds of dogs, including Kerry Blue Terriers, Australian Kelpies, and Irish Setters. The cerebellar breakdown is progressive, meaning it gets worse over time. The progression can be fast, leaving the puppy unable to walk within a few months of the first symptoms, or it can be slow, allowing the puppy to get around adequately for years. There is no treatment for cerebellar degeneration, and afflicted dogs are usually euthanized when they can no longer walk. As sad as it is to put puppies to sleep, the vet at the animal shelter undoubtedly felt they were failing quickly and had no chance for a decent quality of life.

LITTLE WHITE SHAKERS

"My mother bought a West Highland White Terrier puppy from a pet store. When the dog was about a year old, he started shaking and trembling so hard that he could barely walk. My mother is very upset. Is there any hope, or should she put the dog to sleep?"

The disease is an inflammation of the cerebellum, the part of the brain that coordinates balance and movement. The condition is called little white shaker syndrome. It isn't painful, and up to 80 percent of the dogs with this problem get better over time, so there definitely is hope for your mother's dog.

As with so many other neurological problems, what sets off the inflammation is unknown. There must be a genetic component, however, because it's seen most often in Maltese, Westies, and Beagles. Not all of the little white shakers are white; dogs with other coat colors can be affected as well.

Little white shakers develop mild to severe head and body tremors

THE "DOWN DOG"

When a dog suddenly has trouble walking, the owner often assumes the dog has a spinal cord injury. Although that's one possible diagnosis, many other conditions—not all of them nerve-related—also can produce a "down dog."

Extreme weakness is probably the most common cause of a sudden inability or reluctance to walk. If a dog is feeling weak and wobbly, she will sit or lie down. This is akin to a person's sitting down when he feels dizzy or short of breath, and is not necessarily a sign that the legs themselves don't work. Any number of illnesses can make a dog feel weak, including heart disease, diabetes, anemia, or shock. So if your dog, whether young or old, is suddenly reluctant to move, make a quick note of any other symptoms or circumstances and then call your vet or a veterinary emergency hospital for advice on what to do next.

Difficulty walking also can come on gradually. Arthritis of the hips or spine is one common cause. Another possibility, one that's much harder to diagnose, is a slow breakdown of the nerves controlling the leg muscles. The many variations of such diseases are often lumped together under the term "nerve atrophy" or "peripheral neuropathy."

Exactly what causes this nerve degeneration usually can't be determined. Genetic factors do play a part, however, because different breeds of dogs often develop specific forms of these nerve diseases. Breeds that have a higher than average incidence of progressive nerve problems leading to difficulty walking include Boxers, German Shepherds, Golden Retrievers, Alaskan Malamutes, Tibetan Mastiffs, Dalmatians, Leonbergers, Doberman Pinschers, and Rottweilers. The symptoms, age of onset, and speed of progression of these diseases vary widely with the individual dog, and a conclusive diagnosis often requires specialized nerve or muscle testing. If you suspect your dog has a nerve problem affecting his ability to walk, consult with your vet or a veterinary neurologist.

when they are young, usually between the ages of six months and five years. The shakes can be so severe that the dog falls over when he tries to walk. Rarely, dogs with this condition may develop seizures as well as tremors. The shakes lessen when the dog rests or is relaxed.

Little white shakers are often treated with corticosteroids to calm the cerebellar inflammation. Recovery usually takes several weeks, and relapses can occur. Good nursing care by the owner is the most important treatment: stairs and other potential hazards should be blocked off, and the dog should be fed and given opportunities to urinate and defecate more frequently than usual if the trembling makes such activities difficult.

DANCING DOBERMANS

"I used to think a Doberman Pinscher I saw walking in the park was nervous and high-strung, because he constantly shifted from one hind foot to the other. Then I heard from another dog owner that the dog has a 'Doberman disease.' What is it?"

"Dancing Doberman syndrome" is a slowly progressive nerve problem affecting the hind legs of some Dobermans. At first, a young to middle-aged dog will hold up one hind foot while he's standing still. As the disease progresses, the dog will "dance" from one hind foot to the other, and may sit rather than stand to calm the motion. Over months to years, the leg muscles weaken and the dog can start to have trouble walking. Occasionally the problem will spread to the front legs and even to the jaw muscles.

Unfortunately, there is no known treatment for this disorder. However, "dancing Dobermans" can get around well and have a good quality of life for several years after symptoms begin.

HIGH-STEPPING ROTTWEILERS

"My three-year-old Rottweiler has started to lift his front feet like he's trying to step over something when he walks. He also seems clumsier than he used to be. My vet thinks he may have a Rottweiler nerve disease. Can you tell me more about it?"

There's a condition in young Rottweilers in which the insulating layers around the nerves and spinal cord begin to break down. The symptoms are a high-stepping gait, especially in the front legs, and slowly progressive leg weakness. It's diagnosed by ruling out other problems that could cause similar symptoms—particularly a spinal cord injury in the neck—using neck x-rays and possibly a dye study to outline the spinal cord.

There is no treatment for this nerve disease, but it progresses slowly, and many dogs continue to have a good quality of life for months to years after it begins.

RABIES IN THE 21ST CENTURY

"The newspaper recently reported that a puppy sold at a local flea market had died of rabies. Anyone who had petted the puppy was supposed to call a doctor immediately. I thought all dogs and cats were automatically vaccinated against rabies these days, so how could this puppy have caught it? Is it treatable?"

Rabies is very common among certain wild animals, such as raccoons and bats. A bite from one of these animals can transmit rabies to a person, an unvaccinated cat or dog, or any other warm-blooded animal. Most puppies and kittens are vaccinated against rabies at the age of 12 to 16 weeks, but perhaps this puppy was younger than that or hadn't been taken to a vet. There still is no treatment for full-blown rabies, and it is almost invariably fatal to people as well as to animals once symptoms have appeared.

The rabies virus is concentrated in an animal's saliva, so the risk from the puppy at the flea market is limited to anyone the puppy nipped or licked on the mouth, the nose, or an open wound.

A HIGH-TECH LOOK AT THE BRAIN AND SPINAL CORD

These days, computed tomography (CT) and magnetic resonance imaging (MRI) are widely used to diagnose a variety of human injuries and diseases. Although these machines aren't found in neighborhood vet clinics, most veterinary schools and other large veterinary hospitals have a CT or MRI machine on-site or nearby. They can be a real boon for diagnosing ambiguous problems of the brain and spinal cord.

A CT scan is like a series of x-rays all hooked together. X-rays are best at showing dense tissue, such as bone, and CT scans are especially good at highlighting small fractures or bone tumors. Such fractures or tumors can put pressure on a dog's spinal cord and cause pain, leg weakness, or paralysis.

MRI scans are best for looking at soft tissues and fluid. They are state-of-the-art for locating tumors or fluid buildup in the brain, plus soft-tissue tumors, ruptured disks, and blood vessel blockages in the spinal cord.

Most neurological problems can be diagnosed without a CT or MRI scan, but if even the specialists aren't certain exactly what is going on inside your dog's brain or spinal cord (and you can afford the cost of a scan, which may be $1,000 or more), such tests are a good way to get information that will help clarify your dog's treatment options and prognosis.

Any person who was exposed to rabies in this way could be given a rabies vaccine by an M.D. (Rabies shots are no longer given in the abdomen. They're given in an arm or leg muscle and are no more painful than any other injection.) If the vaccine is given before any symptoms of the disease appear, the person is usually fine.

In an animal, rabies often causes a change in behavior, such as unusual friendliness, aggressiveness, or hyperactivity, followed within a few days by a decline from lethargy to stupor, paralysis, and death. Wild animals may lose their fear of people in the early stages of rabies, and be unable to flee in the later stages, which is why you should never approach a wild animal that is acting strange.

The incubation period of rabies—the time between a bite and the onset of symptoms—can be anywhere from three to eight weeks or more, depending on how concentrated the virus was in the animal's saliva and where the victim was bitten. Rabies travels backward from the nerves at the site of the bite to the spinal cord and brain, so a bite on a dog's face or neck will progress faster than a bite on a hind leg.

If a dog that's up-to-date on his rabies boosters is bitten by an animal that might be rabid—a raccoon that was out in broad daylight and acting aggressive, for example—the dog should be given a rabies booster as soon as possible to help fight the disease. If the biter is a stray dog, stray cat, or wild animal that can be safely captured by animal-control officers, then it will be euthanized and its brain will be examined microscopically for signs of rabies. Examining the brain is the only sure test for rabies.

Each state has its own law about how often dogs and cats must be vaccinated against rabies. Once at the age of 12 to 16 weeks, once at the age of one year, and then every three years after that is a typical regimen.

Your local vet can tell you what the law is in your state and what wild animals in your area, if any, are significant carriers of rabies.

A LIMP FRONT LEG

"My dog got hit by a car right in front of my house. At first, I thought he had only scrapes and cuts and possibly a broken front leg. Then the vet said the leg wasn't broken, but the nerves controlling it had been damaged. He said we may not know for months whether the nerves will recover. Please tell me more about the prognosis, if you can."

Each front leg is controlled by a cluster of large nerves called the brachial plexus, which is embedded in the muscles under the dog's "armpit." A dog's front legs are not designed to move to the side, and an injury that forces a leg into that position can stretch and damage the brachial plexus. Your dog's leg was probably jerked to the side as the car hit him or as he hit the ground.

Depending on which nerves in the brachial plexus were damaged and how badly, some or all of the leg muscles may

be paralyzed, and your dog may have lost pain and touch sensation in part or all of the leg. The real difficulty is in determining whether the nerves will recover. Specialized nerve testing is often inconclusive. Your vet will probably recommend that you wait and watch for a minimum of four to six weeks before giving up hope of recovery. In the meantime, your dog will adapt to getting around on three legs, and you can massage the leg and gently flex and extend the joints twice a day to enhance blood circulation and flexibility. Your dog's foot may need to be bandaged if it drags on the ground and becomes abraded.

If, after weeks to months, your dog doesn't regain muscle control or sensation and the foot is dragging on the ground, your vet may recommend amputating the leg to prevent further injury and infection.

TICK PARALYSIS

"My six-year-old retriever mix seemed a little weak in the hind legs one morning, and by that evening his hind legs were completely paralyzed. I rushed him to the vet, who checked him from nose to tail and wound up removing a tick from his belly. The vet said the tick was responsible for the paralysis and my dog should recover quickly. Is this some type of Lyme disease?"

No, tick paralysis is not a form of Lyme disease. It is caused by a toxin secreted by one of several species of wood ticks and dog ticks found throughout the United States. The paralysis begins with the dog's hind legs and progresses forward in just one or two days. If the tick is not found and removed, the dog's diaphragm and chest muscles will become paralyzed and he won't be able to breathe. If the tick is removed, the dog recovers and is able to walk within a day or two.

COONHOUND PARALYSIS

"My 10-year-old dog got weaker and weaker in his hind legs over a couple of days. The young vet at the emergency clinic—I think she just graduated from vet school—said he may have 'Coonhound paralysis.' What's she talking about? My dog is a shepherd mix, not a Coonhound, and we live in Massachusetts, not the South."

Coonhound paralysis doesn't happen only to Coonhounds, or only in the South. It occurs for unknown reasons one to two weeks after a dog has been bitten by a raccoon, or in some cases exposed to another substance that triggers an immune response affecting the spinal cord. It is similar to Guillain-Barré syndrome in people. The disease begins with weakness in the hind legs that spreads over a couple of days to the front legs and sometimes the head. The dog may be paralyzed for days to weeks. There is no treatment except supportive care—helping the dog eat and drink, keeping him clean and free of bed sores, and monitoring him for respiratory and urinary infections—during the illness. Most dogs recover completely within four to six weeks. Usually the breathing muscles are spared, but if not, the dog has to be on a respirator until those muscles recover.

There is no specific test for Coonhound paralysis. It is diagnosed by ruling out other possible causes of sudden paralysis, such as tick paralysis, myasthenia gravis, or botulism poisoning.

DISAPPEARING NERVE SIGNALS

"When my four-year-old Bouvier began to walk slowly and stiffly, I took him to my vet, who was stumped. Finally, the neurologist at the nearby veterinary school diagnosed myasthenia gravis. Can you tell me about this disease? I'm still confused."

Myasthenia gravis is weakness caused by nerve signals not getting through to receptors in the muscles. In dogs that are born with the disease, the problem is either too few receptors or malformed receptors. This inherited form of myasthenia gravis is seen most often in Smooth Fox Terriers, Jack Russell Terriers, and Samoyeds. The symptoms—muscle weakness and regurgitation due to a malfunctioning esophagus—usually appear before the age of six months.

Myasthenia gravis can also develop later in life when, for unknown reasons, the dog's immune system starts attacking the nerve receptors. The symptoms are leg weakness that worsens with exercise and improves with rest; a short, stiff gait; and sometimes weak facial muscles and megaesophagus (a dilated, malfunctioning esophagus).

There are two commonly used tests for myasthenia gravis. One is a blood test that measures antibodies to acetylcholine receptors. In myasthenia gravis, those antibodies are increased. The other is a Tensilon test: the dog is exercised to the point of collapse, then given the drug Tensilon (edrophonium chloride) intravenously. Dogs with myasthenia gravis will regain their strength almost instantaneously (although briefly) when given Tensilon, because it slows the breakdown of acetylcholine, one of the body's key neuromuscular transmitting chemicals, long enough to allow it to interact with the remaining undamaged receptors.

Dogs with myasthenia gravis are treated long-term with medications that block the breakdown of acetylcholine for longer periods of time, such as neostigmine. The disease sometimes goes away after weeks or months of treatment. Dogs that have already developed megaesophagus have a poorer prognosis, because a dilated esophagus is often irreversible and puts the dog at risk of inhaling food or water into his lungs and developing pneumonia.

PARALYZING POISONS

"My four-year-old farm dog suddenly went down on his hind legs. Could he have been poisoned?"

There are a couple of natural toxins that can cause paralysis, particularly tetanus and botulinum. Tetanus bacteria are found in the soil and animal feces and can enter the bloodstream through an open wound, causing muscle rigidity, heart arrhythmias, seizures, and even respiratory arrest. Tetanus toxicity is diagnosed either by the presence of a wound and likely exposure to the bacteria or by a blood test for tetanus. It is treated with an antitoxin, antibiotics, and antiseizure medication if needed. Treatment can be long and expensive.

Dogs most often contract botulism (poisoning by botulinum toxin) from eating dead animals or undercooked meat. Botulism causes muscle weakness that advances over a couple of days from

the hind legs to the front legs and head. The pupils of the eyes may be enlarged and the heart rate abnormally slow, and the dog will be unable to urinate or defecate. The disease is diagnosed by finding the toxin in the dog's blood, feces, or stomach contents, and is treated with botulism antitoxin and nursing care for the two to three weeks it usually takes to recover.

Certain rodent, snail, or insect poisons can cause paralysis, seizures, or muscle twitching in dogs. They include bromethalin, strychnine, metaldehyde, zinc phosphide, organochlorine, and paradichlorobenzene. Tell your vet immediately if your dog may have had access to a poison.

Of course, a spinal cord injury could also produce your dog's symptoms, so your best bet is to have him checked out by your vet as soon as possible.

MENINGITIS AND ENCEPHALITIS

"First my five-year-old Pomeranian started stepping on his own toes and stumbling when he walked, then he started tilting his head to one side and acting dizzy and out of it. After a spinal tap and a bunch of other tests, a veterinary neurologist diagnosed GME. What exactly is that?"

GME is granulomatous meningioencephalitis, an inflammation of the brain and spinal cord that has no discernable cause (such as an infection by a virus, bacterium, or fungus). The symptoms vary with what parts of the nervous system are most affected, and can include sudden blindness, stumbling, weakness, walking in circles, and seizures. GME is diagnosed by a spinal tap, which shows abnormal numbers of white blood cells in the cerebrospinal fluid but no viruses, bacteria, or fungi. The symptoms often can be eased for months or years with corticosteroids, but GME is considered incurable.

Brain and spinal cord inflammation also can be caused by viruses, bacteria, fungi, or other infectious agents.

Dogs are routinely vaccinated against distemper and rabies, two viruses that cause meningitis and encephalitis. Cryptococcus is one fungus that sometimes targets the nervous system, and the tick-borne bacterial diseases Rocky Mountain spotted fever and ehrlichiosis occasionally cause brain and spinal cord inflammation.

CHAPTER 14

The Bladder, Kidneys, and Reproductive Tract

DON'T ALL DOGS KNOW how to pee and procreate? Well, sure, but even the most straightforward process can get complicated. To begin with, you—not your dog— should decide whether you want him or her to reproduce, and if not, you're in charge of taking steps to prevent it. Next, you should learn at least a little about the canine waterworks system, so you can respond appropriately to symptoms that indicate something may be wrong—for example, leaking urine, straining to urinate, blood in the urine, or "drinking and peeing all the time." Your dog's kidneys, and not just your living room rug, may be at stake.

EMERGENCY!

Does your dog need immediate veterinary care? Check this list to help you decide.

TAKE IMMEDIATE ACTION!

Call your vet or an emergency veterinary clinic *now* if your dog is showing any of the following symptoms:

❏ He makes **repeated attempts to urinate** for an hour or more but produces nothing or only a drop or two of urine; he might have a blocked urethra.

❏ She **hasn't been spayed,** was **in heat recently,** has **no appetite,** and is **drinking a lot of water;** these can be symptoms of pyometra, a potentially fatal infection of the uterus.

❏ He may have lapped up some **antifreeze;** this is a deadly poison that causes kidney failure.

❏ She has eaten **grapes or raisins** and **is vomiting, has diarrhea,** or otherwise seems very ill; these fruits can cause kidney failure.

TAKE A MINUTE . . .

Read further in this book and then call your vet during office hours as needed if your dog is showing any of the following symptoms:

❏ She is **drinking and urinating more than usual,** has **blood in her urine,** or is **urinating small amounts frequently** (see the following page).

❏ He has had **several urinary tract infections** in one year (see page 330).

❏ She is **leaking urine** on her bed or around the house (see page 336).

❏ He has **only one testicle** in his scrotum (see page 346).

❏ She **acts like she's pregnant** even though you're certain she couldn't have been bred (see page 341).

❏ She is **going into labor** (see page 344).

❏ He has **blood in his urine** or has **trouble defecating** (see page 346).

Remember, it's never wrong to call your veterinarian if you have a question about your dog's health, or if you're worried about a symptom or your dog's overall condition. That's what we're here for.

URINATING ALL THE TIME

"Lately my 12-year-old mixed breed has been asking to go outside all the time. She's even had a couple of accidents in the house. Does this mean she has a urinary tract infection? Can I drop off a urine sample at the vet's office to find out?"

U rinating more frequently than usual (which is usually accompanied by drinking more water than usual) can be a symptom of a urinary tract infection (UTI). Especially in an older dog, however, it can also be a symptom of kidney disease, diabetes, Cushing's disease, or another illness.

Other common symptoms of a UTI are straining to urinate, painful urination, urinating small amounts frequently, blood in the urine, or urinating in the house. In a male dog, an inflamed or infected prostate gland can also cause these symptoms (see page 346).

Simply collecting a sample of your dog's urine in a jar and dropping it off at the vet's office is not going to reveal what's going on. The definitive test for a UTI is to try to grow bacteria from the urine. The urine in the bladder contains no bacteria unless a dog has an infection. But if a urine sample is a "free catch," meaning the urine was "caught" as the dog urinated in the usual fashion, it will grow bacteria picked up from the dog's skin and hair. For an accurate bacterial culture, the urine must be collected directly from the bladder, via either a sterile catheter threaded through the urethra into the bladder or a sterile needle poked through the abdominal wall into the bladder. The latter procedure, called a cystocentesis, sounds gruesome but is no more uncomfortable than a vaccination.

So the way to find out whether your dog has a UTI is to make an appointment with your vet. An hour or so before the appointment, give your dog a fresh bowl of water to drink and then *do not let her urinate* before the vet examines her. That way her bladder won't be empty when it's time to take a urine sample.

Because of your dog's age and symptoms, the vet will also want to run some blood tests to check for signs of kidney disease, diabetes, or Cushing's disease.

TREATING A URINARY TRACT INFECTION

"My dog has had urinary tract infections a couple of times before, and the vet has always prescribed amoxicillin for them. She has the same symptoms again. Can't I just get some more amoxicillin without the hassle and expense of bringing her in for an exam?"

A sking for an antibiotic without a diagnosis is an especially bad idea *because* your dog has had the same symptoms before and has taken amoxicillin for them. Maybe the problem isn't a urinary tract infection after all, and that's why the symptoms keep coming back. Or perhaps she does have a urinary tract infection, but the bacteria are resistant to amoxicillin.

Your vet needs to get a urine sample directly from your dog's bladder, culture it to see whether any bacteria grow, and find out what antibiotics the bacteria are sensitive to. The vet may still send you home with some amoxicillin to start your dog on while you wait for the results of the bacterial culture and sensitivity test, which usually takes between three and five days.

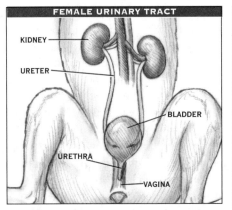

The female dog's shorter, wider urethra makes her more susceptible to urinary tract infections.

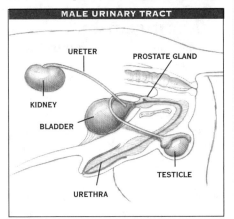

The male dog's longer, thinner urethra makes him more susceptible to blockages by urinary stones.

If no bacteria grow from the urine, your dog doesn't have a urinary tract infection, and you and your vet need to explore further to find out what's causing the symptoms. If bacteria grow and they are resistant to amoxicillin, then the vet can switch your dog to a different antibiotic. If bacteria grow and they are sensitive to amoxicillin, your dog may need to stay on it for longer than she has previously—perhaps for four weeks instead of two weeks—to get rid of the infection. You and your vet should also consider whether your dog has an underlying problem that predisposes her to urinary tract infections (see the following Q&A).

RECURRENT URINARY TRACT INFECTIONS

"My young Miniature Schnauzer has had three urinary tract infections in the past year. The dog I had before this, who lived to the age of 16, never had a single infection. Are some dogs more susceptible to them than others?"

Recurrent UTIs are not the norm, and a dog who has had several in one year should be checked for the following predisposing factors.

"Stones" in the bladder or urethra. Rocklike clumps of minerals can form in a dog's kidneys or bladder and lodge there or in the urethra. One type of urinary stone, struvite, forms when a dog's urine is infected with a certain type of bacteria. The other types of stones can irritate the bladder or urethra, causing the same symptoms as an infection: frequent urination, painful urination, or blood in the urine.

A birth defect in the bladder or ureters. The embryonic bladder is connected to the umbilical cord by a tube called the urachus. Normally this tube closes off smoothly before birth. Occasionally, however, a small pocket remains on the inside of the bladder where the urachus was connected. This pocket, called a urachal remnant, can trap urine and bacteria and lead to recurring UTIs.

The ureters—the tubes that carry urine away from the kidneys—normally connect to the lower part of the bladder. Occasionally one or both takes a slight detour and connects with the urethra (the tube that empties the bladder during urination) instead. This can predispose the dog to a kidney infection by allowing bacteria to pass from the urethra to the kidney. An ectopic ureter, as this condition is called, also can cause constant leaking of small amounts of urine if the ureter connects below the sphincter that controls urination.

A urachal remnant or ectopic ureter is diagnosed using dye-contrast x-rays or an ultrasound exam. A urachal remnant can usually be closed surgically. An ectopic ureter can sometimes be repositioned surgically, depending on how large it is and where it connects. If it can't be moved, then the dog may need to be on antibiotics long-term to prevent a kidney infection.

Kidney infections. Most urinary tract infections involve only the bladder; bacteria from outside the body travel up the urethra, grow in the bladder, and stop there. Occasionally, though, bacteria make their way up a ureter and infect a kidney. Often a dog with a kidney infection will have a fever, back pain, lethargy, loss of appetite, and blood in the urine, but sometimes the symptoms are the same as those of a simple bladder infection. A longer course of antibiotics—four to six weeks instead of two weeks—and sometimes a different antibiotic altogether are needed to eliminate a kidney infection.

A kidney infection is usually diagnosed by compiling information from blood tests, urine tests, and the dog's symptoms. If the infection is affecting the kidneys' ability to do their job, then blood levels of urea nitrogen and creatinine will go up (see page 335). A urine sample may also show microscopic "casts," or collections of white blood cells and debris from the kidneys.

A tumor in the bladder or urethra. A tumor growing in the bladder or urethra can produce the same symptoms as a UTI, such as straining to urinate, blood in the urine, or urinating small amounts frequently. Tumors are diagnosed using dye-contrast x-rays or ultrasound. For more about urinary tract tumors, see page 386.

A disease that makes the body less resistant to infection. Diabetes mellitus and Cushing's disease can predispose a dog to recurrent urinary tract infections. Diabetes is diagnosed by finding high levels of blood glucose on a fasting blood test, and glucose in the urine (see page 291). Cushing's is diagnosed by two special blood tests (see page 300).

VITAMIN C TO PREVENT URINARY INFECTIONS?

"Will putting cider vinegar or vitamin C in a dog's drinking water help prevent urinary tract infections?"

No. Giving a dog vinegar or vitamin C might make her urine more acidic, but that will not prevent UTIs. The pH of a dog's urine normally ranges from 5.0 to 8.0. (A pH below 7.0 is acidic, and one above 7.0 is alkaline.) Acidic urine is not healthier or more desirable than alkaline urine, and a dog can get a UTI regardless of the urine pH.

If your dog had urinary stones, medications to change the urine pH might be used to help dissolve them (in the case of urate or struvite stones) or to prevent them from recurring, but whether you wanted to make the urine more acid or more alkaline would depend on what type of stones they were (see the box on page 333).

BROWN SPOTS ON THE LAWN

"Is there anything that can be fed to a dog to prevent her urine from killing the grass in our yard? Someone recommended tea as a neutralizer."

The high concentration of nitrogen in dog urine is what kills the grass. But in lower concentrations, nitrogen is a fertilizer (you'll notice that the dead brown spots have a ring of lush green grass around them). You can prevent the scald by immediately pouring water on the spots where your dog urinates. But a longer-term solution is prevention. Try designating a corner of your yard as a dog bathroom, using sand, mulch, or a hardy ground cover such as thyme in that area, and training your dog to relieve herself there rather than on the lawn.

Most of the things people suggest feeding a dog to prevent grass scalding—such as tomato juice, vitamin C, and commercial products—acidify the urine. But it's the nitrogen in the urine, not the urine's pH, that causes the scald, so those supplements are unlikely to help.

A gardening aside: some landscapers recommend treating urine-scalded spots with gypsum in the spring and fall. I'm a dog doctor, not a lawn doctor, so I don't know for certain whether this works. You might want to consult a lawn specialist for advice about treating the brown spots you already have.

DALMATIANS AND URINARY STONES

"I recently adopted a Dalmatian, and I've read that the breed is prone to urinary stones. What should I be watching for?"

Dalmatians are prone to forming urate stones in their urinary tract because they have an inborn defect in how they process uric acid. The stones can cause symptoms similar to a urinary tract infection (frequent urination, painful urination, straining to urinate, or blood in the urine); in male dogs, they can also block the urethra and make it difficult or impossible for the dog to urinate.

Urate stones, which account for about 10 percent of all urinary stones in dogs, are not exclusive to Dalmatians. They also occur in other breeds, especially English Bulldogs. For some reason, they are more common in male dogs than in females. Urate stones form more easily in acidic urine and are often invisible on plain x-rays, so an ultrasound exam or dye injected into the bladder are used to diagnose them.

The stones often can be dissolved by medication or a prescription diet (Hill's u/d). Feeding u/d or Royal Canin Urinary SO is sometimes recommended to help *prevent* urate stones from forming as well, so ask your vet what's advisable for your dog.

Another type of urate stone, ammonium urate, is found exclusively in dogs with a liver shunt (see page 263) or severe liver disease. These stones may dissolve on their own if the underlying disease can be controlled, or if the dog is fed u/d.

BLADDER STONES CAUSED BY BACTERIA

"My Shih Tzu has a urinary tract infection, and the vet wants to check her for bladder stones. Is there a connection?"

The most common type of urinary stone—accounting for 60 to 70 per-

CRYSTALS AND STONES IN THE URINARY TRACT

Urine contains a variety of minerals. Some of these minerals form **crystals**—microscopic deposits of an identifiable shape. Crystals are not harmful and can be ignored unless the dog also has bacteria in her urine.

Urinary **stones**—also called calculi or uroliths—are much bigger than crystals. They are visible to the naked eye, ranging in size from a grain of sand to as much as 3 inches in diameter. They can be found in the kidneys, ureters, bladder, or urethra. Urinary stones usually cause symptoms such as frequent urination, straining to urinate, or blood in the urine. A veterinarian sometimes can feel urinary stones in the bladder when palpating a dog's abdomen, but they usually are diagnosed by an ultrasound exam or x-rays.

Dogs can get a half-dozen or so different types of stones, which are identified according to their mineral makeup. Some types of stones show up well on plain x-rays, but others aren't dense enough to be seen that way. The less-dense types of stones are found by ultrasound exam or by filling the bladder with a dye that outlines the stones' shape on x-rays.

A dog may have a single stone or multiple stones. If a urinary stone is found in one location—say, the bladder—then the rest of the urinary tract (kidneys, ureters, and urethra) should be carefully checked for stones as well.

Two common types of urinary stones, urate and struvite, can often be dissolved by giving the dog medication and a special diet for three to six weeks. The other types of stones cannot be dissolved and usually must be removed surgically. Small stones sometimes can literally be squeezed out of an anesthetized dog's bladder or urethra by water pressure, a procedure called hydropropulsion. Lithotripsy, in which kidney stones or bladder stones are pulverized by shock waves, is available at some veterinary-school hospitals.

Dalmatians and English Bulldogs are prone to urate stones. The other types of stones are seen most often in small purebred dogs, such as Shih Tzus, Lhasa Apsos, Miniature Schnauzers, and Yorkshire Terriers.

cent of the cases in dogs—is caused by a bacterial infection. Made of a phosphate compound known as struvite, these stones form when urease-producing bacteria such as staph or mycoplasma infect the bladder, raise the urine's pH, and trigger the formation of phosphate clumps.

Because of their short urethras, female dogs are more prone to urinary tract infections than male dogs, so most struvite stones are found in females. The stones are usually dense enough to show up on plain x-rays. Struvite stones can often be dissolved by giving the dog antibiotics and feeding a special prescription diet (such as Hill's s/d) for three to six weeks, but no other food or treats can be given during that time. The stones can also be removed surgically. They do not recur unless the dog gets another urinary tract infection.

A URINARY STONE BLOCKING THE URETHRA

"My male mixed breed kept acting like he needed to urinate, but nothing would come out. I didn't think much of it until the following day, when he was so weak he could hardly stand. I took him to the vet, who said my dog's urethra was blocked by a urinary stone. How did this happen?"

Urinary stones form in the kidneys or bladder. Sometimes one or more of the stones will enter the urethra (the tube that carries urine out of the body) and block it, making it difficult or impossible for the dog to urinate. This happens more often in male dogs because their urethras are longer and narrower than those of female dogs.

When a dog is unable to urinate, it's a medical emergency because he can die within just a few days from a buildup of toxins in the blood, a ruptured bladder, or kidney failure. A dog whose urethra is blocked will make repeated attempts to urinate, producing only a drop or two of urine or blood. If the blockage continues for a day or more, the dog's belly may appear swollen and he may lose his appetite or vomit. Ultimately the dog may become too weak to stand, as your dog did.

The blockage is treated by anesthetizing the dog, passing a urinary catheter up the urethra to the site of the blockage, and then using saline in a syringe to flush the stone or stones back into the bladder. Once his condition is stable, he will have surgery to remove the stone or stones from his bladder. After the stones are analyzed, he will be put on a prescription diet to help prevent their recurrence.

OTHER TYPES OF URINARY STONES

"When stones showed up in an x-ray of my dog's bladder, my vet said there was a 60 to 70 percent chance they could be treated with antibiotics and a prescription food. That was a month ago, and a new x-ray shows that the stones are still there. Now what?"

If she ate nothing but the prescription food for those four weeks, the bacteria in her bladder weren't resistant to the antibiotic, and the stones are the same size they were when you started treatment, then most likely they're not struvite—the type found in 60 to 70 percent of the dogs with stones. That means hydropropulsion, surgery, or lithotripsy will be required to get rid of them (see the box on page 333).

After removing the stones, your vet can send them to a lab for identification so you can take appropriate measures to prevent their recurrence. They're most likely one of the following four:

Calcium oxalate stones. These account for about 10 percent of the urinary stones found in dogs. They can form in acidic or alkaline urine and are usually visible on plain x-rays. They cannot be dissolved with medication. Once the stones have been removed, a dog may be prescribed potassium citrate or a special diet (Hill's u/d or Royal Canin Urinary SO) to help reduce oxalate crystal formation in the urine. Dogs that have had calcium oxalate stones should not be given foods or supplements rich in vitamin C because it increases oxalate formation in the urine.

Cystine stones. These are found exclusively in male dogs, especially Dachshunds and English Bulldogs, and they account for about 5 percent of all urinary stones. They form more easily in acidic urine and often can't be seen on plain x-rays, requiring an ultrasound exam or dye study to diagnose. They cannot be dissolved with medication, but a low-protein diet and medication to make the urine slightly alkaline can help prevent their recurrence.

Silica stones. These stones account for less than 5 percent of the total and are found more often in male dogs than females. They are visible on plain x-rays and can form in acidic or alkaline urine. They cannot be dissolved. Silica stones can form when dogs eat dirt or food high in corn gluten or soybean hulls, so those factors should be eliminated and the dog given plenty of water at all times to prevent their recurrence.

Calcium phosphate stones. These stones account for a small percentage of the total and are usually seen in dogs who have higher than normal levels of calcium in their blood and urine. They are visible on plain x-rays and can't be dissolved with medication. Treating the cause of the excess calcium in the blood and urine can help prevent the stones from recurring (see page 305).

WHAT IS KIDNEY FAILURE?

"My 14-year-old dog had some blood tests before having her teeth cleaned. The vet told me—rather casually, I thought—that my dog has kidney failure. I'm so upset. Does this mean my dog is going to die soon?"

No, it doesn't mean your dog is at death's door, particularly if she didn't seem ill to you before you heard that diagnosis. "Kidney failure" is a legitimate medical description, but "chronic kidney disease (CKD)" is also accurate and less dire-sounding.

Kidney failure, or CKD, means the kidneys aren't removing waste products from the blood efficiently. It is diagnosed by blood and urine tests. A dog with kidney disease will have higher than normal levels of blood urea nitrogen (BUN) and creatinine, two substances the kidneys are supposed to get rid of, and dilute urine. (A dog with normal kidney function who had high BUN and creatinine levels would have concentrated urine.) Many vets use a numerical system to describe the severity of the disease, based on the creatinine level: from CKD stage 1 to CKD stage 4, with 4 being the worst.

High BUN and creatinine levels plus dilute urine are signs that a dog's kidneys are working at 25 percent of normal capacity or less. That's the bad news. The good news is that many dogs can get along quite well for a long time with only 25 percent kidney function, depending on how they got there and how quickly the problem is progressing. So ask your vet what she thinks may have caused the kidney problem and whether you should be taking steps to treat it.

SYMPTOMS OF KIDNEY DISEASE

"How would I know if something were wrong with my dog's kidneys?"

THE LEAKY DOG

When a dog who is housebroken starts urinating in the house, some detective work is required to determine the cause. First, gather the facts by answering the following questions:

1. When did she start urinating in the house?

2. How often do the accidents occur?

3. Is she urinating large amounts, like a whole bladderful, or leaving smaller spots?

4. When, in general, do the accidents occur? After she has gone to bed for the night? When she is home alone? About how many hours after she last urinated?

5. Is she drinking more water than usual?

6. Is her bottom or tail sometimes wet? Do her bed and other areas where she rests smell of urine?

7. Is she also defecating inside?

8. Is she scuffing her hind feet or having trouble walking? Is her tail limp or droopy?

Next, try to match the facts with one of the following profiles:

A dog who is drinking more than usual and needs to urinate all the time may have a bladder infection, diabetes mellitus, Cushing's disease, or kidney disease. Your veterinarian can run blood and urine tests to find out.

A female dog who leaks urine when she sleeps or rests may have urinary incontinence caused by a weakened urethral sphincter. Her bed will smell of urine and her tail or bottom may sometimes be wet. This type of urinary incontinence is fairly common in older female dogs and can be treated with the drug phenylpropanolamine (PPA), which helps tighten the urethral sphincter. Before starting on PPA, your dog should have a blood test and urinalysis

---

If only a flashing neon sign went on when a dog had kidney disease. Unfortunately, the most common symptoms—drinking and urinating more than usual, loss of appetite, vomiting or diarrhea, sores in the mouth, weight loss, loss of energy—are vague and could be caused by many things other than kidney disease, including diabetes mellitus or Cushing's disease. If something is wrong with your dog's kidneys, your vet will need to run blood and urine tests in order to make a diagnosis.

CAUSES AND TREATMENT OF KIDNEY FAILURE

"What makes a dog's kidneys stop working properly?"

A host of problems can damage a dog's kidneys. Some of them (like antifreeze poisoning) occur suddenly, in a day or two, and others creep up gradually over weeks or months.

Sudden-onset kidney failure may have a clear and obvious cause, such as

to make sure she doesn't also have a kidney problem or a bladder infection.

An older dog who is both urinating and defecating in the house, or wandering and urinating in the house at night, may have canine cognitive dysfunction, or "doggie Alzheimer's" (see page 181).

A dog who urinates when left home alone may have separation anxiety (see page 179).

A new dog added to a household may trigger a "pissing contest" among the housemates to mark their territory and establish who's dominant (see page 195).

A dog who is having seizures may urinate while unconscious (see page 308).

A dog who is having trouble with her hind legs, and urinating or defecating wherever she happens to be, may have a nerve disorder that's affecting her ability to control her bladder and bowels as well as her hind legs (see page 249).

a toxin, infection, heat stroke, or blood clots cutting off circulation to the kidneys. Chronic kidney disease, the type that comes on slowly and gradually, is more of a mystery. In most cases, the underlying cause can't be discovered. When it can be determined, it can be anything from a kidney infection to kidney stones; kidney dysplasia, an inborn kidney defect; an immune-system disease; cancer; or even a rare parasite, the giant kidney worm (*Dioctophyme renale*).

Treating the cause, if it can be determined, is one facet of dealing with kidney disease. The other is easing the burden on the kidneys and related symptoms in any way possible. On an emergency basis, this may include hospitalizing the dog and giving intravenous fluids; stopping any medications that can damage the kidneys, such as the antibiotic gentamicin; and giving antacids and antinausea drugs as needed. Once they are back home, dogs with kidney disease need unlimited fresh drinking water and extra opportunities to go outside to urinate; an antacid such as Tagamet or Zantac if stomach upset is a problem; a diet containing highly digestible protein, reduced sodium, and increased water-soluble vitamins; and sometimes a phosphorus binder or potassium supplement. Stress—which can include boarding, hot weather with no air conditioning, and new animals in the house—should be avoided as much as possible.

Other high-tech treatments for kidney failure are used occasionally in dogs. One is dialysis, in which the blood is filtered through a machine to remove toxins. Dialysis machines are available at only a few veterinary schools and specialty hospitals around the country. Dialysis is expensive, costing thousands of dollars per session, and is used mainly when kidney failure is sudden and potentially reversible, as when a dog has ingested antifreeze or is fighting the bacterial disease leptospirosis.

A few kidney transplants have been performed in dogs, mainly at the University of California's vet school. Only dogs who are young and reasonably healthy—such as those with early signs of an inherited kidney defect—are candidates for a kidney transplant. Tissues are matched with a healthy donor dog. (The owner's other dogs or shelter dogs can be tested for a match. If a shelter dog is used, the owner must adopt and care for him for life.) One of the donor dog's kidneys is removed and transplanted into the recipient. Both the donor and the recipient require extensive follow-up care for life. The small number of surgeons performing the procedure, the health restrictions on the patients, the difficulty of getting a good tissue match, and the price tag of $20,000 or more make kidney transplants extremely rare for dogs.

COMING INTO HEAT

"My Shiba Inu is seven months old, and I'm wondering when her first heat will occur and how long it will last. I'd like to breed her later. At what age should a female dog first be bred?"

A female dog first comes into heat sometime between the ages of 6 and 24 months. Small breeds usually come into heat sooner than large breeds, because small breeds mature faster.

Each heat lasts an average of 18 to 24 days. The first signs are a swollen vulva and bloody discharge from the vulva. For the first week or so that she's in heat, a female dog will attract the attention of male dogs but usually won't allow them to mount her. During the rest of the heat, she will actively court male dogs and stand to be mounted. Her vulva may become slightly smaller and the discharge may stop or change from bloody to clear during this phase, but she is still very much in heat and able to become pregnant.

Sometimes a dog's first heat is a "split heat"—she will develop a swollen vulva and bloody discharge but won't ovulate (release eggs) and won't allow a male dog to mount her. Two to six weeks later, she will come into heat again and this time follow the full cycle.

Dogs come into heat roughly twice a year, five to eight months apart. Older dogs do not go through menopause, but their heat cycles do get farther and farther apart after they're about seven years old.

A dog should not be bred until she has reached physical maturity—which occurs at around 18 months for a small breed, and 2½ years for a large breed—and has demonstrated that she has a good temperament, is an outstanding example of her breed, and does not have any inherited defects. There's no reason to breed a dog who isn't truly exceptional—having a litter won't improve her health or temperament, and there are already far too many purebred and mixed-breed dogs without homes. If you are determined to breed your dog, please consult with a top professional breeder of Shiba Inus first.

WHEN TO SPAY?

"I have a Golden Retriever, and the breeder told me I should wait until she's had her first heat before spaying her. Do you agree?"

In most cases, I recommend spaying a dog *before* her first heat to prevent an accidental pregnancy and give her the most protection against developing breast cancer in the future. One exception is the puppy who has severe puppy vaginitis (see page 54), which can be "cured" by letting her go through one heat before spaying her.

Here are the breast-cancer stats: A dog who is spayed before her first heat has a 0.5 percent risk of developing breast tumors later in life. A dog who is spayed between her first and second heat has an 8 percent risk of developing breast tumors. And a dog that is spayed after her second heat has a 26 percent chance of developing breast tumors, the same as a dog who is not spayed at all.

SPAYING: WHAT'S INVOLVED?

"I always intended to have my Jack Russell Terrier spayed because I know it's healthier for her, but now that she's approaching six months old, I'm feeling nervous about the surgery. What exactly is involved? Will she have to spend the night at the veterinary clinic, or will she come home the same day? Will she be in a lot of pain?"

Spaying a dog may be a routine procedure for a small-animal vet, but it is abdominal surgery, so your questions and concerns are understandable. Here's how it's done:

The dog is put under general anesthesia in the same way a person would be, with a breathing tube in the trachea that's connected to an anesthesia machine. Her heartbeat, breathing, and sometimes blood pressure and body temperature are monitored by machines or by an assistant during the surgery.

The dog is positioned on her back on a heated surgical table. The hair is shaved from her abdomen and the skin is cleaned several times with surgical scrub. The veterinarian wears a surgical mask, head cover, sterile gown, and sterile gloves, and the surgical instruments are sterile as well.

Using a scalpel, the vet makes an incision in the skin of the abdomen, then an incision through the muscle layer that leads into the abdominal cavity. Depending on the size of the dog, the skin incision may be 1½ to 4 inches long. The vet finds the uterus under the urinary bladder and follows each horn of the uterus up to its corresponding ovary. The vet uses surgical clamps and sutures to tie off blood vessels before cutting the uterus and ovaries free and removing them. Then the vet sutures the abdominal muscles back together, and sutures or glues the skin back together. The anesthesia is turned off and the dog is watched closely until she is fully awake; then she's moved to a bed inside a cage for recovery.

Some vets prefer that a dog spend the night in the clinic after being spayed, to "sleep it off" without the excitement of being at home. Other vets will send a dog home late in the day if she was spayed several hours before.

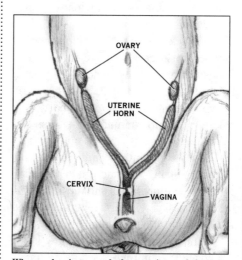

When a dog is spayed, the ovaries and the uterus—which is Y-shaped—are removed.

Most vets give pain medication during or immediately after the surgery and send some home to be given for the first two or three days after surgery. Often the dog will act completely normal the day after surgery, but the usual advice is to restrict her exercise to leash walks and not let her roughhouse with other dogs until her incision has healed, usually in 10 to 14 days.

Most dogs leave the incision alone after the surgery, but once in a while a dog will lick excessively at the area, irritating it, potentially triggering a skin infection, and possibly pulling out the sutures before the skin has healed. A dog who won't let the incision alone will need to wear an Elizabethan collar (see page 427) until she forgets about the incision or it has healed completely.

The most serious potential risk in spaying a dog is death from an unpredictable anesthetic reaction, excessive bleeding, or an abdominal infection. But it is exceedingly rare for a healthy young dog to die as a result of being spayed. Careful monitoring of a dog's heart rate, breathing, blood pressure, and body temperature is the best safeguard against an allergic reaction to anesthetic. Many vets check a dog's blood-clotting ability before surgery to make sure the dog doesn't have an unsuspected bleeding disorder (see page 358). Sterile instruments, sterile surgical garb, and careful skin preparation minimize the possibility of infection.

Other potential surgical complications—pain, fever, or skin irritation from the sutures or a minor skin infection—are slightly more common but fortunately not life-threatening.

Those are the basics of how a dog is spayed. Your own vet will be happy to discuss the details as they pertain to your dog: what blood tests the vet recommends before surgery, what kind of anesthesia is used and how it's monitored, whether dogs usually or sometimes are given pain medication after a spay, whether the dog stays overnight or goes home the same day, and so on. Knowing what to expect is the best way to put your mind at ease.

AN INFECTED UTERUS

"My parents have had a Collie mix for ages. She suddenly stopped eating but drank all the water she could get, and just generally acted sick. My parents took her to the vet, and the next thing they knew she was having emergency surgery to remove an infected uterus. How did she get such a bad infection so quickly?"

Pyometra is the veterinary term for an infected uterus. The condition is very common in older unspayed dogs and can be fatal if the infected uterus isn't removed quickly. In fact, a veterinary adage—"Never let the sun set on a pyometra"—emphasizes the need to get the dog into surgery sooner rather than later.

How a dog develops pyometra has less to do with bacteria and more to do with the hormones involved in the heat cycle. The infection occurs within two to three months after the dog goes into heat, when levels of the hormone progesterone are high even if the dog isn't pregnant. Progesterone closes the cervix (the opening from the uterus into the vagina) and increases the secretion of fluid within the uterus. This fluid provides a perfect growth medium for any bacteria that may have entered the uterus from the vagina.

A dog with an infected uterus may have a bloody or foul-smelling discharge from the vulva, but sometimes the cervix is so tightly closed that no discharge is seen. Often the dog will lose her appetite, drink more water and urinate more than usual, or vomit. Sometimes she will have a fever, but other times her temperature will be normal.

Pyometra is diagnosed by x-rays or an ultrasound exam of the abdomen, which will show an enlarged, fluid-filled uterus. It can't be treated with antibiotics alone because the bacteria produce toxins so rapidly that the dog can easily go into shock and die before the antibiotics have a chance to work. Rather, the infected uterus is surgically removed as quickly as possible to get rid of the toxin-producing bacteria.

The likelihood of an unspayed dog developing pyometra at some point in her life is one of the top medical reasons for spaying any female dog that is not going to be used for breeding. The protection that dogs who are spayed early receive against breast cancer is the other.

"THE PILL" FOR DOGS?

"Is there any kind of birth control for dogs besides spaying and neutering?"

Abstinence works, of course. As for pharmaceutical options, megestrol acetate (Ovaban) and mibolerone (Cheque Drops) are hormones that can be given daily to a female dog to block a heat that is expected to start at least a month later. Ovaban can also stop a heat cycle if it is started within the first three days of vaginal bleeding. These drugs are sometimes given so dogs can be entered in dog shows or used for hunting with-

out coming into heat. The potential side effects make them highly unsuitable as a convenience measure, however. Ovaban can cause increased appetite, lethargy, weight gain, change in hair color, breast enlargement, changes in behavior, and even Addison's disease (see page 304) or breast cancer. Cheque Drops cannot be used in dogs that are still growing because it can make the growth plates in bones close prematurely, leading to stunted or crooked legs. In full-grown dogs, Cheque Drops can cause vaginitis, urine leakage, aggressive behavior, and skin problems.

An implant that blocks hormone release, and therefore fertility, in male dogs was approved for use in Australia in 2004 and is now available in Canada as well. The Peptech product, Suprelorin (deslorelin), is injected under the skin, much like a microchip, and blocks testosterone and sperm production for six months. American vets may be able to obtain these implants from overseas, and the FDA is likely to approve them for direct sale in the United States soon.

Research into vaccine-type injections that temporarily block fertility in male and female dogs and cats is ongoing, and such products are likely to come onto the market within the next decade.

FALSE PREGNANCY

"My 15-month-old dog had her first heat a couple of months ago. As far as we know she wasn't around any unneutered males during that time, but her nipples are bigger, she seems to be producing a little milk, and she has been cuddling her favorite toy and carrying it everywhere. Could she be pregnant? How can I find out?"

The surest way to find out whether your dog is pregnant is to have your vet x-ray or do an ultrasound exam of her abdomen. Pregnancy in a dog lasts for 62 or 63 days; so if your dog did manage to find a male during her last heat, she'd be close to delivering the puppies, and their spines and skulls would be mineralized and visible on x-rays.

Since her sides aren't obviously bulging with puppies, and you don't think she was bred, a more likely explanation is that she's having a false pregnancy. Whether a dog is bred and becomes pregnant or not, levels of the hormone progesterone remain high for about two months after she's in heat. Progesterone can make her breasts enlarge, increase her appetite (possibly causing her to gain weight), and make her more lethargic, just as if she were pregnant. At the end of two months, if the progesterone level drops quickly—as it does when a pregnant dog goes into labor—the dog may make a nest, "adopt" objects, and even produce a little milk.

False pregnancy is not abnormal or harmful unless the dog becomes destructive or aggressive in her efforts to create

A false pregnancy can look decidedly real when a dog's breasts enlarge, her appetite increases, and she gains weight.

a nest or guard her "puppies." If this happens, the hormone mibolerone (Cheque Drops) can be given for five days to break the hormone spell.

SIDE EFFECTS OF NEUTERING

"I have a 14-week-old male Lab who can be quite a handful. My wife thinks we should neuter him when he is about six months old to help calm him down. Will this work? What are the positive and negative effects of neutering?"

Neutering or spaying will not usually make a dog less hyper. The only behavioral changes you should expect or hope for from neutering are that your dog will be less inclined to roam in search of female companionship, and that he'll be less likely to get in fights with other male dogs.

Labs can be very exuberant, to say the least, and your pup will soon grow into a large, strong adult. Your best bet for dealing with his high energy is to make sure he gets an hour or more of leash walks each day and to get serious about obedience training. (Avoid high-impact exercise, however, so you don't promote hip dysplasia—see page 229.) A good trainer can advise you on what kind of collar and reward system will work best with your dog.

Besides lessening the likelihood that your dog will roam, father unwanted pups, and be attacked by other male dogs, neutering eliminates the risk of testicular cancer and significantly reduces the risk of problems associated with prostate enlargement.

Some people worry that neutering a dog will make him fat, lower his self-esteem, and subject him to sexual frustration. Reality check: a dog's self-image is not sexual. He doesn't watch the Playboy Channel, take Viagra, or wonder whether the girls at the dog run think he's studly. Dogs who are spayed or neutered before having had a sexual encounter have no idea what they're missing, and even if they did have a rendezvous or two before surgery, those are not going to be remembered, longed for, or brooded over.

As far as gaining weight, some animals do get heavier after they are "fixed," but usually for other reasons. As they progress from adolescence to adulthood, their growth is also slowing down, so excess calories naturally wind up as excess pounds. If a dog becomes overweight after being spayed or neutered, he should be fed less, switched to a lower-calorie food, or exercised more.

THE OLD NEUTER

"Our puppy is going to be neutered in a couple of days. My husband is worried sick. How bad is the procedure really?"

Not so bad. The thought of it is much harder on some sensitive male dog owners than the procedure is on their dogs. Reassure your husband by telling him as many of the following details as you think he can handle.

Before being neutered, your puppy will be put under general anesthesia, so he won't feel any pain or be aware of the procedure at all. His heartbeat, breathing, and sometimes blood pressure and body temperature will be monitored by machines or by an assistant during the surgery.

After he's anesthetized, he'll be placed on his back on a heated surgical table. The hair will be shaved from a small area in front of where the scrotum meets the sheath of the penis, and the skin will be cleaned several times with surgical scrub. The veterinarian, wearing sterile garb and using sterile instruments, will make a small incision in the scrubbed area—about ½ to 1½ inches long, depending on the size of the testicles. Then he'll push each testicle in turn through the incision, clamp and tie off the attached vessels, cut the vessels, and remove the testicle. The skin incision will be closed with sutures or surgical glue. The anesthesia will be turned off and your puppy will be watched closely until he is fully awake, then moved to a bed inside a cage for recovery.

It's possible to do a vasectomy on a dog—in other words, cut the sperm ducts without removing the testicles—but most vets aren't experienced in that procedure and it doesn't eliminate testosterone production, so a vasectomized dog might still roam, fight, and develop an enlarged prostate when he gets older.

Neutering a male dog is much quicker and less involved than spaying a female dog, because the parts in question are just below the skin rather than inside the abdomen (unless the dog has an undescended testicle—see page 346). Your puppy will probably go home a few hours after surgery, and he's unlikely to be in pain. He'll probably act completely normal the following day, but he should be restricted to leash walks and not allowed to roughhouse with other dogs until the incision heals, in about 10 days.

Most dogs leave the incision alone after surgery, but if he licks excessively at the area, he'll need to wear an Elizabethan collar until he loses interest in the incision or it has healed.

Any time a dog is anesthetized, there is a risk that he could have a serious and unpredictable anesthetic reaction, but such complications are exceedingly rare in a healthy young dog. The most common complication following neutering is minor skin irritation at the incision site. Chances are your puppy will bounce back from his surgery as if nothing had happened.

THE NEW NEUTER

"I read in my newspaper's pet column that puppies can be neutered with an injection. This certainly sounds less drastic than removing their testicles. Does it work?"

Neutersol is the product you remember. It was introduced in the United States in 2003, then withdrawn by the manufacturer in 2005, apparently because of a licensing dispute. It is currently available in Mexico under the brand name Esterisol.

It works like this: Esterisol is injected directly into the testicles of male puppies between the ages of 3 and 10 months. The manufacturer claims "most" puppies don't find the injections painful, but adds that vomiting and diarrhea are potential side effects.

The main drawback of Esterisol is that it leaves dogs with the ability to produce some testosterone—up to 50 percent of normal levels. That means the neutered dog may still be inclined to roam in search of female companionship and get into fights with other male dogs, which are behaviors that most dog owners want to eliminate along with their dogs' ability to impregnate females. The residual testosterone level also puts a dog at higher risk of developing an enlarged prostate later in life than if he had been surgically neutered.

Of course, some owners may prefer chemical neutering because their dogs get to keep their testicles (although Esterisol does shrink them somewhat). For these image-conscious dog owners, there is another option: artificial testicles. Neuticles is the brand name of a line of artificial dog testicles, available in a variety of sizes and textures. (The firmest are the least expensive, but they can cause a tell-tale clicking sound when the dog sits down.) Neuticles can be implanted in a dog's scrotum while he's being surgically neutered. Your veterinarian is unlikely to suggest artificial testicles for your dog—because they are completely unnecessary—but can order your dog a pair if you feel he must have them.

GIVING BIRTH

"Our dog is about to deliver pups, and I need to know what to expect."

Here's a quick course on dog midwifery. Gestation in dogs lasts 63 days. A dog's temperature will drop a degree or two from the normal 101° to 102°F approximately 24 hours before she goes into labor. You can take her temperature once a day starting on day 58 or so, to get advance warning of when she's going to deliver (see page 404). This can be especially helpful if it wasn't a "planned" pregnancy, and you're not sure exactly when she conceived.

Delivery problems are rare in dogs, but if your dog is small compared to the male, or if she or the male have very large heads and narrow hips (English Bulldogs are an extreme example), you should be extra watchful and prepared to take her to the vet if she seems to be having trouble giving birth. Ask your vet if you're unsure whether your dog's size may present problems.

Dogs can have anywhere from 2 to 14 or more pups, depending on the individual and the breed. If your dog has had an x-ray or ultrasound to determine the number of puppies she's carrying, that number should be taken only as an estimate—occasionally an extra puppy or two can be hidden from view.

Uterine contractions start 2 to 12 hours before the first puppy is born. Signs of labor include restlessness, seeking a place to give birth, shivering, and panting. Often you will see some slightly bloody vaginal discharge.

When contractions have moved the first puppy into position to be born, the dog will begin "pushing." She'll strain with her abdomen and hindquarters while squatting or lying down. She may yelp, moan, or whine—this is normal. If she pushes for more than four hours without delivering the first puppy, call your vet or a veterinary emergency hospital to discuss whether you should bring her in for evaluation and possible medical assistance.

Puppies can be born either head first or tail first. When the puppy starts to come out of the birth canal, do *not* try to help things along by pulling on it—that can injure the puppy or the mother. If a puppy is "stuck" partway out for more than 20 minutes, call your vet for advice.

Each puppy will be born partly or totally encased in a membrane sac, with a placenta attached via an umbilical cord. Although many dogs do a fine job of getting their pups out of the sacs and biting off the umbilical cords, first-timers sometimes aren't sure what to do, or they may bite the umbilical cord

too short, causing bleeding. If your dog is hesitant or overly enthusiastic in her efforts, you should take over by removing the sac, drying and massaging the puppy with a towel, gently wiping its nose and mouth clear of fluid, and pinching off the umbilical cord for 15 seconds or so before cutting it with scissors about a half inch away from the puppy's abdomen. If the cord bleeds, simply pinch it for another 30 seconds or so. Then place the puppy near the mother's abdomen so he can root for a nipple and stay warm.

Your dog will probably be interested in eating the sacs and placentas. It's OK for her to eat a couple of them, but eating more than that might make her sick, and it's fine to throw them away.

If a puppy isn't moving or breathing, cup him in your hands, carefully supporting his head and neck, and gently swing him with his head pointing down to help drain any fluid from the nose and throat. Then rub the puppy's sides fairly vigorously with a towel to stimulate him to breathe.

Your dog will rest briefly between births. Call your vet if she pushes for more than two hours before each subsequent puppy is born.

Newborn puppies need to nurse as soon as possible, and they need their mother to stimulate them to urinate and defecate by licking their bellies and bottoms. You can help "steer" a puppy toward a nipple to encourage him to nurse. Call your vet if any pups do not nurse within two hours of birth.

Very rarely, a dog will attack and injure or kill her newborn puppies. During and just after delivery, watch your dog carefully for signs of aggression. If she behaves aggressively toward any of the puppies, put all the puppies in a warm place where she can't reach them and call your vet for advice.

Take the mother and all the puppies to your vet for a postnatal exam within a day or two after they're born. It's normal for a dog to have a reddish, greenish, or dark vaginal discharge for up to five weeks after giving birth. If the discharge is foul-smelling, however, call your vet—that might indicate a uterine infection.

THE HUNT FOR A MISSING TESTICLE

"My vet tells me my Dachshund puppy has only one testicle 'down,' in his scrotum. I hadn't even noticed, and my dog doesn't seem to mind. But my vet is strongly urging surgery to find and remove the other testicle from wherever it is inside my dog's abdomen. Why can't we just leave well enough alone?"

Testicular cancer is relatively common in dogs, and an undescended testicle is about 10 times more likely to become cancerous than a testicle that's in the scrotum. That's why your vet wants to find the "missing" testicle and take it out.

REPRODUCTIVE BIRTH DEFECTS

"When I took my new puppy to the vet, he looked closely at the puppy's private parts, and I was too embarrassed to ask why. What was he looking for?"

Your vet was probably checking for birth defects in the puppy's reproductive equipment. The most common such

birth defect is an undescended testicle (see the previous Q&A). The following abnormalities are also occasionally seen in dogs.

Inguinal hernia. This is a gap in the muscles of the lower abdomen. If the gap is large enough to allow part of the intestine or another abdominal organ to slip through, the puppy should have surgery to close the gap. Inguinal hernias are seen in both male and female puppies.

Hypospadias. This is a urethra that opens somewhere on the underside of the penis instead of at the end. A dog with hypospadias may leak urine.

Hermaphroditism. Occasionally, a dog is born with combined male and female reproductive organs. Hermaphroditism may affect only internal structures (the ovaries, uterus, and testicles) or the external genitalia as well (the vulva, vagina, and penis). "Mixed" internal reproductive organs should be surgically removed to prevent them from becoming cancerous and to correct hormone abnormalities. Mixed genitalia can be left alone unless they interfere with urination.

PROSTATE PROBLEMS

"I have a 10-year-old Lab. This year our new vet checked my dog's prostate. Why?"

Dogs can get enlarged prostates, prostate infections, and prostate cancer. Assessing the size and symmetry of the prostate by palpating it via a gloved finger in the dog's rectum is a quick and easy way of checking for an enlarged or painful prostate. There is no prostate-specific antigen (PSA) blood test for dogs.

Most prostate problems occur in older male dogs who haven't been neutered, but they are sometimes seen in neutered dogs as well. Symptoms of a prostate problem can include straining to defecate (because the enlarged prostate partially blocks the rectum); dribbling urine; bloody urine at the beginning of urination, or a bloody discharge independent of urination; and occasionally fever, lower abdominal pain, or a stiff, painful walk.

Prostate problems are diagnosed using a combination of x-rays, ultrasound, urinalysis, prostatic fluid analysis, and biopsy.

An enlarged prostate need not be treated unless it's making it difficult for the dog to defecate or causing urinary incontinence. If it is causing problems, neutering is the recommended treatment. The prostate begins to shrink within one week of neutering and continues to decrease in size for two to three months after that.

Prostate infections are treated with antibiotics for a minimum of 30 days.

Prostate cancers are often adenocarcinomas, and they spread quickly to other sites in the body, especially the spine. Prostate tumors are extremely difficult to remove without leaving the dog permanently incontinent. Chemotherapy isn't usually effective, but radiation therapy may be helpful. Overall, the prognosis for survival and a good quality of life for a dog with prostate cancer is poor.

CHAPTER 15

Blood and Lymph Disorders

MINUSCULE THOUGH THEY MAY BE, red blood cells, platelets, and clotting factors are crucial to a dog's survival. Even minor deficiencies in these blood components can tax a dog's resources and sap his strength. Red blood cells contain hemoglobin, which binds with oxygen in the lungs and transports it throughout the body. Platelets and clotting factors work continuously to plug blood vessel walls damaged by injuries or simple wear and tear. Leaks can also spring up in the body's other circulatory network, the lymph system. It's the interactions among these constituents and the coordination between these two pipelines that keep a dog's lifeblood flowing.

E M E R G E N C Y !

Does your dog need immediate veterinary care? Check this list to help you decide.

TAKE IMMEDIATE ACTION!

Call your vet or an emergency veterinary clinic *now* if your dog is showing any of the following symptoms:

❏ He may have **eaten mouse or rat poison.**

❏ She has **eaten a penny, diaper-rash ointment,** or something else that contains **zinc or lead.**

❏ He has **eaten large amounts of onions, garlic, or Tylenol.**

❏ She has **diarrhea that's mostly blood.**

❏ He has **blood in his vomit.**

❏ She is obviously ill and **bleeding from the nose, mouth, rectum, or wounds.**

TAKE A MINUTE . . .

Read further in this book and then call your vet during office hours as needed if your dog is showing any of the following symptoms:

❏ She has a **bloody nose;** this could be a sign of a blood-clotting problem (see pages 283 and 357).

❏ His **urine is dark red or brown;** this could be a symptom that red blood cells are being destroyed (see page 353).

❏ Her **skin or the whites of her eyes look yellow;** this could be a symptom that red blood cells are being destroyed (see page 353).

❏ His **gums are very pale pink;** this could be a symptom of anemia (see page 353).

❏ She has **red spots on her skin or gums;** this could be a sign of a platelet problem (see page 357).

❏ He **bleeds a long time** from a minor wound: this could be a sign of a clotting problem (see page 360).

Remember, it's never wrong to call your veterinarian if you have a question about your dog's health, or if you're worried about a symptom or your dog's overall condition. That's what we're here for.

THE MEANING OF ANEMIA

"When my 14-year-old dog lost her appetite and just didn't seem like herself, I took her to the vet. According to a blood test, she was anemic—her packed cell volume was 28—but the vet didn't give her a blood transfusion. Why not?"

Many people think of anemia as a disease in itself, but it isn't—it's a symptom. Mild anemia usually isn't an emergency that warrants a blood transfusion. Rather, it is a signal to hunt for and treat the underlying cause.

Anemia is a shortage of red blood cells, which pick up oxygen from the lungs and transport it to all the cells in the body. The packed cell volume (PCV) is the percentage of the blood, by volume, that is made up of red blood cells. (The rest is plasma, white blood cells, and platelets; see page 352.) A normal PCV is about 35 to 45 percent.

More important than the specific number are clues to how it came about. Those clues are also found on blood tests. If a dog has a low PCV but lots of young red blood cells in circulation (the younger cells are larger and look different from the mature cells), then the bone marrow is working well enough to respond appropriately to the shortage. If the PCV is low and young red blood cells are also scarce, or if the blood contains other, abnormal cells, then the situation is more serious.

In your dog's case, her symptoms, overall condition, and blood test results reassured your vet that a transfusion wasn't required, and he turned his attention to finding out *why* your dog had become anemic (see the next Q&A).

THE CAUSES OF ANEMIA

"Why is my dog anemic? Does she need an iron supplement?"

Anemia is almost never the result of an iron deficiency. Iron is needed to make hemoglobin, the oxygen-carrying compound in red blood cells, but the body recycles and stores iron efficiently. A dog would have to eat a diet containing no iron for many months to become iron-deficient, and all commercial dog foods contain iron.

Anemia indicates a breakdown somewhere in the supply and demand for red blood cells. For a dog to become anemic, the cells are either being replaced more slowly or disappearing more quickly than they should be.

The supply center is the bone marrow. Problems that can hamper the bone marrow's ability to produce sufficient numbers of red blood cells include chronic illnesses, such as kidney disease (see page 355); toxic effects of certain drugs, such as the antibiotic chloramphenicol, the anti-inflammatory phenylbutazone, estrogen, or chemotherapy agents; or cancer of the bone marrow, such as leukemia (see page 376). Your vet will check your dog's history for possible toxic drug exposures and search for evidence of chronic illnesses using blood tests. A bone-marrow biopsy can show how severely blood cell production has been disrupted and whether it is recovering.

In a demand problem, red blood cells disappear from the circulation more quickly than normal. This blood loss can be obvious, as when a dog bleeds severely from a wound, or nearly invisible. Hidden blood losses might include bleeding into the digestive tract from a

BLOOD BASICS

A dog's blood contains the same basic components as human blood: cells (red cells, white cells, and platelets) and plasma (the liquid portion). Plasma is more than just saltwater; it contains blood-clotting factors and other proteins, minerals, glucose and other nutrients, and by-products of metabolism. Here is what the major blood components do and where they come from.

Red blood cells transport oxygen from the lungs to all the cells of the body. They are produced by the bone marrow and have a lifespan of three to four months, after which they are broken down and their components (including iron) recycled. Red blood cells normally make up 35 to 45 percent of a dog's blood by volume. This percentage—which is easily measured by placing a few drops of blood into a narrow glass tube, spinning the tube in a centrifuge, and then comparing the height of the red portion of the spun blood (the red blood cells) with that of the yellowish portion (the plasma)—is called the hematocrit (Hct) or packed cell volume (PCV).

Anemia is a shortage of red blood cells. An excess of red blood cells—a much rarer condition than anemia—is called erythrocytosis.

White blood cells fight infection and other diseases. Like red blood cells, they are also produced by the bone marrow. They are far less numerous than red cells, accounting for only 1 to 2 percent of blood by volume. There are several different types of white blood cell, each with a different function and appearance. The various types are tallied in a complete blood count, or CBC. Increases or decreases in different types of white blood cells can be caused by infection (bacterial, viral, or fungal), inflammation (such as allergies or arthritis), parasites, corticosteroid use, Cushing's disease, diabetes mellitus, or blood cell cancers.

Platelets are tiny cells that quickly attach to the wall of a damaged blood vessel and send signals for a blood clot to form and plug the hole. They are produced by the bone marrow and have a lifespan of about 10 days.

stomach ulcer or a heavy hookworm infestation.

Red blood cells can even be destroyed right in the blood vessels by a variety of problems, including the tick-borne diseases ehrlichiosis and babesiosis; immune-mediated hemolytic anemia (see the next Q&A); a heavy infestation of adult heartworms; certain toxins; and a couple of rare enzyme deficiencies. Blood tests, your dog's history of exposure to potential toxins, physical exam findings, and other evidence will tell your vet whether one of these demand-side problems is responsible for your dog's anemia.

Plasma contains numerous proteins, minerals, and other substances, including the following:

❏ **Albumin,** a protein produced by the liver, holds water inside blood vessels and transports other substances in the blood (such as calcium and thyroid hormone).

❏ **Clotting factors** are proteins produced by the liver that interact to form a clot when a blood vessel is damaged. Deficiencies in clotting factors, which can lead to severe bleeding, can be caused by ingesting mouse or rat poison; liver disease; or hemophilia.

❏ **Electrolytes** are minerals—such as calcium, sodium, potassium, chloride, and magnesium—that are used by cells in chemical and electrical reactions.

❏ **Nutrients and by-products** are transported in molecular form by the plasma. A blood chemistry profile measures some of these substances, including glucose; urea nitrogen and creatinine, which are waste products destined for excretion by the kidneys; enzymes produced by the liver and pancreas; and bilirubin, produced by the breakdown of red blood cells.

IMMUNE-MEDIATED HEMOLYTIC ANEMIA

"My 12-year-old Cocker Spaniel seemed tired and had no appetite for a couple of days, then suddenly collapsed. The vet noticed that the whites of her eyes and the inside of her ears looked a little yellow. After running some tests, the vet said my dog's immune system was attacking her red blood cells. What causes this?"

The cause of immune-mediated hemolytic anemia (IMHA) is usually a mystery. Sometimes a triggering factor can be identified—a bacterial or viral infection, a drug or vaccine the dog has received in the past few weeks, cancer somewhere in the body, an unmatched blood transfusion—but most often it can't. For whatever reason, antigens (foreign proteins) become attached to the dog's red blood cells. These antigens cause the dog's immune system to identify its own red blood cells as "outsiders" and attack them. The red blood cells are destroyed in the spleen or liver or sometimes right in the blood vessels.

IMHA looks the same in many clinical tests as any other disease that suddenly destroys red blood cells. The packed cell volume (PCV) will be low and dropping, sometimes even hourly. There may be hemoglobin (the oxygen-carrying compound found in red blood cells) or bilirubin (a by-product of the breakdown of red blood cells) in the dog's blood and urine. When masses of red blood cells are being destroyed, as in IMHA, more bilirubin is produced than can be processed immediately by the liver. Excess bilirubin and hemoglobin can color the urine dark red or brown.

A quick clue that the anemia is immune-mediated can be gathered by smearing a drop of blood on a slide and looking at it under a microscope. In IMHA, the red blood cells are coated with antigen and antibodies, so they stick together in clumps even when a drop of saline is added to the slide to float them apart. Another specific sign of IMHA is the presence of spherocytes—unusually small, round red blood cells that have had part of their membranes nipped off by white blood cells. Finally, the most definitive test for IMHA is an antiglobulin (Coombs') test, which checks for antibodies attached to red blood cells.

IMHA occurs most often in young adult and middle-aged dogs. It seems to strike a lot of Cocker Spaniels, Poodles, and Old English Sheepdogs, but it can occur in any breed or mix.

The treatment for IMHA is steroids, such as prednisone, to slow the immune system's attack on the red blood cells. For at least the first few days, the dog is hospitalized on IV fluids and her PCV is checked two or three times a day to make sure she is responding to treatment. Blood transfusions are often given if the dog's PCV drops into the teens. Even though the transfused red blood cells are likely to be attacked by antibodies as well, they will provide extra oxygen-carrying capacity for at least a couple of days.

The PCV should level off and begin to rise within a few days of the dog's starting steroids, and she can go home once her PCV is on a strong upward trend. The steroids are continued at a lower dose until the PCV rises all the way to normal—at least 35 percent—which can take many weeks.

If steroids don't halt a plummeting PCV, then a stronger immune-suppressing drug is used, such as azathioprine, cyclophosphamide, or cyclosporine. Removing the dog's spleen can also help slow IMHA because much of the destruction of red blood cells occurs there. Dogs with IMHA are also at risk of developing blood clots

in the lungs (see page 361) or disseminated intravascular coagulation (see page 363), so they may be given heparin to prevent clots.

The overall prognosis for IMHA is highly variable. Up to one-third of dogs with IMHA don't respond to treatment and die, usually within a week after diagnosis. The outlook is much more positive for dogs that respond with a rising PCV within that first week of treatment. Occasionally, dogs will have a relapse and need to be treated for a second bout of IMHA.

TOXINS THAT CAN CAUSE ANEMIA

"When my rambunctious six-month-old puppy had a bad bout of vomiting and diarrhea, the vet discovered that he was also anemic. The vet asked me whether my dog could have eaten onions, pennies, diaper-rash ointment, or Tylenol. Why that strange list?"

Onions, pennies, diaper-rash ointment, and Tylenol are four of the most common household items that can poison red blood cells and cause anemia in a dog. Because many puppies will chew on or eat anything and everything, your vet wanted to explore the possibility that your puppy might have gotten into something that could have caused the anemia as well as the vomiting and diarrhea. Here's what those substances can do to red blood cells.

Onions and garlic in small amounts don't usually cause any problems; but eating large amounts damages the hemoglobin in red blood cells, making them unable to transport oxygen, and breaks up the cells (see page 414).

Pennies and diaper-rash ointment are two common sources of zinc, which can destroy red blood cells. (Pennies minted after 1982 are 88 percent zinc, with a copper coating.) **Lead** can also attack red blood cells. Dogs can ingest lead if they chew on fishing weights, the foil collars from certain wine bottles, or old linoleum floors, caulk, or paint (see page 415).

Tylenol is acetaminophen, which in large doses damages the hemoglobin in red blood cells and breaks up the cells. Because acetaminophen doesn't work well as a pain reliever for dogs anyway, I advise owners not to use it at all (see page 412).

THE BASENJI BLOOD DISEASE

"I'm interested in getting a Basenji, but I hear they can have an inherited blood disease. How common is it? Is there a test for it?"

Basenjis are the breed most closely associated with a rare enzyme deficiency of red blood cells called pyruvate kinase deficiency. Fortunately, veterinarians and breeders have known about this inherited problem since the 1960s, and since then it has been largely eliminated from the breed. In the late 1990s, a DNA test even became available to check whether a Basenji is a carrier of the disease.

Pyruvate kinase (PK) deficiency can also occur in other breeds, including West Highland White Terriers, Beagles, Cairn Terriers, and Miniature Poodles. A DNA test for PK deficiency has been developed for Westies but not for the other breeds. If the disease is suspected in another breed or a mixed-breed dog, special blood tests to measure PK activity can be run.

PK deficiency causes red blood cells to die much more quickly than normal. Affected dogs may seem fine at rest but tire easily with exercise. Often the dog's gums will look pale instead of pink because his blood is only 11 to 25 percent red blood cells instead of the normal 35 to 45 percent. There is no treatment other than avoiding exercise and possibly giving transfusions during crisis periods. Over time, the bone marrow and liver deteriorate from the constant strain of churning out and breaking down red blood cells, and most dogs with a PK deficiency have shorter than average life spans.

A similar condition—phosphofructokinase (PFK) deficiency—affects English Springer Spaniels and American Cocker Spaniels. PFK is needed by both red blood cells and muscle cells, so dogs with a PFK deficiency often collapse, run a fever, and have muscle cramps when they exercise or are stressed by hot weather. Their urine may be colored dark red or brown by hemoglobin and bilirubin during such crises. There is no specific treatment other than avoiding heat and strenuous exercise. Bone-marrow and liver deterioration are less likely with PFK deficiency than with PK deficiency, and dogs with a PFK deficiency may have a close-to-normal life span. A DNA screening test for PFK is available for Springer and Cocker Spaniels, so like PK, the disease is becoming less common.

ANEMIA OF CHRONIC ILLNESS

"My 15-year-old dog has failing kidneys, and my vet says that's why she's anemic. What's the connection?"

BLOOD TRANSFUSIONS

There's no canine Red Cross, but blood transfusions are available for dogs and are often used to treat anemia, shock, and blood-clotting problems.

Dogs have different blood types, as people do. A dog's blood type can be determined by placing drops of blood on a special test card. Unlike people, however, dogs don't have pre-formed antibodies against other blood types, so in an emergency, a dog that has never had a transfusion before can receive a different blood type than his own. After one transfusion, however, the dog may produce antibodies against that blood type, so future transfusions would need to be matched to his own blood type.

Donor dogs provide the blood for transfusions. They may be owned by individuals or by the veterinary hospital. To be a donor, a dog must be healthy and even-tempered, never have received a transfusion himself, and weigh at least 50 pounds. A dog that is healthy and well-nourished and weighs at least 50 pounds can safely donate up to 450 ml (about a pint) of blood once a month. Blood can be stored at near-freezing temperatures for up to a month, or it can be separated into components and frozen for up to one year. Here are the different types of "blood products" used most often in veterinary medicine:

Whole blood contains red blood cells, white blood cells, platelets, and plasma. It is given for blood loss, anemia, or a blood-clotting problem when other blood products aren't available.

Packed red blood cells is blood that has been spun down to separate the red cells from the plasma. It is given for anemia or blood loss (along with IV fluids).

Fresh frozen plasma is separated from packed red cells and frozen within six hours after the blood is collected. Plasma contains platelets and clotting factors, so it is used to treat blood-clotting emergencies.

Oxyglobin is a synthetic blood substitute that can transport oxygen in the blood the way red blood cells do. It can be used to treat anemia or blood loss.

Anemia is a fairly common side effect of kidney disease, because the kidneys produce erythropoietin, a hormone that signals the bone marrow to produce more red blood cells. Kidneys that aren't working well may not secrete normal amounts of erythropoietin, so the bone marrow produces fewer red blood cells. Synthetic erythropoietin can be given to dogs, but unfortunately, over time they often develop antibodies against it, so it's usually used only as a last-ditch measure when a dog with kidney failure becomes severely anemic.

Other chronic illnesses can also make a dog slightly anemic, for reasons that are less clear-cut. Severe hypothyroidism and various kinds of cancer are two examples.

TOO MANY RED BLOOD CELLS

"My seven-year-old dog just had some blood tests to check her health before going under anesthesia for a dental cleaning, and the vet says she has too many red blood cells. What's wrong with that? Isn't it the more, the better?"

An excess of red blood cells is called erythrocytosis. Too many red blood cells is not better, because it makes the blood thick and causes blood vessels to dilate and weaken. The weakened blood vessels can break, causing internal bleeding and possibly blindness (from bleeding in the retinas) or seizures (from bleeding in the brain).

A packed cell volume (PCV) of 65 percent is enough to cause such problems. (A normal PCV is 35 to 45 percent.) Erythrocytosis is rare in dogs, but can occasionally be caused by a long-standing heart or lung problem that deprives the body of sufficient oxygen; a kidney tumor producing excess amounts of erythropoietin, the hormone that signals the bone marrow to produce red blood cells; or unknown factors. The condition is treated by addressing the underlying cause, if one can be found, and by bloodletting: about 10 ml of blood per pound of the dog's body weight are removed, as when people donate blood, and replaced with IV fluids. This proce-

dure can be repeated every two to four weeks to keep a dog's PCV in the high-normal range in order to avoid internal bleeding, eye damage, or seizures.

Erythrocytosis with no underlying cause can also be treated as if it were cancer, using the chemotherapy agent hydroxyurea to decrease the bone marrow's production of red blood cells.

PLATELET PROBLEMS

"My eight-year-old shepherd mix had a bunch of red spots on her belly, so I took her to the vet, who discovered that her platelet count was really low —only 10,000. Can you tell me about this problem and the prognosis?"

Platelets are the first responders when a blood vessel is damaged. When platelet numbers are extremely low, a dog may have small bruises—the red spots you noticed on your dog's belly—or prolonged bleeding from minor wounds. A normal platelet count is between 200,000 and 500,000, and bruising or bleeding is usually seen only when the platelet count is below 75,000.

So what happened to your dog's platelets? A deficiency indicates a problem in supply or demand. Either the bone marrow isn't producing enough platelets, or they're being used up in huge numbers in the circulation. A bone-marrow cancer, such as leukemia, can hamper the production of platelets and other normal blood cells. Your vet would have looked for evidence of leukemia on blood tests and with a bone-marrow biopsy.

On the demand side of the equation, platelets can be used up during unusual bleeding, or they can be destroyed in another fashion. Disseminated intravascular coagulation (DIC) is a severe condition that can use up platelets rapidly, but if your dog had that, she would be obviously and gravely ill (see page 363). Two diseases transmitted by ticks—ehrlichiosis and Rocky Mountain spotted fever—can also deplete platelets. They can be diagnosed through blood tests.

In a dog who seems completely well aside from a low platelet count, an immune-system attack on the platelets is a likely diagnosis. This is called immune-mediated thrombocytopenia (ITP).

ITP is most common in middle-aged female Cocker Spaniels, Poodles, German Shepherds, and Old English Sheepdogs, but it can occur in either sex and any breed. Dogs with ITP may have tiny bruises on their mucous membranes or skin. They may also have nosebleeds or bleed into their digestive tract or bladder. There is no definitive test for ITP; rather, it is diagnosed by ruling out the other potential causes of low platelets described above.

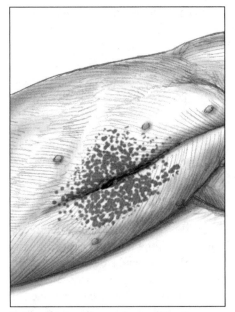

Red or purple spots may be small bruises, which are symptoms of a platelet problem.

The treatment for ITP is prednisone to suppress the immune attack on the platelets. If prednisone is not effective at raising the platelet count, then a stronger immune-suppressing drug is used. The goal of treatment is to raise the platelet count to around 100,000, which is high enough to prevent bleeding. About one-third of dogs with ITP recover permanently with treatment; another one-third recover but relapse at least once; and one-third do not respond well to treatment and die or are euthanized as a result of the disease.

VON WILLEBRAND'S FACTOR

"My six-month-old Dobie mix flunked a routine pre-spay blood clotting test. After checking her platelet count, the vet discovered that she has a deficiency in something called von Willebrand's factor. How common is this?"

Von Willebrand's factor (vWF) is a substance that helps platelets stick together and to the walls of a blood vessel in order to stop bleeding. It's the most common inherited blood-clotting problem in dogs, and has been found in at least 50 breeds. Dobermans, Standard Poodles, Shetland Sheepdogs, and German Shepherds are the most commonly affected. Males and females are affected at equal rates.

Platelets and vWF work in tandem, so a deficiency in one will look the same as a deficiency in the other. Tiny bruises on the skin or mucous membranes, prolonged bleeding time on a lip-stick test, or occasionally nosebleeds are symptoms of either a platelet problem or a vWF deficiency. The lip-stick test involves

SHOCK: A STATE OF BODY, NOT OF MIND

Vets and M.D.s—and the actors who play them on TV—talk all the time about treating patients for shock. But what does that mean, exactly? Because horrifying accidents often lead to victims being treated "for shock," people sometimes assume that it's a mental phenomenon, as in "She's had a terrible shock." In reality, though, shock is a physical condition, not a mental one.

The medical definition of shock is failure of the body to maintain adequate blood flow to supply the organs with oxygen. The main components of this fluid-distribution system are the fluid (the blood), the pump (the heart), and the pipes (the blood vessels). Shock can result from a drop in blood volume, problems with the pumping of the heart, or failure of nerves and neuroreceptors to open and close various blood vessels appropriately.

A dog who is in shock will usually be cold, unable to stand, and breathing rapidly, with pale gums and a fast heart rate. If a dog is in shock, you can bundle him in blankets and prop up his hindquarters to help get blood to the heart and brain, but your main focus should be on getting him to a vet. The vet will give IV fluids, medications, and oxygen as well as treat the condition that put the dog into shock in the first place.

---

pricking the underside of a dog's upper lip with a stylet, then timing how long it takes for the tiny puncture to stop bleeding. Bleeding will stop within four minutes in a dog with normal platelet and vWF activity.

To differentiate between a platelet problem and a vWF deficiency, blood samples are checked for the number of platelets and the amount of vWF. The amount of vWF in a dog's blood is not constant over time—it goes up with stress and exercise, for example—so several blood samples may be checked over a couple of weeks to get the most accurate picture of whether a deficiency exists and how severe it is.

An affected dog may be anything from slightly deficient in vWF to entirely deficient, and it's possible for dogs who are severely deficient to have spontaneous, life-threatening internal bleeding. This severe form has been seen most often in Scottish Terriers, Chesapeake Bay Retrievers, and Shetland Sheepdogs. Fortunately, most dogs with a vWF deficiency have a milder form, and many do very well and have normal life spans when precautions are taken to avoid injuries and control bleeding during any necessary surgery.

When a dog with a vWF deficiency requires surgery, two precautionary measures can be taken. One is to administer the drug desmopressin acetate shortly before surgery. Desmopressin acetate triggers the release of stored vWF from the cells lining blood vessels, temporarily

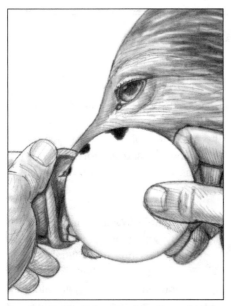

In a lip-stick test, the vet pricks the underside of the lip and then measures how long it takes the wound to clot.

increasing the levels of vWF in the blood. The other is to transfuse the dog with plasma or a plasma concentrate called cryoprecipitate just before and during surgery. Plasma contains vWF, platelets, and other clotting factors and will help the dog's blood to clot normally during surgery.

A vWF deficiency can be passed on to a dog's offspring, so it's especially important to spay or neuter affected dogs, using appropriate precautions against excessive bleeding.

DEFICIENCIES IN MULTIPLE CLOTTING FACTORS

"Shortly after I moved into a new apartment, my four-year-old mixed breed lost his energy and appetite. When the vet drew blood for some tests, the leg kept bleeding for a long time and got a big bruise. The vet said we should run some blood-clotting tests and also start my dog on vitamin K supplements. Is this really necessary?"

Yes. Under the circumstances, I would do the same thing. Excessive bleeding and bruising after a blood test may be the first sign of a blood-clotting disorder. If your dog never had bleeding problems before and was healthy until your move, your vet is probably concerned that he may have found and eaten some mouse or rat poison in your new apartment. Rodenticides use up the vitamin K the liver needs to make certain clotting factors. The prognosis for a dog who has ingested mouse or rat poison is good if the problem is caught early and treated long-term with vitamin K.

Approximately a dozen clotting factors interact to stop bleeding when a blood vessel is punctured or torn. A prothrombin time (PT) test checks for problems with five clotting factors. A partial thromboplastin time (PTT) test checks for problems with eight clotting

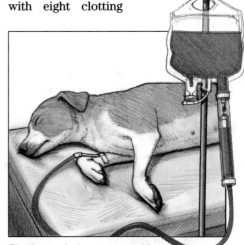

Blood transfusions can provide red blood cells for dogs with anemia, and clotting factors for dogs with hemophilia.

factors—four from the PT test, plus four others. If a dog's PT and PTT are *both* prolonged, then he has a multi-factor clotting problem. A dog with a multi-factor clotting disorder may develop large bruises, bleeding into his joints, and internal bleeding. Rodenticide poisoning is the most common cause of such bleeding disorders in dogs, but severe liver disease or disseminated intravascular coagulation (see page 363) can also result in multifactor deficiencies.

HEMOPHILIA IN DOGS

"If you look up inherited diseases in dogs, it seems that hemophilia is found in practically every breed. Are there really that many dogs out there with hemophilia?"

Hemophilia has been found in many dog breeds, it's true, but it's quite rare in individual dogs.

Hemophilia is an inherited deficiency in a single blood-clotting factor. The two most common types—hemophilia A and hemophilia B—are caused by recessive genes carried on the X chromosome. Females have two X chromosomes, so if they have one normal gene and one abnormal gene they will not show symptoms of hemophilia. Males are XY and get their X chromosome from their mother, so about 50 percent of the male puppies born to a female dog who's a carrier of the hemophilia gene will have the disease.

Symptoms range from mild to severe. A puppy that's severely affected may even bleed uncontrollably from the umbilical cord and die at birth. Other times, puppies will bleed excessively as their adult teeth are coming in

(slight bleeding of the gums is normal in teething puppies). Excessive bleeding during surgery—such as spaying, neutering, ear cropping, or tail docking—is another sign. Dogs with hemophilia may also bruise severely and bleed into their joints, chest, or abdomen.

Hemophilia A is a factor VIII deficiency, and hemophilia B is a factor IX deficiency. Which type a dog has is determined by measuring the amounts of those factors in his blood. Inherited deficiencies of other clotting factors do occur, but they're even rarer than hemophilia A and B.

The amount of factor VIII a dog with hemophilia A produces can range from none to 25 percent of normal. Symptoms vary according to the severity of the deficiency. Dogs with hemophilia B have almost no factor IX at all. Both forms are treated with transfusions of plasma or whole blood as needed to control episodes of bleeding.

STROKES AND BLOOD CLOTS IN THE LUNGS

"I'm the devoted owner of a senior dog. At age 78, I'm a senior myself, and one of my big fears is that I will have a stroke—I take medication for my heart and blood pressure, and coumarin to prevent blood clots. Should I be worrying that my dog could have a stroke, too?"

Spontaneous blood clots are far less common in dogs than in people, and strokes—the blockage of blood flow to some part of the brain, as by a blood clot or ruptured blood vessel—are rare in dogs.

When dogs do form blood clots or break blood vessels, an underlying disease is responsible. Massive bacterial infections, tick-borne diseases, heartworm disease, hypothyroidism, protein loss from the kidneys or intestines, certain heart diseases, and cancer can potentially lead to a stroke. Symptoms of a stroke in a dog are more likely to include bizarre behavior, seizures, or blindness than muscle weakness or paralysis. To help protect your dog against strokes, take her to the vet every six to twelve months for a physical exam and blood tests, so you can catch and treat any predisposing factors early.

Blood clots caused by the diseases listed above can also lodge in the blood vessels of the lungs, causing sudden and severe breathing problems. If that occurs, anticoagulants are added to the treatment for the underlying disease, and the dog is placed in an oxygen cage to help it through the crisis.

LYMPH LEAKS

"My two-year-old Sheltie started coughing about a month ago. He got a little better, then a little worse, and then two nights ago he started gasping for breath. The emergency clinic found that he had fluid in his chest. The vet left a message this morning saying that he was doing well, the fluid was 'from the lymph system,' and she'd call back later to explain. While I'm waiting to talk to her, can you tell us what the lymph system is and what it might have to do with our dog's problem?"

The lymph system is a secondary circulatory system (separate from the blood and blood vessels) that is made up of fluid, nodes, and vessels. The fluid, which is called lymph, seeps out of cells and blood vessels. It's about 95 percent water and 5 percent protein molecules, fat molecules, and white blood cells. Lymph collects in a branching network of lymph vessels and is pushed along passively by contractions of the surrounding muscles. The lymph vessels are dotted with lymph nodes, lumps of tissue containing large numbers of white blood cells that check the lymph for bacteria, viruses, cancer cells, and other invaders. A large lymph vessel called the thoracic duct returns lymph to the vena cava, the major vein that brings blood back to the right side of the heart.

It's that final connection in the chest that apparently has gone awry in your dog. If the thoracic duct is blocked or torn, or if the blood pressure in the vena cava is unusually high, then lymph may leak from the thoracic duct into the chest.

Fluid surrounding the lungs can be seen on x-rays and then removed using a needle and syringe. Fluid collected this way is tested to determine exactly what it is and where it came from. Lymph in the chest cavity is referred to as chylothorax ("chyle" is lymph that contains a lot of digested fat from the small intestines).

What blocked the flow of chyle from your dog's thoracic duct into the vena cava? Your vet will tell you the results of her search for the cause. The thoracic duct can be torn in an accident, such as getting hit by a car, but you don't mention that your dog was injured. It can also be blocked by a tumor in the chest. At age two, your dog would be very young to have a tumor, but if he did have one, it would most likely show up on chest x-rays or an ultrasound exam of the heart. Heart disease, including heartworm infestation, can increase the blood pressure in the vena cava and trigger a backup and leakage of fluid from the thoracic duct into the chest. Again, you don't mention any history of heart problems in your dog, but if he did have one, it would show up on ultrasound. Finally, there's idiopathic chylothorax—that with no discernable cause. Your dog may very well be in this category.

In cases of idiopathic chylothorax, the "lymph leak" usually tapers off and stops within a couple of weeks. In the meantime, your vet can remove the fluid buildup in the chest as often as is necessary to keep your dog breathing comfortably, and put your dog on a low-fat diet to reduce the production of chyle by the small intestines. If the leak doesn't stop on its own, then chest surgery may be recommended to reroute the flow of lymph away from the problem area.

BLOOD CLOTTING GONE HAYWIRE

"I live close to one of the best veterinary schools in the country, and when my 12-year-old Akita collapsed suddenly, I rushed him to the ICU. They started treating him immediately for shock, and then the resident came out and said my dog had something called DIC. He died an hour or so later. Is this anything I could have prevented had I know about it beforehand?"

I am so sorry to hear about your dog's death. I hope you will take comfort from the fact that you couldn't have foreseen or prevented this problem. DIC is disseminated intravascular coagulation—a sudden, fast-moving, often fatal condition that is usually set off by a severe illness or injury, such as an overwhelming bacterial infection, cancer, heat stroke, pancreatitis, hemolytic anemia, blood loss, or shock.

DIC occurs when the blood-clotting system goes haywire. In a healthy dog, a system of checks and balances ensures that blood clots form where they are needed and dissolve when and where they're not needed. In DIC, platelets and clotting factors activate erroneously throughout the body. This in turn overwhelms the body's mechanisms for breaking down such clots safely. The clots begin to lodge in small blood vessels in the lungs, kidneys, and elsewhere. Platelets and clotting factors become depleted within a few hours, and then severe bleeding from the nose or into the lungs or digestive tract can occur.

DIC is diagnosed from blood tests and treated with plasma transfusions and heparin. At the same time, the underlying condition that triggered the DIC—infection, cancer, shock—must be diagnosed and treated to halt the process. Unfortunately, the combination of DIC and the underlying disease often wins, and many dogs with DIC die despite expert care.

CHAPTER 16

Cancer and Cancer Treatment

LET'S BE CLEAR: A diagnosis of cancer is not an automatic death sentence. More than ever, surgery, radiation, chemotherapy, and other measures can relieve symptoms and prolong the life of dogs with many types of cancer. Dogs usually adapt extremely well to these treatments and experience fewer side effects than people do. Before cancer can be treated, however, it must be diagnosed, and that requires more than just a physical exam, or even x-rays or blood tests. In most cases, a biopsy will confirm the diagnosis and determine the best treatment for a dog with cancer.

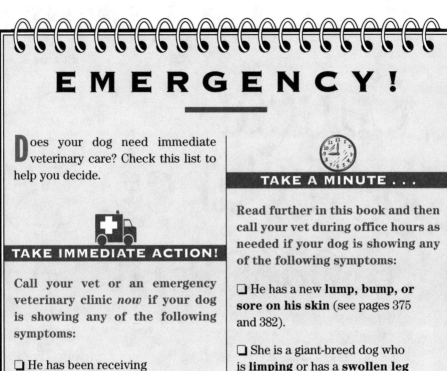

EMERGENCY!

Does your dog need immediate veterinary care? Check this list to help you decide.

TAKE IMMEDIATE ACTION!

Call your vet or an emergency veterinary clinic *now* if your dog is showing any of the following symptoms:

❏ He has been receiving chemotherapy for cancer and has **suddenly collapsed;** a severe drop in white blood cells might be the cause.

❏ She has been receiving chemotherapy for cancer and has **bruised skin, blood in the urine, or unexplained bleeding;** a severe drop in platelets might be the cause.

❏ He has been diagnosed with cancer and has **collapsed;** tumors can release toxins that will make a dog suddenly and severely ill.

❏ She is being treated for cancer and **won't eat, is vomiting, has diarrhea, or seems weak.**

TAKE A MINUTE . . .

Read further in this book and then call your vet during office hours as needed if your dog is showing any of the following symptoms:

❏ He has a new **lump, bump, or sore on his skin** (see pages 375 and 382).

❏ She is a giant-breed dog who is **limping** or has a **swollen leg** (see page 383).

❏ He is an old dog who has had a **seizure** for the first time (see pages 309 and 367).

❏ She has a **bloody nose** (see pages 283 and 369).

❏ He has a new **lump, growth, or sore in his mouth** (see page 371).

❏ She has a **lump, swelling, or thickening near a mammary gland** (see page 384).

Remember, it's never wrong to call your veterinarian if you have a question about your dog's health, or if you're worried about a symptom or your dog's overall condition. That's what we're here for.

BRAIN TUMORS

"Two days ago, our 12-year-old dog had a seizure. When we told the vet that our dog had also been behaving strangely for the past few weeks— barking for no reason, eating less, and wandering aimlessly around the house—he said a brain tumor was a possibility. Can you tell us more?"

The main symptom that might lead a veterinarian to suspect a brain tumor is the onset of seizures in an older dog, especially if the dog's behavior has also changed or his reflexes or coordination are abnormal. A seizure in an older dog is not *proof* of a brain tumor, however, because it could also be caused by a toxin, low blood sugar, or a heart problem, among other possibilities (see page 309). To know for sure whether a dog has a brain tumor requires a CT or MRI scan, which can be done at many veterinary-school hospitals or referral centers. Plain x-rays and ultrasound cannot show the brain clearly because they don't penetrate the skull well.

Some brain tumors, depending on their size and location, can be removed surgically. Such surgery is difficult, and a dog may die from complications during or shortly after the procedure. Some brain tumors respond very well to radiation, and survival times may be as long as one year.

A dog who has a brain tumor can be given corticosteroids (such as prednisone) to relieve brain swelling, and phe-nobarbital or another drug to decrease seizures. These drugs will improve the dog's quality of life but will not extend his life significantly. The survival time of a dog with a brain tumor that is not treated by surgery or radiation is weeks to months.

TUMORS OF THE SPINE

"Our five-year-old Lab mix started limping, then got worse over a few weeks until the tops of her hind feet were scraped raw from being dragged. Our vet sent us to a neurologist, who diagnosed a tumor pushing on the spinal cord. Our dog seems so young to have cancer—does her age improve her prognosis?"

Your dog's prognosis depends on the exact location of the tumor and what kind of cancer it is. The tumor may have originated in a vertebra (bone), in the tissues between the vertebrae and the spinal cord, or in the spinal cord itself. A tumor in any of these areas can put pressure on the spinal cord and produce pain and weakness, or paralysis of the hind legs. A myelogram—dye-contrast x-rays—will sometimes reveal the origin of the tumor; other times, a CT or MRI scan is required.

Roughly half of spinal tumors arise from the vertebrae. These may be osteosarcomas (see page 383), multiple myelomas (see page 376), or another type of cancer. Bone tumors often can be removed surgically. If it's a cancer that has spread to the vertebra from elsewhere in the body, however, the cancer elsewhere will also require treatment, perhaps with chemotherapy.

Tumors of the tissues surrounding the spinal cord often can be removed

A glossary of the cancer terms used in this chapter appears on page 389.

surgically if they haven't penetrated into the spinal cord. Radiation can be used to treat tumors surrounding the spinal cord that can't be removed completely.

Most tumors that arise from within the spinal cord are not treatable, because to remove or radiate them would severely damage the spinal cord and leave the dog paralyzed.

Although at five your dog may seem young for cancer, spinal tumors are seen most often in middle-aged or younger large-breed dogs. The most common signs are back or neck pain, limping, an unsteady gait, or weakness or paralysis of one or more legs. A disk problem can cause the same symptoms (see page 248).

EYE TUMORS

"I recently noticed that my 14-year-old shepherd mix has a black blotch on the iris of his left eye. My sister, who works for an optometrist, says I should get it checked out to make sure it's not some kind of cancer. Could it be cancer?"

I t's possible, and your sister is right—you should have your vet take a look. Most spots or discolorations on the eye are *not* cancer, but once in a while they can be a melanoma, adenocarcinoma, lymphoma, or other tumor. Tumors can occur within the eye as well as on the surface. Tumors on the surface of the eye may cause eye irritation (redness, itching, or tearing) or no symptoms at all; a tumor within the eye may cause glaucoma, eye irritation, or no symptoms.

Spots and growths on the surface of the eye can be scraped with a scalpel to obtain cells to examine for cancer.

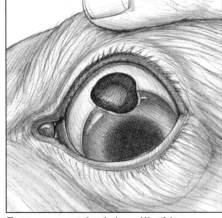

Eye tumors may be obvious, like this one, or small, subtle, and asymptomatic.

Tumors growing inside the eye—which can be seen with an ophthalmoscope after the pupil has been dilated—often are assumed to be malignant without further testing.

Certain tumors on the surface of the eye grow very slowly and don't metastasize. They should be graded by a pathologist and measured, and if they are low-grade and remain the same size, they can often be left alone (see page 209). More aggressive tumors should be removed. Sometimes the tumor alone can be snipped from the surface, and other times the entire eye must be removed. When an eye is removed, there is no pain once the site has healed, and most dogs adapt very well to the loss of vision on one side (see page 214).

A TUMOR BEHIND THE EYE

"A few weeks ago, I noticed that one of my dog's eyes suddenly seemed a little bigger than the other one. Then the eye seemed to bulge out even more, so I took her to the vet. He said my dog has either an abscess or a tumor behind her eye, and we

need to do a biopsy to find out for sure. Is there any other way to find out?"

An infected molar can sometimes cause an abscess behind the eye, as can sharp objects that poke through the roof of the mouth, like a porcupine quill or splinter of wood. A tumor behind the eye can arise from the bones of the skull, the optic nerve, or even a blood-cell cancer like lymphoma.

An abscess will usually be painful, while a tumor usually won't, but for a definitive diagnosis you need a biopsy. A fine-needle aspirate (see page 372) can be obtained either through the roof of the anesthetized dog's mouth or from behind the eye, using an ultrasound probe on the anesthetized eye for guidance. A CT or MRI scan can also show the origin and extent of the abscess or mass.

Most tumors growing behind the eye are aggressive, invasive, and likely to metastasize. Chest x-rays should be checked for signs of metastasis to the lungs. Tumors behind the eye are treated by removing the eye and the tumor. Radiation after surgery may be helpful in killing stray cancer cells and prolonging remission.

TUMORS IN THE NASAL PASSAGES

"My 11-year-old Collie has a bit of a bloody nose. Actually it's more like a runny nose tinged with blood, from just one nostril. The vet wants to anesthetize my dog to look up inside the nose and do a biopsy. Is this really necessary?"

Your dog's age and symptoms do warrant a closer look and a biopsy. Bloody noses are far less common and simple in dogs than they are in people. They can be caused by something stuck in the nasal passages, a fungal infection, a blood-clotting disorder, or a tumor in

SIGNS OF CANCER

When a dog is discovered to have cancer, owners sometimes express remorse or dismay that they didn't somehow "know" their dog had cancer before their veterinarian diagnosed it. But cancer almost never announces its presence loudly and unambiguously. Each organ and body system has a limited vocabulary, so the same outward signs and symptoms can result from a variety of underlying causes: infection, injury, parasite, cancer, and so on. That's why blood tests, x-rays, biop-

sies, and other measures are required to make a definitive diagnosis.

The Q&As in this chapter cite symptoms that *may* accompany specific types of cancer. In addition, cancer can sometimes produce general signs of lethargy, weakness, fever, loss of appetite, or weight loss. None of the symptoms described in this chapter is proof positive of cancer; rather, they are signals for you to call your vet, describe what's going on with your dog, and schedule a physical exam.

the nasal passages. Symptoms of a nasal tumor can include a nosebleed or other nasal discharge, particularly from one nostril only; watery eyes; swelling of the face; and sometimes sneezing, coughing, or difficulty breathing. Your dog's one-sided nasal discharge and his age—at 11, he's a senior citizen for a large-breed dog—heighten the possibility that he could have cancer, so your vet's diagnostic plan makes sense.

Your vet can guide an endoscope—a tiny video camera on a long, flexible tube—through your dog's mouth to the back of the throat and up and back into the nasal passages to find the origin of the bleeding and discharge. The vet may see obvious infection, an object, or a tumor, or the nasal passages may look normal. Tissue samples can be obtained to check for bacteria, fungi, or cancer cells.

Skull x-rays can be used to look for cancer in the nasal passages, but these also require the dog to be under anesthesia, because the x-rays are taken with the dog lying motionless with his mouth open. A nasal tumor will often erode nearby bone, which is visible on x-rays, but since an aggressive fungal infection can do the same thing, a biopsy would still be required to differentiate between those two possibilities.

If a biopsy did reveal cancer, your vet would want to check lymph nodes and chest x-rays to see whether it had spread. Nasal tumors can be treated with surgery plus radiation, or radiation alone. Radiation is necessary because nasal tumors often extend close to the eye or the brain, making surgical removal of every last cancer cell impossible. Approximately 50 percent of dogs with nasal tumors live for a year or more following treatment.

LUNG CANCER

"Dogs don't smoke cigarettes, so how do they get lung cancer?"

People tend to associate lung cancer with smoking, but the disease can strike nonsmokers—both human and canine—as well. Cancer can originate in the lungs, or it can metastasize (spread) to the lungs via the bloodstream from another area of the body, such as a leg bone, the mouth, or the thyroid gland. Metastatic lung cancer is the most common type seen in dogs.

Living in urban areas increases a dog's risk of developing primary lung cancer (the type that originates in the lungs), probably because of exposure to air pollution. Dogs who live with smokers are more likely to get nasal tumors than dogs who live with nonsmokers, presumably because their noses trap many of the carcinogens in cigarette smoke before they reach the lungs.

The most common symptom of a lung tumor is a cough that persists for weeks or months. Oddly, lung cancer can also cause limping because of changes it triggers in the leg bones (see page 251). But about 25 percent of dogs with lung cancer have no symptoms when it is discovered on chest x-rays. There may be one mass or several, large or small, and lymph nodes inside the chest may be enlarged.

When masses and enlarged lymph nodes are seen on chest x-rays, the most likely causes are lung cancer or a fungal lung infection. Those two diseases sometimes can be differentiated by taking a fine-needle aspirate of the mass (see page 372) or examining secretions from the lower trachea or bronchi to look for cancer cells, white blood cells, fungi, or bacteria. Finding fungi and white blood cells makes it likely that the masses are a fungal infection, not cancer; but finding no fungi or cancer cells doesn't rule out cancer, because some cancers don't shed cells into the bronchi.

Surgery is the treatment of choice when cancer is confined to one area of the lung. Metastatic lung cancer can be treated with radiation or chemotherapy. Survival times following treatment range from two months to two years, depending primarily on whether the cancer has spread to lymph nodes or elsewhere in the body before surgery.

MOUTH TUMORS

"My three-year-old dog has a pea-size red growth on her gums. My vet said the growth was probably benign but should be removed anyway. Why?"

An epulis is a tumor that originates from the layer of tissue that lines each tooth socket and holds the tooth in place. Epulides (that's the plural) are technically benign because they don't metastasize, but the most common form of epulis eats away at the underlying bone and over time can cause pain and tooth loss. Any age dog—young or old—can get an epulis. Even though they're benign, epulides should be removed surgically (this may entail removing some of the underlying bone as well) or treated with radiation to prevent future loss of teeth.

Other types of tumors can grow on the gums, lips, tongue, hard palate, or tonsils, usually in middle-aged or older dogs rather than young ones like yours. Symptoms can include bad breath, drooling, bleeding from the mouth, and sometimes difficulty eating. Malignant melanoma is the most common type of oral cancer in dogs, followed by squamous cell carcinoma and fibrosarcoma. Melanomas are sometimes, but not always, black from melanin, the skin pigment they contain; otherwise the tumors look alike and can be positively identified only by biopsy.

Malignant mouth tumors often metastasize quickly to local lymph nodes, the lungs, or other areas of the body, so lymph-node biopsies and chest x-rays should be taken before a treatment plan is made. Surgery plus radiation is the recommended treatment for malignant mouth tumors. Either high-detail skull x-rays or a CT scan is used to plan the extent of surgery. A melanoma vaccine introduced in 2007 has greatly reduced the rate of metastasis and increased survival time in many dogs with this type of cancer. The tumor must first be removed as completely as possible in order for the vaccine to be effective. The vaccine has shown promise in treating malignant melanomas of the nail bed and other areas of the body as well as those in the mouth.

Surgery for a malignant mouth tumor may involve removing large portions of the dog's upper or lower jaw or tongue.

This dog had a large part of his upper jaw removed because of cancer, but he can eat and drink with no trouble.

DIAGNOSING CANCER

One of the cardinal lessons of veterinary medicine is that you can't identify cancer just by looking at it. Cancer is a disease of individual cells, and you can't see cells with the naked eye. Cancer can also spread silently from one site to another, so when a growth is diagnosed as malignant, the rest of the body needs to be scanned for signs of the invader. Here are the tests commonly used to diagnose cancer, and what veterinarians are looking for with each of them.

Biopsy. A biopsy is a sample of a growth or organ that is examined microscopically by a veterinary pathologist to diagnose cancer and other diseases, such as infections. The biopsy sample may be a small snippet of tissue that was removed specifically to obtain a diagnosis, or it may be an entire mass or lymph node that was removed surgically and is checked throughout for cancer cells. If the outer edges, or margins, of a mass contain cancer cells, then another surgery may be required to remove more of the surrounding tissue, or chemotherapy or radiation may be recommended to kill any remaining cancer cells.

❏ **Fine-needle aspiration** (FNA) is a simple type of biopsy in which a needle is inserted into a lump or lymph node and a syringe is used to withdraw a droplet of the contents to be examined for cancer cells.

❏ A **lymph-node biopsy** is the removal and examination of an entire lymph node to check for metastasis (the spread) of cancer from its original site, or for lymphoma (cancer of the lymph nodes).

❏ A **bone-marrow biopsy** is used to check for leukemia and other cancers of the blood cells.

Blood tests. There is no specific "blood test for cancer." Rather, vets use different blood tests to assess the dog's overall health and to look for signs that cancer may be affecting various organs. These signs can include high calcium, low glucose, low red blood cell or platelet counts, low or high white blood cell counts, and high kidney or liver values.

X-rays. Chest x-rays are used to look for primary lung tumors (cancer that originates in the lungs) or lung metastases (the spread of cancer from another site to the lungs). X-rays of bones are used to look for changes characteristic of primary bone cancer or cancer that has spread to bones from another site. Abdominal x-rays will sometimes reveal an obvious tumor or an enlarged spleen, liver, or other abdominal organ, but more often an ultrasound exam, exploratory surgery, or other diagnostic procedure is required to reveal cancer within the abdomen.

Ultrasound exam. An ultrasound exam gives a clearer picture of abdominal structures than x-rays can and is better at finding tumors, swellings, fluid accumulation, and other abnormalities within the abdomen. Ultrasound also can be used to guide biopsies taken with large-diameter needles through the abdominal wall. (A dog is anesthetized briefly for an ultrasound-guided biopsy, so the procedure is not painful.)

Endoscopy. An endoscope is a tiny video camera on a thin, flexible tube that can be inserted into the nasal passages, trachea, esophagus, stomach, or intestines of an anesthetized dog to look for masses, bleeding, and other problems. Biopsies can be obtained through the endoscopy tube.

Exploratory surgery. Cutting a dog open may seem like a drastic way to arrive at a diagnosis, but in certain instances, surgery is the best or only way to find out what is wrong with a dog who's severely ill. Examples include a dog who arrives at a veterinary clinic in shock and is discovered to have blood in his abdomen and a mass on his spleen; or a middle-aged dog who has had persistent vomiting, blood in the vomit, and weight loss, and for whom an ultrasound exam or endoscopy was inconclusive.

Computed tomography (CT) and magnetic resonance imaging (MRI) scans. CT or MRI scans for dogs are available at many veterinary-school and referral hospitals. They are useful for revealing the precise outlines of tumors in areas of the body that are surrounded by bone or air (such as the brain, spinal cord, and lungs), which don't show up well on x-rays or ultrasound.

Dogs adapt surprisingly well to even the more drastic surgeries, learning to eat and drink comfortably despite the loss of part of their jaw or tongue. Owners who fear the surgery will make their dogs look deformed or grotesque often are reassured by looking at before-and-after photos of dogs who have had similar surgeries. A dog will look different after the surgery, to be sure, but once the area has healed, he won't look terrible.

LUMPS ON THE NECK

"When I picked up my 16-year-old Poodle mix from the groomer's, she pointed out some swellings on his neck that had been hidden by the long hair. What could they be?"

The first clue is the exact location of the swellings. Dogs have lymph nodes on the left and right sides of the neck where it meets the lower jaw. Normally you wouldn't see or feel them, but they can enlarge when a dog has an infection, cancer somewhere in the mouth or head, or lymphoma (cancer of the lymph nodes). A swelling near the jaw could also be an infected or cancerous salivary gland. A swelling farther down the neck and in the middle, over the windpipe, could be a thyroid tumor.

Your vet will need to examine your dog, run some blood tests, and possibly do a fine-needle aspirate (FNA) of the swellings to determine exactly what's going on. If the swellings are lymph nodes, an FNA will show whether the enlargement is due to an infection or cancer. Cancer cells in the lymph nodes could be from lymphoma (see the following Q&A) or a nearby tumor.

An enlarged salivary gland is more likely to be caused by a blocked salivary duct or an infection than by cancer. If it is cancer, surgery plus radiation is the recommended treatment.

Thyroid tumors are rare in dogs but common in cats. In cats they are usually benign, but in dogs they are usually malignant. Malignant thyroid tumors metastasize readily and are difficult to remove surgically because they are near—and may even grow into—the jugular veins and carotid arteries. Canine thyroid tumors are treated with surgery, radiation, or chemotherapy depending on the size and invasiveness of the tumor and whether it has metastasized to other sites in the body.

LYMPHOMA, THE "GOOD CANCER"

"My five-year-old Boxer had a lump under his jaw that I thought might be a bee sting. I took him to the vet, who said the lump was actually an enlarged lymph node. She said it was important to do some tests immediately to rule out—or rule in, I suppose—cancer of the lymph nodes. Was she overreacting?"

No, I wouldn't say your vet was overreacting. Lymphoma, or cancer of the lymph nodes, is quite common in dogs. What's more, it progresses rapidly if not treated but often responds very well to chemotherapy, so moving quickly to get a diagnosis is the right thing to do. Because lymphoma in dogs is so treatable, vets sometimes think of it as a "good cancer," comparatively speaking, but early diagnosis and treatment are key.

Lymphoma is a disease of middle-aged dogs, especially large ones. Some researchers feel that Boxers, Bullmastiffs, German Shepherds, Poodles, and Golden Retrievers are predisposed to the disease. Occasionally there is a toxin connection—exposure to the herbicide 2,4-dichlorophenoxyacetic acid (2,4-D) has been associated with an increased risk of lymphoma in dogs *and* people.

There are numerous lymph nodes deep inside the body, as well as some just under the skin. They can enlarge in response to an infection or inflammation (such as an infected tooth or Lyme disease) or because of cancer. When one enlarged lymph node is discovered, the vet checks the size of the other surface lymph nodes as well. She'll take a fine-needle aspirate of any enlarged lymph nodes (see page 372) and draw blood for a complete blood count (CBC) and blood chemistry profile, which can give further clues to whether an infection or cancer is present. High blood calcium levels are often seen in lymphoma.

The pathology report may say that the cells from the fine-needle aspirate look normal. Alternatively, the report may say that the cells are suspicious of cancer or that the diagnosis is not clear. If the initial diagnosis is "bad" or "uncertain," the next step is to remove an entire enlarged lymph node (this requires the dog to be put under general anesthesia) and send it to a pathologist for a complete biopsy. It's possible to miss the cancer when drawing a few cells from a lymph node with a needle and syringe, but much less likely when examining the entire node.

If the diagnosis is lymphoma, then the vet assesses the severity of the disease by surveying internal lymph nodes, the liver and spleen, and the bone marrow for signs of cancer. Chest x-rays, an ultrasound exam of the abdomen, and a bone marrow biopsy are used to determine whether the lymphoma has spread. Lymphoma that is localized to one or a

IS IT A LYMPH NODE?

You've undoubtedly discovered lumps or bumps on your dog before when petting or grooming him. If you ever notice a lump in a spot where there's a lymph node, it's wise to have your vet check it out right away.

The illustration shows the location of the lymph nodes that are closest to the skin. Normal lymph nodes are roughly bean-shaped, ½ to 1 inch long, and a bit squishy. They are under the skin, not attached to it, so you can push the skin back and forth without moving the lymph node.

With practice, you can feel the lymph nodes under your dog's jaw where it meets his neck, and behind his knees (the joint in the hind leg that points forward, like your own knee). The left and right lymph nodes should be about the same size, and an inch long or less.

The other lymph nodes pictured—in front of the shoulder blades, behind the front legs, and in front of the hind legs—usually can't be felt easily. If you notice a lump in one of those areas, show it to your vet.

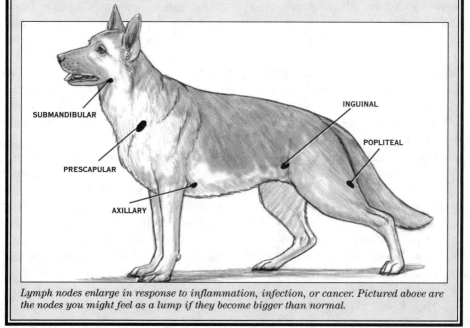

SUBMANDIBULAR

PRESCAPULAR

AXILLARY

INGUINAL

POPLITEAL

Lymph nodes enlarge in response to inflammation, infection, or cancer. Pictured above are the nodes you might feel as a lump if they become bigger than normal.

few lymph nodes has a better prognosis for longer-lasting remission than does lymphoma that has spread to the liver, spleen, or bone marrow.

The treatment for lymphoma is chemotherapy, usually using three or more different chemotherapy drugs in rotation. Chemotherapy is given once a week for 10 weeks; then every two or three weeks for two to four months; and then every other month for a year. Although many dog owners dread the thought of chemotherapy, in dogs the side effects are much milder than they are in people, and most dogs tolerate chemotherapy very well (see page 378). With multi-agent chemotherapy, approximately 75 percent of dogs with lymphoma go into complete remission for six months or more. Dogs that come out of remission can sometimes be put back into remission by a second round of chemotherapy.

DOGS AND LEUKEMIA

"When my five-year-old Lab mix lost her appetite and started limping, I took her to the vet. I was shocked when tests showed that she has leukemia. Can you tell me more about the prognosis?"

Leukemia is cancer of the blood cells, and dogs can get several different types. The most important distinction among these types is whether they are acute or chronic. In acute leukemia, the bone marrow contains many highly abnormal cancer cells, and the blood is deficient in normal cells. In chronic leukemia, the bone marrow contains some cancer cells, but those cells are more normal than those seen in acute leukemia and may even function the way they're supposed to. A dog with chronic leukemia may have normal numbers of the other blood cells.

The type of leukemia is diagnosed by blood tests and a bone-marrow biopsy. Your vet can tell you whether your dog's leukemia is acute or chronic. The two vary significantly in prognosis—dogs with acute leukemia may live for only days to weeks, while those with chronic leukemia may live for months to a year or more.

The outward signs of leukemia are vague at best. Acute leukemia can cause a loss of appetite, weight loss, fatigue, and limping (the changes in the bone marrow may be painful). On physical exam, the vet may notice an enlarged liver and spleen. Blood tests often show deficiencies in red blood cells (anemia) or platelets. White blood cell counts can be low, high, or normal, and cancer cells may be seen in the blood as well as the bone marrow. Acute leukemia can be treated with chemotherapy, but the prognosis for long-term survival is poor.

Chronic leukemia is primarily a disease of older dogs. Often there are no symptoms, and it is discovered because of higher-than-normal white blood cell counts on a routine blood test. Occasionally, however, a dog with chronic leukemia will show the same symptoms as one with acute leukemia— loss of appetite, weight loss, fatigue, or lameness. On physical exam, the vet may notice an enlarged liver and spleen. Red blood cell and platelet counts are usually normal.

The prognosis for chronic leukemia is good. The cancer cells don't usually take over the bone marrow completely, so enough normal cells are produced to fight infection, carry oxygen, and aid in blood clotting. Dogs who have symptoms are treated with chemotherapy, and those with no symptoms may be monitored with blood tests every two or three months and treated only if symptoms appear. Survival times generally range from months to years.

MULTIPLE MYELOMA

"Over a couple of months, my nine-year-old dog became weaker and weaker, until he couldn't climb the

stairs anymore. I thought it was arthritis or a back problem, but the vet discovered that it's a cancer affecting both the blood and the bones. What's the best treatment?"

Multiple myeloma is the cancer you're describing. Cancerous white blood cells take over the bone marrow, activate cells that break down normal bone (leading to pain and sometimes bone fractures), and clog the bloodstream with a flood of unneeded antibodies. Multiple myeloma can be treated with chemotherapy, but the odds of achieving remission are only about 50-50. When remission does occur, however, it can last for a year or more.

Whether to treat multiple myeloma with chemotherapy, simply try to make the dog more comfortable, or euthanize him to avoid further pain and suffering is a difficult choice, one that depends a great deal on your dog's exact symptoms and situation. For that reason, it's wise to consult with a cancer specialist as soon as possible to help you make your decision. Your regular vet can refer you to a cancer specialist in your area.

The symptoms of multiple myeloma, like those of so many cancers, are vague. Often owners will notice, as you did, that their dog seems weak. The dog may even become partially paralyzed if a weakened bone in the spine breaks. What vets discover when they test dogs with multiple myeloma is shortages of red blood cells, platelets, and normal white blood cells, caused by the cancer crowding out normal cells from the bone marrow. X-rays usually show weakened or "moth-eaten" bones in one or more areas of the body. Often there will be high levels of calcium in the blood as well, from the breakdown of bone. Special tests on the

blood and urine can confirm the presence of a surge in one type of antibody produced by a set of white blood cells gone haywire. Infections, bleeding problems, and kidney disease are common complications.

Older, purebred dogs are the ones that get multiple myeloma most commonly. If owners decide against chemotherapy or euthanasia, then antibiotics, IV fluids, and painkillers can be used to make the dog more comfortable.

ANAL-GLAND TUMORS

"The groomer said she felt a lump when she emptied our 12-year-old Poodle's anal glands and suggested we have our vet check it out. The vet suspects a tumor, and he's running tests. Could it be cancer?"

Your dog is probably having an abdominal ultrasound exam, blood tests, and a urinalysis to check for spread of the tumor. Adenocarcinomas—the most common type of anal-gland tumor—are highly metastatic and can spread to lymph nodes early in the course of the disease. In addition, they often secrete a substance that increases blood calcium, and elevated blood calcium can damage the kidneys if it persists for weeks to months.

The primary treatment for anal-gland tumors is surgical removal. The surgery can be difficult because the tumors can be quite large, and nerves and muscles in the area must be preserved so the dog can maintain control over her bladder and bowels. If your dog has enlarged lymph nodes or elevated blood calcium, the nodes should also be removed, and chemotherapy or radiation may be recommended after surgery. The average

(continued on page 380)

TREATING CANCER

Different cancers respond best to different treatments. Before a treatment plan can be made for an individual dog, the cancer must be precisely identified, usually through a biopsy; the extent and possible spread of the cancer must be evaluated, often through x-rays and lymph node or bone marrow biopsies; and the dog's general health and ability to tolerate the proposed treatment must be assessed via a thorough physical exam, blood tests, and sometimes an electrocardiogram (EKG) or ultrasound exam of the heart.

The Q&As in this chapter discuss specific types of cancer and the treatments most often recommended for each type. Here is an explanation of those treatments, the principles behind them, and their potential side effects.

SURGERY

Cancer that consists of a single tumor or is restricted to a small area of the body can often be removed surgically. The main drawback of surgery as a treatment for cancer is that you can't be certain it will remove every single cancer cell from the dog's body, so there's a possibility that the cancer could recur in the future. Chemotherapy or radiation are sometimes used after surgery to kill any remaining cancer cells and reduce the risk of recurrence. *Potential adverse side effects:* Bleeding or anesthetic complications during surgery; postsurgical infection; postsurgical pain; possible loss of function of affected areas. Postsurgical pain can be treated safely and effectively and

need not be considered a deterrent to surgery. The risk of the other complications is low with most surgeries and can be estimated more precisely for a specific dog and procedure by the veterinary surgeon.

CHEMOTHERAPY

Chemotherapy uses drugs to kill or damage rapidly dividing cells. It is used to treat blood-cell cancers, such as lymphoma and leukemia, and cancers that have metastasized or are highly aggressive and likely to metastasize. These drugs may be given orally or intravenously, or injected directly into the tumor. Cancer cells can develop resistance to individual chemotherapy drugs, so often several different drugs are used in rotation. Chemotherapy usually lasts for six to twelve weeks. Intravenous chemotherapy drugs are given in the hospital anywhere from once every three weeks to twice a week, depending on the drug and the cancer being treated. Oral chemotherapy drugs are given at home once or twice a day. *Potential adverse side effects:* Bone-marrow suppression leading to reduced numbers of white blood cells and a risk of infection; nausea, vomiting, or diarrhea; severe chemical burns if IV chemotherapy drugs leak from the vein into surrounding tissues. (Individual chemotherapy agents may have other, specific side effects, which your veterinarian will explain.) Bone-marrow suppression is monitored by running blood tests periodically while a dog is undergoing chemotherapy. If white blood cell levels drop low enough to create a risk of serious infection, chemotherapy is halted for a week or two to allow the bone marrow to catch up in cell production. Antibiotics also can be given to combat infection. Dogs undergoing chemotherapy usually don't develop the severe nausea and vomiting that people sometimes do, but anti-nausea drugs and stomach protectants are given if needed. Dogs rarely lose their hair as a result of chemotherapy.

RADIATION

Radiation kills cancer cells by bombarding them with atomic particles. It is often used to shrink or destroy tumors that are too extensive or inaccessible for surgery, such as tumors of the mouth and throat, nasal passages, or brain. Radiation treatments are given two to five times a week for three to six weeks. Dogs receive a short-acting anesthetic before each treatment to ensure that they don't move once the radiation beam has been precisely aimed at the tumor. *Potential adverse side effects:* Burnlike injuries to normal tissues overlying the tumor; temporary hair loss in the area radiated; mouth pain, drooling, difficulty eating, and loss of appetite when the mouth or throat are radiated. Radiation "burns" are cleaned and protected with a bandage or ointment and usually heal well within a couple of weeks. Mouth pain, drooling, and loss of appetite are treated with mouth rinses and pain relievers; a feeding tube can be placed in the stomach before radiation treatment begins if the dog is likely to have difficulty eating. Mouth irritation usually heals within a couple of weeks after radiation treatment is completed.

CRYOTHERAPY AND HYPERTHERMIA

Freezing (cryotherapy) or heating (hyperthermia) can sometimes be used to kill small (less than $\frac{1}{3}$ inch in diameter) benign or malignant tumors on the surface of the body. Potential advantages of cryotherapy and hyperthermia over surgery are that they are fast and require only local anesthesia. The main drawback is they will not kill cancer cells that have spread beyond the small area frozen or heated. Chemotherapy or radiation is sometimes used afterward to kill stray cancer cells. *Potential adverse side effects:* Cryotherapy and hyperthermia leave a wound about double the size of the original tumor that scabs over and heals, with basic wound care (cleaning and ointment or a bandage), within about two weeks. The hair in that area may grow back a different color or texture than it was originally.

IMMUNE-SYSTEM MODULATORS

A dog's own white blood cells will attack and kill cancer cells—*if* they find them and recognize them as a threat. Immune-system modulators are substances given orally or by injection that rev up the immune system and help it to recognize and target cancer cells. The main drawback is that a dog's immune system is unlikely to be able to kill every tumor cell in a cancer that has already gotten a head start. Therefore, immune-system modulators are most often combined with other cancer treatments such as surgery, chemotherapy, or radiation. *Potential adverse side effects:* These vary with the specific modulator. Some have no adverse side effects.

(continued from page 377)

survival time after surgery for dogs with enlarged lymph nodes or elevated blood calcium is about six months, or only half as long as the survival time of dogs with no obvious signs the tumor has spread.

Anal-gland adenocarcinoma is relatively common among older female dogs. For that reason, all dogs over the age of eight or so should have a rectal exam as part of their annual physical.

A BLEEDING TUMOR

"I adopted an older dog—a shepherd mix—from a shelter. After I'd had him for about a year, his belly started to get big and he began to slow down a little, but I thought it was just his age. Then he collapsed while we were out on a walk. I rushed him to the vet, and they discovered that he had a tumor on his spleen, but he died before they could get him to surgery. Is there anything else we could have done for him?"

From your description, it sounds as if your dog may have had hemangiosarcoma. These tumors are difficult to detect in early stages and difficult to treat, so even if you had known that your dog had it a few weeks before, the outcome, sadly, might have been the same.

A hemangiosarcoma is a malignant tumor that develops from the endothelium, or lining of blood vessels. The spleen is the most common site for a hemangiosarcoma, followed by the right atrium of the heart (see page 270). Because hemangiosarcomas are so intimately connected with blood vessels, and because they often rupture, they spread easily to the liver, other abdominal organs, and the lungs. This rapid spread is what makes them so difficult to treat.

Often there are no outward signs that a dog has a hemangiosarcoma. Your dog's enlarged abdomen may have been caused by the tumor on the spleen, another tumor on the liver, or bleeding from the tumor into the abdomen. However, an enlarged abdomen in an older dog can also be caused by Cushing's disease, congestive heart failure, or—as you probably assumed—weight gain, so it was not an obvious signal.

A vet may happen upon a tumor of the spleen in an otherwise healthy-seeming dog in one of two ways. If the tumor is fairly large—say a couple of inches in diameter—or particularly lumpy, the vet may be able to feel it within the abdomen. Feeling something strange in the area of the spleen (or anywhere else in the abdomen, for that matter) would lead the vet to take x-rays or do an ultrasound scan of the abdomen to see what the lump looked like and what organ it was attached to.

The second clue that a dog might have a hemangiosarcoma is anemia and misshapen red blood cells on a complete blood count (CBC). Dogs with a hemangiosarcoma of the spleen often become anemic because the tumor swells with blood or leaks blood into the abdomen. The tumor can also prevent the spleen from removing misshapen and broken blood cells from the circulation as it would normally, so those cells might turn up in a blood test.

Often, however, there are no obvious signs that a dog has a hemangiosarcoma until the tumor suddenly ruptures and fills the abdomen with blood. Then the dog collapses, as yours did, and goes into shock. Sometimes it's possible to rush a dog to surgery, remove the tumor, and stop the bleeding, but even then the dog often dies within weeks to months because the hemangiosarcoma had already spread elsewhere in the body. To date, chemotherapy has not been effective in prolonging the survival of dogs with hemangiosarcoma.

A lump in the spleen isn't always a hemangiosarcoma. It can be a hematoma (an area of pooled blood, like a bruise), scar tissue, or a pocket of actively growing normal cells. However, between one-third and two-thirds of lumps in the spleen *are* malignant tumors, and most of those are hemangiosarcomas. A biopsy is required to determine whether a lump is benign or malignant.

LIVER SPOTS

"My 12-year-old retriever mix had lost her appetite, and blood tests showed her liver enzymes were elevated. An ultrasound exam of her abdomen showed some 'spots' on her liver, and we're waiting for the biopsy results. Could this be anything other than cancer?"

Yes. Most liver abnormalities are *not* cancer, but it's difficult to know for sure based on symptoms, blood tests, or even the liver's overall appearance on ultrasound. The biopsy results should reveal the cause.

Those "spots" on your dog's ultrasound were areas that looked either darker or lighter than the surrounding tissue. They could be fluid-filled cysts, scar tissue, blood clots, or pockets of infection, or they could be cancer.

Liver cancer usually affects older dogs. A dog with liver cancer may have vague symptoms, such as loss of energy, loss of appetite, excessive thirst and urination, or vomiting, or she may have no symptoms at all. Liver cancer can be a single, often large tumor, or multiple smaller tumors. It often spreads to lymph nodes and other abdominal organs.

A single liver tumor that hasn't metastasized can be removed surgically, and survival times average about one year. Multiple liver tumors or liver cancer that has spread elsewhere in the body does not respond well to chemotherapy and has a poor prognosis.

NUTRITION AND CANCER

"I'm skeptical of many aspects of holistic medicine, but I am intrigued by the idea of cancer-fighting foods. Is there mainstream support for adding antioxidants and so forth to the diet of dogs with cancer?"

Yes. Vets often recommend that dogs who have cancer eat a diet that's higher in fat, lower in carbohydrates, and higher in high-quality, readily available proteins, and that they take antioxidant supplements (such as vitamins A, C, and E and selenium) and omega-3 fatty acids as well.

Many cancer cells need glucose—derived from carbohydrates—for energy and are unable to use fat, so a diet that is lower in carbohydrates and higher in fat will "starve the cancer and feed the dog." High-quality proteins help the body rebuild cells destroyed by cancer and prevent the breakdown of body muscle for its amino acids. Antioxidants support the body's repair mechanisms.

Overdoses of vitamin A can cause painful bone changes, and overdoses of the other antioxidants can cause vomiting, diarrhea, and loss of appetite, so don't exceed the following doses: vitamin A, 625 IU per pound of the dog's body weight per day; vitamin C, 25 milligrams per pound of the dog's body weight per day; vitamin E, 10 IU per pound of the dog's body weight per day; selenium, 2 micrograms per pound of the dog's body weight per day.

SKIN CANCER

"My 10-year-old hound mix recently got a couple of dime-size sores on his belly, and the vet wants to biopsy them to check for cancer. The sores don't look like much of anything to me—could they really be cancer? And if they are, could my dog's fondness for lying in the sun have caused them?"

Dogs get all kinds of lumps, bumps, and sores on their skin, and most are not cancerous, but the only way to know for sure is to do a biopsy. Skin cancer in dogs, especially in the early stages, often *doesn't* "look like much of anything." Your vet may indeed be concerned about these sores because your dog likes to sunbathe—sunlight can trigger some forms of skin cancer in dogs, particularly in areas of the body that are light-colored and don't have much fur, such as the belly. (To reduce the risk of skin cancer, you can rub a baby-safe sunscreen onto thinly haired areas of your dog's skin, and limit his sunbathing time.)

Dogs can get many different forms of skin cancer. Here's what is known about the behavior and treatment of the more common types:

Squamous cell carcinoma (SCC). SCCs can look like sores or lumps. They can be caused by overexposure to the sun. They usually don't metastasize and can be treated by surgical removal, chemotherapy ointments, or cryotherapy. SCCs of the nose, mouth, or nail bed are more problematic. An SCC on the nose can spread rapidly and be extremely difficult to remove. SCCs in the mouth often metastasize and can also be difficult to remove. An SCC of the nail bed may cause nail or toe pain, sores around the base of the nail, or limping. This type of SCC destroys bone and is best treated by amputating the affected toe. Black large-breed dogs, such as Giant Schnauzers and Standard Poodles, are more likely than other dogs to get nail-bed SCCs.

Melanoma. Melanomas range from small black spots to large lumps or bumps. They may be smooth or rough, have hair growing on them or not, and have sores on them or not. They can be any color from light gray to brown to black. Most melanomas in dogs grow slowly and are unlikely to metastasize, except for those in the mouth and on the feet, which often metastasize quickly to lymph nodes and the lungs. They are treated by surgical removal.

Cutaneous hemangiosarcoma. In a hemangiosarcoma, the cells that normally line the inside of blood vessels become cancerous and form a tumor. Most hemangiosarcomas are found on the heart or spleen. They can also form cutaneous (skin) tumors, which are often soft or spongy, rapidly spreading masses that may bleed. These tumors may be metastases from hemangiosarcomas in other areas of the body, or they may occur on their own. A cutaneous hemangiosarcoma that occurs on its own can be removed surgically. Cutaneous hemangiosarcomas can be triggered by sunlight.

Fibrosarcoma. This is a soft-tissue tumor that can occur anywhere in the body, including the skin. Fibrosarcomas quickly infiltrate the surrounding tissue and send out branching tendrils of cancer cells. A fibrosarcoma is usually a single lump, large or small, often with an irregular or bumpy surface. The lump may have sores on it. The best treatment is surgical removal as soon as the fibrosarcoma is discovered. The surgeon must also remove apparently normal tissue from at least 1 inch around and below the tumor to capture the microscopic tendrils of cancer cells. Radiation of the area may be recommended after surgery to kill any remaining cancer cells.

Mast-cell tumor. Mast cells are a type of white blood cell. Mast-cell tumors (MCTs) are usually found on the skin, but they can metastasize to lymph nodes, bone marrow, and other organs. They are more common in Boxers, Pit Bulls, and Boston Terriers than in other types of dogs. An MCT can look like almost anything—a single lump or multiple lumps, large or small, with or without hair or associated irritation and bleeding. They will often grow and then shrink again within days when the mast cells release histamine, a sub-

stance that causes inflammation and swelling. An MCT that is low-grade and hasn't spread beyond the skin can be removed surgically, sometimes followed by radiation. MCTs that are high-grade or have metastasized are extremely difficult to eradicate. Corticosteroids, radiation, histamine blockers, and antihistamines can be used to keep dogs with such tumors comfortable.

Cutaneous lymphoma. Like a mast-cell tumor (above), lymphoma is a cancer of white blood cells. It usually affects lymph nodes, the bone marrow, or internal organs, but it can also appear on the skin. Cutaneous (skin) lymphoma can look like bumps, sores, or even a skin infection and is often itchy. Its behavior is extremely variable—a single mass can sometimes be cured by surgical removal or radiation, but other times the mass recurs or has already metastasized elsewhere in the body. For that reason, chemotherapy is often recommended as part of the treatment.

BONE CANCER

"I recently adopted a four-year-old dog from a Great Dane rescue organization, and the dog's foster owner told me the breed has a higher than average risk of bone cancer. What should I be watching for?"

The most common type of bone cancer, osteosarcoma, is seen mainly in large- and giant-breed dogs such as Great Danes, Saint Bernards, and Doberman Pinschers. They can get osteosarcoma in late adolescence (one or two years old), but it occurs more frequently in middle-aged or older dogs.

Osteosarcoma usually targets a leg bone, so limping, leg pain, or a firm

Most dogs who need to have a leg amputated adapt beautifully.

swelling of a leg bone are the most likely symptoms. Of course, several other diseases or injuries—including Lyme disease, panosteitis, and a torn knee ligament—can cause similar signs, so dog owners shouldn't leap to conclusions about their limping large-breed dogs. (See page 232 for how to assess a limping dog at home.) Osteosarcoma often has a distinctive appearance on x-rays, and the bone can be biopsied to confirm the diagnosis.

Osteosarcoma is a very aggressive cancer, destroying the bone in which it appears and metastasizing quickly to the lungs, and it is often extremely painful as it progresses. Amputation of the affected leg is the standard treatment for osteosarcoma. Dog owners often are apprehensive about such drastic surgery, but in fact most dogs adapt extremely well to getting around on three legs. Thankfully, dogs don't suffer from self-pity or self-consciousness, so their altered appearance doesn't bother them, and they are no longer in pain from the tumor.

Osteosarcoma metastasizes early on, and even amputation can't be considered a complete cure because cancer cells can still form lung tumors weeks or months later. The average survival time of dogs with osteosarcoma following amputation is six months. Chemotherapy after the amputation increases the average survival time to one year, and 20 percent of dogs who undergo chemotherapy after amputation live for two years or longer.

In some instances, limb-sparing surgery can be done as an alternative to amputation: just the obvious bone tumor is removed, and a bone graft and bone plate are implanted to fill in for the missing bone. Chemotherapy is required before surgery, after surgery, or both, and bone infection is a potential complication. The average survival time is about the same as for amputation plus chemotherapy: one year.

Although limb-sparing surgery may sound more appealing than amputation, amputation provides better pain relief and carries a much lower risk of infection, so I encourage dog owners facing that choice to consider both options carefully. A veterinary orthopedic surgeon can show you videos of how well dogs with three legs can get around, and put you in touch with other people whose dogs have had each type of surgery, to help you decide what's best for your dog.

BREAST CANCER

"Do dogs get breast cancer? How is it treated?"

Yes, dogs get breast cancer—in fact, it's the most common type of cancer in female dogs. (Breast cancer also occurs in male dogs, but rarely.) Poodles, terriers, Cocker Spaniels, and German Shepherds have a higher than average incidence of breast cancer.

But breast cancer can be largely prevented by spaying a dog before her first or second heat. (A dog's first heat usually occurs when she is between six months and one year old, and most dogs come into heat twice a year.) Twenty-six percent of dogs that are spayed after their second heat or not spayed at all will develop breast tumors. Spaying a dog before her first heat reduces her risk of developing breast tumors to 0.5 percent, and spaying a dog between her first and second heat reduces her risk to 8 percent.

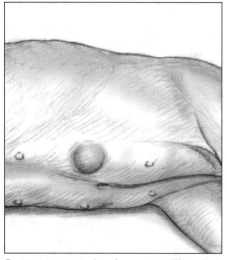

Breast tumors can be a lump or swelling of any size. They occur most often in females who were spayed late or not at all.

Most dogs have five pairs of mammary glands, and breast tumors can take the form of small lumps or large swellings in one or more of these glands. A dog with breast cancer will sometimes produce milk because of hormones secreted by the tumor. About 50 percent of canine breast tumors are benign, and 50 percent are malignant.

The mammary glands on either side are connected by blood and lymph vessels, so malignant tumors can spread from one mammary gland to others or metastasize to lymph nodes or the lungs. Chest x-rays are taken to look for lung metastases, and enlarged lymph nodes can be checked with fine-needle aspiration (FNA) or surgical biopsy. The breast tumor is removed and biopsied via a lumpectomy or mastectomy.

Survival times for breast cancer depend on the stage and grade of the tumor, how large it is, and how long it's been there. High-grade breast tumors are likely to recur; small, low-grade tumors often can be cured by surgical removal.

Spaying a dog who has been diagnosed with breast cancer lowers the risk of recurrence, by reducing estrogen levels.

STOMACH AND INTESTINAL CANCER

"My 12-year-old Pug has been unable to hold down solid food for a month— he vomits if he eats anything besides liquids. X-rays of his abdomen looked normal. Could it be cancer?"

Sudden, severe, and persistent vomiting in an older dog raises concerns of pancreatitis, liver or kidney disease, something blocking the stomach or upper part of the small intestine, or stomach cancer. Your vet has undoubtedly ruled out pancreatic, liver, and kidney disease with blood tests. To look further for a blockage or cancer, I'd recommend a thorough ultrasound exam of your dog's abdomen and an endoscopic exam and biopsies of the stomach and small intestine.

The most common symptoms of stomach cancer are vomiting, weight loss, and loss of appetite; some dogs with stomach cancer will have blood in the vomit. It's primarily a disease of older male dogs—the average age of dogs with stomach cancer is 10, and for unknown reasons males are two or three times as likely as females to get it.

Cancer often penetrates large portions of the stomach wall and metastasizes rapidly to other sites in the body, making it difficult to treat effectively. Smaller, more localized stomach tumors can be removed surgically.

Cancer in the upper part of the small intestine can also cause vomiting. Tumors in the lower part of the small intestine and the colon most often cause diarrhea

MALE AND FEMALE CANCERS

Most cancers of the reproductive tract are preventable by spaying and neutering. Spaying removes the ovaries and uterus, neutering removes the testicles, and what a dog doesn't have can't become cancerous. Except as noted, the reproductive-tract cancers listed below affect only unspayed or unneutered dogs.

KIND OF CANCER	SYMPTOMS	AGE OF DOGS AFFECTED	TREATMENT AND PROGNOSIS
Ovarian	Vaginal bleeding; frequent heats (more than twice a year); or uterine infection.	Older (average age 10).	Surgical removal; prognosis is good if cancer has not metastasized, poor if it has.
Uterine	None; or an enlarged abdomen.	Middle-aged to older.	Surgical removal; prognosis is good if cancer has not metastasized, poor if it has.
Vaginal	A swelling or mass protruding from the vulva; bleeding; occasionally, straining to urinate or defecate.	Middle-aged to older.	Transmissible venereal tumors (see next entry) respond well to chemotherapy; other types are removed surgically; prognosis is good.

and weight loss. Intestinal tumors can sometimes be felt by the veterinarian during a physical exam, or they may show up on x-rays or ultrasound. Some intestinal tumors can be removed surgically, but often they have metastasized to lymph nodes or elsewhere in the body, which reduces the dog's survival time.

CANCER OF THE BLADDER AND URETHRA

"My 10-year-old Scottish Terrier had three or four urinary tract infections in one year. Each time they would clear up on antibiotics, then come back. Recently he had an ultrasound exam, which showed what appears to be a tumor in the wall of his bladder. Were his symptoms typical?"

Recurrent urinary tract infections (UTIs) are the most commonly observed symptom of bladder or urethral cancer. But recurrent UTIs can have other causes as well, such as urinary stones, a birth defect, or diabetes (see page 330). Beagles, Scotties, Shetland Sheepdogs, Collies, and Airedales are at higher risk for developing cancer of the

KIND OF CANCER	SYMPTOMS	AGE OF DOGS AFFECTED	TREATMENT AND PROGNOSIS
Transmissible venereal tumor (TVT)	Single or multiple masses or swellings of the vulva, vagina, or penis.	Young and sexually active.	Can usually be cured by chemotherapy.
Testicular	Often none; or an enlarged or shrunken testicle or enlarged prostate. Estrogen-secreting testicular tumors can make a dog sexually attractive to other males and cause hair loss on the body.	Older (average age 9 to 11) for cancer in a descended testicle; can be much younger for an undescended testicle (see page 346).	Surgical removal of both testicles; prognosis is excellent if cancer hasn't metastasized, poor if it has.
Prostate	Straining to defecate; pain on defecation; dribbling urine; bloody urine.	Older (average age 10). Can occur in neutered as well as intact male dogs, because the prostate isn't removed during neutering.	Possibly radiation or chemotherapy; prognosis is very poor because prostate cancer metastasizes rapidly (see page 346).

bladder or urethra. Tumors of the urinary tract are often multiple—occurring, for example, in both the bladder and the urethra—so the entire urinary tract should be checked carefully via ultrasound before treatment is begun. Urinary tract cancers can also metastasize to lymph nodes and other sites in the body.

Some urinary tract tumors can be removed surgically, but other times such surgery would leave a dog incontinent. Radiation or chemotherapy sometimes can be used to relieve symptoms and prolong the comfortable lifespan of a dog with bladder or urethral cancer.

SHOULD WE TREAT HER OR LET HER GO?

"My dog was just diagnosed with cancer. My vet has told me about treatment options, but I don't know if it's fair to put my dog through all that just to prolong her life for six months or a year. And if I choose not to treat the cancer, should I put my dog to sleep now to spare her any suffering?"

Treating certain kinds of cancer may extend a dog's life only months, it's true. The decision about whether to treat is individual and personal and depends on the specifics of your dog's illness. Basically, you have three broad options: do whatever it takes to get your dog's cancer into remission; relieve as much of the pain or disability associated with the cancer as possible without attempting to put it into remission; or euthanize your dog relatively early in the course of the disease, before her quality of life deteriorates.

Consider scheduling a visit with a veterinary oncologist to discuss your situation. A veterinary oncologist can give you detailed information about treatment and life expectancy for your dog, which will help you decide what to do. (Your regular vet can refer you to an oncologist in your area.) Here are some questions to ask yourself and the vet:

❑ Which treatment has the best likelihood of putting this cancer into remission?

❑ What's the average survival time of dogs who undergo this treatment? Do the specifics of your dog's situation—the stage and grade of her cancer, her age, her overall health—suggest that her survival time might be shorter or longer than that average?

❑ How much would the treatment cost? Cancer treatment can be very expensive, so be realistic: figure out up-front whether you can afford an all-out battle against the cancer. If you carry pet health insurance, be sure to find out

exactly how much the insurance company will cover. Do your best to weigh the cost of treatment with the benefits. And whatever decision you make, don't be hard on yourself for considering the cost of treatment—money is a fact of life for everyone.

❑ What would the treatment schedule be? Chemotherapy or radiation can require multiple visits to the vet's office over several weeks. Can you take that time away from work?

❑ What side effects are expected with the treatment? In many cases, the side effects are milder than dog owners expect.

❑ If you choose *not* to treat the cancer aggressively, how long is your dog likely to live? What symptoms and discomforts is she likely to experience during that time? Can those symptoms and discomforts be relieved by pain medication or other measures?

❑ Is your dog relatively happy and comfortable now, or is she in pain? Is she able to eat, go for walks, sleep, and enjoy your company? Whether a dog is well enough to enjoy her routine canine pleasures is a good measure of whether she's suffering (see page 393).

❑ Do you feel that you need to do everything possible to extend your dog's life before you can accept letting her go?

❑ If you decide not to treat your dog's cancer aggressively, will you later regret not having had the extra time with her?

DEFINING CANCER TERMS

Medical terminology is immensely useful for doctors, who can use it to precisely describe conditions to one another, but it can be confusing to the layperson. Here is a glossary of the cancer terms used in this chapter.

BENIGN: Not malignant; in other words, not cancer.

CANCER: An uncontrolled growth of abnormal cells.

GRADE: How abnormal or aggressive a cancer is, as determined by biopsy. The grade is often a number from 1 to 5, with 1 being the "best," or least abnormal, and 5 being the "worst," but other grading schemes are sometimes used, so ask your vet to explain what the grade of a particular cancer means. The grade of a malignancy, along with its stage (see below), determines what treatment is best and gives a general idea of the dog's prognosis.

INVASIVE: A cancer that spreads outward from its point of origin into adjacent tissues.

LYMPH NODES: Small lumps of tissue containing white blood cells that are found along the lymphatic system, a network of fluid-filled vessels that's separate from the veins and arteries. Cells from a malignant tumor often enter the lymphatic system, so the lymph nodes closest to the tumor—plus any lymph nodes elsewhere that are enlarged—are often biopsied to see whether the cancer has spread.

MALIGNANT: Cancerous.

MASS: A growth or tumor. A mass can be benign or malignant.

METASTASIZE: To spread from one site in the body to a distant site, usually via the bloodstream or the lymphatic system.

NEOPLASIA: Cancer.

ONCOLOGIST: A doctor who specializes in treating cancer.

PATHOLOGIST: A doctor who specializes in examining biopsies, blood, urine, and other tissue samples to diagnose diseases.

PROGNOSIS: The likelihood that a dog's cancer can be treated successfully; a dog's "prognosis without treatment" is how long he is likely to live if the cancer is not treated.

RECURRENCE: A cancer that was once in remission but has now returned.

REMISSION: The disappearance of detectable cancer. "Remission" is used rather than "cure" in discussing cancer because if even one cancer cell remains in a dog's body, it is possible for the cancer to recur in the future.

STAGE: The site of a cancerous tumor and whether it has spread (metastasized) to other sites in the body. The stage may be given in letters, numbers, or a combination of the two.

TUMOR: A mass or growth. A tumor can be benign or malignant; a "fatty tumor" (lipoma) is one common example of a benign tumor.

CHAPTER 17

When the End Is Near

THE AVERAGE LIFE SPAN OF A DOG is much shorter than that of a person, making the death of a canine companion an experience most dog owners will have to face one day. The circumstances of the loss can vary widely. A dog may die suddenly, leaving the owner shocked as well as grief-stricken, or he may have been seriously ill for some time. In some instances, owners are faced with the difficult responsibility of deciding whether to end a beloved pet's suffering through euthanasia. Friends may not know how to respond to someone whose dog has died, and children may need extra care and comforting. This chapter provides practical advice and support to people whose dogs are elderly or terminally ill, as well as to those whose dogs have died.

WHEN YOUR DOG IS VERY ILL

"We are waiting for test results, but the prognosis for my dog is not good. What questions should I ask my vet once the diagnosis has been confirmed? I love my dog and don't want him to suffer."

I'm sorry to hear your dog is ill. You're wise to gather your thoughts before talking to the vet about the test results. It's good to write down your questions beforehand, and also take notes on what the vet tells you so you can refer back to them later. Having a calm and practical friend or relative along during face-to-face meetings or listening in on phone conversations also helps some people think of questions and remember details of what's discussed.

While you are waiting for news, treat your dog with your usual loving care. Dogs don't worry about their health, but they can become anxious if the people around them are acting strangely. So do your best to be your normal self around your dog, and don't lose hope.

When you talk to your vet about the diagnosis, you'll probably want to ask the following questions:

❏ What are the treatment options for this disease? Which of those options might be appropriate for my dog, taking into account the individual details of his disease and his current state of health? Listen carefully as your vet describes the options. Don't make a quick decision about any option without understanding it fully. For example, some dog owners automatically reject the idea of chemotherapy or a leg amputation for treating certain types of cancer, assuming that such procedures would make their dogs miserable. In fact, dogs tend to have far fewer side effects from chemo than people do, and many dogs get along extremely well on three legs. So hear out your vet as he describes the potential treatments, and ask how well he thinks your dog would tolerate them.

❏ How long do I have to make a decision about treatment? A dog owner almost never has to make an instantaneous decision about how to treat a serious illness. Usually you will have at least a couple of days to discuss and think about your options before deciding what to do next.

❏ Do you recommend I talk to a specialist before I make a decision about what treatment to pursue?

❏ Do you think my dog is in pain? What signs should I be looking for to tell me whether he's suffering? Is there any medication that would help him feel better?

❏ What problems and symptoms is my dog likely to encounter if I choose to keep him comfortable for as long as possible without treating the illness aggressively? How many weeks or months is he likely to have before his quality of life becomes poor?

For some people, asking the vet "What would you do if this were your dog?" or "Which treatment do you think would be best for my dog?" helps them sort through their options. Both are completely appropriate questions that vets hear all the time, so don't hesitate to ask them if you think the answers will help you.

Once you have the details of your dog's prognosis, discuss the options with your family and perhaps also a close friend, the same way you would any major decision.

WHEN IS IT TIME TO LET GO?

"I have a 13-year-old male Samoyed who is very arthritic, deaf, and senile. Lately his hind legs have been giving out. Also, when he is lying down, he sometimes whines. But other times he seems bright and happy. How do I know when it's time to let him go? I don't want him to be in pain, but I don't want to lose him either."

One of the hardest things for dog owners to face is the fact that our beloved companions don't live as long as we wish they did. Dog owners also have the weighty and sometimes unwanted responsibility to make choices about ending their dogs' lives. With such an emotional topic, it's helpful to use a rational framework for thinking through the issues. Remember, too, that you don't have to make a decision instantly. Give yourself time to think and discuss your situation with family members and friends. Here are some questions that can help guide you in deciding whether it's time to let go:

❏ How is your dog's overall quality of life? Is he still able to eat, rest, and enjoy your companionship? Does he have more good hours than bad, or more bad hours than good?

❏ What problems lessen his quality of life significantly? Do you have a definite diagnosis for each? Do you know the different treatment options for each? For example, loss of strength in an older dog's hind legs can result from arthritis, or it could be due to overall weakness from heart disease or another condition that could also be treated. Senility, or canine cognitive dysfunction, can sometimes be helped with medication. Talk to your vet to be clear about the causes of each problem and whether different treatments might be worth trying.

❏ Can you adjust your dog's environment to keep him more comfortable? For specific ways to help your dog get around more easily at home, see page 88.

❏ Do you have the physical, emotional, and financial resources to continue to care for your dog? It can be extremely difficult for people who have physical problems of their own to care for a large dog that cannot walk well. You need to be fair to yourself as well as to your dog.

❏ Have you discussed your dog's condition with family members and friends to get their help and emotional support?

Many dog owners feel better about making the decision to euthanize a seriously ill dog when they know they've carefully considered the treatment options available to them and tried the ones with the best chance of success. If you would like to get a second opinion from a veterinarian other than your regular vet—perhaps a specialist in neurology or orthopedics—by all means do so. Your regular vet will understand your desire to get all the information you can about your dog's prognosis.

Pet-loss counseling and support groups can be immensely helpful before a dog has died, while you're caring for a severely ill dog or grappling with a decision about whether to have him euthanized. Ask your vet whether there are pet bereavement groups in your area, and see the box at right for a list of national bereavement hotlines, websites, and books.

All caring dog owners empathize with your pain and your desire to do the right thing. Give yourself as much time as you need to make a decision, and trust yourself to be your dog's loving advocate.

DECIDING HOW FAR TO GO WITH TREATMENT

"Our Cocker Spaniel is 14 years old and in the early stages of congestive heart failure. Should my husband and I be thinking about how far we want to go with medical treatment if he takes a turn for the worse?"

It's a good idea to talk with your husband, any adult children, and other important members of your dog's immediate "family" about how each of you foresees handling a potential medical crisis. If you don't find out one another's feelings now on these issues—such as heroic resuscitation efforts, having your dog hospitalized for days or longer in the hope he'll get better, the potential cost of prolonging your dog's life for a few weeks or months, and euthanasia—then you might find yourselves in sudden and painful conflict if and when a medical crisis does occur. Finding out one another's thoughts is what's most important, although you can also put some guidelines in writing if you want to.

If your dog becomes severely ill, your veterinarian will tell you all the treatment options so you can make a decision about how to proceed. Most veterinary emergency practices and some regular practices will ask you to desig-

nate a resuscitation code for your dog if he is hospitalized with a severe illness. The code tells the vets on duty whether you want them to attempt to restart your dog's heart if it stops beating, and if so, how far their attempts should go (external chest compressions, using a defibrillator, cutting open the chest to compress the heart directly, putting the dog on a ventilator if he can't breathe on his own, and so on).

As your dog's owner and health advocate, you will be asked to make decisions about his medical care, and that will be easier if you and your family have established a framework for how to handle such issues.

EUTHANASIA

"My elderly dog is in the hospital with terminal cancer. I've come to the decision to have her put to sleep, but I haven't yet decided whether to be there with her when it happens. What is the procedure for putting a dog to sleep? Knowing exactly what will happen will tell me whether I can bear to be there or not."

First of all, please accept my sympathy for the loss you are facing. Doing your best to handle these difficult decisions is a sign of the deep love you have for your dog.

Here is what happens during euthanasia. The dog is given an overdose of a barbiturate anesthetic designed for that purpose, injected into a vein in the dog's leg. In my experience, an assistant always holds and comforts the dog while the veterinarian injects the euthanasia solution. The anesthetic is not painful. The dog loses consciousness within a few seconds, and then her heart stops

SUPPORT WHEN YOU'RE GRIEVING

When someone's beloved dog dies, even the person's closest friends sometimes don't know how to respond. They may say "I'm sorry," change the subject, and quickly forget about their friend's loss. What they may not realize is that people often grieve the death of a dog as deeply as if the dog had been a family member—because that's what she was.

Pet bereavement counseling gives you a place to talk about your loss and cope with it in a positive manner. Most veterinary schools have pet-loss websites or hotlines, and many large veterinary hospitals sponsor bereavement counseling—ask your vet about pet-loss groups in your area. The following hotlines and websites also provide support for people whose animals have died.

American Animal Hospital Association
www.healthypet.com/Library_view.aspx?ID=2&sid=1

American Veterinary Medical Association
www.avma.org/careforanimals/animatedjourneys/goodbyefriend/goodbye.asp

ASPCA Pet Loss Hotline
877-474-3310

Chance's Spot Pet Loss and Support Resources
www.chancesspot.org

Delta Society
www.deltasociety.org/AnimalsHealthPetlossResource1.htm

Humane Society of the United States
www.hsus.org/pets/pet_care/coping_with_the_death_of_your_pet/

Iams Pet Loss Support Center
888-332-7738

In Memory of Pets
www.in-memory-of-pets.com

Pet Loss Grief Support
www.petloss.com

Pet Loss Support Page
www.pet-loss.net

beating within a minute or two after that. The veterinarian listens to the heart with a stethoscope to determine that it has stopped. Occasionally a dog will twitch, sigh, or moan as the heart stops, but these are involuntary reactions—she isn't feeling any pain or fear, because she is already deeply unconscious. The dog's bladder and bowels will sometimes leak a bit as her muscles relax.

If you wish to be present when your dog is put to sleep, you will be able to pet her and talk to her in her final moments, and your voice will be the last one she hears. The veterinarian will stay with you and your dog long enough to verify that the dog's heart has stopped, and after that, if you wish, you can spend time alone with your dog for private grieving.

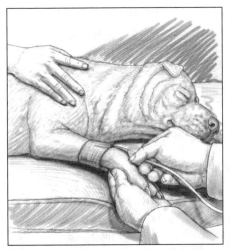

Whether to be with your dog when he is put to sleep is a deeply personal decision.

If you decide to be present for the euthanasia, it's a good idea to have a close friend take you to the veterinary hospital and home again afterward so you can follow your thoughts and emotions without having to worry about driving.

Many vets will make a house call so that a terminally ill dog can be put to sleep in her home rather than in the vet clinic. This may not be an option in your dog's case if she's too ill to be brought home from the hospital, but you could ask your vet whether it's possible.

If you decide not to be there when your dog is put to sleep, you can, of course, spend time with her beforehand to say good-bye. Just let your vet know what you'd like to do. Again, it would be a good idea to ask a close friend to provide transportation so you don't have to think about anything else at an emotional time.

There is no right or wrong decision about being present when your dog is put to sleep, so do what will give you the most comfort when you look back on the end of your dog's life. No matter what,

your dog will not be alone or unloved in her final moments, because the vet and the assistant will pet her, talk to her, and tell her what a good dog she's been and always will be.

SUDDEN DEATH

"When I was a child, we had a dog who simply died one day when she was quite old but not apparently ill. If this had been a person, I'm sure we would have done what we could to determine the cause of death. Is this possible with a dog?"

At the dog owner's request, a vet can do an autopsy to look for a cause of death. Some causes are clearly visible on autopsy, such as a ruptured major blood vessel or obvious cancerous tumors. Others can be determined only by a veterinary pathologist looking at tissue samples microscopically or using chemical tests, and in some cases, no definite cause of death can ever be determined.

It's up to the owner to decide whether they want an autopsy done. Some people want to "know for sure" what happened, and others don't. In the case of your childhood dog, your parents probably figured she had died of natural causes and accepted that as explanation enough.

AFTER A DOG HAS DIED

"What happens to the body after a dog has died?"

Owners decide what they want done. The choices may include burying the body in their backyard (if state and local laws permit it), having the dog buried in a pet cemetery, having the body cre-

BOOKS ABOUT PET LOSS

Dozens of books have been written about coping with the loss of an animal companion. The books vary in tone and approach, so you may want to browse a few at the library or bookstore to find the one that appeals to you the most. Some to consider are *Pet Loss: A Thoughtful Guide for Adults and Children*, by Herbert A. Nieburg and Arlene Fischer; *When Your Pet Dies: How to Cope with Your Feelings*, by Jamie Quackenbusch and Denise Graveline; *Coping with Sorrow on the Loss of Your Pet*, by Moira K. Anderson; *The Loss of a Pet*, by Wallace Sife; *Absent Friend*, by Laura and Martyn Lee; and *Oh, Where Has My Pet Gone?* by Sally Sibbitt.

There are also many wonderful books aimed specifically at children, including *The Tenth Good Thing About Barney*, by Judith Viorst; *When a Pet Dies*, by Fred Rogers; and *I'll Always Love You*, by Hans Wilhelm.

---

mated individually and getting back the ashes, or having the body cremated in a group with other pets. Most veterinary practices have contracts with cremation services that pick up dead animals from the clinics, cremate them in their facilities, and either dispose of the ashes or return them to the dogs' owners. When a dog dies in the hospital, the veterinarian tells the owner the options and asks what she'd like to have done with the body. If a dog dies at home, the owner can call the vet to arrange a cremation, get information about pet cemeteries, and so on.

CHILDREN AND THE LOSS OF A PET

"My husband and I have agreed it's time to have our dog, Sam, put to sleep, because he has a nerve problem that has progressed to the point where he can barely stand or walk. But we haven't decided what we should tell our young children about our decision, and when."

I would tell the children what is going to happen, in a manner appropriate to their age, a day or two before you have Sam euthanized. If you tell them the truth, then they can think about Sam's illness and how unhappy he probably is to be unable to do the things he used to do, and they can say good-bye to him. If you make something up, like Sam "went to live on a farm," you're sending bad messages about responsibility toward animals and how to face difficult or painful situations. If you wait until after Sam has died to say anything, your older children might feel betrayed and sad not to have had a chance to say good-bye.

I don't recommend having children under the age of 12 or so be present for the euthanasia, and older children only if they understand exactly what's going to happen and really want to be there. Witnessing the moment of death and their parents' grief may be upsetting and overwhelming to younger children.

Here are some thoughts to keep in mind when telling a child about the death of an animal:

NINE WAYS TO REMEMBER A WONDERFUL DOG

A dog who has been loved is never forgotten. Here are just a few of the innumerable ways you can create a memorial to a special dog.

1. Take doughnuts and coffee to your late dog's play group, and host an informal wake.

2. Make a special scrapbook of photos and reminiscences about your dog.

3. Ask your children if they would like to write and illustrate a story or book about their dog.

4. Create a memorial in your yard. Plant a flowering shrub, place a sculpture in your dog's favorite spot, or have your children paint stepping-stones to put in a flower garden. Tell your children that they can leave a note or picture in the memorial spot whenever they miss their dog or want to tell him something.

5. Arrange to have a tree planted in your dog's favorite park and invite your dog's friends to a dedication ceremony.

6. Establish or contribute to a medical fund for pets in need at your veterinarian's office.

7. Post your dog's photo and obituary on a pet-loss website.

8. Make a donation in your dog's memory to an animal welfare organization, such as the local animal shelter or the Humane Society of the United States.

9. Make a donation for research or treatment of the illness your dog had to a veterinary school or the Morris Animal Foundation (*www.morris animalfoundation.org*).

Gone, but not forgotten: a tree can be a beautiful living memorial to your dog.

❏ To a toddler or preschooler, you might say, "Sam has been very sick for a long time, and he's not going to get better, so we are going to have the vet help him die. Death means we won't see Sam anymore or be able to pet him. Let's tell Sam how much we love him and are going to miss him."

❏ Avoid using the phrase "put to sleep" with children younger than about 10 years old. A young child can easily confuse that idea with sleeping, and not understand that the dog isn't going to wake up, or else be afraid that they could die when they go to sleep.

❏ With school-age children, you might say something like "We've tried everything we can to make Sam better, but it hasn't worked, and we think he's unhappy and in pain. We're going to take him to the vet on Tuesday so the vet can give Sam a drug that will make his heart and breathing stop, and then Sam will be dead, and we won't see him anymore. We're going to miss him so much, but we don't want Sam to have to hurt anymore. Would you like to do something special to tell Sam good-bye before then?"

Your vet may have a booklet on helping children to cope with the death of a pet. There are also a number of wonderful books on the subject, and pet-loss groups and websites also have information about children and grief (see pages 395 and 397).

Part 3
Quick Reference

CHAPTER 18

First Aid Basics and Poison Control

CUTS, SCRAPES, AND STICKY MESSES—just like children, dogs are magnets for minor injuries and mishaps. A simple canine medical kit and some basic know-how will enable you to handle many first aid problems efficiently at home. Cleaning minor wounds, getting goo out of fur, clipping broken nails, and getting your dog to hold still are all skills that can be easily mastered with a bit of practice. When it comes to poisoning, however, focus your attention on prevention rather than treatment. Dogs will eat almost anything, so it's up to you to learn which substances around your house are most likely to pose a problem—including mouse poison, medicines, toxic plants, and even raisins—and keep them out of reach.

CANINE VITAL SIGNS

If your temperature is 102°F, you have a fever. But what about your dog? At 102°, his temperature is right where it's supposed to be. Here are some tips for checking and interpreting your dog's vital signs.

Normal temperature: From 100° to 102.5°F.

Use a rectal (baby) thermometer. Shake down the thermometer to below 99°F (if it's the mercury type) or turn the thermometer on (if electronic). Lubricate the bulb with a little petroleum or K-Y jelly. Grasp the base of your dog's tail and hold it up firmly (to keep him from sitting on the thermometer). Gently slide the thermometer bulb about 1 inch into the rectum. Keep holding on to the thermometer and your dog's tail to keep everything steady. After 60 sec-

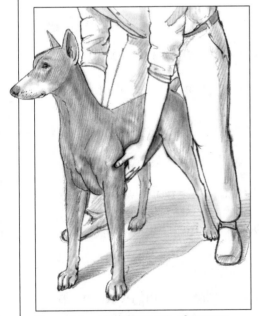

To count your dog's heart rate, place your hands on his ribcage behind the elbows.

onds, remove the thermometer and read the temperature.

Normal resting heart rate: From 70 beats per minute for a large-breed dog to 160 beats per minute for a toy dog (see page 258).

Find a clock or watch with a second hand. Place both hands on your dog's ribs behind his elbows until you can feel his heartbeat easily. Count the number of beats in 15 seconds and multiply by four, or count the number of beats in 30 seconds and multiply by two. With practice, you can also feel a dog's pulse on the sides of his neck, on his lower front legs (the equivalent of your wrists), and on his inner thighs.

Normal resting respiratory rate: From 15 to 30 breaths per minute.

Find a clock or watch with a second hand. Look at your dog's ribcage and count the number of breaths he takes in 1 minute. Don't try to count your dog's respirations while he's panting—pants don't count as breaths. Dogs pant when they're hot, tired, excited, or in pain (see page 285).

BASIC WOUND CARE

Minor wounds can be treated by clipping and cleaning, as described below. But first, here are some signs that a wound is *not* minor and should be treated by a vet:

❏ The wound is bleeding heavily.
❏ Your dog has been hit by a car (he may have internal injuries as well as scrapes or wounds).
❏ The wound is swollen and hot (it may be infected or contain deep debris).

THE CANINE FIRST-AID KIT

A few simple supplies will help you with routine canine care and first aid. Stock the following in a shoebox or similar container so you can find everything quickly when you need it.

Ear-cleaning solution, cotton balls, and cotton swabs, for cleaning ears

Plain saline eyewash, for cleaning discharge or flushing debris from the eyes

Mild dog shampoo, for general clean-ups

Dog nail clipper, for broken nails

Tweezers, for removing ticks and splinters

Electric hair clipper, K-Y jelly, chlorhexidine or povidone-iodine (Betadine) wound cleaner, and gauze squares, for clipping and cleaning wounds

Roll of 2-inch-wide gauze and roll of 1-inch-wide bandage tape, for bandaging leg or tail wounds

Antibiotic ointment, for minor wounds

Hydrocortisone spray or ointment, for itchy wounds or bug bites

3cc oral medication syringe, for giving liquid medication

Muzzle, in case you need to handle your dog when she's frightened or in pain

Diphenhydramine (Benadryl), for insect bites or hives

Rectal (baby) thermometer, for taking your dog's temperature

10cc oral medication syringe, for flushing wounds, rinsing caustic substances from your dog's mouth, or inducing vomiting; a turkey baster can substitute in a pinch but is messier and harder to aim

3% hydrogen peroxide, for inducing vomiting *only when appropriate* (see page 411)

❑ Your dog may have a broken bone.
❑ Your dog is having trouble standing or walking, is panting excessively or breathing strangely, or otherwise seems ill (he may have other injuries besides the obvious wound).

Clipping and cleaning. Contrary to popular belief, letting your dog lick a wound is not the best way to get it to heal. Dog saliva doesn't have magic pow-

ers, and a dog's mouth is not "cleaner than a human's"—it contains just as many, if not more, bacteria. Also, when dogs lick their wounds, they tend to get carried away; persistent licking can prevent a wound from healing and damage the surrounding skin.

The best way to treat minor wounds is to clip the surrounding hair and wash the wound with a diluted antiseptic solution. Clipping the hair lets you assess and clean the wound more thoroughly, and wounds heal more quickly when they're not covered by damp, dirty hair.

To clip around and clean a wound, you'll need an electric hair clipper (the quieter the motor, the better), K-Y jelly, an antiseptic wound cleaner such as chlorhexidine or povidone-iodine (Betadine), a small bowl for mixing the wound cleaner with water, a 10cc syringe for flushing the wound, a washcloth or paper towels, and some gauze squares.

First, coat the wound with a large glob of K-Y jelly. This will prevent clipped hair from getting embedded in the wound. Next, using the electric clipper, clip away all hair from about 1 inch around the wound. Also shorten any long hair that is likely to flop across or get stuck in the wound. When you're done clipping, gently wipe away the hair and the K-Y jelly with some gauze.

Mix a small amount of antiseptic wound cleaner with water in a bowl—just enough cleaner to tint the water a pale color. Draw up the antiseptic solution into the 10cc syringe and squirt it gently all over the wound, mopping up the drips with a washcloth or paper towels. Continue flushing the wound in this way until it seems clean and free of surface debris. Finish by gently patting and wiping the wound with gauze squares soaked in the antiseptic solution. Dry the fur around the wound so your dog doesn't lick up a lot of antiseptic solution.

If the wound is somewhere that your dog can't reach to lick, dab it with a small amount of antibiotic ointment. If the wound is within reach of your dog's tongue, don't use any ointment, because he'll wind up eating it. There's no need to cover or bandage minor wounds.

As a follow-up, gently clean the wound once or twice a day until the skin heals, using gauze pads soaked in a little antiseptic cleaner and water. Call your vet if the wound becomes swollen, hot, or more painful than it was initially.

HOW TO PILL YOUR PUP

Your vet has prescribed 14 days' worth of medication for your dog. Your assignment is to get one of those pills into your dog twice a day for two weeks. Now what?

Some canine medications, such as heartworm prevention and carprofen (Rimadyl), are available as chewable meat-flavored tablets. Most dogs will gobble those right out of your hand as a treat, so be careful to store chewables on a high shelf or some other place your dog can't possibly reach or he may eat the entire supply at once. Call your vet if your dog does get into some medicine, even if it was prescribed for him.

Other medications aren't so tasty, and thus aren't as easy to give. Here are some tips on getting your dog to take his pills:

❑ The classic pilling maneuver is illustrated here. Gently grasp your dog's muzzle from above with one hand. Squeeze gently behind the upper canine ("fang") teeth to get him to open his mouth. With your other hand, quickly pop the pill as far back on the middle of his tongue as you can. (A quick secondary poke with your index finger often will slide the pill back farther. It's virtually impossible to choke a dog with a pill, so don't worry.) Gently hold your dog's mouth closed for a moment to keep him from gag-

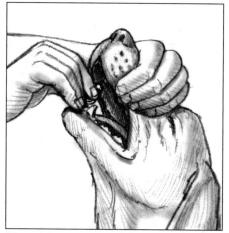

When giving your dog a pill, tip his nose straight up and let gravity help.

ging the pill back out. After he's swallowed it, offer him a treat and a little water to help wash things down. Don't put pills or liquid in the lip pouches on the sides of your dog's mouth, because he'll just spit it out. If a pill sticks to your dog's tongue, you might try lubricating the pill with a dab of butter—although that will also make it slippery for you to hold.

❏ If the classic pilling method just doesn't work for you, buy a piller, which looks like a syringe with a soft rubber end instead of a needle. Put the pill in the rubber end, slip the piller in from the side of the dog's mouth so that the pill is far back in the middle of the dog's tongue, and push the plunger. The rubber is very soft and won't hurt your dog's throat. Your vet may sell pillers, and most pet-supply stores and catalogs carry them.

❏ If you think your dog will gulp down a pill hidden in a tasty tidbit, go ahead and try that method. You want him to swallow the treat whole, not chew it, so use just a dab of food. Try hiding the pill in a half-teaspoonful of Cheez Whiz, liverwurst, canned cat food, or

vanilla ice cream. Don't crush pills and mix them with food. The medicine will make the food taste bad, and unless your dog eats every bit, he won't get the full dose of medicine.

❏ Many pharmacies can create custom-flavored liquid medications—turning your dog's pills into a liver-flavored liquid, for example. But compounded medications are often expensive, and it may be just as difficult to get your dog to swallow a liver-flavored liquid as it is to get him to take a pill.

RESTRAINING YOUR DOG FOR TREATMENT

A dog can become as slippery as an eel when you're trying to get a close look at a wound, clip his nails, or clean his ears. If you can get your dog to hold still, you're halfway done. Here are some professional restraint tips.

❏ Put on your dog's "outside" collar and leash. Most dogs are more cooperative when someone is holding their leash.

A dog-savvy friend can use a "hug hold" to steady your dog in a standing position.

❏ Place small or medium-size dogs on a waist-high table or counter—if your dog isn't likely to throw himself off the table *and* you or an assistant can steady him while you're working.

❏ Back him into a corner in a small room, such as a bathroom.

❏ Use the "hug hold": with your dog standing, have a dog-savvy assistant hold your dog against her body by bringing one arm under the dog's neck and the other arm over the dog's back (see the previous page). The arm around the dog's neck keeps the dog from moving forward or back, and the arm over the dog's back keeps him from moving sideways or up.

❏ Use the "down hold": with your dog standing, have a dog-savvy assistant reach over your dog's back and grasp the front and hind legs on the *assistant's* side. While you hold and steady the dog's head and neck—to keep him from bashing his head on the ground—the assistant pulls the legs away from her body and eases the dog into lying on his side, never letting go of the legs. The assistant holds the dog in this position by keeping one

A helper can use the "down hold" to keep your dog lying on his side.

forearm over the dog's neck (to keep him from thrashing his head) and the other forearm across his flank (to keep his hind end down), while continuously pulling gently on the legs to keep them extended.

PUTTING ON A MUZZLE

When you must handle a dog that's frightened, injured, or in pain, using a muzzle will help protect you and your helpers from getting bitten.

To prevent a dog from biting, a muzzle must fit snugly, extend to the tip of the dog's snout, and be fastened tightly behind the ears. The shorter part of the muzzle goes over the top of the snout, and the longer part underneath. A muzzle that's loose or rides up on the snout won't stop a dog from getting his mouth open far enough to get his teeth into you; and if it's loose behind the ears, he'll quickly shake or paw it off.

Never leave a muzzle on for more than 10 minutes at a time, because the dog won't be able to pant and may become dangerously overheated or have trouble breathing.

To create a muzzle in an emergency, use a 2- to 3-foot-long piece of gauze, a scarf, or similar soft, strong material. Make a half-knot with the ends of the gauze, leaving a large loop in the center. Standing behind the dog, slip the loop over his snout and *quickly* tighten the loop snugly before he can paw it off. Bring the ends of the gauze down and cross them under the snout, then bring the ends to the back of the dog's neck and tie them snugly in a bow behind his ears. (Use a bow rather than a knot so you can remove the muzzle quickly when you need to.)

To make an emergency muzzle, first lasso the dog's snout with a loop of soft cloth.

Quickly tighten the loop, cross the ends under the chin, and tie a tight bow behind the ears.

SLING-WALKING AN UNSTEADY DOG

If your dog has a hind-leg injury or weak hind legs, you can use a sling to help him walk or climb stairs (see the illustration on page 88). Do *not* use a sling to move a dog that may have an injured spine or pelvis. Doing so could cause severe spinal cord damage, pain, or other serious injuries. Use a board or box instead to move a dog whose spine or pelvis may be injured.

To make a sling take a bath towel or similar-size piece of fabric. Loop it under the dog's belly just in front of his hind legs. Hold both ends of the towel in one hand, and lift gently as you walk alongside the dog and steady and support his hind end.

Ready-made walking slings and even dog wheelchairs can also be ordered from many pet-supply catalogs.

GETTING RID OF GOO

Sooner or later, your dog will get chewing gum, tar, tree sap, burrs, or some other sticky or tenacious substance in her fur. To get rid of sticky stuff without cutting the hair, work some vegetable oil into the goo with your fingers. The oil will help break up the goo into smaller pieces, which you can gently pull out of the fur. When you're done, bathe your dog with a mild dog shampoo to remove the vegetable oil.

Never use paint thinner, turpentine, nail-polish remover, or other solvents to remove messes from your dog's fur: they are toxic if licked off or absorbed through the skin.

TRIMMING NAILS

How does nail trimming qualify as first aid? When nails split or break partway, which they frequently do, they can be painful and should be trimmed so they don't snag and pull when your dog walks. That's why I recommend putting a nail trimmer in your canine first-aid kit. And once you have a good nail trimmer, you can also give your dog regular pedicures, assuming that she isn't footphobic. Here's how to get started.

First, make sure you have a strong, sharp nail trimmer that's large enough for the thickness of your dog's nails. I prefer the type that look like pliers over the guillotine type because they're stronger and easier to line up for a straight cut. The blades need to be strong and sharp so they cut the nails cleanly rather than crushing them, which hurts.

Your dog can stand, sit, or lie down while you cut her nails, whichever is the most comfortable for both of you. Having a dog-savvy friend hold and pet your dog while you work on the nails can be helpful. If your dog squirms, have your assistant use one of the restraint holds described on page 407.

The No. 1 goal, especially when you're first learning, is to avoid cutting into the quick. This is the live tissue of the nail, where the blood vessels and nerves are located. If you cut it, it will hurt just the same as if your own fingernail were torn below where it attaches to the skin.

You can see the shadow of the quick inside white or light-colored toenails but not in black nails. If your dog has even one white nail, start with that nail and use it as a guideline for how short to cut the rest. Aim to leave about an eighth of an inch of the nail below the end of the quick, just to stay on the safe side.

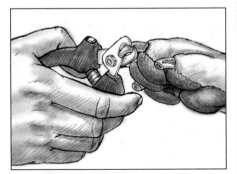

You can see the quick in light nails. Allow an extra eighth of an inch just to be safe.

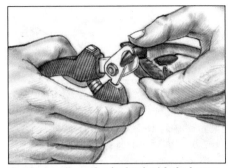

Cut dark nails so they're level with the bottom of the foot pads. Be conservative, not bold.

If all your dog's nails are black, you'll have to guesstimate where the quick is. One trick for doing so is to cut the nail level with the bottom of the pad (the leathery cushion on the underside of the toe). Or you can look to see where the nail tapers to a narrow hook, and just trim off the hook.

When you're ready to start cutting, talk to your dog in a relaxed, calm tone of voice while you pick up a foot and choose a nail to start on. If you're not sure where the quick is, be ultraconservative at first—you can always take off more later. Cut the nail straight across rather than at an angle. Keep talking to your dog in a normal tone of voice to reassure her that everything is OK. If the first nail goes well, trim a few more. Stop whenever you or your dog are feeling stressed—there's nothing wrong with cutting one nail per day if that's how it works best for you. You can also "tip" the nails—trim off just a sliver—once a week, or shorten and smooth the nails with a pumice stone. Praise your dog extravagantly and give her a treat when you're done.

If a nail should bleed, it means you've cut too far and hit the quick. Apologize profusely to your dog and stop the bleeding by applying firm pressure against the cut surface with a tissue or paper towel for a couple of minutes. Styptic or plain bar soap will also stop the bleeding, but they sting.

Remember that your dog's nails are not worth getting hurt over. If you have the slightest inkling that she might snarl or snap at you, then your dog needs to wear a properly fitted muzzle and be held securely by an experienced person while her nails are cut. If that's the case, your best bet is to let a groomer, vet assistant, or other professional handle the job.

WHEN AND HOW TO INDUCE VOMITING

If you know or suspect your dog has eaten something that may make her sick, your first move should be to call your vet or a vet emergency clinic, not to try to make your dog vomit. That's because inducing vomiting is dangerous in certain situations, and useless in many others. So before we get to the how, here's the when-not-to list. Don't give a dog something to make her vomit if:

❑ She is already vomiting.

❑ She is unconscious, too weak to stand, or having trouble breathing.

❑ She has swallowed something caustic that is likely to burn again on the way back up, such as bleach.

❑ She ate the substance more than two hours ago, because it most likely will have passed into the small intestine already, where it can't be vomited back up.

The two situations in which you *should* induce vomiting are (1) when your dog has ingested antifreeze within the past two hours, or (2) when you've talked to a vet on the phone and she has

advised you to induce vomiting. Before you make your dog vomit, give her a few tablespoons of dog food, a slice of bread, or a few crackers if she'll eat. (She'll vomit more easily with a bit of food in her stomach.) Then pour some 3 percent hydrogen peroxide in a bowl and, using a 10cc syringe with no needle on it, draw up about 3ccs of hydrogen peroxide for every 20 pounds of your dog's body weight. Put the end of the syringe in your dog's mouth and steadily squirt the hydrogen peroxide toward the back of her mouth so she swallows it. Wait 10 minutes, and if she hasn't started to vomit yet, repeat the dose. If she still doesn't vomit, call your vet immediately.

Ipecac syrup can also be used to induce vomiting in dogs; follow the label directions for your dog's weight. A dog given ipecac may start vomiting and not stop, however, so be prepared to take your dog to the vet for further care.

14 COMMON HOUSEHOLD TOXINS

Prevention, not treatment, is the key to keeping your dog safe from poisons, and dogs are most likely to be poisoned by substances they encounter in and around their own homes. To prevent poisoning, you need to learn what could be toxic to your dog and keep those substances out of reach. Here are 14 common toxins to watch out for when you're dog-proofing your house and yard; what these toxins do; and what you should do if your dog has been exposed to them.

ANTIFREEZE (ETHYLENE GLYCOL)

Not only is it one of the most toxic substances imaginable, but antifreeze also smells and tastes sweet, making it appealing to dogs and other animals. Dogs can get into antifreeze as it's added to or drained from a car radiator, or by licking spills from a road or driveway. *What it does:* Causes kidney failure. As little as 1 teaspoonful of antifreeze can make a small dog very sick or kill him. *What you should do:* (1) Call your vet or an emergency vet hospital immediately. (2) Induce vomiting; see the previous page. (3) Take your dog to the vet hospital as quickly as possible. *What your vet can do:* Administer 4-methylpyrazole or ethanol intravenously for several days to block the breakdown of antifreeze into its toxic components.

MOUSE AND RAT POISON

These are just as tasty and toxic to dogs as they are to mice and rats. *What they do:* Cause potentially fatal internal bleeding. *What you should do:* If you think your dog may have eaten mouse or rat poison, call your vet or an emergency vet hospital immediately. Don't wait for symptoms to appear—by the time you notice any (such as bruises, nosebleeds, sore joints, bloody vomit, or blood in the feces), your dog will already be in deep trouble. *What your vet can do:* Test for a blood-clotting problem and begin treatment with vitamin K, which helps the liver replenish the body's stores of blood-clotting factors.

OVER-THE-COUNTER PAIN RELIEVERS

People take over-the-counter pain pills so routinely, they may assume such products are safe for dogs as well. They're not. Never give a dog ibuprofen (Motrin, Advil), or naproxen (Aleve), because they are toxic even in low doses. Acetaminophen (Tylenol) is toxic pri-

marily in excessive doses, but it doesn't work well as a pain reliever for dogs anyway, so I advise against using it as well. Buffered or enteric-coated aspirin (Bufferin, Ecotrin) is sometimes used for arthritis pain in dogs, but it should never be given to a dog who is also taking a prescription anti-inflammatory (such as Rimadyl, Metacam, or Deramaxx), and you should of course ask your vet for the proper dosage and frequency. *What they do:* Ibuprofen and naproxen can cause severe, even fatal, stomach ulcers and kidney and liver damage in dogs. High doses of acetaminophen can cause liver and kidney damage, and aspirin can cause stomach ulcers. *What you should do:* If you have mistakenly given your dog ibuprofen or naproxen—even just a child's dose—call your vet or an emergency vet hospital immediately for advice. Be prepared to tell them how

Some of the substances that are toxic to dogs are well known, and others aren't. You've undoubtedly heard about the dangers of antifreeze and chocolate, but what about ibuprofen, garlic, and mothballs?

many milligrams of the drug you gave your dog (check the bottle), and how much your dog weighs. If you have given your dog acetaminophen or aspirin and he has lost his appetite, is vomiting or having diarrhea, or is lethargic, call your vet or an emergency vet hospital. *What your vet can do:* Give activated charcoal to absorb any drug remaining in the digestive tract, IV fluids to help clear the drug from the bloodstream, stomach protectants to guard against ulcers, blood transfusions if needed, and other treatments as needed.

OTHER MEDICATIONS— CANINE OR HUMAN

Just about any drug can be toxic to a dog, especially when eaten in quantity. Heart medications, antidepressants, and Sudafed (pseudoephedrine) are just a few of the common drugs that can make dogs sick. Less common but extremely toxic to dogs are Efudex (fluorouracil) and Dovonex (calcipotriene), two prescription skin creams; and isoniazid, an oral medication for tuberculosis. *What they do:* The adverse effects depend on the medication and how much your dog ate. *What you should do:* Keep all medications—your dog's as well as your own—out of your dog's reach. If you suspect your dog has gotten into any medication, even one that was prescribed for him, call your vet or an emergency vet hospital immediately. *What your vet can do:* Give activated charcoal, IV fluids, or other treatments as needed, depending on the drug.

SLUG AND SNAIL POISON

Slug and snail poison contains the chemical metaldehyde plus sugar or other tasty stuff to make it attractive to slugs—and dogs. *What it does:* Causes tremors, twitching, and seizures. As little as 1 teaspoonful can make a 20-pound dog sick. *What you should do:* Call your vet or an emergency vet hospital immediately. *What your vet can do:* Induce vomiting if appropriate, give activated charcoal and IV fluids, and control seizures.

CHOCOLATE

Chocolate contains theobromine and caffeine, both of which are toxic to dogs. (Carob, white chocolate, and cocoa butter contain little or none of these toxins.) *What it does:* Causes vomiting, diarrhea, pancreatitis, tremors, heart arrhythmias, or seizures. Fortunately, the dose that will cause the most severe symptoms—heart arrhythmias and seizures—is quite high. Unsweetened baking chocolate contains ten times the amount of theobromine and caffeine found in milk chocolate, making unsweetened chocolate the most dangerous. A dangerous dose of unsweetened chocolate is about 1 ounce (one square) for a 20-pound dog, about 2 ounces for a 40-pound dog, and about 4 ounces for an 80-pound dog. In practical terms, this means that if your 80-pound Lab eats half a chocolate cake, he is less likely to have heart arrhythmias and seizures than he is to vomit and have diarrhea. *What you should do:* Call your vet or an emergency vet hospital and tell them how much chocolate your dog ate, what type it was (unsweetened, semisweet, or milk chocolate), and how much he weighs. Watch your dog for vomiting, diarrhea, weakness, tremors, or seizures. *What your vet can do:* Induce vomiting if appropriate; give activated charcoal to absorb any chocolate remaining in the digestive tract and IV fluids to help clear the theobromine and caffeine from the bloodstream; treat seizures and arrhythmias.

XYLITOL

Xylitol is an artificial sweetener found in some sugar-free gum, mints, candy, cookies, and other treats, and some toothpaste. *What it does:* In dogs, xylitol triggers the release of insulin and can cause a severe drop in blood sugar, leading to weakness, collapse, and seizures. At higher doses, it can cause liver failure and blood clotting abnormalities. *What you should do:* Keep all products containing artificial sweeteners away from your dog. If your dog does eat sugarless gum or candy, find the wrapper if possible, estimate the number of pieces your dog may have eaten, and call your vet or an emergency clinic immediately. You may need to take your dog in right away for treatment. *What your vet can do:* Induce vomiting if appropriate. Start intravenous fluids containing dextrose to counteract hypoglycemia. Treat seizures if they occur. Check for liver damage and clotting problems with blood tests, and treat them if they occur.

GRAPES, RAISINS, TOMATOES, ONIONS, AND GARLIC

Many dog owners are surprised to discover that these common foods can be toxic to dogs. *What they do:* Eating 2 ounces or more of **grapes or raisins** per 10 pounds of the dog's body weight can cause kidney failure (that's 4 ounces for a 20-pound dog, and so on.) **Tomatoes and tomato plants** contain atropine, which can cause dilated pupils, tremors, and heart arrhythmias. The highest concentration of atropine is found in the leaves and stems of tomato plants, followed by unripe (green) tomatoes, followed by ripe tomatoes. Eating more than 1 tablespoon of **onion** or 1 teaspoon of **garlic** per 10 pounds of the dog's body weight can destroy red blood cells. *What you*

should do: Keep grapes and raisins away from your dog. Don't let your dog chew on tomato plants or eat green tomatoes. Don't give your dog food that contains large amounts of tomato, onion, or garlic. If your dog has eaten a lot of grapes, raisins, tomatoes, onions, or garlic, and especially if he is vomiting, has diarrhea, or is weak or lethargic, call your vet or an emergency vet hospital immediately. *What your vet can do:* Induce vomiting if appropriate, give activated charcoal and IV fluids, and administer other treatment as needed.

ALCOHOLIC BEVERAGES, COFFEE, TOBACCO, AND MARIJUANA

It probably goes without saying that coffee, bourbon, cigars, and pot aren't good for dogs. But people are sometimes surprised to discover that their dog has cleaned out the ashtrays and polished off the drinks after a party, or eaten some pot. *What they do:* **Alcohol** can cause weakness, depression, and staggering. **Caffeine** can cause tremors, heart arrhythmias, and seizures. **Tobacco** can cause drooling, vomiting, weakness, and coma. **Marijuana** can cause sedation, staggering, and urination. *What you should do:* Call your vet or an emergency vet hospital and tell them how much of the substance your dog has eaten, how much she weighs, and what her symptoms are. *What your vet can do:* Induce vomiting if appropriate, give activated charcoal and IV fluids, and administer other treatment as needed.

CLEANING PRODUCTS

If you have a dog who gets into everything, keep your cleaning supplies locked up as securely as if you had a toddler in the house. *What they do:* Toilet bowl cleaners, automatic dishwasher gels, oven cleaners, drain open-ers, bleach, detergents, and Pine-Sol are just a few of the cleaning products that can burn a dog's eyes, nose, mouth, stomach, or skin. *What you should do:* Don't let your dog drink out of the toilet. Don't leave a bucket of cleaning solution unattended—your dog might stick his nose into it or taste it. Keep dogs off floors that are wet with cleaning solutions. Call your vet if your dog gets into a cleaning product. *What your vet can do:* Treat the chemical burns caused by cleaning products.

MOTHBALLS

These are toxic if eaten, so don't put them anywhere your dog can reach, such as on the closet floor. *What they do:* Mothballs contain either naphthalene or paradichlorobenzene. Naphthalene can cause vomiting, diarrhea, hemolytic anemia, weakness, or collapse. Paradichlorobenzene can cause vomiting, diarrhea, liver damage, staggering, or seizures. *What you should do:* Estimate how many mothballs your dog may have eaten, and if you still have the box, find out what the active ingredient is; then call your vet or an emergency vet hospital. *What your vet can do:* Induce vomiting if appropriate, administer activated charcoal and IV fluids, and treat anemia and seizures.

LEAD AND ZINC

Lead poisoning is a threat to animals as well as children. The main sources of lead poisoning for dogs are painted wood-work, old linoleum, or fishing weights (all of which they chew), or dust from home renovations, which they can eat or inhale. The main sources of zinc poisoning are post-1982 pennies, which are 97 percent zinc; some screws and bolts, including those used in some old pet car-riers; and zinc oxide ointment. *What they do:* **Lead** poisoning can cause vomiting, diarrhea, hemolytic anemia, weakness, blindness, tremors, and seizures. **Zinc** poisoning can cause vomiting, diarrhea, and hemolytic anemia. *What you should do:* Call your vet if you think your dog has eaten something containing lead or zinc, even if he doesn't show any symptoms. *What your vet can do:* Remove pennies or other objects from the digestive tract; give lead-binding medication; treat anemia and seizures.

FLEA AND TICK PRODUCTS

Flea and tick products are safe—if they are used as directed. But applying a product more often than you're supposed to, using several flea and tick products at the same time, or dosing a puppy or small dog with enough flea killer for an 80-pounder can cause problems. *What they do:* Anything applied to the skin, including spot-on flea products and sprays, can cause severe itching in a dog that's sensitive to one of the ingredients. Organophosphate pesticides—mainly used on livestock or for lawn-and-garden insect control, not in canine flea and tick products—can cause tremors and seizures. Permethrin can cause tremors and seizures in cats but is safe when used as directed for dogs. *What you should do:* Read the label carefully every time you use a flea and tick product. Look for what age and size dog the product is intended for, the appropriate amount to use, and how often it can be used safely. If your dog becomes violently itchy after you apply a flea or tick product, bathe him immediately using mild dog shampoo, lathering and rinsing several times, and then call your vet or an emergency vet hospital for advice. Also call your vet or a vet emergency clinic if your dog is weak or disoriented, drools heavily or vomits, or has tremors or seizures after being exposed to a flea or tick product or other pesticide. *What your vet can do:* Administer activated charcoal and IV fluids and control the seizures.

MACADAMIA NUTS

These are toxic to dogs, but the active component hasn't been identified. *What they do:* Cause temporary weakness or paralysis of the hind legs. The toxic dose can be as little as 1 ounce of nuts for a 20-pound dog. *What you should do:* Call your vet or an emergency vet hospital if your dog eats macadamia nuts. *What your vet can do:* Induce vomiting if appropriate, and administer activated charcoal and IV fluids. Fortunately, the paralysis caused by macadamia nuts usually goes away within a few days, but the dog will need help getting outdoors to relieve himself and staying clean and dry until he recovers.

SAFE GARDENING

One of the great pleasures in a dog's life is relaxing in the yard with his favorite people. But gardens and gardening supplies include some canine hazards. Watch out for the following when you're enjoying time outside with your dog:

❏ **Poisonous plants** (see the chart beginning on the following page).

❏ **Mouse or rat poison** (see page 412). Remember that even if you don't have any rodent poison in your house or yard, your dog could find some on a golf course or in a park or other public area.

❏ **Slug and snail poison** (see page 413).

❏ **Pesticides,** especially those containing organophosphates and carbamates, which can cause drooling, vomiting, diarrhea, tremors, or seizures.

❏ **Cocoa-bean mulch.** This contains theobromine, one of the toxins found in chocolate, so if your dog eats a lot of it, he could have heart arrhythmias or seizures.

❏ **Fertilizer.** Dogs love the stuff, but even organic fertilizer—the kind made from bonemeal, blood meal, fish meal, or manure—can cause vomiting and diarrhea, plus tremors or seizures if the fertilizer is moldy. Other types of fertilizer contain high levels of minerals that can burn a dog's mouth or cause vomiting, stomach ulcers, liver damage, hemolytic anemia, or seizures. If you must use fertilizer on, say, your rosebushes, consider putting a fence around them to keep your dog away.

❏ **Compost,** which may contain mold spores that can make a dog severely ill (see page 139).

❏ **Mothballs.** Sometimes used to deter squirrels or other creatures from digging up bulbs, mothballs can cause vomiting, diarrhea, liver damage, hemolytic anemia, or seizures (see page 415).

M (MOUTH): Mouth burns or swelling

S (STOMACH): Vomiting and diarrhea

H (HEART): Heart arrhythmias

K (KIDNEY): Kidney or liver damage

B (BRAIN): Weakness, tremors, or seizures

! (POTENTIALLY FATAL): Severely toxic

POISONOUS PLANTS

Many dogs enjoy chewing on plants, so it's important to know which ones are toxic. The chart that follows lists houseplants, landscaping and gardening plants, and weeds and wildflowers that are known to be harmful to dogs. Bold plants are potentially fatal.

If your dog eats a poisonous plant or one you're not sure about, estimate how much he may have ingested; look inside his mouth for sores; rinse his mouth with water from a slow-flowing garden hose or a turkey baster; note any symptoms he is having (such as drooling, vomiting, or twitching); and call your vet or an emergency vet hospital to discuss what to do next.

The effects of poisonous plants vary. Some are caustic and burn the mouth and throat, while others cause vomiting and diarrhea, heart arrhythmias, kidney or liver damage, or tremors or seizures. Use the key in the box on the previous page to identify the toxin's main targets and symptoms. Photographs of poisonous pants can be found on the ASPCA Animal Poison Control Center website (*www.aspca.org/site/PageServer?page name=pro_apcc_toxicplants*) and the Cornell University Poisonous Plants Informational Database website (*www .ansci.cornell.edu/plants/comlist.html*).

Aloe (*Aloe vera*) S, B
Amaryllis (*Hippeastrum*) S, B
Anthurium (*Anthurium*) M, S
Apple (seeds) B
Apricot (pits) B
Asparagus fern or lace fern berries (*Asparagus setaceus*) S
Autumn crocus (*Colchicum autumnale*) M, S, K, !

Azalea (*Rhododendron*) M, S, H, B, !
Bird-of-paradise (*Caesalpinia gilliesii*) S, B
Bittersweet, American (*Celastrus*) S, B
Bittersweet, European (*Solanum dulcamara*) S, H, B
Bleeding heart (*Dicentra spectabilis*) S, B
Buckeye (*Aesculus*) S, B
Buddhist pine (*Podocarpus macrophyllus*) S
Caladium (*Caladium*) M, S
Calla lily (*Zantedeschia*) M, S
Carolina cherry laurel (*Prunus caroliniana*) B, !
Carolina jessamine or evening trumpet flower (*Gelsemium sempervirens*) B
Castor bean (*Ricinis*) M, S, K, B, !
Ceriman or cut-leaf philodendron (*Monstera deliciosa*) M, S
Cherry (pits and wilting leaves) B
Chinese evergreen (*Aglaonema*) M, S
Christmas rose (*Helleborus niger*) S, B

Eating azaleas or other rhododendrons can lead to mouth burns, vomiting, shock, and death.

Autumn crocus is lovely but can be lethal: it damages the digestive tract, kidneys, and bone marrow.

Clematis (*Clematis*) M, S, B
Cordatum (*Philodendron oxycardium*) M, S
Corn plant or dracaena (*Dracaena*) S, B
Croton (*Codiaeum*) M, S
Cycad (*Cycas* or *Zamia*) S, K, !
Cyclamen (*Cyclamen*) S, !
Daffodil (*Narcissus*) S, H, B
Daphne (*Daphne*) M, S
Dieffenbachia or dumb cane (*Dieffenbachia*) M, S
Dogbane (*Apocynum*) H
Elephant's ear (*Colocasia antiquorum*) M, S
Emerald feather or emerald fern berries (*Asparagus densiflorus*) M, S
English ivy or common ivy (*Hedera helix*) S, B
Euonymus (*Euonymus*) H
Foxglove (*Digitalis*) H, !
Geranium (*Pelargonium*) M, S
Gladiolus (*Gladiolus*) S
Gloriosa or glory lily (*Gloriosa superba*) M, S, K

Heavenly bamboo (*Nandina domestica*) S, H, B, !
Holly (*Ilex*) S
Hurricane plant (*Monstera*) M, S
Hyacinth (*Hyacinthus orientalis*) S, B
Hydrangea (*Hydrangea*) S, H
Iris (*Iris*) S
Jack-in-the-pulpit (*Arisaema*) M, S
Japanese andromeda (*Pieris japonica*) S, H, B, !
Jerusalem cherry (*Solanum*) S, H, B
Kalanchoe (*Kalanchoe*) S, H
Laburnum or golden chain (*Laburnum anagyroides*) B, !
Lantana berries (*Lantana*) M, S
Lily-of-the-valley (*Convallaria*) H, !
Macadamia nuts S, B
Marble queen (*Scindapsus aureus*) M, S
Marijuana (*Cannabis*) B
Mexican breadfruit (*Monstera*) M, S

Lily-of-the-valley contains cardiac glycosides, powerful chemicals that can cause heart arrhythmias and death.

Milkweed (*Asclepias*) S, H, B, !

Mistletoe berries (*Phoradendron*) S, H, B

Morning glory (*Ipomoea purpurea*) S, B

Mushrooms, death cap and death angel (*Amanita*) S, K, B, !

Narcissus (*Narcissus*) S, H, B

Nephthytis (*Syngonium podophyllum*) M, S

Nightshade (*Solanum*) S, H, B

Oleander (*Nerium oleander*) S, H, B, !

Onion (*Allium*) S, K

Peace lily (*Spathiphyllum*) M, S

Peach (pits and wilting leaves) B

Philodendron (*Monstera* or *Philodendron*) M, S

Plumosa fern berries (*Asparagus plumosus*) S

Poinsettia (*Euphorbia*) M, S

Potato (leaves, stem, and green skin) S, H, B

Pothos or devil's ivy (*Epipremnum aureum*) M, S

Rhododendron (*Rhododendron*) M, S, H, B, !

Rhubarb (leaves) M, S

Rosary pea or precatory bean (*Abrus precatorius*) S, B, !

Sago palm (*Cycas* or *Zamia*) S, K, !

Schefflera (*Brassaia*) M, S

Snake plant or mother-in-law's tongue (*Sansevieria*) M, S

Snakeroot (*Eupatorium rugosum*) S, K

Spurge (*Euphorbia*) M, S

Stinging nettle (*Urtica*) M, S

Swiss cheese plant (*Monstera deliciosa*) M, S

Taro vine (*Scindapsus*) M, S

Tomato (leaves, stem, and green fruit) S, H, B

Tulip (*Tulipa*) S

Yew (*Taxus*) H, B, !

Yucca (*Yucca*) S, B

SAFE PLANTS

If you're planning a landscaping or decorating project and you want to choose plants that are safe for your dog, check the following websites for extensive lists of plants that are recognized as nontoxic:

www.aspca.org/site/PageServer? pagename=pro_apcc_nontoxicplants

www.VeterinaryPartner.com/Content .plx?P=A&S=0&C=0&A=1217

Be aware, however, that eating *any* plant can cause an upset stomach (in other words, vomiting and diarrhea), so discourage your dog from nibbling on greenery. Also keep in mind that common names of plants can be confusing—a single plant may have several common names, and several different plants may have the same common name. For example, dozens of plants are known as jasmine or jessamine, and some are safe while others are poisonous. When in doubt, check the plant's botanical name.

CHAPTER 19

ABC Guide to Injuries and Emergencies

TAKE A DEEP BREATH—that's the first thing to do in an emergency. No matter how severe the problem appears, remain calm, keep thinking, and focus on how you can help. In many cases, the proper response to an emergency counts for more than the speed of response. So call a vet if you can—or better yet, have someone nearby call for you—and then use the alphabetical list in this chapter to get specific instructions on what to do for your dog's injury. If you are not alone, delegate tasks. Others can help by bringing you supplies, writing down information, or getting a car to take your dog to the hospital. But if you are by yourself, take *two* deep breaths, and just do your best to provide the treatment your dog needs.

ANTIFREEZE POISONING: If your dog has gotten into antifreeze within the past two hours, induce vomiting by squirting about 1 tablespoon of 3 percent hydrogen peroxide per 20 pounds of your dog's body weight into her mouth with a turkey baster or oral medication syringe. Then call your vet or a veterinary emergency hospital immediately, and be prepared to rush your dog there as soon as you hang up the phone. Antifreeze poisoning can be fatal if not treated right away.

ARTIFICIAL RESPIRATION: See page 426.

BANDAGING A LEG OR TAIL: If you want to keep your dog from licking a wound on her leg or tail, consider buying or making an Elizabethan collar instead of bandaging the wound (see page 427). If you need to bandage a leg or tail for some other reason, here's how:

1. You'll need scissors, a roll of 1-inch bandage tape, antibiotic ointment, enough gauze squares or Telfa pads to cover the wound, and some rolls of 2-inch gauze, plus a roll of elastic bandage material (such as Vetrap), if possible.

2. Start with a clean wound (see page 404).

3. A leg bandage should extend all the way from the joint below the wound to the joint above it, in order to stay on without slipping off. A tail bandage should include the base of the tail.

4. Spread antibiotic ointment on the wound and cover it completely with gauze squares or Telfa pads.

5. Hold the pad in place by wrapping it with 2-inch gauze from the roll. This is easiest if you hold the roll "inside out"

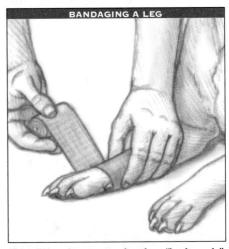

BANDAGING A LEG

Unspooling the gauze or bandage "backwards" onto the leg is faster and easier.

Make sure the tape isn't too tight, or you'll cut off the circulation.

(see the illustration above). Overlap each layer of gauze by about half its width. Stretch the gauze a bit as you wrap it so it puts a bit of pressure on the area, but don't pull too hard or you'll cut off the blood circulation.

6. Continue wrapping gauze around the leg or tail until you've covered the leg joint above the wound or, on the tail, the base of the tail; then switch wrapping directions and wrap back down

over the wound and past the leg joint below it, or to about 3 inches below a tail wound. If your gauze roll runs out, start another.

7. If you have elastic bandage wrap, use it to cover the gauze from bottom to top with a single layer. Hold the roll "inside out," and stretch the wrap a bit, but not so much that you cut off the circulation.

8. Tape the end of the bandage wrap or gauze.

9. Tape the top and bottom of the bandage to your dog's skin. Don't pull the tape too tight—you don't want to cut off the circulation.

10. Change the bandage whenever it gets wet or dirty, or at least every three days.

BEE, HORNET, OR WASP STING: If a stinger is visible in the skin, flick it out with the edge of a credit card. Don't use tweezers or anything else that may squeeze the stinger and inject more toxin into the skin. If your dog's face is swollen, if he is having trouble breathing, or if he passes out after a bee sting, take him to a vet immediately—he may be having a potentially fatal allergic reaction. The vet can give him epinephrine to counter the reaction and oxygen to help his breathing. If the bee sting is swollen, hot, and painful, but your dog seems comfortable otherwise, bathe the area in cool water, dab it with hydrocortisone cream or an anesthetic skin lotion, and give your dog 1 mg per pound of his body weight of diphenhydramine (Benadryl)—in other words, 10 mg for a 10-pound dog, 25 mg for a 25-pound dog, and so on. Depending on your dog's weight, you may find it more convenient to use the children's-strength chew-

able tablets (which contain 12.5 mg of diphenhydramine) rather than the adult-strength tablets (which contain 25 mg of diphenhydramine). There should be much less swelling, heat, and pain within 24 hours. If not, call your vet.

BIRTH OF PUPPIES: See LABOR AND DELIVERY.

BITE WOUNDS: If you don't know what bit your dog, be aware that it could have been an animal carrying rabies. Your dog probably has been vaccinated against rabies, but *you* could get rabies from the rabid animal's fresh saliva if it gets into a cut on your skin or into your nose, mouth, or eyes while you're examining and treating your dog's wounds. Wear rubber gloves and wash your hands thoroughly after you're finished.

It's best to have a vet treat bite wounds. If that's not possible, clip and clean the wounds as described on page 404. Bite wounds can easily become infected, so call a vet if they become swollen or hot, or ooze clear fluid or pus. Don't let your dog lick his wounds excessively, because that will irritate the skin and delay healing. Use an Elizabethan collar if necessary to keep him from licking the wounds.

BLEEDING, SEVERE: Place a thick layer of clean, absorbent cloth over the wound and press down firmly with your hand. Don't remove the cloth; if it becomes saturated with blood, add more layers on top. Transport the dog as quickly as possible to a vet. Avoid using a tourniquet, except on a leg you're certain will have to be amputated anyway, because a tourniquet cuts off blood flow in the undamaged blood vessels as well as in the torn vessel. The vet will clamp off and suture torn blood vessels, give

Apply firm, direct pressure with a cloth to stop bleeding from a wound.

IV fluids and medications for shock, and give a blood transfusion if necessary.

BLOAT: If your dog's abdomen seems swollen or distended and she seems very uncomfortable, call a vet immediately. Bloat, or gastric dilatation and volvulus (GDV), is a life-threatening emergency in which the stomach distends with gas and twists out of position, cutting off blood flow to the stomach and other organs. If your dog has GDV, the vet will pass a tube from your dog's mouth into the stomach to relieve the gas pressure, and then will most likely do emergency surgery to untwist the stomach. (See page 136 for how to prevent GDV.)

BLOOD IN URINE: This is not an emergency unless (1) the dog is clearly trying to urinate but is able to pass only a few drops of bloody urine, which could mean his urethra is blocked; (2) the dog has been hit by a car or had a similar accident that could have ruptured her bladder; or (3) she is an unspayed female who was in heat a month or so before and therefore might have an infected uterus (pyometra). In those situations, call a vet immediately. Blood in the urine can also be caused by a urinary-tract infection, "stones" (mineral deposits) in the urine, a tumor in the bladder or urethra, vaginal discharge in an unspayed female in heat, or a prostate problem in a male dog. Call your vet during office hours for an appointment. Give your dog plenty of fresh water to drink and take her outside frequently, but try not to let her pee within an hour before your vet appointment so her bladder will be full for a urine test.

BLOOD IN VOMIT: This can be red or brownish black, like coffee grounds. Call a vet immediately. An ulcer in the stomach or small intestine or a bleeding disorder could be the cause; these are serious problems that need to be treated right away.

BLOODY DIARRHEA: A few streaks of blood in diarrhea is a sign of colitis (an inflamed colon), which is not an emergency. Call your vet during office hours for an appointment. But if the diarrhea seems like it's mostly blood, if your dog is weak or lethargic, or if he's vomiting as well even though he hasn't had any food or water for four hours or more, call a vet immediately. Diarrhea that's mostly blood is a sign of parvovirus, hemorrhagic gastroenteritis, or another serious illness and should be treated right away.

BROKEN BONE: If the end of the bone is sticking through the skin, cover it with a clean cloth soaked in clean water. For a broken leg, tape or tie a rolled newspaper or magazine around the break to limit the motion of the bone ends. Transport the dog to a vet as quickly as possible. Use a blanket or board as a stretcher if necessary.

BROKEN NAIL: If the nail is still partly attached, put a muzzle on the dog and cut off the broken piece using dog nail clippers or strong scissors (see page 409). To stop the bleeding, put a folded paper towel or tissues against the broken surface and press firmly for five minutes. Don't remove the paper towel or tissue, because that might disturb the blood clot and start the bleeding again—let it fall off on its own later. You can also apply styptic or bar soap to a broken nail to help stop the bleeding, but they sting. If the bleeding won't stop, call a vet.

BURNS: Immediately rinse the burns with large amounts of cool, clean water, and call a vet immediately. Even burns that look minor can be dangerous.

CAR, HIT BY: Call a vet immediately. Even a dog that has no obvious injuries may have a collapsed lung or ruptured bladder from the impact, so she should be evaluated as soon as possible by a veterinarian.

CARBON MONOXIDE POISONING: Dogs can be exposed to carbon monoxide from car fumes or propane fumes in a garage or other enclosed area. Signs of carbon monoxide poisoning include weakness and staggering, unconsciousness, seizures, or sometimes bright red gums. Remove the dog from the source of exposure immediately and call a vet. If the dog is not breathing and has no heartbeat, do chest compressions (see the box on page 426) while rushing her to the vet.

CHOCOLATE POISONING: Estimate how many ounces of chocolate your dog ate, what kind of chocolate it was (unsweetened baking chocolate, semi-sweet chocolate, or milk chocolate), and how much your dog weighs. Note any symptoms your dog is having, such as vomiting, diarrhea, or tremors, and call a vet. See page 413 for more on chocolate toxicity.

CHOKING: If the dog has a small ball or other object lodged in his windpipe and is having trouble breathing, do the Heimlich maneuver immediately (see the box on page 429). If the Heimlich maneuver doesn't work, rush him to a vet.

If the dog is gasping for breath, cool him if he's hot, calm him, and transport him to a veterinary hospital immediately.

If the dog is able to breathe but is pawing at his mouth and shaking his head, he may have something stuck in his mouth. Open his mouth—if you can do so without getting bitten—to look for an object stuck there, and remove it if possible. If the dog has something caught crosswise against the roof of his mouth, you may have to push the object back toward his throat (where the jaw is wider) in order to dislodge it. Be careful not to push it down his throat. If you can't get the object out, call a vet.

If the dog is coughing, hacking, or gagging but seems to be getting enough air in and out, he may have a cold, a collapsing trachea, or another respiratory or heart ailment. This is not an emergency unless the dog is weak and lethargic, won't eat, or otherwise seems very ill. Call your vet during office hours for an appointment.

COLLAPSE: A dog who is unconscious and twitching or paddling her legs back and forth may be having a seizure; see SEIZURE. A dog who has collapsed in hot conditions may be suffering from heat stroke; see HEAT STROKE.

CARDIOPULMONARY RESUSCITATION

Dog owners who know how to do cardiopulmonary resuscitation (CPR) on people often wonder whether similar techniques can be used on dogs. The short answer is yes, they can, but their usefulness in canine emergencies is extremely limited.

First, a common situation in which you definitely should *not* attempt mouth-to-nose respiration: when a dog is conscious and gasping for breath. You will not be able to blow more air into his lungs than he can inhale on his own, and he will be terrified at your efforts. When a dog is **struggling to breathe,** do the following instead:

1. Perform the Heimlich maneuver if you know he has an object stuck in his trachea (see page 429).

2. If he is hot, cool him down by spraying or wiping him with water or moving him to an air-conditioned location.

3. Calm him as best you can.

4. Get him as quickly as you can to a vet clinic or other source of oxygen. (A kindhearted ambulance crew may let you use their oxygen tank.) Hold an oxygen mask close to the dog's nose but not so tightly against his muzzle that he struggles against it, or hold just the oxygen tube in front of his nostrils.

If a dog is **unconscious, not breathing, and has no heartbeat,** forget about mouth-to-nose breathing and concentrate your efforts on chest compressions—which help push blood to the brain and internal organs —while rushing the dog to the nearest veterinary hospital:

1. Lay the dog on his side.

2. Place the heel of one hand in the middle of the dog's ribs with the other hand over it.

3. Push down hard enough to compress the dog's ribs by 1 or 2 inches, once per second.

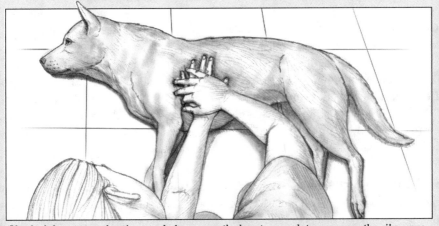

If a dog's heart stops beating, push down over the heart, enough to compress the ribs, once per second, while you rush him to the nearest veterinary hospital.

A host of other illnesses could also cause sudden, extreme weakness or unconsciousness, so your best bet is to call a vet immediately.

CONVULSION: See SEIZURE.

COONHOUND PARALYSIS: This is a disease that can occur for unknown reasons one to two weeks after a dog has been bitten by a raccoon or exposed to another immune-system trigger. It usually starts with weakness in the hind legs that progresses within two or three days to paralysis of the hind legs and then the front legs. Tick paralysis causes similar symptoms, so check your dog carefully for ticks, and if you find any, remove them (see TICK PARALYSIS). Then call a vet.

DIABETES EMERGENCY: Low blood sugar (from too much insulin and not enough food) and high blood sugar (from too little insulin) can cause the same symptoms—lethargy, weakness, staggering, or seizures. So don't give a weak or lethargic diabetic dog more insulin or sugar, because you may make the problem worse. Call a vet instead.

DIARRHEA: If the diarrhea looks like it's mostly blood or your dog is weak or lethargic or just seems really sick, call a vet right away. Otherwise, give your dog all the water she wants but no food for 12 hours, then start her on the bland diet described on page 122. If the diarrhea doesn't improve within one day of the bland diet, or isn't at least 80 percent better by the end of three days, call your vet.

DOG FIGHT: Use extreme caution in breaking up a dog fight, because you may get bitten. Dowsing the dogs' heads with water from a hose or bucket sometimes distracts them enough for the owners to be able to separate them. Or you and the other dog owner may be able to pull the dogs away from each other by their tails. It's best to have a vet treat bite wounds, but if that's not possible, clip and clean the wounds as described on page 404. Bite wounds can easily become infected, so call your vet if they become swollen or hot, ooze clear fluid or pus, or continue bleeding for more than one hour.

DROOLING: See SALIVATION, EXCESSIVE.

DROWNING: If the dog is conscious, keep him warm and quiet and watch him closely for two hours. Call a vet if he has trouble breathing or seems very ill. If the dog is unconscious, hold him head-down by the hind legs (if he's small) or waist (if he's large) to drain water from his mouth and lungs. If he's not breathing and has no heartbeat, do chest compressions while you rush him to the nearest veterinary hospital (see the previous page).

ELECTRIC SHOCK: Biting an electric cord can cause mouth burns, lung damage, or even cardiac arrest. If your dog has received an electric shock, call a vet. Even if the dog seems OK, he may have a lung injury that isn't obvious at first but can worsen without treatment.

ELIZABETHAN COLLAR (E-COLLAR): Use an E-collar to prevent a dog from licking a wound or rubbing an injured eye. You can buy an E-collar at a pet-supply store or make a temporary one from cardboard. Cut a fan-shaped piece of cardboard and tape it into a cone. The small end should fit around the upper part of your dog's neck with just an inch or so of slack. The cone should be long enough to extend past your dog's nose. Tape the edges so they're smooth. Punch several holes in the neck end of the

An E-collar must fit tightly on the neck and extend past the nose to be effective.

cone and thread gauze strips, pieces of string, or shoelaces through them. Slip the cone over your dog's head and tie the gauze, strings, or shoelaces to his collar, using bows rather than knots so you can remove the E-collar easily when you need to.

EYE DISCHARGE: If your dog is squinting or rubbing at her eye as if it were painful, call a vet immediately. Otherwise, flush the eye with plain saline eyewash squirted directly from the bottle, and see page 205.

EYE INJURY: Call a vet immediately. Eye injuries are extremely painful and can result in blindness if not treated appropriately.

EYE OUT OF THE SOCKET: If the eye is still attached (by muscles and the optic nerve), a vet can sometimes put it back in the socket. Keep the eye moist by holding a clean cloth soaked in water or saline eyewash over it. Take the dog to a veterinary hospital as quickly as possible. The vet will put the eye back in the socket and stitch the eyelid closed to hold it in place while it heals. If the eye

and optic nerve aren't severely damaged, the dog may regain some vision in the eye after it heals.

FEVER: A dog's normal temperature is between 100° and 102.5°F. Take the temperature rectally, using a baby thermometer (see page 404). If a high body temperature was caused by hot conditions or heat stroke, cool him off by bathing him in cool—not icy—water. Do not use rubbing alcohol; it's absorbed by the skin, and it's toxic. Offer the dog plenty of water to drink. If he seems ill and has a fever of 103°F or higher, call a vet. Don't give aspirin or other medications to reduce the fever; aspirin can cause stomach ulcers and mask other symptoms, and other fever reducers can be toxic to dogs.

FISH HOOK IN MOUTH OR SKIN: If the hook is not embedded deeply in the skin, you may be able to pull it out gently. If the hook doesn't come out readily, push the barbed end all the way through the skin, cut off the barb with wire cutters, and pull the rest of the hook out of the skin. Clip and clean the area as described on page 404.

FOAMING AT THE MOUTH: See SALIVATION, EXCESSIVE.

FOOT WOUND: Rinse the area thoroughly with water and look for glass, splinters, or other debris stuck in the wound. Remove any debris, and soak the foot for a minute or two in water with a bit of mild soap added. Dry the foot gently after soaking it. If the foot is bleeding, put a folded paper towel over the area and press firmly for five minutes. Don't remove the paper towel after that; let it fall off on its own. Soak foot wounds twice a day in slightly soapy water, drying the foot well afterward,

THE HEIMLICH MANEUVER

If you know your dog has a small ball, toy, piece of food, or other object stuck in his trachea (windpipe) and he can't breathe, do the Heimlich maneuver immediately.

1. Stand (if he's a tall dog) or kneel (if he's a small or medium dog) behind the dog, with the dog facing away from you.

2. Put your arms around the dog's waist. Make a fist with one hand and place your fist, thumb side up, on the dog's abdomen just below his ribs. Wrap your other hand around that fist.

3. Give a hard, fast jerk or squeeze upward, toward the dog's backbone. Apply enough force to move the dog's whole body. (If he's a very small dog, place two knuckles of one hand on the abdomen just below the ribs and the other hand flat on the dog's back to help steady him, then give a quick, hard poke upward with your knuckles.)

4. If the object does not come out of the dog's mouth on the first try, give another hard jerk. If after three or four jerks the object still has not come out or the dog still can't breathe, rush him to the nearest veterinary clinic, where a vet can do a tracheotomy (cut a hole in the dog's windpipe below the obstruction) to get air into the lungs and then remove the object surgically.

Use the Heimlich maneuver to dislodge an object that's blocking your dog's airway.

until they heal. Cover the foot with a plastic bag (taped to the dog's leg to hold it on) or a boot from a pet-supply store to protect it when you take the dog outside, but remove it when the dog is indoors. Foot wounds that bleed profusely need stitches, so call a vet right away.

FROSTBITE: A dog's ears, tail, and toes can freeze if he's exposed to extreme cold. Frostbitten skin can be hard, shriv-eled, red, or dark. Get the dog to a warm location. Wrap him in blankets or towels that have been warmed in a clothes dryer, if possible. Warm frostbitten areas with warm (not hot) water. Don't rub frostbitten skin, because that will cause more damage. Call your vet during office hours for an appointment.

GDV (GASTRIC DILATATION AND VOLVULUS): See BLOAT.

HEART FAILURE: Dogs don't have heart attacks, so a cardiac crisis is more likely to be caused by an arrhythmia or congestive heart failure. If a dog is unconscious and has no heartbeat, do chest compressions while rushing him to the nearest vet (see page 426). If the dog is conscious and you suspect a cardiac emergency, call a vet immediately.

HEAT STROKE: Dogs can cool themselves only by panting, so they can overheat even more quickly than a person might. Symptoms of heat stroke can include weakness, staggering, drooling, or unconsciousness. Move the dog to a cooler area, pour cool—not icy—water over his body, and check his temperature rectally using a baby thermometer, if possible. Call a vet immediately if you're not able to reduce the dog's body temperature to 103°F within 20 minutes, or if he can't stand or otherwise seems very ill even after his temperature goes down.

HIVES: Hives are fluid-filled bumps caused by an allergic reaction. If your dog has hives, give him 1 mg per pound of his body weight of diphenhydramine (Benadryl)—in other words, 10 mg for a 10-pound dog, 25 mg for a 25-pound dog, and so on. Call your vet if your dog is still extremely itchy or uncomfortable two hours after taking the diphenhydramine. If your dog's face is swollen or he's having trouble breathing, call a vet immediately—he may be having a life-threatening allergic reaction.

HOT SPOT: A hot spot is a local skin infection that often seems to pop up overnight. Clip and clean the area as described on page 404. Put an Elizabethan collar on your dog if the hot spot is in an area she can lick. See page 98 for more about hot spots.

HYPOTHERMIA: Symptoms can include shivering, staggering, lethargy, unconsciousness, or seizures. Move the dog to a warm location. Dry him if he's wet, and wrap him in blankets or towels that have been warmed in a clothes dryer, if possible. If he's conscious, offer him warm water or warm chicken soup to drink. Fill an empty liter soda bottle or hot-water bottle with warm (not hot!) water, wrap it in a towel, and place it next to the dog's belly. If you have a heating pad, turn it to the lowest setting, place it over (not under) the dog, and check every few minutes to make sure it's not too hot. Remove the hot-water bottle or heating pad as soon as the dog's body temperature reaches 100°F.

INSECT BITE OR STING: See BEE, HORNET, OR WASP STING.

ITCHING, SEVERE: Bathe the area in cool water, dry it, dab it with hydrocortisone cream or an anesthetic skin lotion, and give your dog 1 mg per pound of his body weight of diphenhydramine (Benadryl)—10 mg for a 10-pound dog, etc. Put an Elizabethan collar on your dog if he's licking the area. Call your vet during office hours for an appointment.

LABOR AND DELIVERY: Pregnancy lasts 63 days. Usually dogs give birth on their own with no problems. Signs of labor—panting, shivering, restlessness, hiding, nesting, and possibly a blood-streaked vaginal discharge—begin 2 to 12 hours before the first puppy is born. When the first puppy has moved into position, the dog will begin pushing—she will strain with her abdomen and hindquarters while squatting or lying down. Call your vet or a veterinary emergency hospital if any of the following occurs: (1) your dog pushes for more than four hours without delivering the first puppy; (2) a puppy is stuck partway out of the birth canal for more than 20 minutes (don't pull the puppy—this can injure him or the mother); or (3) your dog pushes for more than two hours before delivering each subsequent puppy. See page 344 for more on the birth process.

LAMENESS OR LIMPING: Examine your dog as described on page 232, and call your vet during office hours if warranted.

LYME DISEASE: See TICK REMOVAL.

MAGGOTS ON THE SKIN: These are a symptom of an underlying wound or skin infection. Keep the dog in a screened area where flies and other insects can't get to him. Bathe him if he's dirty, and clean the skin wound as described on page 404. Call your vet during office hours for an appointment, and see page 170 for more information on maggots.

MATING, UNWANTED: If your dog has mated and you don't want her to have a litter of puppies, the best way to terminate the pregnancy (and prevent any others) is to have her spayed as soon as possible. Otherwise, the safest course of action is to simply let her carry the puppies to term.

If she's a show dog and you insist on terminating the pregnancy without spaying her, hormone injections can be used to induce abortion. However, these injections have side effects that are extremely unpleasant and potentially dangerous. See page 341 for more on the injections.

MOUSE OR RAT POISON: If you think your dog may have eaten mouse or rat poison, don't wait for symptoms to appear—call a vet immediately. Rodent

poison can cause fatal internal bleeding if it's not treated promptly. See page 412 for more information.

MOUTH, PAWING AT: If the dog is able to breathe but is pawing at his mouth and shaking his head, he may have something stuck in his mouth. See CHOKING.

NOSEBLEED: If your dog has a nosebleed after being hit by a car or injuring her head, call a vet right away. If he has a nosebleed for no apparent reason, call your vet during office hours for an appointment. Spontaneous nosebleeds in dogs are not common and should be checked out by a vet (see page 283).

PANTING, EXCESSIVE: Dogs pant when they're excited, hot, short of breath, or in pain. If your dog may be overheated, bathe her in cool—not cold—water or move her to an air-conditioned location. If she's panting for no apparent reason and is also weak, having trouble walking, or too uncomfortable to eat, call a vet.

PARALYZED LEG OR LEGS: The potential causes are so numerous, this is a problem for a professional. If the paralysis has come on suddenly, call a vet right away. In case your dog has a spine injury, use a blanket or board as a stretcher to move him, and avoid bending or flexing his neck and spine.

PARVOVIRUS: The symptoms of parvovirus are severe bloody diarrhea, vomiting, and weakness. Parvo can occur in dogs that haven't been vaccinated against it or haven't received a full set of vaccinations. If you think your dog may have parvo, call a vet immediately—it's often fatal if not treated promptly. For more about parvo, see page 121.

POISONING: If you think your dog may have ingested something toxic, do not induce vomiting—this is often useless or harmful. Instead, estimate how much of the substance your dog may have eaten; check her quickly for symptoms such as vomiting, diarrhea, or tremors; and call a vet and tell him what your dog ate, how much, what her symptoms are, and how much she weighs. For tips on poison prevention, see page 411.

PORCUPINE QUILLS: Removing porcupine quills is very painful and is best done under anesthesia, so call a vet.

PREGNANCY, UNWANTED: See MATING, UNWANTED.

PUNCTURE WOUND: Clip and clean as described on page 404. Look carefully for embedded material and remove it if possible. If you can't remove the material, call your vet during office hours for an appointment. Puncture wounds often become infected, so watch the area closely for swelling, redness, or oozing, and call your vet if you see any of those signs.

RABIES: Rabies is a virus transmitted by saliva-to-blood or blood-to-blood contact with an infected animal. Raccoons, skunks, bats, and feral cats are some of the animals most commonly diagnosed with rabies. Since you could get rabies if a rabid animal's saliva gets in a cut on your skin or in your nose, mouth, or eyes, don't handle wild animals, and wear rubber gloves while examining and treating your dog if he has bite wounds from an unknown animal. If you suspect that your dog or a wild animal in your neighborhood may have been exposed to rabies, call a vet or your local animal-control office immediately. For more about the disease, including its symptoms, see page 320.

SALIVATION, EXCESSIVE: Drooling or even foaming at the mouth may be caused by nausea, something stuck in the mouth, or an inability to swallow. Open the dog's mouth (if you can do so without getting bitten), look for an object stuck there, and remove it if possible. In the following situations, call a vet immediately: if you see an object stuck in your dog's mouth but can't remove it; if your dog may have eaten something toxic; if her sides are swollen as if she may be bloating (see page 424); or if she's unable to swallow anything (saliva, water, or food).

SCORPION STING: While most scorpion stings are not highly toxic to dogs, they are extremely painful. The area is likely to swell, and if the sting is on a leg or foot, the dog may limp for a day or two. A dog stung by a more toxic species of scorpion may drool, vomit, become feverish, collapse, or have a seizure. Call a vet immediately if you see any of those symptoms.

SEIZURE: Look at a clock or watch to time the seizure. If the dog is unconscious and making involuntary movements for five minutes or more, or has three or more seizures right after each other, call a vet immediately. Do not put anything in the dog's mouth; he won't choke on his tongue. Move him only if he's in a dangerous location, such as at the top of a flight of stairs. If it's the first time the dog has had a seizure, call your vet within 48 hours to report the seizure and to discuss possible causes; see page 309.

SHAKING OR SHIVERING: See TREMBLING.

SHOCK: Shock is a shortage of oxygenated blood reaching the brain, heart, kidneys, and other vital organs. It can be caused by blood loss, internal bleeding, heart failure, toxins, and other problems. The symptoms are weakness, panting, pale or bluish gums, collapse, or unconsciousness. Prop up your dog's hindquarters to help blood reach her heart and brain, cover her with a warm blanket, and rush her to a vet.

SHOCK, ELECTRIC: See ELECTRIC SHOCK.

SKUNK SPRAY: If your dog has been sprayed in the face, rinse the eyes well by squirting plain saline eyewash directly from the bottle. Rinse out your dog's mouth with water squirted from a turkey baster or slow-flowing garden hose. If your dog is still squinting or rubbing his eyes after you rinse them, call a vet right away.

Numerous concoctions are reported to help remove the skunk smell from a dog's fur, but the most effective "active ingredient" is simply washing the dog many times, in whichever remedy you prefer, until the smell is tolerable. Here are some options:

❏ Pet-supply stores and many vets sell deskunking shampoos. Lather your dog, leave the suds on for five minutes, rinse, and repeat until the smell is tolerable.
❏ Soak the dog in tomato juice for five minutes, then lather him with dog shampoo and leave the suds on for five minutes. Rinse and repeat as needed.
❏ Soak the dog in a baking soda or vinegar douche solution (like Massengill) for five minutes, then lather him with dog shampoo and leave the suds on for five minutes. Rinse and repeat as needed.

❏ Mix 1 quart of 3 percent hydrogen peroxide, ¼ cup of baking soda, and 1 teaspoon of dish soap in a bucket (it will foam up). Soak your dog in this mixture for five minutes, then lather him with dog shampoo and leave the suds on for five minutes. Rinse and repeat as needed.

SMOKE INHALATION: Remove the dog from the source of exposure and call a vet. If the dog is not breathing and has no heartbeat, do chest compressions (described on page 426) while rushing her to the vet.

SNAKEBITE: Most snakes found in the United States are not venomous. Treat a bite from a nonvenomous snake as an ordinary wound (see page 404). Rattlesnakes, copperheads, water moccasins, and coral snakes are venomous and are found primarily in the Southwest, Northeast, and East. Symptoms of a venomous snakebite are extreme pain, rapid swelling and bruising of the area around the bite, drooling, panting, a rapid heart rate, and possibly collapse. If your dog shows any of these symptoms, call a vet immediately. A vet can treat the dog for shock (with IV fluids, oxygen, and medications) and possibly administer an antitoxin.

SWALLOWED OBJECT: If your dog has eaten an object that's fairly small, reasonably smooth, and may pass through the digestive tract, feed her normally and watch for vomiting, diarrhea, or loss of appetite. If any of those problems occurs, call a vet and report what your dog ate, how long ago, and what the symptoms are. If your dog eats cloth or string, however, call a vet right away; cloth and similar materials can get hung up in the digestive tract and cause serious damage.

Facial swelling can quickly progress to throat swelling or shock, so call a vet right away.

SWOLLEN FACE: This can be the onset of a potentially fatal allergic reaction. Call a vet immediately.

SWOLLEN JOINT: This can be caused by an injury, infection, Lyme disease, or other problem. Call your vet during office hours for an appointment.

TICK PARALYSIS: Some ticks secrete a toxin that can cause paralysis. It usually starts with weakness in the hind legs that gets worse and progresses to the front of the body. If your dog is suddenly weak or paralyzed, check him carefully for ticks, remove any that you find, and then call a vet immediately. See page 322 for more information.

TICK REMOVAL: Remove ticks as soon as possible to avoid transmission of tick-borne diseases, such as Lyme, babesiosis, ehrlichiosis, and Rocky Mountain spotted fever. A tick needs to be attached and feeding for about 24 hours before it can transmit a disease. Put a tick-killing collar (one that contains amitraz)

on your dog or pull off the ticks using tweezers or a tick remover. For detailed instructions, see pages 170 and 171.

TOAD POISONING: Most toads found in the United States taste terrible but are not toxic. Biting a toad will make a dog drool and vomit but usually doesn't cause serious damage. Rinse the dog's mouth with a slow stream of water from a garden hose and call your vet if vomiting persists for more than four hours. Bufo toads are highly toxic, however, and can kill a dog that bites or mouths them. *Bufo marinus* is known as the cane, marine, or giant toad and is found primarily in Florida, the Caribbean, and south Texas. *Bufo alvarius* is known as the Colorado River or Sonoran Desert toad and is found primarily in the Southwest. Toxins secreted by bufo toads' skin can cause seizures, heart arrhythmias, shock, and death if ingested. If your dog bites or mouths a bufo toad, his first symptoms are likely to be heavy drooling or even foaming at the mouth and retching or gagging. If he is salivating and retching but still conscious and not having a seizure, rinse his mouth with a slow stream of water from a garden hose, then take him to a vet immediately for further treatment.

TOOTH, BROKEN: Call your vet during office hours for an appointment. In the meantime, feed your dog canned food if eating dry food is uncomfortable.

TREMBLING: Dogs tremble, shiver, or shake when they're cold, excited, anxious, or in pain. If your dog is trembling in a way that's unusual for her, check her carefully for signs of an injury, note any other symptoms she may be having (such as loss of appetite, diarrhea, or limping), and call a vet if she seems ill or injured. A few neurologic problems can also cause twitching or tremors, but these are rare—see page 311.

UNCONSCIOUSNESS: If the dog is paddling his legs back and forth, he may be having a seizure (see page 432). If he is unconscious, is not breathing, and has no heartbeat, do chest compressions (see page 426) while rushing him to the nearest vet. If he is unconscious but breathing, call a vet immediately.

URINATION: If your dog hasn't urinated in 24 hours, or tries to urinate but can't or produces only a drop or two of urine, he might have a blocked urethra—call a vet immediately. If he's urinating more than usual or has blood in his urine, call your vet during office hours for an appointment. Give your dog plenty of fresh water to drink and take him outside frequently, but try not to let him pee within an hour before the vet appointment so his bladder will be full for a urine test.

VACCINE REACTION: After receiving a vaccine, a dog may have mild swelling, heat, or pain at the site of the injection, a slight fever, and mild fatigue or listlessness. These symptoms usually go away on their own within a day or two. Don't give your dog any pain relievers, and call your vet during office hours to report the symptoms. A severe vaccine reaction will usually occur within minutes to an hour after a vaccination. Symptoms are extensive swelling, difficulty breathing, and collapse. Rush your dog back to the vet immediately if this happens. Your vet will give your dog epinephrine and IV fluids and place him on a respirator if necessary. See page 48 for more information on vaccine reactions.

VOMITING: If your dog is vomiting and may have eaten something toxic, call your vet or a veterinary emergency hospital right away. Also call right away if your dog is vomiting and seems weak, lethargic, or simply very ill. Otherwise, when your dog vomits, fast her for 12 hours—this means no food *or water*—and follow the instructions on page 134. If your dog is still vomiting four hours after she last had any food or water, call a vet.

WORMS IN VOMIT OR FECES: This is not an emergency unless the puppy or dog is also weak or lethargic, vomiting repeatedly, having watery diarrhea, or not interested in food. If any of those symptoms are present, call a vet immediately. If your dog seems well aside from the worms, make an appointment to take him and a stool sample to the vet—your dog may have more than one kind of parasite. Don't give an over-the-counter dewormer, because it may not be effective against the type or types of worms your dog has.

Part 4

Healthy Dog Resources

A P P E N D I X A

Pet Health Insurance

Most people have to consider what they can afford when making decisions about medical treatment for an ill or injured dog. That's why vets like pet health insurance—it lightens the financial burden on dog owners and allows them to focus on what's best for their dog rather than how much they have in their bank account. The main difficulty with pet health insurance is comparing different plans' costs and coverage so you can pick the policy that makes the most sense for you.

Things to Consider When Shopping for Pet Health Insurance

Health insurance policies vary widely, from coverage only for accidental injuries to complete coverage for everything from preventive care (such as vaccines and heartworm tests) to prescription medications to illnesses and injuries. To decide what's best for you, calculate how much you spent on different categories of veterinary care over the past year and think about what kinds of medical treatment your dog is most likely to need in the next year or two. Here are some specific health factors to consider:

❏ If you're getting a puppy, look for a policy that covers puppy vaccinations, spaying or neutering, deworming, and ID microchips, as well as injuries and illnesses.

❏ If you spend a lot on prescription medications, look for a policy that covers all or part of that cost. Many policies do not.

❏ If you have an older dog, look for a policy that covers routine dental cleaning, prescription medications, and diagnostic tests such as blood work, EKGs, and x-rays.

❏ If your dog has a chronic or recurring condition, look for a policy that covers preexisting problems. Many policies don't cover hereditary or congenital defects. Others will cover preexisting problems only if the dog has not needed treatment for the problem in at least six months. If your dog's breed is predisposed to an inherited health problem—such as hip dysplasia—be sure to find out whether that problem is covered.

❏ If you favor alternative treatment, look for a policy that covers acupuncture, chiropractic work, and holistic medicine.

Pet Health Insurers

Pet health insurance companies and their policies can change in the blink of an eye, so use the following information only as a starting point for your own research. Look for a health insurer that has been in business for at least a couple of years, ask your vet and other pet owners for recommendations, and search the Internet for complaints against or praise for the company. Above all, read policies carefully for conditions and exclusions before enrolling. Prices vary depending on your dog's breed and age and where you live, so call the companies or visit their websites to obtain current rates and specific details.

VETERINARY PET INSURANCE

www.petinsurance.com
800-872-7387

VPI STANDARD PLAN

Owner pays a $50 deductible for each incident. After that, owner is reimbursed for cost of treatment up to a set limit for each covered accident or illness. Yearly limit is $9,000.

Medical care included: Treatment for "over 6,400 medical problems and conditions related to accidental injuries, poisonings and illnesses (including cancer)"; diagnostic tests; prescription medications; hospitalization; office visits; surgery; acupuncture and chiropractic treatments by a licensed veterinarian; euthanasia.

Medical care excluded: Annual physical exams, vaccinations, and dental cleaning (unless you also buy Vaccination & Routine Care Coverage—see below); some preexisting conditions; knee ligament injuries that occur during the first 12 months of coverage; prescription foods; behavior treatment; elective procedures; congenital or hereditary defects, including hip dysplasia; expenses related to pregnancy or whelping.

Age restriction: No.

Breed restriction: No.

Preexisting condition restriction: Yes.

VPI SUPERIOR PLAN

Owner pays a $50 deductible for each incident. After that, owner is reimbursed for cost of treatment up to a set limit—

higher than that for the VPI Standard Plan, above—for each covered illness or accident. Yearly limit is $14,000.

Medical care included: Treatment for "over 6,400 medical problems and conditions related to accidental injuries, poisonings and illnesses (including cancer)"; diagnostic tests; prescription medications; hospitalization; office visits; surgery; acupuncture and chiropractic treatments by a licensed veterinarian; euthanasia.

Medical care excluded: Annual physical exams, vaccinations, and dental cleaning (unless you also buy Vaccination & Routine Care Coverage—see below); some preexisting conditions; knee ligament injuries that occur during the first 12 months of coverage; prescription foods; behavior treatment; elective procedures; congenital or hereditary defects, including hip dysplasia; expenses related to pregnancy or whelping.

Age restriction: No.

Breed restriction: No.

Preexisting condition restriction: Yes.

VPI VACCINATION & ROUTINE CARE COVERAGE

Set amounts will be reimbursed for an annual physical exam, fecal test, deworming, heartworm test, heartworm prevention, microchipping, vaccines, prescription flea control, and one of the following: spaying or neutering; dental cleaning; or a "comprehensive health screening," such as a complete blood count and blood chemistry test, urinalysis, and EKG reading.

PREMIER PET INSURANCE

www.ppins.com
877-774-4671

PREMIER BASIC PLAN

Owner pays a $100 deductible each year. After that, owner is reimbursed for 80 percent of cost of treatment up to a limit of $1,500 for each covered illness or injury. Yearly limit is $8,000.

Medical care included: Treatment for illnesses and injuries, including surgery; spaying or neutering; diagnostic tests; hospitalization; prescription medications, except for heartworm prevention; treatment for abscessed, diseased, or broken teeth; euthanasia.

Medical care excluded: Annual physical exams and "routine checkups"; vaccines; dental cleaning; prescription foods; expenses related to breeding and whelping; acupuncture and other alternative treatments; behavior treatment; organ transplants; heartworm prevention; cosmetic surgery (such as dewclaw removal, tail docking, and ear cropping).

Age restriction: Must be between 8 weeks and 8 years old when first enrolled; coverage may be renewable for dogs age 8 and older who are already enrolled, at a higher charge.

Breed restriction: Shar-Peis and Shar-Pei mixes are covered for spaying or neutering and injuries only.

Preexisting condition restriction: PPI will not insure dogs who have been diagnosed with a "chronic or terminal" illness such as cancer, diabetes, seizures, or untreated hip dysplasia. Other, non-chronic and non-terminal preexisting injuries and illnesses may be covered beginning 90 days or 180 days after the most recent treatment, depending on what state you live in—check on your dog's specific preexisting condition. Conditions that are congenital (present at birth) are not covered.

PREMIER PLUS PLAN

Owner pays a $100 deductible each year. After that, owner is reimbursed for 80 percent of cost of treatment up to a limit of $3,500 for each covered illness or injury. Yearly limit is $11,000.

Medical care included: Same as Premier Basic Plan, plus one annual physical exam and preventive care including DHLPP and coronavirus vaccines and puppy boosters; rabies vaccine; and heartworm testing.

Medical care excluded: Dental cleaning; prescription foods; expenses related to breeding and whelping; acupuncture and other alternative treatments; behavior treatment; organ transplants; heartworm prevention; cosmetic surgery (such as dewclaw removal, tail docking, and ear cropping).

Age restriction: Same as Premier Basic Plan.

Breed restriction: Shar-Peis and Shar-Pei mixes are restricted to Premier Basic and will be covered for spaying or neutering and injuries only.

Preexisting condition restriction: Same as Premier Basic Plan.

PREMIER PLATINUM PLAN

Owner pays a $100 deductible each year. After that, owner is reimbursed for 80 percent of cost of treatment up to a limit of $5,000 for each covered illness or injury. Yearly limit is $13,000.

Medical care included: Same as Premier Plus Plan, plus Lyme and bordetella vaccines and puppy boosters; heartworm prevention; fecal test; flea treatment and prevention; and one dental cleaning per year.

Medical care excluded: Prescription

foods; expenses related to breeding and whelping; acupuncture and other alternative treatments; behavior treatment; organ transplants; cosmetic surgery (such as dewclaw removal, tail docking, and ear cropping).

Age restriction: Same as Premier Basic Plan.

Breed restriction: Shar-Peis and Shar-Pei mixes are restricted to Premier Basic and will be covered for spaying or neutering and injuries only.

Preexisting condition restriction: Same as Premier Basic Plan.

PREMIER ULTIMATE PLAN
Owner pays a $100 annual deductible, then is reimbursed 80 percent of cost of treatment, up to a limit of $2,500 for each covered illness or injury. Yearly limit is $13,000.

Medical care included: Same as Premier Plus Plan, plus coverage for some chronic and long-term conditions.

PET ASSURE
www.petassure.com
888-789-7387

Pet Assure is a pet-care discount club. Owner pays a membership fee of $99 per year for the first pet and $79 per year for each additional pet, and receives a 25 percent discount on medical care by 2,500 Pet Assure veterinarian providers.

Medical care included: All, including physical exams and vaccines; diagnostic tests; treatment for illnesses and injuries, including preexisting conditions; hospitalization; dental care; elective procedures; treatment for hereditary diseases, including hip dysplasia; holistic care (by

member providers); prescription medications, including heartworm prevention.

Nonmedical care included: Pet Assure non-veterinarian providers offer a 30 percent discount on dog care and products such as boarding, training, grooming, pet sitting, food, beds, toys, crates, and treats.

Age restriction: No.

Breed restriction: No.

Preexisting condition restriction: No.

Veterinarian restriction: Yes; website has a directory that lets you search by zip code for enrolled veterinarians near you.

PETCARE
www.petcareinsurance.com
866-275-7387

QUICKCARE
Owner pays a $50 deductible for each accident. After that, owner is reimbursed for cost of treatment up to a set limit for each covered accident. No yearly limit.

Medical care included: Diagnostic tests and treatment for covered accidental injuries, including object ingestion requiring surgical removal; motor vehicle accidents; bone fractures; poison ingestion; lacerations, bite wounds, and abscesses; burns; allergic reactions to insect bites or stings.

Nonmedical care included: Reimbursement of dog's original purchase price in case of accidental death, up to $500.

Medical care excluded: All other, such as preventive care (checkups, vaccines) and treatment for illnesses.

Age restriction: Must be at least 8 weeks old.

Breed restriction: No.

Preexisting condition restriction: Yes.

QUICKCARE OPTIMUM

Owner pays a $100 deductible for each covered injury and then is reimbursed 90 percent of the cost of treatment, up to $2,000 per incident. For a "first-time illness," the owner pays a $100 deductible and then is reimbursed 90 percent of the cost of treatment, up to $1,500. For annual wellness visits, there is no deductible, and the owner is reimbursed up to $150.

Medical care included: Same as QuickCare, plus an annual exam; DHLPP and rabies vaccines; spaying or neutering; heartworm testing and prevention; and a dental cleaning. The limit on annual wellness visits is $150.

Medical care excluded: All other vaccines, and flea and tick prevention.

Nonmedical care included: Advertising or a reward for a lost animal, $150 limit. Euthanasia and cremation or burial, $100 limit.

Age restriction: Must be between 8 weeks and 6 years old.

Breed restriction: Shar-Peis are eligible for accident coverage only (i.e., the QuickCare policy).

QUICKCARE GOLD

Owner pays a $100 deductible and then is reimbursed 70 percent or 90 percent (depending on the premium level), up to a limit of $3,000 per injury and $3,000 for each of 12 "illness categories." The lifetime illness limit is $72,000.

Medical care included: Same as QuickCare, plus diagnostic tests and treatment for 12 illness categories,

including blood tests, x-rays, hospitalization, surgery, prescription medications, chemotherapy, and holistic treatments such as acupuncture and chiropractic. The disease categories are cardiovascular and respiratory system; digestive system; urogenital system; musculoskeletal system; nervous system; eyes; ears; skin; endocrine system; blood and lymphoid system; infectious diseases; and cancer.

Medical care excluded: Preventive care, such as annual physical exams and vaccines.

Nonmedical care included: For accidental death, reimbursement of the animal's purchase price, up to $500. Boarding kennel fees up to $250 if the owner is hospitalized for more than 48 hours and can't care for the animal. Advertising or a reward for a lost animal, up to $150. Euthanasia and cremation or burial, up to $100.

Age restriction: Must be between 8 weeks and 6 or 8 years old, depending on breed.

Breed restriction: Breed-based age restriction; certain breeds pay a higher monthly premium; Shar-Peis are eligible for QuickCare only.

Preexisting condition restriction: Yes.

QUICKCARE COMPLETE

Annual wellness visits have no deductible and are reimbursed up to $150. For accidents and illnesses, owner pays a $100 deductible per incident and then is reimbursed 70 percent of the cost of treatment, with a limit of $5,000 per injury or illness category and a $60,000 lifetime limit.

Medical care included: Same as QuickCare Gold, plus an annual physical exam; DHLPP and rabies vaccines; spaying or neutering; heartworm testing and prevention; and dental cleaning. The limit on annual wellness visits is $150.

Medical care excluded: Any other vaccines; flea and tick prevention.

Nonmedical care included: Same as QuickCare Gold.

Age restriction: Same as QuickCare Gold.

Breed restriction: Same as QuickCare Gold.

Preexisting condition restriction: Yes.

QUICKCARE SENIOR

Medical care included: Owner pays a $200 deductible and then is reimbursed up to $2,000 per illness for treatment for strokes, seizures, heart disease, and cancer not noted, diagnosed, or treated in the previous 36 months. Accident and injury coverage as in QuickCare.

Medical care excluded: All other illnesses and preventive care, such as wellness exams, vaccines, and heartworm testing and prevention.

Nonmedical care included: Same as QuickCare Gold, plus $500 to cover the cost of canceling a trip if your dog requires life-saving medical treatment up to 7 days before or during your vacation, and a $200 bequest to the guardian of your dog if you die.

Age restriction: Must be at least 8 weeks old. No upper age limit.

Breed restriction: Shar-Peis are eligible for accident coverage only. Certain breeds pay a higher monthly premium.

Preexisting condition restriction: Yes.

EMBRACE PET INSURANCE

www.embracepetinsurance.com
800-511-9172

Customizable coverage, with a range of deductibles ($100, $200, or $500 per year), copays (10, 20, or 30 percent), and annual limits ($2,000, $5,000, or $10,000).

Medical care included: Accidents, injuries, and illnesses; many genetic and congenital diseases; alternative and complementary treatments, such as acupuncture and hydrotherapy.

Medical care excluded: Annual physical exams and vaccines; cosmetic procedures; pregnancy; spaying or neutering. Coverage for prescriptions, dental care, and chronic illnesses (those lasting more than 12 months) can be added at an additional cost.

Age restriction: Purebred dogs must be between 8 weeks and 6 years old. Mixed-breed dogs must be between 8 weeks and 8 years old.

Breed restriction: Different breeds pay different monthly premiums.

Preexisting condition restriction: Some; check website for specifics.

PURRFECT PET INSURANCE

www.purrfectpetinsurance.com
877-440-PETS

PROTECT 1 PLAN

Owner pays an annual deductible ranging from $100 to $200, depending on the age of the dog and area of the country. Copayment for each injury or accident ranges from 20 to 40 percent. The per-incident limit is $1,500 and the annual limit is $8,000.

Medical care included: Diagnosis and treatment of injuries and accidents.

Medical care excluded: Holistic treatments and rehabilitation. All other illnesses and preventive care, such as annual exams and vaccines.

Nonmedical care included: Euthanasia when required for humane reasons. Reimbursement of the dog's purchase price, up to $200, for death resulting from injury. An optional benefit provides up to $200 for death due to illness in a dog 8 years old or younger.

Age restriction: Deductibles and copays increase with age.

Breed restriction: No.

Preexisting condition restriction: Yes.

PROTECT 2 PLAN
Owner pays an annual deductible ranging from $100 to $200, depending on the age of the dog and area of the country. Copays range from 20 to 40 percent. The per-incident limit is $1,500, and the annual limit is $10,000.

Medical care included: Same as Protect 1 Plan, plus diagnosis and treatment of illnesses.

Medical care excluded: Holistic treatments and rehabilitation; preventive care, such as annual exams and vaccines; special diets or supplements; behavior consultation or treatment; elective or cosmetic surgery.

Nonmedical care included: Euthanasia when required for humane reasons. Reimbursement of the dog's purchase price, up to $250, for death resulting

from injury. An optional benefit provides up to $250 for death due to illness in a dog 8 years old or younger.

Age restriction: Deductibles and copays increase with age.

Breed restriction: No.

Preexisting condition restriction: Yes.

PROTECT 3 PLAN
Owner pays an annual deductible ranging from $100 to $200, depending on the age of the dog and area of the country. Copays range from 20 to 40 percent. The per-incident limit is $2,500, and the annual limit is $13,000.

Medical care included: Same as Protect 2 Plan, plus optional coverage for dental extractions and preventive health care, including an annual exam; DHLPP, coronavirus, and rabies vaccines and puppy boosters; fecal test; and heartworm test.

Medical care excluded: Dental cleaning; Lyme and bordetella vaccines; heartworm prevention; flea and tick treatment and prevention; holistic treatments and rehabilitation; special diets or supplements; behavior consultation or treatment; elective or cosmetic surgery.

Nonmedical care included: Euthanasia when required for humane reasons. Reimbursement of the dog's purchase price, up to $500, for death resulting from injury. An optional benefit provides up to $500 for death due to illness in a dog 8 years old or younger.

Age restriction: Deductibles and copays increase with age.

Breed restriction: No.

Preexisting condition restriction: Yes.

PROTECT 4 PLAN

Owner pays an annual deductible ranging from $100 to $200, depending on the age of the dog and area of the country. Copays range from 20 to 40 percent. The per-incident limit is $3,500, and the annual limit is $15,000.

Medical care included: Same as Protect 3 Plan, plus Lyme and bordetella vaccines, annual vaccine titers, heartworm prevention, flea and tick protection, an annual blood test for dogs age 8 years or older, an annual dental cleaning, holistic treatments, and rehabilitation.

Medical care excluded: Special diets or supplements; behavior consultation or treatment; elective or cosmetic surgery.

Nonmedical care included: Euthanasia when required for humane reasons. Reimbursement of the dog's purchase price, up to $750, for death resulting from injury. An optional benefit provides up to $750 for death due to illness in a dog 8 years old or younger.

Age restriction: Deductibles and copays increase with age.

Breed restriction: No.

Preexisting condition restriction: Yes.

PETSHEALTH CARE PLAN

www.petshealthplan.com
800-807-6724

ACCIDENT ONLY PLAN

Owner pays a $100 annual deductible, then is reimbursed 80 percent of allowable charges. Per-incident limit is $2,500, annual limit is $8,000.

Medical care included: Diagnosis and treatment of accidents and injuries.

Medical care excluded: Treatment or surgery for knee ligament damage that occurs or is symptomatic within the first 12 months of coverage. More than one incident of foreign body ingestion in a 12-month period. Costs related to breeding or pregnancy. Treatment for illnesses; preventive care and vaccines; holistic treatment; and rehabilitation.

Age restriction: Must be between 8 weeks and 13 years old.

Breed restriction: No.

Preexisting condition restriction: Yes.

BASIC PLAN

Owner pays a $100 annual deductible, then is reimbursed 80 percent of allowable charges. Per-incident limit is $1,500, annual limit is $8,000.

Medical care included: Same as Accident Plan, plus treatment for illnesses that occur at least 30 days after the start of the plan.

Medical care excluded: Treatment or surgery for knee ligament damage that occurs or is symptomatic within the first 12 months of coverage. More than one incident of foreign body ingestion in a 12-month period. Costs related to breeding or pregnancy. Preventive care and vaccines; dental cleaning; holistic treatment; and rehabilitation.

Age restriction: Must be between 8 weeks and 13 years old.

Breed restriction: Shar-Peis are eligible for the Accident Plan only.

Preexisting condition restriction: Yes.

VALUE PLAN
Owner pays a $100 annual deductible, then is reimbursed 80 percent of allowable charges. Per-incident limit is $3,500, annual limit is $11,000.

Medical care included: Same as Basic Plan, plus spay or neuter; DHLPP, coronavirus, and rabies vaccines and puppy boosters; an annual physical exam, fecal test, and heartworm test.

Medical care excluded: Other vaccines. Treatment for illnesses that occur within the first 30 days of coverage. Treatment or surgery for knee ligament damage that occurs or is symptomatic within the first 12 months of coverage. More than one incident of foreign body ingestion in a 12-month period. Costs related to breeding or pregnancy. Dental cleaning, holistic treatment, and rehabilitation.

Age restriction: Must be between 8 weeks and 13 years old.

Breed restriction: Shar-Peis are eligible for the Accident Plan only.

Preexisting condition restriction: Yes.

CHOICE PLAN
Owner pays a $100 annual deductible, then is reimbursed 80 percent of allowable charges. Per-incident limit is $5,000, annual limit is $13,000.

Medical care included: Same as the Value Plan, plus Lyme and bordetella vaccines, heartworm prevention, flea and tick protection, and an annual dental cleaning.

Medical care excluded: Other vaccines. Treatment for illnesses that occur within the first 30 days of coverage. Treatment or surgery for knee ligament damage that occurs or is symptomatic within the first

12 months of coverage. More than one incident of foreign body ingestion in a 12-month period. Costs related to breeding or pregnancy. Holistic treatment and rehabilitation.

Age restriction: Must be between 8 weeks and 13 years old.

Breed restriction: Shar-Peis are eligible for the Accident Plan only.

Preexisting condition restriction: Yes.

BEST PLAN
Owner pays a $100 annual deductible, then is reimbursed 80 percent of allowable charges. Per-incident limit is $2,500, annual limit is $13,000.

Medical care included: Same as Choice Plan, plus treatment for chronic and long-term illnesses.

Medical care excluded: Same as Choice Plan.

Age restriction: Must be between 8 weeks and 13 years old.

Breed restriction: Shar-Peis are eligible for the Accident Plan only.

Preexisting condition restriction: Fewer restrictions than with the other plans. Check the website for details.

PETFIRST HEALTHCARE
www.petfirsthealthcare.com
866-937-PETS (7387)

BASIC PLAN
Owner pays a $50 deductible for each accident or illness, then is reimbursed 90 percent of the remaining cost up to $1,500 per incident. The annual maximum is $7,000. There is no deductible for preventive care, but the maximum reimbursement is $100 per year.

Medical care included: Diagnosis and treatment of injuries and illnesses. An annual physical exam; DHLPP, bordetella, Lyme, coronavirus, and rabies vaccines; heartworm testing and prevention; and flea and tick protection.

Medical care excluded: Spaying or neutering; dental cleaning; routine blood tests; fecal test; treatment of anal sacculitis or surgical removal of anal sacs; special diets or supplements; treatment of behavior problems; treatment of a knee ligament injury that occurs within the first 12 months of coverage.

Nonmedical care included: Advertising or a reward for a lost dog, $250 limit; boarding kennel fees up to $250 if owner is hospitalized for more than 96 hours and can't care for the animal.

Age restriction: Must be between 8 weeks and 10 years old.

Breed restriction: No.

Preexisting condition restriction: Yes.

PREFERRED PLAN
Owner pays a $50 deductible for each accident or illness, then is reimbursed 90 percent of the remaining cost up to $2,500 per incident. The annual maximum is $10,000. There is no deductible for preventive care, but the maximum reimbursement is $220 per year.

Medical care included: Same as Basic Plan, plus spay or neuter; an annual dental cleaning; fecal testing; and annual screening tests such as blood tests, urinalysis, and an EKG.

Medical care excluded: Treatment of anal sacculitis or surgical removal of anal sacs; special diets or supplements; treatment of behavior problems; treatment of

a knee ligament injury that occurs within the first 12 months of coverage.

Nonmedical care included: Behavioral training; advertising or a reward for a lost dog, $250 limit; reimbursement of purchase price, up to $250, of a lost pet; boarding kennel fees up to $500 if owner is hospitalized for more than 96 hours and can't care for the animal; up to $500 for trip cancellation fees if your dog has emergency surgery up to 7 days before or during your trip.

Age restriction: Must be between 8 weeks and 10 years old.

Breed restriction: No.

Preexisting condition restriction: Yes.

PREFERRED PLUS PLAN
Owner pays a $50 deductible for each accident or illness, then is reimbursed 90 percent of the remaining cost up to $3,500 per incident. The annual maximum is $13,000. There is no deductible for preventive care, but the maximum reimbursement is $220 per year.

Medical care included: Same as Preferred Plan.

Medical care excluded: Same as Preferred Plan.

Nonmedical care included: Behavioral training; advertising or a reward for a lost dog, $400 limit; reimbursement of purchase price, up to $500, of a lost pet; boarding kennel fees up to $500 if owner is hospitalized for more than 96 hours and can't care for the animal; up to $500 for trip cancellation fees if your dog has emergency surgery up to 7 days before or during your trip; $100 toward burial or cremation.

Age restriction: Must be between 8 weeks and 10 years old.

Breed restriction: No.

Preexisting condition restriction: Yes.

PETPARTNERS INC.
www.ncfbph.com/BHIACMS/
800-956-2495

ACCIDENT PLUS
Owner pays a $75 deductible and a 10 percent copay per incident, then is reimbursed up to $2,000 per incident and $8,000 per year.

Medical care included: Diagnosis and treatment of accidents and injuries.

Medical care excluded: Treatment for knee ligament injuries, illnesses, injuries connected with pregnancy or grooming, and behavior problems; alternative treatments; preventive care.

Age restriction: No.

Breed restriction: No.

Preexisting condition restriction: Yes.

ESSENTIAL
Owner pays a $125 deductible and 10 percent copay per incident and then is reimbursed up to $1,500 per incident and $11,000 per year.

Medical care included: Same as Accident Plus, plus treatment for illnesses, including cancer; and euthanasia when medically warranted.

Medical care excluded: Treatment for illnesses that occur in the first 30 days of the policy period; many "congenital" illnesses (read the Exclusions list carefully); treatment for knee ligament injuries, injuries connected with pregnancy or grooming, and behavior problems;

alternative treatments; preventive care; spaying or neutering.

Age restriction: Must be less than 9 years old.

Breed restriction: No.

Preexisting condition restriction: Yes.

ESSENTIAL PLUS
Owner pays a $125 annual deductible, plus a 20 percent copay for each illness or injury. Per-incident limit is $3,000, and yearly limit is $11,000.

Medical care included: Same as Essential.

Medical care excluded: Treatment for illnesses that occur in the first 30 days of the policy period; many "congenital" illnesses (read the Exclusions list carefully); treatment for knee ligament injuries, injuries connected with pregnancy or grooming, and behavior problems; alternative treatments; preventive care; spaying or neutering.

Age restriction: Must be less than 9 years old.

Breed restriction: No.

Preexisting condition restriction: Yes.

WELLNESS
Owner pays a $125 annual deductible and a 20 percent copay per incident or illness. Per-incident limit is $5,000, and annual limit is $13,000.

Medical care included: Same as Essential, plus preventive health care, including an annual physical; DHLPP, coronavirus, bordetella, Lyme, and rabies vaccines and boosters; heartworm testing and prevention; flea and tick protection; and an annual dental cleaning.

Medical care excluded: Treatment for illnesses that occur in the first 30 days of the policy period; many "congenital" illnesses (read the Exclusions list carefully); treatment for knee ligament injuries, injuries connected with pregnancy or grooming, and behavior problems; alternative treatments; spaying or neutering.

Age restriction: Must be less than 9 years old.

Breed restriction: No.

Preexisting condition restriction: Yes.

WELLNESS PLUS
Owner pays a $125 annual deductible and a 20 percent copay per incident, with a per-incident limit of $5,000 and an annual limit of $13,000.

Medical care included: Same as Wellness, plus spaying or neutering.

Medical care excluded: Treatment for illnesses that occur in the first 30 days of the policy period; many "congenital" illnesses (read the Exclusions list carefully); treatment for knee ligament injuries, injuries connected with pregnancy or grooming, and behavior problems; alternative treatments.

Age restriction: Must be less than 9 years old.

Breed restriction: No.

Preexisting condition restriction: Yes.

PETPLAN
www.gopetplan.com
866-GO-PETPLAN (866-467-3875)

BRONZE PLAN
Customizable coverage, with deductibles ranging from $50 to $200 and copays ranging from 0 to 20 percent. Annual limit is $8,000.

Medical care included: Diagnosis and treatment of illnesses and injuries, including alternative and complementary therapies.

Medical care excluded: Preventive care, such as annual physical exams and vaccines; spaying or neutering.

Age restriction: Upper age limit of 5 or 8 years, depending on breed.

Breed restriction: Wolves, wolf hybrids, and cloned dogs are not eligible. Certain breeds may have age limits or other restrictions.

Preexisting condition restriction: Yes.

SILVER PLAN
Customizable coverage, with deductibles ranging from $50 to $200 and copays ranging from 0 to 20 percent. Annual limit is $12,000.

Medical care included: Same as Bronze Plan.

Medical care excluded: Preventive care, such as annual physical exams and vaccines; spaying or neutering.

Nonmedical care included: Advertising or reward for a lost dog, $250 limit; reimbursement of purchase price up to $250 for a lost dog; boarding costs up to $250 if owner is hospitalized.

Age restriction: Upper age limit of 5 or 8 years, depending on breed.

Breed restriction: Wolves, wolf hybrids, and cloned dogs are not eligible. Certain breeds may have age limits or other restrictions.

Preexisting condition restriction: Yes.

GOLD PLAN

Customizable coverage, with deductibles ranging from $50 to $200 and copays ranging from 0 to 20 percent. Annual limit is $20,000.

Medical care included: Same as Bronze Plan.

Medical care excluded: Preventive care, such as annual physical exams and vaccines; spaying or neutering.

Nonmedical care included: Advertising or reward for a lost dog, $500 limit; reimbursement of purchase price up to $500 for a lost dog; boarding costs up to $500 if owner is hospitalized; purchase price of animal, up to $1,000, if it dies as a result of illness or injury; reimbursement of trip cancellation fees, up to $1,000, if animal becomes seriously ill while you are away.

Age restriction: Upper age limit of 5 or 8 years, depending on breed.

Breed restriction: Wolves, wolf hybrids, and cloned dogs are not eligible. Certain breeds may have age limits or other restrictions.

Preexisting condition restriction: Yes.

PETS BEST INSURANCE
www.petsbest.com
866-929-3807

PETS BASIC

Owner pays a $100 deductible per incident, and then is reimbursed 80 percent. The per-incident limit is $2,500. There is no annual limit, but the lifetime limit is $42,000.

Medical care included: Treatment for accidents, injuries, and illnesses, including holistic care. Reimbursement for treatment for behavior conditions, pregnancy, and hereditary conditions is limited to $40 to $100 each, once per lifetime.

Medical care excluded: Reimbursement for a knee ligament injury that occurs within the first year of the policy is limited to $50. Preventive care, such as annual exams and vaccines. Dental cleaning.

Nonmedical care included: A $50 reimbursement for cremation or burial costs.

Age restriction: Must be at least 7 weeks old. No upper age limit.

Breed restriction: No.

Preexisting condition restriction: Yes.

PETS FIRST

Owner pays a $75 deductible per incident and then is reimbursed 80 percent. The per-incident limit is $7,000, there is no annual limit, and the lifetime limit is $100,000.

Medical care included: Same as Pets Basic. Reimbursement for behavior conditions, pregnancy, and hereditary conditions is limited to $100 to $200 each, once per lifetime.

Medical care excluded: Reimbursement for a knee ligament injury that occurs within the first year of the policy is limited to $100. Preventive care, such as annual exams and vaccines. Dental cleaning.

Nonmedical care included: A $50 reimbursement for cremation or burial costs.

Age restriction: Must be at least 7 weeks old. No upper age limit.

Breed restriction: No.

Preexisting condition restriction: Yes.

PETS PREMIER
Owner pays a $300 deductible per incident and then is reimbursed 80 percent. The per-incident limit is $14,000, there is no annual limit, and the lifetime limit is $100,000.

Medical care included: Same as Pets Basic. Reimbursement for behavior conditions, pregnancy, and hereditary conditions is limited to $200 to $300 each, once per lifetime.

Medical care excluded: Reimbursement for a knee ligament injury that occurs within the first year of the policy is limited to $200. Preventive care, such as annual exams and vaccines. Dental cleaning.

Nonmedical care included: A $200 reimbursement for cremation or burial costs.

Age restriction: Must be at least 7 weeks old. No upper age limit.

Breed restriction: No.

Preexisting condition restriction: Yes.

BESTWELLNESS
Owner pays no deductible, and is reimbursed up to set limits for each included procedure. Annual limit is $440. This plan cannot be purchased separately—it must be added on to one of the Pets Best accident and illness plans listed above.

Medical care included: Annual exam, spay or neuter, dental cleaning, blood and urine tests, heartworm test, fecal test; rabies, DHLPP, coronavirus, bordetella, Lyme, and giardia vaccines.

Medical care excluded: All other.

Age restriction: Must be at least 7 weeks old. No upper age limit.

Breed restriction: No.

Preexisting condition restriction: Yes.

PURINA CARE
www.purinacare.com
877-8-PURINA (878-7462)

Owner pays a $250 annual deductible and then a 20 percent copay per incident. There is no per-incident limit, and the annual limit is $20,000.

PURINACARE
Medical care included: Diagnosis and treatment of injuries and illnesses, including alternative care if prescribed and performed by a licensed veterinarian in a clinical setting.

Medical care excluded: Preventive care, including annual exams and vaccines. Dental cleaning. Spaying or neutering. Pregnancy-related illnesses.

Age restriction: Must be at least 8 weeks old. No upper age limit.

Breed restriction: No.

Preexisting condition restriction: Yes.

PURINACARE PLUS PREVENTIVE CARE
Medical care included: Same as PurinaCare, plus an annual exam, vaccines, fecal test, heartworm test and prevention, flea and tick protection, spay or neuter, microchip implant, and dental cleaning.

Medical care excluded: Breeding and pregnancy-related illnesses.

Age restriction: Must be at least 8 weeks old. No upper age limit.

Breed restriction: No.

Preexisting condition restriction: Yes.

———

TRUPANION
www.trupanion.com
800-569-7913

Animals must be between 8 weeks and 1 year old to enroll. Owner selects a per-incident deductible and pays a 10 percent copay. No per-incident or annual limit; lifetime limit is $20,000.

Medical care included: Diagnosis and treatment of injuries and illnesses, including most congenital and hereditary disorders.

Medical care excluded: Treatment for hip dysplasia, unless owner buys the optional additional coverage. Veterinary exam fees. Preventive care, including vaccines and heartworm prevention. Dental cleaning. Treatment for behavior problems. Alternative therapies. Illnesses related to breeding or pregnancy.

Age restriction: Must be between 8 weeks and 1 year old to enroll. No upper age limit for continuing an existing policy.

Breed restriction: No.

Preexisting condition restriction: Yes.

Alternative and Complementary Medicine

The popularity of alternative and complementary medicine for companion animals has grown steadily over the past two decades. Even the American Veterinary Medical Association, that staunch guardian of traditional veterinary education and practice, has officially recognized alternative medicine by publishing guidelines for its use in animals. In addition, many vets have undergone special training in alternative and complementary therapies and now incorporate them into their practices.

This appendix gives a quick overview of acupuncture, chiropractic, herbs and Bach flower remedies, holistic medicine, homeopathy, and massage and other physical therapies, plus resources for further information and help in finding practitioners. My intention is to describe the different therapies, not to prescribe them for an individual dog or a particular illness.

ACUPUNCTURE

Acupuncture is the stimulation of various points on the body to unblock the flow of energy along meridians, or pathways, corresponding to the internal organs. Thin needles are placed in the skin, and sometimes mild electric current or heat is applied to the needles. Lasers, magnets, and ultrasound may also be used to stimulate acupuncture points.

Acupuncture has been shown to increase blood circulation and the release of natural pain-killing substances by the body. For that reason, it can be helpful in the management of chronic pain in dogs, such as that from arthritis. Acupuncture also has been used to treat seizures in epileptic dogs and many other illnesses. Those uses are more controversial.

Some practitioners combine acupuncture with the use of Chinese herbs, a pairing known as traditional Chinese medicine, or TCM. Other practitioners use acupuncture as an adjunct to Western medicine.

The International Veterinary Acupuncture Society (IVAS), founded in 1974, trains and certifies veterinary acupuncturists. The society's website includes a list of IVAS-certified acupuncturists: *www.ivas.org*.

The American Academy of Veterinary Acupuncture (AAVA), an affiliate of IVAS founded in 1998, also has a directory of veterinary acupuncturists: *www.aava.org*.

A valuable resource for information on veterinary acupuncture is the website of Allen Schoen, D.V.M., a pioneer in the field: *www.drschoen.com/therapies_L2_acu.html*.

CHIROPRACTIC

Chiropractic medicine focuses on skeletal alignment, particularly that of the spine. The theory is that misaligned vertebrae can put pressure on the spinal cord and nerves, potentially blocking nerve impulses and causing pain.

BEFORE YOU GO "ALTERNATIVE"

Before committing to any alternative therapy, get a traditional diagnosis. You should have as much information about your dog's ailment as possible before making decisions about treatment. It wouldn't make sense to give a dog who has started urinating in the house an herbal remedy for separation anxiety when the real problem is diabetes mellitus. Talk to your vet, do tests if necessary to arrive at a diagnosis, and discuss the traditional treatment options. Alternative-medicine practitioners will also use the results of diagnostic tests such as x-rays, blood chemistry profiles, or bacterial cultures to help determine a treatment plan. Then follow these guidelines:

❏ **Tell your vet you want to take a holistic approach.** Most health problems have a range of possible treatments. If your vet knows you'd prefer not to give your dog antibiotics, for example, he might recommend medicated baths and a hypoallergenic diet for treating a skin infection, or time in a steamy bathroom and lots of fluids for a case of kennel cough.

❏ **Don't abruptly stop giving traditional medications.** Talk to your vet if you plan to switch from traditional medications to an alternative therapy. She can advise you on how to taper off the medication, if necessary, and tell you about any danger signs you will want to watch for.

❏ **Ask your vet to recommend alternative-medicine practitioners.** Many mainstream vets incorporate alternative therapies into their practice or know colleagues who do. Your vet may also have other clients who can give you their recommendations.

❏ **Ask alternative-medicine practitioners about their training and background in treating dogs.** Dogs, horses, and humans differ physiologically from one another, and you want a practitioner who knows the species in question. Many different associations now offer training and certification in alternative therapies, but remember that membership in a group is not a guarantee of an individual's ability. Talk to the practitioner to make sure you feel comfortable with his experience.

❏ **Ask the alternative-medicine practitioner what results to expect, and when you might see them.** As with prescription medicines, every alternative therapy will not work for every dog. Ask the practitioner what the likelihood is that your dog's condition will respond to the alternative therapy and how long a trial period to give the treatment.

Chiropractors use their hands and other tools to help correct skeletal alignment. Veterinary chiropractic has caught on especially for horses, whose backs withstand enormous stresses, but it is also used on dogs for back pain, lameness, neurologic problems, and rehabilitation following injuries.

The American Veterinary Chiropractic Association, founded in 1989, trains veterinary chiropractors. Its website contains a directory of members and other referral information: *www.avcadoctors.com.*

The American Holistic Veterinary Medical Association's website lists members who practice chiropractic as well as numerous other alternative-medicine therapies: *www.ahvma.org.*

HERBS AND BACH FLOWER REMEDIES

Herbalists use plants for medicinal purposes, believing that they help heal and balance the mind as well as the body. There are many different branches of herbal medicine, including Ayurvedic (from India), Western, and Chinese (which is often paired with acupuncture). Veterinary herbalists may draw from one or more of these approaches.

Bach flower remedies are based on the teachings of Edward Bach, a British physician who lived in the early 1900s. He believed that negative emotional states such as sadness, fear, and impatience cause disease, and that a balanced mental state will help individuals restore themselves to physical health.

One of the best-known Bach flower mixtures is Rescue Remedy, a combination of five flower extracts that is said to fortify the emotions against physical and mental emergencies (see page 196). Other flower remedies are recommended for many other physical and mental conditions, including grief over the loss of a companion or stress from being boarded.

The Veterinary Botanical Medical Association has a directory of veterinary herbalists: *www.vbma.org.*

The American Holistic Veterinary Medical Association's directory lists veterinarians who use Bach flower remedies, Chinese herbs, and Western herbs, along with other alternative therapies: *www.ahvma.org.*

HOLISTIC MEDICINE

Holistic medicine looks at every aspect of a dog's health and well-being and combines elements of traditional and alternative medicine in a treatment plan. For example, a holistic treatment plan for a dog with lymphoma might include traditional chemotherapy plus a specially designed natural diet, herbs to bolster the immune system and counter stress, and massage and acupuncture to increase strength and relieve discomfort.

The American Holistic Veterinary Medical Association, founded in 1982, publishes a directory of members and their areas of interest on its website: *www.ahvma.org.*

HOMEOPATHY

Developed by the German physician Samuel Hahnemann in the early 1800s, homeopathy uses the principle of "Like cures like." Since symptoms are seen as the body's attempt to overcome an illness, the notion is that they should be stimulated rather than suppressed. This is done by giving minuscule amounts of substances that in larger doses would produce the same symptoms. For example, a dog with car sickness might be given a homeopathic dilution of ipecac, which is used in concentrated form to induce vomiting.

Many homeopaths feel that their methods should not be combined with traditional medicine or even with other alternative therapies such as acupuncture. Combining therapies is felt to alter the animal's natural responses to illness or to set up conflicting energy flows.

The Academy of Veterinary Homeopathy trains and certifies veterinary homeopaths. The Academy's website contains its Standards of Practice and Purpose and a directory of homeopathic practitioners: *www.theavh.org.*

MASSAGE AND PHYSICAL THERAPY

Various forms of healing touch, physical therapy, hydrotherapy, and massage are practiced on dogs. They can be particularly helpful for rehabilitation from broken bones and other injuries; after back, hip, or knee surgery; and for arthritis. For referrals to a physical therapist in your area, talk to your vet or a veterinary orthopedic surgeon.

Two popular forms of what might be called "alternative massage" are Reiki and Tellington TTouch. "Reiki" comes from the Japanese words for "universal life force." Practitioners use their hands and energy to unblock the flow of *ki,* or *chi,* much like in acupuncture. This is believed to speed healing and increase a dog's energy and sense of wellbeing. The American Holistic Veterinary Medical Association's website lists members who practice Reiki as well as other alternative-medicine therapies: *www.ahvma.org.*

Tellington TTouch was developed specifically for animals by Linda Tellington-Jones. Her website describes her methods, which are said to be effective for behavioral problems such as fearfulness and aggression as well as physical conditions such as wounds or nerve damage. The website also sells her books and lists Tellington TTouch practitioners: *www.lindatellingtonjones.com.*

Finding a Veterinary Specialist

Most small-animal veterinarians are general practitioners—they earned their doctorate, passed the national and state veterinary licensing exams, and perhaps did a one-year internship at a teaching hospital before entering private practice. But just as in human medicine, there are also veterinary specialists—vets who went on to study a particular area of medicine, such as cardiology, cancer treatment, or ophthalmology, in depth for several years *after* earning a doctorate. Veterinary specialists are usually found at veterinary teaching hospitals or specialty centers rather than in neighborhood practices.

WHEN SHOULD YOU CONSULT A SPECIALIST?

Specialists are a terrific resource for vet general practitioners as well as for their clients and patients. Your vet will refer you to a specialist when your dog needs diagnostic tests or treatments that require special equipment or expertise, such as an MRI scan, cataract removal, or radiation therapy. A vet may also refer especially complicated cases to a specialist, sending a dog with difficult-to-control seizures to a neurologist, or a dog with severe and persistent skin problems to a dermatologist.

As your dog's owner and health advocate, you can also ask your vet to refer you to a specialist. You may want to consult a specialist for a second opinion on treating a life-threatening illness or a longstanding and vexing health problem. If you feel frustrated or uncertain about your dog's illness, do ask your vet for a referral. That way your vet can send the specialist a summary of your dog's previous treatment and test results to avoid confusion and unnecessary repetition of diagnostic procedures.

Remember, though, that "vet hopping" is not the same as consulting a specialist. Taking your dog from one general practitioner to another in the hope of resolving a health problem is expensive and unrewarding because each vet will be starting from scratch, and tests and treatments are bound to be duplicated. If you're truly dissatisfied with the medical care your vet is providing, ask for a referral to a specialist for the immediate medical problem, and meanwhile search carefully for a new regular vet to provide routine care (see page 60). Once you have settled on a new vet, ask your previous vet to send him a copy of your dog's medical record and x-rays.

VETERINARY SPECIALTIES

The treatment-oriented specialties currently recognized by the American Veterinary Medical Association are dermatology; cardiology; neurology; internal medicine; oncology (cancer treatment); ophthalmology; radiology; surgery; behavior; dentistry; nutrition; and theriogenology (reproduction). All veterinarians are trained in diagnosing and treating problems within those areas of medicine and do so every day, of course, but to legitimately call oneself a specialist, a veterinarian usually must be board certified. Board certification involves extensive training over several years and testing by other experts in the field. To locate a specialist in your area, either ask your veterinarian for a referral (the easiest and best way) or search the websites listed below.

American College of Veterinary Dermatology
www.acvd.org

American College of Veterinary Internal Medicine
Specialties: Cardiology, neurology, oncology (cancer treatment), internal medicine
www.acvim.org/index.aspx?id=244

American College of Veterinary Ophthalmologists
www.acvo.com

American College of Theriogenologists
Specialty: Reproduction and infertility
www.theriogenology.org

American College of Veterinary Behaviorists
www.veterinarybehaviorists.org

American College of Veterinary Nutrition
www.acvn.org

American College of Veterinary Radiology
Specialty: Diagnostic imaging, including ultrasound, CT, and MRI scans
www.acvr.org

American College of Veterinary Surgeons
www.acvs.org

American Veterinary Dental College
www.avdc.org

VETERINARY SCHOOLS IN THE UNITED STATES AND CANADA

The 32 veterinary schools in the United States and Canada are excellent places to find veterinary specialists and state-of-the-art diagnostic and treatment facilities. In most cases, you need a written referral from your regular veterinarian before scheduling an appointment with these specialists. Below are phone numbers and websites (where available) providing information about the veterinary teaching hospitals and their specialties. These schools are not the only places where veterinary specialists can be found, however, so if you don't live near a vet school, simply ask your vet for a recommendation or check the appropriate specialty-board website above for help in locating practitioners.

ALABAMA
Auburn University College of Veterinary Medicine
Small Animal Teaching Hospital
Auburn, Alabama
334-844-4690
www.vetmed.auburn.edu

**Tuskegee University School of
Veterinary Medicine, Nursing,
and Allied Health**
Veterinary Teaching Hospital
Tuskegee, Alabama
334-727-8436

ALBERTA
**University of Calgary Faculty of
Veterinary Medicine**
Calgary, Alberta
403-210-3961
www.vet.ucalgary.ca

CALIFORNIA
**University of California School of
Veterinary Medicine**
Small Animal Clinic, Veterinary Medical
Teaching Hospital
Davis, California
530-752-1393
*www.vmth.ucdavis.edu/vmth/
clientinfo/org.html*

COLORADO
**Colorado State University
College of Veterinary Medicine &
Biomedical Sciences**
James L. Voss Veterinary Teaching
Hospital
Fort Collins, Colorado
970-221-4535
www.csuvets.colostate.edu/appt.htm

FLORIDA
**University of Florida College of
Veterinary Medicine**
Veterinary Medical Teaching Hospital
Gainesville, Florida
352-392-2235
*www.vetmed.ufl.edu/patientcare/
medicalcenter/*

GEORGIA
**University of Georgia College of
Veterinary Medicine**
Veterinary Medical Teaching Hospital
Athens, Georgia
706-542-2895 or 800-542-9294
*www.vet.uga.edu/hospital/
smallanimal/index.php*

ILLINOIS
**University of Illinois at
Urbana-Champaign College
of Veterinary Medicine**
Veterinary Teaching Hospital
Urbana, Illinois
217-333-5300
http://vetmed.illinois.edu

INDIANA
**Purdue University School
of Veterinary Medicine**
Veterinary Teaching Hospital
West Lafayette, Indiana
765-494-1107
www.vet.purdue.edu/vth/

IOWA
**Iowa State University College
of Veterinary Medicine**
Veterinary Teaching Hospital
Ames, Iowa
515-294-4900
http://vth.cvm.iastate.edu/VMC

KANSAS
**Kansas State University
College of Veterinary Medicine**
Veterinary Medicine Teaching
Hospital
Manhattan, Kansas
785-532-5690
www.vet.ksu.edu/depts/VMTH/

LOUISIANA
Louisiana State University
School of Veterinary Medicine
Veterinary Teaching Hospital & Clinic
Baton Rouge, Louisiana
225-578-9600
www.vetmed.lsu.edu/vth&c/default.htm

MASSACHUSETTS
Tufts University School of
Veterinary Medicine
Foster Hospital for Small Animals
North Grafton, Massachusetts
508-839-5395
www.tufts.edu/vet/sah

MICHIGAN
Michigan State University College
of Veterinary Medicine
Veterinary Teaching Hospital
East Lansing, Michigan
517-353-5420
www.cvm.msu.edu/hospital

MINNESOTA
The University of Minnesota
College of Veterinary Medicine
Veterinary Medical Center
St. Paul, Minnesota
612-626-8387
www.cvm.umn.edu/vmc/forclients/
home.html

MISSISSIPPI
Mississippi State University
College of Veterinary Medicine
Animal Health Center
Starkville, Mississippi
662-325-1351
www.cvm.msstate.edu/ahc/index.html

MISSOURI
University of Missouri College of
Veterinary Medicine
Small Animal Clinic

Columbia, Missouri
573-882-7821
www.vmth.missouri.edu

NEW YORK
Cornell University College of
Veterinary Medicine
Companion Animal Hospital
Ithaca, New York
607-253-3060
www.vet.cornell.edu/hospital/
companion.htm

NORTH CAROLINA
North Carolina State University
College of Veterinary Medicine
Veterinary Teaching Hospital
Raleigh, North Carolina
919-513-6670
www.cvm.ncsu.edu/vth/appointments
.html

OHIO
The Ohio State University College
of Veterinary Medicine
Veterinary Teaching Hospital
Columbus, Ohio
614-292-3551
www.vet.ohio-state.edu/27.htm

OKLAHOMA
Oklahoma State University College
of Veterinary Medicine
Boren Veterinary Medical Teaching
Hospital
Stillwater, Oklahoma
405-744-7000, option 1
www.cvm.okstate.edu

ONTARIO
University of Guelph Ontario
Veterinary College
Veterinary Teaching Hospital
Guelph, Ontario
519-823-8830
www.ovc.uoguelph.ca

OREGON
Oregon State University College of Veterinary Medicine
Veterinary Teaching Hospital
Corvallis, Oregon
541-737-4812
http://oregonstate.edu/vetmed/small/small.htm

PENNSYLVANIA
University of Pennsylvania School of Veterinary Medicine
Matthew J. Ryan Veterinary Hospital
Philadelphia, Pennsylvania
215-746-8387
www.vet.upenn.edu/ryanhospital.aspx

PRINCE EDWARD ISLAND
University of Prince Edward Island Atlantic Veterinary College
Veterinary Teaching Hospital
Charlottetown, Prince Edward Island
902-566-0950
www.upei.ca/avc/teaching_hospital

QUEBEC
University of Montreal Faculty of Veterinary Medicine
Saint-Hyacinthe, Quebec
450-773-8521
Google "University Montreal Veterinary" and click on "translate this page"

SASKATCHEWAN
University of Saskatchewan Western College of Veterinary Medicine
Veterinary Teaching Hospital
Saskatoon, Saskatchewan
306-966-7126
www.usask.ca/wcvm/vth/sac/about.php

TENNESSEE
University of Tennessee College of Veterinary Medicine
Veterinary Teaching Hospital Small Animal Clinic
Knoxville, Tennessee
865-974-8387
www.vet.utk.edu/clinical/sacs/index.php

TEXAS
Texas A&M University College of Veterinary Medicine
Veterinary Teaching Hospital
College Station, Texas
979-845-2351
http://vmth.tamu.edu/index.shtml

VIRGINIA
Virginia-Maryland Regional College of Veterinary Medicine
Veterinary Teaching Hospital
Blacksburg, Virginia
540-231-4621
www.vetmed.vt.edu/vth/sa/index.asp

WASHINGTON
Washington State University College of Veterinary Medicine
Veterinary Teaching Hospital
Pullman, Washington
509-335-0751
www.vetmed.wsu.edu/depts-vth/

WISCONSIN
University of Wisconsin-Madison School of Veterinary Medicine
Veterinary Medical Teaching Hospital
Madison, Wisconsin
608-263-7600
http://vmthpub.vetmed.wisc.edu

A P P E N D I X   D

Helpful Websites for Dog Owners

A s anyone who has ever typed the word "dog" into a search field knows, the web contains innumerable sites devoted to our canine companions. The following list is limited to only the most authoritative, reliable, and useful sources of information on canine health care.

The American Kennel Club
www.akc.org
Information on choosing, finding, and caring for purebred dogs, including breed-related health concerns, tips on finding good breeders, and links to breed rescue organizations.

The American Society for the Prevention of Cruelty to Animals
www.aspca.org/site/PageServer
Information on pet care, behavior, and disaster preparedness, plus a link to the Animal Poison Control Center, which includes lists of poisonous and nonpoisonous plants, tips on poison-proofing your home, and more.

Animal Health Care Canada
www.animalhealthcare.ca
The Canadian Veterinary Medical Association's website for animal owners. Includes information on vaccines, diseases, nutrition, kids and dogs, and a host of other topics.

The Canadian Kennel Club
www.ckc.ca
Information on selecting a dog; breed standards; canine news, events, and legislation; and more.

Care for Animals
www.avma.org/careforanimals/default.asp
The American Veterinary Medical Association's website for animal owners. Information on animal adoption, health care, training, pet loss, kids and animals, and becoming a vet.

Healthypet.com
www.healthypet.com
The American Animal Hospital Association's website for animal owners. Articles and FAQs on pet care and behavior, videos on acupuncture, dog behavior, and other topics, and a photo gallery.

Healthy Pets Healthy People
www.cdc.gov/healthypets/index.htm
Information from the federal Centers for Disease Control and Prevention on diseases that can be transmitted from animals to people and how to avoid them.

The Humane Society of the United States
www.hsus.org/pets
Pet-related news updates plus information on animal adoption and care, puppy mills, cloning, dog-fighting, and other topics.

**Public Health Agency
of Canada**
www.phac-aspc.gc.ca/index-eng.php
Information on pet food recalls and diseases affecting both dogs and people, such as rabies, tick-borne illnesses, and salmonella.

**Urbanhound: The City Dog's
Ultimate Survival Guide**
www.urbanhound.com
Although targeted primarily to residents of New York City, Chicago, and San Francisco, this award-winning website contains valuable information and ideas for dog owners across the country, organized into categories such as Hound Play, Hound Health, Hound Manners, and Hound Law. *The Complete Healthy Dog Handbook* originated with my Q&As for the Hound Health section of Urbanhound.

**The U.S. Food and Drug
Administration's Center for
Veterinary Medicine**
www.fda.gov/cvm/default.html
Up-to-the-minute information on pet food recalls, drug approvals, disease outbreaks, and other public health and animal health issues.

VeterinaryPartner.com
www.veterinarypartner.com
Health care information for animal owners that's written by veterinarians and other professionals. VeterinaryPartner is run by Veterinary Information Network, a comprehensive database and learning center for veterinarians. The dog section of VeterinaryPartner includes a Pet Health Care Library; drug information; a Pet Nutrition Corner; a Canine Behavior Series; a Dental Care Series; and a First Aid and Emergency section.

Index

VETERINARY EMERGENCY NUMBERS

When a dog is sick or injured, the most important first-aid equipment to have on hand is a telephone and the right phone numbers. Copy this chart, fill out the information, and post it on the refrigerator, inside a kitchen cabinet, or wherever you will be able to find it quickly if an emergency arises.

Dog's name:_____
_____

Year of birth:_____
Breed and weight:_____
_____

Recent or ongoing medical problems (arthritis, heart disease, allergies, etc.):_____
_____
_____
_____

Current medications and supplements:_____
_____
_____

Feeding schedule (kind of food and amount):_____
_____
_____

Date last seen by vet and reason for that visit:_____
_____

Most recent vaccinations (date and type—rabies, distemper, etc.):_
_____
_____

Vet's name:_____
Address:_____
_____

Phone:_____
Hours:_____

Emergency veterinary clinic (the one your regular vet recommends for after-hours emergencies):_____
_____

Address:_____
Phone:_____
Hours:_____

Nearest 24-hour pharmacy:___
_____
_____

Address:_____
Phone:_____

ASPCA Animal Poison Control Center: 888-426-4435
www.napcc.aspca.org
Call the Animal Poison Control Center only if you can't reach your regular vet or emergency clinic for advice about a possible poison exposure. You will be charged a fee for the call.